HOW TO INCREASE
READING ABILITY

HOW TO INCREASE READING ABILITY

A GUIDE TO DEVELOPMENTAL AND
REMEDIAL METHODS

Albert J. Harris
and
Edward R. Sipay

107760

SIXTH EDITION
Revised and Enlarged

DAVID McKAY COMPANY, INC.
NEW YORK

HOW TO INCREASE READING ABILITY

First Edition January 1940
Four Printings
Second Edition January 1947
Ten Printings
Third Edition June 1956
Six Printings
Fourth Edition April 1961
Eight Printings
Fifth Edition January 1970
Revised and Enlarged
Five Printings
Sixth Edition April 1975
Third Printing April 1977

isbn: 0–679–30277–8
library of congress catalog card number 70-92514
Printed in the United States of America

Design by Bob Antler

To
EDITH

Preface to the Sixth Edition

Although only five years have passed since the publication of the Fifth Edition, the very large volume of writing and research about reading during those years has made another thorough revision necessary. Our study of the literature, which resulted in the compilation of about 3,500 reference cards, includes references as recent as May 1974; the great majority of the nearly 1,200 references actually used were published since 1969. In addition to incorporating the best of the recent work, the book contains new terminology, new concepts, new illustrations, and new materials.

Despite this comprehensive updating, the basic character of *How to Increase Reading Ability* has remained unchanged. The continuing popularity of the book, which has had 5 editions and 33 printings since the First Edition appeared in 1940, has encouraged us to maintain the same objectives as in the previous editions. The four guiding principles remain: scope, balance, practicality, and clarity.

Breadth of scope has made the book useful in a variety of ways. It meets the need for a textbook for graduate students in courses on reading diagnosis and remediation, and as a desk reference for reading teachers, remedial specialists, and supervisors; yet it has also been used successfully in undergraduate courses on the teaching of language arts and reading. It is on many reference lists for courses in special education, particularly those dealing with learning disabilities.

A second continuing principle is the maintenance of a balanced point of view. On important controversial issues we explain the opposing viewpoints, cite the most important relevant research, point out what we believe to be the strengths and weaknesses on each side, and state our own opinion. We believe that excellence in teaching, and especially in remedial teaching, involves the selection of diagnostic procedures and teaching methods and materials that are best suited to the individual student. There is no one predominant cause for reading disabilities and no one panacea for treating them.

The third guiding principle is to make this book helpful and practical. Diagnostic procedures, tests, specific teaching methods, and specific teaching materials are described succinctly, and are related to underlying theory to provide guidelines in making choices. Brief illustrative cases are utilized to give concrete meaning to many of the ideas.

The fourth main objective has been to write as clearly and understandably as possible. We have tried to state ideas in plain nontechnical language whenever possible, to define and explain technical terms, to avoid ambiguity, to give examples and illustrations, and to provide answers to the important questions that teachers ask.

The general plan of the book remains as in the Fifth Edition. The first third of the book (Chapters 1–6) describes the developmental reading program from readiness through college, with emphasis on ways to provide for individual differences. The middle third (Chapters 7–12) covers evaluation and diagnosis. The treatment of evaluative and diagnostic procedures has been substantially expanded and now fills three fairly long chapters. Discussion of correlated factors and causal theory includes considerable new material and also takes three chapters. The final third of the book (Chapters 13–19) considers in detail both developmental and remedial teaching based on a comprehensive set of reading objectives. After a chapter on basic principles of remedial teaching, the developmental and remedial teaching of word identification, comprehension, study skills, interests, and rate of reading are dealt with in turn.

All chapters have been considerably revised. Some topics have been thoroughly rewritten; others are completely new. The special problems of disadvantaged minority-group children in learning to read are more adequately treated. The relation of reading disability to learning disabilities in general and to neurological problems is discussed at some length. Recent contributions from related disciplines such as neurology, linguistics, and cognitive psychology are described. Criterion-referenced testing, behavioral objectives, and behavioral modification techniques have been given due consideration as important recent developments.

Most of the illustrative material in the figures is new; even those that may look familiar to users of previous editions are often taken from a newly revised edition of the source. Lists of references, workbooks, commercial remedial materials, and so forth, include a great many new items as well as revised versions of items previously listed. We have tried to be selective; every item listed seems to us to have some potential usefulness with some remedial cases. Despite this effort, the lists are considerably longer, due to the continuing outpouring of new and revised materials.

The appendixes have been thoroughly revised. Most of the test descriptions in Appendix A are either new or revised. Appendix B lists series of books written with content that is more mature in interest appeal than in vocabulary used, and therefore is usable in remedial programs. The listing of individual trade books has been discontinued. Appendix C gives current names and addresses of publishers of materials mentioned in the text.

An important feature included for the first time is the presentation in Appendix D of two previously unpublished readability formulas developed by A. J. Harris and Jacobson. Complete step-by-step directions for using the formulas are given, supplemented by information about their validity, reliability, and utility. Use of these formulas will allow a teacher to measure the difficulty of reading material before using it with children, and enable a writer to determine if material is at the desired level of difficulty before it is set in type. We are grateful to Dr. Milton D. Jacobson for his cooperation in allowing these formulas to be first published here.

The very large number of references cited in the text has made it impractical to continue the policy of giving each reference in a footnote on the page where it is mentioned. Instead, a Bibliography of more than 1,100 items follows Chapter 19. References are identified in the text by placing author's name and date of publication in the text in parentheses, using lower-case letters to identify an item when the author had more than one item in print in that year. Even this large number of references represents careful selection, as more than two references were discarded for each one cited. Documentation is selective, calling attention to the better and more recent references on a topic.

The ideas in this book have come from our combined experience of more than forty-five years in working directly with teachers of reading and children with reading problems; and from hundreds of people, including authors of books, writers of research papers and journal articles, lecturers at professional conferences and conventions, our former teachers, and our present and former colleagues. To list a few of those whose thinking and research has helped us would be to be ungrateful to many others.

Several of the figures were drawn by Mrs. Stella F. Rapaport. The section on vision has again been reviewed by Bernard Fread, M.D., an ophthalmologist. Mrs. Edith Harris has helped in a great many ways as with previous editions, and her perspective as an experienced classroom and remedial teacher has helped us to focus on telling what teachers need to know in a way that they can understand. Our gratitude is also extended to Barbara M. Steger who offered many valuable suggestions based upon her expertise as a classroom teacher and reading specialist in a learning disabilities center. Thanks also go to Joseph Fusaro for his assistance in completing the references, and to Mary Unser for her expert typing.

We acknowledge our indebtedness to the many publishers who have permitted us to use quotations or samples from tests or teaching materials. These permissions are acknowledged with gratitude and appreciation at the appropriate places in the text.

ALBERT J. HARRIS
EDWARD R. SIPAY

January 1975

Contents

Tables

Illustrations

HOW TO INCREASE
READING ABILITY

1

Reading: Ability and Disability

I. IMPORTANCE AND STATUS OF READING IN OUR SOCIETY

The importance of reading ability increases as a democratic society such as ours becomes more complex and industrialized. A literate population is a necessity if the processes of democracy are to function properly. As Jennings pointed out:

> If democratic living is valuable to us as individuals and as members of groups, then we have to make certain that every generation will grow beyond our grasp and understanding. Techniques are not enough and the expansion of scientific knowledge is never sufficient. We need to develop the kind of living understanding of the relations of our daily experiences to the total experience of the human race. We need to be able to read widely and wisely in the library of "all our yesterdays" to keep the record of our achievement straight. We need to be able to read accurately the words and features, the hopes and plans of ourselves and our fellowmen. (1965, p. 191)

As technology advances, more occupations tend to require higher levels of education or specialized training in which improved reading ability plays a vital role. Automation has eliminated the jobs of many unskilled or semi-skilled workers, many of whom were not even functionally literate and became unemployed or chronically unemployable because they did not possess the minimum reading skills required for success in other positions. Few realize the level of reading competency needed in certain occupations.

For example, Sticht, Caylor, Kern, and Fox (1972) determined that the minimum literacy levels for army cook, repairman and armor crewman, and supply clerk were reading grade levels of 7.0, 8.0, and 9.0 respectively. Literacy is essential if loss of self-esteem and permanent relief status is to be avoided. In these efforts, reading ability is centrally important, since without it little academic learning can go on (Luke, 1967).

If one considers what happens in our culture to children who fail to read adequately, the importance of reading ability becomes even more obvious. As they get older, poor readers, and particularly nonreaders, are increasingly handicapped by their lack of reading ability. They are almost sure to repeat grades, and if they get into high school, they are practically certain to drop out before graduation. Thus many desirable occupations are closed to them, and the pattern of failure and its consequences are repeated.

There also are noneconomic benefits of reading. To a large extent, non-readers (those who cannot read, and also those who can but choose not to) are cut off from cultural activities and find it difficult to mingle with educated people. Furthermore, reading can fulfill emotional and spiritual needs.

As compared to movies, radio, and television, reading has certain unique advantages. Instead of having to choose from a limited variety made available to him by courtesy of the advertising sponsor, or from the currently available films, the reader can select from the finest writings of the present or past. He can read in a place and at a time chosen for his own convenience. He can go at his own pace and can slow down or speed up, take an intermission, reread, or pause and think, at his own pleasure. He can read what, when, where, and how he pleases. This flexibility insures the continuing value of reading both for education and for entertainment.

If reading ability is so important in our culture, how well, how much, and what do Americans read? Three current studies provide some information about the reading achievement of Americans. In one study (Schaie and Roberts, 1970) a standardized word recognition (pronunciation) test was administered to over 7,000 children aged 6 to 11 who were representative of our school population. Their data indicate a wide range of achievement at each age level which must be taken into account when planning reading programs. For example, although 35 per cent of the 10-year-olds and 25 per cent of the 11-year-olds correctly recognized only as many words as the average 9-year-old, approximately 10 per cent of the 7-year-olds and 30 per cent of the 8-year-olds scored as well as the average 9-year-old.

The National Assessment Study (Gadway, 1972) examined the trends of the reading knowledges, understandings, and skills of approximately 100,000 individuals at four age levels (9, 13, 17, young adult). The study found that, with a few exceptions, individuals read all types of materials better than the exercise developers anticipated. Among the findings of interest were:

1] Almost 60 per cent of the 17-year-olds discerned that a passage about Helen Keller's life referring in almost every sentence to particular years was organized as a chronological narrative, rather than as a diary, a flashback, an interview, or an eyewitness account.

2] More than half of the 17-year-olds understood that Shakespeare in his 29th sonnet used "deaf Heaven" to refer to a God who does not hear.

3] Nearly half the 13-year-olds and more than 25 per cent of the 17-year-olds (and this group is only one year away from voting age) were unable to read a passage containing two conflicting statements and arrive at the conclusion that one of them had to be wrong.

4] More than 15 per cent of the adults and 17-year-olds, one-third of the 13-year-olds, and nearly two-thirds of the nine-year-olds had difficulty reading and then answering questions about a common daily TV schedule. (Justus, 1972, p. 12)

The Survival Literacy Study (L. Harris and Associates, 1970) attempted to determine how many Americans were prevented by reading deficiencies from filling out application forms for such common needs as a social security number, a personal bank loan, public assistance, Medicaid, and a driver's license.[1] This survey estimated that 13 per cent (18.5 million) of the adult population failed to complete the forms with fewer than 10 per cent errors, with 3 per cent (4.3 million) making errors on more than 30 per cent of the blanks on the forms. Even 8 per cent of the college-educated adults failed more than 10 per cent of the items. This latter finding, coupled with the fact that thousands of high school graduates in the army scored below seventh-grade level in reading (Sticht and others, 1972), indicates that educational level is not necessarily an indication of reading ability.

Although increased book sales and library transactions might make it appear that Americans have a rather substantial commitment to reading, other data indicate otherwise. For example, only 26 per cent of interviewed adults claimed they had read a book in the last month (Meade, 1973), and 75 per cent of all paperbacks were bought by only 10 per cent of our population (Jennings, 1965). The average adult spends one hour and 46 minutes per day reading. However, there is great variability as to reading time, and few read for relatively long periods (Sharon, 1973–1974).

Information such as the preceding has created a justified concern regarding the status of reading in the United States. This concern is reflected by the National Right to Read Effort (Allen, 1970; Holloway, 1973), the tremendously increased attention recently given to reading and reading disability in the professional literature of various disciplines and in the popular press, the increased quantity and quality of research in reading (N. B.

1. Of course there is always the question as to how clearly the forms are written.

Smith, 1971), and by accountability for reading instruction (Ruddell, 1973). Literacy and the teaching of reading are also receiving increased international attention (Downing, 1973).

II. THE NATURE OF READING

No one fully understands the extremely complex process we call reading. During the 1950's and 1960's increased attention was given to definitions and explanations of reading (Clymer, 1968). The 1970's have seen much more complex model building and theoretical constructs which primarily draw from four sources: developmental psychology, information-processing, psycholinguistics, and linguistics (see, *e.g.*: Athey, 1971; Carver, 1971; F. Davis, 1972; J. E. Mackworth, 1972; F. Smith, 1971a; Venezky and Calfee, 1970; Weaver and Kingston, 1972). Many of the existing theories and models have been summarized (Geyer, 1972; Harker, 1972; Williams, 1973). Williams summarized her review of the literature as follows:

1] Models at present focus on cognitive aspects of reading; little attempt has been made to incorporate affective aspects into the models.
2] Several different theoretical positions within psychology, representing a wide variety of points of view, have been used in the development of models of reading, whereas transformational-generative grammar is the only theory from linguistics that is represented in recent attempts at comprehensive model building.
3] There seems to be a rapprochement among theorists toward a view of reading as both a complex cognitive skill, the goal of which is obtaining information, and a complex language system.
4] Most models focus on the reading process *per se*. This is due in large part, of course, to the theorist's specific interest in skilled reading. However, the emphasis on proficient reading is also the result of the opinion that in order to understand the acquisition process, we must first study the skill as it appears in final form.
5] Most models of the acquisition phase focus on decoding and its prerequisite abilities. The mechanisms involved in making correspondences between orthography and sound cannot, however, be characterized in terms of simple associative learning. Rather, basic knowledge of language is intimately involved, as well as the utilization of complex active perceptual and cognitive strategies.

The view has been advanced by some that reading is simply the recognition or identification of the words represented by the printed symbols, regardless of whether or not meaning is achieved. Thus Flesch wrote: "I once surprised a native of Prague by reading aloud from a Czech newspaper. 'Oh, you know Czech?' he asked. 'No, I don't understand a word of it,' I answered. 'I can only read it' " (1955, p. 23). Somewhat similarly, some linguists distinguish between "reading" and "understanding." Reed stated: "Anyone who has learned to read can read many sentences whose meanings are almost completely unknown to him" (1965, p. 847). Writers who define reading as simply the production of spoken words or linguistic forms which correspond to the printed symbols usually advocate that the recognition skills should be taught thoroughly before any attention is given to comprehension.

Most reading specialists regard reading as a synthesis of recognizing and comprehending, in which the absence of either makes true reading impossible. From this standpoint, making sounds in response to the print on a Czech newspaper is making noises, not reading. Even the beginning reader seeks for meaning; and when he makes errors, the sentence as read usually makes sense, even if not the sense intended by the writer. The prevalence of "context errors" (reasonable but incorrect responses to unknown printed words on the basis of the rest of the sentence) is familiar to every primary teacher.

A psycholinguist has emphasized this seeking for meaning to the point of calling reading a psycholinguistic guessing game. On the basis of detailed analysis of fairly typical oral reading miscues, Goodman offered the following definition: "Reading is a selective process. It involves partial use of available minimal language cues selected from perceptual input on the basis of the reader's expectation. As this partial information is processed, tentative decisions are made to be confirmed, rejected, or refined as reading progresses" (1967, p. 126). This statement, when compared to Reed's, indicates how far linguists and psycholinguists are from agreement among themselves. Goodman's analysis corresponds closely to the viewpoint of most reading specialists.

As used in this book, *reading is the meaningful interpretation of written or printed verbal symbols*. It can apply also to the interpretation of mathematical symbols, musical notation, codes, and other symbolic systems; but we are not concerned with them. Reading is an extension of oral communication and builds upon listening and speaking skills.

In the beginning stages, learning to read means learning that queer-looking marks stand for speech, although, as linguists have pointed out, writing systems are an imperfect representation of speech (*e.g.*, there are no marks for pitch, stress, and the like). The child "reads" when he is able to say the words that are represented by the printed marks. The child may say the words out loud, or he may say them to himself; in either case, reading means saying the correct words. The child's response to the first words sets up an anticipation of meaning which, if correct, aids in identifying the following words. If he says the wrong words, if he has to leave out too many words because he does not recognize them, if his recognition is so slow and halting that the words are not heard as coming in meaningful sequences, or if he runs sentences together and frequently misphrases, the approximation to heard speech will not be good enough to convey the intended meaning.

That reading is a process involving meaning is self-evident, but it can hardly be overemphasized that meaningful response is the very heart of the reading process. "It can and should embrace all types of thinking, evaluating, judging, imagining, reasoning, and problem-solving" (Gates, 1949, p. 3). Not only are intellectual meanings involved; feelings of considerable intensity may be aroused and emotional attitudes may be profoundly altered through reading.

Skill in the recognition of words continues to develop as the child's reading ability matures. Recognition of common words becomes faster and more accurate. New words are continually being added to the child's store of sight words. Gradually the child becomes able to recognize short, familiar phrases as meaningful units. Skill in decoding new words is acquired concurrently, so that the child does not have to be told each new word. The necessity for translating the printed symbols into the corresponding speech sounds recedes; reading becomes inaudible, noticeable lip and tongue movements cease, and to many an expert reader the meaning seems eventually to leap from the printed page with scarcely any awareness of inner speech.

As the child gets beyond the beginning stages in reading and the task of recognizing words becomes more nearly automatic, he finds his reading material becoming more complicated. Ideas are introduced which are outside the range of his experience, and words are employed which he has never heard spoken. Sentences become longer, and their structure grows more complex. Finding out what the book means becomes harder because the language is more involved than the conversation to which the child is accustomed. To keep up with his reading the child must increase his vocabulary, enlarge and refine his store of concepts and ideas, and develop his mastery of more complex forms of expression.

The child meets a variety of reading materials and finds that he reads to satisfy many different needs and purposes. Story-type reading becomes differentiated from work-type reading. In pleasure reading, exclusive concern with the plot becomes gradually enriched by the development of appreciation for humor, characterization, accuracy and vividness of description, and the sheer beauty of artistic expression. In work-type reading, study skills and habits must be formed. They differ from subject to subject, and different methods of study must be learned to cope with the different phases of one subject. The efficient student learns how to locate what he needs, to distinguish major from minor points, to follow directions, to interpret, to summarize, to outline, and to utilize the information.

Finally, reading becomes reflective and evaluative. To grasp the meaning and organization of a writer's ideas is important, but not sufficient. The mature reader brings his previous knowledge and experience into relation with his present reading, compares the facts and arguments presented by one author with those of another, and is on the alert for errors in logical reasoning. He has learned to distinguish factual reporting from biased propaganda and objective reasoning from wishful thinking.

To summarize, we may define reading as the act of responding with appropriate meaning to printed or written verbal symbols. For the beginner, reading is mainly concerned with learning to recognize the printed symbols which represent speech and to respond intellectually and emotionally as he would if the material were spoken rather than printed. The reasoning side of reading becomes increasingly important as recognition is mastered. As proficiency in reading increases, the individual learns to adapt his method of reading in accordance with his purpose for reading and the restrictions imposed by the nature of the material. The nature of the reading task, therefore, changes as the learner progresses from less mature to more mature levels. Reading is not one skill, but a large number of interrelated skills which develop gradually over a period of many years.

Reading is a very complex process in which the recognition and comprehension of written symbols are influenced by the perceptual skills, the decoding skills, the experience, the language background, the mind set, and the reasoning ability of the reader, as he anticipates meaning on the basis of what he has just read. The total process is a *Gestalt* or whole in which a serious flaw in any major function or part may prevent adequate performance.

III. OBJECTIVES OF READING INSTRUCTION

When teachers of reading are asked to state their objectives, the answers are frequently very general. Many teachers do not get beyond the statement that their aim is to help children become better readers. This praiseworthy desire is much too broad and vague to be helpful in the specifics of teaching.

It is important to be as definite as possible about educational objectives. Teachers who set up as a major objective the development of a love for reading as a form of recreation can find many different ways of working toward it, and each can achieve substantial success. But if developing a love for independent reading is not one of the teacher's goals, it is unlikely that his pupils will acquire such an attitude as a result of his efforts. Having the right goals and knowing what they are is the necessary first step in working out a sound reading program.

Some objectives should characterize the reading program as a whole. In setting down a list of eight major criteria of a sound reading program, the Yearbook Committee of the National Society for the Study of Education pointed out the interrelationship between the reading program and the school program as a whole and emphasized that reading must fit harmoniously into the total plan of a good educational program. According to this committee, a good reading program in an elementary school

1] Is consciously directed toward specific valid ends which have been agreed upon by the entire school staff

2] Coordinates reading activities with other aids to child development

3] Recognizes that the child's development in reading is closely associated with his development in other language arts

4] At any given level, is part of a well-worked-out larger reading program extending throughout all the elementary and secondary school grades

5] Provides varied instruction and flexible requirements as a means of making adequate adjustments to the widely different reading needs of the pupils

6] Affords, at each level of advancement, adequate guidance of reading in all the various aspects of a broad program of instruction: basic instruction in reading, reading in the content fields, literature, and recreational or free reading

7] Makes special provisions for supplying the reading needs of cases of severe reading disability; in other words, the small proportion of pupils whose needs cannot be satisfied through a strong developmental program

8] Provides for frequent evaluation of the outcomes of a program and for such revisions as will strengthen the weaknesses discovered (Whipple, 1949)

These eight criteria describe very well the broader aspects of the reading program. Each of them needs to be spelled out in greater detail for its applications to be clear. These applications are developed in later chapters. At this point it seems desirable to point out in expanded degree the meaning of the sixth criterion, which mentions different aspects of a broad reading program.

The teacher of reading wants his pupils to be able to read, to use reading effectively as a learning tool, and to enjoy and appreciate reading. Using somewhat more technical language, we can talk about developmental reading, functional reading, and recreational reading. *Developmental reading* activities are those in which the main purpose of the teacher is to bring about an improvement in reading skills—activities in which learning to read is the main goal. *Functional reading* includes all types of reading in which the primary aim is to obtain information; in other words, reading to learn. Some writers prefer to call it study-type reading or work-type reading. *Recreational reading* consists of reading activities that have enjoyment, entertainment, and appreciation as major purposes.

A somewhat more detailed analysis of these three types of reading, stated as general outcomes in terms of learner behavior, is as follows:

A. Developmental Reading
    1] Mechanics of reading
        a) Has a large sight vocabulary
        b) Flexibly uses a variety of skills to decode unknown words
        c) Has good eye-movement habits
        d) Reads silently with speed and fluency
        e) Reads orally with proper phrasing, expression, pitch, volume and enunciation
    2] Reading comprehension
        a) Has a rich, extensive, and accurate reading vocabulary
        b) Interprets non-literal and figurative language
        c) Grasps the meaning of units of increasing size; phrase, sentence, paragraph, whole selection
        d) Finds answers to specific questions
        e) Selects and understands main ideas
        f) Understands a sequence of events
        g) Notes and recalls details
        h) Follows directions accurately
        i) Grasps the author's plan and intent
        j) Understands the techniques by which the author attempts to create his effects
        k) Anticipates outcomes
        l) Makes inferences
        m) Relates the ideas found within paragraphs to the ideas presented in other paragraphs
        n) Notes cause-effect relationships
        o) Evaluates what is read
        p) Coordinates rates with comprehension
        q) Remembers what has been read
B. Functional Reading
    1] Locates needed reading material
        a) Uses indexes

           b) Uses tables of contents
           c) Uses dictionaries
           d) Uses encyclopedias
           e) Uses other bibliographic aids
           f) Skims in search for information
     2] Comprehends informational material
           a) Understands technical and specific vocabulary
           b) Applies the general comprehension skills listed under A, 2, above
           c) Uses the specific skills needed by special subject matter, *e.g.*.
               (1) Reading of arithmetic problems
               (2) Reading of maps, charts, and graphs
               (3) Conducting a science experiment from printed directions
           d) Reads independently in the content subjects
     3] Selects the material needed
     4] Records and organizes what is read
           a) Takes useful notes
           b) Summarizes
           c) Outlines
C. Recreational Reading
     1] Displays an interest in reading
           a) Enjoys reading as a voluntary leisure-time activity
           b) Selects appropriate reading matter
           c) Satisfies present interests and tastes through reading
     2] Improves and refines reading interests
           a) Reads various types of material on a variety of topics
           b) Reads materials which reflect more mature interests
           c) Achieves personal development through reading
     3] Refines literary judgment and taste
           a) Establishes differential criteria for fiction and nonfiction, prose and poetry, and drama
           b) Appreciates style and beauty of language
           c) Seeks for deeper symbolic messages

These three major types of reading cannot and should not be kept entirely separate. In a developmental lesson children must read material that is either recreational or functional in character. An enjoyable story may be used for the cultivation of particular reading skills, and developmental lessons should be planned to help pupils in their reading of content subject material.

A sound reading program must have balance among these major types of reading. If the desire to read for fun is killed by overemphasis on drills and exercises, one of the major aims of reading instruction is defeated and the result is the pathetic graduate who never opens a book after commencement. The relative balance changes grade by grade. For the beginner, nearly all reading activities are primarily developmental; by the upper elementary grades, functional reading is most important and developmental lessons take the least amount of time.

The general learning objectives stated above are anticipated general outcomes of a reading program. These general objectives may be subdivided and stated in varying degrees of specificity. Such specific objectives are commonly known as "behavioral" or "performance" objectives, the writing of which has been described in detail (*e.g.*, Mager, 1962; Gronlund, 1970). Although there are variations in style, a behavioral objective usually states the condition under which a specified behavior will occur (external conditions), the type of behavior that is to occur as a result of planned instruction (terminal behavior), and the performance level that will be accepted (acceptable performance) (Norris and Bowes, 1970). Some writers do not suggest stating external conditions. A behavioral objective is the result that is to follow from instruction, not the instructional activity itself (McNeil, 1970). That is, the behavioral objective should be stated in terms of learner behavior (the anticipated produce or outcome) rather than in terms of teacher behavior (the process of what the teacher does with the learner).

To illustrate, the general objective "Evaluates what is read" is a complex objective that calls for the use of critical thinking in reading. A number of more specific learning outcomes can be listed under this general objective:

1] Distinguishes between facts and opinions
2] Distinguishes between facts and inferences
3] Identifies cause-effect relations
4] Identifies errors in reasoning
5] Distinguishes between relevant and irrelevant arguments
6] Distinguishes between warranted and unwarranted generalizations
7] Formulates valid conclusion from written material
8] Specifies assumptions needed to make conclusions true (Gronlund, 1970, p. 14)

Adding external conditions to the first specific outcome would result in: Given an editorial, the learner can underline statements of opinion. Then adding a criterion for acceptable behavior, the behavioral objective would read: Given an editorial, the learner can underline at least 9 of the 10 statements of opinion without misidentifying any statements of fact.

More specificity could be added, for example the qualifier "written at the sixth reader level" might be added after "editorial." It is easier to determine when cognitive objectives have been met than affective objectives.

The sequence in using behavioral objectives is: 1) to state the objective; 2) to select and use appropriate procedures, content, and methods; and 3) to test to determine if the criterion for mastery has been met. Thus, by clearly stating what the learner can do under given conditions when he has achieved the objective, the teacher can determine the extent to which a given specific skill has been mastered.

From a teacher's standpoint, it is helpful to distinguish between outcome objectives and process objectives. Behavioral objectives are outcome objectives. The teacher is at least equally interested in formulating a process objective—a statement of what the teacher can do to bring about the desired outcome. Thus, "To introduce the consonant cluster *sm*" is a process objective, which can be amplified by a detailed lesson plan. The desired outcome can be formulated as a behavioral objective, such as: "Identifies five of six one- and two-syllable words beginning with *sm*." The process objective identifies the means, while the outcome objective identifies the desired result; both are needed for effective teaching.

IV. A BRIEF HISTORICAL OVERVIEW[2]

The first published report of a case of reading disability was made by W. Pringle Morgan, a British ophthalmologist, in 1896; he described a 14-year-old boy who had not learned to read although he seemed otherwise intelligent (Morgan, 1896). The term "congenital word blindness" was used and continued to be popular in Europe for many years. Most prominent among the early investigators in Great Britain was Hinshelwood, a Glasgow eye surgeon, whose monograph attracted international attention (Hinshelwood, 1917). The early interest in reading problems on the part of medical men in Great Britain attracted relatively little notice from psychologists and educators.

The first published report in the United States of an attempt to diagnose individual reading problems and prescribe treatment was by Uhl (1916). The following year, Bronner (1917) made some interesting observations about reading problems. The first two books on reading disability in America were published in 1922 (C. T. Gray, 1922; W. S. Gray, 1922). Meanwhile, a practical phonic method for teaching nonreaders had been described by Schmitt (1918), and the kinesthetic method had

2. For details about early developments in reading diagnosis and remediation, see Critchley (1970), Thompson (1966), and A. J. Harris (1968b), and refer to Hallahan and Cruickshank (1973) for a historical account of learning disabilities.

been outlined by Fernald and Keller (1921). The first battery of reading diagnosis tests was developed by Gates (1927). The first clinics specializing in reading difficulties, at schools like the University of Chicago and Boston University, became centers for the training of reading specialists and remedial teachers. The first large-scale remedial reading program in a public school system was begun in New York City in the mid-1930's, as a project of federal antidepression agencies.

Although reading disability received a little notice from American physicians as early as 1906, Samuel T. Orton, a neurologist, was the first whose work attracted wide attention. While he recognized that there were multiple causes for delay in learning to read, Orton was mainly interested in *"the* reading disability." He considered the primary symptom to be a severe reversal tendency, explained this as based on a failure to establish clear dominance of one cerebral hemisphere over the other, coined the term "strephosymbolia" (twisted symbols) as a preferred name for the condition, and recommended a systematic sounding-blending type of phonics teaching (Orton, 1937).

Since the beginning of the study of reading disability, there have been two opposed tendencies. Physicians have postulated a basic constitutional condition, often hereditary and usually accompanied by other communication difficulties (in speech, spelling, handwriting, composition). While admitting that cases of reading disability may stem from other causes, they have preferred to concentrate on the constitutional issue.

Educational psychologists, on the other hand, have tended to be impressed by the wide range of physical, psychological, emotional, sociological, linguistic, and educational handicaps that may be found in poor readers, and have tended to favor a pluralistic theory of causation. Without denying the possibility of specific subgroups, they have emphasized the wide range of handicaps to be found in school and clinic populations and the continuity of problems from mild to most severe disabilities.

For about a twenty-year period (1935–1955), psychoanalysts and clinical psychologists sought to explain reading disability as a symptom of emotional disturbance and to suggest psychotherapy as a preferred mode of treatment. There is little doubt that the great majority of children with reading disabilities who come to the attention of psychologists and psychiatrists have emotional symptoms and problems. In individual cases, however, it is often very difficult to determine whether the emotional problem is a cause of the reading disability or a result of it. Psychotherapy alone seems to be an adequate method of treatment in only a small minority of cases.

Since 1955 there has been an accelerating interest in reading disabilities in the United States. This resulted in a vast expansion of remedial programs, a shortgage of qualified personnel, and an upsurge in research.

Under provisions of the National Defense Education Act many workshops and institutes were held. Funds from Title I and Title III of the Elementary and Secondary Education Act of 1965 financed a great many new and innovative remedial reading programs, and federal funds were largely responsible for the increased volume of research. The 1960's were noted for the emergence of, and resulting controversies about, such terms as *dyslexia* and *learning disability*, and a renewed interest in determining the nature of the disability.

V. INCIDENCE OF READING DISABILITY

Definitive information on the frequency of reading disability is not available for several reasons. First, the definitions (*e.g.*, reading retardation, dyslexia, specific reading disability) used to define the populations vary considerably; thus the figures are of doubtful comparability. Second, even when similar terms were employed, the criterion used to set a cutoff point has varied from one investigator to another. Finally, it is reasonable to expect that populations will differ somewhat and that age of school entrance, socioeconomic background, method of teaching, and degree of regularity in the symbol-sound relationships of the language will produce variations.

The per cent of reading disability reported in various countries ranges from one per cent in Japan (Makita, 1968) to approximately 8 per cent in Sweden (Malmquist, 1958) and West Germany (Weinschenk, 1970) through 10 per cent in England (Newton, 1970), 14 per cent in Argentina (de Quiros and Della Cella, 1959), 15 per cent in Scotland (Clark, 1971) to as high as 22 per cent (4 per cent having "severe dyslexia") in Austria (Schenk-Danziger, 1960). Makita attributed the low rate of disability in Japan to the nature of Japanese orthography and concluded that reading disability is more of a philological than a neuropsychiatric problem.[3] In his sample of 425 Chinese children simultaneously learning to read and write in English and Chinese, Kline and Lee (1970) found the incidence of reading disability to be similar in both languages. Also of interest was his finding that the incidence in these bilinguals was not higher than in monolingual children (Kline and Lee, 1972).

A comprehensive survey of available evidence of the incidence of reading disabilities in the United States resulted in the conclusion that about 15 per cent of schoolchildren have reading disabilities. "Eight million children in America's elementary and secondary schools today will not learn to

3. At the International Reading Congress in Vienna in August 1974, Makita repeated his low estimate and was supported by T. Sakamoto. Both attributed this low incidence to the ease of learning *Kana*, the Japanese syllabic alphabet, and in part to almost universal parental teaching before children enter school. The *Kana* writing system is apparently much easier to learn than the ideographs used in both Chinese and Japanese.

read adequately. One child in seven is handicapped in his ability to acquire essential reading skills. This phenomenon pervades all segments of our society—black and white, boys and girls, the poor and the affluent" (National Advisory Committee on Dyslexia and Related Reading Disorders, 1969, p. 7).

The per cent one finds depends on the criteria used as well as on the population studied. The data in Table 3 (p. 89), based on the recent restandardization of a widely used series of reading tests, indicate that about 30 per cent of fourth graders and about 35 per cent of sixth graders are one or more years below the norm in reading. If two-thirds of them are generally slow learners and one-third are disabled readers, one gets a figure of 10 to 12 per cent with reading disability. The true per cent is probably between 10 and 15 per cent. Boys usually comprise between 65 and 90 per cent of the reading disability population; the reasons for this markedly higher incidence in males are still obscure.

VI. ADAPTED, CORRECTIVE, AND REMEDIAL READING PROGRAMS

About 25 per cent of American children have IQ's below 90. These slow learners need a reading program geared to their abilities, one that accepts their limitations, sets reasonable expectations that are neither too high nor too low, and is designed to meet their needs and interests. Such an *adapted reading program* should differ from the typical developmental reading program mainly in its slower pace and use of different materials and interests. The materials more closely resemble these found in remedial reading programs because the slow learners' interests are often more mature than their reading ability. Mentally handicapped children can learn reading skills (Aaron, 1971). Research regarding reading and the slow learner has been reviewed by Cegelka and Cegelka (1970) and various programs and materials that may be used have been discussed by Lazar (1971). A good adapted program includes adjustments in the slow learner's entire academic program, not just for reading.

Children who are reading below their potential (disabled readers and underachievers in reading) should have reading programs that are planned to teach them the specific reading skills not yet mastered, using the best methodology, materials, and motivation possible. Efforts to help these children are broadly described as *remedial reading*. Within this broad heading a distinction often is made between *corrective reading* and *remedial reading* programs. Theoretically, the two differ in four respects: 1) where the treatment takes place, 2) who provides the treatment, 3) the number of children treated in a session, and 4) the severity of the problems treated. Corrective reading occurs within the framework of regular class instruction and is conducted by the classroom teacher for groups or subgroups whose reading-skill weaknesses are uncovered in the daily or periodic assessment of skill development. Remedial reading occurs away from the regular classroom, in or outside the school, and is conducted by a teacher with special training in reading for small groups or on a one-to-one basis.

In actuality, the distinction between corrective and remedial reading is somewhat artificial. The problems treated are more likely to differ in degree than in kind, and whether a child receives corrective or remedial reading help may depend more on the resources available than on the nature of his reading problem or the nature of the instruction best suited to his needs (Clymer, 1967). Furthermore, as pointed out in the next section, corrective teaching should be a normal part of good teaching.

It is tempting to speculate on the results that would be achieved if all teachers could come close to perfection in the teaching of reading. Under these conditions, reading problems that are presently the result of faulty educational practices would not arise. Would the need for remedial reading disappear?

It seems probable that even in an educational Utopia, some children would have neurological handicaps, visual handicaps that resist correction, emotional problems arising out of early family experiences, and so on. These children would need diagnostic study of a depth beyond most classroom teachers' capabilities, and many of them would need, as they do now, an amount and kind of individual help that is very difficult to provide in a classroom situation. Utopian teaching would lessen the number of reading difficulties but would not eliminate them, and some need for special remedial facilities would remain.

At present, and at least for the next decade or two, most reading programs will continue to fall short of Utopia. With the best of teacher efforts to meet individual needs, thousands of children will get lost in the early stages of reading instruction. We can be sure that most of these children will not just outgrow their reading problems; the large number of severe disability cases of secondary school age proves this conclusively. The need for corrective and remedial teaching is not likely to diminish soon.

Light is cast on this issue if we compare it with the situation in the field of physical health. There is no argument over the principle that great emphasis should be placed on hygienic living and that with proper attention to the teaching of principles of nutrition and safety education, much poor health and many accidents can be avoided. This does not mean that first aid becomes unnecessary. Accidents will continue to happen, and germs will continue to circulate. Knowledge of what to do for common, minor physical ailments and mishaps is just as important as ever. Finally, when a serious illness or accident occurs, nobody denies the need for the diagnostic skill of a capable physician or the expert care of trained nurses. There is a need for all three: general practice of hygienic living, widespread knowledge and use of approved first-aid practices, and expert medical care.

The situation with regard to the teaching of reading is similar. There can be no quarrel with the proposition that major efforts should be devoted to improving the general efficiency of classroom teaching. As this takes place, the frequency of reading disabilities will diminish. Nevertheless, under the best of teachers, children will continue to be handicapped by physical defects, to miss school because of illness, and for other reasons to fall behind. Detecting weak points in the child's achievement and helping the child to overcome these weaknesses are integral parts of the effective classroom teacher's method. This corrective instruction is a sort of educational first aid. It is, of course, remedial teaching, but remedial teaching conceived of without capital letters, as a normal part of good methodology. As corrective teaching in its simpler forms becomes taken for granted because it is part of every good teacher's procedure, the need for calling it by a special name diminishes. In this sense, remedial reading is losing its distinctive character by becoming normal rather than unusual procedure. Finally, a small percentage of children will continue to have special handicaps in reading that will require the application of refined diagnostic procedures by experts and individual teaching by skilled remedial teachers. There is, then, no conflict among the three phases of a good reading program: superior first teaching which is adapted to the needs and individual abilites of the children, frequent classroom use of simple corrective procedures as they are needed, and careful diagnosis and special remedial help for the disabled reader.

SUGGESTED ADDITIONAL READING

BOND, GUY L. & TINKER, MILES A. *Reading difficulties: their diagnosis and correction* (3rd ed.). New York: Appleton-Century-Crofts, 1973. Chaps. 1, 4.

DOWNING, JOHN (Ed.). *Comparative reading: cross-national studies of behavior and process in reading and writing.* New York: Macmillan, 1973.

DURKIN, DOLORES. *Teaching them to read* (2nd ed.). Boston: Allyn and Bacon, 1974. Chap. 1.

HARRIS, ALBERT J. & SIPAY, EDWARD R. (Eds.). *Readings on reading instruction* (2nd ed.). New York: McKay, 1972. Chaps. 1, 2.

SCHELL, LEO M. & BURNS, PAUL C. (Eds.). *Remedial reading: classroom and clinic* (2nd ed.). Boston: Allyn and Bacon, 1972. Pp. 1–43.

SEBESTA, SAM L. & WALLEN, CARL J. (Eds.). *The first R: readings on teaching reading.* Chicago: Science Research Associates, 1972. Pp. 7–38, 68–147.

SINGER, HARRY & RUDDELL, ROBERT B. (Eds.). *Theoretical models and processes in reading.* Newark, Del.: International Reading Association, 1970.

SMITH, FRANK. *Understanding reading: a psycholinguistic analysis of reading and learning to read.* New York: Holt, Rinehart and Winston, 1971.

2

Readiness for Reading

Until about two generations ago, a child who got off to a poor start in the first grade was considered lazy or stupid or both, and was required to repeat the year. When school surveys disclosed that nonpromotion in first grade was as high as 30 to 40 per cent in many communities (Caswell, 1933), educators began to realize that perhaps the school was more responsible than the child. They began to be concerned with the tremendous differences to be found among young children of about the same age. They started to study the nature of the maturities that are important in learning to read, how to measure those characteristics, and what can be done to prevent failure and give children a better start in reading.

I. THE NATURE OF READING READINESS

Readiness for reading is a complex concept involving many different contributing factors and developing through the intimate interplay of learning with biological growth. It depends also, in part, on the fit between the child's abilities and the way he is taught. Thus a child of below-average intelligence may fail in a fast-moving group or succeed in a group taught slowly and patiently; and children with serious visual defects may learn to read normally if the print is made large enough.

Reading, like walking, can be mastered only after a long process of growing and learning has taken place. It is a much more complex activity than walking and requires both a much higher level of general growth and brain development and a host of specific learnings. Some of the traits involved depend primarily on the growth potentialities of the child as determined largely by constitutional makeup. Other traits, equally important, develop through learning from everyday living. The intimate interplay of inner growth and environmental stimulation is present in all aspects of child development, and readiness for reading is no exception.

Reading readiness may be defined as a state of general maturity which, when reached, allows a child to learn to read without excess difficulty. It is a composite of many interconnected traits. A child may be more advanced in some aspects of reading readiness than in others. The major characteristics that are important in reading readiness are age, sex, general intelligence, visual and auditory perception, associative learning, physical health and maturity, freedom from directional confusion, background of experience, comprehension and use of oral English, emotional and social adjustment, and interest in reading. These are discussed below in the order in which they have just been listed.

The Age Factor

In most school systems children are accepted into the first grade once a year, and there is a minimum age limit. The entering class is likely to vary almost a full year in age, from the child just barely old enough to the child who was almost old enough the year before. If the minimum entering age is 5 years 9 months, the age difference of almost a year between youngest and oldest amounts to about 16 per cent. Such a difference in chronological age is highly significant because general development takes place rapidly during this period, and a difference of 10 per cent or more in age between two children is likely to be accompanied by important differences in the levels of physical, intellectual, linguistic, and emotional maturity attained.

Age is of significance, not in itself, but because of the changes that take place as children get older. A mature younger child will learn faster than an immature older child. Wide differences in achievement are found, whether reading is taught at age 5 as in Scotland, at age 6 as in the United States, or at age 7 as in Sweden. Age is, therefore, a convenient but very inaccurate way of determining when children are ready for reading; it has the practical advantage of being completely objective and impartial in its application and is therefore favored by many school administrators.

The Sex Factor

Girls tend to become ready for reading a little earlier than boys, and at the same age fewer girls are low in reading readiness. Girls tend to reach puberty about one and a half years earlier than boys, and throughout childhood there are detectable differences in physiological maturity, as shown by age of eruption of teeth and X-ray studies of bone development. Girls tend to begin to talk earlier than boys, have larger vocabularies, and do more talking (McCarthy, 1953). Girls spend more time in sedentary activities that have some relationship to schoolwork. Girls tend to make higher average reading scores in the primary grades, and a much smaller proportion develop reading disabilities; they constitute about one-third of the milder cases and between 10 and 25 per cent of the severe cases.

Sex differences in readiness as shown by tests, however, tend to be small and do not always favor girls. In the combined Cooperative First-Grade Studies, the average for girls was higher than the average for boys on five of seven readiness tests (Bond and Dykstra, 1967). In the CRAFT Project, a large-scale study of disadvantaged urban black children, the boys had slightly higher means on three readiness measures and the girls on three other readiness tests; however, the girls were slightly ahead in reading by the end of second grade and increased their lead in third grade (A. J. Harris, Morrison, Serwer, and Gold, 1968). It would seem possible, therefore, that sex differences in reading achievement are due more to school-related factors than to biological factors.

Intellectual Factors

General Intelligence. The most important factor in reading readiness is general intelligence, which, being an average of many phases of mental growth, is significantly related to most of the other factors. The results of tests of general intelligence for children are usually expressed in terms of Mental Age (MA) and Intelligence Quotient (IQ). Saying that a child has an MA of 6 years 0 months means that his score on a particular intelligence test is equal to the average score of children who are exactly 6 years old. The MA is a measure of degree or level of mental maturity that tends to increase steadily as the child gets older, until mid-adolescence. The IQ is a measure of brightness or rate of mental growth and tends to remain fairly stable as children get older, although marked changes happen occasionally. About 50 per cent of children fall within the average IQ range of 90-110, while about 25 per cent are bright (110 and above) and 25 per cent are dull or slow (below 90). Of the two measures, the MA tends to give the better short-range prediction of performance during the next few months, while the IQ gives the better long-range prediction.

It is generally recognized that the IQ is influenced by environmental factors as well as by heredity, although the argument about the relative importance of each continues. For children who grow up in an environment different from that of the children on whom an IQ test was standardized, the test is probably not a fair measure of brightness or potential for learning. Nevertheless, differences in IQ scores within a disadvantaged group of children can predict differences in future achievement fairly well (Lessler and Bridges, 1973). When a reading-readiness test and an intelligence test are both given at the beginning of the first grade, the readiness test usually has slightly higher correlations with reading achievement at the end of first grade; but the IQ test tends to have higher correlations with reading in higher grades.

Correlations between intelligence test scores and reading achievement in the first grade tend to be substantial in size, although not as large as in higher grades. In the Cooperative Studies of First-Grade Reading sponsored by the United States Office of Education, for example, the combined results of fifteen projects were grouped according to six methods of instruction. Correlations between raw scores on the *Pintner-Cunningham Primary Test of Mental Ability* and *Stanford* Paragraph Meaning ranged from .42 to .56, with a median of .50 (Bond and Dykstra, 1967). For an *r* of that size the forecasting efficiency of a test is 25 per cent, allowing predictions for groups, but indicating that the reading scores of individual children cannot be predicted with much accuracy.

The oft-repeated statement that a minimum mental age of 6 years is necessary for success in beginning reading is not correct. With individual instruction and much patience, even children with mental ages of 4 can learn the beginnings of reading (Davidson, 1931). What is true is that the child's intelligence is one of the main factors influencing the rate at which the child can learn to read. As Gates sensibly pointed out many years ago, if the pace of instruction is faster than the child's learning rate, failure is very probable (Gates, 1937).

The way in which mental age is related to both chronological age and IQ is shown in Table 1. If we assume that an MA of at least 6 years 0 months is desirable (although not essential) for beginning reading, a bright child with an IQ of 130 has reached it by the age of 4 years 9 months, while a dull child with an IQ of 80 does not reach it until the age of 7 years 9 months. If we assume that an MA of 5 years 0 months is sufficient, about one-quarter of beginning kindergartners (those with IQ's of 110 and up) have already reached it, while the approximately 10 per cent with IQ's below 80 are older than 6 years 3 months when they reach it. For many teachers it is difficult to realize the size and importance of such differences in mental maturity.

Durkin followed up two groups of children who learned to read before entering school and found no evidence that the experience was harmful to them. Although most of the children were bright, a few were of average intelligence and many came from working-class families. Most of them learned to read from their mothers or from playing school with an older

TABLE 1. *Reading readiness: relation of mental age to chronological age and intelligence quotient*

| | | | | Intelligence Quotient | | | |
	70	80	90	100	110	120	130
Chronological Age				Corresponding Mental Age			
4 yrs. 9 mos.	3–4	3–10	4–4	4–9	5–3	5–9	6–2
5 yrs. 3 mos.	3–8	4–2	4–9	5–3	5–9	6–4	6–10
5 yrs. 9 mos.	4–0	4–7	5–3	5–9	6–4	6–11	7–6
6 yrs. 3 mos.	4–5	5–0	5–8	6–3	6–9	7–6	8–2
6 yrs. 9 mos.	4–9	5–5	6–1	6–9	7–5	8–1	8–9
7 yrs. 3 mos.	5–1	5–10	6–6	7–3	8–0	8–8	9–5
7 yrs. 9 mos.	5–5	6–2	7–0	7–9	8–6	9–4	10–1

NOTE: *Mental ages for other chronological ages and IQ's may be computed with the formula: Mental Age = Chronological Age times IQ. One must remember that the IQ is really a decimal fraction. For example: To find the MA of a child who is 6 years 6 months old and has an IQ of 85, 78 mos. × .85 equals 66.3 mos. which equals 5 years 6 months.*

sister (Durkin, 1966). The few inner-city black children in the CRAFT Project who could recognize a few words when they entered first grade were not only superior on readiness tests, but also showed an advantage in reading scores which increased each year from first through third grade (Morrison, A. J. Harris, and Auerbach, 1971).

What this shows is that some children are ready for reading early, and when they are given an opportunity to learn to read, they do. Opinions differ on when it is advantageous to start systematic reading instruction for all children. In Great Britain it is common to begin the teaching of reading at the age of 5, while in Sweden and Russia systematic instruction starts at the age of 7. Any decision based on age rather than on the readiness of individual children is likely to delay some children unnecessarily, while finding others to be still not ready.

The fact that some children are ready to learn to read at an early age should not deflect attention from the fact that other children are lacking in reading readiness when instruction normally begins. Spache and his coworkers tested the effects of readiness programs in eight Florida counties in parallel white and black schools. Pupils in the top quarter were started on reading in September. The second quarter started reading in November, the third quarter in January, and the lowest quarter in March. Specific materials to develop visual and auditory perception skills were used flexibly in the readiness groups. The effectiveness of the readiness program appeared to increase as the ability levels of the pupils decreased. In the two lowest black quartiles, the experimental children who started reading late in the year scored higher on reading tests than the control black children who had several more months of reading instruction (Spache and others, 1966).

The following conclusions concerning the relationship of mental ability to beginning reading seem justified: 1) There is a substantial relationship between mental age and ease of learning to read; most children who fail in reading in the first grade have mental ages below 6 years. The more mature children not only learn more easily but also retain what they learn better than the less mature children. 2) Most 6-year-old children who have IQ's within or above the normal range and are free from special handicaps can be successfully taught to read in the first grade. 3) It is not possible to set a definite minimum mental age for learning to read because too many other factors are involved. Children with mental ages as low as 5 years can be taught to read first-grade materials provided that they are ready in other respects. 4) A program of systematic readiness training preceding the beginning of reading instruction enables some children to make faster and easier progress in reading when they do start, but is not needed by all children; many are ready before the first day of school. A delayed start without specific efforts to improve readiness has little to recommend it.

Specific Mental Abilities. It is natural to suppose that when children whose general intelligence seems adequate for the requirements of learning to read fail to do so, they may have some special kind of mental defect that prevents them from making progress. Intelligence tests contain many different kinds of items, and it seems possible that the child's total score might be good while he might do very poorly on some one type of question. The best available evidence indicates that in most young children such traits as memory and attention are not separate, but are closely interrelated and are not clearly distinguishable from general intelligence. It does not rule out the possibility of finding an occasional child who shows very poor memory, perceptual difficulty, inability to concentrate and pay attention, or difficulty in following directions, which is in marked contrast to otherwise satisfactory mental ability.

Visual Discrimination. Even if visual acuity is normal, the child may have immature visual perception. Seeing a thing does not always mean noticing its details. Many young children pay attention only to the main characteristics of visual stimuli—the size, shape, and color—and ignore the details. When asked to match letters or words they make many errors, not because of faulty vision, but because they do not notice differences that are obvious to older children.

Prominent among the perceptual tendencies of immature children is the tendency to make *reversal* errors. To such children, *b, d, p,* and *q* are

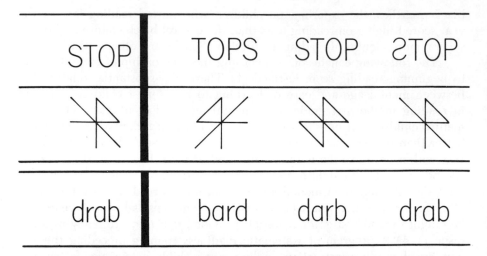

FIGURE **2.1** Samples of readiness test items for visual discrimination. The child is to mark the choice to the right of the heavy line that is the same as the stimulus on the left. Reproduced from *Metropolitan Readiness Tests*, copyright © 1965 by Harcourt, Brace and World, Inc. Reproduced by permission of the publisher; reduced in size.

the same; the differences are ignored. The letters *m* and *w* may be confused; this is an example of a vertical reversal. Pairs of words, such as *on* and *no*, *saw* and *was*, *tap* and *pat*, also tend to be confused, since the children have not yet learned to look at a word always from left to right. Studies have shown that reversal errors are very common among young children, tending to decrease as children get older, and that children with marked reversal tendencies make less than normal progress in the first grade (Potter, 1939; Goins, 1958; Jansky and De Hirsch, 1972).

Because the ability to perceive visual similarities and differences is so consistently related to progress in reading, items designed to measure this ability are found in all reading readiness tests.

Barrett (1965), in a thorough review of the value of visual perception tests in predicting first-grade reading, concluded that: 1) visual discrimination of letters and words has a somewhat higher value than visual discrimination of geometric designs and pictures; and 2) several tests that utilize geometric designs and pictures have predictive possibilities that warrant additional study.

Auditory Discrimination. Inability to distinguish between words that sound somewhat alike may prove a severe handicap in learning to read. In some children it is due to faulty hearing. In others hearing acuity may be normal, but the child has not learned to perceive the differences in the sounds of the words. Deficiency in auditory sensation or perception often results in the persistence of infantile pronounciation. If a 6-year-old still pronounces his *r*'s like *w*'s or mixes up his *th* and *v* sounds (*muvver* for *mother*), or slurs and mispronounces words of more than one syllable, the chances are good that he does not notice the difference between his pronunciation and the correct pronunciation. If a child does not notice the difference between two spoken words, he may have difficulty associating each with its visual equivalent.

Research on the significance of auditory discrimination in beginning reading was summarized by Dykstra (1966). In general, correlations with first-grade reading scores have been low to moderate. His own results showed rather low intercorrelations among seven different measures of auditory discrimination, and the highest correlations with reading were in the .40's. More recently, some higher correlations with first-grade reading have been reported (A. J. Harris and Sipay, 1970).

Deutsch (1964) found that auditory discrimination as measured by readiness tests is particularly poor among disadvantaged black children; this has been confirmed in several other studies. Linguists have pointed out that this apparent difficulty is the result of a tendency of the children to hear words as they are pronounced in black English (Baratz, 1970; Labov and Cohen, 1973). Thus many black children will report that *pin* and *pen*

FIGURE **2.2**   Samples of readiness test items for auditory discrimination. Item 2 directions: "Now, put your marker under the next row. Listen to the first sound in *bike*. I will say *bike* every time I name a picture. If the name begins with the same sound as *bike*, make a mark on the picture. "*Bike-pig.*" Pause 5–8 seconds. "*Bike-baby.*" Pause. "*Bike-rocket.*" Pause. "*Bike-boat.*" Pause. For item 13, the task is to mark the two pictures whose names rhyme with *tool*. From the *Macmillan Readiness Test*, Revised Edition, 1970, by permission of the Macmillan Publishing Co. Reduced in size.

sound the same, since there is no discernible difference in the way speakers of black English pronounce these words. Black children tend to have much difficulty distinguishing among final consonants, because their own speech has a strong tendency to diminish or completely elide such sounds. Spanish-speaking children also have difficulties with auditory discrimination of the sounds of standard English because of dialect differences. For such children, the validity of typical auditory discrimination tests is questionable.

Associative Learning. The ability to learn relatively simple associations, such as between a printed letter and its spoken name or between a printed word and its spoken equivalent, is essential to learning to read. Even with the effects of intelligence controlled, intersensory transfer (ability to match visual and auditory patterns) shows significant relationships with success in learning to read (Jones, 1972).

If a child can name many of the alphabet letters before reading instruction begins, it shows that: 1) his visual discrimination among the shapes of the letters is satisfactory; 2) he has learned the correct association between shape and letter name; 3) he has had opportunity and probably encouragement to learn these associations, at home or at school; and 4) he has had the motivation to persist with the task. It should not be a surprise, therefore, that ability to name letters has consistently ranked high among measures of reading readiness (Bond and Dykstra, 1967; Lowell, 1971). On the other hand, teaching the names of letters in kindergarten or early in first grade does not seem to improve reading scores (Samuels, 1971).

Physical Fitness

In some school systems, every child entering the first grade is given a comprehensive examination by a physician. This is a desirable practice which should be more widely followed. A school is negligent when it allows children to flounder along handicapped by physical defects that are correctible. The physical defects that interfere most frequently with beginning reading are poor vision and poor hearing. Benger (1968) found, in screening first graders for participation in a research study, that about one in eleven had a hearing deficiency while one in nine had a visual defect, all previously undetected.

Any marked departure from normal vision may give a child hazy or incorrect images when he looks at words. Few first-grade children are nearsighted, but the majority of them are farsighted and tend to outgrow the condition as they get older (Shaw, 1964). Astigmatism and poor coordination of the eyes are also common in 6-year-olds.

Judy was a total loss in the first grade. She not only failed to make any progress in reading but also was quite a nuisance in the classroom. That summer her mother took her to a reading clinic. There it was found that Judy had normal intelligence (IQ 104) but poor visual acuity. She had probably been unable to see charts or the blackboard clearly from her seat and so had missed much of the instruction. Provided with suitable glasses and given some individual help, Judy began to make good progress in reading. Judy's poor vision should have been discovered at the beginning of her year in the first grade, not at the end.

When a medical examination is not possible, an alert teacher can still notice many signs that suggest physical problems and are unfortunately overlooked very often. A child whose eyes turn pink and begin to water in the classroom may need glasses. The child who looks stupid may have a hearing defect. No child is intentionally clumsy; when motor incoordination is very marked, it may be caused by something wrong in the child's nervous system, making a neurological examination desirable. Listlessness, laziness, and lack of effort may be related to anemia, malnutrition, and endocrine disorder, or to a focal infection, such as diseased tonsils.

According to Kephart, consistent and efficient motor patterns permit a child to explore his environment and systematize his relationship to it. Perceptual data are similarly systematized by comparing them with this motoric system; babies, for example, learn up and down, near and far, from relating what they see with what happens when they reach for things. Through matching perceptual experience with motor experience, the perceptual world and motoric world of the child come into agreement, and this provides a foundation for the development of symbolic and conceptual thinking (Kephart, 1964; Dunning and Kephart, 1965).

Kephart's ideas have grown out of a background of work with brain-injured and mentally retarded children, and the degree to which they apply to children of normal intelligence is still not clear.

Lateral Dominance

One issue concerning reading about which there is still much disagreement is the importance of hand and eye dominance in relation to reading progress. This issue, a complex one, is discussed in greater detail in Chapter 11. Part of the problem lies in an ambiguous terminology. The term "mixed dominance" has been used to include three quite different conditions: directional confusion, shown in inability to identify left and right correctly; mixed or incomplete handedness, ranging from ambidexterity in which both hands seem equally proficient and are equally preferred to a partial preference for one hand; and crossed dominance, in which the preferred hand and preferred eye are on opposite sides. Evidence has been accumulating that it is a mistake to lump these three conditions together.

Directional confusion and delay in establishing a consistent preference for one hand seem to be significantly related to difficulty in learning how to read (Clark, 1970; Cohen and Glass, 1968; A. J. Harris, 1957). On the other hand, several recent studies, including the three just cited, have found no significant relationship between crossed dominance and success in reading (Stephens, Cunningham and Stigler, 1967; Robbins, 1966).

Experience

The general cultural level of a child's home is the most important determiner of the adequacy of his background of knowledge and experience. The young child whose parents are educated and cultured grows up in a home that provides many opportunities for favorable development. He is surrounded by adults who speak standard English with a rich vocabulary, and naturally he tends to develop the same kind of speech. Through trips and excursions he is provided with broadening experiences. Books and magazines in the home attract him with their bright pictures, and the stories that are read or told to him tend to develop an early interest in books and reading. Such a home is valuable in providing the child with a background of knowledge that will aid him in reading (Almy, 1949). Many children who are normal in intelligence come to school from homes that are quite lacking in intellectual stimulation. Nevertheless, it is a mistake to assume that if a child grows up in an economically poor home, he is necessarily educationally disadvantaged.

Since 1960 a greatly increased interest has been shown in educational handicaps related to economic and cultural disadvantage. Special emphasis has been placed on compensatory education for disadvantaged preschool children, mainly through the federally supported Head Start program. Preliminary evaluations indicate that effective pre-kindergarten programs can result in significant initial gains in intelligence, language proficiency, and reading readiness and that the most effective pre-kindergarten programs are those with specific and structured cognitive activities (Stanley, 1972). However, these gains tend to "wash out" or disappear during the primary grades.

Language Factors

Adequate mastery of spoken language is important for progress in reading. The major aspects of language that seem most significant in reading readiness are: 1) the child's vocabulary, which is basic both to his understanding of what is said to him and to his ability to communicate; 2) mastery of sentence structure, shown most clearly in the child's spontaneous conversation; and 3) clarity of pronunciation. Since typical first-grade reading material employs only a few hundred words and the typical 6-year-old understands the meaning of thousands of words, deficiencies in sentence structure and clarity of speech are more likely to be handicaps at the beginning level than a restricted vocabulary.

Mastery of language is dependent on many factors. The most important of these are intelligence, hearing, and home environment. The genuinely dull child is slow at learning to talk because language is a highly intellectual acquisition. There is in general a close relationship between a child's intelligence and his mastery of speech. When children of normal intelligence and background are retarded in speech it is usually because of a special handicap, such as defective hearing, or a neurological difficulty.

Labov (1973) has challenged the idea that nonstandard "black English" is less grammatical or less suitable for logical reasoning than standard English. He and other linguists (Baratz and Shuy, 1969) argue that black English is a legitimate dialect with its own rules of grammar and pronunciation. Problems arise when the teacher makes it clear that she considers such speech incorrect, and the child stops trying to communicate in class; or when teacher and child fail to understand each other because of "mismatches" between their dialects. Similar problems arise when children who know little English enter school.

Emotional and Social Maturity

The social and emotional development of first-grade children is just as varied as their mental development. Some newcomers to school are cheerful, stable, self-reliant children who fit into the new routine without difficulty. Others are very babyish. They may show immaturity in a great variety of ways: they cannot take off or put on their outer clothing; they need help in the toilet; they cannot play independently; they do not know how to get along with other children; they are extremely timid; they are too shy to open their mouths in class; they do not know what it means to take orders or obey; they are crybabies; they talk baby talk; or they try to monopolize the teacher's attention. These and many other forms of immature behavior may be found in varying degrees of severity and in many combinations. It is not uncommon to find a bright child who is quite immature in nonintellectual traits and consequently makes less progress than one would expect from his mental test scores.

Three aspects of emotional and social maturity are significant in reading readiness. The first of these is emotional stability. The unstable 6-year-old has not outgrown the emotional volatility that characterizes the child of nursery school age. Among the ways in which he may show his instability are rapid changes of mood, crying at the least provocation, and fits

of temper or tantrums. Difficulties in the home situation are usually responsible for marked instability in young children.

The ability and desire to help oneself, or self-reliance, is another aspect
of social maturity that is significant in school adjustment. Some children
have parents who wisely encourage their first fumbling efforts at feeding,
dressing, and washing themselves, choosing their playthings, and solving
their own problems. Some neglected children develop self-reliance to a
high degree through necessity. Other children are still very helpless when
they enter school, often because their mothers baby them and do everything for them.

The ability to participate actively and cooperatively in group activities
is a third extremely important aspect of social development. So much of
the learning in the primary grades is done in groups that a child who is
too shy, too restless or too antagonistic to take a normal part in group
activities is bound to miss a great deal. Children who are emotionally or
socially immature can learn to read in a classroom where the teacher makes
special adjustments for them.

Interest in Books

One of the most important aspects of readiness is the desire to learn to
read. Children who have spent many pleasurable hours listening to stories
and looking through picture books usually look forward to reading with
eager anticipation.

Children's expectations about reading are strongly influenced by what
they hear at home. In one study, 700 kindergarten children were interviewed shortly before promotion to the first grade (Brumbaugh, 1940).
More children expected reading to be hard than expected it to be easy.
Often their expectations were based on what they were told by older
brothers and sisters. Some were discouraged before they even started:
"You make mistakes and the teacher hollers at you." For a few children
who are trying to maintain a babyish dependence in their home relationships, learning to read means growing up and is therefore put off as long
as possible.

The attitudes that the child brings to the first grade are quickly modified by his experiences in school. A good first-grade program satisfies those
who expect to like reading and want to read, and changes the attitudes of
those whose attitudes are negative or indifferent.

II. METHODS FOR EVALUATING READING READINESS

In the preceding section, it was pointed out that reading readiness is a
combination of many different characteristics. Some of these can be meas-

ured by standardized tests, some can be judged from information obtained from the child's family, and some can be noted only by observing the child in his daily behavior.

Use of Intelligence Tests

Since general intelligence is the most important factor in readiness for reading, it is obvious that intelligence tests are useful for appraising certain phases of readiness to read.

Most schools rely on group intelligence tests. These tests are comparatively simple and economical. They can be given and scored by a classroom teacher and so are practical for routine use. Group intelligence tests for first-grade children are all somewhat alike. Directions are given orally, and the children indicate their answers by making marks on pictures. No reading ability is involved. Items commonly included are intended to measure such abilities as range of information, understanding of single words and sentences, memory, ability to follow directions, recognition of similarities and differences, and logical reasoning. The following group tests are recommended for use near the end of kindergarten or beginning of the first grade: the *Pintner-Cunningham Primary Test*,[1] the *Otis-Lennon Mental Ability Test, Primary I*, the *SRA Primary Mental Abilities*, the *California Test of Mental Maturity, Pre-Primary Battery*, and the *Kuhlmann-Anderson Measure of Academic Potential*, grade 1A.

In comparative studies, group tests have sometimes shown higher correlations with achievement in the first grade than individual intelligence tests. This is probably because the child's ability to conform to the group situation influences both his classroom learning and his score on a group test.

To obtain a measure of mental ability that is as nearly as possible a measure of the child's mental capacity, uninfluenced by emotional and social factors, it is necessary to use an individual intelligence test. In such a test the examiner can watch what the child is doing all the time and has a better chance to keep the child doing his best throughout the test. He can also observe the child's attentiveness, effort, or carefulness. The two individual intelligence tests most widely used for children in kindergarten or first grade are the *Revised Stanford-Binet Intelligence Scale* and the *Wechsler Intelligence Scale for Children* (WISC), which provides separate Verbal and Performance IQ's as well as a Total IQ. The *Wechsler Preschool and Primary Scale of Intelligence* (WPPSI) is gradually replacing the WISC at this level. These tests should always be administered by a person with special training; they take about 30 to 60 minutes for each child.

1. A descriptive list of all the tests mentioned in this book will be found in Appendix A.

The *Slosson Intelligence Test* is an individual test that does not require a highly trained examiner; it has sufficient agreement with the *Revised Stanford-Binet* and WISC to justify its use as a screening test.

For most schools the practical procedure, if intelligence tests are to be given to entering children, is to give a group test. The few children whose scores are quite low, or who are thought to be brighter than the test results indicate, should then be retested individually or in a small group with another test that a teacher can give. If there is still doubt about the accuracy of a child's results, or if his score is so low that special class replacement must be considered, the child should be referred to a psychological examiner for individual examination.

Tests of Specific Abilities

The *Illinois Test of Psychologinguistic Abilities*, Revised Edition (ITPA), is an individually administered test battery that attempts to provide a diagnostic analysis of a child's performance in receiving information (decoding), association, and expressing information (encoding); in three channels of communication (visual, auditory, and motor); and at two levels of organization (automatic-sequential or representational). It contains ten subtests and two optional subtests, providing a total score and twelve subscores. It has been enthusiastically welcomed by clinicians, and in the ten years following its publication in 1961, over 250 research reports appeared. Recent critical reviews by J. B. Carroll (1972) and Chase (1972) point out that the test battery is heavily loaded with vocabulary and general information, has a middle-class bias, probably taps only three or four interpretable factors, and has some subtests with rather low reliability. According to Carroll, ". . . its main contribution might be to differentiate deficits in the 'auditory' and 'visual' areas, with secondary values in cases of poor verbal expression."

The *Frostig Developmental Test of Visual Perception* (DTVP) has subtests intended to measure five aspects of visual perception: eye-hand coordination, figure-ground, form constancy, position in space, and spatial relations. The total score correlates with first-grade reading achievement almost as well as a good reading-readiness test does. However, factor-analysis studies show that the test has one main factor and possibly a second factor (Hammill, Colarusso, and Wiederholt, 1970), and follow-up studies do not show the expected relationships between specific subtests and later specific reading difficulties (Olson, 1966a). Thus the diagnostic value of differences among subtest scores is questionable; particularly in view of their rather low reliabilities (Mann, 1972).

The Behavior Tests used at the Gesell Institute have been described in detail by Ilg and Ames (1964). These individual tests include measures of writing, copying designs, completing drawings, laterality and direction-ality, visual perception, and vocabulary, and they stress clinical evaluation as well as scoring. Data showing a substantial relationship between kin-dergarten developmental ratings and educational status in the sixth grade have been presented.

The *Purdue Perceptual-Motor Survey* is a series of individually admin-istered tests of aspects of physical coordination and perceptual-motor inte-gration, considered by Kephart to be basic for the development of academic achievement (Roach and Kephart, 1966).

Reading-Readiness Tests

A number of tests are available that are designed specifically to meas-ure readiness for reading. These are similar to intelligence tests in many respects, but there are also important differences. While intelligence tests attempt to measure general mental ability, readiness tests attempt to measure the particular phases of mental functioning that are most closely related to success in reading. Some of the subtests in readiness tests are measures of acquired information, such as knowledge of the names of the letters of the alphabet.

In selecting a readiness test, attention should be paid to the following questions: 1) How good is the test's validity in terms of predicting reading achievement? This is by far the most important question. 2) Does the test have adequate reliability? For satisfactory measurement of individual chil-dren the reliability coefficient should be at least .90. 3) Are the norms satisfactory? Are they based on a sufficiently large and representative num-ber of children? Are there norms for the separate parts as well as for the total score? 4) Are the directions for administering and scoring the test clear and complete? 5) How time-consuming is the test to give and score? Tests which have parts that must be given individually to each child are generally quite time-consuming. 6) Does the test provide helpful diag-nostic information? Does it show specific weaknesses of individual chil-dren? A very large number of brief subtests is not necessarily an advantage, since the parts may be so short and unreliable as to be quite undependable measures when considered separately.

Among the many readiness tests now available, the following are rec-ommended: *Gates-MacGinitie Readiness Skills Test, Harrison-Stroud Read-ing Readiness Profiles, Macmillan Reading Readiness Test, Metropolitan Readiness Tests, Clymer-Barrett Prereading Battery,* and *Murphy-Durrell Reading Readiness Analysis.* Most of the correlations reported between total scores on these tests and reading scores at the end of first grade are between .50 and .70. Correlations of this size are substantial and allow good prediction of the rate of progress for a group, but do not provide accurate predictions for individual children. The *Monroe Reading Aptitude Tests* are very comprehensive, with seventeen subtests, but several parts require individual administration and therefore the total time required is impractical for most schools.

The *Walker Readiness Test for Disadvantaged Preschool Children* is an individually administered test taking about 10 minutes per child. It was developed to be as culture-fair as possible and was standardized on nearly 12,000 Head Start and Day Care Center children. Norms are given for six-month intervals from ages 4 to 6 years 6 months.

The *Kindergarten Evaluation of Learning Potential* (KELP) consists of lessons to be used daily in kindergarten with structured observations and a final test providing the evaluation. Further research is needed before a judgment can be made about the value of such learning-testing programs as compared with conventional readiness tests. Certainly the process is infinitely more time-consuming, but it may prove to be worth the trouble, particularly with disadvantaged children.

Although standardized readiness tests have been criticized as being biased against minority-group and disadvantaged children, one study found that the *Metropolitan Readiness Test* correlated .76 with end-of-first-grade reading scores for a population of rural first-grade children, one-third of whom were black, and continued to have good prediction for second-grade reading scores. (Lessler and Bridges, 1973). The cutoff point for failure was lower, however, than for a middle-class population. One study found that Spanish-surname children did not score higher on a Spanish translation of the *Metropolitan Readiness Test* than on the regular version (Davis and Personke, 1968), and another study found that the regular *Metropolitan* given before reading instruction had substantial predictive value for third-grade reading, for Mexican-American children (Mishra and Hurt, 1970). The case against readiness tests has been exaggerated.

Predicting Failure in Reading

There have been several efforts to develop procedures that can detect children who are likely to fail in learning to read. The emphasis is on locating children who are "at risk" and distinguishing them from children likely to succeed.

An important pioneering study was carried out by de Hirsch, Jansky, and Langford (1966). Starting with 39 tests given individually to kindergarten children, they used failure by the end of the second grade as the main criterion. In their first study they developed a Screening Index of 10 tests which predicted the failures among a middle-class population quite well. In a second study, in which disadvantaged children were also used, they cut the Screening Index to 5 tests: Letter Naming, Picture Naming,

Gates Word Matching, Bender Gestalt, and Binet Sentence Memory (Jansky and de Hirsch, 1972). This Index predicted failure for 77 per cent of the children who did fail, and for 19 per cent of those who passed. They also developed a Diagnostic Battery of 19 tests covering 4 factors determined by factor analysis: visuo-motor organization, oral language, pattern matching, and pattern memory.

The original Predictive Index has been compared with the *Metropolitan Readiness Tests* in two studies. In one study in which reading tests were given late in the first grade, the two procedures did not differ significantly in predictive power; the *Metropolitan* correctly classified 89 per cent of the children while the Predictive Index correctly classified 87 per cent (Zaeske, 1970). Using end-of-second-grade reading test results, the Predictive Index did slightly better than the *Metropolitan* in identifying future failures, but the authors doubted that the slight increase in accuracy justified the expense of individual testing (Askov, Otto, and Smith, 1972). Jansky has recommended that the Predictive Index be used with a flexible pass-fail cutoff that depends on local school standards, and in conjunction with teachers' ratings.

McLeod developed a *Dyslexia Schedule* of 23 items based mainly on parents' reports of the child's preschool experience and history. This identified 20 or 23 dyslexic children and only one of 23 nondyslexic children, in Australia (McLeod, 1966).

Hoffman (1971) developed a Learning Problem Indication Index by comparing parental information on the early development of 100 children with severe learning disabilities, and 200 controls. Large differences were found on the following items: difficult delivery, prolonged labor, cyanosis, prematurity, blood incompatibility, adoption, late or abnormal creeping, late walking, tiptoe walking for more than one month, late or abnormal speech, and ambidexterity after age 7. A criterion of two or more signs was present for 72 per cent of the disability group and only 6.5 per cent of the controls. It seems evident that this Index selects mainly children whose learning problems have neurological correlates.

Banks developed a Kindergarten Behavioral Index (KBI) based on a follow-up study of 2,304 Australian children. Out of 63 items tried, 37 differentiated poor readers from good readers. These 37 items, which are reproduced in Figure 2.3, "represent a diffuse syndrome of developmental functions involving sensori-motor abilities, language, perception, cognitive abilities, social attributes, and behavioral patternings" (Banks, 1970). In two samples, a cutoff score of more than three checks correctly identified 78 and 82 per cent of those who became poor readers in first grade, and mis-identified 15.5 and 10 per cent of the successful readers. The Banks KBI seems quite promising as a screening instrument. It is also a practical instrument, as it can be filled out by a kindergarten teacher near the end

Kindergarten Behavioural Index

Enid M. Banks

INDIVIDUAL RECORD

Name ....

Date of Birth................................... Age .... Date of Recording.............................

☐   1   Does not know own age
☐   2   Is ambidextrous—uses left hand for some activities, right hand for others
☐   3   Puts shoes on wrong feet
☐   4   Has difficulty in hopping, changing from one foot to another
☐   5   Reverses letters and numbers when copying or writing
☐   6   Slow and fumbling putting on shoes, coat, etc.
☐   7   Has difficulty doing up buttons
☐   8   Clumsy—trips over, bumps into, knocks over, objects
☐   9   Holds pencil awkwardly
☐ 10   Has difficulty controlling pencil—presses hard—messy work
☐ 11   Cannot keep within lines when colouring in
☐ 12   Has difficulty using scissors
☐ 13   Lacks sense of rhythm—keeping in time with music in running, clapping, etc.
☐ 14   Has difficulty pronouncing all sounds, e.g. 'wed'–'red', 'fink'–'think', 'muver'–'mother', etc.
☐ 15   Uses 'baby talk', e.g. 'me'–'I', 'runned'–'ran', 'dood'–'did'
☐ 16   Lacks verbal fluency—speaks mainly in words or phrases
☐ 17   Mixes up words, e.g. 'applepine' for 'pineapple'
☐ 18   Mixes up order of words in a sentence
☐ 19   Stutters
☐ 20   Has difficulty ordering thoughts when describing or discussing a topic
☐ 21   Loses main thread and goes into irrelevant details when telling a story or talking
☐ 22   Forgets an instruction or message and has to ask again
☐ 23   Cannot write own name correctly from memory
☐ 24   Has difficulty remembering poems, rhymes, etc.
☐ 25   Cannot count up to 20
☐ 26   Confuses names of colours
☐ 27   Avoids talking in front of class
☐ 28   Cries easily
☐ 29   Appears to be shy
☐ 30   Daydreams
☐ 31   Slow in carrying out commands
☐ 32   Overactive—always on the move
☐ 33   Has difficulty sitting still for very long
☐ 34   Fidgets with things
☐ 35   Lacks concentration—does not pay attention
☐ 36   Loses interest quickly—moves from one activity to another
☐ 37   Frequently loses belongings
☐   TOTAL

Comments..
....
....

Published by Australian Council for Educational Research, Frederick Street, Hawthorn, Victoria 3122.
Copyright © Enid M. Banks 1972.

FIGURE 2.3   The Banks Kindergarten Behavioral Index, reproduced by permission of *The Slow Learning Child* and Enid M. Banks.

of the year, or by a first-grade teacher three or four weeks after the beginning of the school year. A follow-up study of the children tested by Banks has shown that the KBI has a substantial correlation with failure in grades 1–4 (J. Miles, Foreman, and Anderson, 1973).

It may be noted that the more efficiently a teacher helps a child to improve his readiness for reading, the more inaccurate a low readiness score will be. The presence of children who succeed in learning to read despite predicted failure may show good teaching rather than a shortcoming in the test. Similarly, when children do well on a readiness test but subsequently fail to learn to read, poor instruction rather than inaccurate measurement may be responsible. This applies to any measure of reading readiness.

Teacher Judgment

Teachers have always tended to form judgments about the rate of progress different pupils would achieve. With the development of standardized intelligence and reading-readiness tests, some first-grade teachers have become hesitant to trust their own opinions about pupils. The judgment of a reasonably competent teacher who has had a few weeks in which to observe the daily behavior of her pupils is by no means to be disregarded.

This should not be taken to mean that all teachers are perfect judges or that tests are useless. The tests provide the teacher with a quick, convenient, standardized basis for judging the status of the children in certain highly important intellectual abilities. They help the teacher to locate quickly most of the pupils who require further careful study. When test results and teacher observations agree, the teacher naturally feels more confident in her opinion; when they disagree, the need for further consideration is shown. Moreover, there are some aspects of reading readiness that tests do not measure, for which teacher judgment, based on observation and interviews, is needed.

It is comparatively easy to form a general overall impression of a child. It is somewhat more difficult, but also more rewarding, to try to analyze the child's strong and weak points. The teacher who does that can determine what specific handicaps may interfere with the child's progress and in many instances can take measures to strengthen the weak abilities.

Two validated forms for recording teachers' judgments about children's readiness for reading are the Banks KBI, discussed above, and the Rating Scale which is Test 1 of the *Macmillan Reading Readiness Test*. The latter has shown high correlations with total readiness test scores and substantial correlation (.44 to .55 in different groups) with reading scores at the end of first grade (A. J. Harris, 1966b; A. J. Harris and Sipay, 1970).

Whether the teacher records her opinions on a form or keeps them in her head, it is advisable for her to reconsider them and revise the ratings that are no longer correct. Many changes will result from growth or improvement in the pupils. Some changes may involve the revision of an opinion that proved to be incorrect. By amending her ratings as the children overcome or outgrow their difficulties, the teacher can keep track of the progress of her pupils and at any time can get a bird's-eye view of her readiness problems.

Planning the Evaluation of Reading Readiness

Many schools routinely test all children for readiness. Although it is possible to give the tests near the end of the kindergarten year and might be advantageous to do so in some schools, it is ordinarily better to wait until the children are in first grade, especially if a substantial number of children enter school without having attended kindergarten. The best time is usually two or three weeks after the beginning of the school year. This allows time for the children to get accustomed to classroom activities and teacher directions and at the same time is early enough to make the results useful in decisions about such matters as how to group the children and when to start reading.

For this testing either a group intelligence test or a group readiness test can be used. Not more than ten or twelve first-grade children should be tested as a group, so arrangements need to be made to take care of part of the class while the rest are being tested. The test should be administered by the teacher or a person known to the children, and the directions in the manual should be followed as exactly as possible. After the test papers have been scored, at least a sampling of them should be rescored by another person, since scoring errors are made with deplorable frequency even by experienced scorers.

Using the test results in combination with the teacher's observations, an estimate of each child's readiness can be made which will prove accurate in most cases. If the test and teacher judgment disagree, further study of the child is needed and further testing may be arranged. Individual testing by a school psychologist is desirable for children whose scores on two or more group tests are very low.

III. DEVELOPMENT OF READING READINESS

Reading readiness is best developed in a class atmosphere that provides optimum conditions for physical, intellectual, and social development. There should be a rich variety of stimulating and informative experiences which encourage children to look and listen attentively and to express their thoughts and feelings in many ways.

In a first-grade class some children are usually ready for reading before the year begins (a few may have already learned to read), others are nearly ready and can benefit from spending a few weeks in readiness activities, and a small number are so immature that they may not become fully ready until quite a long time later.

The particular kinds of readiness that need greatest emphasis will vary from one group of children to another. The extent to which experiential and ideational enrichment is needed tends to vary with the social and economic background of the children; the more underprivileged they are, the more enrichment is likely to be needed. Language development is particularly important to those whose language or dialect interferes with communication between them and the teacher. Practice to improve visual and auditory discrimination is usually necessary. The left-to-right progression requires more emphasis with some children than with others.

Many aspects of a well-rounded kindergarten program have some value in building readiness for reading. In such a program the child engages in both group and individual activities. Eyes and hands are trained through work with blocks, clay, crayons, paint, scissors, weaving, and so on. Language growth is stimulated in many ways, including listening to stories, discussing experiences, conversation, "show and tell," rhymes and poetry, and dramatization. New ideas and concepts are introduced through many kinds of experiences, including trips and visits. Among the very important social learnings are learning to live in a group, to take one's turn, to curb one's temper, to listen attentively, to follow directions.

Within this framework it is possible to incorporate activities planned to develop specific aspects of readiness in which growth may be needed. Table 2 takes up the various aspects of reading readiness discussed earlier in this chapter, lists for each aspect the kinds of evidence that point to a need for improvement, and provides a few practical suggestions concerning what can be done to foster progress. More detailed descriptions of readiness activities can be found in the references listed at the end of this chapter.

Reading-Readiness Workbooks

In a readiness program the teacher's task can be lightened somewhat by making use of readiness workbooks. Every modern set of primary readers now has at least one readiness workbook, with an accompanying teacher's guide or manual containing suggested lesson plans. These workbooks provide colorful, interesting pictures which can serve as a basis for description, discussion, storytelling, and learning new concepts and vocabulary. They also contain graded series of exercises for making comparisons, noting

TABLE 2.   *Reading-readiness handicaps and their correction*

Handicap	*Evidence of handicap*	*Helpful procedures*
Low in general intelligence	MA is below 5–0	Mental age will increase steadily as child gets older.
	IQ is below 90	If child has been handicapped by poor environment, sometimes shows increase in IQ with good schooling.
	Seems lacking in curiosity Ideas seem vague and confused Comprehension is poor Range of information is poor Unable to give explanations Language development is retarded	If MA below 5–0 or IQ below 80, may take a year or more to become ready for reading instruction. Reading readiness program leading into slow, gradual reading program with continuing readiness work.
Poor memory	Forgets instructions	Give motive for wanting to remember; send on errands with oral messages.
	Unable to recall events of story	Tell a simple story; ask child to retell the story after other children have done the same.
	Memory span below 4 digits or words Poor memory for visual details Memory is tested in various ways in the ITPA and *Detroit Tests of Learning Aptitude*	Play memory games: One child says something, second tries to repeat it; if correct, he takes lead. Several objects on table. Child who is "it" turns back, tries to tell which one was removed. Have children inspect picture. Remove picture, ask for list of things in the picture.
Inability to follow directions	Needs repetition of directions Becomes confused if given more than one direction at a time	Give directions slowly and clearly. Gain the child's attention before starting. Have him repeat them.

TABLE 2. *Reading-readiness handicaps and their correction (Continued)*

Handicap	Evidence of handicap	Helpful procedures
	Look for evidence of low intelligence, language handicap, or poor hearing Difficulty in following directions on any readiness or intelligence test	Play "following directions" games. At first, give one direction at a time, then two, then three. Allow children to take turns in giving directions for games and other classroom activities.
Poor attention	Does not listen when directions are given Tires of an activity quickly Is very distractible Seems dreamy, absorbed in own thoughts	Check for possible hearing difficulty. Watch for signs of restlessness and change to another activity. For individual activities, give a seat away from other children. Give opportunity to tell his stories and ideas. In general, provide interesting activities. Children are attentive when their interest is aroused.
Poor visual perception	Insensitive to similarities and differences in pictures, words, letters Draws and copies drawings poorly All readiness tests contain subtests to measure visual discrimination *Frostig Developmental Test of Visual Perception*	Check for possible visual difficulty. Practice in clay modeling, drawing, cutting around outlines. Assembling picture puzzles. Finding missing parts in pictures. Describing pictures in detail. Exercises for noting visual similarities and differences, such as those in reading readiness workbooks: use letters, words. If very poor, use kinesthetic procedures.
Poor auditory perception	Seems to have poor hearing but does well on hearing test	Provide a good model of speech.

TABLE 2. *Reading-readiness handicaps and their correction (Continued)*

Handicap	Evidence of handicap	Helpful procedures
	Speech is indistinct or defective	Encourage accurate pronunciation. See suggestions under "Defective speech" below.
	Does not recognize rhymes	Much use of rhymes, jingles, poems, and songs.
	Is insensitive to similarities and differences in word beginnings or word endings	Call child's attention to the difference between two words which he confuses.
	Cannot recognize (or blend) a word if it is sounded out	Play "word family" games. One child says a word; the next child has to say a word which begins (or ends) the same way.
	Tests of auditory discrimination are included in many reading-readiness tests	Say a list of words. Have child listen for the one that does not sound like the others. Many teachers do much of their training in auditory or phonic readiness after the children have begun to read.
Poor general health	One or more of these: overweight; underweight; pale, looks anemic; listless; tires easily; frequent colds; mouth breather; poor posture; other signs of poor health	Recommend a thorough medical examination. Take special precautions to avoid strain and fatigue for frail or sickly children. Give rest period. Discuss with mother the child's eating and sleeping habits.
	Report from physician or nurse	Check up to see if defects are corrected.
Physical immaturity	Child is very short for age	In some cases where evidence of endocrine deficiency is present, medical treatment speeds up growth.
	Child looks much younger than his age	Child should not be teased or made to feel conspicuous.

TABLE 2.   *Reading-readiness handicaps and their correction (Continued)*

Handicap	Evidence of handicap	Helpful procedures
		If child is generally immature, retention in kindergarten may be advisable.

Poor vision	Does poorly on vision tests
	Teacher observes that:
	  eyes tear or become bloodshot
	  child squints or closes one eye to see better
	  gets close to board or chart to see
	  complains of headaches
		Refer for eye examination. If glasses are needed, see that they are obtained and used. Orthoptic training is sometimes needed.
		Place in a favorable seat.
		If difficulty is severe, sight-saving activities and materials may be necessary.

Poor hearing	Does poorly on audiometer test
	Teacher notes that child:
	  has a chronic ear infection
	  seems inattentive
	  misunderstands directions
	  asks to have statements repeated
	  comprehends better in conversation than at usual classroom distances
		Refer to an ear specialist or hospital clinic.
		Give child a favorable seat.
		Speak distinctly to the child.
		Speech training or lip reading may be needed.
		Emphasize visual approach in reading.
		Poor hearing is no reason for delay in starting reading, unless other handicaps are present.

Poor coordination	Clumsy: poor at walking, running, skipping, hopping, dancing, climbing stairs, throwing, catching Often drops and spills things Poor hand-eye control in using scissors, crayon, pencil Neurological examination	Be patient; clumsiness and slowness are not intentional. Lack of coordination may be a sign of a neurological difficulty. Refer for medical examination. Rhythmical games to music: dancing, skipping, etc., Rhythm band. Show careful ways of holding objects.

TABLE 2. *Reading-readiness handicaps and their correction (Continued)*

Handicap	Evidence of handicap	Helpful procedures
		Simple types of handiwork: cutting, pasting, coloring, clay or plasticine, weaving, construction.
		Use of manipulative toys: pegboards, form boards, etc.
Different cultural background	Parents are undereducated Only foreign language is spoken at home Low priority placed on education Home is lacking in common cultural assets: telephone, radio, magazines, books, television, etc.	If possible, encourage parents to take adult education courses. Provide a good model. Give rich oral language activities (see below). Explain to parents the desirability of child's hearing and speaking English at home. Provide rich, varied experiences (see below).
Meager background of experience	Child's experience is confined to his own neighborhood Common concepts unknown Unacquainted with traditional rhymes and stories Range of information very limited Does poorly on information and vocabulary tests	Plan a sequence of visits: the school itself, stores, fire station and other points of interest in the neighborhood, more distant parts of the community, the zoo, a farm, etc. Develop new concepts and vocabulary during the trip and in subsequent discussion. Make use of pictures and film strips. Provide rich experiences in the classroom. Encourage children to bring pets and possessions to school, sharing experiences. Have appropriate, simple units of activity. Read and tell stories and poems to children. Children retell and dramatize stories.

TABLE 2. *Reading-readiness handicaps and their correction (Continued)*

Handicap	Evidence of handicap	Helpful procedures
Limited vocabulary	Limited comprehension Has difficulty finding words to express his ideas; uses circumlocutions Nearly all readiness and intelligence tests contain vocabulary subtests	Vocabulary develops normally out of rich, varied experiences (see above). Acting games. Teacher says a sentence, children (taking turns) act it out. Different games can be played in which children act out nouns (animals, etc.), verbs (walk, run, hop), adverbs (quickly, quietly), prepositions (under, behind, in). Pictures are used for introducing new concepts. Children list all the words they know of one type (toys, pets, flowers, etc.). Those not generally known are described and illustrated.
Limited use of standard English	Speaks in one or two words, or in fragmentary sentences Uses immature speech forms ("I runned" etc.) Uses awkward or confused word order	Put child's idea into a complete sentence, have him repeat it. Praise for ideas and imitation of teacher's sentence. Provide opportunities for natural growth in language ability through free conversation, group discussions, "telephone conversations," "radio broadcasts," composing group stories, telling experiences, dramatization of stories.
	Uses nonstandard speech forms which are characteristic of his cultural background	Respect and accept child's language. Convey idea that "street talk" and "school talk" are both good and one needs to know both. Develop comprehension of standard English through storytelling and reading to children, talking slowly, pointing out different ways of saying same idea.

TABLE 2.   *Reading-readiness handicaps and their correction (Continued)*

Handicap	Evidence of handicap	Helpful procedures
Defective speech	Speaks too fast, runs words together Lisping Baby talk; defective pronunciation of consonant sounds Marked hesitation, stammer, or stutter	Speak slowly and distinctly to children. Encourage child to take his time. Promote relaxation. Lisping is normal in children who have lost front baby teeth. If marked, defective pronunciation requires special training in production of speech sounds. Mild cases usually clear up without special attention. Stuttering is a problem for a speech correctionist or psychologist. Classroom teacher should encourage relaxation, rhythmical activity, freedom from strain.
Emotional immaturity	May be shown in: excessive shyness, timidity, self-consciousness quick temper, tantrums stubbornness, negativism extreme restlessness extreme sensitivity; crybaby specific nervous habits poor concentration	Do not rush timid child into group activities; give him time to become used to school. Remove overexcited, rebellious, stubborn, or angry child from group temporarily; provide a quiet individual activity. Teacher should show warmth, liking for the child, appreciation. Severe cases of emotional instability should be referred to a psychologist or mental hygiene clinic.
Lack of self-reliance	Child makes excessive requests for help	Encourage child to try to do things. Provide help and support when needed. Praise generously for effort.

TABLE 2.   *Reading-readiness handicaps and their correction (Continued)*

Handicap	Evidence of handicap	Helpful procedures
	Child gives up quickly when he meets difficulties	Build self-confidence through experience of success in a graded series of activities, starting with very easy ones.
Poor group participation	Child is bossy; picks fights and quarrels Submissive, shy, afraid to speak up Unable to wait for his turn	Remove from group temporarily. Explain standards for group behavior calmly and patiently. Praise generously any slight improvement. Ask the child easy questions. Praise generously. If too shy to talk in front of group, allow to recite to teacher privately. Encourage participation in puppetry.
Bad family situation	Interview with mother or older children in family. Look for evidence of: Poor discipline—too harsh, too lax, or inconsistent Quarreling and dissension Child is unloved Child is overprotected	When family situation is very bad, parents should be encouraged to seek help of a social service agency or mental hygiene clinic. Some mothers are receptive to tactfully given suggestions concerning discipline and child management.
Lack of interest in reading	Child seems restless, uninterested, when teacher reads or tells stories Child shows no interest in books or in learning to read	Language may be too difficult or ideas too strange for child's comprehension. Vary the type and difficulty of stories. Provide library table with interesting picture and storybooks. Read stories from books in class library. Have a bulletin board. Post simple notices, etc. Build simple reading stories from children's own experiences. Praise generously the first signs of interest or attempts to read.

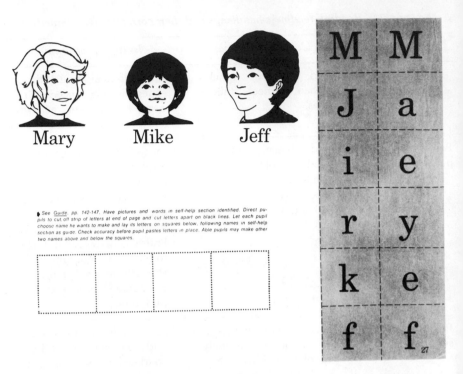

Mary   Mike   Jeff

▶ See *Guide*, pp. 142-147. Have pictures and words in self-help section identified. Direct pupils to cut off strip of letters at end of page and cut letters apart on black lines. Let each pupil choose name he wants to make and lay its letters on squares below, following names in self-help section as guide. Check accuracy before pupil pastes letters in place. Able pupils may make other two names above and below the squares.

FIGURE 2.4 An exercise combining word discrimination, letter matching, practice in left-to-right sequence, and development of fine motor coordination through cutting and pasting. Reproduced from *Teacher's Annotated Edition and Guide to Accompany WE BEGIN*, the readiness book of the Macmillan Reading Program, Revised Edition, 1974, by permission of the Macmillan Publishing Co. Reduced in size.

similarities and differences, and learning to observe in a left-to-right direction. The newer readiness workbooks tend to stress visual discrimination of letters and later of words, and auditory discrimination of words and of sounds within words, such as initial consonants and rhyming endings. Letter names are also taught in some workbooks.

No materials can be expected to produce miracles in slow-maturing children, even though specific, well-planned learning experiences can help somewhat. Furthermore, a readiness program can fulfill only a few of its many aims by relying on a workbook. These materials are useful, but only as a part of a rich and varied program. The suggestions for supplementary and enrichment readiness activities in the teacher's guides for some readiness books can be very helpful to teachers. Teachers must avoid the temptation to let the workbook carry the full instructional load.

There is some evidence that use of a workbook for certain specific readiness objectives may be more efficient than teacher-planned lessons based on the same objectives. Hillerich (1965) found that learning to use initial-consonant associations and context was more effective with a workbook than without one and lasted over the summer; also, children who received formal readiness work in kindergarten were better readers at the end of first grade than children who did not have such training.

Special Readiness Procedures

Kephart, developing his principles out of a background of work with brain-injured children, has emphasized the desirability of helping children to achieve mastery over basic perceptual-motor skills as a prerequisite for academic learning. His program involves practice in coordinated acts such as hopping, skipping, and balancing while walking on a narrow plank, training to improve laterality and directionality, and training in ocular control and visual perception (Kephart, 1960; Ebersole, Kephart, and Ebersole, 1968).

Klesius (1972) reviewed 38 studies investigating the influence of perceptual-motor development programs of the Kephart type, of which 11 met his criteria for acceptable research; in 6 of these no significant differences were found, and in 5, there were significantly greater gains in the experimental than in the control groups. He concluded: "The hypothesis that perceptual-motor development programs positively influence reading achievement can neither be confirmed nor denied on the basis of the research reviewed here."

The *Frostig-Horne Program for the Development of Visual Perception* (published by Follett) provides practice in the five aspects of visual perception measured by the Frostig tests, supplemented by directions for physical exercises similar to those recommended by Kephart. The Frostig program has been widely used in preschool and first-grade programs, and numerous research studies on its effectiveness have been carried out with Head Start, kindergarten, and first-grade children. Two recent analyses of this literature (H. M. Robinson, 1972; Wiederholt and Hammill, 1971) conclude that in general the Frostig training program produces improved scores on the Frostig tests; sometimes, but not always, produces improvement on reading-readiness tests; and usually fails to do better than, and sometimes does not do as well as, conventional readiness and beginning reading programs. "The use of this program as a supplement to traditional readiness activities or as a method to facilitate the mastery of reading or arithmetic does not appear to be warranted" (Wiederholt and Hammill, 1971).

Training in visual and auditory perception was emphasized years ago by Durrell and Murphy (1953) as important for first-grade reading success and now forms an important part of the readiness procedures of most basal reader programs. It seems probable that when this perceptual training uses letter and word forms, and spoken words from the beginning reading vocabulary, its transfer value to reading is enhanced. It is doubtful that intensive auditory discrimination training beyond what is provided in conventional programs benefits early reading attainment for most children, although it can improve auditory discrimination scores (Jeffares-Fast and Cosens, 1970). McNeil (1967) found that Mexican-American and black children trained to hear phonemes within words did show some gain in reading, however.

Special emphasis on language enrichment has not shown a real advantage in reading readiness work with disadvantaged children. Use of the *Peabody Language Development Kit* has been found to improve some language skills of disadvantaged children but does not improve reading performance in the primary grades (Dunn, Pochanart, Pfost, and Bruininks, 1968). A kindergarten program intended to improve black children's mastery of speaking as well as listening to standard English did not show an advantage in readiness scores over a program confined to listening (Strickland, 1973a). It would seem to be common sense that improving the language proficiency of children should benefit their reading, but each technique for doing so needs to be evaluated carefully.

In general, the research reviewed above is in harmony with long-established findings about transfer of training, which have shown that the more closely a learning activity resembles the activity to which transfer of learning is desired, the more likely it is for useful transfer to take place. Thus visual discrimination practice using letters and words is more transferable to reading than discrimination of geometric forms. Auditory discrimination of words and phonemes is more transferable to reading than discrimination of nonverbal sounds. The transfer to reading of gaining skill in large-muscle and small-muscle activities is doubtful. Developing listening comprehension seems more relevant to reading than becoming a competent speaker of standard English is. Viewed in the light of transfer, the research on what pays off in readiness training makes sense.

Reading Readiness and Beginning Reading

Beginning reading can be started quite gradually and informally with children who do not seem to be ready; this is preferable to complete postponement. Labels can be placed on each child's desk, chair, coat hook, and so on. Colorful pictures can be displayed, with a brief title below each. A bulletin board can be kept with weather reports, special events, and messages for individual children, which can be read to them if they cannot do the reading themselves. Informal experience stories provide an interesting and easy introduction to reading (see p. 67) and can be used with all the children. Gradually the immature ones begin to recognize some words, and this indicates that they are becoming ready. Meanwhile, they have had the feeling of being part of the reading program and not having been excluded from reading. Readiness activities can go on after as well as before these reading activities begin.

Recent research does not give a blanket endorsement to readiness practice in kindergarten, but specific kinds of readiness activities that are directly related to the reading methodology to be used later may be beneficial. There seems to be no good reason to exclude systematically planned reading-readiness activities from the kindergarten, and many schools, particularly in suburban areas with advantaged populations, have moved the readiness program from the beginning of first grade to the latter part of the kindergarten.

The question of whether or not to begin reading instruction before first grade is equally complicated. As was shown earlier in this chapter, children with IQ's of 110 and over (comprising about 25 per cent of the child population) all have mental ages over 5 years when they begin kindergarten, and most of the 10 per cent with IQ's of 120 or over have mental ages of 6 years or over at kindergarten entrance. However, some of them have good perceptual and memory abilities and probably could master reading easily during that year, while others may have specific immature abilities that would seriously hold down their learning rates. Prediction of individual success in beginning reading cannot be done accurately in first grade; it should be considerably less accurate a year earlier. Thus, an early start may succeed very well with some children, while exposing others to early and unnecessary failure. Such decisions should be made on an individual basis in which the interest as well as the maturity of the child is taken into consideration.

The notion that when children do not seem to be ready one should just wait until they show a spontaneous desire to begin reading has unduly delayed the start of reading for many children. Similarly, there is little justification for an extended readiness period for those who are definitely quite ready. Much of the criticism of the readiness idea in recent years has been due to unnecessary delays in the beginning of systematic instruction. The combination of the improvement of beginning reading materials with improved methods of instruction, aided perhaps by the stimulating effect of television, makes extended delays less necessary than they seemed twenty years ago.

A special kind of class called a "transition class," for first-grade entrants who are quite lacking in readiness, was tried out successfully in some large cities around 1940 but has not been widely adopted. Such a class should have a specially trained teacher, be limited in size, and have a carefully planned readiness program leading gradually into reading. In such a class the majority usually are promoted to first grade, while some do so well that they can enter second grade after it. The transition class as a way of providing for unready children has been strongly recommended by Ilg and Ames (1964), who found a large percentage of middle-class children to be lacking in some aspects of readiness, although of at least average intelligence. In our opinion, the transition class deserves a wider tryout.

An alternative for children whose IQ is normal or higher, but who seem unready for reading in certain respects, is to organize special first-grade classrooms for them in which reading is taught by methods similar to those used with severe-reading-disability cases. East (1969) reported a third-grade follow-up on children with a mean IQ of 110 who had been placed in Specific Language Disability first grades in Renton, Washington, and taught by the Slingerland adaptation of the Orton-Gillingham methods (for description, see Chap. 15). By the end of third grade this group achieved as well in reading as a control group of equivalent age, sex, and IQ. The criteria for placement in the special classes were not specified.

Systematic reading instruction for all kindergartners, as Brzeinski and Elledge (1972) advocate, probably benefits the many who are ready before the end of the kindergarten year, but probably makes it even harder for those who are lacking in readiness or desire to read. For the latter group, reading instruction before first grade does not make sense. In the present state of partial knowledge, a good case can be made for either of two alternatives for such children: 1) a somewhat delayed start in reading, with specific training in areas of readiness in which needs are evident; and 2) slow, careful reading instruction which includes much readiness development as part of the reading program. Ollila (1972) concluded, after reviewing the evidence on teaching four- and five-year-olds to read, that the whole issue of early reading remains unsolved. A definitive statement on this issue does not seem justified at this moment.

SUGGESTED ADDITIONAL READING

BOND, GUY L. & WAGNER, EVA BOND. *Teaching the child to read* (4th ed.). New York: Macmillan, 1966. Chap. 2.

DALLMAN, MARTHA; ROUCH, ROGER L.; CHANG, LYNETTE Y. C.; & DEBOER, JOHN J. *The teaching of reading* (4th ed.). New York: Holt, Rinehart and Winston, 1974. Chaps. 4A, 4B.

DURKIN, DOLORES. *Teaching them to read* (2nd ed.). Boston: Allyn and Bacon, 1974. Chaps. 5, 6, 7.

HARRIS, ALBERT J. & SIPAY, EDWARD R. (Eds.). *Readings on reading instruction* (2nd ed.). New York: McKay, 1972. Chap. 3.

HEILMAN, ARTHUR W. *Principles and practices of teaching reading* (3rd ed.). Columbus: Charles E. Merrill, 1972. Chap. 4.

RUDDELL, ROBERT B. *Reading-language instruction: innovative practices.* Englewood Cliffs, N.J.: Prentice-Hall, 1974. Chap. 4.

SMITH, NILA B. *Reading instruction for today's children.* Englewood Cliffs, N.J.: Prentice-Hall, 1963. Chaps. 15, 16.

TINKER, MILES A. & MCCULLOUGH, CONSTANCE M. *Teaching elementary reading* (3rd ed.). New York: Appleton-Century-Crofts, 1968. Chaps. 3, 4, 5.

3

Beginning Reading Instruction

Over a half century ago, the National Committee on Reading issued a report in which the process of learning to read was categorized in five stages, a classification that remains useful: 1) readiness for reading, 2) beginning to read, 3) rapid development of reading skills, 4) wide reading, and 5) refinement of reading (W. S. Gray, 1925). Reading readiness has been discussed in Chapter 2, and the last three stages will be described in Chapter 4. In this chapter, which is concerned with the crucially important stage of beginning reading, a brief historical review of past methods is followed by a discussion of current beginning reading approaches, an evaluative comparison of these approaches, and programs for educationally disadvantaged children. The possible contributions of linguistics and psycholinguistics to learning to read are interwoven among these topics.

I. A BRIEF LOOK AT THE PAST

Fashions do not change in education as quickly as in women's clothing; yet many methods for teaching beginners to read have been introduced as revolutionary improvements, have held the stage (or part of it) for a while, and in turn have been displaced by newer methods. Many of these stemmed from dissatisfaction with a prevailing method, and excesses in one direction have at times been replaced by equally objectionable swings toward the opposite extreme. Detailed and quite interesting historical accounts may be found in Huey (1908), N. B. Smith (1965), and Mathews (1966).

The comparative evaluation of teaching methods is not easy. The majority of children can learn to read by a variety of methods. The skill of teachers, pupil abilities, and the learning environment have been shown in a number of research studies to be more important than differences in methodology. Methods may vary in effectiveness depending upon local conditions, making it dangerous to generalize from a limited sample; procedures that work well in a prosperous suburb may not suit the needs of children in an impoverished neighborhood. And only recently has research on beginning reading been conducted on a large enough scale and with sufficient skill in research design and statistical analysis to provide some basis for conclusions.

Synthetic Methods

Methods that start with small parts (alphabet letters) and move to larger units (word, phrase, sentence) are called *synthetic methods.*

The alphabet-spelling method was universally used from ancient times well into the nineteenth century. First, weeks or months were spent in memorizing the alphabet. Then two-letter combinations were drilled, the letters being named and the unit pronounced, and eventually the child got to words and meaningful sentences. In studying a word, the letters were named in sequence, and then the word was pronounced over and over until learned. In most languages this is an effective procedure because the letter names are essentially the same as their sounds. In English, however, naming the letters of *cat* and putting them together gives something like *seeaytee.* The alphabet-spelling method was mechanical, uninteresting, and difficult. "The value of the practice in learning to spell doubtless had much to do with blinding centuries of teachers to its uselessness for the reading of words and sentences" (Huey, 1908, p. 266).

A number of phonic methods were developed during the nineteenth century. Their common characteristic was that they started with the sounds represented by the letters (rather than the names) and then proceeded to the sounding of consonant-vowel and vowel-consonant combinations: *ba, ca, da . . . ab, ac, ad . . .* , to syllables, and then to words. When a child came to a new word he was expected to sound it letter by letter (or by letter groups) and fuse or blend the sounds mentally to get the sounds of the whole word.

Critics of the synthetic alphabet and phonic methods have emphasized several shortcomings: 1) The English language has so many irregularities in its sound-symbol relationships that an adequate phonic system has to be quite complicated and difficult. 2) The synthetic methods tended to produce slow, labored reading. 3) These methods encouraged attention to the mechanics of word recognition and did not give enough attention to the thought-getting side of reading. 4) It is impossible to pronounce a word one sound at a time with accuracy, and many children have great difficulty identifying a word after sounding it (O'Neil, 1972).

One kind of effort to standardize the sound-symbol relationship was to employ diacritical markings, similar to those in the pronunciation keys of dictionaries. Mathews (1966) has reproduced a page from a book published as long ago as 1644, in which long vowels and silent letters were marked. Around the beginning of the twentieth century, diacritical markings were used in the very popular Ward Readers and Pollard Readers.

Another effort to reduce phonic difficulties was to modify the alphabet by adding new letter forms, so as to have a separate letter to represent each sound. A modified alphabet devised by Isaac Pitman was tried in a few American school systems during the mid-nineteenth century, but although the reports of its results were favorable, it failed to make headway and died out. This was the ancestor of the current Initial Teaching Alphabet. A "scientific alphabet" was used for many years in readers and dictionaries published by Funk and Wagnalls.

Analytic Methods

Methods that start from larger wholes and proceed to the study of parts are generally called *analytic methods*; they are sometimes referred to as *global methods*. They include word, sentence, and story methods.

The word method was advocated by Horace Mann before the middle of the nineteenth century, and primers using this method began to be used in some schools around 1850. The method is based on the idea that a written word is not merely a sequence of letters but has a distinctive recognizable character of its own. The classical example was that a cow is not seen as a head, body, four legs, and tail, but as an animal with a distinctive appearance. The usual procedure was for the teacher to print or write a word on the board, pronounce it, and then combine it with other words to form various sentences. Word-picture associations were employed, and flash cards were often used for drill.

Mathews (1966) has pointed out that there were two main variations of the word method: a *words-to-letters* method, in which words were analyzed and studied sound by sound shortly after they were introduced, and a *words-to-reading* method, in which word analysis was postponed for varying periods of time; often analysis was not begun until a substantial sight vocabulary had been learned. The *words-to-reading* method was used in most basal reader systems until the mid-1960's when the pendulum again began to swing toward use of the words-to-letters method. Because of the critical importance in this method of building an association between the appearance of the printed word and its spoken equivalent, it is often referred to as the "look and say"[1] method or "whole-word" method.

The *sentence* method was first advocated in the United States around 1870. Its proponents argued that since the sentence is the smallest complete unit of meaning, the child should first be taught a whole sentence at a time. The same words were presented in many different sentence arrangements, but the need for continuity of meaning from one sentence to the next was ignored in some of these systems.

The *story* method attempted to correct the weakness of the sentence method by introducing a whole story at a time. The teacher would read a story, usually a cumulative folk tale such as "Chicken Little" or "The Gingerbread Boy," over and over to the children until many of them had memorized it. She would then present the first few sentences in print and have them recite the memorized lines as they looked at the print; in this way, recognition of words was developed. This method assumed that the child would look at the words in proper sequence and in time with the story; failure to do this produced many cases of pseudo reading in which the children would be able to recite the story perfectly page by page without having learned to recognize individual words.

Proponents of the synthetic methods stressed the child's need to be able to work out the pronunciation of unfamiliar words. Proponents of the analytic methods emphasized the need for meaningful reading and for immediate sight recognition of words and phrases. Current methodology tries to utilize the good features of these older methods and to combine them into a comprehensive, flexible program that is adaptable to individual differences.

II. CURRENT APPROACHES TO TEACHING BEGINNING READING

Over a hundred commercially prepared beginning reading programs are available (Aukerman, 1971). A number of influences—dissatisfaction with the results of the older basal readers, new interest in the teaching of reading on the part of educational psychologists and linguists, agitation by pressure groups who are sure that a particular approach will provide a panacea to make every child a superior reader, government support for reading materials and research—converged to make the 1960's and 1970's a time of innovation in the teaching of reading. As one examines the "new" methods, some of them seem quite familiar to those who are acquainted with the history of reading instruction. The discussion below focuses on six

1. Because the task is to associate the printed word with its spoken counterpart, "look while you say" would be a more appropriate term. Unless the child is attending to the printed word while it is being said, the association will be weak or nonexistent.

approaches into which most of these programs can be classified, although some programs do not fit into one category: 1) meaning-emphasis approaches, 2) code-emphasis approaches, 3) programmed approaches, 4) special alphabet approaches, 5) language-experience approaches, 6) individualized reading.

Basically, most approaches differ in two or three of the following ways: 1) how a child is first taught to read words, 2) the initial emphasis placed on comprehension versus decoding, and 3) the preplanned structure.[2] Furthermore, not only are there marked differences as to basic philosophy, methodology, and materials among approaches, but wide variations also exist among programs categorized within the same approach.

Meaning-Emphasis Approaches

Programs that initially stress meaning typically focus initial instruction on teaching children to associate printed whole words with their spoken counterparts. The rationale for this procedure is that recognition of whole words whose meanings are probably known by most children permits quicker introduction to sentences and stories from which meaning can be derived.

Basal reader programs are not simply series of books and accompanying materials. They are preplanned, sequentially organized, detailed materials and methods used to teach and to learn the skills of developmental reading.

The pattern of a graded series starting in first grade, with a controlled vocabulary, gradually increasing difficulty, and a variety of content, has not changed greatly since the McGuffey Readers first appeared in the 1830's. For the past fifty or so years, most basal reader systems have been eclectic, trying to achieve a balanced reading program with a broad and varied set of objectives. Until the mid 1960's, most of them used a look-and-say procedure for developing initial reading vocabulary, with phonics and other word-identification skills taught gradually, mainly with the second- and third-grade readers. Since then, however, there has been a decided trend toward more and earlier stress on teaching decoding skills. The following discussion deals with the eclectic basal readers that have been popular since the 1930's and the recent changes in them (A. J. Harris, 1972a).

Materials. A representative series starts with one or more readiness books, usually in workbook form. The first actual reading materials are usually three thin paperbacks, called pre-primers. To dispel the mistaken

2. The need for systematic reading instruction has been pointed out by Cane and Smithers (1971), A. J. Harris (1972b), and Southgate (1973).

idea that a given book should only be used in a particular year in school, however, increasingly series are numbering their books by levels. For example, a first pre-primer following two readiness books would be labeled Level 3. The pre-primers (Levels 3, 4, and 5)[3] are followed by the first hard-covered book (Primer 1^1 or Level 6), and a first reader (1^2 or Level 7) which completes the program covered by most first graders. There are usually two second reader books (2^1 and 2^2 or Levels 8 and 9), two third reader books, (3^1 and 3^2 or Levels 10 and 11) and one thick reader in each of grades 4, 5, and 6. Since the mid 1960's, there have been some departures from this traditional format, such as a choice between a conventional hard-covered reader and the same content bound in two or more paperback units. Also, a few programs now utilize a systems approach; *i.e.*, they provide a large number of components that, through skillful management, can be used to allow for individual differences. The efficacy of such systems has yet to be adequately tested.

Each book in the series is accompanied by a consumable workbook, some of which provide self-help cues at the top of the pages, or have taped directions and answers for self-correction. Other accessory materials may include exercises printed on duplicating stencils; large cards for group practice with phonic elements, words, and phrases; introductory story cards or charts; correlated filmstrips and recordings; and supplementary paperback storybooks. The recent trend in enrichment is to provide the kinds of materials just mentioned in convenient packages as optional supplements.

Each reader is accompanied by a guide or manual which details the teaching method. Most manuals present a general plan and then give a detailed lesson plan for each selection. The manual, which is really a handbook on how to teach with the pupil book, is either a separate book or is bound together with a copy of the reader. Manuals usually provide more suggestions for skills development and enrichment than are needed for most children, while extra practice is needed for some children. The teacher must therefore judiciously select activities based on the children's needs, as well as determine the appropriate rate of presentation for different groups.

The trend in basal readers to have progressively smaller vocabularies (which extended from the 1920's through the 1950's) has been reversed. New series of the 1960's and 1970's tend to have somewhat richer vocabularies than their predecessors and also give increased attention to critical reading and the development of creative thinking through reading.

The language of first-grade basal readers has often been criticized as artificial, stilted, monotonous, and unduly repetitious. "Oh, oh, look, look," has been the subject of many jokes. This criticism, although aimed at basal

3. The numbering of levels varies from series to series depending on the number of books in the program.

readers in general, has always taken its examples from pre-primers, in which the vocabulary restrictions are most severe. Similar criticism can be leveled at phonic and linguistic programs that control the vocabulary on the basis of phonic regularity or spelling patterns. Even at pre-primer level, different series vary greatly in their degree of success at approximating the natural spoken language patterns of childhood.

Prior to the mid-1960's, the content of most first-grade materials centered around one suburban family comprised of a boy and girl of primary school age, a younger child, their parents, a dog, and a cat. Since then, marked changes in regard to characters and environment have occurred. There has been a rather general effort to replace the suburban middle-class white stereotype with ethnic and environmental pluralism. More emphasis has been placed on urban settings, members of minority groups, and problems related to limited income. The one-family theme has sometimes been dropped, allowing more variety in content. Old folk and fairy tales, poetry, anthropomorphic animal stories, and space-age stories are prevalent. The increased amount of nonfiction, particularly in the intermediate grades, makes it possible to teach basic study skills with appropriate content.

Methodology. The structure of a typical basal-reader lesson consists essentially of three steps: 1) preparation, 2) reading the story, and 3) follow-up activities.

PREPARATION. Preparing to read a new story involves three main phases. The first is arousal of interest, which is given extra attention when a new group of stories is begun. The second is the teaching and clarification of ideas, concepts, and meanings that may be unfamiliar to some of the children. The third is presentation and pre-teaching of new words. Although some basal readers still stress a look-and-say procedure, others do much of their phonics teaching and practice at this point.

GUIDED READING AND REREADING. The teacher usually leads some discussion of the story title and first illustration and then asks a question. The children read silently to find the answer, then discuss it, and often read orally the sentence or two that contains the answer. The amount read silently may vary from one or two lines in the earliest pre-primer to a complete story unit. After a first silent reading followed by some discussion, there is often oral rereading of the selection. Manuals provide varied purposes for oral rereading: to find out how different characters feel, to find the sad parts or happy or funny parts, to find facts to use in a picture, to take parts in a dramatization of the story, and so forth.

FOLLOW-UP ACTIVITIES. Follow-up activities are of two main kinds: skills development and enrichment activities. In some basal reader programs the major parts of instruction in decoding skills is located after reading and discussion. Additional practice in specific comprehension skills, and use of workbook pages that incorporate a variety of skills, also usually come after reading and rereading.

Usually the manual provides suggestions for varied kinds of enrichment. There are recommendations for stories that the teacher can read to the children, songs that can be sung (the music may be provided), poems with related themes, jingles and rhymes, and related art and handiwork. As children become able to do some independent reading, specific supplementary reading selections may be recommended.

When a teacher is using basal readers and has the class divided into groups, it is difficult to find the time to cover all parts of the lesson plan. Preparation and guided reading are usually covered fairly well. Follow-up activities are most likely to be neglected. Thus one can see how a basal reader series may have quite adequate provisions in its manuals for the teaching of phonics and other word-identification skills, but these plans may not be adequately carried out in many classrooms. Similarly, enrichment activities may be omitted by a teacher who is anxious to keep to a pre-set schedule.

Code-Emphasis Approaches

Code-emphasis programs place initial stress on teaching decoding skills. Although many programs that employ special alphabets or are programmed could be classified as having a code emphasis, only two major code-emphasis approaches are discussed here—phonics programs[4] and linguistic programs.

Phonic Approaches. Phonics materials have been used in many first-grade classes to supplement the use of basal readers by teachers who wanted to teach phonics somewhat earlier and more intensively than their basal reader plans provided. Most of these materials shared several characteristics: 1) they were intended as preliminary or supplementary materials rather than as a total reading program; 2) they stressed learning grapheme-phoneme relationships, *i.e.*, the sounds represented by letters and letter groups; 3) several of them were in consumable workbook form; 4)

4. *Phonology* is the scientific study of speech sounds, including phonetics and phonemics. *Phonetics* is the branch of phonology dealing with the study of the sounds of speech, including their production, combination, description, and representation by written symbols. *Phonemics* is the study and establishment of the sounds (*phonemes*) of a particular language. *Phonics* is the study of the relationship of phonemes to the printed or written symbols that represent them (letters and letter strings, called *graphemes*) and their use in discovering the pronunciation of printed and written words. Phonics is therefore the part of phonology and phonetics that is most involved in reading instruction.

they tended to stress phonic generalizations and ignore the exceptions (*e.g.*, a final magic *e* is silent and makes the vowel before it say its name; when two vowels go walking, the first does the talking); 5) they provided some practice in applying phonic knowledge in reading sentences. Some of them emphasized the study of words in list form, while others emphasized the use of picture and sentence contexts. Some materials used a whole-word phonics or word-to-sounds method similar to that employed in basal readers, while others used a synthetic sounding-blending procedure.

An intermediate step was the appearance in the 1950's of a phonic series complete from pre-primer through third reader, which was recommended for use alternately with an eclectic basal reader series: first the phonic pre-primer, then the basal pre-primers, then the phonic primer, the basal primer, and so on. There are also phonic programs intended to be self-sufficient and to replace basal readers.

Recent phonics basal reader programs take the more conventional basal reader format but start with heavy emphasis on teaching symbol-sound associations; this is followed by instruction in blending the sounds into words, and then introduction of meaningful context. In these programs, the beginning reading material is composed of words that utilize only the grapheme-phoneme elements taught up to that point. A relatively new phenomenon is the development of phonics-based reading programs by research-and-development centers (Beck and Mitroff, 1972; Cronnell, 1973).

Phonic methods have in common a stress on word recognition through the learning of the phonemic equivalents of letters and letter groups and the application of phonic generalizations. They differ among themselves on many important issues, such as whether to begin with consonants or vowels, whether to teach short vowels before long vowels or vice versa, how many generalizations to teach, which generalizations and in which order, whether to use a whole-word phonics procedure or a synthetic sounding-blending procedure, when to introduce meaningful material, and so on. While the placing of emphasis on phonics may be described as an approach to the teaching of beginning reading, there is little agreement among phonic methods on details.

Linguistic Approaches.   Leonard Bloomfield, a noted linguist, became interested in the teaching of reading in the late 1930's and wrote an essay on the subject which appeared in 1942. Materials based on his ideas were not published until 1961, however (Bloomfield and Barnhart, 1961). Bloomfield was highly critical of phonic methods, particularly those using a synthetic sounding-blending procedure, and even more critical of the whole-word method, which he likened to the study of Chinese ideographs. Very briefly, his recommended procedure included the following ideas:

1) start with teaching the identification of all alphabet letters by name (not by sound); 2) begin with words in which each letter represents only one phonemic value, avoiding words with silent letters or less common sounds, so that the beginning words consist of three-letter words with a consonant-vowel-consonant pattern containing only short vowels; 3) use the principle of minimal variation, employing a list of words alike except for one letter, such as *ban, Dan, can, fan, man*, and the like; 4) do not teach rules about letter-sound correspondences, as the children will evolve correct responses when sound and spelling correspond in regular fashion; 5) employ learned words in sentences, such as "Nan can fan Dan."

Since 1961 several basal reader series based on linguistic principles have appeared. They have in common agreement that "decoding," or translating the printed words into their spoken equivalents, is the first and most important goal of a reading program. Most of them also agree on using whole words and the principle of minimal variation, rather than a synthetic sounding-blending procedure. Programs differ on such factors as the use and teaching of high utility words (*e.g.*, the word *the*) which are not phonemically regular. Some use illustrations from the beginning; others consider them distracting and harmful. Just as with programs in other approaches, no two linguistic series agree very closely on details.

There is some question as to how well young children abstract letter-sound associations without direct instruction (Bishop, 1962) and the possible adverse effects of not establishing a "set for diversity" caused by the use of a tightly controlled vocabulary based on a one-to-one letter-sound correspondence in set spelling patterns (Levin and Watson, 1962). Questions regarding linguistic reading programs also have been raised by linguists (Wardhaugh, 1969) and psycholinguists (F. Smith and Goodman, 1971; K. Goodman, 1972), who state that there is no such thing as a linguistic reading program, but only reading programs written by linguists.

Special-Alphabet Approaches

Although English is an alphabetic language, it has many irregularities in the relationships between alphabet letters and the sounds they represent. "For example, the letter *e* has at least ten vowel sounds, as well as possessing consonant values in combination with certain letters, such as *t* (righteous) and *d* (grandeur). It is frequently silent. Moreover, sounds which could be consistently spelled even with our inadequate alphabet are spelled in many ways. The long *e* sound is spelled 14 ways in common words and only about one fifth of the time with *e* alone" (E. Horn, 1960).

Since the middle of the nineteenth century there have been many efforts to promote a phonetically regular alphabet for the English language, in which each letter symbol would always represent one sound, and each sound would be represented by only one symbol. If the proponents of this idea had been able to agree on one alphabet, they might have succeeded. As it is, however, the supporters of simplified and regularized spelling are still arguing among themselves about details. Most of the new alphabets that have been devised have been intended to supplant the present 26-letter alphabet.

Meanwhile, prominent linguists have recently been defending the present writing system as more useful and beneficial than a phonetically regular alphabet would be: "conventional English orthography in its essentials appears to be a near-optimal system for representing the spoken language" (Chomsky, 1970, p. 4). Most of the examples used by such linguists as Chomsky and H. L. Smith (1968) involve related words in which the written forms show a similarity in meaning despite accent shifts and changes in vowel values (*courage, courageous; history, historian*). This underlying regularity is more useful to mature readers than to beginners (Francis, 1970).

In the 1960's a new idea came forward: use an alphabet with regular sound-symbol correspondence to develop initial reading and writing skills, after which a transition can be made to the conventional alphabet (sometimes called "traditional orthography"). The main advocate of this idea, Sir James Pitman, was responsible for the development of the Initial Teaching Alphabet (i/t/a) and for marshaling support for large-scale experimental tryout of teaching beginners with i/t/a in Great Britain.

While some have thought of i/t/a as a method of instruction, it should be emphasized that it is not an instructional method, but rather a 44-character alphabet which can be used in a variety of ways (Downing, 1964). The i/t/a readers that have been most widely used in Great Britain employ an eclectic methodology similar to that of most American basal readers, while the i/t/a series most used in the United States follows an alphabet-phonic procedure. This alphabet has a number of interesting features: 1) capitals are like lower-case letters in shape, only larger; 2) there is a separate symbol for each of 44 consonant and vowel sounds; and 3) many present letters are retained, and new characters have been designed to facilitate transition to the conventional alphabet.

Downing (1970) has offered a psycholinguistic theory for i/t/a and discussed needed improvements in its alphabet, and has also suggested that combining an alphabet modification with use of a language-experience approach should facilitate learning to read by providing a close match between the language of the reading instruction and the child's own language (Downing, 1972).

UNIFON is a phonetically regular 40-capital-letter alphabet designed so that the characters can be read by a computer, like the digits on a bank check. Whether transition to the conventional alphabet can be made as easily from UNIFON as from i/t/a has not yet been determined (Malone, 1963; Medcalf and Ratz, 1972).

There is some evidence that learning to read is easier and can be accomplished more quickly when there is a consistent correspondence of symbol and sound. It is also clear that much, if not all, of this advantage is lost in the process of transferring from one alphabet to another. The desirability of using a transitional alphabet is still an open question. (Downing *et al.*, 1967; Dykstra, 1967; Warburton and Southgate, 1969; Wapner, 1969)

Another special-alphabet system is *Words in Color* (Educational Solutions), a synthetic alphabet-phonic system in which sound-symbol correspondence is provided through the use of color rather than additional graphemes. Each of 47 consonant and vowel sounds is assigned one hue, and various spellings which may represent that phoneme in different words are all printed in that color. Thus the color, rather than the grapheme, is the main clue at the beginning. The use of color cues is gradually phased out. Three comparative studies have not shown *Words in Color* to have any advantage over other reading programs (Dunn, *et al.*, 1967; Lockmiller and DiNello, 1970; Hill, 1967).

Two other programs that employ color cues have been published (Jones, 1967; Bannatyne, 1973). The only available assessment of either was reported by Jones (1968) who indicated that in England his *Colour Story Method* produced better results than i/t/a for the top third of the experimental groups.

Programmed Approaches

Programmed materials are designed so the user 1) encounters a series of small tasks on which he is very likely to be successful, 2) is involved in the learning process through actively responding, and 3) receives immediate feedback as to the correctness of each response. In theory, programmed materials should greatly facilitate individualized instruction because they should allow each student to be working almost independently with material suitable for his needs, proceeding at a pace commensurate with his abilities and interest.

Two programmed reading series each consists of 23 consumable workbooklike texts with accompanying manuals and accessory materials. Their basic method is best described as a phonic/linguistic one, and both programs are linear. The limited research findings regarding the relative effectiveness of these programs is mixed. One preliminary report (Della-Piana and Hogben, 1968) stated that 12 classes using programmed reading did as well or better than control classes using an undescribed method, except for children with low readiness scores and excepting accuracy of oral reading. Another study, with recognized limitations, found that use of programmed instruction to supplement the basic reading program produced significantly higher achievement-test scores than the basic reading program alone (Feldhusen, Lamb, and Feldhusen, 1970). However, two other studies found that programmed reading did not produce significantly different results as compared to other beginning reading programs (Hammill and Mattleman, 1969; Woodcock, 1967).

Pioneering work in the development of computer-assisted beginning reading instruction (CAI) has been carried on by Atkinson and Fletcher (1972). His equipment presents visual material on a screen, which is the face of a cathode-ray tube, and auditory stimuli by means of a tape recorder. Responses are made with a light-pen; when that touches the face of the tube, the computer determines from the location of the touch whether the response is correct or not. A branching type of program is used which allows faster or slower progress through skipping or repeating items, and can switch the learner to additional practice if needed. A number of children can be working individually at different steps of the program with one computer. The technology is not tied to any one teaching methodology, but Atkinson's approach is based on teaching decoding, and is considered a supplement to classroom instruction on other aspects of reading. An evaluative study (Atkinson, 1972) revealed significantly higher achievement by first graders who used CAI for about 12 minutes daily for 5 months. Atkinson estimated that learning with a computer is about equal to learning through individual tutoring, and would cost approximately $70 per child annually for schools located near the computer. Another CAI system has been described by Serwer and Stolurow (1970). A small computer is also employed with the Edison Responsive Environment "talking typewriter" (Moore and Andersen, 1967).

A different kind of programmed approach has been used by Ellson, who programmed the teacher rather than the materials (Ellson, P. Harris, and Barber, 1968). Each tutor (usually a person not trained as a teacher) was given extremely specific step-by-step written directions on how to tutor a child who had made poor progress because of low mentality or educational disadvantage. The procedure was based on a state-adopted basal reader series. The tutors following the programmed directions achieved better results than other tutors given direction and supervision by experts. Materials based upon these procedures are available for use with three widely used basal reader programs (Ginn, Macmillan, Harper & Row).

It would be unfair to judge the future potentialities of programmed and computerized approaches to beginning reading on the basis of the limited available evidence. Future developments in this technology deserve to be watched closely.

Language-Experience Approaches

As early as the 1890's, some experimental schools were using little stories dictated by the children and written down by the teacher as beginning reading materials (A. J. Harris, 1964). Such "experience stories" have been used widely for decades to provide an informal introduction for basal readers. They have also been used by many teachers as supplementary reading material, with particular reference to experiences in science and social studies. The experience method, now renamed the language-experience approach, rarely has the preplanned structure associated with other approaches. Like individualized reading, therefore, it almost defies description. Generally, however, a language-experience approach is one in which

> . . . emphasis is placed on the teaching of reading in close correlation with the related language-arts activities of listening, speaking, and writing. Children are encouraged to express their thoughts, ideas, and feelings, often stimulated by a specific experience guided and developed by the teacher. The verbal productions of the children are written down by the teacher in the early stages, and are used as the earliest reading materials. Pupil expression is encouraged through the use of a variety of media such as painting, speaking, and writing. Gradually the program moves from exclusive use of reading material which is developed out of the oral language of the children, into a program of reading in which increasing emphasis is placed upon a variety of children's books. (A. J. Harris and Serwer, 1966a)

The implementation of a language-experience approach requires a great deal of teacher initiative, creativity, and planning. Helpful suggestions for implementing such a program can be found in a number of sources (Lee and Allen, 1963; Hall, 1970; Stauffer, 1970; Humphrey and Redden, 1972). Themes for experience stories are developed from trips, science (weather, pets, plants), social studies (holidays, elections, famous people, current events), and interesting happenings at home, at school, or in the neighborhood. The teaching method tends to resemble that of the old story-memory method, going from the teacher's reading of the entire story, to the reading of single lines, to phrases and words. Word-recognition and word-analysis skills are developed from words used in the experience stories and usually are introduced as the teacher perceives a need and an opportunity rather than in a preplanned sequence. Gradually, as sight vocabulary grows, easy first-grade books are introduced, and a transition may be made either to a basal reader program or to an individualized reading program.

Individualized Approaches

Certainly programmed reading approaches and computer-assisted instruction can be classified as individualized approaches; just as might such skills-centered approaches as the Wisconsin Design for Reading Skill Development (Otto and Askov, 1972). In effect, the recent use of behavioral objectives and criterion-referenced tests are attempts to individualize reading instruction. Nevertheless, only two approaches are mentioned here: 1) individualized developmental reading, which is discussed more fully in Chapter 5; and (2) Individually Prescribed Instruction (IPI).

In an individualized developmental reading program children must be able to read and to work independently for periods of time. Because many beginning first graders are immature and often depend on the teacher for guidance and structure, and beginning reading materials specifically planned for individualized progress are not widely available, it seems reasonable to conclude that a highly individualized reading program is less feasible in first grade than in later grades.

In Individually Prescribed Instruction (Beck and Bolvin, 1969), objectives are arranged in sequential order by area of study. Placement tests are used to determine where each child should begin in each area. As the child progresses through his individual prescriptions (programmed readers were used primarily during the decoding stages), progress is measured with diagnostic and mastery tests. Individually Prescribed Instruction must be still considered to be in the development stage.

III. ADJUSTING TO THE NEEDS OF DISADVANTAGED LEARNERS

Evidence from many studies has shown that the children of the poor not only tend to get off to a bad start in first-grade reading, but also tend to fall farther back as they proceed in school. Several recent publications have presented a variety of points of view on how best to meet the reading needs of such children (Baratz and Shuy, 1969; T. Horn, 1970; Figurel, 1970; DeStefano, 1973a).

One explanation offered for the quite general reading retardation of children belonging to disadvantaged groups is that the disparities between their dialects and standard English create linguistic barriers that interfere with learning to read (Goodman, 1965). A remedy strongly urged by some linguists is to provide such children with beginning reading materials in their own dialect (Baratz, 1970). As yet, no experimental evidence shows that pre-primers printed in children's dialect make it easier to learn to read standard English later. Reasons why this approach is impractical have been advanced by Venezky (1970).

In addition to the problems occasioned by the need to provide for various dialects (Mitchell, 1972) and parental opposition, three studies (Nolen, 1972; I. Ramsey, 1972; Hall, Turner, and Russell, 1973) found that black children were no more successful understanding material in their dialect than in standard English. Davino (1971) and Erickson (1969) suggest that standard English should be learned as an alternate dialect needed for effective communication. A bi-dialectal reading program has been developed (Davis, Gladney, and Leaverton, 1969). Another alternative would have children, particularly those whose dialects deviate markedly, first learn to speak standard English before initiating reading instruction with materials that employ standard English (Venezky, 1970). A fourth suggestion (Goodman, 1965) recommends that material written in standard English be used, but that teachers accept the child's rendition into his own dialect. Still others (Serwer, 1969; Cramer, 1971) urge use of a language-experience approach, although research regarding its use for such children is limited and inconclusive (Hall, 1972).

Although there is some indication that massive intervention may not be as successful as hoped for with first-grade disadvantaged children (Goolsby and Frary, 1970), evidence exists that such children can achieve in reading in response to good teaching (A. J. Harris, Morrison, Serwer, and Gold, 1968). A viable program might incorporate a number of suggestions, such as teaching the children and teachers to be bi-dialectal, *initial* use of a language-experience approach coupled with a structured skill development program, and acceptance of dialect in oral reading and discussion, all under the direction of a skilled teacher.

Non-English-Speaking Children. Attempts also have been made to lessen failure in learning to read by American children whose native (or strongest) language is not English. Instructional reading materials that are conceptually attuned to the cultures of such children have been developed in the hope that they would be more understandable and interesting to the children, as well as reflect their cultural heritage.

Until fairly recently, most programs simply employed English as the language of instruction and utilized materials written in English. The limitations of such an approach are obvious. Newer programs have either 1) taught the children to read first in their native language, concurrently teaching or following up with teaching receptive and expressive English-language skills; or 2) taught the children to understand and to speak English before initiating reading instruction in English. Some movement also exists toward bilingual education. As yet, no clear research evidence favors any of these approaches.

In a beginning reading project, Spanish-speaking children of Puerto Rican origin in New York City were tested individually with the WISC and obtained approximately the same verbal IQ when tested in Spanish as when tested in English; in both languages verbal IQ was on the average substantially lower than performance IQ (Goldberg and Taylor, 1970). Vocabulary was particularly low in both languages. It would seem that helping such children improve their comprehension of English might be more relevant than teaching them to read Spanish before English.

It seems probable that nonstandard speakers learn to derive the deep meaning of standard English communications despite the surface-structure differences which characterize their own dialects. Learning to comprehend standard English is important for learning to read; learning to speak standard English correctly does not seem very relevant for reading comprehension, although it may have economic and social values later in life.

IV. EVALUATION OF BEGINNING READING APPROACHES

There are numerous small-scale comparisons of methods of teaching beginning reading in the research literature, some of which have been mentioned in this chapter. A review of the available studies led Chall to conclude:

> It would seem, at our present state of knowledge, that a code emphasis—one that combines control of words on spelling regularity (although not complete control of one sound for one symbol), some direct teaching of letter-sound correspondences, as well as the use of writing, tracing, or typing—produces better results with unselected groups of beginners than a meaning emphasis, the kind incorporated in most of the conventional basal-reading series used in the schools in the late 1950s and early 1960s. (Chall, 1967, pp. 178, 179)

She also concluded that there was no experimental basis for preferring one code-emphasis method over another. Chall's procedures and conclusions have been questioned (Strang, 1968b; Evertts, 1968; Ramsey and Burnett, 1969), with perhaps the most cogent criticism being that she did not differentiate between good and poor research in reaching her conclusions. Also, it should be noted that Chall's major conclusion was stated very cautiously, to the effect that methods which paid more and earlier attention to word-identification skills than the basal readers of the 1950's and early 1960's tended, on the whole, to come out with better results than the basal readers. It was not a blanket endorsement of procedures that ignore meaning for weeks while drilling on letters and words. She also carefully discussed the great variations in results which different teachers obtain with the same method, the favorable but transient effect of novelty, the significance of the effort put forth by teachers volunteering to use a new method, the tendency to spend extra time with a new method, and other complicating factors. Accepting her main conclusion without carefully studying the many qualifications can produce a dangerously inaccurate oversimplification of a very complex problem.

The U.S. Office of Education mounted a major effort to get a conclusive answer to the question of the merits of beginning reading approaches when it supported 27 coordinated first-grade research studies in 1964–1965. Report summaries written by the authors of all the projects appeared in *The Reading Teacher* (May and October, 1966; May and October, 1967) and have been gathered together in a paperback book (Stauffer, 1967). Results from the projects that utilized representative children and studied methods that were also employed in other projects were drawn together in a composite statistical analysis, summarized in two reports: the first covers 15 first-grade studies; the second, 13 studies that continued through the second grade. In the summary of the first-grade report, 15 numbered conclusions were offered. Of these, the following seem most significant:

1] Word study skills must be emphasized and taught systematically regardless of what approach to initial reading instruction is utilized.

2] Combinations of programs, such as a basal program with supplementary phonics materials, often are superior to single approaches. . . .
   The addition of language experiences to any kind of reading can be expected to make a contribution.

3] It is likely that basal programs should develop a more intensive word study skills element, while programs which put major emphasis on word recognition should increase attention paid to other reading skills.

4] On the average, boys cannot be expected to achieve at the same level as girls. . . .

6] Reading programs are not equally effective in all situations. Evidently factors other than method, within a particular learning situation influence pupil success in reading. . . .

9] . . . The tremendous range among classrooms within any method points out the importance of elements in the learning situation over and above the methods employed. To improve reading instruction it is necessary to train better teachers of reading rather than to expect a panacea in the form of materials.

10] Children learn to read by a variety of materials and methods. . . . Furthermore, pupils experienced difficulty in each of the programs utilized. No one approach is so distinctly better in all situations and respects than the others that it should be considered the one best method and the one to be used exclusively.

11] The expectation of pupil accomplishment in initial reading instruction probably should be raised. . . .

13] A writing component is likely to be an effective addition to a
primary program.

14] It is impossible to assess the relative effectiveness of programs
unless they are used in the same project. Project differences are
so great even when readiness for reading is controlled that a program utilized in a favored project would demonstrate a distinct
advantage over one used in a less favored project regardless of the
effectiveness of the program. (Bond and Dykstra, 1967, pp. 210–
212)

The second-grade report from the Coordinating Center essentially supported and repeated the conclusions of the first-grade report (Dykstra,
1968a). Limitations of these studies have been pointed out (Sipay, 1968;
Lohnes and Gray, 1972; Lohnes, 1973).

Although at the end of the second year these studies appeared to support Chall's conclusion concerning the superiority of code-emphasis programs, Dykstra (1968b) cautioned that there was no clear evidence that
the early emphasis on code *per se* was the only or even the primary reason
for the relative effectiveness of the code-emphasis approaches. Other characteristics of these programs may have been more crucial in determining
pupil achievement.

Eight of the original 27 projects followed their pupils through the third
grade. These projects included a variety of methods, including basal readers, i/t/a, linguistic readers, diacritically marked readers, supplementary
phonics, language-experience, and phonic/linguistic readers. In 7 of these
projects, the reading test results at the end of the third grade showed no
consistent and statistically significant superiority for any of the methods
being compared. (Fry, 1967; A. J. Harris, *et al.*, 1968; Ruddell, 1968; Schneyer
and Cowen, 1968; Vilscek and Cleland, 1968; Sheldon, *et al.*, 1967; Stauffer
and Hammond, 1969). In the eighth project, the meaning of the results is
obscured by the fact that the phonic/linguistic method that achieved the
highest mean adjusted reading scores in second and third grades also had
markedly higher nonpromotion rates in the first and second grades; removal
of the poorest readers in that method by nonpromotion would seem to
have affected the results (Hayes and Wuest, 1967).

Thus the most recent large-scale studies done in America indicate no
consistent advantages for any of the methods studied, when the pupils are
followed through the third grade. There is strong evidence that the qualities of the school system, of the particular school, of the teacher, and of
the pupils far outweigh differences in methodology in their influences on

reading achievement. There is also strong evidence that none of the methods studied was able to eliminate failure.

In Great Britain a large-scale study by Morris was cited by Chall as favoring a phonics-first method over a word method (Chall, 1967, pp. 130, 157). Morris has since issued a report following the pupils through the sixth year of school. By the end of the sixth year the pupils who started with the word method were slightly ahead of the phonics-first group, thus reversing the findings at the end of three years of schooling. Morris emphasized that the characteristics of the community, the quality of school leadership provided by the "head" (principal), and the quality of teaching had much more effect on results in particular schools than whether they began with phonics or with words (Morris, 1966).

Thus the results of many years of research indicate that the quality of administrative leadership, of teaching skill, and of pupil ability (in turn related to characteristics of home and neighborhood) are much more important in determining the results of beginning reading instruction than differences in methodology and materials.

It is also noteworthy that no approach has been able to lessen significantly the proportion of children who make disappointing progress in beginning reading. Some children may fail with one approach who might not have failed with another approach. The time has come to end the quest for *the* best method of teaching reading. Gross comparisons of beginning reading approaches have yielded little useful information.

Efforts should concentrate on determining which program(s) works best with which children when used by certain types of teachers under given conditions, and why. Research has begun in such areas as attempting to match learner characteristics with the demands made on the learner by various methods. For example, studies have shown that, in general, matching visual or auditory modality preference to reading method does not result in better achievement (Bateman, 1968; Bruininks, 1968; Freer, 1971; Neville, 1971; H. M. Robinson, 1972b; Waugh, 1973). Similar negative results are reported for attempts to match sensory-integration abilities (matching stimuli presented in different modalities) with beginning reading approaches (Thom, 1971; Pressman, 1973).

Until more evidence is available, it seems that for most children a balanced eclectic approach that uses visual, auditory, touch and kinesthetic cues in combination, and develops word identification and comprehension simultaneously seems safer and less likely to produce difficulties than any method that relies primarily on one sensory avenue or stresses one important side of reading while neglecting another. When a child continues to fail in a given reading program, consideration should be given to employing a program with him that utilizes different methodology.

SUGGESTED ADDITIONAL READING

AUKERMAN, ROBERT C. *Approaches to beginning reading.* New York: John Wiley and Sons, 1971.

AUKERMAN, ROBERT C. (Ed.). *Some persistent questions on beginning reading.* Newark, Del.: International Reading Association, 1972.

FRY, EDWARD. *Reading instruction for classroom and clinic.* New York: McGraw-Hill, 1972. Chap. 3.

HARRIS, ALBERT J. & SIPAY, EDWARD R. *Effective teaching of reading* (2nd ed.). New York: McKay, 1971. Chap. 3.

HARRIS, LARRY A. & SMITH, CARL B. *Reading instruction through diagnostic teaching.* New York: Holt, Rinehart and Winston, 1972. Chaps. 3, 4.

HEILMAN, ARTHUR W. *Principles and practices of teaching reading* (3rd ed.). Columbus: Charles E. Merrill, 1972. Chaps. 5, 6, 9.

SOUTHGATE, VERA & ROBERTS, GEOFFREY R. *Reading—which approach?* London, England: University of London Press, 1970.

VILSCEK, ELAINE C. (Ed.). *A decade of innovations: approaches to beginning reading.* Newark, Del.: International Reading Association, 1968.

WITTICK, MILDRED L. Innovations in reading instruction: for beginners. In Helen M. Robinson (Ed.). *Innovations and change in reading instruction,* 67th Yearbook of the National Society for the Study of Education, Part II. Chicago: University of Chicago Press, 1968. Chap. 3.

4

Toward Mature Reading

A half-century ago the process of learning to read was subdivided into five stages, a differentiation that still has merit (W. S. Gray, 1925). In addition to reading readiness and beginning reading, which have already been discussed in Chapters 2 and 3, three later stages were identified: rapid development of reading skills in grades 2 and 3; wide reading, characteristic of grades 4 through 6; and refinement of reading at secondary, college, and adult levels. This chapter briefly discusses the main characteristics of these stages and then considers certain special problems and issues in reading instruction.

I. LATER STAGES IN READING INSTRUCTION

Although the three stages discussed below have distinctive features, each blends into the following one, with considerable overlapping. The range of individual differences at each grade is such that some of the children are still reading at the preceding stage, while a few may have made such rapid progress that they are ready for reading activities more typical of the following stage.

Stage 3. Rapid Development of Reading Skills

The reading program of the second and third grades is of crucial importance, since in these grades the foundation for later reading should become firmly established and rapid progress is normally achieved in all important phases of reading. By the end of this period the child should be able to recognize at sight a large number of words, should be able to work out successfully the pronunciation of many unfamiliar words, should read orally with fluency and expression, should read silently with good comprehension and at a rate equal to or faster than oral reading, should be able to do factual reading at a simple level in textbooks and references, and should be well started on reading for pleasure.

In this stage developmental reading lessons still form the major part of the reading program, although functional reading and recreational reading gradually increase in importance. For developmental reading the class is usually divided into groups reading at different levels of difficulty. Problems of group instruction are considered in detail in Chapter 6. Alternative forms of more highly individualized reading instruction are described in Chapter 5. Reading instruction tends to occupy a larger part of the school day than any other part of the curriculum, averaging around ninety minutes a day.

Basal readers for these grades generally are collections of short stories arranged in groups with similar themes. Some readers put major emphasis on enjoyable fiction, while others stress the social studies value of their content. One finds stories about the farm and city; about trips to various places by plane, train, and boat; animal stories of both the "talking animal" and realistic types; folk tales and fairy tales. Vocabulary is fairly carefully controlled. Illustrations are colorful and plentiful but no longer tell a major part of the story. Correlated workbooks are supplied and can be quite helpful in providing useful supplementary silent reading activities (A. J. Harris, 1972a). Supplementary readers, phonics workbooks, tapes, recordings, filmstrips, a class library for individualized reading, textbooks in other curriculum areas, and informational books related to units or special projects are desirable in addition to the basal readers.

For those using basal readers, the general structure of lesson planning remains basically the same as at first-grade level: preparation, silent reading, oral rereading, related activities, and enrichment activities. In preparatory work, teaching the meanings of unfamiliar ideas increases in importance, although providing motivation and presenting new words continue to be essential. Silent reading is usually a few pages at a time, followed by answering questions (which may be provided in the workbook), oral discussion, and oral rereading. Systematic teaching of decoding techniques is a very important related activity. Enrichment activities are expanded in scope by the growing ability of the children to read independently.

Functional reading increases in importance in these grades. In some schools this mainly takes the form of the reading of textbooks in various subjects. In other schools it consists chiefly of reading in varied sources to obtain the information needed in the carrying on of units or projects. Weekly newspapers provide a basis for current events and other phases of the social studies in many schools.

As children become better able to read, the range of possible recreational material increases markedly. At first-grade level the classroom library consists mainly of picture books, books at pre-primer, primer, and first reader levels, and books for the teacher to read to the class. At second-grade level many children can read simple story books for pleasure, and at third-grade level there is a wide range of books and stories suitable for individual reading.

Stage 4. Stage of Wide Reading

The reading program at fourth-, fifth-, and sixth-grade levels is characterized mostly by a broadening scope of reading, with diminishing emphasis on developmental reading and growth in importance of both functional reading and recreational reading.

Developmental reading activities are concerned primarily with the further refinement and improvement of skills already well started. Time devoted to developmental reading lessons decreases to about five hours a week in fourth grade, four hours in fifth grade, and three hours in sixth grade. While the basic outline of a complete reading activity persists as a desirable general plan, considerable flexibility is in order. Preparation and oral reading usually take proportionally less time than in the primary grades. Word study is concerned more with meanings than with pronunciation. Decoding skills involve review of the primary grade decoding program, the teaching of syllabication, and systematic teaching of the use of the dictionary for both pronunciation and meanings. Silent reading is done in large units, often a complete story or selection, and comprehension questions may be given either before or after the first reading. Comprehension may be checked by written answers to questions as well as in oral discussion, and an attempt is made to develop skill in answering different kinds of questions and in reading for different purposes. Rate of reading deserves some attention, and some practice to speed up silent reading may be appropriate for those who have reached an adequate level in other skills.

In these grades the basal reader is still the primary focus of developmental reading. The readers are typically collections of selections which have been shortened and adapted from the original or written expressly for the reader. An increasing amount of factual material may be included. A representative fifth reader presents stories in the following general categories: animal stories, stories about young Americans, inventions, funny stories, children in other countries, old tales, sea stories, and stories about hunting for gold. Workbooks to accompany the readers are available. Manuals are somewhat less detailed than those for the primary grades.

Functional reading of many kinds occupies much of the time devoted to other curricular areas, since children in these grades get much of their information and instruction through reading. Materials for functional reading include textbooks in various subjects, pamphlets, informational books, magazines, newspapers, encyclopedias, and so on. Frequently a textbook in a content field requires more advanced reading skill than many of the pupils possess, requiring use of the textbook in ways different from those intended by its author. Most children in these grades need guidance in learning how to adapt their general reading skills to the specific requirements of these special kinds of reading matter. This guidance may be incorporated in the content work such as social studies or science, using the regular text material. Techniques of locating information and of summarizing and organizing it in various ways should also be taught in these grades (McCullough, 1972).

As children become more competent in reading, their capacity for independent reading grows. Much can be done in these grades to strengthen children's interest in reading for pleasure. A rich variety of good books should be made available, and time for pleasure reading should be provided in school, in addition to stimulating the use of leisure hours at home for reading. Through this independent, individualized reading a major part of the child's reading improvement and general educational growth can take place.

Stage 5. Refinement of Reading

As a student progresses through junior high school, senior high school, and college, the reading he is expected to do increases both in amount and in difficulty. There is definite need for continued guidance in reading, although this need is not recognized in many schools (Artley, 1972). The adaptation of reading to the study requirements of different kinds of courses is achieved by many students without special help; but others including many bright students, need assistance in learning how to study effectively.

Since at these levels reading is usually no longer a separate subject in the curriculum, definite planning for the provision of reading guidance is needed; otherwise it is everyone's responsibility in general and no one's responsibility in particular. At junior high school level, developmental reading and recreational reading are usually the responsibility of the English teacher. Increasingly it is recognized that guidance in functional reading is the responsibility of every subject-matter teacher, since efficient learning requires different reading patterns in science, mathematics, history, and other subjects. Developmental reading may center around the use of basal readers, of which there are several appropriate for junior high school use. Anthologies of literary selections are widely used. The poorer readers at junior high school level are still reading at various elementary school grade levels, and therefore the junior high school teacher of reading needs to understand the reading methodology of the first six grades and should be prepared to analyze the reading problems of the pupils and provide special help when needed. Recreational reading is usually a combination of the rather intensive reading and discussion of selected "classics" and individualized outside reading.

At senior high school and college levels the early remedial programs for poor readers have led into a concern for improving the reading of all students. Developmental reading programs are relatively new and take many forms. The study of literature to a large extent replaces wide, uncritical reading for pleasure, and specific training in thoughtful reading of many kinds is provided. In the improvement of rate of reading, considerable use is made of projectors and devices for controlling the speed of reading (see Chap. 19). There has also been a great expansion in the provision of courses in literacy instruction and reading improvement at the adult level, sponsored by the government, armed services, business, and industry.

II. SOME SPECIAL PROBLEMS AND ISSUES

Although each stage of reading instruction has distinct features, certain problems and issues are present at all levels and stages. A few of these are now discussed.

Oral Reading

Many years ago, instruction in reading was predominantly oral. When research began to show that children taught in this way tended to be slow, laborious readers, silent reading became the vogue. In many schools the pendulum swung so far that oral reading was almost completely neglected above the first-grade level. This tendency in turn had its bad effects, among which was inaccurate word recognition.

The traditional oral reading lesson was one in which all the pupils had the book open at the same place and were expected to follow along as each one rose in turn, read two or three sentences, and sat down as quickly as possible. Such a procedure has only a limited utility, as a rapid method of testing. Each oral reading lesson should have a specific goal and should be planned to contribute a definite value to the reading program.

It is now recognized that oral reading contributes to the total development of the child in many ways. Among them, the following are noteworthy: 1) oral reading gives the teacher a quick and valid way to evaluate progress in important reading skills, particularly those of word recognition and phrasing, and to discover specific instructional needs; 2) oral reading provides practice in oral communication for the reader and in listening skills for the audience; 3) oral reading aids in the development of effective speech patterns; 4) oral reading provides a vehicle for dramatization and effective portrayal of stories in situations where memorization would not be practical; and 5) oral reading provides a medium in which the teacher, by wise guidance, can work to improve the social adjustment of children, particularly those who are shy and retiring (Shane, 1955).

Although in the usual pattern of developmental reading lessons it is desirable for silent reading to precede oral reading, there are some situations in in which oral reading at sight is preferable. One of these is for diagnosis, when the teacher wants to get a clear picture of the child's word-recognition skills. In remedial or corrective reading, difficulties in word recognition can be corrected more quickly when the first reading is oral, since a recognition error made in silent reading goes unnoticed by the teacher. In group reading, children may enjoy from time to time getting away from the usual pattern and reading the story aloud at sight; this is particularly true of the better readers. What may be undesirable as routine procedure has real value as an occasional variation.

A partial list of types of oral reading lessons that seem to have real worth follows.

1. Taking Turns in a Small Group.   The bad effects of taking turns, as described above, are minimized if the child is a member of a small group who are similar in reading ability. Expecting a turn soon, each child is more likely to pay attention. He has a turn oftener and gets more practice in oral reading than in a whole-class lesson. Self-conciousness on the part of a poor reader is less likely because the rest of the group are not markedly better than he is. This type of oral reading activity is especially important with retarded readers.

2. Individual Reading to the Teacher.   Oral reading gives the teacher an opportunity to observe and note pupils' errors and reading habits that need correction. Having the child read a fairly long, representative selection out loud is an important phase of checking up on the pupil's reading abilities.

3. Finding and Reading Answers to Questions.   After the silent reading of a selection, some kind of checkup on comprehension has become a nearly universal practice. One procedure which brings in oral reading in a natural and significant way is to ask the children to locate in the selection the answers to specific questions. The answers are then read aloud. This provides purposeful review in silent reading as well as desirable practice in oral reading and may serve as a stimulus for interesting discussions about the correctness of the answers.

4. Audience Reading. Each pupil is given a chance to choose and prepare a selection to read to the class, preferably from material that is *not* familiar to the other pupils. After considerable practice at home, and if possible, a preliminary rehearsal with the teacher, the child reads his carefully prepared selection to his classmates. Since the material is new to them and well presented, the interest of the class is usually well sustained and the pupil experiences satisfaction from a job well done. Many good teachers of reading make a period of audience reading a weekly event.

5. Choral Reading. Certain definite values can be derived from occasional periods in which the class reads aloud in unison. The better readers carry along the poorer ones, who may gain a better appreciation of pronunciation, phrasing, rhythm, and interpretation. This kind of oral reading is especially suitable for poetry and other strongly rhythmical material.

6. Reading Parts in Radio Scripts or Plays. There is no type of oral reading that is more interesting to children or that helps them more to read with natural expression than reading a part in a play. When children are allowed to read their parts from the script, plays can be prepared and presented in a fraction of the time formerly required.

7. Reading with Varied Intonation Patterns. To get across the idea of how meaning varies with intonation, and how the same sequence of words can convey quite different meanings, it is desirable occasionally to have children read a sentence, placing stress on different words and changing the intonation pattern, and then explaining what the specific meaning of each rendition is. For example, *What* am I doing? What *am* I doing? What am *I* doing? What am I *doing?*

The Eye-Voice Span. There has recently been renewed interest in the eye-voice span. To determine a person's span roughly, cover the material suddenly while he is reading orally; the eye-voice span is the number of words he can say after the text has been concealed. In other words, it is the amount by which the reader's eyes are ahead of his voice. The eye-voice span, which is normally the amount the person can read in one second (Geyer, 1968), shows that already perceived material is stored in short-term memory until the vocal response is made. The eye-voice span is longer for sentences than for unrelated words, and with meaningful material the span tends to stop at a phrase boundary rather than within a phrase, showing that it is controlled somewhat by the apprehension of meaning (Levin and Kaplan, 1970). A large eye-voice span tends to accompany superior reading; a small span often goes with slow, choppy, word-by-word reading. This is in harmony with evidence that good readers tend to respond to cues at the intersentence, sentence, phrase, and word levels while poor readers tend to respond mainly to part-word and word cues (Clay and Imlach, 1971).

The length of the eye-voice span also has been studied in terms of the number of words. For example, Levin and Turner (1966) found the average eye-voice span was approximately 3 words for second graders and 4½ words for fourth graders. The eye-voice span tends to increase with age (Buswell, 1920; Levin and Cohn, 1968), and is influenced by the meaningfulness of the material (Lawson, 1961; Morton 1964), and linguistic constraints (Wanat and Levin, 1970; Fusaro, 1974).

Silent Reading

Changes have also taken place in the teaching of silent reading. One of them is the tendency to think in terms of specific kinds of reading and to plan lessons designed to improve a particular reading skill. One lesson is designed to give practice in finding the central idea of a selection, another to improve ability at locating answers to specific questions, a third to develop ability to remember the sequence of events, and so on. Each lesson should have a definite aim or aims. Reading for appreciation and pleasure is clearly distinguished from work-type reading or study. Dissection of plot and characters is avoided in pleasure-type reading because of its tendency to spoil enjoyment, while habits of careful and accurate reading are built up with carefully planned exercises in the reading of informational material.

Another trend in silent reading has been toward increasing the amount and broadening the scope of the reading done in the schools. The use of basal readers is supplemented by wide reading in a variety of sources. Magazines, pamphlets, and newspapers are brought into the classroom and used as instructional materials. The "classics" have had to make room for a large amount of reading that is intimately related to contemporary life. Functional reading of many varied types absorbs a major part of the total time spent in school.

Comprehension after Silent and Oral Reading and Listening

Whether one comprehends better in oral reading, silent reading, or listening seems to be related to how well one can read. In grades 2, 3, and

4, below-average readers tend to comprehend best after listening, next best after oral reading, and worst after silent reading (Swalm, 1972). Average readers may comprehend better in oral than in silent reading (Morris, 1970) or do about equally well in both (Swalm, 1972). In grades 2 to 4 oral reading, and silent reading followed by oral, both provided higher comprehension than silent reading alone, and were about equal; there were, however, marked individual differences and some pupils did best after silent reading only (Glenn, 1971). Above fourth grade, one should not be surprised to find that poor readers do best in listening, below-average readers are helped to comprehend by oral reading, and good readers read with better comprehension as well as more rapidly in silent reading.

Decoding

The research evidence (reviewed in Chap. 3) has failed to indicate a marked superiority for any one approach in beginning reading. In recent studies a variety of methods which introduce word-identification skills earlier and more intensively than meaning-emphasis basal readers have produced results as good as, or better than, those of basal readers. So did the language-experience approach, in which phonic skills tend to be given less systematic attention than in basal reader teaching. No one approach has succeeded with all children.

Efficient reading requires both that the reader develop an extensive sight vocabulary and that he be able to work out the pronunciation and meaning of unfamiliar words he meets while reading. Fluency requires fast recognition of hundreds, and later thousands, of words. It is also necessary that children should learn how to figure out unknown words without help from the teacher. The greater the emphasis that is placed on wide independent reading, the more urgent it is for children to be able to decode unfamiliar words. Formerly, reliance was placed exclusively on the teaching of phonic sounding and blending as the major aid in unlocking new words. Today it is recognized that there are many ways of decoding words and that a good reader is not dependent on any one of these procedures, but has several techniques and makes use of the one that best fits the situation. The term *decoding* is used to include all methods by which a word can be divided and its pronunciation worked out.

Modern teaching of decoding makes use of four main approaches, which are applied in conjunction in solving an unknown word, not as alternatives. First, children are helped to make intelligent use of the context or meaningful setting in which the new word appears. Second, children are taught to apply structural analysis techniques of several kinds— recognition of root words and endings (play-ing), prefixes, roots and suffixes, separation of a word into known parts, and syllabication. Third, phonics is definitely taught, since knowledge of the sound equivalents of letters and letter combinations is essential. And last, the use of the dictionary is taught as a dependable aid in determining the pronunciation, meaning, and correct spelling of words.

Words are to be analyzed when they cannot be recognized as wholes, and the analysis need be carried only so far as necessary to solve the word. Thus, it would be foolish to attack the word "schoolmaster" one phonic element at a time if a child already has "school" and "master" in his sight vocabulary. Structural and phonic clues should be used in combination with the context, and therefore instruction should not be concerned primarily with words in lists, but rather should emphasize meaningful material.

When a child has done very poorly with the word-identification skills he has been taught in a developmental program, it is often desirable to use a quite different method of instruction in remedial teaching. Thus the remedial teacher needs to understand and be able to teach several different approaches to the development of word-recognition skills and to select the most effective one for a given child.

The improvement of word recognition and decoding is considered in Chapters 14 and 15.

Reading in Content Areas

Some children whose reading is satisfactory in basal readers and in self-chosen library books run into difficulty in applying their reading skills in content areas such as science, mathematics, and social studies. This is sometimes due to a misfit between book difficulty and reader competence. Many content textbooks are substantially more difficult by conventional measures of readability than basal readers intended for the same grade level, and children for whom the basal reader is at their instructional level may run into frustration when trying to read a difficult text or reference book. Sometimes the child attempts to read the content textbook in the same way that he reads a story in a reader, resulting in superficial comprehension and poor retention.

The improvement of functional reading in content areas is considered in greater detail in Chapter 17.

Recognition of Individual Differences

Even more significant than the specific changes in teaching procedures has been the increasing awareness of the importance of individual differences as a factor in reading. Some teachers still seem to believe that if their teaching is good it should bring all or nearly all their pupils up to a fairly uniform level of achievement. The schools are realizing more and more the falsity of this belief. Children when they enter school differ widely in their abilities and in their potentialities for future development. With efficient instruction, these differences should increase rather than decrease as they progress through school. Even when the truly dull child is brought by highly efficient instruction up to the highest level that his capacity allows, he will still be far behind his bright classmates. Uniformity of achievement in a class is more apt to indicate neglect of the abler pupils than generally effective teaching.

This recognition of the significance of individual differences has brought about all sorts of attempts to adjust the school program to the varying abilities of the pupils. These have included plans for classifying pupils into instructional groups on the basis of general reading ability and plans that attempt to provide complete individualization of the reading program. Realization of the importance of meeting the needs of each pupil has brought remedial instruction into the foreground. This should not be conceived too narrowly. The aim of the teacher should be not merely to help those who are poor in reading but rather to help every pupil, the good as well as the poor, to develop the maximum power in reading of which he is capable. Ways of providing for individual differences are discussed in Chapters 5 and 6.

Major Concerns of Classroom Teachers about Reading

One hundred elementary and junior high school teachers were asked to complete the statement, "My greatest problem in teaching reading is . . ." The most frequently mentioned problems were: 1) finding enough time to do the job, 2) meeting individual needs, 3) motivating pupils to want to read, 4) finding suitable materials, 5) diagnosing reading problems, 6) getting pupils to use their work-attack skills, and 7) providing meaningful seatwork (Schubert, 1971). These concerns seem quite typical, and similar to the responses of groups of teachers of whom the present writers have asked similar questions.

III. SOME GENERAL CONSIDERATIONS

There is no one plan for teaching reading that is ideally suited to meet the needs of all teachers. Classes of pupils differ in mental ability, in background, in previously acquired skill in reading, and in the amount of variation in the class. The availability of materials also differs; some teachers have nothing to use except one set of readers, while others are provided with extensive and varied instructional material. Finally, teachers themselves vary in many significant ways: in amount and kind of training, in resourcefulness, in energy, in temperamental characteristics. The best program for a particular teacher to follow is one that is adapted to his pupils, makes efficient use of his materials, and is suited to his abilities as a teacher.

There are, however, certain general principles that should be incorporated into any method of teaching reading. While specific applications may and should differ according to circumstances, these principles are fundamentally important and provide a basis for evaluating the probable effectiveness of any plan.

1. Reading must be made an enjoyable activity. Methods that conceive of reading narrowly as a collection of word-recognition and comprehension skills, to be taught by drill methods, often fail to achieve this important goal. If pupils are to develop a genuine liking for reading, provision must be made to encourage large amounts of silent reading in materials that are interesting and of suitable difficulty. Every reading plan should try to build up the habit of reading for fun.

2. Systematic training must be given in the mastery of specific reading skills. In the primary grades much emphasis has to be placed on the acquisition of a fundamental reading vocabulary, on the development of accuracy and independence in word recognition, and on reading for meaning. Above the primary level, attention should be given to the continued expansion of vocabulary, the refinement of comprehension, and the mastery of the many varied skills that are required in work-type reading and study.

3. A good reading program is balanced and contains varied activities. The relative emphasis to be placed on silent and oral reading, on specific practice and unsupervised reading, on recreational and informational reading, naturally differs according to local conditions. A program that emphasizes any one phase of reading to the virtual exclusion of all others, however, is practically certain to produce a corresponding lack of balance in the reading abilities of the pupils.

4. Provision must be made for individual differences. Pupils differ widely in every significant trait that can be observed. An effective plan of teaching reading must take account of variations in intelligence, in language and conceptual skills, in maturity, in interest, and in the presence or absence of handicaps to learning. If a reading program is to succeed with all pupils, it must be flexible enough to give different pupils the kinds of instruction they need.

5. Special attention must be given to pupils whose reading is below normal. Every teacher should be alert to notice the difficulties of individual children and should arrange his teaching so as to leave time for giving these pupils the assistance they need. It does not matter very much whether this assistance is given individually or in small groups, by the regular teacher or by a special remedial teacher, so long as it is based on an intelligent diagnosis of his needs and helps to overcome his difficulties.

6. *Ideally there should be a planned reading curriculum extending from kindergarten through high school.* With clearly stated objectives arranged by skills and by grades or levels, each teacher can know what pupils should have learned in previous years, and what this year should prepare them to do in following years. Instruction can be adapted to individual needs without losing sight of overall goals.

SUGGESTED ADDITIONAL READING

ARTLEY, A. STERL. *Trends and practices in secondary reading: a review of the literature.* Newark, Del.: International Reading Association, 1968.

GOODMAN, KENNETH & NILES, OLIVE. *Reading: process and program.* Urbana, Ill.: National Council of Teachers of English, 1970.

GUSZAK, FRANK J. *Diagnostic reading instruction in the elementary school.* New York: Harper & Row, 1972. Chap. 12.

HARRIS, ALBERT J. & SIPAY, EDWARD R. *Effective teaching of reading* (2nd ed.). New York: McKay, 1971. Chap. 5.

HEILMAN, ARTHUR W. *Principles and practices of teaching reading* (3rd ed.). Columbus: Charles E. Merrill, 1972. Chaps. 10, 12.

HUUS, HELEN. Innovations in reading instruction: at later grade levels. In Helen M. Robinson (Ed.). *Innovation and change in reading instruction,* 67th Yearbook of the National Society for the Study of Education, Part II. Chicago: University of Chicago Press, 1968. Chap. 4.

SMITH, RICHARD J. & BARRETT, THOMAS C. *Teaching reading in the middle grades.* Reading, Mass.: Addison-Wesley, 1974.

TINKER, MILES A. & MCCULLOUGH, CONSTANCE M. *Teaching elementary reading* (3rd ed.). New York: Appleton-Century-Crofts, 1968. Chaps. 22, 23, 24, 25.

5

Meeting Individual Needs in Reading

Among conscientious teachers of reading, dissatisfaction with the degree to which they succeed in meeting the instructional needs of every pupil is almost universal. Whether the teacher is in a conventional graded school or an ungraded school, teaching children of widely varying reading abilities or a group brought together because of similar reading skills or needs, he usually finds that not all pupils respond with substantial improvement. Many solutions to this problem have been tried, but a fully satisfactory answer is still an unreached goal. The issues involved in attempting to provide reading instruction suited to every child are so many, and the proposed solutions so numerous, that it will take this chapter and Chapter 6 to explore them.

I. THE SIZE OF INDIVIDUAL DIFFERENCES IN READING

The data in Table 3 are based on the standardization data for the 1973 revision of the *Stanford Achievement Tests*, Reading Comprehension.[1]

1. The following information is quoted by permission of Harcourt Brace Jovanovich, Inc., from the *Manual Part II: Norms Booklet for Stanford*: "A total of 109 school systems drawn from 43 states participated; over 275,000 pupils were tested in the three standardization programs. . . . The standardization samples were selected to represent the national population in terms of geographic region, size of city, socioeconomic status, and public and non-public schools."

Looking at the data for the end of grade 4, one can see that the full range is from below second grade to ninth grade and above; leaving out the top 10 per cent and bottom 10 per cent, the range of the middle 80 per cent is still over five years. If one were to divide this population into a top 30 per cent, middle 40 per cent, and bottom 30 per cent, the top group has reading grade scores of 6.0 and up, a range of at least three years; the middle group ranges from 3.9 to 5.9, a range of two years; and the bottom group ranges from 3.8 down to 1.0 or complete nonreader, a range of nearly three years. The scores for grade 6 are even more spread out; for grade 2, slightly less so.

Findings such as these, repeated in survey after survey, have produced determined efforts to provide school situations that can deal with the realities of individual differences. These efforts have been of two major kinds. One kind includes many types of administrative attempts to reduce the range of differences in a class to teachable levels. The other kind includes the various ways of adapting instruction within the classroom to individual differences.

TABLE 3. *Grade equivalent scores on the Stanford Achievement Reading Comprehension Test corresponding to selected percentile ranks, Form A*

Percentile Ranks	Grade Equivalent Scores		
	Primary Level End of Grade 2	Intermediate Level I End of Grade 4	Intermediate Level II End of Grade 6
99	7.0+	9.5+	10.5+
90	4.6	7.7	10.5+
80	4.0	6.7	10.2
70	3.5	6.0	8.6
60	3.2	5.5	7.6
50	2.9	4.9	6.9
40	2.6	4.4	6.4
30	2.4	3.9	5.7
20	2.1	3.3	4.9
10	1.6	2.5	3.9
1	1.0−	2.0−	3.0−

Goals for Differentiated Reading Instruction

Before taking up the details of plans that aim at meeting the problem of wide individual differences in reading ability, it is desirable to consider what the specific objectives should be for any plan of differentiated reading instruction. Such objectives fall naturally into four categories.

There is, first of all, the objective of providing opportunities for the maximum growth of each child in the important phases of reading. A plan that is concerned only with developmental reading is too limited in scope; recreational reading and functional reading must be given careful consideration also.

Second, a sound plan for reading instruction must necessarily be one that favors the social and personal adjustment of all the children and helps to foster the development of truly democratic attitudes and practices. Many complaints against specific classification or grouping procedures have arisen from experiences in which snobbishness, social ostracism, defeatism, and bitter resentment seemed to result from the procedure. A sound plan should be acceptable to administrators, teachers, pupils, and parents. It should be one in which children are helped to become happier and more secure, as well as better in reading skills.

In the third place, the plan should be one which can be carried out by teachers of average training and ability. Some of the plans that have been praised in the professional literature portray an exceptionally expert and creative teacher carrying out a program that requires a great deal of planning and preparation. Exhorting average teachers to adopt such a plan sometimes discourages them from trying anything new, because they feel quite unable to meet the requirements. Realistic plans must be usable by most teachers, and at the same time provide scope for creative work by superior teachers.

Finally, a good plan should fit the school and its pupils. Some good plans are workable only in large schools with hundreds of pupils. Others require an abundance and variety of materials far beyond the resources of the typical school. The little red schoolhouse, with eight grades in one room, enforced a kind of differentiated instruction rarely seen in graded schools. Each school has to appraise its own situation and work out solutions that fit its own needs.

II. ADMINISTRATIVE PROVISIONS FOR READING INSTRUCTION

Retardation and Acceleration

Fifty years ago, it was still common to find 30 to 40 per cent of first graders required to repeat the year, with smaller but still substantial percentages of nonpromotion in higher grades (Caswell, 1933). By 1950 many school systems were promoting children regardless of achievement, relying on research that had shown that nonpromotion neither improved achievement nor reduced the range of individual differences; the nonpromoted child was more likely to leave school early, to be a discipline problem, and to have social difficulties (Anderson and Ritsher, 1969).

On the other hand, so-called "one hundred per cent promotion" plans also have been disappointing. New York City, after trying a "continuous progress" plan involving less than 2 per cent nonpromotion for a dozen years, officially restored nonpromotion as an approved policy in 1958, with reading performance more than two years below grade level as the recommended criterion. This was to be considered an opportunity to provide intensive help to the child, not just repetition of the same program.

Ideally, promotion policy should allow each child to be with the group in which he can make the best total adjustment, socially and educationally. This is usually—but not always—his own age group. Children of exceptional all-round maturity usually benefit from some acceleration, and children who are quite immature in general may be better off in a younger group. The extent to which instruction can be provided at the child's functioning level is also an important factor in the decision.

Postponing Reading for All Children

John Dewey was one of the earliest proponents of the idea that reading is taught when children are too young. In 1898 he stated that "present physiological knowledge points to the age of about eight years as early enough for anything more than an incidental attention to visual and written language-forms" (quoted in Huey, 1908, p. 306). Considering the difficulties of the phonic methods popular at that time and the high rate of failure then prevalent, his proposal does not sound unreasonable; but methods of instruction have changed. In Sweden, beginning reading instruction at the age of 7 has not prevented the occurrence of reading disabilities (Malmquist, 1958, 1969). Postponing reading for all does not abolish or even lessen individual differences; it simply delays the time at which adjustment to varied learning rates will have to be made.

Homogeneous Grouping

In the first wave of efforts to cope with individual differences, many plans of "homogeneous grouping" were tried out. Classes at the same grade level were organized on the basis of ability. Grouping was based on intelligence, reading achievement, average achievement, teacher judgment, or some combination. In some schools all classes covered the same curriculum, but at different rates of speed; in relatively few were there real differences in content and methodology. When achievement in homogeneous classes was compared with that in ungrouped schools, differences were found to be slight. It was found that when a class was made homogeneous in one trait, the children still tended to be quite varied in their other traits. In many places complaints developed about unfavorable attitudes of teachers and pupils toward the slower classes. A recent review finds the evidence about homogeneous grouping's effects on learning to be mixed and inconclusive with regard to achievement, and to show reduced self-esteem of children assigned to low-ability groups (Esposito, 1973). As subgrouping within classes became popular, many schools discontinued homogeneous grouping. It is still practiced in many junior and senior high schools and in some large elementary schools. After more than thirty years in use, homogeneous grouping still fails to show an advantage in educational growth (Justman, 1968).

The Special Class for Poor Readers

Some large elementary schools have tried the idea of gathering together into one room all the poorest readers at a particular grade level, while the rest of the school has heterogeneous classes. Such a special class is kept small (preferably under twenty), the teacher is selected on the basis of ability to work with poor learners, extra materials are supplied, and the teacher is free to deviate from the usual curriculum of the grade. Such classes are often called "opportunity classes," although it is probably better not to give them a special designation. If such a class is set up and works well, it may be desirable to keep the teacher and children together for a two-year period.

One of the major advantages of this plan is that it relieves the other teachers of the children who require a disproportionate share of the teacher's time and energy in a regular class and reduces individual differences in the regular classes to the point where teachers feel competent to deal with them.

The special class, of course, requires a teacher whose skills include a practical working knowledge both of mental health principles and of corrective and remedial techniques. Even with such a teacher, the special reading class may become very difficult to manage if it is overloaded with children who are severely maladjusted.

Cross-Grade and Cross-Class Grouping for Reading

Plans in which children are grouped homogeneously only for reading instruction have been in operation for over thirty years. Such plans involve the giving of reading tests to all the children in the grades in which the plan is to be used. On the basis of test results and teacher judgment the pupils are divided into reading classes, all of which are scheduled for reading at the same time. When the bell rings, each child goes to his reading teacher, and when the reading period is over he returns to his homeroom. Plans of this sort are often referred to as Joplin Plans, since a variation of the plan used in Joplin, Missouri, received wide publicity in 1957.

In a small school with one class per grade, such a plan would require cross-grade grouping, with, for example, the reading scores for all pupils in grades 4, 5, and 6 placed in a single rank order. The sixth-grade teacher could have the upper group for reading, the fifth-grade teacher the middle group, and the fourth-grade teacher the lowest group, which might be a little smaller than the other two. In a large school with several classes at each grade it is possible to have cross-class grouping for reading within each grade.

In a plan of this sort the range of reading scores is reduced from about six years to two to three years; it is still far from real homogeneity, since not only is there still a two-year or more span of reading levels but also individual pupils with similar scores may have different kinds of reading problems. However, it does come closer to placing each child in a reading situation in which he can experience some success.

Cushenbery (1967) described the plan as it operated in Joplin and reviewed the relevant research. Although he found the plan to have limitations as well as advantages, he concluded: "The Joplin Plan of grouping for reading instruction is one of the most significant advances in attempting to meet the needs of children in reading instruction. The advantages of the plan appear to outweigh the limitations, particularly when the procedures are introduced in a careful, systematic manner into a given school system." On the other hand, two reviewers have concluded that once the newness of the plan wears off, the improved reading found during the first year or two tends to disappear (Newport, 1967; W. Miller, 1971).

When the plan includes some differentiation of instruction within the reading class, increased expenditures for reading materials, conferences between teachers, and enthusiastic administrative support, as is said to be true in Joplin, the results can be highly satisfactory. Nevertheless, several limitations, if not forestalled, can limit the effectiveness of the plan. There is a temptation to treat the reading class as if it were truly homogeneous. When reading is taught by one teacher and the other curriculum areas by another teacher, there may be interference with the correlation of the work of the pupils. There may be little opportunity to combine word recognition with spelling, to utilize social studies material for practice in work-type reading, and so on. The rigidity of a set time schedule also imposes some limitations. The reading teacher who has a child only for the reading period may not get to know him very well. The fact that reading is a tool more than a subject tends to be obscured. The plan gives teachers an opportunity; how that opportunity is used determines whether the results are superior or mediocre.

Classification for Reading in Secondary School

Grouping plans similar to those employed in elementary schools have been employed successfully in some secondary schools as an aid to more effective work in teaching reading. In secondary schools reading is not usually considered a separate subject, but is included in the English curriculum.

At junior high and senior high school levels, concern about reading first took the form of remedial programs for the disabled reader. The trend in recent years has been toward increasing recognition of the need to continue to refine and improve reading skills beyond the elementary school level. While primary responsibility at secondary school level tends to be placed with the teacher of English or of a core combining English with one or more other subjects, many attempts have been made to draw the teachers of other subjects into taking an active part in refining reading skills. The slogan "Every Teacher a Teacher of Reading" has not yet been fulfilled by any means, but progress toward this ideal is being made. Since training in the teaching of reading has not been part of the professional preparation of most secondary school teachers, it is going to take some time and much in-service staff training before the objectives of such an ideal are satisfactorily achieved.

So many different kinds of programs for reading have been evolved in secondary schools that it is impossible to review them here; the reader is referred to the books listed at the end of the chapter.

The Nongraded School

The ideas that each child should be able to move ahead in school at his own rate of learning and that yearly grades are too coarse a basis for pupil classification have resulted in nongraded plans of organization, usually restricted to the primary years (Goodlad and Anderson, 1959). Pupil classification is usually based mainly on reading. The primary reading curriculum is usually divided into eight to twelve instructional levels; a twelve-level plan includes readiness, three pre-primer levels, and then levels for primer, 1^2, 2^1, 2^2, 3^1, 3^2, 4, and 5 (as in basal reader series). Usually the child's assignment to a level is based mainly on informal reading tests and teacher judgment, tempered by considerations of age, social maturity, and progress in other curricular areas. Each teacher usually has not more than three adjacent levels in a self-contained classroom. A child may move to the next higher level at any time during the year, whenever he completes the program for the present level. There is continuous progress in that no child is ever required to repeat, although children move through the levels at different speeds. Thus most children complete the primary program in three years; some take four years; a few may complete it in two years.

Because children who are at the same instructional level may have different patterns of reading skills and needs, a considerable amount of individualization is necessary in a nongraded plan. Careful diagnosis and planning for individuals are desirable in any plan for reading instruction; the need seems to be more clearly recognized and more vital for success in a nongraded plan than in a conventional school. "The nongraded requires a very definitive method for the identification and inventorying of a pupil's achievements. It requires a knowledge and specificity about each child which was not somehow necessary under the graded situation. Teachers must know exactly what skills a youngster has mastered in each curricular area before he can proceed from one sequential learning level to the next" (Glogau and Fessell, 1967). Research thus far has failed to demonstrate improved reading achievement in nongraded as compared to conventional schools (Di Lorenzo and Salter, 1965; McLoghlin, 1967). Apparently what happens in the nongraded classroom often falls short of the hopes of the plan's supporters.

As one reads about the various administrative plans that have been tried, the striking fact is that all of them seem to have produced quite favorable results in the local situations in which they were developed. Probably the enthusiasm and ability of the people operating the plan and the appeal of novelty will give any sensible innovation an advantage over what was done before. In this, as in many other important questions about reading instruction, research has produced no final answers.

III. DIFFERENTIATED LEARNING WITHIN THE CLASSROOM

If a reading program is to be richly varied in its objectives and learnings, it is reasonable to expect that no one way of organizing the class will serve all these purposes equally well. A well-rounded reading program includes several different kinds of class organization, each used for the reading activities for which it is best suited. The question is no longer one of choosing between individualization and grouping, but rather of how to combine several kinds of organization, including whole-class activities, individualized reading, and group reading, into a harmonious whole.

Whole-Class Reading Activities

Several kinds of reading activities can profitably be carried on with the entire class. They include audience situations, common new learnings, current events reading, "open-book" textbook sessions, and choral reading. Each of these has a legitimate place in the total reading program.

Audience Situations.   One type of oral reading approved for modern schools involves the presentation to the class of an oral reading selection which has been prepared and rehearsed. Materials can include poems, jokes, selections from stories and books, radio scripts, or short plays. The presentation may be by an individual or small groups. Sessions in which children give oral book reports or present reports based on individual or committee reading also can provide whole-class audience situations. The two important features are 1) advance preparation, so that the performance is reasonably good; and 2) the class does not read along silently, but is a real audience.

Common New Learnings.   There are many occasions when a new reading skill can be introduced to the whole class, even though not all will learn it with equal rapidity. Alphabetizing, the use of such aids as the table of contents, index, dictionary and encyclopedia, and new phonic principles and word meanings are among the reading skills that can be introduced in this way.

Current Events.   School newspapers provide opportunities for current event periods in which all can participate. Weekly graded editions make it possible for all to do the same kind of reading together, while some may be reading an advanced edition and others an edition intended for lower grades. In the primary grades, experience stories can be used for the same purpose.

Textbook Reading.   When a textbook is the focus of a particular curriculum area, it may be necessary to have open-book sessions in which the textbook is used like a basal reader. Often the unavailability of simpler textbooks makes it necessary to use the one book with the entire class. The poorer readers get the content mainly by listening and are called on only for comparatively easy passages or questions. Better ways to take care of the needs of pupils for whom the content textbook is frustratingly difficult are discussed on pages 495–496.

Choral Reading.   The occasional use of choral reading not only is helpful for the appreciation of poetry and rhythm but also assists in developing the spirit of belongingness and group cohesion in the class.

Group Reading Activities

The essential character of a group reading activity is that a number of children carry on a reading activity together. Usually all are using the same material. Groups may be set up according to reading level, specific needs, or interests; the activity may be carried out with the teacher present, with a pupil acting as leader, or as silent seatwork. The major part of reading instruction in the elementary schools of the United States is carried on in groups. Since group reading instruction is discussed in detail in the following chapter, it is only mentioned at this point.

Individualized Reading Activities

A completely individualized reading situation is one in which no two children in the class are reading the same thing at the same time. Individualized reading makes it possible to provide maximum flexibility in adjusting reading to individual abilities, interests, and needs. It naturally requires an abundance of varied materials. An entire class may be engaged in individualized reading at one time, or part of the class may be reading individually while other children work in groups. Individualized procedures have been developed for four different kinds of reading activity: recreational reading, research reading, practice in reading skills, and developmental reading.

Individualized Recreational Reading. Periods for recreational reading in which each child is free to read what he pleases (from the materials available) have been called *free-reading* periods. During such a period the teacher can circulate among the class, spending a minute with one child and five minutes with another. These individual contacts can be spent in discussing a book already finished, considering with the child what he might like to read next, finding out more about the child's interests or problems, listening to some oral reading, providing help on a specific difficulty, and so on.

Since in a free-reading program the pupils read only what they like, there are great possibilities for developing and broadening interest in reading. Extensive reading will in itself bring about some enrichment of vocabulary and improvement of speed and comprehension. It is necessary, of course, to have books available covering a wide variety of subject matter and of suitable difficulty. Arrangements can often be made to borrow an appropriate collection of books from the school library or from a public library; librarians are ordinarily glad to cooperate with teachers. A given amount of money can go farther if much of it is spent on paperbacks. The teacher employing free reading must always keep in mind that the success of the method depends on the extent to which it builds more favorable attitudes toward reading and gets the pupils to read more.

Individualized Research Reading. Modern teaching procedures create many occasions for a child to read by himself to find needed information.

For good readers this highly functional reading provides multiple opportunities for intellectual enrichment and personal development. For the poor reader, the absence of relevant material simple enough for him to comprehend is often a cause of frustration and the decline of intellectual curiosity.

Individualized Skills Practice. There can be a place in the schedule for periods in which each child can work on particular reading skills in which he needs to improve. For this to be effective one must have ways of determining individual needs, making individual assignments, and providing practice materials which have been set up with clear, self-administering directions and scoring keys.

IV. TYPES OF INDIVIDUALIZED READING PROGRAMS

Individualized Developmental Reading

Since 1950, much has been written about a form of developmental reading instruction in which major reliance is placed on each child reading self-selected books by himself, with periodic conferences with the teacher. This has been variously called Individualized Reading (in capitals), IRP (Individualized Reading Program), or personalized reading. It is here called "individualized developmental reading" to distinguish it from other forms of instruction in which individualized procedures are employed.

Individualized developmental reading is characterized by eliminating systematic instruction with basal readers and using individual reading in a variety of reading materials as the core of method rather than as a supplement. The basal reader method (see Chap. 3) generally has a succession of steps: preparation, guided reading and discussion, oral reading, related skills practice including word attack, and enrichment. Most of these steps are eliminated in individualized developmental reading.

Each child selects a book that he wishes to read, sometimes with help from the teacher. During reading periods he reads ahead in the book silently, getting help from the teacher or another pupil if he needs it. At intervals (usually once or twice a week) he has an individual conference with the teacher, which may involve discussion of what he has been reading, some oral reading, and perhaps some skills teaching. Preparation for reading is almost completely eliminated. Reading is usually not guided by any specifically stated purposes except interest in the book. Comprehension is checked occasionally, and usually on the general plot rather than on details or inferences. Rereading is usually eliminated in favor of doing a large amount of varied reading. Workbooks usually have no place in such a program. Training in word recognition and decoding consists of help given to a child as opportunities occur during the conferences, and sometimes groups are formed who need help on specific reading skills.

Three words often repeated by exponents of individualized developmental reading are *seeking, self-selection,* and *pacing.* These imply that the child is to explore a wide range of available reading material, choose his own reading, and proceed at his own pace. Great stress is placed on the importance of these factors in developing a spontaneous love for reading and in allowing reading to fit harmoniously into the unique pattern of growth of each child. The gradual, steady introduction of new words that can be obtained by reading a series of readers in sequence is considered unnecessary.

Jacobs (1958) listed the following teacher characteristics as important: the teacher recognizes that learning to read is a continuous, cumulative accomplishment; is well-informed about reading skills; provides ample time for individual reading and for various kinds of group reading; arranges for individual skills reading as well as for independent recreational reading; provides time for children to share their reading experiences; provides a varied, extensive collection of reading matter, including practice and self-testing materials; encourages the child to select reading matter that extends his growing edges; develops an adequate system of record keeping; utilizes appropriate evaluation procedures; and makes appropriate arrangements for independent work for others while an individual is working with the teacher.

There are many differences of opinion on the details of individualized developmental reading. Procedures at first- or second-grade level naturally would be somewhat different from those at higher grade levels. Most of the reports have described programs in the middle elementary grades.

Some of the important issues will now be discussed:

1. *Class Size.* Obviously the smaller the class, the easier it is to operate an individualized program. Most of the successfully individualized classes known to us have had fewer than twenty-five children. Veatch (1958) stated, however, that a successful program can be managed with a class of forty or more.

2. *Time Necessary.* It is usually recommended that between one and two hours a day are needed, which may be divided into morning and afternoon periods.

3. *Books Needed.* It seems to be generally agreed that a classroom library should contain at least three times as many books as there are children in the class; there should be great variety in both content and difficulty. The class library contents should be changed periodically.

INDIVIDUAL CONFERENCE RECORD

Name _____ *Sue* _____   Date _____ *8/29* _____
Book *Where's the Bunny?*   Pages _____ *8–12* _____

Oral reading

Generally fluent; phrasing ability has improved markedly.

May have some difficulty decoding words containing vowel combinations.

Comprehension

Easily answered all comprehension questions, including inferred main idea which used to cause her difficulty.

Able to relate to past experiences.

Observations and Plans

Seems to enjoy this type of story; check with librarian for other suggestions. Also try humorous stories.

Overall oral reading ability continues to improve; she seems much more relaxed and confident.

Check ability to make symbol – sound associations for common and consistent combinations.

FIGURE 5.1   Record of Sue's individual reading conference. This, or a
similar form, may be used for record keeping in individualized developmental reading or remedial reading.

4. *Record Keeping.* The teacher has to keep a cumulative record for each child, noting the date, the book he is reading, the page he is on, and any special points to keep in mind. The pupil also usually keeps a record of books finished.

5. *Independent Activities.* In the first or second grade the teacher must be skilled at setting up a variety of self-directing nonreading activities at which children can keep busy for fairly long periods. The few children who will read to the teacher that day read silently near her while the rest paint, work in clay, and so on. From the third grade up this may not be necessary.

6. *Group Activities.* Children may be brought together by the teacher on the basis of a common need for help or may spontaneously form a group on the basis of a common interest. Groups are temporary and are disbanded as soon as the specific purpose is accomplished.

7. *Scheduling Conferences.* There is a general preference for spending about ten minutes with each child. Allowing time for meeting with groups and for sessions in which children discuss and share their reading with one another, most teachers try to get around the class in three or four days. Some teachers arrange the conference schedule themselves and post the names for the day on the board, while others prefer to have the children volunteer, which means that the less interested come least often.

8. *Teaching of Skills.* Phonic principles are usually taught by pointing out features of words to an individual child during a conference, and comprehension is also checked mainly by discussion during the individual conferences. Provision of special materials for practice on specific skills, as suggested by Jacobs (1958), does not seem to be a common practice. Some teachers do a good deal of skills teaching with small groups, while some introduce new skills in whole-class sessions.

9. *Evaluation Procedures.* Most emphasis is given to the quantity and quality of books read and to children's expressed feelings about the books. Analysis of skills is usually based on informal observations during the individual conferences. There are relatively few reports of standardized test results. Children are encouraged to be evaluative in regard to their own performances.

While a large number of studies involving Individualized Reading have appeared, many of them are faulty. "Much of the reported research suffers from poor research design, inadequate sampling, careless measurement, and a biased attitude on the part of the investigator" (Duker, 1968). The following quotation seems to be a fair evaluation of the results of the research on Individualized Reading:

> An examination of the research reports leads to these tentative conclusions about individualized reading instruction: 1) Individualized reading can be

somewhat successful under certain conditions. 2) It requires highly competent teachers, and those who are not particularly capable should not be asked
to adopt it. 3) Children usually enjoy the personal attention of the individual
conference and, as a result, develop favorable attitudes toward reading. 4)
They often, but not always, read more books. 5) The less capable pupils and
those having special problems are likely to be less successful in individualized
reading than in more structured programs. 6) The lack of a sequential skills
program and opportunities for readiness instruction cause teachers to feel
doubtful about the adequacy of skills learning. 7) Teachers are constantly
pressed for time to provide conferences that pupils should have. (Sartain,
1969)

It seems unlikely that the kind of individualized developmental reading discussed above will ever achieve wide acceptance, although it can produce excellent results when all conditions are favorable. "Seeking, self-
selection, and pacing" are very well adapted to recreational reading, however, and it is quite probable that an individualized, free-reading approach
to recreational reading will be an integral part of the total reading program
in more and more schools.

Reading in Informal or Open Schools

There has recently been much discussion of a variety of primary and
elementary school programs that have the common element of replacing
planned curriculum sequences with child-centered and, to a large extent,
child-initiated learning activities. Essentially this is a reformulation of what
used to be called Progressive Education (A. J. Harris, 1964). Much of the
present interest has been generated by a desire to emulate the British
informal infant and junior schools. The ideal classroom is seen as an active,
busy place where children choose their activities and engage in them individually or in small, temporary groups. The teacher's role is that of a
helper and resource person more than as a director of learning. "Rather
than a disseminator of knowledge, the new teacher must be one of many
resources available to the youngster as he acquires knowledge" (Ross,
1972).

These schools have been variously called *open* or *informal* or *free
schools*; the latter term has been used mainly for private schools modeled
more or less after the permissiveness of Summerhill. Usually the classes
are nongraded and often include children with an age range of two or three
years. Team teaching and open work areas are other features often included
(Congreve and Rinehart, 1972).

Reading instruction in such schools tends to be a combination of language experience and Individualized Reading procedures, with relatively
little systematic attention to skills development (Moss, 1972; Watters,

1971). In other schools, however, diagnosis and individually prescribed instruction are stressed (Klausmeier, Sorenson, and Quilling, 1971); this approach is discussed below.

Evaluations of reading growth in informal reading programs have not been encouraging. Jonathan Kozol, a critic of public education and strong advocate of free schools, reported sadly that private free schools had lasted an average of only nine months, and attributed this to their neglect of teaching basic skills such as reading (Kozol, 1972). Southgate (1973), in presenting a generally sympathetic description of language arts instruction in British informal primary schools, also reviewed research in which the largest-scale studies found somewhat better results in schools with formal reading instruction, and concluded that reading instruction is slighted in some informal schools.

The Systems Approach: Diagnostic and Prescriptive Instruction

Since the advent of programmed instruction in the 1950's there has been a gradual increase of interest in a kind of individualization that stresses careful diagnosis of each learner's status and needs, and individualized skills development based on the diagnostic findings. This is part of a broader effort to apply the systems approach to education (Twelker, Urbach, and Buck, 1972). It is sometimes described as *diagnostic and prescriptive reading instruction.*

Such teaching involves the following steps: 1) A comprehensive list of behavioral objectives is set up. 2) Pretests and posttests for each specific objective, and mastery tests covering groups of objectives, are constructed or selected. These are criterion-referenced tests with arbitrarily set passing standards rather than tests with norms. 3) If pretests show a lack of readiness for a particular skill, readiness training is provided and the pretest is given again. 4) Practice materials based directly on the objective are provided, with instruction by the teacher only when necessary. Usually this practice is individualized and often it is programmed or provided with a self-scoring device. 5) A posttest is given after completion of the assigned practice. If the pupil passes it he takes the next pretest. If he fails it, he is given additional practice, preferably somewhat different but based on the same objective, and followed by another posttest. 6) Mastery tests which cover broader areas of skills are given from time to time and review work is assigned if needed.

The teacher's main role in diagnostic and prescriptive reading instruction emphasizes selecting, administering, and scoring tests or other diagnostic procedures; arriving at diagnostic conclusions; assigning appropriate practice as indicated by the diagnosis, securing, organizing, and keeping track of a wealth of material; giving help to individuals as they need it;

maintaining motivation and order; and keeping adequate records. This would leave little or no time for telling, explaining, questioning, leading group discussions, and other common instructional procedures, unless teacher aides, machine scoring of tests, and perhaps computer management of records are part of the system. Since very few teachers have been trained for this kind of teaching role, adoption of a systems approach requires intensive retraining of participating teachers.

Although this approach is still quite new, several reading systems of this kind are already commercially available. They include the Wisconsin Design for Reading Skill Development (Otto and Askov, 1972), Individually Prescribed Instruction (IPI) developed at the University of Pittsburgh (Glaser, 1968; Scanlon, 1970), SCORE (Westinghouse Learning Corp.); and PLAN (Flanagan, 1971). Each of these includes a set of behavioral objectives and criterion-referenced tests which parallel the objectives. Because of the large amount of testing required, test-scoring services are available. The tests for Individually Prescribed Instruction can be scored by a computer, which automatically adds the results to previous information about the pupil and provides the teacher with a printout that can be used in deciding what the pupil is to do next (Richardson, 1969). The Wisconsin Design, SCORE, and PLAN provide machine scoring services for their tests.

There seems to be fairly general agreement that the testing program in a systems approach is too heavy for a teacher to handle unaided. "Some teachers who initially embraced a systems approach later were inclined to feel trapped by it. The amount of testing, observational note taking, and general bookkeeping has, in some cases, approached the point of absurdity" (Carner, 1973). Providing the teacher with extra help to lessen the burden, whether by using a computer, machine scoring, or hand scoring by a clerk or teacher aide, involves extra expense which many school systems cannot afford.

Another problem with diagnostic and prescriptive instruction is the danger that it may become quite mechanical. Counting right answers to a test is less important than discovering why a child has made the kind of errors he committed, and scoring by machine provides little qualitative information. Similarly, assigning a child to a particular kind of exercise without finding out why he did poorly on a pretest sometimes can lead to mere blind repetition of the same kind of error, with declining motivation.

Systems approaches are still very new and evaluations of their results in carefully controlled longitudinal comparisons with other teaching approaches are not yet available. Usually results are reported in terms of the criterion-referenced tests that are part of the system, and do not allow comparisons with other approaches. In comparative studies, one finds little more than the following: "Additionally, RBS (Research for Better Schools) conducted a series of 'school comparison' tests on IPI reading in the fall of 1970. Among the results, it was discovered that IPI students scored better than, or equal to, non-IPI pupils on several standard tests" (Research for Better Schools, 1971). It will be several years before a satisfactory evaluation of the systems approach in reading instruction will be possible.

Individualized Progress in Basal Readers

Although much of the writing about Individualized Reading gives the impression that basal readers are not to be used, a survey of 124 individualized reading programs in Iowa found that 75 per cent of the teachers used basal readers in one or more ways (Blakely and McKay, 1966). Readers were used by some teachers as self-selected or required reading material, as a source of skill lessons, as a source of exercises, as a common base for discussion, as a beginning reading program, and as a basis for informal reading tests. Individualized progress through sequential levels of a basal reader program is common in nongraded schools. Sucher (1969) has briefly described several programs in which individualized use of basal readers has been combined with other types of reading activities.

The possibility of applying a modified systems approach to basal readers has also been explored (Bruton, 1972). Bruton selected nine major objectives, formulated them in behavioral terms, and constructed pretests and posttests for them. Exercises directly related to the nine objectives were removed from the workbooks, mounted, and arranged in sequence. In a small-scale tryout with a few children, they showed "reasonable gain." This kind of partial adaptation to a systems procedure would be easy for basal reader publishers to provide, and would probably be far less taxing on teachers than a full-fledged systems approach.

Individualization and Teacher Training

One of the major problems in developing any form of individualized reading program is that most teachers have never had any experience in individualized learning as students. It is noteworthy, then, that efforts to individualize courses in methods of teaching reading are beginning to be described (Yarington and Boffey, 1971; Braun, 1972). Teachers who have experienced individualized learning themselves may be more inclined to individualize than teachers whose only acquaintance with individualization is through reading about it.

The Future of Individualized Reading Instruction

True individualization is present when the child's instructional needs are understood, the materials he uses are appropriate in difficulty and content, he is guided effectively in learning progressively more advanced and more refined reading skills, he is helped to overcome difficulties that he may encounter, he feels that he is successful in reading, his attitudes toward reading become and remain positive, he learns to apply reading effectively in studying, his tastes become more mature, and he develops the habit of reading for pleasure. Individualization means a close fit between child and program, and is not an exclusive concomitant of any one system of classroom organization and management.

A fundamental necessity for effective individualization is a teacher or specialist who is really able to diagnose pupil needs, abilities, and interests, and plan appropriate learning activities based on this understanding. Diagnostic skills have not been given much attention in teacher-education programs, and the present level of diagnostic proficiency among classroom teachers leaves much to be desired. In one of the Cooperative First Grade reading projects, in which individualized and group instruction were compared, the teachers who taught on a one-to-one basis were found to be no more accurate in their knowledge of the achievement of individual pupils than the teachers who taught groups (Macdonald, T. L. Harris, and Rarick, 1966). Even teachers near the end of a six-credit course in remedial reading in which they tutored individual children have been found to be not very accurate in their diagnostic interpretations (Emans, 1965). There is good reason to question whether past or present teacher-education programs equip teachers with the diagnostic skills needed to make individualized guidance of pupils effective. The trend toward "competency-based" teacher-education programs may help to overcome this shortcoming.

It seems probable that setting aside substantial time periods for free reading accompanied by teacher-pupil conferences will become part of the total reading program in more and more classrooms. As practice materials for the development of specific skills on an individual basis become more available, they will probably be widely used as supplements to the basal program. More schools may be expected to try out a systems approach, even before the efficiency of each such approach has been evaluated. Conventional exercises with answer keys for pupil use, self-correcting programmed materials, and perhaps, if the cost can be reduced sufficiently, computer-assisted instruction may aid individualization in more schools. Increased use of teacher aides, interns, undergraduate students, volunteers, and older pupils can provide more children with individualizd help in the form of tutoring. Programmed tutoring can provide step-by-step guidance for the tutor without professional training (see p. 66).

This chapter started with evidence of the very wide range of reading performance to be found at each age or grade in the elementary school. Different kinds of administrative provisions designed to reduce this range to proportions more manageable by teachers were reviewed, none of which provides a panacea. The importance of the social aspects of learning arrangements was stressed. The functions of whole-class, group, and individualized reading were discussed, and several kinds of individualization described. Group reading procedures are discussed in the next chapter.

SUGGESTED ADDITIONAL READING

HAFNER, LAWRENCE E. & JOLLY, HAYDEN B. *Patterns of teaching reading in the elementary school.* New York: Macmillan, 1972. Chaps. 9, 10.

HARRIS, ALBERT J. & SIPAY, EDWARD R. (Eds.). *Readings on reading instruction* (2nd ed.). New York: McKay, 1972. Chap. 7.

HOWES, VIRGIL M. (Ed.). *Individualized instruction in reading and social studies: selected readings on programs and practices.* New York: Macmillan, 1970.

HUNT, LYMAN C. JR. (Ed.). *The individualized reading program: a guide for classroom teaching.* Newark, Del.: International Reading Association, 1967.

MIEL, ALICE (Ed.). *Individualizing reading practices.* New York: Teachers College Press, Columbia University, 1958.

RAMSEY, WALLACE Z. (Ed.). *Organizing for individual differences.* Newark, Del.: International Reading Association, 1967.

ROBECK, MILDRED C. & WILSON, JOHN A. R. *Psychology of reading: foundations of instruction.* New York: John Wiley and Sons, 1974. Chap. 12.

ROBINSON, H. ALAN (Ed.). *Meeting individual differences in reading,* Supplementary Education Monographs, No. 94. Chicago: University of Chicago Press, 1964. Chaps. 15, 16, 17.

SARTAIN, HARRY W. Organizational patterns of schools and classrooms for reading instruction. In Helen M. Robinson (Ed.). *Innovation and change in reading instruction,* 67th Yearbook of the National Society for the Study of Education, Part II. Chicago: University of Chicago Press, 1968. Chap. 7.

VEATCH, JEANETTE. *Reading in the elementary school.* New York: Ronald Press, 1966.

6

Efficient Reading Instruction in Groups

This chapter continues the discussion of ways of taking care of individual differences in reading instruction. In Chapter 5 the different kinds of activities that can be carried on with a whole class, with groups, and with individual pupils were described and several kinds of individualization were discussed in detail. The present chapter provides answers to the many questions that teachers ask about group instruction.

I. PRACTICAL ISSUES IN GROUP INSTRUCTION

The main problems considered in this section are those concerned with time allotments, group organization, scheduling, assignments, use of helpers, group names, and needed supplies and equipment.

Time Allotments

For the reading program to be effective, a substantial portion of the school day should be scheduled for reading. Sometimes instructional methods or materials are blamed for mediocre results, when the real trouble is insufficient time. In a large-scale study of first-grade reading, a significant relationship was found between time spent on reading and reading test results, while time spent on other language arts or on related activities such as art and music was not significantly correlated with growth in reading (A. J. Harris and Serwer, 1966b).

Time allotments for reading as recommended by 100 reading specialists and as reported from 1,224 schools were summarized by Brekke (1963). Table 4 contains a slightly simplified version of his results. At first grade, 90 minutes a day were reported for basal reading (over 99 per cent of the schools utilized basal readers), decreasing gradually to 40 minutes per day in grades 7 and 8 (these were apparently eight-grade elementary schools; the results may not be representative of junior high schools). There was fairly close correspondence between reported practice and recommended practice, with reported practice slightly higher in the primary grades and slightly lower in the middle grades.

With regard to "other reading," recommended time exceeded reported time at all grade levels. "Other reading" includes experience chart reading, independent reading, library reading, reading in school of textbooks in other curricular areas, reading of weekly or daily newspapers, and so on. At first grade about half as much time was reported spent on "other reading" as on "basal reading"; the ratio changed gradually, so that by fourth grade "other reading" time exceeded "basal reading" time, and it was nearly double "basal reading" time by the eighth grade. The experts did not want "basal reading" time decreased, but did recommend more time for "other reading" than was reported to be typical practice.

TABLE 4. *Reported and recommended mean time allotments for reading in elementary schools*[a]

Minutes per day

	Basal reading		Other reading	
Grade	Reported	Recommended	Reported	Recommended
1	90	85	45	55
2	85	80	50	60
3	75	65	60	65
4	55	60	70	80
5	50	60	75	85
6	50	55	75	90
7	40	40	75	100
8	40	40	75	100

[a] *Based on Brekke's data. Minutes per week have been changed to minutes per day and rounded to the nearest five-minute interval.*

Organization of Groups

Because classes differ so widely, no one plan for grouping fits every need. A method of grouping that may be appropriate for one class may not adequately meet the needs of another class. The range of ability within the class, the age of the pupils, the previous experience of the pupils in working in groups, the materials available, and the teacher's competence all have to be considered. Grouping children for reading is not an end in itself, but a means for achieving desirable objectives of learning and adjustment.

A clearer understanding of the instructional problem requires a consideration of the range of differences in reading ability to be found in normal classrooms. Let us assume that we are studying a school in which the children are representative of the general population in intelligence, there is one class at each grade, all children are promoted regularly regardless of achievement, and reading instruction is of average quality. In such a school, the distribution of reading ability would correspond closely to the figures given in Table 5. This table includes the second, fourth, and sixth grades; results in other grades would be similar.

At the beginning of each grade, half of the children in such a school are reading at or above the grade norm and half are reading below the grade norm. In the second grade, the range is likely to be from children still in the readiness stage to at least third-grade level. At the beginning of the fourth grade, the range is likely to be from low second-grade level to sixth-grade level. At the beginning of the sixth grade, the range is likely to be from third- to ninth-grade level. If the school is one in which the child who does poorly is not promoted, there will be fewer pupils with low reading scores in each grade, but a corresponding number of older

TABLE 5. *Probable distribution of reading abilities in the second, fourth, and sixth grades of an elementary school*

IQ	Approx no. of pupils in a class of 36	Beginning of year Reading grade levels		
		Grade 2	Grade 4	Grade 6
120 and up	3	2.9 up	5.2 up	7.5 up
110–119	6	2.4–2.8	4.6–5.1	6.7–7.4
100–109	9	2.0–2.3	4.0–4.5	6.0–6.6
90–99	9	1.5–1.9	3.4–3.9	5.2–5.9
80–89	6	1.0–1.4	2.7–3.3	4.5–5.1
Below 80	3	Readiness	Below 2.7	Below 4.5

pupils. If the school as a whole is above or below average, the distribution of reading ability will show about the same range, but will be shifted up or down. If pupils are arranged in "homogeneous" classes for reading instruction, the range may be reduced to a year and a half or two years.

Grouping by Reading Level

When the range of ability in each class is wide, as in the example just cited, it is usually advisable to set up reading groups primarily on the basis of reading grade levels. When the range of ability is comparatively small, because of homogeneous grouping or excessive nonpromotion, grouping can be done on the basis of other characteristics.

The simplest form of grouping divides the class initially into two groups; those who can do the normal reading for the grade and those who cannot. The groups will vary in size according to the ability of the class. In an average class it is usually desirable to place about two-thirds of the class in the upper group and about one-third in the lower group. The upper group can use reading material normal for the grade, and the lower group preferably should use a reader of a difficulty level appropriate for the average child in the group. If there are one or two children in the low group who cannot cope with that reader, they will need individual consideration.

This kind of grouping, into two groups, is probably the most effective kind for the teacher who is just learning the technique of group instruction. As the teacher becomes more skilled, he can increase the number of groups, or supplement the plan with a greater amount of individualized work, or both.

There is nothing magical about the number three. Two groups will often suffice, especially if combined with some individualized reading. On the other hand, sometimes three groups are not enough.

Durrell has been an innovator in developing new patterns of classroom organization. In 1940 he advocated using five or more reading groups, with many activities led by pupil leaders, the teacher supplying the plans and materials and exercising general supervision (Durrell, 1940). In 1956 he recommended a varied pattern of class organization, involving whole-class activities, some individualized reading, heterogeneous groups for project work, small reading groups with pupil leaders, and practice on skills in pairs or groups of three (Durrell, 1956). In 1959 he reported the outcome of a one-year project in which team learning in groups of three to five pupils was stressed; the results showed no significant change in reading improvement from the preceding year in grades 4 and 5, although there was an improvement in grade 6. Better results were obtained in spelling and arithmetic (Durrell, 1959).

Grouping According to Specific Needs

When the range of reading ability in a class is comparatively narrow, it may be desirable to organize the main grouping on the basis of special needs rather than on levels. The particular needs would be determined by the teacher and would vary from class to class. Thus a second-grade class could have one group working on phonics, one for more natural expression and phrasing in oral reading, and one for getting main ideas. A sixth-grade class might be divided into the generally competent readers, the accurate but slow, the rapid but inaccurate, and the generally poor readers. As the purpose for a particular skills group is accomplished, that group can be disbanded and a new group set up to focus on another skills area.

Sometimes the main grouping should be by levels, but can profitably be supplemented by one or more special needs groups. In a fourth-grade class this might include those whose phonic knowledge needs improvement, and one or two of the better readers might be in it, as well as most of the poorest readers. In a sixth grade a special group might be formed for extra practice in alphabetizing or in following directions. Such groups should usually be temporary and be disbanded as soon as their purpose has been accomplished.

Temporary special needs groups are also used as a regular feature of Individualized Reading. When skillfully employed they can counteract to a considerable extent the weakness in skills development that is sometimes characteristic of that approach.

Grouping According to Interests

A teacher may find that a few children in the class have a hobby or interest in common, such as raising tropical fish, collecting stamps, having dogs or cats as pets, and so on. Such a group can be encouraged to meet, discover common problems, find reading material related to their special interest, read it, exchange information, and report to the class. Several interest groups may be set up in a class, with membership entirely voluntary. Such groups would not have to meet often; once a week or even once in two weeks might be sufficient.

Reading in Heterogeneous Groups or Committees

Many projects, units, or activities are organized on a committee basis in modern schools. Each committee usually takes responsibility for one part of the total project. Within the committee the questions to be answered are decided on, and each member has his allotted responsibilities. Committees are usually set up by the teacher so that each contains a cross section of the class in abilities.

When reading is to be done to find the answers to questions, a project committee consults as wide a variety of sources as it can. The better readers tackle the hard references; the less capable readers pore over the simpler books. Those whose reading is very limited can contribute information learned from illustrations. Each finds what he can to contribute. Ideally this can be an excellent way of individualizing functional reading. In practice it is often hard to find any relevant material that is easy enough for the poorest readers to read.

Size of Groups

Since the distribution of reading ability within a class varies so much from one class to another, the size of the groups should also vary. It would be undesirable to fix arbitrary rules concerning group size. Some guiding principles, however, can be set down.

A group in which the children require a good deal of individual attention should preferably be kept small; one capable of much individual or self-regulated activity can be larger. When in doubt about the best group placement for a child, it is usually better to place him in the lower of the two groups being considered; this more nearly insures successful participation and allows him to be moved up later if he seems ready. If a class has two groups, it is generally desirable for the lower group to be the smaller; similarly, the lowest of three groups should usually be smaller than the middle group. Groups set up on the basis of special needs or special interests can be of any size. Groups of two children can be effectively used for such activities as testing each other on word or phrase cards and for some kinds of reading games. One of the pair should know the answers or be provided with them.

Group size is sometimes restricted by equipment. If listening to tapes or records through earphones is one of a group's activities, the number of headsets available limits the size of the group for that activity. To use six sets, a group of ten to twelve can be divided into two subgroups. One subgroup listens during the first half of the period while the other does a workbook page or some other independent activity. Then the subgroups exchange activities for the rest of the period. If there is only one set of earphones, one child at a time can leave the group activity to take his turn.

Flexibility in Grouping

Although there is general agreement that flexibility in grouping is highly desirable, some striking examples of inflexibility can be found. In one school, achievement tests were given in May, and on the basis of the reading scores, the principal divided each class into groups which the teachers were not allowed to modify until the next reading tests were given the following May. This is about as bad a misuse of the idea of grouping as one can find. Flexibility in grouping can be of two main kinds.

1. Changing Group Placements.   Children should be moved from one group to another whenever it becomes evident that their reading needs can be better met in the new group. Children differ in their rates of progress; some outgrow a slow group, while others are unable to keep up with a faster group. Sometimes a child who has been floundering as the poorest reader in a group takes on a new lease on life when he finds that he is one of the best readers in his new group. Similarly, a child who glides through his group assignments with a minimum of effort may respond with redoubled energy to the challenge of working at a higher level of difficulty. In making such decisions, it is often desirable to consult the child and respect the child's desires concerning his group placement.

2. Using Different Groupings Simultaneously. At least two different forms of groupings should be in operation. In classes with a wide range of ability, grouping for developmental reading should be according to reading level, with some use of special needs grouping as special needs become apparent. Grouping for functional reading can often be in heterogeneous groups, especially if a project or activity unit plan is followed. Recreational and functional reading both provide opportunities for setting up interest groupings. When children belong now to one group and now to another, the possibility of developing a rigid caste system in which the poorest readers become "untouchables" is held to a minimum.

An unchanging three-group plan was compared to a very flexible grouping at fourth-grade level. Despite the fact that the teachers spent an average of 100 minutes a week or more in planning when using very flexible grouping, there were no significant differences between the two procedures in reading gains or in pupil attitudes, while discipline was more difficult with the flexible plan. At the end of the project the teachers, each of whom had tried both procedures, preferred a combination of a three-group plan with a moderate degree of flexibility (Eberwein, 1972).

One must avoid the danger of assuming that flexibility is an end in itself, since that leads to the changing of groupings just for the sake of change. Under such a system it is hard to see how either the teacher or the children would be able to settle down and get much work done. Flexibility has value when it improves learning conditions and social interrelationships, and too much change can be as undesirable as too little.

A Whole-Class Procedure Using Groups

A plan tried out in a special education class seems worth a tryout in regular classes also (Wu, 1971). The teacher had three groups, reading at primer, first reader, and second reader levels. Keeping the whole class together, the teacher first led preparation and guided reading for the slowest group. The other two groups listened during oral reading and joined in discussion and decoding practice. Next the selection for the middle group was covered in the same way, with the low group participating as they could. When the high group's selection was covered the low group listened, the middle group tried to read the selection silently and followed along during oral reading, and all joined in the discussion. Thus each child participated in three group lessons rather than one, and the interruptions so common when low groups are not yet really capable of independent work were minimized.

Individualized Reading within a Group

A teacher who generally likes to organize reading instruction on a group basis in preference to an individualized program may find it appropriate to consider the use of individualized reading with one group rather than with the entire class. For example, a third-grade teacher was satisfied with the way her high and middle groups were working. The low group, however, included eight children ranging from pre-primer to first reader level, and it was impossible to make group lessons profitable for all. With a primer, two children were at a frustration level and three were unchallenged; only the three children actually at primer level seemed to be profiting. She therefore tried an individualized approach with these eight children. In a twenty-minute period with this group she was able to spend about two minutes with each child, and the others read ahead silently, asking for help when they met new words. Each child progressed at his own rate, and no two were at the same point. Four or five minutes were used for group discussion, motivation, words difficult for several children, and the like. She reported a tremendous improvement in interest and a doubled rate of reading growth for this group. Whenever the range of individual abilities in a group is so large that it is impossible to choose a basal reader for the group that is reasonably satisfactory for all members of the group, the possible advantages of using an individualized approach with that group should be given serious consideration.

Equipment and Materials

A suitable classroom for instruction by groups should be large enough so that the groups can be separated physically, and classroom furniture should be movable so that it can be rearranged in many patterns. For any group activity involving intercommunication, the group should be seated so that all can see one another; a rectangular arrangement with desks pushed together as if to make a large table and a circle or semicircle of chairs is often used. A large area of chalkboard and bulletin board is desirable. There should be convenient shelving for books and supplies. A library corner should have in it not only space for books but also a table and chairs to encourage browsing and a colorful display of books or book jackets. These are desirable features, but none of them is absolutely essential.

Materials for a rich, well-rounded reading program should include:

1] Several sets of basal readers, in numbers appropriate for the groups using them, ranging in difficulty from readers appropriate for the lowest group to readers appropriate for the highest group.

2] Workbooks which accompany the readers. Without these, the teacher has a heavy additional burden of creating suitable comprehension questions and other kinds of written questions or duplicated seatwork.

3] Reading games and puzzles. These can be used when an assignment is finished early, or in a free-reading period instead of a book; some simple group games are also desirable.

4] A classroom library of at least fifty books, covering a wide range in difficulty and interest appeal, and changed at least several times during the year.

5] Reference works. In primary grade rooms, picture dictionaries should be available. Above the primary grades there should be an encyclopedia, dictionaries, atlases, an almanac, and the like.

6] Special teacher-devised materials, to fill gaps in the available commercial materials.

7] Children's magazines and picture magazines. These have a place on the library table.

8] Workbooks not correlated with specific readers. These can be helpful in providing additional practice material for particular reading skills.

9] Related pictures, filmstrips, slides, recordings, and movies to help provide ideational background.

10] Materials which are self-administering and/or self-correcting. These may include programmed materials, boxes of exercises with answer keys, commercial or teacher-prepared lessons on tape, and so forth.

The teacher in a school where supplies are meager should not feel utterly discouraged about being able to provide some differentiated instruction in reading, but it is unquestionably more difficult with insufficient materials.

Choosing Reading Materials for Groups

In most plans for grouping by reading levels, at least two different basal readers are required: one of below-grade difficulty and one of normal difficulty for the grade. The below-grade book should be at the instructional level of the average child in the low group. If there are middle and high groups it is probably better for them to be in different books, with the high group using either a comparatively difficult basal reader intended for that grade or a reader intended for the next higher grade. It is also possible to teach effectively with the middle and high groups using the same basal reader. In that case, the high group is given less preparation, works more independently, moves more rapidly, and has more time for supplementary and independent reading.

Many school systems use one basal series for low groups, another for middle groups, and a third series for high groups, through the grades. This has the advantage that no group has heard a story read and discussed by another group before getting to it. When the series are similar in difficulty and in teaching plans, this may be the best procedure. When the series chosen are quite different in their teaching plans, however, the teacher has to keep track of the skills covered in each group.

Some teachers lose practically all the potential benefits of grouping by levels by having all groups use the same basal reader. This is probably even less efficient than whole-class instruction, for not only are most of the children using material too easy or too hard for best results but also the amount of direct instruction each child receives is less than in whole-class instruction. For within-class ability grouping to be reasonably effective, the reader must be suitable in difficulty for at least a majority of the group.

One of the major sources of difficulty in group management arises from giving a group a basal reader that is too difficult. This encourages restlessness, inattention, excessive requests for help, and whispering. The writers have often found, when consulted about a classroom in which group reading was not working well, that excessively hard material was the main source of trouble, and that the vocabulary and skills presented were not learned.

Assignments

In group instruction, while the teacher is working directly with one group, the other group or groups must have definite assignments which they can carry on without help from the teacher.

At the earliest levels, it is often true that one or more groups are unable to carry on any kind of reading activity without the active participation of the teacher. When this is the case, it is desirable to alternate reading with other kinds of activity that the children are able to carry on independently. At first-grade level, independent activities include play in a dollhouse corner, painting at easels, clay, weaving, crayons, cutting and pasting pictures, and so on. These can be combined with reading in a rotating plan so that the group reads only when the teacher is with them and engages in quiet self-directed activities when the teacher is with another group. This procedure is essential in the first grade and is often needed in grades above the first for one or more groups.

Before starting the group activities of the day it is helpful to take a few minutes to go over the specific assignments for all groups. A group should always have supplementary activities to which they can turn if they finish an assignment before the end of a period. It is helpful to have, for each group, a poster which they can consult if they forget what to do next. The following list was drawn up by one group in a fifth-grade class:

1] Read the pages in your book.
2] Write the new words in your notebook.
3] Look them up in the dictionary.
4] Write answers to the questions.
5] Read a library book, *or*
6] Draw a picture about the story.

With such a plan, it was easy for the group to keep busy for a thirty- or forty-minute period. The faster readers had more time than the others for reading their library books.

Interference between groups should be kept at a minimum. When working with a group, the teacher should keep his voice low; the children soon learn to speak quietly also. Routines for distributing and collecting books, workbooks, paper, and other supplies quietly and efficiently need to be developed and practiced.

Time Schedule. It is necessary to consider with care the total amount of time to be devoted to the reading program per day and per week, the duration of reading periods, and appropriate spacing of reading periods in the school day. In the primary grades the developmental reading program should take about an hour and a half per day. From the fourth grade on the amount of time specifically scheduled for developmental and recreational reading decreases grade by grade (see p. 109), but the amount of time spent in functional reading in a variety of curricular fields more than makes up the difference.

Each teacher has to experiment to determine the length of period that seems to work best in the particular class. When periods are too short, so much time is spent in getting materials out, warming up to the task, and putting things away again that inefficiency results. When periods are too long, children get fatigued or bored, and their increasing restlessness and noise signal to an alert teacher the fact that effective learning has stopped. Young children, with their brief attention spans, need somewhat shorter periods than older children; in consequence, the teacher may find it desirable to have two or three short periods a day with a group, rather than one long one. Periods devoted to easy, pleasurable activities can be relatively prolonged; periods requiring intense concentration on difficult tasks should be comparatively brief.

Many teachers plan their reading as a solid block of an hour or more, during which they work with each group in turn. The known facts about the psychology of learning indicate that it is efficient to separate periods of similar activity by periods in which quite different activities are carried on. "If one period of study is to be followed immediately by another, we should arrange our schedule so that we may switch to the lesson that is least similar to the one on which we have been working" (Kingsley, 1946, p. 485). In the planning of a reading program it would seem desirable to interpolate nonreading activities between reading periods or to follow one reading activity by another quite different kind of reading activity.

Group Names. Some teachers are quite concerned about what to call their groups. They think of them as "the high group" or "the low group," but they realize it would be bad for morale to use such terms with the children. Numbering the groups is not very desirable for the same reason. The assignment of names that imply relative size, speed, or competence is to be avoided, as in Eagles, Robins, and Sparrows, or Jets, Trains, and Cars. Teachers should be sensitive to the feelings of the children about the traits implied by group names: Roses, Pansies, and Lilies may be quite acceptable to girls, but certainly would arouse strong objections in boys. Children are quite aware of the comparative proficiencies of groups. "The teacher calls us the red, white, and blue groups, but she might as well call us the fruits, vegetables, and nuts." Choosing names wisely does not eliminate this awareness; it merely avoids rubbing it in.

One way of selecting group names that is quite popular is by discussion and voting, allowing each group to choose its own name. During a unit on Indians, for example, the groups may wish to choose the names of Indian tribes. This procedure avoids the dangers cited above. It sometimes gives the groups an implication of permanence and stability that one may prefer to avoid. It has, however, worked very well for many teachers.

Perhaps the best way of treating this problem is to make it as casual as possible. Thus, groups with chairmen can be referred to as Billy's group or Annette's group, or the group can be named accordingly to the color of the cover of the book they are currently using. The less fuss made about group names, the better.

Chairmen and Helpers. There are many group activities in which pupils can act as group leaders, making it unnecessary for the teacher to be with the group for that activity. Often a few of the best readers are assigned by the teacher to be the leaders of the less capable groups. Sometimes this privilege is rotated among several children so that no one child gets conceited or misses too much of his own group's reading activities. An alternative is to let each group select its own chairman, or to have the chairmanship rotate among the members of the group, with each child having a turn. The chairman who is a member of a group is often accepted with better grace than the leader who comes from another group. When a group is not yet able to function without help, it may be possible to have a chairman from within the group, who assigns turns to read and keeps order, and a helper from a higher group, who can supply unknown words and correct errors.

Helpers can be used during silent reading or workbook practice, as well as during oral reading. One child can be the helper for a group, or each child who needs help may be allowed to select another child as his personal helper. In the latter case, the helper and the child helped may be assigned neighboring seats.

Children do not naturally know how to be effective chairmen or helpers. Sometimes they will give too much help or too little, or they may become officious or sarcastic. It is desirable to train helpers or chairmen for their jobs, and it is certainly necessary to keep an eye on how they carry out their functions. Since many children consciously imitate their teacher when placed in a teaching role, evaluation of child leadership performance sometimes leads to modification of teacher behavior.

Use of Teacher Aides. Sometimes it is possible to have two or more adults present during reading instruction. The extra people may be student teachers, volunteers, or teaching aides. Team teaching also makes possible situations in which more than one group at a time has adult leadership. Careful planning is necessary to insure that what the assistant teachers do will be beneficial to the learning of the children.

II. ILLUSTRATIVE GROUP PLANS

For many years the writers have discussed grouping problems with classroom teachers in graduate courses, presented specimen plans to them for criticism, and encouraged them to develop program plans that fitted their own classes. From this we have become convinced that classes at the same grade level vary tremendously, so that it is impossible to present a plan for a given grade that will suit all classes. The plans described below are intended to be used as sources of ideas, not as specifications to be followed exactly.

In these specimen plans an attempt has been made to adhere to five basic principles. 1) Each plan combines reading by groups with some whole-class and some individualized reading. 2) The teacher is with the group for those activities for which he is most needed. 3) Expectancy concerning what a group may be able to do without the teacher (but with a chairman or helper) is realistic. 4) Length of periods has some relationship to the maturity and attention span of the children. 5) All groups get a reasonable share of the teacher's attention.

Figure 6.1 shows a sample plan for the latter part of the first grade. In it there are three periods for group work and one whole-class period every day, and both developmental basal reader activities and some other kinds of reading and nonreading activities are included. The plan assumes that the high group can do some independent reading in easy books that are below their instructional level, but that the low and middle groups require teacher guidance for nearly all reading activities. Some workbook and seatwork periods are scheduled without the teacher, on the assumption that a teacher aide or pupil helper can be with the group; if this is not possible, there would need to be additional periods of nonreading activities for these groups, and it would take a day or two longer to complete each story.

Directions should be given to all groups at the beginning of the school day. At the start of each group period the teacher should spend a couple of minutes with each group that is to work without her, making sure that they have the right materials and know what to do.

The low group is guided by the teacher through the essential steps of a typical basal reader developmental teaching plan: preparation, guided reading and discussion, oral rereading, and related skills. It has several periods of nonreading activities, but may be able to do workbook and seatwork pages with an aide or helper.

The middle group also has teacher direction through the cycle of preparation, guided reading and discussion, oral rereading, and related skills. Without the teacher it does workbook and seatwork pages, cuts, pastes, and labels entries for a picture dictionary, and the like, but probably needs a helper for these. Nonreading activities fill in the gaps.

The high group has teacher guidance for preparation, discussion of story and oral reading, and checking workbook and seatwork pages. On its own it does silent reading in the reader, workbook, and seatwork as well as some individualized independent reading.

Low Group *(pre-primer)*	Middle Group *(primer)*	High Group *(first reader)*

MONDAY

Nonreading activities	T Preparation for new story	Indvidualized silent reading
T Preparation for new story	Teacher-prepared seatwork or workbook	Workbook
Teacher-prepared seatwork or nonreading activities.	Cut pictures from old magazines for picture dictionary	T Check workbook Preparation for new story

Whole Class: Initial consonant *f*: auditory perception games, listing words beginning with *f* underlining the *f*. Teacher reads story.

TUESDAY

Seatwork to sharpen visual discrimination	T Guided reading and discussion	Silent reading of story Workbook
T Guided reading and discussion	Workbook	Supplementary reading or nonreading activities (through second period)
Workbook or nonreading activities	Mount and paste pictures	T Check workbook Discussion of story and selective oral reading

Whole Class: Teacher reads a poem. Children volunteer poems and rhymes they know. Children listen for rhyming words and teacher lists them on chalkboard.

WEDNESDAY

Nonreading activities	T Oral rereading Check workbook	Individualized silent reading Word games
T Oral rereading Check workbook	Duplicated seatwork	Nonreading activities (through second period)
Word games or nonreading activities	Draw a picture about the story	T Preparation for new story

Whole Class: Review *f*, introduce another initial consonant as on Monday. Choral reading of duplicated poem read by teacher on Tuesday.

THURSDAY

Cut pictures from magazines	T Check seatwork Related skills: phonics, comprehension	Individualized silent reading Workbook
T Related skills: phonics, comprehension	Labeling pictures for picture dictionary	Word games or nonreading activities (through second period)

Low Group (pre-primer)	Middle Group (primer)	High Group (first reader)
Draw a picture about the story	Duplicated seatwork	T Check workbook Discussion of story and selective oral reading

Whole Class: Develop experience story about some new experience, practice reading it. Review the two new initial consonants.

	FRIDAY	
Nonreading activities	T Check seatwork Preparation for new story	Duplicated seatwork Independent silent reading
T Preparation for new story	Nonreading activities	Word games or nonreading activities
Seatwork to sharpen visual discrimination	Silent rereading in preparation for dramatization	T Check seatwork Preparation for new story

Whole Class: Review the two initial consonants introduced during the week.
One group dramatizes a story
Teacher reads a story

FIGURE **6.1**   A three-group plan for the latter part of the first grade. T indicates the group with which the teacher is working. The three periods each day are 20–30 minutes each and the whole-class period is about 30 minutes.

Whole-class activities include phonics, teacher reading to the class, choral reading, experience stories, and dramatization of stories. Phonic skills introduced and reviewed with the whole class have additional review during "related skills" periods for the low and midde groups.

A plan appropriate for many fourth- and fifth-grade classes is shown in Figure 6.2. Each day there are two periods for group activity and one whole class period. The plan covers developmental reading, in addition to which there is much reading done in other curricular areas. In this plan the teacher works with the low group every day, with the middle group three times a week, and with the high group twice a week.

The teacher closely supervises the low group's reading and goes over its workbooks and seatwork with the members, in addition to being with them for preparation, discussion and oral reading, and related skills. The low group does not require the teacher's direct supervision for silent reading or for work on workbook and seatwork pages. The low group has independent reading during two whole-class periods.

The middle group is scheduled for somewhat more self-directed read-

Low Group	Middle Group	High Group

Whole Class: Directions and assignments are given to each group each day.

MONDAY

Low Group	Middle Group	High Group
T Discussion and oral reading of story read silently on Friday	Silent reading, preparation on Friday	Silent reading of new story (no preparation) Related workbook
Related workbook	T Discussion and selective oral rereading	Check workbook, group chairman Independent reading

Whole Class: Read and discuss weekly newspapers, different editions

TUESDAY

Low Group	Middle Group	High Group
T Check workbook Related skills: phonics and comprehension	Related workbook Check workbook, group chairman; reread to verify answers	Silent reading of new story (no preparation)
Seatwork reinforcing related skills	Independent reading	T Discussion of two stories Selective oral reading Related skills

Whole Class: Independent reading period; teacher circulates and has individual conferences or works with a group that has a special need in common

WEDNESDAY

Low Group	Middle Group	High Group
T Check seatwork Preparation for new story A related skill	Plan dramatization of story, group chairman	Comprehension exercises from independent workbook or exercise collection; self-correction
Silent reading of new story	T Check plan for dramatization Preparation for new story	Independent reading

Whole Class: Decoding: phonics, syllabication, structural analysis, dictionary guide to pronunciation

THURSDAY

Low Group	Middle Group	High Group
T Discussion and oral rereading A related skill	Silent reading of new story	Same plan as on Monday
Related workbook	T Discussion and selective oral rereading A related skill	

Whole Class: Some plan as on Tuesday; or special interest groups

Low Group	Middle Group	High Group
	FRIDAY	
T Check workbook Preparation for new story	Check workbook, group chairman Reread portions to verify answers	Independent workbook or seatwork; self-correction
Silent reading of story	Quietly rehearse dramatization	T Discussion of story, selective oral rereading Related skills

Whole Class: (afternoon) book club meeting, audience reading, choral reading of poetry, dramatization, oral reports

FIGURE **6.2**   A three-group plan for a heterogeneous fourth or fifth grade. Periods are 20–30 minutes each.

ing than the low group. The teacher is with it for preparation, discussion and selected oral reading, and some related skills practice. The members are expected to carry on with a group chairman such activities as correcting workbooks and planning and rehearsing the dramatization of a story they have finished. They fill in with independent reading when they complete an assignment early, in addition to the two whole-class periods scheduled for independent reading. The privilege of presenting a story dramatization, shown for the middle group in this plan, should rotate among the groups and may be omitted in some weeks.

The children in the high group, all of whom probably score above grade level on standardized reading tests, are expected in this plan to be able to read a selection silently with no preparation, or with a very abbreviated preparation during the giving of assignments. They correct their own workbooks and other seatwork with a group chairman. They have two group periods of independent reading in addition to the two whole-class periods.

The whole-class periods accommodate a wide range of activities, not all of which can be shown in one plan and not all of which would be scheduled every week. This plan shows current events reading, individualized independent reading, decoding skills development, teacher-pupil conferences, book club meeting, oral book reports, audience reading, choral reading, and dramatization. Special needs groups and special interest groups can be fitted into periods when most of the class are doing independent reading. Teacher-pupil conferences and some individualized diagnostic testing and corrective teaching can also occur during periods of independent reading.

Combining Whole-Class, Group, and Individualized Reading

The plans described above have suggested ways in which a sequential program of reading instruction in groups based on reading level can be combined with whole-class activities, groups based on special needs, groups based on common interests, and periods of completely individualized reading. Teachers who want to try more individualization than is provided in these plans can do it in more than one way: 1) The reading activities of one group can be individualized. This is easiest to do with the best readers. They can often finish the basic readers for the grade early in the spring; for the rest of the year they can be given individualized reading. Sometimes the poorest readers are just too different from one another to be taught as a group, requiring that their reading be individualized (see p. 115). 2) Additional periods of individualized reading can be provided for the entire class, devoting more total time to the reading program. 3) It is possible to alternate days of group instruction with days of individualized reading. In one elementary school, the principal is enthusiastic about the results of a plan in which group reading activities are scheduled three days a week and the other two days of reading are individualized. This kind of plan, maintaining the program of systematic instruction, but incorporating much more individualized reading than is common at present, deserves serious consideration.

III. SPECIAL PROVISIONS FOR REMEDIAL READING

The programs for differentiating and individualizing reading instruction discussed above are based on the assumption that a good developmental reading program must provide for marked differences in rate of learning. Children are expected to progress at individual rates of speed, and a child is not considered in need of remedial help just because he is not up to the majority of his classmates. These plans also include provisions for giving specific corrective help as needed, which can take place during a whole-class activity, during a group session, or during a period of individualized reading. In this way much of what formerly was considered to be remedial activity is now provided for in the framework of the regular classroom program.

Even in schools where well-differentiated reading programs are in operation, the need for special remedial help for a few pupils is not eliminated. The program of the lowest reading group in the class may still be at a frustration level for the poorest readers, and the teacher may find it impossible to give them enough individual attention to meet their needs. A second difficulty is the necessity for detailed diagnosis when dealing with severe cases of reading disability. A classroom teacher, even when able to carry through such a diagnosis, may not be able to spare the time required. A third, and probably crucial, difficulty is the fact that some children just are unable to concentrate in the face of the many kinds of stimulation and distraction present in a typical classroom. This inability to resist distracting stimulation is found in restless, hyperactive, nervous chldren, some of whom show signs of neurological difficulty. For some disabled readers the embarrassment of being watched or overheard by the other children is a severely inhibiting factor.

A good total reading program needs to provide special facilities for children with reading disabilities. Special provisions for diagnosis should be made. At a first level, a reading consultant or remedial teacher can make an intensive analysis of the child's reading performance and can outline a specific program of corrective instruction for the classroom teacher to carry out. At a second level, the child may be referred to a school psychologist for testing of intellectual and personality characteristics and to an eye specialist or other medical services for study of possible health problems. At a third level, it should be possible to refer the child to a child guidance or mental health clinic where an intensive social, psychological, and psychiatric study can be made.

Many school systems have remedial reading teachers who work with children in small groups. A special room is set aside, and the teacher works with one group or one child at a time. The group (often called a "reading club") is usually no larger than five or six children and has two to five sessions a week with the remedial teacher. Many remedial teachers divide their time between two schools, spending three days in one and two days in the other. As pupils become able to function in their regular classrooms, they are discharged and replaced by other children. The successful remedial teacher often finds his position expanding to include consultations with classroom teachers and leadership in curriculum reconstruction and in-service training (Price and Layton, 1968). A recent publication of the International Reading Association provides helpful information about graduate programs for those wishing to become reading specialists (Wanat, 1973).

Where there is a reading supervisor or reading consultant, but no remedial teacher, the procedure is somewhat different. The reading consultant or supervisor has responsibility for the total reading program, including the developmental as well as the remedial activities. Usually the consultant does a more thorough diagnostic study than the classroom teacher can carry out and on the basis of this confers with the teacher and suggests methods and materials which the classroom teacher can use with the child. When the difficulty seems too severe to respond to individualized help in the classroom, the consultant may see the child individually for a while, but transfers responsibility to the teacher as soon as possible. Reading consultants should be well trained in remedial as well as in developmental reading; sometimes their duties include supervision of remedial teachers.

Another plan often used in the elementary school involves the creation of a learning-disability homeroom. The most severe disability cases from a range of two or three grades are gathered together under a specially qualified teacher and stay in that class throughout the day; reading is given a very prominent part in the class program, but other subjects are not neglected. The class should be small. Necessarily the teacher of such a class must be well versed in methods of individualized instruction, not only in reading but in other curriculum areas as well, and must be able to cope with deviant behavior.

The Reading Center or Laboratory. In departmentalized schools, a reading center or laboratory may provide an effective way to combine remedial with developmental reading. Crawford and Conley (1971) have described a reading laboratory in a middle school for grades 6 to 8. Two laboratories take care of the total student population of about 1,200 students. Each laboratory is staffed with a reading specialist, assisted by a corps of student aides, and is located in a large room divided into a number of work areas. It provides three kinds of programs: 1) an extra help program (remedial), with individual diagnosis and instructional sequences planned by the teacher; 2) a variety of short, self-administering minicourses for students of average or above reading ability who wish to improve in specific skills areas; and 3) an informal recreational reading program open to all students during their free periods. Students in all three programs use the laboratory simultaneously, and the teacher moves from one program to another as needed.

Faced with a shortage of reading specialists, many school systems have selected a good classroom teacher, sent him or her to an intensive brief conference, and put him or her to work as a remedial teacher or reading consultant (Brown, 1972). Many of these people have eventually become competent specialists, particularly when they recognized their need for additional professional training and continued to study. Minimum standards have been established by the International Reading Association for Special Teacher of Reading, Reading Clinician, Reading Consultant, and Reading Supervisor. The current version of these standards, which are revised periodically, may be obtained by writing to the International Reading Association for the brochure entitled "Roles, Responsibilities, and Qualifications of Reading Specialists."

The pioneering efforts of people like Donald D. Durrell at Boston University, Emmett A. Betts at Temple University, Helen M. Robinson at the University of Chicago, and Arthur I. Gates and Ruth Strang at Teachers

College, Columbia University, in establishing reading clinics with accompanying training programs in remedial reading have borne fruit in the rapid increase in the number of reading clinics and reading laboratories in operation. Most of these are connected with colleges or universities; a few have become integral parts of local school systems.

In practically every remedial program a few children (usually 5 to 10 per cent) are found who do not improve under good remedial teaching. While these failures are sometimes the result of injudicious remedial methods, they are probably more often cases in which causal factors such as unsuspected neurological injuries or deep-lying emotional difficulties are present. To care for such cases there should be available in the community a clinic whose staff of psychiatrists, psychologists, and social workers can make a more intensive and thorough diagnosis than can be expected of a remedial teacher.

Treatment of these cases may require psychotherapy, or completely individual remedial teaching, or a combination of the two. A growing number of well-trained private remedial teachers, whose background should include supervised practice in a good reading clinic, can be called upon for help with many of these cases.

Provisions in Secondary Schools

Homogeneous grouping based largely on reading proficiency is more prevalent in junior and senior high schools than in elementary schools. The classes lowest in reading ability at each grade usually contain considerably more than an average number of students with problems of truancy, disorderly behavior, and general academic failure. Often slow learners, students with average ability but some reading retardation, and bright boys and girls with serious reading disabilities are placed in the same group, and the teacher is unaware of their differences.

A comprehensive reading program in a secondary school should have several components. There should be a developmental reading program for most students, in which general reading skills either are taught in a separate course or are given an important place in the English curriculum. There should be a simpler reading curriculum in a special track for generally slow learners. There should be a corrective reading program for intellectually normal students with moderate reading retardation. There should be a special remedial program for those with severe disabilities. There should also be an elective program for good readers who wish to become superior readers in preparation for college. Finally, every subject teacher should take responsibiity for helping his students develop the specialized vocabulary needed in his subject and for adapting general reading skills to the methods of study found to be most effective in that subject.

The range of individual differences among children in reading proficiency is large at every age from 6 on, and increases as children get older. Administrative procedures for pupil classification can make it a little easier for teachers to cope with this range by reducing it somewhat in specific classes, but even within "homogeneous" groups one usually finds both a range in general reading ability and differing patterns of skills needs. The rigid three-group instructional plan should be superseded by flexible combinations of whole-class reading, group reading activities of several kinds, and individualized reading. Even with highly skilled teachers some children fail to respond to corrective help within the classroom, and the total reading program should include provisions for detailed diagnostic study and special remedial instruction for such children.

SUGGESTED ADDITIONAL READING

BOND, GUY L. & WAGNER, EVA BOND. *Teaching the child to read* (4th ed.). New York: Macmillan, 1966. Chap. 16.

DURKIN, DOLORES. *Teaching them to read* (2nd ed.). Boston: Allyn and Bacon, 1974. Chap. 3.

DURRELL, DONALD D. *Improving reading instruction.* New York: Harcourt, Brace, and World, 1955. Chaps. 6, 15.

HARRIS, ALBERT J. & SIPAY, EDWARD R. *Effective teaching of reading* (2nd ed.). New York: McKay, 1971. Chap. 7.

————. *Readings on reading instruction.* New York: McKay, 1972. Chap. 6.

HARRIS, LARRY A. & SMITH, CARL B. *Reading instruction through diagnostic teaching.* New York: Holt, Rinehart and Winston, 1972. Chap. 5.

KENNEDY, EDDIE C. *Classroom approaches to remedial reading.* Itasca, Ill.: Peacock, 1971. Chap. 7.

MAY, FRANK B. *To help children read: mastery performance modules for teachers in training.* Columbus: Charles E. Merrill, 1973. Module 9.

ZINTZ, MILES V. *The reading process: the teacher and the learner.* Dubuque, Iowa: Wm. C. Brown, 1970. Chaps. 4, 5.

7

Reading Disability, Dyslexia, and Learning Disabilities

The next six chapters are devoted to diagnosing reading problems. They are concerned with determining: 1) whether a learner has a reading problem, and if so, how serious it is; 2) the learner's general level of reading ability; 3) the learner's specific reading-skill strengths and weaknesses; and 4) the correlates of reading disability.

Chapter 7 addresses itself to the first question. After discussing the nature of diagnosis, the various and often confusing terms found in the literature are defined and brought into proper perspective. Finally, the authors' viewpoint regarding causation and an objective definition of reading disability are presented.

I. THE NATURE OF DIAGNOSIS

Diagnosis is a word that comes from two Greek roots, *dia* meaning through or thoroughly, and *gnosis* meaning knowledge; its literal meaning is to know thoroughly. Its medical meaning is determining, by examination, the nature and circumstances of a diseased condition. A definition more suitable to its meaning in the study of reading disabilities is "a determining or analysis of the cause or nature of a problem or situation" (*Random House Dictionary of the English Language*, 1966).

Learning to understand a child who is having trouble in reading is a challenging and exciting task, like any other form of exploration. This learning process, which we call diagnosis, can be carried out to different degrees of completeness by teachers, by remedial specialists, and by special clinical centers. It is not expected that a classroom teacher should make a thorough diagnosis of every pupil; such an undertaking would leave little time or energy for teaching. Fortunately many of the simpler difficulties in reading can be corrected by direct teaching of the missing skills, without an intensive search for reasons why the skills were not learned before. Teachers, nevertheless, should know the factors that can contribute to reading difficulties and should be able to carry out the simpler parts of a diagnostic study.

In the process of making a diagnosis it is necessary to collect facts, and tests can contribute many of the facts needed. But the heart of diagnosis is not testing. It is, rather, the intelligent interpretation of the facts by a person who has both the theoretical knowledge and the practical experience to know what questions to ask, to select procedures (including tests) that can supply the needed facts, to interpret the meaning of the findings correctly, and to comprehend the interrelationships of these facts and meanings. The natural outcome of a diagnostic study is a plan for treatment that involves two parts: a plan for correcting or minimizing the handicapping conditions that are still interfering with learning; and a plan for remedial instruction that is most likely to be successful in the light of what has been found.

The kind of search for causal or contributing factors that one conducts in a specific case is strongly influenced by one's belief about the causation of reading disabilities. For example, neurologists have tended for over fifty years to postulate a basic constitutional condition (usually called *congenital word blindness* or *dyslexia* by them), often hereditary, and often accompanied by other communication difficulties (in listening, speaking, spelling, handwriting, and written composition). While most of them admit that some reading disabilities have other types of causation, the neurologists have concentrated on this group (Penn, 1966; Gomez, 1972; Rosenthal, 1973).

On the other hand, the majority of educational psychologists and reading specialists in the United States and Great Britain dislike terms such as *dyslexia* and *learning disability* because of their varying meanings and because of the variations in symptoms among cases given these labels (Burt, 1966; Reid, 1968; Botel, 1969).

Because of this basic disagreement it seems wise to take a detailed look at the various terms found in the literature.

II. TERMINOLOGY[1]

Although failure in reading has been intensively studied for many years, terminology has not yet been standardized. Thus, depending on who examines him, the same child might be called a case of reading disability or reading deficiency, a retarded reader, an underachiever in reading, or a dyslexic. More recently, the labels *perceptually handicapped* or *learning disability* would be applied by some.

The terms used by others to describe severe reading disability fall into two broad classifications: 1) etiological and 2) behavioral.

> Medical terminology tends to label learning disorders in terms of etiology (causation) and generally relates them to deficits in the brain. Terms such as brain injury, brain damage, minimal cerebral dysfunction, neuropsychological dysynchrony, organic disorder, central nervous system disorder, psychoneurological disorder, etc., are terms which imply a neurological etiology as an explanation for the deviation in development.
>
> Behavioral terms attempt to label the disordered function according to behavioral manifestations. These behavioral terms include: perceptual handicap, conceptual disorders, reading disability, dyslexia, catastrophic behavior, developmental imbalance, learning disability, and various subcategories of the term "aphasia." (Kirk and Kirk, 1971, p. 6)

Numerous other terms can be found in the literature. This proliferation of terms, particularly since the early 1960's, has lead to confusion and has complicated communication within and between professions (Whitcraft, 1971). The common element among the various terms is agreement that there are learners whose progress in reading is unsatisfactory when compared to their potential. Beyond this there is insufficient agreement; the same term is used with different meanings, and the same condition is given various labels by different writers. As Brown and Botel (1972) pointed out, the problems created by use of diverse terms and definitions is further complicated by the confusion of etiologies, or search for causes, with symptoms, diagnostic criteria, and correlated characteristics.

A Glossary of Terms

Although it does not contain all the terms found in the literature, the following glossary illustrates the confusion that exists. It also may serve as a useful reference by those reading the literature.

Alexia: loss of ability to read, partially or totally, usually as a result of brain injury or disease.

1. Much of the material in this section is based on A. J. Harris (1968a).

Backward reader, backwardness in reading: terms used primarily in England to indicate individuals whose reading ages (based on test scores) fall below the average performance of children of their chronological age; intelligence or potential for learning is *not* considered (Vernon, 1960, pp. 3, 5).

Brain damage: any injury to the brain structure. Alternate terms: brain injury, organic brain damage, brain lesion (Strang, 1968a).

Congenital alexia: synonym for developmental dyslexia.

Congenital word blindness or *word blindness:* synonym for dyslexia once favored by some European medical writers (*e.g.,* Hinshelwood, 1917; Hermann, 1964).

Dyslexia: defective reading. The reading defect may represent loss of competency following brain injury or degeneration; or, it may represent a developmental failure to profit from reading instruction (Money, 1962). Dyslexia has been qualified as *specific* (meaning reading failure in contrast to general learning failure) or *developmental* (in contrast to acquired, or loss of previously acquired skill). Usually it implies a constitutionally based reading disability in an individual who is free from mental defect, serious neurotic traits, and gross neurological deficits; and frequently heredity is emphasized in discussing its causation (Critchley, 1970).

Hyperlexia: uneven reading skills in which word recognition is at a much higher level than comprehension (Niensted, 1968; Silverberg and Silverberg, 1968).

Learning disabilities: as with *dyslexia* there is no universally accepted definition. The National Advisory Committee on Handicapped Children (1967) defined it as: "a disorder in one or more of the basic psychological processes involved in understanding or in using spoken or written languages. These may be manifested in disorders of listening, thinking, talking, reading, writing, spelling, or arithmetic. They include conditions which have been referred to as perceptual handicaps, brain injury, minimal brain dysfunction, dyslexia, developmental aphasia, etc. They do not include learning problems which are due primarily to visual, hearing, or motor handicaps, to mental retardation, emotional disturbance or to environmental disadvantage."

Legasthenia: a term that has largely replaced dyslexia in German-speaking countries (Klasen, 1972).

Maturational lag: a concept introduced by Bender (1957) to indicate slowness in certain specialized aspects of neurological development.

Minimal brain damage, minimal brain dysfunction, minimal cerebral dysfunction: implies that causation is brain damage, or disordered functioning for which brain damage is inferred. Diagnosis is often based on "soft neurological signs"; that is, signs of doubtful validity.

Perceptually handicapped: indicates a learning problem due to a perceptual problem, most often noted as visual or auditory, or to a combination of problems such as visual-motor.

Primary and secondary reading retardation: terms proposed by Rabinovitch (1968). *Primary* indicates that the capacity to learn to read is impaired, with the reading retardation reflecting a definitive neurologic dysfunction in the absence of history or signs of brain injury; the concept is essentially the same as Critchley's use of *dyslexia*. Rabinovitch delineated two types of *secondary reading retardation:* 1) *secondary to exogenous factors* means that the capacity to learn to read is intact, but is impaired by such external factors as emotional or environmental influences; 2) *secondary to brain injury* means that the capacity to learn to read is impaired by frank brain damage manifested by clear-cut neurologic deficits or lesions. He used *retardation* in the same sense in which we use *disability* in this text.

Psycholinguistic learning disability: term employed by Kirk and Kirk (1971) to refer to an individual's weaknesses as assessed by the *Illinois Test of Psycholinguistic Ability*.

Psychoneurological learning disability: term coined by Myklebust to describe learning disabilities in which the causation is a combination of psychological and neurological factors. It includes speech, writing, and nonverbal disabilities as well as reading disabilities, and represents conditions in which the central nervous system is not functioning efficiently in sensory-motor, perceptual-motor, or language functions, whether due to genetic, maturational, or traumatic conditions, sociocultural deprivation, emotional problems, or a combination of some of these (D. J. Johnson and Myklebust, 1967; Denhoff, Hainsworth, and Siqueland, 1968).

Reading disability: reading is significantly below expectancy for both age and intelligence and is also disparate with the learner's cultural, linguistic, and educational experience.

Reading disorder: term used as a synonym for reading disability.

Reading retardation: cases whose general level of reading ability is significantly below age and grade norms, regardless of such factors as their potential or intelligence; equivalent to British backwardness in reading. Some medical writers use "retardation" as equivalent to "disability." In Great Britain, however, reading retardation usually means reading below expectancy.

Reading-skill deficiency: regardless of the individual's general level of reading ability, he is weak in one or more reading skills.

Slow learner in reading: general level of reading is below grade and age level but commensurate with the individual's somewhat limited learning potential.

Specific language disability: a concept similar to *dyslexia* or *primary reading disability* but broadened to include spelling, writing, and speech problems referable to the same constitutional origin. A term often found in the Orton Society literature (Gallagher, 1960; Rawson, 1971).

Underachiever in reading: reading may be average for age and grade but is significantly below expectancy for intelligence.

Cautions in Using Technical Labels. When considering terminology, it is wise to consider Samuels admonition regarding labels as pseudo-explanations:

> By identifying the problem, giving it a name, and putting the students into a diagnostic category, many educators and psychologists delude themselves into believing that they have gained insight into the causes of the problem. If we ask, "Why is the student failing in reading?" we often get the answer, "He is unable to learn because he has a learning disorder." This answer tells us nothing about the actual sources of difficulty the students are experiencing. In fact, the answer implies circular reasoning since it is largely because of the presence of academic retardation that the label is ascribed.
>
> Actually, labels such as learning disorder, dyslexia, etc. provide no useful information as to why students are failing. . . . The labels do not in any way indicate where the student is having trouble, nor do they provide a clue as to how the difficulty may be overcome. (Samuels, 1973b, p. 203)

Two terms, *dyslexia* and *learning disabilities*, have received considerable attention in recent years. Therefore they, and a related term, *maturational lag*, are discussed in more detail.

Dyslexia

There is no unanimity concerning the meaning of dyslexia (Reid, 1968). Some employ it broadly as the equivalent of reading disability (Money, 1962). Yet others offer diverse definitions which include: 1) presence of brain damage, 2) observation of behavioral manifestations of central nervous system dysfunctions, 3) indication of genetic or inherited cause, 4) inclusion of a general language disability along with a reading problem, 5) presence of a syndrome of maturational lag, 6) synonym for reading retardation, and 6) the child who is unable to learn to read through regular classroom methods (Lerner, 1971a).

Although there are some (*e.g.*, Morris, 1966, pp. 303–304) who do not believe that a condition such as dyslexia exists, evidence suggests that, regardless of the label attached to it, there is a basic disability in some disabled readers that lies outside the normal range of variation (Vernon,

1971, p. 176). We presently know little about the precise nature of this disability, however.

Critchley, an influential British neurologist, stated his conception of "developmental dyslexia" as follows:

> Neurologists believe that within the community of poor readers there exists a hard core of cases where the origins of the learning defect are inborn and independent of any intellectual shortcomings which may happen to co-exist. Such are the cases which neurologists speak of as examples of specific, or developmental dyslexia. . . . To identify these cases of specific developmental dyslexia among the multitude of poor readers is no easy task . . . for there is no single clinical feature which can be accepted as pathognomic. (1970, pp. 101–102)

Rabinovitch explained his concept of primary reading retardation, which is quite similar to Critchley's dyslexia, as follows:

> Capacity to learn to read is impaired without definite brain damage being suggested in the case history or upon neurological examination. The defect is in the ability to deal with letters and words as symbols, with resultant diminished ability to integrate the meaningfulness of written material. The problem appears to reflect a basic disturbed pattern of neurological organization. Because the cause is biological or endogenous, these cases are diagnosed as *primary reading retardation*. (Rabinovitch, 1962, p. 74)

Rabinovitch and Critchley both opposed ascribing severe reading disabilities to "minimal brain damage," a term with which there was much dissatisfaction, partly because it implies a knowledge of etiology that does not exist. They were more sympathetic to the concept of a *maturational lag*, or slowness in certain specialized aspects of neurological development (Bender, 1957). Satz (1973) similarly postulated that specific reading disability reflects a lag in the maturation of the left hemisphere of the brain.

Recognizing that the diagnostic differentiation of maturational lag from minimal brain damage is difficult and uncertain, Clements (1966) proposed a term which begs the question, "minimal brain dysfunction syndrome":

> These aberrations may arise from genetic variations, biochemical irregularities, perinatal insults or other illnesses or injuries sustained during the years which are critical for the development and maturation of the central nervous system, or from unknown causes. The definition also allows for the possibility that early severe sensory deprivation could result in central nervous system alterations which may be permanent. During the school years, a variety of learning disabilities is the most prominent manifestation of the condition which can be designated by this term. (Clements, 1966, p. 13)

Those who accept Clements' concept may prefer to call it "delayed and irregular neurological development" as both conveying the central idea more clearly and being far less threatening to children, parents, and teachers. This term was first suggested to one of us by A. Abrams (1968).

Our present knowledge concerning dyslexia was well summarized by Vernon:

> As to the precise nature of the disability we know little, and much further experimental investigation is required to define this and to demonstrate exactly how it operates in creating reading difficulties. And as to the ultimate cause of the disability, the evidence is too weak and conflicting to do more than suggest certain highly speculative hypotheses. . . .
>
> It is difficult in the present state of our knowledge to differentiate dyslexia from non-dyslexic backward readers. Indeed it may be impossible to do so with any precision. (Vernon, 1971, pp. 176–178)

The National Advisory Committee on Dyslexia and Related Reading Disorders (1969) concluded that *dyslexia* does not seem to be a useful term. A similar committee in England came to the same conclusion (Tizard, 1972). Adams (1969, p. 618) reviewed twenty-three attempts to define dyslexia and found little agreement. He concluded: "But sometimes a word gets born which, rather than live as servant to man, moves out in life like a Frankenstein wreaking havoc in the discourse of sensible men. *Dyslexia* is such a word. Its meaning is obscure and it has divided the efforts of professional men when collaboration would have been the better course." For this book the preferred is *reading disability* or *disabled reader*, qualified with whatever descriptive terms may help to clarify the particular case.

Learning Disabilities

Because of the confusion as to what dyslexia means, its use has been declining, only to be supplanted by an even broader and vaguer term— learning disability. Indeed, *dyslexia* and *learning disability* are used almost interchangably in much of the literature. However, *learning disability* appears to be a more encompassing term. The broadness of the term is best illustrated by the definition suggested by Kirk and Bateman (1962):

> A learning disability refers to a retardation, disorder, or delayed development in one or more of the processes of speech, language, reading, writing, arithmetic, or other school subjects resulting from a psychological handicap caused by a possible cerebral dysfunction and/or emotional or behavioral disturbance. It is not the result of mental retardation, sensory deprivation, or cultural or instructional factors. (p. 73)

A somewhat similar educational definition was offered by Kass and Myklebust (1969):

> Learning disabilities refers to one or more significant deficits in essential learning processes requiring special education techniques for remediation.
> Children with learning disability generally demonstrate a discrepancy between expected and actual achievement in one or more areas, such as spoken or written language, reading, mathematics, and spatial orientation.
> The learning disability referred to is not primarily the result of sensory, motor, intellectual, or emotional handicap, or lack of oportunity to learn. (pp. 39–40)

The field of learning disabilities grew phenomenally during the 1960's (McCarthy, 1969; Lerner, 1971b; Hallahan and Cruickshank, 1973). By 1968, approximately two-thirds of the states made provisions for children with learning disabilities either directly through law or indirectly through inclusion in the term "handicapped child." Only one-fifth of them had specific legislation for children with learning disabilities. The definitions and diagnostic procedures included in these laws varied considerably (Kass, Hall, and Simches, 1969). A federal learning disabilities act was passed in 1969 (Yarborough, 1969).

This rapid growth has not been without its problems. McCarthy (1969) summarized the "progress" made in the field of learning disabilities to that date:

> Methodologically, we started with visual perception, then went to sensori-motor training, then to ocular pursuit, then to the establishment of cerebral dominance, then to stimulus reduction, then to auditory perceptual or language training, then to multisensory training, then to integration of sensory stimuli, then to an analytic approach, and then to behavior modification. Academically, we have gone from Orton to Fernald to Gillingham to Spaulding to SRA to BRL, to Phonovisual, to the Language Master, to ITA, and now to any reading method which has a decoding emphasis. The focus of remediation has been passed from the social worker to the pediatrician to the psychiatrist to the psychologist to the neurologist to the endocrinologist and now back to the teachers. (p. 36)

More recently, Hallahan and Cruickshank (1973) wrote:

> All is not well in the learning disability fraternity. It is an area in education and psychology which can be characterized, as Winston Churchill once did in speaking of a colleague, as "profoundly superficial." . . .
> Despite the lack of a large reservoir of trained professionals in this field and the dearth of research and writing to provide a common definition, children with all sorts of problems, related or unrelated, were placed into classes

for the "learning disabled" under the guidance of inadequately trained teachers. Personnel conducting diagnosis and placement often had no adequate concept of the problem. . . .

Reading problems, emotional problems, management problems, intellectual problems, speech problems, handwriting problems, and others, irrespective of their etiology or symptomatology are found grouped together on the premise that each is a learning problem. . . . Thus, the practical result of the new term went far beyond its original conceptualization. . . . Indeed, the popularization and misuse of the term could easily undermine its usefulness. . . . Confusion is everywhere. (pp. IX, 8–9)

Thus, unless there is a drastic change in the field, the term *learning disability* appears headed for the same fate as dyslexia.

Often there is confusion, consternation, or even friction when deciding whether a case of reading disability falls within the purview of the reading specialist or the learning-disability specialist. As Hartman and Hartman (1973a) pointed out, there is little if any difference between many children labeled as being learning disabled and those seen by reading specialists. A false dichotomy has arisen because the two specialists employ different terms, diagnostic approaches, and remedial procedures. Learning-disability specialists tend to focus on factors within the child that they believe are causing the reading disability, and to treat these factors. Reading specialists usually seek to determine the child's reading skills, and to teach those skills felt to be weak or nonexistent. The personal experience of the authors has indicated that some reading teachers are intimidated by the mystique of learning disabilities and that many learning-disability teachers know little about diagnosing and treating reading problems.

Terms Used in This Book

Labels can be useful when they accurately communicate meaning, but the lack of agreement as to what many terms mean suggests the need for fewer terms that are more clearly understood and accepted. Less concern should be focused on terminology and more effort focused on answering two general questions. Because not all children reading below age level have a reading problem, and some children reading at or above grade level do, the first general question becomes: Is this child reading about as well as can reasonably be expected? Use of the terms *disabled reader, underachiever in reading,* and *slow learner in reading* should assist in answering this question.

Not all children of a given age can read at the same level, nor will they learn as quickly or as much. Furthermore, children reading at the same reader level are not equally proficient in all reading skills. To deny these facts is to deny individual differences. Inclusion of the term *reading skill deficiency* recognizes that, regardless of a child's general level of reading ability, he may be weak in one or more reading skills.

The second general question becomes: What can we do to help this child improve his reading skills? This leads to two subquestions: 1) What are his needs?, and 2) How can we best teach him?

The following terms are used in this book:

Disabled reader or *reading disability:* designates individuals whose general level of reading ability is significantly below expectancy for their age and intelligence, and also is disparate with their cultural, linguistic, and educational experience. The latter part of this definition suggests that factors other than chronological age and intelligence must be considered.

Severely disabled reader or *severe reading disability:* refers to disabled readers whose general level of reading ability is extremely below expectancy. Some writers apply labels such as *dyslexia* or *learning disability* to these cases.

Slow learner in reading: indicates children who, although reading below age level, are generally functioning in reading close to their somewhat limited learning potential.

Underachiever in reading: applies to those children who, although reading at or above age or grade level, are reading significantly below their own potential or expectancy level which is well above average.

Reading skill deficiency or *difficulty:* indicates that, regardless of the child's general level of reading ability, he is weak in one or more reading skills. In some cases, the deficiency may be quite specific and may not lower the general level of reading ability. Naturally, if there are a number of skill deficiencies, if they are in basic skills, or if the skills are severely deficient, the child's general level of reading ability will be adversely influenced.

Both the disabled reader and the underachiever in reading are working below capacity. The basic difference between the two is that the disabled reader is functioning below age level whereas the underachiever in reading is not. A child of below-average intelligence can also be a disabled reader if his general level of reading ability is below his potential. Somewhat similarly, a disabled reader is likely to have more severe reading-skill deficiencies than a child reading at grade level.

Moreover, some children do not achieve in school despite adequate reading ability. Their inability to function academically in school, therefore, cannot be attributed to a reading disability. There may be a lack of positive motivation or interference from emotional problems. These are cases for the psychologist or counselor rather than for the reading specialist.

The terms *disabled reader, underachiever in reading,* and *slow learner in reading* can be useful in that they draw attention to three types of learners who generally need differing treatment. Disabled readers often need intensive specialized treatment. Underachievers in reading usually need either to be better motivated or to be allowed to use "above grade level" materials. They rarely receive attention because they are functioning at grade level.

Once such children have been identified, attention should be focused on helping each individual attain realistic goals. Underachievers should be aided, but not pushed continuously to attain unreasonable levels of achievement. Slow learners should not be expected to reach grade level in reading, nor should they be written off as unable to learn. Both underachievers and slow learners can be misclassified by test scores; expert judgment must also be given consideration. Whatever their classification, most children, including truly slow learners, can learn more if we can determine how to teach them; and often we do not gain such information unless we *attempt* to teach them and to analyze these attempts. As Adelman (1971) and Wagner (1971) have pointed out, a disability or learning problem may be the result not only of the subject's characteristics, but also of the task characteristics as well as the teaching procedures and setting. An interaction of deficiencies in both the learner and the task may seriously hamper progress.

III. VIEWPOINTS REGARDING CAUSATION

Much of the controversy regarding the nature of reading disability, particularly severe disability, is reflected in the numerous and varied terms found in the literature. Often the definitions of these terms reveal the writers' beliefs as to what caused the disability. In turn, the reason(s) ascribed to the disability determine how it should be treated. The following section briefly summarizes these opinions.

Single-Factor Theories

Various writers believe that all or most cases of reading disability can be attributed to a single cause. Some (*e.g.*, Hallgren, 1950; Hermann, 1959, 1964; Michal-Smith, Morgenstern and Karp, 1970; Critchley, 1970; Symmes and Rapoport, 1972; Bakwin, 1973) believe that the disability is genetically linked and therefore inherited. They often consider the presence of similar difficulties in other family members to be an important factor in diagnosis. However, studies in this area do not agree on all points "and it is by no means proved that a single dominant gene is involved. In fact, it has not been strictly shown that the tendency for dyslexia to run in families is even partly due to genetic rather than psychological causes" (Thomas, 1973, p. 39).

Terms such as *brain damage* imply a cortical or neurological basis. Yet actual injury in particular areas of the cortex occur in only a few cases (Vernon, 1971), and it is very difficult to establish any detailed neuroanatomy and neurophysiology relevant to severe reading disability (Buchanan, 1968).

Reed, Rabe, and Mankinen (1970) examined the literature on teaching reading to brain-damaged children for the period 1960 to 1970. They concluded: "the criteria for diagnosing brain damage was generally inadequate or nonexistent. There was little evidence to suggest that children diagnosed as brain-damaged require or benefit from teaching procedures that differ greatly from those used with reading disability cases without brain damage."

Similarly, *minimal brain damage* suggests a neurological problem whose existence is suggested but cannot be proved by existing medical tests. The difficulties in making such a diagnosis have been discussed by Dunn (1968). And although the basic cause was still believed to be neurological, Delacato (1966) believed that reading disability was caused by a lack of neurological organization, rather than being inherited or caused by some damage or deficit.

The term *maturational lag* suggests a slowness in certain specialized aspects of neurological development; *i.e.*, a delay in development rather than a deficit or loss. A somewhat similar developmental point of view holds that the outstanding cause of school failure in general is immaturity (Ames, 1968). Delayed maturation implies that, given the opportunity for learning, a normal level of function will ultimately be achieved (Naidoo, 1971).

Another single-factor theory was that of D. E. P. Smith and Carrigan (1959) who suggested that reading disability was due to a biochemical imbalance which results in a deficit in the transmission of neural impulses across synapses in the brain. Other theorists postulate that perceptual-motor deficits (Cruickshank, 1961; Kephart, 1960, 1964; Barsch, 1965) or visual-motor deficits (Frostig, 1964; Getman, 1965) are the major causes of reading or learning disabilities. "The motor development view suggests that the study of human movement is inseparable from the study of learning because as man moves, he learns. An understanding of the dynamics of learning thereby necessarily involves the understanding of movement and motor development. Motor learning, thus, becomes the foundation for later learning of other kinds" (Lerner, 1973). Many of these later theories seem to stem from the early work of Werner and Strauss (Werner and Strauss, 1939; Strauss and Lehtinen, 1947). Still other single-factor theories stress defects of attention (Dykman, *et al.*, 1971; Stott, 1973).

A Pluralistic Viewpoint

In our opinion, and that of others (*e.g.*, H. M. Robinson, 1946; J. C. Reed, 1968; J. C. Abrams, 1969; Malmquist, 1971), most cases of reading disability cannot be attributed to any *one* cause. It is more likely that differing interrelated factors or combinations of factors cause, or contribute to, a vast majority of the cases. The point of view is more fully discussed in Chapter 10.

Nevertheless, we do believe that there are cases of severe reading disability in which constitutional predisposition is strong. If one assumes for the sake of argument that these account for somewhere between 10 and 25 per cent of all reading disabilities, they are the cases most likely to make slow or no progress with the best help school can give and thus most likely to be referred to a clinic, a neurologist, or a residential treatment center. In a school-based survey of reading disability, however, they would be outnumbered at least three to one by nonconstitutional cases with varied causation. Since there is no easy or sure way to identify the constitutionally based cases from other types of reading disability (Lannay, 1971) and often the child with a constitutional basis has other, more clearly identifiable handicaps as well, their presence in the larger school group could easily be overlooked by an investigator. At present there is no sure way to differentiate between or among those whose severe disability is inherited or caused by some neurological damage, deficit, dysfunction, or delay.

The problems involved in determining the causal or contributing factors in a given case are numerous, and not without pitfalls. Our present state of knowledge does not allow us to make accurate differential diagnoses.

One pitfall that should be avoided is the mistaken belief that a single label can be used to describe a case accurately. As Dunn (1968) pointed out, the diagnostic category selected may depend on the training, philosophy, and predisposition of those making the diagnosis. Depending on their biases, three different diagnostic teams could label the same child as brain injured, emotionally disturbed, or mentally retarded. One suspects that diagnostic labels are sometimes self-fulfilling prophecies. Furthermore, quite often a child may fit two or more labels. For example, a mentally retarded child may have "dyslexia" (Thompson, 1971). To complicate matters further, a particular label may be deceptive. Although there is a high incidence of reading disability in low socioeconomic areas, one cannot be certain that reading disability is caused by low socioeconomic status. Even if one were considering this population in general, and not just a single case, he could not be certain whether the disability was attributable to genetic factors, linguistic factors, or poor nutrition (Hallahan and Cruickshank, 1973); or, to what extent the reading problem was the result of emotional problems, home environment, poor motivation, or inadequate teaching. Nor can anyone state positively how probable contributing factors interact to create the problem.

IV. AN OBJECTIVE DEFINITION OF READING DISABILITY

In determining whether or not an individual has a reading disability, his present level of reading ability is compared with an estimate of his reading expectancy. However, there is little agreement on what to use as measures of reading achievement or reading potential, how to express the relationship of attainment to expectancy, or how large a difference constitutes a disability (A. J. Harris, 1971a; Bruininks, Glaman, and Clark, 1973).

Even if agreement existed regarding what formula to use and the amount of difference that indicates a disability, a number of unsolved measurement problems must be considered. First, no test is a perfectly reliable measure. A test score should be considered as falling within a range of scores that is estimated by using the test's standard error of measurement, rather than as a specific and exact point on a scale. Second, use of different tests probably will influence decisions, particularly when the scores are close to whatever cutoff criterion is used to indicate a disability. Third, a difference between scores on two tests with acceptable reliability may have substantially lower reliability than either of the tests taken individually. Fourth, the relationship between intelligence test scores and reading test performance becomes stronger at older chronological ages. Therefore, use of capacity minus reading achievement scores for selecting remedial cases becomes a less valid procedure as CA (chronological age) increases (Farr, 1969). Thorndike (1973) has provided useful tables for finding the odds that a difference between scores on two tests is real, for different combinations of test reliability and correlation between the tests. Generally a difference has to be at least one standard deviation to have much probability of being real. These and other reasons have led some writers to question the usefulness of existing procedures (Farr, 1969; Jerrolds, Callaway, and Gwaltney, 1971).

There are instances when the evidence for the presence of a reading disability is so clear as to be self-evident. For example, if a child is known to have at least average intelligence and his reading is three years below normal for his age, everyone would agree that he is disabled in reading. No computation is needed to arrive at this decision. But more exact procedures are necessary for a variety of purposes, such as: 1) to arrange a number of children in order of severity of reading disability, 2) to assist in determining eligibility for inclusion in a remedal program, 3) to make statistical studies of the frequency of occurrence of reading disability, 4) to match groups of disabled readers for experimental purposes, and 5) to determine the need for remedial personnel in a school system.

The procedures described below are suitable for use in satisfying each of these purposes. They provide an objective numerical measure of severity of disability (the Reading Expectancy Quotient); set a specific cutoff point (an R Exp Q of 90); and differentiate among disability, under-achieving, and slow learners in reading (using the Reading Quotient).

These procedures should be used with a full understanding of their limitations. They should not be employed as the sole basis for determining whether or not efforts are to be made to assist an individual to improve his reading ability or skills (*e.g.*, admission to a remedial reading pro-gram). Furthermore, it should be realized that although an individual's Reading Expectancy Quotient may fall within normal limits, indicating he should not be classified as a disabled reader, he may have reading skill deficiencies which could be improved and therefore should be treated. The same is true for underachievers and slow learners.

Determining General Level of Reading Ability

Standardized reading tests or well-constructed informal reading in-ventories may be used to estimate an individual's present general level of reading ability. In either case, the reading score should represent, as accurately as possible, the individual's instructional level. The uses and limitations of such tests for this purpose are discussed in Chapter 8.

For children who are reading below the fourth-grade level and seem to have problems in reading, equal weight should be given to silent reading and oral reading in arriving at a composite reading score. For those reading at or above fourth-grade level, only a silent reading score may be used, but oral reading should be given at least qualitative consideration. "It is better for two reasons to use a composite of oral reading and silent reading scores, than silent reading alone. The first is that difficulties in word identification are central in many reading disabilities, and low compre-hension scores may be the result of inability to recognize the words. The other is that poor readers tend to get many of their correct answers on multiple-choice tests by guessing, making their scores on such tests less dependable than the scores of normal readers" (A. J. Harris, 1971a).

Reading Age. Many reading tests provide grade norms, but not age norms. For the computational procedures described below it is necessary to have a reading-age score. Since the typical child in American public schools enters first grade at the age of 6.2 years (the usual minimum is 5 years 8 or 9 months) and is promoted regularly, there tends to be a regular difference of 5.2 years between chronological age and grade placement. When a reading test does not provide age norms, reading-grade scores may, for the purpose of these computations, be changed into reading-age scores by adding 5.2 years. Reader levels for informal reading inventories (IRI) may be treated similarly. Because scores yielded by the IRI typically are in reader levels rather than grade-equivalent scores, the following arbitrary grade-equivalent scores may be assigned to the instructional levels derived from the administration of an IRI:

pre-primer = 1.2	low third reader = 3.2
primer = 1.5	high third reader = 3.7
first reader = 1.8	fourth reader = 4.5
low second reader = 2.2	fifth reader = 5.5
high second reader = 2.7	sixth reader = 6.5; and so on

Determining Reading Expectancy

Reading expectancy should be an informed estimate of the level of reading achievement that can realistically be expected of an individual when the relevant facts are known. Intelligence test scores are commonly used to estimate reading expectancy which is sometimes referred to as *reading potential* or *reading capacity*. Expectancy levels vary with the test used to measure reading potential (Bliesmer, 1956; Reed, 1970). These estimates should therefore be tempered by knowledge of the child's chronological age, motivation, amount and quality of education, and familiarity with standard English, as well as his conceptual and experiential background. Most frequently, reading expectancy levels are based on measures of intelligence, learning potential, or listening comprehension (auding).

Intelligence Tests. When intelligence or learning potential is used in arriving at an estimate of reading expectancy, priority should be given to the results of verbal and nonverbal intelligence tests. The correlation between mental ability and reading comprehension is substantial at all ages. Correlations are generally in the .40's and .50's in the first grade (Bond and Dykstra, 1967), rise into the .70's by the fourth grade (Allen, 1944), and tend to remain at about .70 for group verbal tests into the freshman year of college (Thorndike, 1963). Verbal mental-ability tests correlate more highly with reading comprehension than they do with average achievement scores or school marks.

Nonverbal tests tend to have lower correlations with reading than verbal mental-ability tests do. For example, for 113 disadvantaged black pupils in seventh grade, the WISC Verbal IQ (based on individually administered tests which do not require reading) correlated .78 with *Metropolitan Reading*, while the WISC Performance IQ correlated .53 and the *Cattell Culture Fair* (a nonverbal group test) correlated .56 with the same reading test (Downing and others, 1965).

Poor readers tend to make significantly lower scores on intelligence tests that require reading ability (Neville, 1965). A child who cannot read the test items cannot score well on the test, thus being unable to display whatever potential he has. Therefore, in testing children with reading difficulties, use of intelligence tests that require reading ability should be avoided. This eliminates many popular group intelligence tests used beyond the primary grades. Because use of such tests may underestimate the poor reader's potential, he may be prevented from receiving remedial assistance either because he obtained a score below that set as a minimum for acceptance into the special program, or because the depressed score results in the incorrect conclusion that he is working up to his expected level. Children who have the potential to learn may not score well even on individual intelligence tests, for reasons such as expressive-language-skill deficits or poor motivation. If there is reason to believe that an individual has the potential to improve his reading skills, he should be given the opportunity to do so regardless of his intelligence test scores.

Individuals who have trouble learning to read sometimes show marked differences between their scores on verbal and nonverbal intelligence tests or subtests. Some score substantially higher on nonverbal measures; for others, the reverse is true. There is some opinion that when a discrepancy of this sort exists, the higher of the two scores, whether verbal or nonverbal, should be used as an indicator of reading potential (Myklebust, 1968). The rationale is that, although this may sometimes result in overestimating reading expectancy, such "errors" are less serious than underestimating it. However, because verbal scores tend to correlate much higher with reading achievement than nonverbal scores do, they generally are better predicators of reading potential. Reading is a highly verbal ability; therefore it may be unrealistic to expect the individual to achieve at a level in reading commensurate with a high nonverbal score. Nonverbal tests may not adequately measure the type of mental abilities related to success in learning to read. On the other hand, a high nonverbal IQ shows the presence of some good abilities which may compensate to some extent for verbal weaknesses. For these reasons, we suggest using the mean of verbal and nonverbal scores, or a total score based on both, in determining reading potential.

Tests that contain both verbal and nonverbal subtests include: 1) individually administered tests such as the WPPSI *(Wechsler Preschool and Primary Scale of Intelligence)*, WISC *(Wechsler Intelligence Scale for Children)*, WISC-R *(Wechsler Intelligence Scale for Children—Revised)*, and the WAIS *(Wechsler Adult Intelligence Scale)*; and 2) primary grade group tests whose verbal tests *do not require reading ability,* such as the *California Test of Mental Maturity,* the *Kuhlmann-Anderson, Analysis of Learning Potential,* and others.

Verbal tests whose scores may be averaged with nonverbal scores in estimating reading expectancy include: 1) the *Revised Stanford-Binet Intelligence Scale,* 1972 Norms Edition, or the *Slosson Intelligence Test;* 2) primary-grade levels of group tests not requiring reading such as *Pintner-Cunningham Primary,* the *Otis-Lennon,* and others; and 3) vocabulary tests that do not require reading, such as the *Ammons Picture Vocabulary Test* and the *Peabody Picture Vocabulary Scale.*

Usable nonverbal tests include: 1) individually administered performance scales, such as the *Arthur Point Scale of Performance Tests;* 2) group nonverbal tests, such as the *Cattell Culture Fair Intelligence Tests* and the *Raven Progressive Matrices;* and 3) for younger children, the *Goodenough-Harris Drawing Test.*

When a reading test and an intelligence test have been normed on the same population, the chances that a difference between a person's scores on the two tests might be due to differences in test standardization are minimized. There is still the problem that some intelligence tests require reading skill to discover the questions, however, and thus are reading tests for poor readers. Test pairs that may be considered include: *Gates-MacGinitie, Survey* Form F and *Lorge-Thorndike; Comprehensive Test of Basic Skills* and *California Short Form Test of Mental Maturity; Stanford Reading Tests* and *Otis-Lennon; Iowa Tests of Basic Skills* and *Lorge-Thorndike; California Reading Tests and Short Form Test of Academic Aptitude.*

Listening Comprehension. Listening comprehension, sometimes referred to as *auding,* is recommended by some as the most satisfactory measure of reading potential. The general technique is to find the highest level at which the child can comprehend material read to him and compare that with his reading level on similar material. Durrell and Hayes stated:

> This ability to understand spoken English demonstrates that the child has the intelligence and perceptual abilities to handle words and sentences, the basic for all later communication skills. . . . Listening comprehension is more directly related to reading than are most tests of intelligence. Intelligence tests measure a variety of mental functions which have varying degrees of relationship to reading. Listening comprehension measures *language* acquisition, the knowledge of the very same words and sentences which are to appear later in reading. (1969, p. 12)

The rationale for checking an individual's comprehension of material read to him is that if he understands orally presented material at a particular level he should be able to comprehend similar printed material at that level if he does not have difficulties with the special skills required in reading. There are standardized tests of listening comprehension such as the *Durrell Listening-Reading Series* and the Listening Test of the *Sequential Tests of Educational Progress*. Some standard reading achievement tests (e.g., *Stanford*) include listening-comprehension subtests. Such tests should measure understanding of connected discourse in order to be used for the purpose suggested here. Listening-comprehension scores also may be obtained from informal reading inventories or standardized measures such as the Spache's *Diagnostic Reading Scales* (DRS).

There are some limitations with using listening comprehension as an indicator of reading potential. Apart from the measurement problems inherent in any test, there is evidence that for some children, particularly bright children in the upper grades, reading ability may exceed listening ability (Durrell and Hayes, 1969).

Auditory handicaps and unfamiliarity with standard English may lower a listening-comprehension score. Therefore, a listening-comprehension score should be considered as a temporary estimate. The possibility that a pupil's potential might change should be determined by careful evaluation. Factors such as his learning experiences (or lack of them), his verbal and nonverbal mental ages, and the stimulation of his environment must be considered. A child should not be excluded from a remedial program because of a low listening-comprehension score alone. Only when the preponderance of the evidence clearly suggests that he does not have the potential to improve should such a decision be made (Spache, 1972). Finally, there is the possibility that listening-comprehension scores may be influenced by the presence or absence of prior training; or by the fact that it is that last ability tested when a series of tests is administered and is adversely influenced by fatigue.

The correlations between listening and reading comprehension are somewhat similar to those found between intelligence and reading, ranging from .45 to .70 with a mean of .58 (Strang 1968a). The tests employed appear to be a factor in the obtained correlations.

Estimating Mental Age and Listening Age

If an intelligence test is employed to estimate capacity, it may be necessary to compute the child's present mental age. If a listening-comprehension test is used, his present listening age may have to be determined in order to utilize the suggested reading expectancy formula.

Estimating Present Mental Age. Although the majority of intelligence tests provide norm tables for both mental age (MA) and intelligence quotient (IQ), there are two reasons why it is often necessary to compute an estimated present mental age: 1) some tests provide IQ's but not MA's; and 2) since MA increases with chronological age (CA) up to about age 15, it is necessary to estimate a present mental age if the test was given more than a month or two ago.

When the available information includes the child's CA and a usable IQ, present MA can be estimated with the formula:

$$MA = \frac{CA \times IQ}{100}$$

CA can be expressed either in years and tenths, or in months; the resulting MA will correspond. When the estimate of mental maturity is a grade-equivalent score, one can convert it into an estimate MA by adding 5.2 years.[1]

Direct Comparison of Mental Age with Reading Age. Prior to the fifth edition of this book, the direct comparison of MA with RA was recommended, with disability indicated at most grade levels when MA is a year or more higher. The Reading Expectancy Quotient described below is more accurate than this simple comparison, particularly in three kinds of circumstances: 1) when there are more candidates for remedial help than can be accommodated and one wants to set up a rank order for degree of severity of the problem; 2) when one needs a statistical measure of degree of disability for use in research; and 3) when one wants to check whether or not remedial help is bringing children closer to their expected reading levels.

Estimating Present Listening Age. Age-equivalent scores for listening-comprehension tests may be used rather than MA. When the listening-comprehension score is in grade equivalents, it can be converted to an age score by adding 5.2 years. If an informal reading inventory or standardized test such as the DRS is used, 5.2 may be added to the reader-level designation suggested on page 147.

Maturity as a Factor in Reading Expectancy

General intelligence, or listening comprehension, is only one of many factors that are relevant to an individual's progress in reading. Assuming that the average correlation between intelligence or listening comprehen-

---

1. While CA and MA are usually expressed in years and twelfths, grade-equivalent scores are stated in years and tenths. To ease comparisons and computations, all age scores are expressed in years and tenths in this discussion.

sion and reading comprehension is between .60 and .75 at most grade levels, this provides a little less than half of the information needed to predict reading performance with complete accuracy. Other factors that influence reading expectancy include errors of measurement and a variety of traits or abilities that improve or grow with increasing age, such as visual and auditory perception, general information, grasp of linguistic and syntactic relationships, vocabulary, and amount of reading instruction and practice. An estimate of reading expectancy based only on intelligence or listening comprehension is likely to be less accurate than one that also gives some weight to general maturing.

Although chronological age (CA) is not in itself closely correlated with growth in reading when other factors are held constant, age provides a time dimension within which a variety of maturing traits have the opportunity to develop. Thus CA can function as a common denominator for a variety of factors which influence growth in reading and which increase or develop as children get older. These may include thinking abilities such as judgment, evaluation, and conceptual foresight, which are not included in some measures of general intelligence (Harootunian, 1966).

A Recommended Formula for Reading Expectancy

Reading Expectancy Age. A simple formula that gives priority to the importance of intelligence, but also recognizes the presence of other age-related characteristics in reading expectancy, involves giving mental age twice the weight of chronological age. The formula may be written:

$$\text{Reading Expectancy Age (R Exp A)} = \frac{2MA + CA}{3}$$

In this formula MA and CA should be expressed in years and tenths, giving R Exp A also in years and tenths.

The statistically minded reader may note that this formula for R Exp A gives essentially the same results as those obtained from using a simple regression equation for predicting reading age from mental age alone, assuming an average correlation of .67 between MA and RA.

Reading Expectancy Quotient. A quotient that expresses how a child's present general level of reading ability compares with his expected reading level may be obtained by dividing attained reading age by expectancy age. In formula form:

$$\text{Reading Expectancy Quotient (R Exp Q)} = \frac{RA \times 100}{R \text{ Exp A}}$$

The difference between reading performance and expectancy is considered to fall within normal limits when the R Exp Q is between 90 and

110. A cutoff score of 90 takes into account that much of any obtained difference may be an artifact based on chance errors of measurement. An R Exp Q below 90 indicates failure to read up to expectancy and therefore presence of a disability or underachievement with very little likelihood that the difference is due to chance errors of measurement.

The lower the R Exp Q, the more severe the disability. In general, an R Exp Q of 85 to 89 indicates the presence of a disability and an R Exp Q below 85 indicates that the disability is severe. It may be noted that for a child totally unable to read (RG = 1.0, RA = 6.2), the higher his R Exp A, the lower his R Exp Q. Thus, with an R Exp A of 7.7, his R Exp Q is 80; with an R Exp A of 9.7, his R Exp Q is 63; and with an R Exp A of 11.7, his R Exp Q is only 52. If a child's reading does not improve, his disability becomes progressively more severe.

Quotients above 110 indicate that reading is above expectancy, usually a sign of much greater than average effort and practice or of very superior instruction; or they may be artifacts of the tests employed (Maginnis, 1972).

Distinguishing among Disabled Readers, Underachievers, and Slow Learners

It is worthwhile to make as accurate a distinction as possible among: 1) disabled readers who are unable to function academically at grade level because of their poor reading ability; 2) underachievers whose reading ability is sufficient for grade-level requirements although well below their own expectancy; and 3) slow learners whose reading ability is below age level but is in keeping with their somewhat limited learning capacity. This may be accomplished by using the *Reading Quotient*, which is simply RA (multiplied by 100 to eliminate the decimal point) divided by CA. Thus the formula for comparing the individual's present level of reading performance with that of others of his chronological age is:

$$\text{Reading Quotient (RQ)} = \frac{\text{RA} \times 100}{\text{CA}}$$

When an individual's R Exp Q and RQ are both below 90, he is reading significantly below both his own expectancy and the normal performance for his age. Therefore he is properly classified as a case of reading disability. Those whose R Exp Q is below 90 but whose RQ is 90 or above are usually able to cope with their reading assignments in school, although they probably are not making full use of above-average or superior potential or aptitude; for them the term "underachiever" seems preferable. An individual whose A Exp Q is 90 or above, but whose RQ is below 90, is reading generally about as well as can be expected of one with somewhat limited potential. An individual with below-average intelligence may more properly be classified as a disabled reader than as a slow learner in reading when he is functioning significantly below his potential.

Some Examples. Bill is 10 years 7 months old (CA = 10.6), has an IQ of 105 and is in the fifth grade. His reading grade-equivalent scores are: silent reading, 4.3; oral reading, 3.1 (therefore a composite reading grade of 3.7 which yields an RA of 8.9 (3.7 + 5.2).

$$MA = \frac{10.6 \times 105}{100} = 11.1$$

$$R \text{ Exp } A = \frac{2(11.1) + 10.6}{3} = 10.9 \text{ years}$$

$$R \text{ Exp } Q = \frac{8.9 \times 100}{10.9} = 82$$

$$RQ = \frac{8.9 \times 100}{10.6} = 83$$

Since Bill is well below the critical value of 90 on both R Exp Q and RQ, there should be no hesitancy in classifying him as a case of reading disability.

Mary, a sixth grader, has an MA of 14.5 years based on her CA of 11.6 and IQ of 125. Her silent reading grade-equivalent score of 6.0 yields an RA of 11.2.

$$R \text{ Exp } A = \frac{2(14.5) + 11.6}{3} = 13.5 \text{ years}$$

$$R \text{ Exp } Q = \frac{11.2 \times 100}{13.5} = 84$$

$$RQ = \frac{11.2 \times 100}{11.6} = 97$$

Mary is definitely below expectancy in reading with an R Exp Q of 84, but her RQ of 97 indicates that her reading is very close to average for her age so that she should be called an underachiever in reading rather than a case of reading disability.

Peter, who is in third grade, has an MA of 7.2 years based on his CA of 9.0 and IQ of 80. His silent and oral reading grade-equivalent scores of 1.8 and 2.6 yield a composite reading grade of 2.2 and an RA of 7.5.

$$R \text{ Exp } A = \frac{2(7.2) + 9.0}{3} = 7.8 \text{ years}$$

$$R \text{ Exp } Q = \frac{7.5 \times 100}{7.8} = 96$$

$$RQ = \frac{7.5 \times 100}{9.0} = 83$$

Although Peter is well below the average in reading for his age (RQ of 83), his R Exp Q of 96 is above the cutoff score of 90. Therefore, he is properly classified as a slow learner in reading.

Using a Reading Expectancy Age Table. The computations explained and illustrated above can be greatly shortened by use of Table 6. Knowing the IQ and CA of a child, his R Exp A can be read from Table 6. If the child's IQ or CA falls between two values given in the table, use the nearest value and the result will usually be correct within two-tenths of a year. For greater accuracy one can interpolate, or do the arithmetic as explained above. The use of the table may be illustrated with the three examples given below.

For Bill, CA 10.6 and IQ 105, the nearest CA column is 10.7 and there is an IQ 105 row; these intersect to give the value of R Exp A as 11.0. Since the CA value used in the table was high, the estimate is slightly higher than the 10.9 computed. For Mary, CA 11.6 (nearest, 11.7) and IQ 125, the table gives the R Exp A as 13.5 years, the same as computed. For Peter, CA 9.0

TABLE 6. *Reading expectancy ages for selected combinations of chronological age and intelligence quotient*

	Chronological age												
IQ	7.2	7.7	8.2	8.7	9.2	9.7	10.2	10.7	11.2	11.7	12.2	12.7	13.2
140	9.1	9.6	10.3	10.9	11.6	12.1	12.9	13.4	14.1	14.7	15.4	15.9	16.7
135	8.8	9.4	10.1	10.6	11.3	11.8	12.5	13.1	13.8	14.3	15.0	15.5	16.2
130	8.6	9.1	9.8	10.3	11.0	11.5	12.2	12.7	13.4	13.9	14.6	15.1	15.8
125	8.4	8.8	9.5	10.0	10.7	11.2	11.9	12.3	13.0	13.5	14.2	14.7	15.4
120	8.1	8.6	9.3	9.7	10.4	10.9	11.5	12.0	12.7	13.1	13.8	14.3	14.9
115	7.9	8.3	9.0	9.4	10.1	10.5	11.2	11.7	12.3	12.7	13.4	13.8	14.5
110	7.6	8.1	8.7	9.2	9.8	10.2	10.9	11.3	11.9	12.4	13.0	13.4	14.0
105	7.4	7.9	8.4	8.9	9.5	9.9	10.5	11.0	11.5	12.0	12.6	13.0	13.6
100	7.2	7.7	8.2	8.7	9.2	9.7	10.2	10.7	11.2	11.7	12.2	12.7	13.2
95	6.9	7.4	7.9	8.3	8.9	9.3	9.7	10.4	10.8	11.3	11.8	12.2	12.7
90	6.7	7.1	7.6	8.0	8.6	8.9	9.5	9.9	10.4	10.8	11.4	11.7	12.3
85	6.4	6.8	7.4	7.7	8.2	8.6	9.1	9.5	10.0	10.4	10.9	11.3	11.8
80	6.2	6.6	7.1	7.4	7.9	8.3	8.8	9.2	9.7	10.0	10.5	10.9	11.4
75	6.0	6.3	6.8	7.2	7.6	8.0	8.5	8.8	9.3	9.7	10.1	10.5	11.0
70	5.7	6.1	6.5	6.9	7.3	7.7	8.1	8.5	8.9	9.3	9.7	10.1	10.5
65	5.5	5.9	6.3	6.6	7.0	7.3	7.8	8.1	8.6	8.9	9.3	9.6	10.1
60	5.3	5.6	6.0	6.3	6.7	7.0	7.5	7.8	8.2	8.5	8.9	9.2	9.8

NOTE: *Any expectancy age in the table can be changed into an expectancy grade equivalent by subtracting 5.2 years.*

and IQ 80, the nearest CA column is 9.2 and there is an IQ 80 row; these intersect at 7.9, slightly higher than the computed R Exp A (7.8).

Using a Reading Expectancy Quotient Table. Finding Reading Expectancy Quotients can also be speeded up by using Table 7. In the left-hand column find the number nearest to the child's RA. Read across on that line to the right to where it meets the vertical column closest to the child's R Exp A; the number at that intersection shows his approximate R Exp Q. The numbers in bold type fall within the normal range of 90–110. Numbers below 90, in the upper-right section, indicate that reading is significantly below expectancy. Numbers in the lower-left section, from 111 up, indicate that reading is significantly above expectancy. When the R Exp Q obtained from the table is close to 90 it is advisable to go through the arithmetic operations to get a more accurate result.

Reading Quotients can also be read directly from Table 7. Interpret the heading *Reading Expectancy Age* to mean *Chronological Age*. Find the number in the left-hand column that is closest to the child's RA and read across horizontally to where the row intersects the CA column closest to his CA; at the intersection one finds the number closest to his RQ.

The objective definitions of reading ability and disability based on the learner's R Exp Q and RQ are summarized in Table 8. Any of these interpretations may not be valid if either the reading expectancy score or the reading score is of doubtful validity.

TABLE 7. *Reading expectancy quotients for selected combinations of reading expectancy age and reading age*

Reading Age	Reading expectancy age											
	6.7	7.2	7.7	8.2	8.7	9.2	9.7	10.2	10.7	11.2	11.7	12.2
6.2	**92**	86	80	75	71	67	63	60	57	55	52	50
6.7	**100**	**93**	87	81	77	72	69	65	62	59	57	54
7.2	107	**100**	**93**	87	82	78	74	70	67	64	61	59
7.7	114	**106**	**100**	**93**	88	83	79	75	71	68	65	63
8.2	122	113	**106**	**100**	**94**	89	84	80	76	73	70	67
8.7	129	120	112	**106**	**100**	**94**	**90**	85	81	78	74	71
9.2	137	128	119	112	**106**	**100**	**95**	**90**	86	82	79	75
9.7	145	135	126	118	111	**105**	**100**	**95**	**91**	87	83	80
10.2	152	142	132	124	117	111	**105**	**100**	**95**	**91**	87	84
10.7	160	149	139	130	123	116	**110**	**105**	**100**	**96**	**91**	88
11.2	167	156	145	137	129	122	115	**110**	**105**	**100**	**96**	**92**
11.7	175	163	152	143	134	127	121	115	**109**	**104**	**100**	**96**
12.2	182	169	158	149	140	133	128	120	114	**109**	**104**	**100**

TABLE 8.   *Summary of objective definitions of reading ability and disability*

Classification	R Exp Q[a]	RQ[b]
Normal reader	90 or above	90 or above
Disabled reader	below 90	below 90
Underachiever in reading	below 90	90 or above
Slow learner in reading	90 or above	below 90

[a] *Expresses how a learner's present general level of reading ability compares with his expected reading level.*
[b] *Expresses how a learner's present level of reading ability compares with that of others of his chronological age.*

Alternative Procedures

Monroe used a Reading Index in which reading age was divided by the average of mental age, chronological age, and arithmetic computation age (Monroe, 1932). This had the advantage of an index in quotient form, but the inclusion of arithmetic in the formula and the giving of equal weight to CA and MA seem questionable. Somewhat similarly, Cleland (1964) and Wilson (1972) suggested adding a listening-comprehension (auding) score which would be given equal weight with MA, CA, and arithmetic computation age.

Bond and Tinker recommend computing reading expectancy by the following formula: years in school multiplied by IQ, plus one year (Bond and Tinker, 1973). For a child with an IQ of 75 at the end of the second grade, their formula gives $2 \times .75 + 1 = 2.5$, or middle second grade. If such a child is exactly 8.0 years, his MA is 6 years 0 months, and according to the expectancy formula recommended above, his R Exp A is 6.7, corresponding to a grade score of 1.5. So it makes a great deal of difference which method one chooses, when the IQ is well above or well below average.

The Bond and Tinker formula sets unduly high expectancies for the dull, and low expectancies for the bright. Their expectancy figures actually come out close to the accomplishments obtained in many schools today; it is true that many slow children (whose parents and teachers put on pressure) do slightly better in reading than their mental ages would lead one to expect (especially in oral reading) and that bright children usually score above average but not up to mental level. We believe that insufficient challenge is all too often given to very bright children, who should more commonly read close to their mental ages, and that the value of trying to force the truly dull child to an achievement level well above his general level of mental functioning is questionable.

Myklebust (1968) suggested using age scores rather than grade scores. In his formulas, learning expectancy age is computed by giving equal weight to MA, CA, and Grade Age. Reading age (or any other achievement age) is divided by expectancy age to get a learning quotient. A learning quotient below 90 indicates a disability; 85 to 89, borderline; and below 85, severe.

The various available methods of estimating reading potential do not yield comparable results (Simmons and Shapiro, 1968; Burge, 1971; Heydenberk, 1971). Rather than use expectancy formulas, some writers suggest using a differences of two or more stanines between achievement and potential as an indication of reading disability (Winkley, 1962). Others (Crowley and Ellis, 1971) recommend use of Durost's "reading reinforced method" (examiner reads an alternate form of a reading test as the child reads it silently) to select children for special reading services.[2]

Determining Reading Disability for Adolescents and Adults. The procedures described above do not apply well at and above the age of 14 because mental ability does not continue to grow in approximately linear fashion during adolescence. When the reading grade score is below eighth grade and a satisfactory IQ is available, however, the procedures described above will not be greatly in error if the CA is used up to the age of 15 and a CA of 15.0 is used for all ages from 15.0 up.

When aptitude and reading tests used in secondary school and college do not have age or grade norms, it is more appropriate to use a regression equation based on the correlation between the particular aptitude and reading tests employed than just to compare percentile or standard scores on the two tests (Thorndike, 1963). After a predicted reading score has been obtained for an individual, it is compared with his obtained reading score; if the discrepancy is at least as large as its standard error, the chances are at least five to one that a genuine failure to read up to expectancy exists. Of course, if the aptitude test score is quite high and the reading test score is quite low, one does not need elaborate computations to see that a disability is present. Another method that will work above the age of 15 is to take the difference between stanines on tests of reading and potential, with a disability indicated when potential is two or more stanines higher than reading.

2. Honel (1973) compared eight reading expectancy formulas and concluded that "the R Exp Q (Harris) appeared to have the broadest application and consequently was deemed to be the preferred formula."

SUGGESTED ADDITIONAL READING

BANNATYNE, ALEXANDER. *Language, reading and learning disabilities: psychology, neuropsychology, diagnosis and remediation.* Springfield, Ill.: Charles C Thomas, 1971. Chap. 1.

BATEMAN, BARBARA (Ed.). *Learning disorders: reading.* Vol. 4. Seattle, Wash.: Special Child Publications, 1971.

BOND, GUY L. & TINKER, MILES A. *Reading difficulties: their diagnosis and correction* (3rd ed.). New York: Appleton-Century-Crofts, 1973. Chap. 4.

CALKINS, ELOISE O. (Ed.). *Reading forum: a collection of reference papers concerned with reading disability.* Bethesda, Md.: National Institute of Neurological Diseases and Stroke, U.S. Department of Health, Education, and Welfare. NINDS Monograph No. 11. n.d.

CHALFANT, J. C. & SCHEFFELIN, A. *Central processing dysfunctions in children.* Bethesda, Md.: National Institute of Neurological Diseases and Stroke, 1969.

HALLAHAN, DANIEL P. & CRUIKSHANK, WILLIAM M. *Psycho-Educational foundations of learning disabilities.* Englewood Cliffs, N.J.: Prentice-Hall, 1973.

INGRAM, THOMAS T. S. The nature of Dyslexia. In Francis A. Young and Donald B. Lindsley (Eds.). *Early experience and visual information processing in perceptual and reading disorders.* Washington, D.C.: National Academy of Sciences, 1970. Pp. 405–444.

KALUGER, GEORGE & KOLSON, CLIFFORD J. *Reading and learning disabilities.* Columbus, Ohio: Charles E. Merrill, 1969. Chap. 3.

KEENEY, ARTHUR H. & KEENEY, VIRGINIA T. (Eds.). *Dyslexia: diagnosis and treatmeat of reading disorders.* St. Louis: C. V. Mosby, 1968. Chaps. 1, 3, 5, 7, 9, 11.

LERNER, JANET W. *Children with learning disabilities: theories, diagnosis, and teaching strategies.* Boston: Houghton Mifflin, 1971.

MYKLEBUST, HELMER R. (Ed.). *Progress in learning disabilities.* Vols. I and II. New York: Grune and Stratton, 1968, 1971.

REID, JESSIE F. (Ed.). *Reading: problems and practices.* London, England: Ward Lock Educational, 1972. Pp. 125–196.

STRANG, RUTH. *Diagnostic Teaching of Reading* (2nd ed.). New York: McGraw-Hill, 1969. Chap. 4.

VERNON, M. D. *Reading and its difficulties: a psychological study.* London, England: Cambridge University Press, 1971.

8

Assessing Reading Performance, I

Before one can adjust reading instruction to group and individual needs, as discussed in Chapters 5 and 6, one must know what those needs are. The best instructional plans can fail if the teacher assigns reading material that is much too difficult or attempts to develop a skill for which the learners have no background.

This chapter and Chapter 9 discuss in detail the measurement and evaluation of reading skills. Attention is given to both informal and standardized procedures.

The evaluation of reading involves considerably more than the collection of scores on reading tests. Evaluation means arriving at judgments about the degree to which the objectives of the reading program are being achieved. Evaluation can make use of data from many sources: standardized test scores, observation of pupil performance during reading lessons, workbook exercises, evidence of reading interests derived from discussion periods or written compositions, reports on independent reading, success in using subject-matter textbooks, and so on. The important thing is to have some usable evidence concerning the degree to which each important objective is being reached.

The term *diagnosis* is used when a difficulty is discovered and explored. Diagnosis means a careful study of the condition to determine its nature and find out about factors that may be contributing to it, with the aim of correcting or remedying the difficulty. The first part of diagnosis, studying the nature of the reading difficulty, is taken up in these two chapters; the correlates of reading difficulties and methods for studying them are discussed in Chapters 10, 11, and 12.

I. SOURCES OF INFORMATION

Information regarding the learner's reading ability may be obtained from informal and standardized measures, both of which should be employed to obtain the best possible estimate of reading ability (Farr, 1969).

Standardized or Norm-Referenced Tests

The general characteristics of standardized tests and methods of constructing them have been admirably described in some of the recent books on testing. Here it is important to note only those characteristics that must be understood for intelligent use of such tests.

The material in a standardized test is selected after careful analysis of the kind of reading that a pupil in the grades for which the test is intended may be called upon to do. Since the test is designed for use in a wide variety of school systems, it must not parallel too closely the content, style, or vocabulary of any one published reading program. It must also include a wide enough range of difficulty so that poor readers in the lowest grade for which the test is intended can get some answers right and so that the best readers in the highest grade for which the test is intended probably cannot get a perfect score. Nearly always, two or more forms are provided which are comparable in type of question and in difficulty. This makes it possible to retest a pupil without using the same material.

Every standardized test is accompanied by a manual of directions which tells in detail exactly how the test should be given and scored. It is essential to follow these directions closely. If this is not done, the norms will not be applicable because they are based on performances under standard conditions.

Test users should have at least minimal understanding of three concepts: *reliability, validity,* and *norms.*

Reliability means the degree to which the test gives consistent results. The question that reliability answers is: How much would the test score vary if the test were given repeatedly? Put another way: How sure can one be that the obtained score won't vary greatly from the learner's true score? Test reliability is usually stated either as a correlation coefficient or as a standard error of measurement.

Test users should be aware that test reliability is affected by such factors as the number of items in a test, the range of achievement of the population tested in the variable measured (the more restricted the range, the lower the reliability coefficient), and the characteristics of the group tested. Although the total score of a standardized test usually shows high reliability, the subtests may not have sufficient reliability for diagnostic use with individuals.

No test is a perfectly reliable measure; chance errors in measurement and fluctuations in individual performance preclude this. For any test, the average scores of groups are more reliable than the scores of individuals. For individual assessment, such as that employed in making a diagnosis, a test should have a reliability coefficient of at least .90 for a single age or grade level (coefficients based on a wide range of ability or characteristics tend to be spuriously high), or a standard error of measurement of not more than three months for scores given as grade or age equivalents.

The standard error of measurement indicates the variation in test scores to be expected if that test were given repeatedly to the individual. By adding and subtracting the standard error of measurement to and from the obtained score, one can determine the range of scores in which the individual's true score probably lies. Thus, if a learner obtained a grade-equivalent score of 4.3 on a test with a standard error of measurement of 0.2, the chances are about 2 to 1 that his "true" score lies somewhere between 4.1 and 4.5 (4.3±0.2) and about 19 to 1 that it is between 3.9 and 4.7 (4.3±twice the standard error). The lower the standard error of measurement, the more reliable the test.

Validity is the degree of accuracy with which a test measures what it is intended to measure. There are at least four types of validity, each of which answers a somewhat different question about the test (Katz, 1973).

If a test has low reliability it cannot be very valid, but a high reliability does not insure validity. Evidence about the validity of a test should be given in the test manual. Such evidence need not be accepted at face value, however; rather, the test should be carefully inspected to determine if the items seem to measure the phases of reading that one wants to measure. Impartial opinions about the test may be obtained from such sources as Buros (1968, 1972).

Norms are the statistics that describe the test performance of the groups on whom the test was standardized. After a test has been constructed it is given to large numbers of pupils, chosen to be representative of those for whom the test is intended. Norms are simply statements of the results obtained in this initial testing, and may be used as a basis for interpreting results on the test when given to other pupils. Norms never should be considered to be a desired standard of achievement (Massad, 1972). The kinds of norms used in reading tests are grade-equivalent scores, reading age, percentiles, standard scores, and stanines.

Grade-equivalent scores are based on raw scores (number of correct responses). A grade equivalent represents the year and month of school (grade level) for which that raw score is the median score. For example, if the median raw score of all children in the norming sample who were in the first month of fifth grade was 46, any child getting 46 correct answers is given a grade equivalent of 5.1. Grade-equivalent scores are usually given in terms of years and tenths, because there are ten months in the school year.

The limitations of grade-equivalent scores have been well enumerated (Angoff, 1971), yet they continue to be badly misinterpreted. It makes little difference which items are answered correctly, so that the child who answers correctly all 10 items he attempts obtains the same grade equivalent as one who guesses at 40 items and gets 10 correct. The same limitation also is true for other types of norms. Furthermore, a grade-equivalent score does not necessarily mean that reading material at that level is suitable for his reading instruction. Nor does it indicate that the pupil has mastered all the reading skills taught in his reading program up to the grade level indicated by the test score. About the only thing one can be certain of is that the pupil correctly answered the same number of items as the average student in the norming sample at that grade level.

Reading age, which is not found on many tests, is similar to the grade equivalent except that the norms are based on the age of the child rather than on his grade position. Thus a reading age of 9-7 (9 years and 7 months) means the child's score is equal to the median score of children who are 9 years and 7 months old. Reading ages are usually expressed in years and twelfths.

Percentiles indicate how a pupil compares with other children of his own age or grade. A percentile score of 89 means that the pupil did as well as or better than 89 per cent of those with whom he is being compared. It does *not* represent the percentage of correct responses. A scale of percentiles is not of equal measuring units. In terms of raw scores, a given percentile difference is larger at the extremes than it is at the middle.

Standard scores are normalized scores; that is, they have been transformed to a normal distribution, the mean (usually 50 or 100) and standard deviation (usually 10 or 15) being preassigned. A standard score of 50 indicates average performance. Because standard scores represent equal units, they can be used to compare performances on different tests.[1]

Stanines are normalized standard scores with a mean of 5 and a standard deviation of 2. The scale ranges from a low of one through a high of 9, with 5 indicating average performance. Stanines are equal units (*i.e.,* a

1. The Anchor Test study (Jaeger, 1973) provides the means for translating intermediate grade students' scores on any of nine widely used standardized reading tests to corresponding scores on any of the other tests.

stanine of 6 is as much better than one of 5 as stanine 3 is better than 2). Students with extremely low or high stanines need to increase their scores by many raw score points to go up from one stanine to another; those around the average stanine need increase only a few points. When comparing stanines for an individual, at least a two-stanine difference must occur before one can be reasonably certain that a real difference exists between the skills or abilities tested.

Factors to Be Considered in Selecting and Interpreting Standardized Tests. There is some question as to what reading tests really measure. As Tuinman (1973) pointed out, it has been repeatedly shown that subjects are able to guess correct answers to multiple-choice reading-comprehension questions with a degree of success that considerably exceeds chance.

There are large changes in the content of reading tests, most obviously in vocabulary subtests, from the first grade to later grades (MacGinitie, 1973c). These content changes may at least partially account for the higher correlations between reading tests and group intelligence tests above the primary grades.

Farr (1969) indicated that the most serious deficiency in using standardized tests to diagnose reading achievement is the lack of discriminant validity (the validity of tests as measures of distinct skills or abilities) for the various subtests.

A frequently voiced complaint is that standardized tests are biased against nonstandard-English-speaking urban children (Meier, 1973; Adler, 1973) and that there should be "dialect fair" tests (Hutchinson, 1972). Nevertheless, a study by Hockman (1973) found that there were no significant differences for either black or white urban children given alternate forms of a standardized test, each written in black dialect or standard English. If the children could read the selection, they found the questions easy to answer regardless of dialect. Admitting that standardized test items do not adequately reflect lower socioeconomic status and urban experiences of many children and that they are not written in black English, MacGinitie (1973b) raised a basic question: "Should they be?" His contention was that a reading test should measure the pupil's ability to deal with materials he will read in school. MacGinitie felt that urban children would not be well served by special testing that deceived the nation into believing that they can read well when they cannot. If we were not aware that many minority children do not read well compared with children in our country at large, little might be done about the situation.

There is also some question regarding how accurately standardized tests measure the reading ability of pupils who are actually reading way above or way below the grade levels for which the test is intended. One solution to this limitation is "out-of-level" testing; that is, having the pupil take the level of test commensurate with his estimated level of reading ability or past test scores. For example, a fifth grader reading at the second reader level should be administered the primary level (for grades 1–3) rather than the intermediate (for grades 4–6) level of the test (Ayrer and McNamara, 1973).

Criterion-Referenced Tests

Criterion-referenced tests (CRT) have gained increased attention in recent years. Whereas norm-referenced tests relate test performance to relative standards (How well does the test-taker's performance compare with that of others?) criterion-referenced tests relate test performance to absolute standards (Can the test taker meet a given performance criterion?). In short, a CR test indicates whether or not the test taker has mastered a specific skill, rather than how well his performance compares with that of others. "A criterion-referenced test is one that is deliberately constructed to yield measurements that are directly interpreted in terms of specified performance standards" (Glaser and Nitko, 1971). Criterion-referenced tests can be tailor-made to assess mastery of specific objectives, and therefore can be useful in individualizing instruction. Thus a criterion-referenced test standard might read: Given 10 paragraphs written at the fourth reader level, the learner can correctly determine the implied main ideas of at least 8.

Criterion-referenced tests have limitations and unresolved questions. For example, good tests will do nothing to overcome the problem of poor objectives (Otto, 1973). There is also some question as to whether CR tests can measure complex domains such as reading comprehension adequately (Jackson, 1970). There is a danger that factors in the affective domain (*e.g.*, appreciation or attitudes) might be overlooked because they are difficult to measure. Furthermore, objectives involving retention and transfer of what is learned may become secondary to the one-time demonstration of mastery-stated objectives (Otto, 1973).

The level of success demanded before a learner is allowed to move on to new content is perhaps one of the most unwieldy issues of criterion-referenced measurement (Prager and Mann, 1973). Often the passing level is set arbitrarily at 80 or 90 per cent.

Which type of test is best? The answer depends largely on the purpose of testing. Norm-referenced tests can be used to compare performances, to provide a basis for judging how much pupils have gained in achievement, and whether they are achieving at a level expected on the basis of measured scholastic aptitude. Criterion-referenced tests are best when the teacher wants to know if a pupil has acquired a particular skill or knowledge (Millman, 1972). Use of CR or NR tests should not be an either/or proposition.

Both have utility and the information gained from each should be used to complement the other. Fremer (1972) suggests ways in which norm-referenced tests might be used to gain information similar to that obtained from criterion-referenced measures.

Various programs employ criterion-referenced measurement. Four of these, *Individually Prescribed Instruction, Comprehensive Assessment Monitoring, Precision Teaching,* and the *Individual Achievement Monitoring System,* have been described by Prager and Mann (1973). Others have been described by Klein and Kosecoff (1973). Commercially prepared criterion-referenced tests available include: *Criterion Reading* (Random House), *Fountain Valley Support System in Reading* (Zweig) the *Prescriptive Reading Inventory* (McGraw-Hill), and *Wisconsin Tests of Reading Skill Development* (Interpretive Scoring Systems). All but the latter have been described and their limitations indicated by Thompson and Dziuban (1973). Banks of behavioral/criterion-referenced tests are available from some state education departments, or from such places as Educational Testing Services (Fremer, 1973) and the University of California (see Niles, 1973). Appropriate items may be chosen from such collections to construct tailor-made criterion-referenced tests, or test users may wish to construct their own items using such sources as the text by Gronlund (1973).

Informal Assessment

Informal assessment is needed to obtain information unavailable from other sources or to supplement available data. NR and CR tests do not always yield the desired information, nor is any one measure a perfect indicator of a learner's reading ability. An important aspect, the functional and realistic application of reading skills, can be measured only through informal testing (Bliesmer, 1972). Furthermore, other useful information can be obtained only through skilled observation. Informal assessments are often more valid measures than standardized reading tests because they employ a wide variety of procedures to assess reading performance over a number of different occasions (Farr, 1969). The more behaviors sampled, the more likely the assessment is to be accurate.

Otto (1973) outlined the following steps for informal assessment: 1) decide exactly what information is desired and what this means in terms of observable behavior; 2) devise new or adapt existing test items, materials, or situations to sample the behavior to be evaluated; 3) keep a record of the behavior evoked in the test situation; 4) analyze the obtained information; 5) make judgments as to how the information fits the total picture and how well it fills the gap for which it was intended.

Informal assessment may take many forms—observations, teacher-made tests, brief skill tests found in teachers manuals or in other reading materials such as workbooks, check lists which provide for systematized behavioral observations, and anecdotal records. Teacher-made tests may be brief, or as extensive as a complete mastery test or an informal reading inventory.

Pupils' self-evaluations of their reading abilities have not proved to be a useful source of information (Farr, 1969; Jason and Dubnow, 1973).

II. DETERMINING GENERAL LEVEL OF READING ABILITY

One of the most important questions to answer about a learner's reading ability is: What level of reading material is appropriate for a given purpose? Answering this question not only aids in forming instructional groups, but also in selecting material appropriate for an individual, whether for use in a developmental, corrective, or remedial reading program. Furthermore, the answer should assist in choosing material that the learner can read independently and may help to determine whether the pupil can profit from using a particular content subject text.

The answer to this question varies somewhat according to the kind of reading and the degree of perfection in reading that is expected. In general, material that is to be read under the guidance of the teacher can be somewhat more difficult than material that the child is to read independently.

More Than One Level of Reading Ability

Levels of reading competence originally described by Betts (1946) are functionally useful. The *independent* reading level is the highest level at which a child can read easily and fluently: without assistance, with few word-recognition errors, and with good comprehension and recall. The *instructional* level is the highest level at which the child can do satisfactory reading provided that he receives preparation and supervision from a teacher: word-recognition errors are not frequent, and comprehension and recall are satisfactory. The *frustration* level is the lowest level at which the child's reading skills break down: fluency disappears, word-recognition errors are numerous, comprehension is faulty, recall is sketchy, and signs of emotional tension and discomfort become evident.

This is a very useful set of concepts and has helped to clarify thinking about the meaning of "reading level." For example, a child may be able to read fifth reader[2] material with considerable strain, difficulty, and inaccuracy (frustration level); fourth reader material with acceptable accuracy

2. Many current commercially prepared reading programs label their texts by level designations that indicate their sequence rather than the intended grade or reader level, but indicate the grade for which the book is primarily intended, in the teacher's guide.

and comprehension after the teacher explains new words and concepts and provides guiding questions (instructional level); and third reader material with ease, fluency, and almost complete accuracy (independent level). If the teacher assigns him to a group using a fifth reader and expects him to do supplementary reading in fourth reader material, his effort and accomplishment are likely to be disappointing. If he is placed in a group using a fourth reader and encouraged to read independently in material of third reader level, the results are apt to be gratifying. If all his reading is at fourth reader level, he will probably do reasonably well in group lessons but engage in a minimum of other reading. If all his reading material is third reader in difficulty, he may complain about a lack of challenge and maturity in his reader, while enjoying storybooks at that level.

A Quick Class Survey

A quick screening test may be used by classroom teachers: 1) to obtain a rough estimate of the suitability of a given book for instruction, or placement in a reading group; or 2) to locate poor readers who need a more thorough diagnosis. The following procedure is a modification of one proposed by Dolch (1953):

1] Tell the class a) they are going to become acquainted with a new book; b) you want to know how difficult it is, so they will take turns reading it aloud.
2] Have each child read three or four sentences at sight.
3] If the child refuses to read, say "All right," and call on the next child.
4] If a child reads with great hesitation and difficulty, supply any aid he needs and go on to the next child.
5] At a later time, retest the children located in steps 3 and 4 with easier material.

Judgment as to mastery of the mechanics of reading is subjective, and because the procedure does not include any comprehension check, it can disclose only one aspect of reading ability.

A quick test on comprehension can also be given for preliminary screening of the pupils unable to get adequate meaning from a particular book. One can choose a short selection (four or five pages) from near the beginning of the book and ask the children to read it silently. As each pupil finishes, he closes the book and looks up; in this way the slowest readers can be spotted easily. When all have finished, the teacher can read a list of questions, to which the pupils write their answers. For this kind of brief test, short-answer questions are generally preferable to objective-type questions. The children who are unable to score at or above 70 per cent are likely to have difficulty understanding the book.

A combination of a quick oral reading survey and a silent comprehension test provides a good way to locate the children for whom a particular book is too difficult. It not only discloses the children who are not ready for the book, but also indicates if the book is suitable for the majority of the class. If teachers will take the trouble to "try the book on for size" (Chall, 1953), not only with basal readers but also with textbooks in such content areas as social studies and science, many frustrating learning experiences can be prevented.

The Informal Reading Inventory

The most straightforward way to learn if a child can read successfully in a book is to try him out on a representative sample of the book. An informal reading inventory (IRI) is a series of graded selections used to determine what level of material is most suitable for a given pupil. The techniques suggested for the construction, administration, and interpretation of the informal reading inventory may be adapted to test the suitability of any single book, including subject texts and library books. IRI's for science and mathematics material have been constructed by E. Smith, Guice, and Cheek (1972).

Preparing Materials. The teacher should start with a well-graded series of readers. The selections chosen should be near the beginning of the book and should be representative of reader material of that level in language and vocabulary. It is usually advisable to start at the beginning of a story. The teacher should mark the starting place in the margin in pencil and then count off 25, 50, 100, and 200 words, marking each place with a vertical pencil line and the number of words in his own copy. Usually 50-word selections are sufficient at pre-primer level, 100-word selections at primer and first reader levels, and 200-word selections at and above second reader level. Sometimes a short sample is enough to show that the material is very easy or too hard, but usually samples of the lengths suggested are little enough on which to base a judgment. If quite a few children are to be tested, it is advisable to prepare two or three selections of comparable difficulty in each book and to use them in rotation.

When an IRI is to be used many times, as in a reading clinic or by a remedial teacher, a somewhat more time-consuming method of preparation is worthwhile.

A word-recognition test that can be used to determine the reader level at which to begin testing may be formulated by randomly selecting 10 to 20 words introduced in each text. These words are typed or printed on separate cards, or as word lists.

Before choosing the reading selections, a readability formula can be applied to about five selections from the text.[3] From the selections whose readability has been determined, choose one to three selectons of comparable difficulty that come closest to the mean readability score (it may be necessary to draw other samples). Although only one sample at each level is needed for oral reading, it is wise to have at least one other available either for silent reading, as a retest to obtain additional information, or to alternate if quite a few children are to be tested.

For each selection, an introduction should be prepared. This statement should provide a brief background for the selection. It also should contain a motivating question (*e.g.*, "Read this story to learn how the boy escaped") and directions as to whether the child should read orally or silently. At the first- and second-grade levels, proper names of characters should be included and pointed out.

If a free-response kind of comprehension check is to be used, an outline of the selection should be made so the concepts can be checked off as the student relates the story. If specific comprehension questions are to be asked, five to ten questions should be prepared. Both factual and inferential questions should be used, with fewer inferential questions occurring at the lower reader levels. The wording should be clearly understood by the pupils, trick questions should be avoided, and the difficulty of the questions should approximate that of the selection. Suggestions for formulating comprehension questions are offered by Valmont (1972).

It is often very difficult to frame a given number of good questions on short selections, and variations in the difficulty of questions make the exactness of per cent scores on them highly questionable. For these reasons, some examiners prefer the free-response kind of comprehension check. Even when the free-response format is used, however, some criterion must be used to determine whether the student successfully understood the selection. Any selection or comprehension-check item that proves unsuitable should be replaced.

Administration.   If a word-recognition test has been constructed, it may be used to determine where to initiate testing. Present the word lists in increasing order of difficulty until the pupil fails to respond correctly to at least 80 per cent of a list. Oral reading may be begun at the highest reader level at which 80 per cent of the words on the list were recognized

3. There are two reasons for using readability formulas: 1) to select samples that are representative of the book, and 2) to assure that the selections chosen for the IRI are of increasing difficulty. Application of a readability formula also may reveal that: 1) a text is not at the level indicated by the publisher; 2) there is a narrow or wide spread of difficulty within the text; and 3) the selections do not necessarily progress from "easy" to "more difficult" from the beginning to the end of the book. See Appendix D.

correctly. If a word-recognition test is not used, it is desirable to start with a reader level expected to be very easy for the child and to go up through the series one book at a time until a frustration level is reached. Starting with a very easy book helps the child to overcome initial nervousness and to settle down in performance before reaching the difficulty levels at which he meets a real challenge.

The teacher should try to put the child at ease and to keep the procedure as relaxed and informal as possible. Before reading each selection, a look at the pictures and a bit of discussion help to maintain similarity to a guided reading lesson. The child is then asked to read the selection out loud from the book as well as he can, with no preceding silent reading. If he pauses for five seconds or asks for help, he is told the word. When the child finishes the selection he is asked to tell the story that he read. If his account is sketchy or incomplete, supplementary questions are asked. Or, if specific questions have been prepared, they are asked orally and his responses recorded. If the child meets the criteria, the next higher level is presented.

The teacher should select a time when about fifteen minutes will be available without interruption, either during a quiet seatwork period for the entire class or preferably when the class is out of the room. Teacher and child should sit side by side. Voices are kept low so as not to disturb the other children. If the class can overhear, they learn the selections and the test is spoiled—and the child may not perform well if he thinks his peers are listening.

When pupils are able to read at or above the third reader level, it is desirable to test both oral and silent reading. The oral test is given as described, with the addition that the number of seconds needed to finish the selection is timed with a watch. Silent reading testing should be initiated one reader level below the highest level at which the oral reading criteria were met. The child's silent reading should be timed and testing continued upward until the comprehension criterion is not met. If comprehension has been checked with similar types of questions on oral and silent reading selections of the same levels, the results can be compared, and one can draw some conclusions about the child's relative rate and comprehension in silent and oral reading (at about the third reader level, silent reading rate should begin to exceed oral rate). This may cast light on some factors contributing to slow silent reading.

The IRI also may be employed to obtain an estimate of the child's listening comprehension. After testing silent reading, the examiner reads the selections to the child, beginning at the level at which the child failed the silent reading criterion. Comprehension is checked in the same manner as if the pupil had read the selection, and testing continues until he fails to meet the comprehension criterion.

Name **HARRY** Date _____

First Reader (A Way to Win) 100 word sample: pp. 8-12

Said	For	Words Aided
fix	far	far
so	soon	
you	yellow	**Omissions**
		little

Word recognition: 95% Comprehension: good   Level: instructional

Low Second Reader (Here Today) 50 word sample: pp. 17-18

Said	For	Words Aided
big	dig	Singing
ast	fast	
Summer	Singing	**Insertions**
riden	river	
garden /	yard	big
we	I	our
Later	Late	
everything	overnight	
covered	come	
our	the	
was	had	
in	a	
friends	family	
the	of	

Word recognition: 68%   Comprehension: fair   Level: frustration

FIGURE **8.1**   Record of oral reading samples of Harry, a 10-year-old with a severe reading disability. The word-recognition miscues were scored according to the procedure outlined on page 173. Only a fifty-word sample was obtained at the second reader level because it was obvious that he had reached his frustration level.

Recording.   Clinics and reading specialists often mimeograph the selections used so that an examiner can use the mimeographed copy as a record form. Classroom teachers, however, may prefer the following simpler procedure.

Use a blank sheet of paper for each book tried. At the top enter the child's name, date, name of book, selection used, and number of words read. An example of this kind of record is shown in Figure 8.1. If no analysis is to be made of the errors, simply keeping a tally of the number of errors may suffice.

Mispronounced words are recorded in two columns, the word said by the child on the left (under *Said*) and the correct word to its right (under *For*). Words pronounced by the examiner are listed in a third column, labeled "Words aided." Repetitions, omissions, other types of errors, and qualitative comments are recorded below. When an error or miscue is made a second time, a check mark is made to the right of the first entry. Comprehension is briefly rated as good, fair, or poor; if a series of prepared questions is used, the per cent score can be entered. At the bottom one can enter the number of errors in word recognition, the accuracy per cent (errors divided by number of words), and one's conclusion as to whether the book is at the independent, instructional, or frustration level for this child. If a parallel silent reading sample is taken, all one needs to record is the rate, comprehension rating, and qualitative observations such as the presence of lip movements.

Scoring. Because a distinction between major and minor miscues should be made, the following scoring procedure is suggested.

1] Count as one miscue each: a) any response that deviates from the printed text and disrupts the intended meaning; b) any word pronounced for the child after a five-second hesitation.
2] Count as one-half miscue each: any response that deviates from the printed text but does not disrupt the intended meaning.
3] Count as a total of one miscue, regardless of the number of times the behavior occurs: a) repeated substitution such as *a* for *the*; b) repetitions.
4] Do not count as miscues: a) miscues that conform to cultural or regional dialects, b) self-corrections made within five seconds, c) hesitations, d) ignoring or misinterpreting punctuation marks.
5] Count repeated errors on the same word as only one miscue, regardless of the type of error made.

Interpretation. Essentially the teacher has to decide, for each selection tried, which of three possibilities is correct: 1) the child can read this book independently with good fluency, accuracy, and comprehension; 2) the child can read the book with instructional guidance; or 3) the child is not ready for the book and shows a frustration pattern when trying to read it. In arriving at conclusions, the following criteria can be applied.

For independent reading, oral reading at sight is fairly fluent. Miscues are not common, and should total not more than 5 per hundred words up to the second reader level and no more than 2–3 errors per hundred words above the second reader level. The child is able to continue reading after a miscue without feeling blocked. The major parts of the story are recalled spontaneously and correctly, and additional details can be supplied in answer to supplementary questions. The child feels that the selection is easy.

For the instructional level, word-recognition errors usually total between 3 and 5 per cent.[4] Comprehension is mostly correct, but free recall is incomplete and some details are forgotten or recalled incorrectly. Reading is mostly fairly fluent, but slows down or becomes hesitant when word-recognition or comprehension difficulties are encountered, and some repetitions and omissions may appear. The child's feeling is that the selection is not easy, but that he can handle it.

The frustration level is most clearly evident in the qualitative pattern of the reading. Fluency tends to break down, and hesitations, repetitions, and word-by-word reading are common. Signs of emotional tension or distress can be found in the child's color, breathing, facial expression, voice, and so on. He makes mistakes not only on unknown words but also on some words that he usually recognizes without difficulty. If not helped, he becomes blocked and has trouble continuing; when allowed to stop, he shows relief. Comprehension generally ranges from fair to poor, although bright children sometimes can understand quite well selections through which they stumble with great difficulty. Most children begin to show signs of frustration when word-recognition errors rise above 5 per cent. When they are highly motivated or the selection is very interesting, some children can cope with material of 5 to 10 per cent difficulty without getting upset. Material of higher than 10 per cent difficulty is nearly always frustrating on materials above the second reader level. Below that, some children are not frustrated until a 14 per cent miscue ratio is reached.

The specific errors recorded during these book samplings provide material for a qualitative analysis of the child's oral reading problems. Specific suggestions on how to make such an analysis are found in the next chapter.

No short sample of reading matter used as a test can give perfectly accurate results. Even if the child is not nervous and reads as he usually does, marked variations are found among books that are all supposedly at the same grade level and even among different stories or chapters in the same book. Estimates of a child's reading level, based on a series of short samples, should therefore be recognized as approximations. The child's subsequent degree of success in reading the assigned books should be watched, and easier or harder material substituted if it seems necessary.

4. The 3 to 5 per cent criterion is based on Cooper's (1952) results, which showed that when miscues rise above 5 per cent, the rate of improving in reading declines. Powell (1973) recommends the following: up to second reader level, 6 to 13 per cent miscues; third to fifth reader levels, 4 to 8 per cent; sixth reader and above, 3 to 6 per cent. These criteria are based mainly on absence of symptoms of frustration. For successful learning it is not safe to assume that if a child does not feel frustrated the material is most appropriate; especially at primary reading levels, instructional material should maximize the child's ability to learn and retain the new vocabulary.

Comparison of IRI Results and Standardized Test Scores. Since Sipay (1964) first reported his findings, most studies have found that some standardized tests tend to give grade equivalents higher than the instructional level as determined by an IRI. It should be realized, however, that the results of any such comparisons will be influenced by 1) the standardized test used, 2) the material on which the IRI is based, 3) how well the IRI is constructed, 4) the criteria used to determine the functional reading levels, and 5) the ability of the examiner to administer and score the IRI.

Some writers suggest subtracting a constant (*e.g.,* one year) from grade equivalent scores to arrive at the learner's instructional level. MacGinitie (1973a), however, pointed out that such a procedure is not accurate.

There also have been attempts to use a cloze test to estimate functional reading levels. The main claimed advantage is that, when using a cloze test, no extraneous questions of unknown difficulty act as an unassessed and intervening variable (Pennock, 1973). This issue is discussed further in Chapter 18.

Tests That Accompany Reading Programs. Most commercially prepared reading programs provide tests that are specifically geared to their program. Some provide oral reading tests to assist in placing the learner in the appropriate level text. Such oral reading tests are most often of one of two types: 1) a single selection to determine whether the book from which the selection is taken is suitable for the child's reading instruction, or 2) what amounts to an informal reading inventory based on their reading series (see Fig. 8.2). Almost all published programs have silent group mastery or achievement tests that are administered after the book has been completed. Some teachers manuals contain informal CR tests for assessing skill development.

III. SILENT READING

Silent reading ability is far more frequently measured than oral reading, primarily due to the fact that it is less time-consuming and requires less expertise. Because silent reading tests are employed so often, it is important to understand what they really do measure, as well as their limitations.

What to Evaluate in Silent Reading

The most important silent reading characteristic to evaluate is the *level of difficulty* at which the child can comprehend. This can be better determined by means of book samples, as discussed in the preceding section, than by means of standardized tests. The tests designed to measure this

ORAL READING

Selection 7
*First Reader * ***

INTRODUCTION. Nat can't find something. He thinks Jerry might know where it is. Read these two pages out loud to find out what happens when Nat sees Jerry.

WRE: Not more than (5)　　**6**

Nat began to yell at Jerry.
"Jerry!" he yelled.
"Come back (here) with my fish!
We must eat that fish!"

Jerry yelled back at Nat.
"I didn't take your fish!"
"Then who did take it?" (took)
Nat yelled.

"I don't know," yelled Jerry.
"But I know I didn't."

Comp.: At least (6)　　**8**

Two policemen went by.
One policeman said, "Here, boys!
Stop that yelling right now!
What is the yelling about?" (for)

Nat began to cry.
"I want my fish!" he said.
"It is for my mother and sister, too. (my)
Make Jerry give it back
to me!"

"I didn't take the fish,"
said Jerry.
"I can't give it back."

FACTS

† 1. What did Nat yell to Jerry? (Come back with my fish)
✚ 2. What was Nat going to do with the fish? (eat it, or take it home)
† 3. What did Jerry say after Nat told him to come back with the fish? (I didn't take your fish)
† 4. What did Nat ask after Jerry said he didn't have the fish? (then who took it?)
½ 5.* What did Jerry yell after Nat asked, "Then who did take it"? (I don't know; I didn't)
✚ 6. Who went by? (two policemen)
† 7.* What did the policeman say? (stop yelling; what's that yelling about?)
½ 8.* What did Jerry say at the end of the story? (I didn't take fish; I can't give it back)

INFERENCE

† 1.* Did Nat believe that Jerry didn't have the fish? (No) How do you know? (told policeman to make Jerry give it back)

_____ COMP. =_____ FACTS + _____ INFERENCE

*Both parts needed for full credit
The Macmillan Company, for excerpts from "Nat" from **Lands of Pleasure, The Macmillan Reading Program, Primary Grades, First Revised Edition, copyright © 1965, 1970 by The Macmillan Company.

FIGURE **8.2**　Sample page from the Record Booklet, *Reader Placement Test*, Form 2, Revised Edition, Copyright © 1972 by the Macmillan Publishing Co. Reproduced by permission of the publisher; reduced in size.

The symbols indicate: *here* was omitted; *did take* was read as *took* (technically 2 errors because 2 words were replaced); *Two policemen* was repeated; *went* was pronounced for the child; *about* was initially read as *for*, but self-corrected (no error); and *my* was inserted. Although the child technically failed the word-recognition criterion, the nature of his errors and his high comprehension score indicate that material at the first reader level is probably not too difficult for this child.

aspect of reading consists of a series of graded selections, varying in difficulty from easy to hard, and usually covering a difficulty range of several
grades. One or more questions are asked about each paragraph. Either there
is no time limit or enough time is allowed so that most pupils have done as
much as they can before time is called.

Because vocabulary is so important in reading comprehension, most
standardized silent reading tests include a separate section for measuring
it. In primary-grade tests the child is usually asked to mark the one word
out of several that corresponds to a picture. In vocabulary tests above the
primary level, each test word is usually presented in a short sentence,
with several possible synonyms from which the correct one is to be
selected.

Rate of silent reading should be measured on material which is of the
same level of difficulty throughout. There are two plans commonly used in
measuring rate. One is to use a test containing a large number of short
paragraphs of equivalent difficulty, with a question to be answered on
each paragraph. Such tests employ a time limit, and the rate is determined
from the amount read in the time allowed. Sometimes the score is called
"rate of comprehension" and is based on the number of correct answers,
rather than on total number of answers; this is neither a pure rate score
nor a very good comprehension measure. The other plan presents a fairly
long selection of several hundred words, and the time required to finish is
recorded, or time is called and the child marks the last word read. Informal
teacher-constructed rate tests as well as standardized tests can be built on
this basis.

Accuracy in silent reading is measured in terms of the proportion of
correct answers to the total number of answers attempted. Although few
standardized tests provide norms for accuracy, the person scoring tests
should make note of a test paper in which unusually high or low accuracy
is shown, as this characteristic often has diagnostic significance.

Informal Appraisal of Reading Comprehension

The most important use of comprehension testing is in connection with
daily work in silent reading. Much of this is done by means of oral questions
and answers. In the early grades, it is often desirable to ask questions that
will disclose whether each line or sentence has been understood.

In first-grade reading, the teacher should attempt to insure an active
interest in the story by proper preparation. There is an introduction for
each story and for each page in the story. In modern sets of primary
readers, the teachers' manuals often contain excellent detailed suggestions
on how to proceed, step by step, through the introduction of new words
and ideas, motivated silent reading, checking on comprehension by means

of thought questions, rereading to select parts for oral reading, and the like.

Usually the first step in checking comprehension involves giving the children a purpose for reading in the form of a guiding question. After silent reading, that question is discussed before proceeding to a more detailed consideration of the story.

The following excerpt from the teacher's guide for a current third reader shows the use of a guiding question:

> Write the title of the first section of the story "Down, Down the Mountain" on the board and have the children locate it under "Contents," page 6.
>
> Discuss the picture on page 53. "What does it tell you about the place where these children lived?"
>
> Explain that the children in this story have a problem. "Read the story to find out how they tried to solve it."
>
> After the silent reading ask "What problem did Hetty and Hank have?" . . . "How did they try to solve it?"[5]

Silent reading is followed by oral reading, during which more detailed comprehension questions are often used. Sometimes the form of answer requested is to read a sentence or two that gives the answer. The lesson plan for the same story about Hetty and Hank begins the section entitled "Guided Oral Reading" as follows:

> Pages 53–57. "Why didn't Hetty and Hank have shoes?" . . . "Read why the children's father wouldn't buy them shoes." (Page 54) . . . "Read what Granny told them to do." (Page 55) . . . "Was this a good way for Hetty and Hank to get shoes?" . . . "Read the part that tells why the children had trouble getting to sleep." (Page 55)[6]

Silent reading may also be followed directly by discussion in which oral reading plays no part. This is more common in the intermediate grades than in the primary grades.

Grasping the central idea of a paragraph, understanding the feelings of the characters, and being able to anticipate what is likely to happen next in a story are some of the aspects of comprehension that can be checked by oral questions and answers. Even when the reading matter is factual in nature, many varied kinds of questions can be asked. Oral questioning has several advantages: 1) the question can allow freedom in response, while questions requiring written answers of equal length

5. Alice M. Scipione, *Teacher's Annotated Edition and Guide to Accompany Better than Gold,* The Macmillan Reading Program, Revised Ed.; Albert J. Harris and Mae Knight Clark, Senior Authors, p. 139. Copyright © 1974 Macmillan Publishing Co., New York. Quoted by permission of the publishers.

6. *Ibid.*

would usually be too time-consuming, and difficult for those with poor spelling and/or penmanship; 2) errors in understanding can be immediately detected and corrected; and 3) socialized discussions and exchanges of opinion are possible. The major disadvantage, of course, is the fact that usually only one child has a chance to answer a particular question.

There are many occasions on which a written comprehension test is desirable. This is particularly true when the teacher assigns a selection for silent reading by one group while the teacher works with another group. Usually the teacher provides the group that is working independently with a set of questions to answer. The questions at the end of stories in some readers, or in their correlated workbooks, may be used to good advantage. In general, short-answer or objective questions are more efficient for this purpose than questions that call for answers in sentence or paragraph form because they take up much less time. Completion and multiple-choice items allow less opportunity for guesswork than yes-no or true-false items and are therefore somewhat more satisfactory. On the other hand, free-response questions should be employed part of the time, to develop ability to explain and defend answers. Workbook exercises and standard test items may be used by the teacher as models for framing questions.

Measuring Rate of Reading

Informal tests of reading rate are easy to give and should be administered from time to time as a routine procedure in reading instruction above the primary grades. The selection used should be easy for the group and should be of approximately uniform difficulty throughout. The proper length varies with the grade level of the pupils; in general, one should use a selection long enough to take the average child in the class five to seven minutes if one wants a fairly accurate measure.

Perhaps the simplest way to measure rate is to start the pupils off together and measure the time necessary for each child to finish the selection. The pupils should be instructed to read at their normal rate and should be informed that they will be questioned about the selection after they finish. They should be told to look up as soon as they finish and copy on their papers the number that is written on the board or displayed on a card. The teacher should expose a new number at regular intervals; every ten seconds will give sufficient accuracy. Knowing the number of words in the selection, the teacher can prepare in advance a little table which gives in words per minute the rate corresponding to each number.[7] If the selection is a long one, some time can be saved by

7. If the number is changed six times a minute, the rate in words per minute for any number is obtained by multiplying the number of words read by six and dividing by the number.

finding the average number of words in a sampling of ten lines from different parts of the selection and multiplying by the total number of lines to get the approximate number of words.

Another technique that can be used is to say "Mark" at the end of each minute and have the pupils mark the last word they read before the signal. The number of words read in each minute can then be counted and averaged. Another variation is to give only one signal to mark and divide the number of words read by the number of minutes allowed. This procedure is especially suitable for use with selections found in some readers and workbooks in which the cumulative total of words is given at the end of each line. After the rate test is over, the slower pupils should be allowed to finish the selection so as to have a fair chance in the comprehension test.

When a pupil is being tested individually, it is a simple matter to get the total time for reading the selection, using a stopwatch or a watch with a second hand, and to divide the number of words by the time to get the rate in words per minute. Norms for rate of reading are given in Table 12 on page 549. Since speed of reading varies greatly according to the material read, any norms for rate must be considered rough approximations.

Standardized Silent Reading Tests

Standardized silent reading tests may be classified according to the grade levels for which they are intended and according to the reading functions they purportedly measure. Under the second method of classification, the major divisions include survey tests, analytical tests, and tests of a single function such as vocabulary or rate.

The major purpose of a survey reading test is to give a fairly accurate measure of a pupil's general level of silent reading ability as compared to that of others who take that test. These tests generally have sufficient time limits so that inability to complete the test is usually due to the increasing difficulty of the items rather than to not having enough time to demonstrate ability. Most survey tests have two parts, vocabulary and comprehension; the latter includes sentence and/or paragraph meaning, depending on the grade level for which the test is intended.

Analytical tests have the potential advantage over general survey tests of providing the teacher with a profile of the silent reading skills of the pupil in which his relatively strong and weak points may be discovered. Care should be exercised in interpreting the subtest results, however, especially for individuals, because there is some question as to whether or not they measure discrete skills, and if they are reliable enough. In judging one of these tests several points should be kept in mind. If the number of subtests is very large, the separate parts may be too short to be accurate measures, even though the total score may be highly reliable. The time limits for the subtests may be so brief as to place an unwarranted premium on rate of reading. The test may require a very long time to score. Finally, in the attempt to provide easy scoring, types of items may be used that do not resemble closely the kinds of reading that pupils ordinarily do. These criticisms do not apply to all analytical tests, but should be kept in mind when making a selection.

Hayward (1968) has suggested three criteria as guidelines for reviewing standardized diagnostic reading tests:

1] How does the test measure the component skills, and do the subscores represent areas for providing remedial instruction?
2] Are the subscore reliabilities sufficiently high (above .90) for individual use?
3] Are the intercorrelations among subtests sufficiently low (below .65) to warrant differential diagnosis?

It is quite important to try to determine exactly what the test really measures. Several tests may have the same subtest label yet measure different abilities. For example a "syllabication" test may require the child: 1) to draw diagonal lines between the syllables in a word, 2) to indicate the number of syllables in a word, or 3) to pronounce a polysyllabic word. Clearly, the demands made on the learner differ on three such tests. Decisions also should be made about the relevance of the skill measured to the ability under consideration. For instance, a subtest of a published word-recognition test asks the child to encircle an item if he can hear the little word that has been boxed in a "big word" (*e.g.*, fol[low], b[us]y). In order to perform this task, he must recognize the whole word. If he can already do so, what need is there to determine whether part of the word is pronounced in a given way? Also, subtests should be examined to determine if more than one skill is required (*e.g.*, to indicate his knowledge of a sound-symbol association, a child may have to write the letter). Failure to make a correct response may be due to a weakness in either or both skills, therefore making it difficult to assess specific skill strengths or weaknesses accurately. Of course, at times the child's ability to combine skills may need to be measured.

Because the results of diagnostic tests are meant to be used for individuals, it is important that the subtest scores provide reliable measures. Diagnostic tests often contain many more items that sample a given skill than do survey tests, because reliability is a function of test length.

If the component parts of a test are to be differentially useful, each subtest should measure a relatively independent skill. The higher the cor-

People buy me.
I am mailed with a letter.
I am found on an envelope.
What am I?

○ **newspaper**   ○ **stamp**   ○ **words**

A few years ago most freight was sent by railroad, but
now a lot of it is sent across the country in trucks.
Goods sent by railroad can go only where   **40**   have
been laid, but goods sent by   **41**   can reach any
point to which a **42**   runs.

40 ○ **roads** ○ **tracks** ○ **highways** ○ **paths**

41 ○ **truck** ○ **rail** ○ **freight** ○ **airplane**

42 ○ **track** ○ **phone** ○ **road** ○ **rail**

FIGURE 8.3   Samples of paragraph-comprehension test items for primary
grades. Top, reproduced from *Metropolitan Achievement
Tests*, Primary I, copyright 1970 by Harcourt Brace Jovano-
vich. Bottom, reproduced from *Stanford Diagnostic Reading
Test*, Level I, copyright 1966 by Harcourt Brace Jovanovich.
Both reproduced by permission of the publisher.

relations between subscores, the more likely it is that the subtests are measuring similar abilities. In diagnostic tests intended for poor readers, the
desirability of low subscore intercorrelations may be of less importance than
the other criteria of meaningful and reliable subtest scores.

Norms are not absolutely necessary for diagnostic tests because we are
more concerned with how a child's skills differ among themselves than with
how his score deviates from the norming population.

Because the primary purpose of this section is to acquaint the reader with the characteristics of silent reading tests rather then serve as a test catalogue, no attempt has been made to include descriptions of all available tests. Only standardized (norm-referenced) tests are discussed. Many of the tests mentioned have levels appropriate for use at various grade designations and have alternate forms available at each level.

Primary-Grade Tests. Among the widely used primary-grade tests are the reading tests that form part of achievement test batteries such as the *Stanford Achievement Test,*[8] 1973 edition, the *Metropolitan Achievement Tests,* the *Comprehensive Tests of Basic Skills,* and the *Iowa Test of Basic Skills,* 1970 edition. Included in these reading tests are measures of reading vocabulary, comprehension, and word analysis. The *Gates-MacGinitie Reading Tests* provide separate booklets for grades 1, 2, and 3. Each booklet contains tests of vocabulary and comprehension, using pictorial clues. Items are arranged in order of increasing difficulty, and scores are corrected for guessing. There is also a separate speed and accuracy test for advanced second and third grade. Other reading tests that contain vocabulary and comprehension subtests are the primary levels of the *New Developmental Reading Tests* and the SRA *Assessment Survey.* On some tests, such as the *California Reading Tests,* 1970 edition, the vocabulary subtest actually includes items that sample word-analysis skills. In some subtests labeled "vocabulary," word recognition rather than word meaning is being measured.

Examples of tests intended to give a more detailed analysis of silent reading include the *Primary Reading Profiles* and the *California Primary Reading Test* (1957 edition, 1963 norms). The former test includes subtests labeled Aptitude for Reading, Auditory Association, Word Recognition, Word Attack, and Reading Comprehension; in the latter, the items measuring a given area are scattered throughout the test.

Intermediate- and Upper-Grade Tests. A representative sample of survey-type reading tests above the primary level is the *Metropolitan Reading Test,* 1970 edition. Its elementary (3.5 to 4.9) and intermediate (5.0–6.9) levels each have two parts: reading vocabulary (word knowledge) and paragraph comprehension. The word-knowledge test requires the student to select synonyms, antonyms, or word classifications for the stimulus words which appear in short phrases. Comprehension questions follow each reading selection and cover a variety of comprehension skills, although no breakdown of which items sample specific types of comprehension is provided. Comprehension and vocabulary items are of the multiple-choice type.

A slightly different format is found in the 1973 edition of the *Stanford Reading Test.* In the vocabulary test, the word being tested is in an incom-

8. A descriptive list of all tests mentioned in this book will be found in Appendix A.

Read this

Dear Jean,

My birthday is Friday, October 20. I am going to have a
party at 4 o'clock. Your mother said she would drive you over.
You should leave by 2 o'clock if you want to get here in time.
It is going to be a Wild West party, and everything is going
to be Western. Be sure to wear the right clothes.

Your cousin,

Dick

23 How will Jean get to the party?	School bus	Car	Walk
24 Where must Jean live?	Many miles from Dick	In the Wild West	A few blocks from Dick
25 What are the right clothes?	A sheet and mask	A pretty party dress	A cowgirl dress
26 Jean is Dick's . . .	sister.	cousin.	You can't tell from the letter.
27 When do you think Dick wrote this letter?	Early in October	October 20	Early in November

FIGURE 8.4   Paragraph-comprehension items for primary grades. Reproduced from the *Cooperative Primary Tests*, Reading, Form
23A, copyright 1965 by Educational Testing Service. Reproduced by permission of the publisher. Reduced in size.

plete sentence; the task is to select from four words the one that best completes the sentence. Some items require choosing a synonym; others, a
definition. The comprehension test consists of a series of short paragraphs,
in most of which a number of words have been left out. Comprehension,
which is checked by a modified cloze procedure, is shown by selecting the
correct word for the blank space. For a few paragraphs, comprehension is
checked in the more conventional way described above. A word-study skills
test is also included in the two intermediate levels (grades 4.5 to 5.4 and
5.5 to 6.9) of this test.

Most survey tests for the intermediate and upper grades follow a pattern similar to that of the *Metropolitan* test, although there are differences
in the kinds and types of items used to measure vocabulary and comprehension. They include the *Sequential Tests of Educational Progress* (STEP),
the *Iowa Tests of Basic Skills* (ITBS), the *Nelson Silent Reading Test*, the
SRA Assessment Survey, and the *Comprehensive Tests of Basic Skills*.

Africans were among the first people to use iron successfully. African blacksmiths of long ago learned how to smelt iron from iron ore and then make tools and ornaments from it. Some historians believe that iron was used in Africa before it was used in Europe and Asia. Also at an early date, the African metal-worker used gold, silver, bronze, and copper in making jewelry and other ornaments.

24 Early Africans probably used iron mainly for —
    5 iron ore
    6 horseshoes
    7 railroads
    8 tools

24 (5) (6) (7) (8)

27 The early Africans appear to have been advanced in the field of —
    1 theology
    2 astronomy
    3 mathematics
    4 metallurgy

27 (1) (2) (3) (4)

28 Early Africans must have had great skills in the field of —
    5 machinery
    6 oil drilling
    7 agriculture
    8 mining

28 (5) (6) (7) (8)

FIGURE **8.5** Sample of paragraph-comprehension test items for intermediate grades. Two comprehension-check questions have been omitted here to save space. Reproduced from *Stanford Achievement Test*, Intermediate Level I. Copyright 1972 by Harcourt Brace Jovanovich. Reproduced by permission of the publisher.

Tests that include measures of rate and accuracy as well as vocabulary and paragraph comprehension are the *Gates-MacGinitie Reading Survey*, usable in grades 4–6 and 7–9, and the lower level of the *Diagnostic Reading Tests, Survey Section*.

4. The loon is a bird with a mysterious cry. It is the size of a large duck and swims very fast under water to catch its food. What does the loon eat?

E	F	G	H
nuts	corn	fish	bread

5. Plants die without light. One way of killing a small patch of poison ivy is to cover it with heavy paper. Soon it will die because it can get no

A	B	C	D
soil	paper	light	leaves

31. Almost all paper is made from wood. Hemlock, spruce, and balsam are often used. These are all soft woods. What kind of wood is hemlock?

A	B	C	D
red	hard	spruce	soft

32. London, the capital of Great Britain, is on the Thames River. Florence, in Italy, is on the Arno River. What river runs through the City of London?

E	F	G	H
Arno	Britain	Thames	Florence

FIGURE 8.6 Sample items for measuring speed and accuracy of reading in grades 4, 5, and 6. Reproduced from the *Gates-MacGinitie Reading Tests*, Survey D, copyright 1964 by Teachers College Press, Columbia University. Reproduced by permission of the publisher.

Level 1 (grades 6–9) of the 1973 revision of the *Iowa Silent Reading Tests* contains tests of vocabulary, comprehension (including items on which the student is not allowed to look back at the selection), directed reading (work-study skills including locational skills, skimming and scanning), and reading efficiency (rate and accuracy).

The *Iowa Tests of Basic Skills* include long and reliable measures of vocabulary and comprehension, and a work-study skills test that has sections on use of references, the index, and dictionary; and the reading of maps, graphs, charts, and tables. Absence of a rate-of-reading test is the major shortcoming of this battery. Although not true of the 1970 edition, each of the elementary and intermediate levels of the *California Reading Test* (1957 edition, 1963 norms) had four vocabulary subtests and three

---

TEST #4.   IDENTIFYING THE CAUSE OF A DETAILED EVENT

Objective: The student is able to identify the most logical cause to explain an event, described in a short written paragraph.

Sample Item:

    Directions.   Read the paragraph and the question which follows it. Mark an "X" on the line next to the answer to the question.

    Example: The sky was black. The wind began to blow, and the rain began to fall. During the storm, the tree blew down.

    Why did the tree blow down?

        _____   a) The clouds were black.
        __**X**__   b) The wind was strong.
        _____   c) The tree had no leaves.

Amplified Objective:

    Testing Situation.
    1. The child will be given a paragraph of no more than four sentences describing an event.
    2. Sentences may be simple, compound, or complex.
    3. The paragraph will contain at least two details (in addition to the actual cause of the event) about the event.
    4. The paragraph will be followed by a question concerning the cause of the event and three options from which the student will choose the most logical answer.

    Response Alternatives.
    1. All options will be single sentences. They may be simple, compound, or complex.
    2. Distractors will offer causal explanations which are irrelevant to the event (e.g., John can run well because he is four years old.)

    Criterion of Correctness.
    1. The correct answer will be the one which provides the most plausible answer to the causal question posed, based upon common experience and awareness of natural phenomena.
    2. Causes may be either physical conditions (e.g., The tree was blown down by the windstorm.) or psychological motivations (e.g., Tom did not like Halloween because he was afraid of the jack-o-lanterns.)

FIGURE 8.7   Sample objective-based test of comprehension. Reproduced from the manual for IOX Objectives-Based Test Set entitled Reading Comprehension Skills (K-6). The actual test is comprised of 5 paragraphs similar to the sample. Copyright 1973 by the Instructional Objectives Exchange. Reproduced by permission of the publisher.

comprehension subtests, one of which sampled work-study skills. Part scores were intended for diagnostic purposes.

Norms also are provided for each part score and the sum of certain part scores for the *New Developmental Reading Test*, intermediate-grade level (4–6). In addition to a measure of vocabulary, subtests include reading for information, reading for relationships, reading for interpretation, and reading for appreciation. There is a creative comprehension score based on reading for interpretation and appreciation, with the general comprehension score being based on all four comprehension subtests.

The *Monroe-Sherman Group Diagnostic Aptitude and Achievement Tests* have been used for many years in some reading clinics. Paragraph meaning, rate, word discrimination, spelling, and arithmetic are included in the achievement tests. The aptitude part includes measures of visual memory, auditory memory, discrimination, motor speed, and vocabulary. Being group tests, these are suitable for use in classrooms.

High School, College, and Adult Tests. Tests at the high school level and above which are composed of vocabulary and comprehension subtests include *TASK* for grades 8–10 and 11–13 (the items that sample different types of comprehension skills are identified in the manual); the *California Reading Test*, 1970 edition, for grades 9–12; the *Iowa Tests of Educational Development* (ITED), for grades 9–12; the *Comprehensive Test of Basic Skills*, for grades 8–12; and the STEP, for grades 10–12 and college freshmen and sophomores.

The *Iowa Silent Reading Tests*, Level 2, intended for use with high school and community-college students, includes tests of vocabulary, comprehension, directed reading, and reading efficiency. Level 3, meant for college students and other adults, does not contain a directed reading subtest.

Tests that include measures of rate and accuracy as well as comprehension and vocabulary are the *Gates-MacGinitie Reading Survey*, usable in grades 10–12; the *Nelson-Denny Reading Test* (1973 edition), for grades 9 through college; the *Traxler Silent Reading Test* (1969 edition), for grades 7–10; the *Traxler High School Reading Test* (revised 1967); the *Diagnostic Reading Test, Survey Section*, upper level, for grades 7–13; the *Cooperative English Tests: Reading*, one level for high school and another for college; the *Davis Reading Test*; and the reading test of the *McGraw-Hill Basic Skills System*.

Among the reading tests that may be used for adult basic education classes are the *Tests of Adult Basic Education* (TABE), the *Adult Basic Learning Examination* (ABLE) whose vocabulary subtest measures listening vocabulary, and the *Adult Basic Reading Inventory* (BRI).

Published Group Tests of Decoding Skills

Some standardized norm-referenced reading achievement tests contain word-analysis subtests at the primary levels (*e.g., Metropolitan, California*) or at the primary- and intermediate-grade levels (*e.g., Stanford*). Mastery or achievement tests that accompany reading programs also contain word-analysis subtests, the level at which they are tested being dependent upon the reader level at which they are taught. These achievement tests sub-scores, in effect, provide only a *survey* of word-analysis skills. They do not provide reliable information regarding specific skills.

There are also tests designed specifically or primarily to provide diagnostic information. Some of these are briefly described below. The task(s) required of the child by each subtest should be examined before making diagnostic or remedial decisions. Success on some subtests is dependent on the ability to perform tasks other than those suggested by the subtest title or in the manual. For instance, part of one test labeled "Whole Word Recognition" actually requires only visual discrimination.

The *Stanford Diagnostic Reading Test* has two forms at each of two levels (Level I for grades 2.5 to 4.5; Level II for grades 4.5 to 8.5). In addition to comprehension and vocabulary subtests at both levels (a rate subtest is included at Level II), there are subtests of syllabication, phonics, and blending. Stanine and percentile scores are reported for each of the subtests, and guidelines for interpreting the subtests are presented.

The *McCullough Word Analysis Tests*, designed for use in intermediate grades, primarily measure phonic and visual analysis skills. Remedial work is suggested for skills in which the subtest score is one standard deviation below the mean for a given subtest. Most of its 7 subtests have good content validity but low reliability.

The *Silent Reading Diagnostic Tests*, 1970 edition, have 8 subtests designed to sample visual analysis, phonics, and blending skills. Intended for use in grades 2 through 6, it provides a graphic profile chart which depicts strengths and weaknesses in various word-recognition skills and patterns.

In addition to norm-referenced tests such as those mentioned above, there are also criterion-referenced word-analysis tests. Probably the most comprehensive of these is the *Cooper-McGuire Diagnostic Word Analysis Test* which specifies varying criterion scores for each subtest. The test is divided into 3 sections, each containing a number of subtests, a few of which must be administered individually. Subtests of letter names, letter shapes, auditory discrimination, and sound blending are found in the "Readiness for Word Analysis" section. The phonic analysis section contains 17 subtests and the structural analysis section 10. Directions are given as to which subtests should be administered.

The *Doren Diagnostic Reading Test of Word Recognition,* 1973 edition, contains 12 subtests, each having from 20 to 90 items. Designed for use in primary grades and above, it primarily measures phonic skills that are sampled in various ways. As with any test that contains a broad range of subtests, it would seem prudent to administer only those deemed appropriate, rather than to administer the entire test. Scoring is based on the number of wrong items; subtests on which more than 7 errors are made (no indication is given as to the derivation of this cutoff score) indicate skills which need remedial teaching.

The *Fountain Valley System* contains a number of single-page self-scoring tests of phonic and structural analysis. Criteria for each behavioral objective are indicated on the answer sheets. Thirty-eight word-analysis skills commonly taught in the primary grades are assessed at four different levels of the *Wisconsin Tests of Reading Skill Development: Word Attack.*

Selection of Silent Reading Tests

As there are many satisfactory tests available, the selection of tests naturally depends on the purpose for testing, and to some extent, on the amount of time available for testing and scoring, the money available for purchasing tests, and other practical considerations. If the school can provide for the use of only one silent reading test, the test selected should be of high reliability, match the objectives of the reading program as closely as possible, and include as a minimum good measures of vocabulary and level of paragraph comprehension. The use of several relatively short and inexpensive tests measuring different functions is sometimes preferable to a single test that is supposedly highly analytical. When it is intended to use a single test to select poor readers for more intensive study, a test emphasizing comprehension may be best.

Before ordering any test in quantities, it is desirable to check expert opinion in such sources as Buros (1968, 1972), Farr and Anastasiow (1969), Blanton, Farr, and Tuinman (1972), and Griffin, Hibbard, and Muldoon (1972) to make a tentative selection of a few tests that might be suitable and to order a specimen set of each of those tests. Careful inspection of the test blanks and manuals of directions will usually show one of the tests to be the most desirable one in that situation.

How to Interpret Silent Reading

All the educational testing in the world would be of no practical value if it did not lead to a better understanding of pupils and their instructional needs. Too often in the past, tests have been given, scored, tabulated, and then filed away and forgotten.

In the hands of the school administrator, silent reading tests are useful as instruments for measuring the effectiveness of instruction and as a basis for the classification of pupils according to their abilities.

Teacher's Use of Silent Reading Tests. The classroom teacher may use reading tests to determine the average and range of reading ability in the class, to divide the class into smaller groups for instructional purposes, to determine the specific phases of silent reading in which the class as a whole and individual pupils need more instruction, to aid in the selection of reading materials of appropriate difficulty, and to measure progress. When used as part of the diagnostic procedure in studying individual cases of reading disability, silent reading tests furnish valuable clues about the nature of the child's difficulties, help determine the level at which remedial teaching should start, and serve as a means of checking up periodically to determine whether the remedial work is properly directed.

One of the important steps in planning remedial teaching is to determine what materials the pupil is capable of reading. In remedial work it is often desirable to start with materials that are one or two grades below the indicated grade-equivalent score, so as to insure a feeling of success from the start.

General Observations. The teacher should be alert to the presence of behaviors that may interfere with efficiency in silent reading. Many of the behaviors discussed for oral reading (see pp. 197–201) also may be observed during silent reading.

One of the most common interfering habits is the tendency to make lip movements during silent reading. When children begin to read, they pronounce each word as they read it. Early silent reading is usually quiet oral reading. With further practice this becomes reduced to inner speech; the person "hears" the words as he reads, but does not say anything. There is a gradual reduction from complete pronunciation through successive stages until completely silent reading is attained. Many children, even in the upper grades and high school, mumble or move their lips when they are supposed to be reading silently. These movements prevent them from reading silently at a faster rate than they can read orally. Lip movements retard speed when they occur above the third-grade level. They can be easily detected simply by watching the child in silent reading. Other habits that interfere with rate of reading and can be observed easily are vocalization or audible whispering, keeping the place with a finger or pencil, and turning the head instead of moving the eyes as one reads.

Lip movements or vocalization also may be symptoms that the material is difficult for the reader. Perhaps "hearing" the material is an aid to comprehension. Vocalization also may be due to lack of experience in silent reading.

The reading difficulties of some children are aggravated by their inabilty to concentrate on the reading matter. They are restless and fidgety in their seats and often interrupt their reading to look around the room or out of the window, or to whisper or get into mischief. In many cases such behavior is not a cause of their difficulties, but a natural result of giving them reading matter which is uninteresting or too difficult, and it disappears when more appropriate materials are used. In other cases close checking on their accomplishments by frequent comprehension questions is needed. Restlessness and inattention are significant and should not be ignored.

It is not necessary for the classroom teacher to observe the eye movements of most of his pupils, as the information to be gained is not ordinarily of sufficient importance to justify the large amount of time required to observe each child separately. The teacher of reading should, however, know how to observe eye movements and should for his own information try the procedure with a few pupils so as to get a clearer understanding of the way the eyes work in reading. Methods for observing eye movements are described on pages 550–556.

Standardized Compared to Informal Tests. Although in using book samples it is not difficult to differentiate the child's grade levels for independent and instructional reading and to determine his frustration level, standardized silent reading tests as yet do not provide a similar differentiation. Standardized test grade-equivalent scores tend to overestimate the instructional level. Children whose reading skills are poor tend to guess more than good readers do, and their scores, based less on reading and more on guessing, may at times overestimate the instructional level by a year or more. On the other hand, when a child misses many easy items but gets harder ones correct, or when he gets upset and stops before reaching his frustration level, the score may underestimate his reading ability. Standardized tests are, then, less accurate for poor readers than for good readers. When there is a disagreement between the estimate provided by a standardized test and the results of an IRI, the latter is usually a more dependable guide in the choice of reading materials, provided it is well constructed, administered, and interpreted.

Interpretation of Silent Reading Patterns. Suppose that in your reading you came across the following sentence: "The _____ led _____ _____ of _____ _____, which _____ in the _____ _____." It is very doubtful that you could make much sense out of it. If, however, the sentence read as follows: "The road led _____ fields of rippling wheat, which _____ in the bright sunlight," you would get the general idea, even if the words you filled in were not the exact ones intended. Children who depend almost entirely on this kind of guessing process are called *context readers*, because they depend on the context or general setting of a word when they cannot recognize it.

Using the context as a clue to the meaning of words is in general a desirable practice. Most good readers make use of it frequently and to good effect. If the reader has no other method of attack on unknown words, however, he will be helpless when the number of unknown words in a selection is large.

Several characteristics serve to distinguish the context readers as a group from other types of reading cases. Their performance is usually better on tests of paragraph reading than on tests of vocabulary or word recognition, as there are usually more clues in a long selection than in a short one. They generaly score higher on a test which involves finding the central idea of a selection than on one which calls for painstaking attention to details. Their scores on rate tests are usually higher than on tests of level of comprehension. Their reading tends to be rapid and somewhat inaccurate. They are apt to do markedly better on tests of silent reading than on oral reading tests. They are usually of average or above-average intelligence, since considerable mental ability and experience with language is necessary to be able to make correct guesses.

In general, context readers need training in word-recognition techniques and in careful, accurate reading. Suggestions for remedial treatment of such cases are found in later chapters.

For some children the reading of paragraphs is a very difficult task. They can do fairly well on short units such as brief sentences, but get lost as soon as the material gets long or complex. In many such cases it is found that the child is reading each word separately. Word-by-word readers usually do better on vocabulary or sentence reading tests than on tests of paragraph meaning. Their speed is usually low and below their level of comprehension. They can read orally with fair accuracy material which they cannot comprehend. Many of them move their lips while reading silently and point with a finger to each word in succession. It is often necessary for them to reread material before it conveys any meaning to them.

These children need training designed to teach them to recognize phrases and thought units, improve their rate of reading, and give training in reading for meaning.

Some children's reading is slow, but otherwise fairly satisfactory. They may be detected by comparing their scores on level of comprehension tests with scores on rate tests. Such children are not very much handicapped on tests like the *Stanford* or *Metropolitan*, because of the generous time limits. They score considerably lower on tests in which speed plays a large part in determining the total score. On such tests they often get right most of

Iowa Silent Reading Tests

Level __1__ [ISRT] Form __E/F__   **PUPIL PROFILE**

Name __Rob__

Teacher _____ School _____

School System _____

City and State _____

Date of Testing __9/12/73__ Reference Group __Grade 8__
            __4/11/74__

SCORE DETAIL

Reading Power				= Vocabulary (50 Items)			+	Reading Comprehension (50 Items)			
Raw Score	Standard Score	%ile Rank	Stanine	RS Items Attempted	Standard Score	%ile Rank	Stanine	RS Items Attempted	Standard Score	%ile Rank	Stanine
73	137	47	5	41/43	147	61	6	32/34	135	32	4
90	164	81	7	46/50	164	81	7	44/48	169	77	7

Directed Reading* (44 Items)				Directed Reading Part A (24 Items)	Directed Reading Part B (20 Items)	Reading Efficiency (40 Items)				R·E Index
Raw Score	Standard Score	%ile Rank	Stanine	RS Items Attempted	RS Items Attempted	RS Items Attempted	Standard Score	%ile Rank	Stanine	
26	144	52	5	18/20	8/16	17/18	117	19	3	F_s
38	170	82	7	21/24	17/20	32/34	161	71	6	H

STANINE PROFILE

TEST SCORE	STANINE 1 2 3 Below Average	4 5 6 Average	7 8 9 Above Average
Reading Power (Vocabulary + Reading Comprehension)	1 2 3	4 ⑤ 6	[7] 8 9
Directed Reading* (Part A + Part B)	1 2 3	4 ⑤ 6	[7] 8 9
Reading Efficiency	1 2 ③	4 5 [6]	7 8 9
Vocabulary	1 2 3	4 5 ⑥	[7] 8 9
Reading Comprehension	1 2 3	④ 5 6	[7] 8 9
	Below Average	Average	Above Average

FIGURE 8.8   Silent reading profile of Rob before and after corrective help. Reproduced from *Iowa Silent Reading Tests*, copyright 1973 by Harcourt Brace Jovanovich, by permission of the publisher. Reduced in size.

the questions that they answer, but are able to complete only a small part of the test within the time limit. Observation of their eye movements usually discloses a short recognition span, many fixations, and frequent regressions. They often make movements of the lips and head and point to each word with a finger as they read.

Figure 8.8 shows the *Iowa Silent Reading* scores of Rob, a bright boy and good student in the eighth grade. Although on the first testing all but one of his scores fell within the average range, an analysis of his performance indicated that his problem was mainly one of slow rate. The pretest stanines are circled and the retest scores, after seven months of corrective help stressing improvement of concentration and speeding up without sacrificing comprehension, are marked with boxes. On the retest he was above average in all areas except Reading Efficiency which was average. His reading efficiency index changed from "fairly efficient" to "highly efficient."

Many reading disability cases do equally poor work on all types of silent reading. These cases show more extensive disability than the groups already described and need training designed to improve all aspects of reading. In addition to the meager vocabulary, slow speed, and poor comprehension which silent reading tests can disclose, the word-recognition techniques used by these children are usually discovered to be sadly deficient when their oral reading is examined.

SUGGESTED ADDITIONAL READING

See references listed at end of Chapter 9.

9
Assessing Reading Performance, II

The reason for a particular wrong answer to a comprehension question based on silent reading is not easily located through a study of silent reading only. Faulty comprehension may result from errors in word recognition, lack of understanding of word meanings, incorrect phrasing or misinterpretation of punctuation, the difficulty or strangeness of the thought being presented, and so on. Some of these possibilities, such as word-recognition and phrasing difficulties, are most easily studied through oral reading. In oral reading one can follow a child's reading word by word and phrase by phrase, and the errors are clearly in evidence. Even when one's intention is primarily to find out the reasons for comprehension difficulties in silent reading, an analysis of oral reading performance is likely to be helpful.

I. WHAT TO LOOK FOR IN ORAL READING

Behavioral Observations

Observing the learner's behaviors may provide insights into his reading problem, as well as yield information about how his reading performance might be improved. Some behaviors appear whether the learner is reading orally or silently; others are manifested only during either mode. Behaviors observable during either oral or silent reading, and those seen only during oral reading, are discussed below. Those more relevant to silent reading were discussed in Chapter 8.

Oral and Silent Reading Behaviors

The following behaviors may occur either when the learner is reading orally or silently.

Lateral Head Movements. These may interfere with speed of reading because the eyes can move much more rapidly than the head. If the head movements are quite pronounced or if they continue during long periods of reading, the back neck muscles may become fatigued and the learner may unconsciously learn to associate the discomfort with reading, and thus to avoid reading. Head movements are more likely to occur in silent reading.

Finger Pointing. This may be manifested in various ways which may have different meanings. Some students point to each word. If word-by-word reading is also observed, the examiner's task then becomes one of determining whether the word-by-word reading is the cause or the effect of the word-by-word pointing, or if both behaviors are caused by a third factor, such as weak word recognition or difficulty in keeping the place. Other types of finger pointing include moving the finger or an object under one phrase at a time as an aid to phrasing, moving the finger under the line of print without pausing, using the hand or finger as a marker under each line of print, or marking the beginning of each line with the finger. These all may indicate that the learner is having difficulty keeping his place on the page. Such behaviors may be helpful in avoiding faulty return eye sweeps and omissions of phrases or lines.

Finger pointing is often a needed crutch, and premature removal of the crutch (insistence that the child stop the behavior) may have adverse effects. No effort should be made to stop it while reversal errors or losing the place continue. When it is time to wean the child from finger pointing, allow him to use a marker, then gradually reduce the use of the marker.

Inappropriate Rate. This may involve either reading too slowly or too rapidly. In either case, the reasons should be investigated. Excessively slow reading may be the result of weak word recognition, poor comprehension, inattention to the task, behaviors such as finger pointing and head movements, a compulsion to obtain perfect comprehension, or simply never having been instructed in reading faster. Reading too rapidly is probably either a result of the desire to get through the material as quicky as possible, or the learner's mistaken belief that all reading should be done as rapidly as possible. Excessively rapid reading often results in poor compre-hension and recall. In such cases, it is important to learn what happens if the student attempts to read more slowly. If slowing down improves com-prehension and recall, there is a need to modify his attitude regarding reading speed. During oral reading, too rapid a rate is quite obvious; dur-ing silent reading, it may be indicated by a combination of a brief reading time and low comprehension. It is difficult to determine the extent to which lack of attention or concentration plays a role in either too slow or too rapid silent reading. In cases where oral reading comprehension is markedly better than silent reading comprehension, it may well be that there is a lack of attention or concentration.

Tension Signs.   These may take many forms: facial tics, voice tense or tremulous or almost inaudible, wiggling and squirming, shuffling of the feet, body rigidity, crying, and outright refusals to continue. Such signs are most often indications that the pupil finds it difficult to cope with the mate-rial or with the situation in general.

Concentration/Task Orientation.   As has been pointed out in Chapter 8, the reading difficulties of some children are aggravated by their inability to concentrate on the reading matter. Such behavior may be a natural result of giving them reading matter that is uninteresting or too difficult, and may disappear when more appropirate materials are used.

Inability to maintain attention to the task also may be caused by physiological or emotional problems. A child who is easily distracted by various stimuli *may* have a neurological disorder. A child who is worried about something may find his mind wandering because at that time his problem is much more important to him than reading. Other children are not task oriented, but rather avoid any self-investment in the learning situa-tion. Others have never learned to assume the responsibility required in learning.

Personality Problems.   An impulsive child may respond quickly with-out giving any thought, while a compulsive child may perform poorly because he does not move ahead unless he is certain that all his answers are correct. Strong anxiety can interfere with performance on tests or in class-room activities.

Some children appear to lack motivation. The reasons for this lack of motivation should be determined. Certain pupils have little interest in learning school-related subjects in general; others lack motivation to learn because the reading material is dull or uninteresting or too difficult, or because they have failed repeatedly in learning to read. Some of these pupils have learned, "If I don't try, I won't fail." Such attitudes are difficult to overcome, but until they are, it is not likely that much reading progress will take place.

Occasionally, one encounters a child whose responses or behaviors are bizarre or extremely unusual, or one who seems lacking in emotional responsiveness or refuses to communicate. In such cases, a psychological or psychiatric referral should be made.

Vision/Eye Movements. While the student is reading, the distance from his eyes to the book should be noted. Normal reading distance is approximately 12 to 18 inches. Holding the book below or above these distances may indicate a visual problem. Likewise note such behaviors as moving the book forward and backward from the eyes, reading with the head markedly tilted to one side, holding the book at unusual angles, and covering one eye. Even if the child's reading is adequate his vision may need professional care.

Posture. Few teachers need to be reminded to observe the posture of their children as they read. It is important for general hygiene, and particularly to avoid eyestrain, that the child should sit or stand in a natural, easy posture while reading, with his back reasonably straight, and the book held firmly or supported a proper distance from his eyes, on a proper level, and with adequate light that is devoid of glare.

Oral Reading Behaviors

The following behaviors are readily observable when the child is reading orally in either a lesson or a testing situation.

Fluency, Phrasing, and Expression. Deficiencies in fluency, phrasing, and expression are readily observed in oral reading. Jerkiness, hesitations, and repetitions are other defects in fluency that are easily detected. In some children these are simply indications of nervousness or self-consciousness, or are symptoms of too-difficult material. In many cases, however, hesitations and repetitions are accompaniments of slowness in word recognition and are employed to gain more time to decode the next word or two.

One of the common defects in fluency is *word-by-word reading.* The word-by-word reader plods along slowly, tending to make a noticeable pause after each word. When he does attempt to phrase his reading, he may group the wrong words together and may disregard or misinterpret punctuation marks. The voice is usually monotonous. Keeping place with a finger is fairly common. Recognition may be slow even for known words. Some word-by-word readers have marked deficiencies in their word-recognition techniques while others have learned to decode fairly well but have not outgrown the habit of reading one word at a time. Some teachers are satisfied if children pronounce the words correctly and never attempt to help them overcome their word-by-word reading. The behavior also may be caused inadvertently by the teacher who bounces her pointer in staccato fashion from one word to another on the chalkboard or experience chart story. If a child reads smoothly in easy material but word by word in harder material, the word-by-word reading is only a symptom that the material is too difficult.

Understanding and recall of the material is often poor in word-by-word readers. Even if such were not the case, word-by-word reading may interfere with comprehension of conceptually more difficult material or make reading a distasteful activity. This is particularly true of older students who can understand and recall material even though they read word by word. Such students often give the impression that their general level of reading ability is even weaker than it is because of their "choppy" reading.

In contrast to the word-by-word reader, the *context reader* may be fairly fluent although quite inaccurate. He goes merrily along, skipping words, adding words, substituting one word for another, and when there are too many unknown words he may invent a new story as he proceeds. His reading is marked by carelessness and inattention to details. He can often reread a sentence correctly after being told that he misread it. Some context readers are unable to decode a word that is not in their sight vocabularies by any method except guessing from the context.

Inadequate Phrasing. This means that the pupil is not grouping the words correctly in thought units. Lack of understanding may contribute to inadequate phrasing. Inadequate phrasing may disrupt comprehension.

Slow, Halting Reading. This suggests that the learner's phrasing is adequate but the oral reading is drawn out by elongated pronunciation of the words or pauses between the phrases. Such behavior is usually habitual and may reflect the learner's oral speaking pattern or dialect.

Oral reading is a more difficult task than silent reading, because the learner must not only understand the material, but also must have additional skills that allow him to transmit that understanding to others. The vehicle for doing so is his use of voice. *Inadequate use of voice* may take many forms: reading in monotone, volume too loud or too soft, poor enunciation, lack of expression, not speeding up or slowing down to portray the tempo of the story, tense or high-pitched voice. The latter is usually a symptom of the difficulty of the material. Most of the other behaviors, however, can be attributed to a lack of training, tenseness when reading orally, or the fact that reading is done at sight (see below).

Some pupils tend to *ignore or misinterpret punctuation marks*, particularly commas and periods. These behaviors may adversely affect comprehension, especially when phrases, clauses, or sentences are run together. Disregard of or misinterpretation of punctuation marks usually is a result of lack of training in their use, or of anxiety manifested by rushing through the selection.

Speech. The classroom or reading teacher cannot help noticing salient facts about the child's clarity of speech and use of his voice while listening to him read. Major speech faults such as stuttering, stammering, and lisping are, of course, very easily detected. Unclear enunciation and faulty pronunciation should also be noted. The quality, pitch, and intensity of the child's voice also deserve attention. A weak, tense, strained, or high-pitched voice may be a highly significant indication that the child is nervous in the reading situation. Excessively loud, nasal, and singsong voices may also be encountered. The former may indicate a hearing loss.

None of the above behaviors is mutually exclusive. They often occur together. A child may read word by word in a voice almost too soft to be heard. These behaviors may occur only when the child is reading before a group, particularly one composed of his peers, but not in a one-to-one situation. Not only may there be a marked difference in overt behavior, but also in word recognition and comprehension. Such a situation usually suggests that the child is anxious when reading orally to a group.

It also should be realized that some of their behaviors may be the result of having the student read orally at sight. To check out this possibility, some material at the learner's instructional level should be preread silently and then reread orally.

Decoding

An examination of a learner's word-recognition errors and his attempts at word analysis may be quite revealing. Several methods may be used by a child in attempting to decode a word that is not immediately recognized. The word may be guessed from the context in which it is found. If it has been taught in spelling lessons, or if the child has been taught to read through a linguistic approach, spelling the word may stimulate recall. The phonemes may be sounded and then blended to get the pronunciation. The size and shape of the word may serve as clues, or the resemblance of the word to an already known word may be noticed. A good reader is resourceful. If one method of attack does not succeed, he tries another. He knows how to utilize the context, how to blend, and how to employ visual resemblances. Poor readers often restrict themselves to one method of attack and employ even that method poorly. It is important to find out what method or methods a child tries to use, or does not use, as well as how successful he is.

Some children have apparenty never learned any technique of word analysis thoroughly enough to use it successfully. They know the sounds represented by only a few letters, or cannot blend the phonemes even when they succeed in making the symbol-sound associations. They have not learned to look for common recognizable parts or phonograms in a word, or to look for resemblances to words they know. They have laboriously acquired a small stock of sight words which is quite inadequate for their needs. They may or may not try to make use of the context and language cues. In these cases remedial teaching must necessarily start at the beginning and should include a thorough and systematic teaching of the necessary decoding skills.

Word-Recognition Miscues. Deviations from the printed text are commonly referred to as *word-recognition errors.* The term *miscue* suggested by K. Goodman (1969) is more appropriate in that it suggests that some "errors" reflect the translation of the language of the writer into the reader's dialect, or show good grasp of the meaning.

There is not complete agreement as to what should be classified as a word-recognition miscue or error. More importantly, most scoring schemes do not distinguish between major and minor errors and the relationship of the miscue to the rest of the sentence (whether it fits grammatically and meaningfully or ruins the intended meaning). Typically, all miscues are given equal weight in scoring. For the word *kitten,* either a response of *cat* or *stop* could be counted as one error. Similarly a badly mispronounced word, an addition of a letter, an omission of a small word, or a repetition would each be counted as one error. A scoring procedure that distinguishes between major and minor miscues has been suggested on page 173. Elaborate procedures for analyzing and interpreting reading miscues have been developed by K. Goodman (1969) and Y. Goodman and Burke (1972), the latter being the less complex.

Mispronunciations. On some words, the learner does not give the response indicated by the printed text. Dialectal or regional variations should not be considered mispronunciations. Mispronunciations may involve whole words (*dog* for *cat*), word parts in various positions (*sat* or *cot* or *cap* for *cat*) or combination of word parts (*cup* for *cat*). Some writers distinguish between *mispronunciations* and *substitutions*, the latter usually indicating that the response made sense in the sentence. Mispronunciations may be caused by inadequate word recognition, weak decoding skills, overreliance on the initial elements of words, inattention to word parts, or overreliance on context. Responses that do not make sense in the sentence and/or are grammatically incorrect indicate that the pupil is not using context or language clues; whether or not he can needs to be determined.

The technique of observing the first one or two letters of a word and guessing the rest is quite common. The intelligent context reader is often surprisingly successful with his guesses because his facility with language allows him to "fill in" anticipated words. Duller children and those with weak language skills also attempt to use this technique, but their guesses may be quite inappropriate syntactically or semantically. Among the commonest errors made by children who rely on this procedure are confusions of words that begin with *wh* or *th* (*who, when, where, which;* or *them, then, the, there, these*).

Errors on the beginnings of words are less common than errors on the middles of words and on word endings. Many children ignore endings such as *es, ed, ly,* and *ing*. The middles of words are especially apt to be misread. Confusions in symbol-sound associations are common. Among the most common confusions are *b, d, p,* and *q; u* and *n; l* and *i; h* and *n; m* and *w;* and vowel errors.

Dialect Variations. We do not all pronounce words, or the sounds in words, in the same way. These variations are the result of our exposure to regional and cultural dialects and to personal idiosyncrasies. Most of these differences occur on vowel sounds. For example, it is common in the South to pronounce long /i/ as /ah/. In many parts of the United States, *path* and *sat* are pronounced with the short vowel sound /a/. Many New Englanders, however, pronounce *path* and *laugh* with an /ä/ as in *father*, while no /r/ is heard in words like *yard* and *Harvard*. Short /e/ is indistinguishable from short /a/ in some places and from short /i/ in others. Those who work with children who speak divergent dialects must familiarize themselves with the special characteristics of those dialects. Sometimes words that rhyme in standard English do not rhyme in a particular dialect, while words that do not rhyme in standard English may rhyme in the dialect. When a child reads orally in accordance with his dialect, the deviations from standard English should not be considered reading errors.

Other Common Miscues. *Words pronounced* for the learner after a five-second hesitation are major miscues. A pupil may be unable to respond to a word because he does not recognize it or cannot decode it; or the student may be afraid to respond unless he is certain that his answer will be correct.

Omissions may involve a whole word, word parts, or groups of words. As with other miscues, the seriousness of the omission depends on the degree to which it disrupts the intended meaning. Leaving out a key word is a more serious miscue than omitting an adjective or final plural *s*. On the other hand, omitting a single letter (*sat* for *scat*) may be more serious than leaving out a word such as *a* or *the*. Omissions usually are caused by carelessness or inattention. However, the pupil may omit words or word parts because he cannot recognize or decode them.

Additions usually are minor miscues. Students may insert words or word parts that are in line with previous miscues, or that reflect language experiences (*e.g.*, they anticipate words occurring in certain patterns, and therefore insert words even though they are not in the printed text).

Reversals almost always affect the intended meaning and therefore usually are major miscues. There are four types of reversals: 1) whole word (*was* for *saw*), 2) single letter (*b*et for *p*et), 3) letter order (*cl*am for *cal*m), and 4) word order (*I was* for *Was I*). The possible causes of reversals are discussed on page 412.

Repetitions may involve word parts, single words, or groups of words. In most scoring systems, repetitions of one word or less are not counted as errors. Repetitions may be made: 1) in correcting an error, 2) to aid comprehension, 3) to regain the train of thought, or 4) to stall for time while attempting to decode a following word. The first possible cause suggests that the learner recognized the error, most probably through the use of context, and went back to correct his initial response. The other three may be indications that the material is difficult for the pupil. Faulty eye movements may cause repetitions. Repetitions may be habitual in that the behavior persists after the original causes are no longer present.

In some scoring systems, if the learner does not respond immediately to a word, it is counted as a *hesitation* error. Or, if the student ignores or misinterprets punctuation marks, each occurrence is counted as one error. Self-corrections, regardless of how soon they are made after the initial response, are sometimes considered errors. Whether or not such behaviors are considered errors may affect test results. Dunkeld (1970) found that the word-recognition score based on a miscue count of mispronunciations, substitutions, words pronounced for the learner, insertions, and reversals showed a higher correlation with comprehension than any other combination of miscues.

The Relative Frequency of Different Oral Reading Errors

The frequency of different kinds of faults in oral reading varies with the abilities of the children, the grades studied, and the methods of teaching that have been employed. It also varies with the error classification that one uses. Weber (1968) analyzed over fifty studies of oral reading errors. She pointed out that lack of agreement in the categories used by different investigators makes it difficult to compare their results. What is called a "substitution" in one scheme may be called a "mispronunciation–several parts" in another. One scheme may note consonant and vowel errors, while another stresses where the error occurs: at the beginning, the end, or in the middle of a word.

Despite these difficulties, it is safe to conclude that the most frequent oral reading difficulty is inadequate word recogniiton. Other faults that are quite common include poor enunciation, inadequate phrasing (including word-by-word reading), errors on common little words (*a, the,* and others), lack of expression, and habitual repetition.

II. HOW TO APPRAISE ORAL READING

Informal Appraisal of Oral Reading

The practice of calling upon children to read orally, one after the other, hopefully has lost its former place as the major activity in reading lessons and has been largely supplanted by more dynamic types of learning activities. Preparation is usually followed by guided silent reading, and oral reading is usually a form of rereading for a definite purpose (see pp. 79–82). The teacher may, for example, ask a child to read the sentence that contains the answer to a specific question. Under these conditions, the teacher and the pupil are both likely to focus their attention on the appropriateness of the choice more than on the qualities of the oral reading. When one wishes to evaluate oral reading as such, the oral reading activity should be planned to provide optimum conditions for a careful appraisal.

The use of book samples to determine the child's independent and instructional levels has been described on pages 169–174. By using a somewhat similar technique, a teacher can make a satisfactory detailed analysis of the oral reading difficulties of each child in a class without using special material.

Each child can be called to the teacher's desk in turn to read ahead at sight. Since preliminary silent reading would give the child an opportunity to decode some of the words, or reread when it does not make sense, this kind of oral reading should be done at sight; preparatory silent reading might conceal some of the children's initial problems from the teacher. It is these problems that are the most revealing. The child should read for a long enough time to give the teacher a good picture of his oral reading; one to three minutes will usually suffice. Most of the good readers in the class will not show many or serious faults, and for them a minute apiece should be ample. A written record of mispronunciations, nonrecognitions, and so on can be taken in the same way as in determining reading level (see Fig. 8.1). While one child is reading to the teacher, the rest of the class can be busy with seatwork or free reading.

The teacher's first problem is to get a survey of the major kinds of faults the child shows in his oral reading. For this purpose, a check list like the one given on pages 208–210 can be conveniently used. Copies of the check list can be mimeographed, and as the child reads, or immediately after he has finished, the teacher writes the child's name and the date on a

	Name							
W O R D R E C O G N I T I O N	Inadequate sight vocabulary							
	Many hesitations							
	Errors on common little words							
	Weak symbol-sound associations							
	Difficulty blending sounds							
	Tends to guess unknown words							
	Overdepends on context							
	Ignores context							
	Many repetitions							
B E H A V I O R	Weak Comprehension							
	Poor enunciation							
	Lack of expression							
	Volume too loud or soft							
	Word-by-word reading							
	Ignores/misinterprets punctuation							
	Tense							
	Finger pointing							
	Loses place							
	Book held too close/far							
	Poor reading posture							
	Comments							

FIGURE 9.1   A check list for recording oral reading characteristics.

copy of the check list and runs down the list, marking items that are characteristic of the child's reading with a check mark, or a double check if the tendency is outstanding.

Some teachers prefer to use a briefer check list, so that the results from the whole class can be summarized on one sheet of paper. A form convenient for this purpose is shown in Figure 9.1. Teachers are welcome to copy this form. After each child finishes reading, the teacher marks the particular faults that he shows, by making checks or double checks in the appropriate columns. From a record sheet like this it is easy to select the names of children who have a particular fault in common and therefore should be brought together in a special group of remedial work to correct this fault.

Mother likes to cook for her family. She prepares delicious meals for them. On certain holidays she cooks special foods which are family favorites. In the warm summer season, there are numerous picnics in the back yard. Father often builds the fire for these outdoor meals. Mary and Dick assist him by gathering wood. The entire family insists that food tastes much better when it is cooked and eaten in the fresh air.

TIME_____Seconds

1. What does Mother like to do?
2. When does Mother cook special foods?
3. How does Father prepare for the outdoor meals?
4. How do Mary and Dick help Father?
____ **5.** Why does the family like food cooked outdoors?

ERROR RECORD	Number
Substitutions	
Mispronunciations	
Words pronounced by examiner	
Disregard of punctuation	
Insertions	
Hesitations	
Repetitions	
Omissions	
Total Errors	

FIGURE 9.2 Portion of the record blank of the *Gilmore Oral Reading Test*, Form C, copyright 1968 by Harcourt, Brace and World, Inc. Reproduced by permission of the publisher.

Many teachers are skeptical of the value of systematically recording observations about oral reading behaviors, as suggested in the paragraphs above. They are confident in their ability to remember the important facts about their pupils without having to write them down. If such a skeptical teacher will take the trouble to employ the check-list system once, he will, if he is honest, be amazed at the number of specific faults he has either overlooked or forgotten during weeks or months of work with his pupils.

For a more detailed study of word-recognition errors, it is desirable to list the errors the child makes as he goes along in his reading. It is most convenient to have a duplicate copy of the reading selections, on which the child's errors can be marked as they occur, using a scheme like the one set up for standardized oral reading tests (see Fig. 9.2). With experience, a fairly accurate list of the child's errors can be written in column form on blank paper for later analysis, as shown in Figure 8.1, p. 172. Trusting to one's general impression about the kinds of errors made is considerably less satisfactory than making a record. Another procedure is to mimeograph copies of a selection from a book; this should not be done without permission from the publishers. Or the teacher may make up a test selection of his own, or use one of the published oral reading tests. Methods of analyzing specific errors in word recognition are taken up later in this chapter, following a discussion of the available published oral reading tests.

Taking the trouble to make a careful appraisal of each child's oral reading at intervals during the year does not tend to make a teacher less sensitive to the characteristics of the oral reading done during regular reading activities. On the contrary, practice in the use of a detailed check list, and familiarity with the main characteristics to be noted in oral reading, lead to improved clarity of perception and greater skill in noting significant facts in any oral reading activity. The kind of informal appraisal recommended here is a supplement to, not a replacement of, the teacher's daily observation.

The time that should elapse between one fairly thorough oral reading appraisal and the next should vary according to circumstances. Children whose progress is poor need to be checked more frequently and more carefully than those making good progress. Once a child has reached a high level of fluency and accuracy in oral reading, thorough periodic rechecks on his oral reading may be a waste of time. If a child does extremely well or very poorly in an oral reading appraisal, the teacher should try him out on a harder or easier book. Two-month intervals will prove sufficient in many situations.

An Oral Reading Check List

The following oral reading check list does not attempt to provide a complete and exhaustive list of all the possible miscues, errors, and behaviors found in oral reading, but rather to direct attention to significant patterns of response frequently found in oral reading. A single check may be used to indicate presence of the behavior; a double check to indicate a marked presence.

1] *Word recognition, general*
___ a) Inadequate sight vocabulary
___ b) Errors on high utility words

___ c) Omits: ___ whole words; ___ final word elements
___ d) Inserts: ___ whole words; ___ final word elements
___ e) Doesn't attempt to decode unknown words
___ f) Tends to guess unknown words; ___ overrelies on initial elements
2] *Use of context*
___ a) Relies heavily on context
   ___ (1) Substitutes words of similar meaning
   ___ (2) Substitutes words that are grammatically correct
   ___ (3) Reads words correctly in context which he misreads in isolation
___ b) Inadequate use of context
   ___ (1) Substitutes words of similar appearance but different meaning
   ___ (2) Substitutes words that spoil or change meaning
   ___ (3) Makes errors which produce nonsense
3] *Decoding procedures*
___ a) No method of word analysis
___ b) Unsuccessfully attempts to decode
___ c) Breaks words into syllables
___ d) Uses morphemic analysis: ___ inflected endings; ___ compound words; ___ prefixes; ___ root words; ___ suffixes
___ e) Looks for little words in big words
___ f) Spells
___ g) Attempts to sound out: ___ single letters; ___ phonograms; ___ syllables
___ h) Overrelies on configuration, size, and shape
___ i) Attends mainly to one part of word: ___ initial; ___ medial; ___ final
___ j) Lacks flexibility in decoding
4] *Possible specific decoding difficulties*
___ a) Visual analysis skills
___ b) Symbol-sound association skills: ___ consonants, ___ single, ___ blends, ___ digraphs; ___ vowels, ___ single; ___ short; ___ long; ___ final silent *e*; ___ vowel digraphs; ___ diphthongs
___ c) Blending: ___ single letters into syllables; ___ syllables into words
___ d) Reversal tendency
___ e) Letter confusions
5] *Comprehension*
   a) Main ideas: ___ strength; ___ weakness
   b) Facts: ___ strength; ___ weakness
   c) Inferences: ___ strength; ___ weakness
6] *Fluency*
___ a) Word-by-word reading
___ b) Phrases poorly
___ c) Hesitations

___ d) Repetitions

___ e) Ignores/misinterprets punctuation: ___ commas, ___ periods, ___ question marks, ___ other

___ f) Inappropriate speed: ___ too fast; ___ too slow

___ g) Rapid and jerky

7] *Use of voice*

___ a) Monotone: lack of meaningful inflection

___ b) Enunciation generally poor

___ c) Slurs and runs words together

___ d) Sound substitutions

___ e) Stuttering or cluttered speech

___ f) Nervous or strained voice

___ g) Volume: ___ too loud; ___ too soft

___ h) Pitch: ___ too high; ___ too low

___ i) Peculiar cadence

8] *Behaviors*

___ a) Finger pointing: ___ word-by-word; ___ by phrases; ___ by lines; ___ line marker

___ b) Head movements

___ c) Tension signs

___ d) Vision: holds book ___ too close, ___ too far away, ___ at odd angle; ___ covers left/right eye; ___ loses place often; ___ skips lines

___ e) Poor concentration

___ f) Poor task orientation

___ g) Impulsive behavior

___ h) Compulsive behavior

___ i) Lack of motivation

___ j) Unwillingness to try

___ k) Possible emotional problems

___ l) Poor posture

The teacher who wants to get a less detailed picture of the oral characteristics common to several of the pupils may prefer to use a check list such as the one shown in Figure 9.1. Each vertical column records the problems of one child. By reading across a line, the children who need extra help on that problem can be identified and brought together as a special needs group.

Published Reading Inventories

There are at least three published oral reading inventories that are similar in organization to an informal reading inventory. Validity and reliability data are reported for only one of these individually administered tests—the *Standard Reading Inventory* (McCracken, 1966). Its materials include a manual, reusable stories, word cards, and a record booklet for each of the two forms. There are eleven word lists, pre-primer to grade 7, for testing word recognition in isolation. On the basis of word-recognition performance a beginning level is chosen for oral and silent reading. There are nineteen passages, eleven for oral reading and eight for silent reading, pre-primer to grade 7. Comprehension of each passage is tested with questions on details and inferences.

In scoring, specific standards are given for the following levels: frustration, instructional (questionable, definite), and independent. Separate ratings are made for vocabulary, errors, comprehension, and speed. Each level at which the child has been tested is rated, and a composite judgment is made. A listening-comprehension level can be obtained by starting at the frustration level, reading the passages to the child, and rating his comprehension. The record booklet includes a "comparative strength chart" and a fairly detailed check list.

There are three forms of the *Classroom Reading Inventory* (Silvaroli, 1969), the first of which is meant for testing oral reading. The other forms may be used as alternate oral reading selections or for measuring silent reading or the learner's capacity level. Each form contains eight word tests ranging in difficulty from the pre-primer to the sixth-grade level, ten paragraphs whose readability ranges from pre-primer to eighth reader level, and a graded spelling survey that can be group administered. Provisions are made to determine the child's reading rate. The results are expressed in terms of the child's functional reading levels, with the instructional-level criteria stated as a minimum of 95 per cent correct word recognition and 75 per cent comprehension. However, the manual indicates that 60 per cent comprehension may be acceptable. For each selection there are five comprehension questions which include factual, inference, and vocabulary items, the number of each type varying from selection to selection.

The *Reading Placement Inventory* (Sucher and Allred, 1973) has only one form composed of twelve word lists and selections ranging in difficulty from primer to ninth reader level. The fifth reader selection may be more difficult than suggested. The instructional-level criteria are: word recognition between 92 to 96 per cent, and comprehension accuracy falling between 60 to 79 per cent. Every selection has one question each of the following types: main idea, factual, sequence, inference, and critical thinking. Space is provided on the cover page for summarizing the findings including the number of each type of word-recognition and comprehension errors.

Tests That Accompany Reading Programs. The task of selecting passages, counting words, and preparing comprehension questions can be eliminated by using a published set of book samples. A number of basal reading programs have what amounts to an IRI constructed specifically for their program (see Fig. 8.2, p. 176). Other publishers have a sample selection in the front of each text that may be used to determine the suitability of that book for instructional purposes with a particular child or group.

Standardized Oral Reading Tests

The *Gray Oral Reading Tests* are available in four equivalent forms. Each form has a spiral-bound booklet containing thirteen passages; each passage is printed on a separate page, in type suitable for the grade level. The passages range in difficulty from pre-primer to college level. There is an examiner's record booklet for each form, containing a copy of each passage with wide spaces between lines for recording errors, four recall questions (the responses to these questions are not considered in determining the test score, however) and a classification of errors. Testing is usually begun two passages below the level corresponding to the pupil's grade; the procedure is explained in the manual. The reading of each passage must be timed, and the passage score is based on a combination of number of errors and time; the passage scores are summed to get a total score. The manual gives separate grade norms for boys and girls, for each form. The test was standardized on a population of 502 children with an average IQ of 110, and so the grade scores obtained are probably a little lower than they should be. The error classification includes the following headings: word aided, gross mispronunciation, partial mispronunciation, omission, insertion, substitution, repetition, and inversion.

Although the *Gray Standardized Oral Reading Paragraphs* have not been changed since their publication in 1915, they are still used in some reading clinics. A four-page booklet contains twelve paragraphs ranging from first grade to high school in difficulty. A second copy is used by the examiner as a record form for errors and time; there is no comprehension check. This test has been popular for a long time, but it is now surpassed by newer tests.

The *Gilmore Oral Reading Test* was revised in 1968 and has two new forms, C and D. The material includes a manual, a spiral-bound booklet containing the reading passages for both forms, and a separate examiner's record booklet for each form. Each form contains ten passages ranging from pre-primer to high school in difficulty. The examiner records errors, time per passage, and answers to five comprehension questions (see Fig. 9.2). Norms for accuracy and comprehension (really factual recall) are given in the form of grade equivalents, stanines, and "performance ratings." Rate is not combined with accuracy, but is given a separate rating as slow, average, or fast. The test was standardized using 4,455 pupils in six widely separated communities.

The most helpful *Gilmore* score is the one for accuracy, since the comprehension score, based entirely on recall of details, is not comparable to scores on silent reading comprehension tests. Although rate is not counted directly in the accuracy score, it appears indirectly since hesitations, repetitions, and self-corrected mispronunciations are counted as errors. The error classification used is: substitutions, words aided by examiner, mispronunciations, disregard of punctuation, insertions, hesitations, repetitions, and omissions. The pupil reads all selections between one which he can read with no more than two errors and one on which he makes ten or more errors. This usually provides a sufficient record for qualitative analysis of oral reading, as well as for scores.

Section IV of the *Diagnostic Reading Tests* includes a graded series of paragraphs for oral reading. There are two levels of difficulty, Lower and Upper. The other tests of this battery are for group administration.

Other tests of connected oral reading are included in the *Gates-McKillop, Durrell,* and *Spache* diagnostic batteries, which are described below.

Diagnostic Oral Reading Test Batteries

The *Monroe Diagnostic Reading Tests* employ the *Gray Standardized Oral Reading Paragraphs* (described above) for measuring oral reading of connected material and two word lists called the *Iota Word Test* and the *Word Discrimination Test* for detecting difficulties in word recognition. The three oral reading tests are used to get a profile of errors. Supplementary tests include a mirror-reading test, a mirror-writing test, an auditory word discrimination test, a visual-auditory learning test, a sound-blending test, and tests of handedness. The material is put up in the form of an individual record blank and a set of test cards. A manual of directions is provided.

The *Monroe* battery contains several tests that are still useful, although they have never been revised since they were published in 1928.

The *Gates-McKillop Reading Diagnostic Tests* are the 1962 revision of a diagnostic battery first issued by Arthur I. Gates in 1927. The materials include a manual, reusable spiral-bound booklets presenting visual material for Forms I and II, exposure cards for words and phrases, and a separate record booklet for each form. The record booklets contain stimulus materials for some of the tests which are given orally, in addition to record forms for all the tests.

There is an oral reading test with seven paragraphs of increasing difficulty, telling a continuing story. This is used both to obtain a grade score for accuracy in oral reading and to provide material for a classification of errors. There is no comprehension check. A word list of forty words is exposed for one-half second each, to get a measure of immediate sight vocabulary. Then the same words are presented with no time limit, and the child is encouraged to try again when he makes a mistake. The untimed test has a parallel list of forty words which can be given in addition, for greater reliability. A phrase recognition test is given with half-second exposures. There are several tests of skills important in word analysis. These are grouped under knowledge of word parts (recognizing and blending common word parts, giving letter sounds, naming capital and lower-case letters); recognizing visual forms representing sounds (nonsense words, initial letters, final letters, vowels); auditory blending; and a set of supplementary tests including spelling, oral vocabulary, syllabication, and auditory discrimination. The oral vocabulary test is intended for use as a measure of reading capacity. The auditory discrimination test, along with the auditory blending test, provides helpful information for judging the child's readiness for phonic instruction.

The *Durrell Analysis of Reading Difficulty* was issued in 1937 and revised in 1955. It was the first diagnostic battery to organize the passages to be read by the pupil in a durable spiral-bound booklet. In addition to the manual and pupil booklet there is a record booklet for the examiner, which contains several check lists, norms for the tests, and room for supplementary information, in addition to record forms for the various tests. There is one form.

Word recognition is tested with several lists, ranging in difficulty from first to sixth grade. These are printed on long, narrow cards and are exposed for approximately half a second by moving the shutter up or down. If the child does not recognize the word, the shutter is opened and he is encouraged to try to figure out the word. In our experience, the Durrell tachistoscope does not work well when one gets near the bottom of a list. There are separate grade norms for flashed and untimed presentations.

There are four sets of eight reading passages each, ranging in difficulty from first to sixth grade. One set is for oral reading, which is timed and scored on the basis of rate, with no scoring for errors. There are four to seven comprehension questions after each passage. A grade level is assigned for each passage, and the median of these is the grade score for oral reading. A second set of passages is used for timed silent reading, after which the pupil is asked to retell the story; grade norms are given for rate and for number of ideas recalled. A third set of passages is marked "supplementary" and can be used as an alternate form for either oral or silent reading. The fourth set is to be read to the pupil, and his answers to comprehension questions form the basis of a listening comprehension grade score.

There are numerous supplementary tests. These include naming, matching, and writing alphabet letters; visual memory of words; learning sounds in words; learning to hear sounds in words; sounds of consonant letters (vowels are ignored); learning rate for words; spelling; and handwriting.

The *Durrell* battery has been widely used for many years. As with the *Gates-McKillop,* an experienced examiner will only rarely use the entire battery.

The *Spache Diagnostic Reading Scales,* revised in 1972, have two main parts, word recognition and connected reading, supplemented by tests of phonic skills. Test material includes a manual, a reusable booklet for the pupil, and a record booklet for the examiner. There is one form, but there are two selections at each reader level.

The examiner has a choice of three word lists, one of first- and second-grade difficulty, the next ranging from second to fifth grade, and the highest, from third to sixth grade. Although the words are not flashed, the examiner notes sight vocabulary and analyzes the pupil's methods of decoding from his performance on the word recognition test. An estimate of instructional level is also obtained, which indicates where to start in the reading passages. Eight supplementary phonics tests may be used for additional information about decoding skills.

There are eleven reading passages, ranging in difficulty from primer to eighth reader level, in each of two parallel scales. Each passage is followed by comprehension questions. The passages are evaluated as in an informal reading inventory rather than scored like a standardized test. The instructional level is defined as the highest reader level at which the pupil can meet the criteria when reading orally. Independent reading level is judged on the basis of comprehension of the silent reading passages. These definitions differ from those put forth by most writers. Spache advocates a minimum standard of 60 per cent comprehension for the instructional and independent reading levels. Most reading authorities use quite different standards: a minimum of 70 per cent for instructional level and 85 to 90 per cent for independent level. One can, if one wishes, use the Spache testing material and apply one's own standards in interpreting the results. A capacity level score can be obtained by reading passages to the child and checking his listening comprehension.

The *Botel Reading Inventory* is intended primarily for determining instructional levels of pupils and group instructional needs rather than intensive individual diagnosis. The material includes a manual, answer sheets for three group tests (phonics mastery, word opposites reading, and word opposites listening), and pupil cards and examiner's scoring sheet for an individually administered recognition test. There is one form.

The Phonics Mastery test includes subtests on consonant sounds, consonant blends, consonant digraphs, rhyming words, long and short vowels, other vowel sounds, number of syllables, accented syllable, and recognition of nonsense words. A class summary sheet is provided on which each child's answers are recorded to show which phonic elements he knows. The Word

Opposites Test is a multiple-choice group test in which a printed word is given and the pupil chooses one of the four words as being opposite in meaning; it is very similar to the reading vocabulary subtests in many silent reading tests. However, the items are arranged in levels corresponding to reader levels and provide a measure of comprehension level. An equivalent word opposites list is read to the pupils and used as a measure of listening comprehension. The Word Recognition Test is arranged in reader levels, twenty words at each level from pre-primer to grade 4. Instead of norms, standards of accuracy are provided for free reading level (95–100 per cent), instructional level (70–90 per cent), and frustration level (65 per cent and below).

Botel (1969) has presented evidence that his Inventory provides more accurate estimates of children's reading levels, as determined by teacher judgment, than silent reading tests do. According to W. Ramsey (1967) the Phonics Mastery Test is superior to most such tests, but the Inventory as a whole does not provide discrete enough information for planning individual remedial programs. However, the fact that only the Word Recognition test requires individual administration makes this Inventory far less time-consuming for the busy classroom teacher than the more comprehensive diagnostic batteries.

Evaluation of Diagnostic Reading Tests

W. Ramsey (1967) has suggested and used several criteria for judging diagnostic reading tests. By *reality* he means that an ability should be tested in much the same manner as it is used in reading. By *guessing* he means that correct guessing should not be possible; this is a general objection to objective items of the multiple-choice type. By *active* he means that the pupil should have to respond with overt, observable behavior. By *specificity* he means that success or failure on an item should be attributable to one ability rather than to a combination of abilities. By *comprehension* he means that questions on comprehension should require understanding and interpretation rather than just recall of directly stated details. According to these criteria, none of the present diagnostic reading test batteries is fully satisfactory. However, this does not prevent them from being very helpful to those who understand their uses and limitations.

Of the four major batteries—*Monroe, Gates-McKillop, Durrell,* and *Spache*—the *Gates-McKillop* and *Spache* batteries test adequately over the widest range of reading ability. The *Monroe* is useful mainly for children reading at first- and second-grade levels; the *Durrell* is most effective for those reading at or above third-grade level.

Those who do diagnostic testing learn to derive more insights from a test battery as they become increasingly familiar with it. It is more practical, therefore, to become thoroughly familiar with one diagnostic battery and to use it repeatedly than to attempt to master them all. Very experienced diagnosticians often use informal tests of their own devising in preference to published diagnostic tests.

As a final note, it should be realized that, despite high correlations among diagnostic tests, there are significant differences between the grade-level scores yielded by various tests (Eller and Attea, 1966). It also should be noted that the grade-level designations for selections indicated in the manuals of published oral reading tests may not be accurate (Daines and Mason, 1972).

Recording Performance on Oral Reading Tests

Some published tests of oral reading require that each paragraph be timed. For this it is desirable to use a stopwatch, although a watch with a second hand can be employed. The examiner follows along in a second copy of the test material, either a copy of the test or a record form which contains a reproduction of the test material. The manual for each test contains directions as to how to record errors and what to count as an error. There are differences on what constitutes an error—for example, hesitations, ignored pronunciation marks, and self-corrected mispronunciations are not counted as errors in the *Gray* tests, but are counted in the *Gilmore*—so that it is necessary to follow carefully the directions in the manual of the test being used. For informal testing the following short cuts are helpful: use a wavy line under repetitions, a check mark to indicate a hesitation, a *P* when the word has to be pronounced by the examiner; encircle omissions, put parenthesis marks around self-corrected mistakes, write in mispronunciations, substitutions, and insertions and use slashes to indicate phrasing pauses. As yet no standardized test has attempted to refine its scoring by distinguishing between minor errors, such as omitting a final *s* or substituting *a* for *the*, and major errors. If a large proportion of the errors are minor in character, the resulting grade score probably underestimates the level at which the child can cope with a book.

Classifying and Scoring Errors in Word Recognition

There is no general agreement about the way errors in word recognition should be classified. Monroe uses a classification with ten divisions: vowel errors, consonant errors, addition of sounds, omission of sounds, substitutions, repetitions, addition of words, omission of words, refusals, and words aided. Gates and McKillop use omissions, additions, repetitions, mispronunciations, whole reversals, part reversals, wrong order, wrong beginning, wrong middle, wrong ending, and wrong several parts.

It is more important to understand the child's errors than to count them. It is helpful to analyze word-recognition difficulties along the lines suggested in the "How to Interpret Oral Reading" section on page 234. The important questions to answer are: 1) To what extent, and how successfully, does the child make use of the context? 2) How does he attempt to attack new words, and with what degree of success can he employ various methods of attack? 3) What specific kinds of errors does he make that may require specific remedial attention? Finding the answers to these questions is not an automatic result of counting different kinds of errors, but involves an attempt to understand what the child is *trying* to do as he reads, as well as noting what he does. It is a qualitative rather than a quantitative method of analysis that is most helpful.

Learning to Give Oral Diagnostic Tests

Recording the child's performance as he reads orally requires speed in the use of a variety of symbols used to represent different kinds of errors. Beginners usually cannot record as fast as the child reads, and their records are usually both incomplete and only partially accurate. For the inexperienced tester it is therefore highly advisable that the child's oral reading be taken down on a tape recorder and scored later at leisure, when parts of the record can be played as many times as necessary to resolve questions. Even for an experienced examiner, use of a tape recorder may allow him to pay more attention to the observation of the child's behavior during reading without distracting the child, who may try to watch what the examiner is writing. It also allows the child to listen to his own performance and, by later comparing with a recording after remedial help, to note his own progress.

III. ADDITIONAL TESTS USEFUL IN READING DIAGNOSIS

Word Recognition'

The importance of appraising the ability to recognize words is obvious. The interpretation of word-recognition errors made during connected oral reading has already been discussed. The cleverness that some children show in using the context makes it possible for them to conceal many of the uncertainties that plague them in attempting to recognize or decode words. To get a true picture of sheer word-recognition ability, one has to test for ability to recognize words when they are out of any meaningful context. For this purpose, one asks the child to read a list of unrelated words.

In using a word list one usually has two purposes. First, one wants to know if the child can recognize the word at sight, with little or no

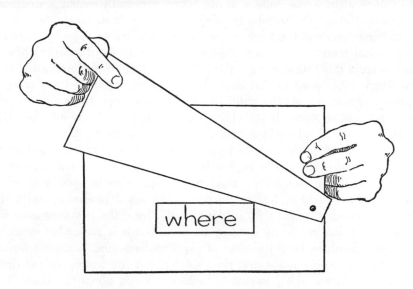

FIGURE **9.3** A simple hand tachistoscope. This can be made in sizes to fit the use of 4 x 6 or 3 x 5 in. index cards. The shield and shutter can be cut out of stiff cardboard or the sides of a grocery carton with a sharp razor blade. To use, hold the shield upright on table top with the left hand. Pick up a card with the right hand and place it against the shield, with the botton of the card resting on the table, so that the material to be exposed is in the opening. Place the left thumb against the card, holding it in place. With the right hand lift the shutter quickly until its lower corner is level with the top of the shield and let go; this gives a fairly rapid exposure. Very rapid exposures can be obtained by placing the left index finger across the top of the shield and bouncing the shutter against it.

hesitation. If the child does not recognize the word at sight, the next question is whether he can work out the pronounciation. In this, an understanding of the child's method of approach to an unknown word, and of the factors contributing to success or failure, is more important than getting a score. If the child does not recognize a word immediately, one should encourage him to do his thinking out loud as he tries to figure it out. A child staring blankly at a page does not reveal very much, but if he can verbalize his thoughts, one can find out what he is trying to do and perhaps why he succeeds or fails.

Teacher-made word-recognition tests are easy to construct. The extent to which a child can recognize the words in a given book often is more informative than a vocabulary grade score, especially when a decision is being made about the suitability of that book for him. Most basal readers list the new words at the back of the pupil book, either page by page or in alphabetical sequence (as in a glossary). A twenty-word sample chosen at random from this listing gives a short list that is quite representative of the new words introduced in that book. It helpful to prepare several copies on a primer typewriter. As the child reads from one copy the examiner notes errors on another copy. If the child is asked to read the words directly in the book list, the "said–for" method of recording can be used.

The idea of testing a child for both quick recognition and careful analysis of words is a good one. Flash cards, with a word or phrase printed on each card, have long been used to give practice in speedy word and phrase recognition. For testing purposes, the usual procedure with these cards—covering the card with a blank card, lifting the covering card for a moment and then replacing it—may be used, but it is somewhat crude and makes it difficult to keep the time of exposure constant. A simple tachistoscope can be readily made and then used either for testing or for drill.

An illustration of a homemade tachistoscope is given in Figure 9.3. It consists of a sheet of stiff cardboard with an opening cut in it, and another piece of cardboard fastened to the first by a brass paper fastener so that it serves as a shutter. The material to be exposed is printed on index cards. Any flash-card material can be used in a device like this.

Tests That Accompany Reading Programs.   Most tests that accompany reading programs at primary levels contain subtests of word recognition. They sample the words introduced at a particular reader level in that program. Word recognition is usually measured in group mastery or achievement tests by having the child match a picture with the word that best describes the picture, or mark from a number of choices, the word pronounced by the examiner. Scores on such tests are influenced by the degree to which the distractors (incorrect answers) resemble the correct response. If the distractors differ greatly (*e.g., ox, elephant, dog,* when the correct response is *cat*) the child need key in on only certain cues (*e.g.,* the initial sound) in order to arrive at the correct response. In such cases some children are able to score well on the test who may not be able to pronounce the words correctly during oral reading. The task on such word-recognition tests is easier than having to pronounce the word acceptably. Standardized group tests of word recognition suffer from the same limitation.

A possible follow-up to a weak performance on a group word-recognition test is to point to each correct answer on the test and have the child attempt to pronounce it. An analysis of his errors may provide clues to the reasons for his problem.

Word-recognition tests more broadly indicative of instructional reading levels may be constructed by taking random samples from a graded vocabulary list. For example, the ten-word lists in Figure 9.4 were constructed by taking random samples from the Harris-Jacobson Core Lists, which are arranged by reading levels (A. J. Harris and Jacobson, 1972). At pre-primer and primer levels, which have 58 and 62 words, every sixth

SAMPLE GRADED WORD LISTS

Preprimer	*Primer*	*1st Reader*	*2nd Reader*
big	away	before	breakfast
did	car	color	dance
funny	good	first	few
help	house	hard	honey
little	man	laugh	lunch
no	one	night	people
said	saw	rabbit	seat
the	some	still	start
we	too	took	trick
you	word	window	young

3rd Reader	*4th Reader*	*5th Reader*	*6th Reader*
bubble	brain	bracket	acknowledge
certain	county	consent	consequence
fasten	fallen	emotion	embarrassment
history	happening	grace	horizontal
manage	lighthouse	kindness	miniature
pilot	ornament	noble	possibility
rule	relation	pursue	resemblance
spent	smear	shred	speculate
ticket	thicket	thermometer	testimony
yesterday	wreck	yonder	victories

FIGURE 9.4   Ten-word lists at eight reader levels. The difficulty levels are not indicated on copies presented to the pupil. These words were taken from the Harris-Jacobson Core Lists (1972). The highest level at which the child can recognize or decode seven or eight of the words is suggestive of his instructional level.

word was chosen; at first reader level, with 211 words, every twenty-first word was picked; and so on. These short lists of ten words each, prepared on a giant primer typewriter, have proven quite useful in clinical practice. If a child has difficulty with more than three words in any list, he is likely to find many unknown words in typical books of that vocabulary level. If he misses two or three words, the rating for that level is "doubtful."

Standardized Word-Recognition Tests. Many of the primary-grade levels of standardized silent reading achievement tests contain subtests of word recognition. The word-recognition tests found in standardized oral reading tests make different and more revealing demands on the test taker in that they require him to pronounce the word orally. There are also tests that measure only word recognition such as the reading part of the *Wide Range Achievement Test* (WRAT). This test of 128 words contains a larger number of difficult words than any of the others and provides grade norms from kindergarten to college-graduate level. It is therefore usable in upper grade, secondary school, and college levels for which the other word lists are too easy. It is, however, not a satisfactory measure of the learner's general level of reading ability, despite the fact that it has been used for that purpose in several research studies, because it does not measure comprehension.

Other standardized word recognition tests with fairly broad ranges of norms are the subtests of the *Gates-McKillop, Durrell,* and *Spache* diagnostic tests, the *Peabody Individual Achievement Test* (PIAT), and the *Slosson Oral Reading Test* (SORT). Despite its title, the latter is similar to the WRAT in that only recognition of words presented in isolation is measured.

Some clinics test poor readers on all 220 words of the *Dolch Basic Sight Vocabulary* list (see page 361), using a printed list rather than individual word cards. We prefer to try only a small sample of the Dolch list to determine if work on it will or will not be needed, leaving to the remedial lessons the identification of the specific words that need to be learned. Tryout on the entire list is unnecessarily tedious and frustrating for most children with severe reading disabilities.

Tests of Decoding Skills

There are three main subskill areas of decoding: visual analysis, phonic analysis, and blending. A good reader usually inspects the unknown word for parts that he can utilize, makes any necessary symbol-sound associations, blends the parts into a whole word and checks for meaning. It is quite possible for different learners to employ different processes and/or information to arrive at the same final response (Sipay, 1971).

The term *visual analysis* is somewhat misleading because although visual components are involved, the process takes place mentally. The visual stimulus is almost always the whole word; it is not divided into parts by spaces or lines. As he views the unknown word, the reader employs his visual-analysis skills to divide it into parts which are recognized as units or to which he can apply his symbol-sound association skills. Phonic analysis refers to the skills needed to make the necessary grapheme-phoneme associations. *Blending,* at times called *synthesis* or *fusion,* is the ability to blend sounds into syllables and syllables into whole words.

A learner who cannot decode words may be deficient in any or all of the skill areas, with symbol-sound association weakness and blending weakness occurring most frequently. The examiner's task is to determine which weaknesses in skills are creating the problem. An apparent deficiency may in fact be caused by a weakness in another area. For example, a student cannot utilize his blending skills if he cannot make the necessary symbol-sound associations.

Although group-administered decoding tests may suffice for some general classroom purposes, they do not provide the information needed to pinpoint the specific needs of disabled readers who have decoding problems. The assumptions upon which most group decoding tests are based, particularly in the area of phonics, are not valid (W. Ramsey, 1972). Group tests have a number of limitations, among which are the following:

1] The manner in which visual-analysis skills such as syllabication are sampled (*e.g.,* drawing lines between syllables) does not allow the examiner to determine why the child divided the word as he did; and more importantly, whether the pupil can or does employ the skill in decoding unknown words.

2] The task involved in "phonics" tests usually require the child to associate oral stimuli with letters (sound-symbol association) whereas in decoding, the letters are the stimuli to which he must associate sounds (symbol-sound association). Primary-grade children tend to score higher on phoneme-grapheme tests than on grapheme-phoneme tests (Hardy, Smythe, Stennett, and Wilson, 1972). Making sound-symbol associations is easier than making symbol-sound associations. For one thing, the child must choose a response from only a limited number of choices. When faced with letters, especially vowels, he must decide which of a number of possible sounds they represent in this unknown word.

3] Some tests require the student to write the letters that represent the sound they hear. This requires an additional motor skill, a deficiency in which may make it impossible for the student to display his phonic skills.

4] Most group tests contain too few items to provide a reliable measure of a specific skill. To provide a reliable indicator, a skill should be sampled by at least three items.

5] It is extremely difficult to measure blending skills on a group test.

6] Group tests do not measure adequately the ability to combine all the skills needed for decoding. Usually the subtests measure just one aspect (*e.g.*, syllabication or sound-symbol associations).

7] It is almost impossible to make a valid analysis of the basis for errors because group tests are read silently.

Informal Appraisal.   Some information regarding a learner's decoding skills may be obtained by analyzing his word-recognition errors as suggested on page 234. However, there may be a need to follow up the leads obtained in this manner in order to obtain more specific information. The analysis may reveal a probable weakness in making vowel symbol-sound associations, but not indicate in which specific associations the weaknesses exist or why they occur. In such cases more detailed testing is necessary. For example, if the child continually gives the hard sound of *c* when its soft sound is more appropriate, the examiner must determine whether the learner knows: 1) that *c* may represent a sound other than /k/; 2) that *c* also may represent /s/; 3) when *c* probably represents its hard or soft sound (the learner may be able to verbalize the generalization but not utilize it either because he does not understand the terms *hard* or *soft* or cannot make the necessary associations). Application of a generalization is a two-step process. The learner must determine: 1) what principle probably applies (*e.g.*, the vowel probably represents its long sound because it is in an open syllable); and 2) what that sound is (*e.g.*, the long sound of *e* is /ē/. A breakdown in any of the steps produces errors.

An informal check of visual-analysis skills may be made by presenting words to the child and asking where he would divide them and why. Directions should be worded so the child understands what is expected of him.

Symbol-sound associations may be tested by presenting letters in isolation or in words. If words are used, they should not be in the child's sight vocabulary. There is no need to make symbol-sound associations if the stimuli are recognized immediately. Pupils may be generally deficient or have specific symbol-sound association weaknesses. A very brief test of symbol-sound knowledge is presented in Figure 9.5.

If the child can make symbol associations, his blending skills may be tested. Depending upon which skills one wishes to sample, single letters (*g a m*), a single letter and a phonogram (*g am*), or syllables (*gam ble*) may be presented. Probably it is easiest to blend syllables into whole words, followed by blending a consonant with a phonogram. If the child is unable to blend when presented with visual stimuli, his auditory blending should

TEST OF PHONIC KNOWLEDGE

by ALBERT J. HARRIS

h	s	v	c	z	k	w	r	f	q
g	l	b	m	d	n	y	p	j	
bl	st	ch	dr	wh	fr	th	pl	sh	
str	scr	spl	spr	kn	wr	gn	thr		

ea	oa	ai	ie	oo	ow	oy

pan	dote	her	jut	rime	weed
pane	dot	here	jute	rim	wed

de-	un-	re-	im-	col-	pre-
-sion	-ity	-or	-ition	-ily	-ous

FIGURE **9.5** A brief informal test of phonic knowledge.
Directions: The child looks at one copy while the examiner records on another. For each phonic element the child is given credit if he is either able to say a word that contains the corresponding sound, or to pronounce the phonic element by itself. The consonants in the top line are tested by asking the child to tell you a word beginning with that letter. If he cannot, ask him what sound the letter stands for. Give the next three lines in the same way. For the vowel pairs, ask for a word that has the sound in it. The two lines of words testing knowledge of long and short vowels are read in horizontal sequence. For children who do well, a few common prefixes and suffixes are given.

be tested. The same stimuli can be pronounced for the child, with brief pauses representing the spaces, to see if the child can achieve a mental fusion which suggests the appropriate word or syllable. Inability to blend is a major problem in many cases of severe reading difficulty.

Published Tests of Decoding Skills. The *Sipay Word Analysis Tests* (SWAT) contains sixteen diagnostic subtests which measure specific visual analysis, phonic analysis, and blending skills, with the majority sampling the ability to utilize symbol-sound association skills. A word analysis survey test is also included. In addition to a general test manual, there is a mini-manual for each test that contains an overview of the skill(s) being measured, specific directions for administering, scoring, analyzing and interpreting the test performance and follow-up suggestions. Only selected subtests need be given.

The *Tests of Phonic Skills* contain nineteen subtests most of which sample symbol-sound association skills. Only the appropriate tests need be administered. This test employs nonsense words. Although only the response to the element under consideration is scored (*e.g.,* responses to the medial vowel and final consonant are not considered in the initial consonant tests), it should be realized that difficulties with other elements may cause errors on the skill under consideration. This is most likely with final elements in which errors may occur because the learner has difficulty with the preceeding vowel symbol-sound association. A unique feature of this battery is the auditory discrimination test for which taped directions in nine different geographic regional dialects and a Spanish dialect are available. However, the manual does not contain data or suggestions for interpreting any of the test scores.

The *Woodcock Reading Mastery Tests* consist of five normed individually administered tests for use from kindergarten through high school. In addition to tests of Letter Identification, Word Identification, Word Comprehension, and Passage Comprehension which is a modified cloze test there is a Word Attack Test. The latter uses fifty nonsense words to measure the subject's ability to decode monosyllabic and polysyllabic words. Although the test does sample many consonant and vowel symbol-sound associations as well as common affixes, it contains too few samples of any one item to provide reliable diagnostic information. Therefore the Word Attack Test would best be used as a screening test and/or to obtain information for comparing the decoding performances of subjects.

Some examiners may prefer to use less detailed individual tests which, although not as comprehensive as the above and lacking in interpretative data, are less time consuming. The *Roswell-Chall Diagnostic Reading Test* is a quick, convenient test for analyzing a child's word-attack skills. It contains short tests of knowledge of letter and phonogram sounds, solving one-syllable words, short and long vowels, and syllabication. Total time is usually around five minutes. Another brief test is the *Phonics Criterion Test* which samples ninety-nine phoneme-grapheme correspondences.

Some of the above mentioned tests and others contain tests of visual blending. As previously noted, visual blending also requires the ability to make the necessary symbol-sound association; whereas auditory blending does not. The *Roswell-Chall Auditory Blending Test* is a brief standardized test of auditory blending ability of demonstrated validity (Chall, Roswell, and Blumenthal, 1963). It should be noted that some children who can make symbol-sound associations are unable to blend sounds into syllables or syllables into words.

Use of Context and Language Clues. Use of context and language clues can aid word recognition and analysis. Minimal visual input may be needed to determine an unknown word if the context and the sentence structure offer strong clues as to what the word probably is. In both cases experiential background plays a role. In the sentence, "The bone was eaten by the _____," the child's past experience, real or vicarious, with animals will suggest the final word. Experience with language suggests that only certain types of words are likely to occur in a given pattern. Thus, the unknown word is likely to be a noun. Context and language clues often are combined with other word-recognition or decoding skills.

If the ability to use context or language clues is measured, the test material should be at the child's instructional level. It is difficult to use context clues if a number of words are not recognized, and impossible to do so if most words are unknown. Some of the aforementioned tests do contain measures of the ability to use context, or the teacher may design her own test.

Follow-up to Decoding Tests. The best way to determine if a child needs to, or can, learn skills in which tests or observations have shown him to be deficient is to try to teach him those skills. If the initial lessons indicate that the tests were in error, there is no need to continue teaching a skill for which a child demonstrates mastery. If the child cannot learn the skill after a reasonable length of time, the teacher should attempt to determine what factors are contributing to the problem. These factors may be external or within the child. Emotional stress caused by events at home or in school may be curtailing his ability or desire to learn in general. Or, something within the way in which the skill is being presented may be a factor. Perhaps the child does not understand the directions (what he is to do), or there is an attempt to teach too much at once, or the pace of the lessons is too rapid, or there is a need for additional reinforcement. A child who cannot learn to make symbol-sound associations may be weak in underlying skills. In such cases it is advisable to check the child's auditory and visual discrimination, acuity, and memory. Suggestions for doing so have been provided by Sipay (1971).

Testing Specific Comprehension Skills

Experts differ as to whether there are statistically identifiable separate reading-comprehension abilities. At best, there seem to be between two and five distinct types, with most authors leaning toward two: understanding factual material and making inferences. Yet as Berg pointed out:

Even though the results from standardized tests of comprehension may not measure separately the several skills they claim to measure, it is possible from a pragmatic or practical point of view such tests may have some value for reading instruction. Obviously, teachers do not teach "pure" skills in isolation any more than tests can measure them. Therefore, it is possible that the teacher who gives the tests gets from the data the kind of information needed to improve instruction, even though neither the test results nor his teaching deal with precisely defined or measured skills. (1973, p. 30)

A few of the silent reading tests described in Chapter 8 have separate subtests that purport to measure different types of comprehension (*e.g., New Developmental Reading Test,* intermediate level) or provide an indication as to which items tap given types of comprehension (*e.g., California Reading Test,* 1957 edition). Tests that accompany reading programs are more likely to specify which types of comprehension are sampled by given items (*e.g., Macmillan Reading Mastery Tests*) or to have separate subtests for each type (*e.g., Reading for Different Purposes*). The *Diagnosis: an instructional aid, Reading* lab includes separate criterion-referenced tests for nine different types of comprehension. The lab also contains CR tests of phonic analysis, structural analysis, vocabulary and use of sources.

Rarely do tests even suggest that they sample the ability to read critically. If such information is desired, the examiner will have to determine what type of comprehension is being sampled by the items and then analyze the child's performance accordingly.

IV. DIAGNOSTIC USE OF SAMPLE LESSONS

In some of the early approaches to diagnosing reading disabilities, tests of associative learning were used to try to give a clear picture of why the child had trouble learning to recognize words. Tests were used that involved the associating of nonsense syllables with geometric forms, meaningful words with geometric forms, real words with squiggles that looked something like printed words, and so on (Gates, 1927). These tests fell into disuse when most users found that the results were of little help in planning a remedial approach. Nevertheless, the idea that it is desirable to test the child's ability to learn by trying him in genuine learning tasks has real merit.

The idea of using miniature sample lessons as a diagnostic procedure for reading was developed by the senior author and his colleague Florence Roswell (A. J. Harris and Roswell, 1953). It is now sometimes known as trial teaching and may be used to determine a viable approach for teaching word-recognition or decoding skills to severely disabled readers; or adapted for use to determine which beginning reading approach is more likely to succeed for given children. The directions for five different methods are as follows:

The entire session is informal and permissive. There is a considerable amount of give-and-take and flexibility in approach.

The examiner should note qualitative observations about the child's ability to profit from reading instruction. Such factors as quick or slow grasp; tempo of work; need for repetition of instructions; degree of motivation required; resistance to specific materials; ability to exert effort; to give sustained attention; and to recall what is taught; are significant in interpreting the results of sample lessons.

Several procedures should be tried until success with at least one method is clearly apparent. If time allows, a variety of materials should be presented so as to obtain some impression of the child's reactions to readers, workbooks, and game-type devices. Any success should be liberally praised and failure minimized. In one such period we have been able to demonstrate to many children that they have the ability to learn to read. We have found that, in most cases, this experience has proved to be a powerful motivating force for future reading instruction.

The procedures described below are to be used at the discretion of the examiner, following careful analysis of the diagnostic reading test results. Thus, which methods to use and what level at which to begin the sample lessons will be based on an appraisal of the child's basic reading skills as indicated on the tests.

1. *Visual (whole-word) Method.* For the child who is a nonreader or almost a nonreader it is advisable to begin with a simple visual approach to word recognition which is essentially one of learning words by means of picture clues. Words that the child wants to learn may be used, thus supplying additional motivation.

For materials, one needs several cards, each with one picture illustrating a well-known object such as a cake, a window, a table, a book, and so on. The word is printed or typed under the picture. On another set of cards the words are printed without pictures. Make sure that there are no marks, smudges, and the like, on the cards which could be used as cues. Test the child to make sure he does not already know the words, and select five for teaching. Follow-up may indicate that this is either an appropriate number or that it is too few or too many for the child to learn and recall in one session.

Present the first picture card, point to the word, and tell the child the word. Ask him to say the word several times while looking carefully at the card. Then ask him to find the non-illustrated card with the same word on it. When the child thinks he has learned the word, proceed to the next illustrated word. After the second word has been learned, shuffle the two non-illustrated word cards and present each in random order three times. A record of this mixed practice will provide information as to the need for reinforcement, the number of words that can be introduced before the child becomes confused, and perhaps what visual cues the learner is employing. Teach a third word, followed by mixed practice with the previously taught words. Follow a similar procedure until all five words have been taught. Then shuffle the five non-illustrated cards and test him on them by presenting each three times in random order. If he is successful, retest about thirty minutes later. Retention also should, if possible, be checked one, three, and seven days later because long-term memory is vital in the use of a whole-word approach.

It may be desirable to follow up by teaching a few words from the material being considered for instructional use, followed by reading the corresponding material. If the child objects to this material, it may be necessary to avoid using any book in the early stages of remedial instruction.

Some children are distracted by the use of pictures in learning to recognize words through a whole-word approach. If use of the preceding procedure suggests this, it may be well to repeat the lesson with different words without the use of pictures.

2. *Single-Letter Phonics Method.* The ability to synthesize or blend sounds into whole words is vital to this method. If the child shows some auditory-blending skill, it is safe to try a single-letter phonics approach. Auditory blending may be checked with one of the available tests or informally by presenting five to ten three-letter words in the following manner: Tell the child you are going to pronounce the parts of a word for him and that you want him to listen carefully so he can tell what word you said. No visual stimuli are employed. Pronounce the sounds separately with about a half-second pause between each (*e.g.,* /o/–/n/, /b/–/a/–/t/, distorting the consonants as little as possible. After each presentation, ask the child to tell what word he heard. A reasonable criterion for adequate performance is at least 80 per cent correct, but any correct responses indicate that a method relying on blending is not impossible.

Teach or review the symbol-sound associations of from three to five consonants and one single short vowel (*e.g., m, c, t, s, d* and *a*). Each symbol-sound association is presented singly as follows: Show the letter *m* (use lower-case letters). "This is *m* (use letter name) and the sound it makes is /m/, the sound that you hear at the beginning of *man* (slightly emphasize the /m/). Listen for the /m/ sound at the beginning of each of these words. *meat, my, milk.* Can you hear the /m/? Now give me some words that begin with /m/." Help with suggestions if necessary. Auditory discrimination (an important subskill in this method) may be informally checked by pronouncing sets of three words and having the child raise his had when he hears a word that does not begin with the sound being taught. Proceed the same way with *c, d, t, s* and *a.*

"Now I'm going to say a word, then its parts slowly, and the whole word again. Listen carefully. Mat; /m/–/a/–/t/; mat. This is how the word *mat* looks." Use separate large letter cards to form the word, first saying the whole word, then each sound as the letter is put in place, and finally the whole word again. Repeat the word, sound by sound, moving your finger under each letter in the word as the sound is pronounced. Hand him the appropriate letters and say, "Put these together to make 'mat.' " Ask him to sound out the word as he does so. Help him, if necessary. Then show him how to change *mat* to *cat* and *sat.*

Write a sentence containing the words, such as "The cat sat on the mat," and have him read it, providing help as necessary.

Show him how to change the final sounds to form new words: *mat* to *mad*, *sat* to *sad*. Then provide practice in using the symbol-sound association to form the five words taught.

At the end of the session, present the five words in random order three times in a manner similar to that described for the visual method. If he reads four of them successfully, he is likely to succeed with a phonic program that employs a very similar method.

If a child is weak in auditory discrimination, blending ability, or learning symbol-sound associations, it is advisable to postpone phonics instruction. The number of associations presented in one session and the way in which the associations are taught are variables that can be manipulated and that may influence the success or failure of this method.

There are variations of the phonic method in which the symbols differ from traditional orthography (i/t/a and UNIFON) or in which color is provided as an additional cue (*e.g.*, Words in Color). The above outlined procedure may be employed with these approaches, but it is advisable to utilize those suggested in the manuals that accompany the specific program. Some disabled readers respond well when a "new" alphabet is used.

3. *Word Family (linguistic) Method.* This technique of word recognition or analysis is especially useful for those who possess only rudimentary blending ability and are unable to cope with the single-letter phonics method described above. If used solely, however, it affords a limited degree of independence in word analysis.

Present a well-known word such as *man*. Then teach or review separately three consonant symbol-sound associations (*e.g.*, *r*, *f*, *p*) that can be used in the initial position to form other common words. Demonstrate how initial consonants may be substituted to form or to recognize new words. Provide practice in utilizing this technique, followed by mixed practice with the three words formed with the introduced consonants. Repeat the procedure for a different phonogram and the same initial consonants. Learning and retention may be checked using the procedure described above for the visual method.

As with the other methods, teaching variations may be tried to determine their possible effect on learning. For example, rather than use a word like *man* as a starting point, a phonogram that is a commonly known word (*e.g.*, *an*) may be employed, and the child taught to form new words by appending initial consonants. Most linguistic reading programs do not provide direct teaching of symbol-sound associations.

4. *Visual-Motor Method.* Choose about three words with which the child is unfamiliar (about 5 to 8 letters in length) such as *friend, airplane, pilot.* Present each word separately. Print the word clearly on a card. Say, "This word is 'friend.' Take a good look at it. What is the word? Now close your eyes. Can you see it with your eyes closed? Look again. What is the word?" Remove the word and ask him to write it. Have him compare his word with that on the card. If incorrect, repeat the above procedure, present the word, pronounce it, have him try to visualize it and then write it again. Sometimes it is necessary to show the card several times before he is able to write it. If

he has much difficulty with a word, try another. If he reproduces the word correctly, have him write it again, covering up his previous writing so as to be sure he is recalling the word from memory rather than merely copying it. Check each time to see that it is done correctly. After a period of time has elapsed, review the words. A more detailed description of this procedure appears on page 358.

5. *Kinesthetic Method.* The brief summary given below is based on the method fully described by Fernald (see page 393). Only the initial stages used in teaching by kinesthetic procedure are presented here.

A short period of orientation is suggested. Tell the child that you are going to teach him to read by means of an entirely new method. Assure him as to its value by telling him that other people who have had difficulty with their reading learned in this way. Describe the procedure to him. Ask him to suggest a word he would like to learn.

Write the word with a crayon on paper in large-size script (letters approximately 2 inches high). The child traces the word with his index finger (or index finger and thumb, if he wishes) saying the word as he traces it. He repeats this as many times as necessary in order to write the word without looking at the original one. When he appears to know it, he writes it on another sheet of paper. In cases of error or if the child hesitates and seems unable to complete the word, he retraces the word as a whole. He is not permitted to erase in order to correct errors. If he has difficulty recalling the word he should be encouraged to trace it over and over and then to write it without consulting the original writing.

It is evident that any approach may be used as a starting point so as to insure success in learning to read from the very outset of remedial instruction. Before long, however, such procedure must be supplemented by others because a successful reader must have a variety of techniques at his command. It is not necessary to try all five methods listed above. It will be found that most children can learn by at least one of the first four methods. In such cases it is usually unnecessary to try Procedure 5. However, in cases of severe disability where children cannot learn by a simple visual approach and cannot synthesize sounds together as required in a phonic procedure, the kinesthetic method should be tried. Trial lessons may be used similarly at all levels and should be varied according to the needs of the case.

The principle of sample word-study lessons has been developed into a standardized technique by Mills (1956). Four methods are used: visual, phonic, kinesthetic, and combined. The examiner spends fifteen minutes with each method, teaching ten words. While his adaptation seems to us to be quite time-consuming and very fatiguing to the child, reading clinics and remedial teachers may find it a real addition to available diagnostic procedures. The picture-word cards at primer, first-, second-, and third-grade levels which form part of the Mills test material are in themselves well worth having.

The Learning Rate test which is part of the 1955 edition of the *Durrell Analysis of Reading Difficulty* utilizes only a purely visual method of word study and presents too much material to be learned for one lesson. A good result on this test is probably a safe indicator that the child can build a sight vocabulary by visual study, but a poor result may be ambiguous.

The essence of the sample lesson is a situation in which the child's behavior as a learner can be carefully observed and evaluated. Qualitative observation and interpretation are more important than numerical scores or ratings. Such characteristics as interest, attentiveness, distractibility, perseverance, effort, reaction to success, reaction to failure, anxiety, discouragement, and efforts to evade the task are some of the characteristics which may be observed and judged. A standardized procedure and scoring may not draw one's attention away from these qualitative factors, but the temptation to rely on scores is strong. For these reasons it is preferable to use sample lessons in a flexible, unstandardized way.

V. HOW TO INTERPRET READING PERFORMANCE

Oral Reading

In interpreting oral reading one must keep in mind that understanding the pupil's difficulties is the important goal. The errors made should be carefully inspected for the information that they may give about fluency, about the utilization of meaning or context, about the pupil's method of attack on words, and about the particular errors in word recognition that he is most prone to make. These findings must be considered in relation to his silent reading and the other information available about the pupil.

A few cases will be presented at this point to illustrate different kinds of errors in oral reading and the procedure followed in interpreting them.

A record of Harry's reading in book samples of high first-grade and easy second-grade material is shown in Figure 8.1, page 172. Although he made five errors in the first-grade sample, only four different words were involved, since *far* was missed twice. This material can be judged to be near the upper limit of his instructional level. In the second-grade sample the excessive number of errors in the first fifty words made it painful and unnecessary to proceed any further; the frustration level had obviously been reached.

Inspection of the errors shows that Harry made some use of initial consonants and occasionally (*ast* for *fast*, *garden* for *yard*) recognized a word-family phonogram. Most of his errors were substitutions involving guesses from context. In the first-grade material some of the words he read correctly were probably good guesses from context. In material as full of unknown words as the second-grade sample he made many errors in his anticipation of meaning so that many of his substitutions ruined the sense; other substitutions, however, like *friends* for *family* and *garden* for *yard,* combined partial cues in combination with context to keep the meaning essentially correct. It was evident that Harry had no consistent methods for attacking unknown words, had a very small sight vocabulary, and depended mainly on guessing from context.

Floyd was a boy 8 years and 9 months old, with an IQ of 105, in the high third grade. His average silent reading score on the *Gates-MacGinitie Primary* tests was 3.0, and on the *Gray Oral* he scored below the norms for the middle of the second grade. His reading was slow and inaccurate in both silent and oral reading. Nearly all his errors in oral reading were mispronunciations; there were no omissions or additions of words, and he tried to pronounce every word. A collection of his miscues from this test and other samples of his oral reading includes the following:

almost	*for*	among		first	*for*	front
party	*for*	pretty		grass	*for*	glass
rigs	*for*	rags		window	*for*	windows
were	*for*	will		her	*for*	hear
hiding	*for*	hidden		pin	*for*	pine
stood	*for*	stone		feets	*for*	feet
every	*for*	very		spot	*for*	spots
well	*for*	wall		five	*for*	four
want	*for*	wants		like	*for*	likes
cold	*for*	cool		those	*for*	these
that	*for*	there		had	*for*	has
for	*for*	from		slow	*for*	slowly
these	*for*	lies		back	*for*	black
clamb	*for*	climb		neck	*for*	kick

A classification of errors by position shows one complete mispronunciation (*these* for *lies*), three wrong beginnings (*every* for *very,* *grass* for *glass,* *back* for *black*), six medial errors (such as *well* for *wall*), two wrong endings (*hiding* for *hidden,* *had* for *has*), ten wrong several parts (such as *party* for *pretty*), five omissions of final elements (such as *want* for *wants*) and one addition of a final element (*feets* for *feet*).

From a more useful point of view, it appears that Floyd 1) had difficutly making symbol-sound associations for initial blends containing *r,* blends containing *l,* but not blends containing *s;* 2) had difficulty making symbol-sound associations for final blends; 3) had difficulty making symbol-sound associations for single vowels, vowel combinations, and vowels followed by *r;* and 4) tended to rely too much on the initial consonant(s) and guess unknown words. He apparently did not have much difficulty with single consonants or consonant digraphs.

The tabulation given above did not supply an immediately meaningful interpretation of Floyd's difficulties in word recognition. For this a different approach was needed. It was noted that in all but two of these words Floyd got the beginning of the word right. He evidently looked mainly at the first letter or two, got a vague impression of the rest of the word, and said a word he already knew which looked like the one before him and started with the same letter. In order to determine whether the vowel and consonant errors were due to lack of knowledge of letter sounds or carelessness, it was necessary to test his ability to give the sounds represented by the letters when presented in isolation. These showed confusion about vowel symbol-sound associations but no errors on single consonants. It was also noted that he made poor use of the context, as half of his errors spoiled the sense of what he was reading. The conclusion was drawn that major emphasis should be placed on exercises to develop the habit of paying attention to the whole word rather than just the beginning, on teaching symbol-sound associations for vowels and consonant blends and providing exercises for overcoming confusions, and on getting him to use the context more effectively when faced with an unknown word.[1]

Theresa, a girl of above-average intelligence in the high sixth grade, obtained a grade score of 5.8 on the *Metropolitan Intermediate Reading Test*. In oral reading her performance was at the fourth reader level for comprehension and third reader level for word recognition. Her errors showed considerable variety, including omissions, additions, and substitutions of words, reversals of word order, and mispronunciations of polysyllabic words. In reading isolated words, her performance was far more accurate than in reading connected material. She had a good phonic background and could work out the pronunciation of long and difficult words. When she came to an unknown word in connected reading, however, her usual tendency was to guess from the context rather than observe the word carefully and work it out. In addition to this habit of depending too much on the context, she read slowly and in a monotonous voice, phrased incorrectly, and sometimes skipped lines. She needed training to improve phrasing and expression and directed practice in utilizing her phonic knowledge.

Philip's errors in oral reading included many reversals of letters (*bid* for *did, baby* for *body*), reversals of words (*top* for *pot, on* for *no*), reversals of word order (*there was* for *was there*), and errors on the beginnings of words (*hand* for *land, father* for *mother*). He had difficulty keeping the place and would sometimes jump from the middle of one line to the middle of the next line. These errors were judged to indicate a failure to establish consistent left-to-right eye movements, and training was instituted to encourage proper direction in reading and placing emphasis on the beginnings of words.

Comparison of Oral and Silent Reading

The discussion of oral and silent reading testing in these two chapters has made it evident that somewhat different aspects of reading are accessible to appraisal in oral as compared to silent reading. In general, silent reading is better for investigating comprehension skills and oral reading for studying word-identification skills and fluency.

1. Remedial procedures for improving word recognition are discussed in detail in Chapter 15.

The direct comparison of oral and silent reading test scores is complicated by the fact that the populations used for developing the norms for oral reading tests are in general of unknown comparability to the populations used for norming specific silent reading tests. For example, a grade score of 2.4 on the *Stanford Primary* may or may not be equivalent to a grade score of 2.4 on the *Gray Oral;* as yet no study has been conducted to study the comparability of widely used oral and silent reading tests.

One way to avoid this problem of noncomparability is to use equivalent selections in an informal reading inventory of both silent and oral reading.

Differences of two or more years between the silent and oral scores of an individual are, however, unlikely to be due solely to differences in the test norms. Some disabled readers show very large disparities. In a published case, vocabulary and silent comprehension reached college level after several years of remediation, but oral reading never rose above fifth grade (Preston and Willson, 1970).

When silent reading seems to be significantly better than oral reading, the following possibilities should be considered:

1] The reader has good language skills and is expert at using context clues, thus achieving comprehension despite weaknesses in word-identification skills.
2] The reader is self-conscious when reading orally, but is more relaxed in a silent reading situation.
3] The reader has benefited from extensive guessing when taking the silent reading test, artificially raising his score.
4] The reader can reread at will in silent reading, but is penalized for repetitions in oral reading.
5] The reader is so concerned about word identification and "expression" in oral reading that his comprehension suffers as compared to silent reading. These possibilities can occur in combination as well as singly.

Children whose oral reading is superior to their silent reading abilities are usually comparatively good in word recognition. Their oral reading difficulties are likely to be deficiencies in fluency, phrasing, and expression or in comprehension rather than in pronouncing the words. Because of this fact, a detailed analysis of the word-recognition skills of these children is often unnecessary. The oral reading of most retarded readers, however, is at least as poor as their silent reading, and in a great many cases it is much worse. Since word-recognition errors make up the majority of the errors of these children, a careful analysis of word-recognition difficulties is usually profitable when one is working with disabled readers.

In these two chapters the analysis of reading performance has been treated in some detail. Consideration has been given both to informal teacher-constructed procedures and to standardized tests. Methods were considered for determining reading level, comprehension, and rate, fluency and accuracy in oral reading, word-recognition skills and learning potentialities in word recognition. These techniques form an important part of reading diagnosis. Equally important is the study of the types of handicaps which may create or intensify a reading problem. This important question is taken up in the next three chapters.

SUGGESTED ADDITIONAL READING

BANNATYNE, ALEXANDER. *Language, reading and learning disabilities: psychology, neuropsychology, diagnosis and remediation.* Springfield, Ill.: Charles C Thomas, 1971. Chap. 14.

BOND, GUY L. & TINKER, MILES A. *Reading difficulties: their diagnosis and correction* (3rd ed.). New York: Appleton-Century-Crofts, 1973. Chaps. 7, 8, 9.

DE BOER, DOROTHY L. (Ed.). *Reading diagnosis and evaluation.* Newark, Del.: International Reading Association, 1970.

DELLA-PIANA, GABRIEL M. *Reading diagnosis and prescription: an introduction.* New York: Holt, Rinehart and Winston, 1968. Chaps. 6, 7, 8.

DURKIN, DOLORES. *Teaching them to read* (2nd ed.). Boston: Allyn and Bacon, 1974. Chap. 16.

DURR, WILLIAM K. (Ed.). *Reading difficulties: diagnosis, correction, and remediation.* Newark, Del.: International Reading Association, 1970. Pp. 67–132.

FARR, ROGER. *Reading: what can be measured?* Newark, Del.: International Reading Association, 1969.

FARR, ROGER (Ed.). *Measurement and evaluation of reading.* New York: Harcourt Brace Jovanovich, 1970.

FRY, EDWARD. *Reading instruction for classroom and clinic.* New York: McGraw-Hill, 1972. Chaps. 2, 6.

GUSZAK, FRANK J. *Diagnostic reading instruction in the elementary school.* New York: Harper & Row, 1972. Chaps. 9, 11.

HARRIS, ALBERT J. & SIPAY, EDWARD R. (Eds.). *Readings on reading instruction* (2nd ed.). New York: McKay, 1972. Chap. 5.

MAC GINITIE, WALTER H. (Ed.). *Assessment problems in reading.* Newark, Del.: International Reading Association, 1973.

OTTO, WAYNE; MC MENEMY, RICHARD A.; & SMITH, RICHARD J. *Corrective and remedial teaching* (2nd ed.). Boston: Houghton Mifflin, 1973. Chaps. 3, 5.

ROBECK, MILDRED C. & WILSON, JOHN A. R. *Psychology of reading: foundations of instruction.* New York: John Wiley and Sons, 1974. Chap. 10.

ROSWELL, FLORENCE G. & NATCHEZ, GLADYS. *Reading diagnosis and treatment* (2nd ed.). New York: Basic Books, 1971. Chaps. 2, 3.

SCHELL, LEO M. & BURNS, PAUL C. *Remedial reading: classroom and clinic* (2nd ed.). Boston: Allyn and Bacon, 1972. Pp. 159–256.

ZINTZ, MILES V. Corrective reading (2nd ed.). Dubuque, Iowa: William C. Brown Co., 1972. Chaps. 2, 11.

10

Correlates of Reading Disability, I: Cognitive Factors

After one has determined that an individual has a reading disability (see Chapter 7), diagnosis involves two main undertakings. The first is evaluation of his reading skills and instructional needs, which has been considered in detail in Chapters 8 and 9. The second is inquiry into the factors that may help to understand the cause of the disability and call attention to handicaps, within the individual or in his environment, that need correction. If the condition cannot be corrected, it can at least be taken into consideration. Many factors in the individual's past history, in his present environment, and in his personal characteristics may be associated with his problems in learning to read. These factors, and methods for studying them, provide the subject matter for this chapter and Chapters 11 and 12.

I. DIAGNOSIS, CORRELATION AND CAUSATION

Chapter 7 pointed out that diagnosis as related to reading involves the intelligent interpretation of relevant facts by a person who knows what questions to ask, what procedures to employ to secure needed facts, how to interpret each bit of information, and how to fit together the many findings in order to gain understanding of the child's problems and needs. Coming to a conclusion about which cause or causes were responsible for the child's poor start is less important than coming up with two plans: one for correcting or minimizing the effects of the conditions, within the individual or in his environment, that still present barriers to learning; and one for a remedial teaching-learning plan that is likely to be successful with this particular child.

Correlation and Causation

The notion of causation has bothered philosophers for centuries. Two kinds of actions, events, or traits can be observed to occur together far more often than can be expected on a pure chance basis. If one of them consistently precedes the other, it is tempting to assume it to be a cause, and the other, an effect. However, correlation—the fact that two or more measurable characteristics tend to be found together—does not prove causation.

In studying people, it is not often that a simple and direct causal relationship can be established, and this is particularly true of reading disability. For example, if one studies a broad range of children one finds a definite relationship between height and reading; taller children tend to be more capable readers. The taller children also tend to be older than the shorter children, and it seems more reasonable to conclude that the increased years of schooling and greater mental maturity which accompany increasing age are the factors causally related to the better reading of taller children than to attribute causal significance to their height, which is another concomitant of increasing age. A correlated factor may or may not have causal significance.

In a particular child with a reading disability several characteristics may be found, each of which has been shown by research to be somewhat correlated with reading disability. To determine which of these characteristics may have interfered with the child's learning to read, and their relative importance in this case, is a difficult detective job at best and often cannot be solved.

For this reason, it is safer to discuss the correlates of reading disability than the causes. Correlation can be readily demonstrated or disproved; causation is much more difficult to establish.

Another issue that complicates the drawing of conclusions about cause and effect is compensation: the probability that strength in one trait related to reading ability can make up for weakness in another relevant trait. In some recent studies, disabled readers differed from good readers primarily in the number of abilities in which they showed special immaturities rather than by showing weakness in particular abilities (White and White, 1972; Bell and Aftanas, 1972). A combination of weak abilities may have combined causal effect which no one of the weaknesses could produce by itself. In, diagnosis it is important to look for strengths that can be used in remediation, as well as to locate weaknesses (Kasdon, 1971).

A Pluralistic View of Causation

In Chapter 7 the question of single or multiple causation of reader disabilities was discussed (see pp. 142–145) and the viewpoint of this book was described as favoring pluralistic causation. Some further evidence on this issue, and some implications that can be drawn from it, are presented below.

One of the most intensive studies of causal or contributing factors in reading disability to date is H. M. Robinson's study (1946) of thirty cases of severe reading disability. A social case history was taken by a trained social worker, and the child was examined by a psychologist, a psychiatrist, a pediatrician, a neurologist, an ophthalmologist, an otolaryngologist, a speech pathologist, and an endocrinologist. After the examinations had been completed a case conference was held on each child, at which the specialists came to a group decision concerning which factors were causal and which were merely concomitants of the reading problem. Treatment was supervised in twenty-two of these cases. After the results of treatment were known, another conference was held at which the conclusions previously reached about causation were reviewed and sometimes changed. A summary of causal factors was then made, based on both diagnosis and remediation. The number of probable causal factors ranged from one to four. The most frequent were social problems and visual difficulties, followed by emotional maladjustment, neurological difficulties, speech or discrimination difficulties, school methods, auditory difficulties, endocrine disturbances, and general physical difficulty. Each handicap was present more often than it was judged to have causal significance, and each handicap was considered by the specialists to be a possible cause before remediation in more cases than it was judged to be a probable cause after remedial treatment.

Malmquist made an intensive study of 399 first-grade children in two Swedish cities, among whom there were 34 with IQ's of 90 or above and very poor reading ability. He concluded:

> On the basis of our results, it appears reasonable to draw the important conclusion that to attempt to find a single factor which will entirely explain the occurrence of reading errors is, in the great majority of cases, a vain endeavor. Most frequently there appear to be several factors in constellation which are related to reading failure. Many of these factors seem to be closely

interrelated. There appears to be an interplay between the child's general physical, intellectual, emotional and social development, and the development of his reading ability. (1958, p. 390)

The factors that seemed to Malmquist most significant were: intelligence; ability to concentrate, persistence, self-confidence, and emotional stability; spelling ability; visual perception; social status and educational level of the parents; and the teaching experience of the child's teacher (Malmquist, 1958, p. 387).

These studies, and others (Park and Linden, 1968; Ingram, 1971; Naidoo, 1972), lead to the conclusion that while there are some cases in which reading disability is a result mainly of neurological immaturity, damage, or dysfunction, there are many other factors that can handicap a child in learning to read. The more comprehensive the diagnostic study, the larger the number of handicaps discovered that seem to have some causal or contributing significance. Thus when a child fails to respond to appropriate remedial instruction, a comprehensive search for significant handicaps should be undertaken. Due to the complex nature of reading disability, research efforts would seem to require cooperative interdisciplinary teams.

In 1972 the Delegates Assembly of the International Reading Association approved the following statement, which had been prepared by the Disabled Reader Committee:

There is no single cause for reading disabilities. Reading problems can be caused by a multiplicity of factors, all of which are probably interrelated. Just as there is no single etiology, there is no one choice of intervention. For these reasons we deplore the action of those individuals and institutions who suggest that their methods are infallible, appropriate and optimal for every child, and universally efficacious. (International Reading Association, 1972)

That resolution states the point of view of the authors of this book quite well.

In practice, the identification of the causes of severe reading disability is complicated by two problems. The first is that some (but not all) of the described symptoms are present in a given case, and there is no invariable common core except for the learning difficulty. The second is that "pure" cases are hard to find. Rabinovitch said: "Despite the neatness of all our attempted theoretical formulations, I must confess that in practice our group not infrequently arrives at a diagnosis such as 'secondary [reading] retardation with a touch of primary disability'" (1962, p. 76). Since some of the symptoms thought to indicate primary disability are usually found along with some of the factors included under secondary disability, differential diagnosis is not easy; and skepticism about the reality and nature of constitutional reading disability remains a tenable scientific position.

Because differential diagnosis is very unreliable at the present time and opinions as to causation remain in the realm of unproved hypotheses, most reading specialists and teachers would be well advised to employ the following sequence in dealing with children who appear to have a reading problem: 1) determine the individual's general level of reading achievement and compare it with his potential; if a reading problem exists, 2) determine the learner's specific reading skill strengths and weaknesses; 3) determine which factors are most probably hampering the child's ability to learn *at that time;* 4) remove or lessen those factors that can be controlled or corrected, either before or during remedial treatment; 5) select the most efficient and effective way to teach the needed skills; 6) conduct a program of skill mastery; and 7) refer to an appropriate clinic or agency any child who does not respond to treatment after a reasonable period of time. Time spent on attempting to determine etiology can often be more profitably spent on helping chidren to overcome their present problems.

The preceding statements should not be misconstrued to indicate that the search for etiology or types of reading disabilities is irrelevant or impossible. To the contrary, because the determination of etiology is important from the standpoint of possible prevention and correction, more research is needed to build upon existing evidence in this area.

II. INTELLIGENCE AND READING

Intelligence has been defined as "the aggregate or global capacity of the individual to act purposefully, to think rationally and to deal effectively with his environment" (Wechsler, 1944). Most intelligence tests include several subtests of different kinds, including verbal, numerical, and spatial materials and requiring different kinds of responses. By including a variety of kinds of tasks, the possibility of the result being strongly influenced by a special talent or deficit is minimized. Factor-analysis studies have shown that there is a common factor underlying all kinds of intelligent performances, and this is usually labeled g; there are also several broad areas of somewhat special abilities, and numerous highly specialized abilities which in some cases have only low correlations with g. Most psychologists believe that the intellectual functioning of an individual involves the intimate interplay between an inborn potential for development, which varies from one person to another, with environmental conditions which strongly influence the degree to which this potential is realized.

Individually administered intelligence tests are generally considered more valid than group tests, partly because the examiner is better able to motivate the child or to note behavior that casts doubt on the validity of the results, and partly because such tests are less dependent on scholastic skills than most group tests. The most widely used individual intelligence tests for children are the *Revised Stanford-Binet Intelligence Scale* and the *Wechsler Intelligence Scale for Children* (WISC-R). The latter, consisting of eleven subtests, allows scoring for three IQ's, Verbal, Performance, and Full Scale, and also permits analysis of patterns of high or low scores on specific subtests. Despite the popularity of the WISC, some psychologists insist that the *Stanford-Binet* is superior in coverage of abilities that are relevant to learning to read (Grassi, 1973). The *Wechsler Preschool and Primary Scale of Intelligence* (WPPSI) is similar to the WISC but is for ages 4 through 6. *The Wechsler Adult Intelligence Scale* (WAIS) is a similarly organized test for older adolescents and adults.

Most intelligence tests can be scored both for mental age (MA) and intelligence quotient (IQ). Mental age is a measure of the level of mental maturity reached at the time of measurement. A bright child, an average child, and a dull child could all have the same mental age of 9 years, but the bright child would reach it in less than nine years, the average child would take nine years, and the dull child would take more than nine years. The IQ therefore shows the average rate of mental development, or brightness. The mental age is the better measure for indicating present expectancy and short-term prediction; the IQ is the better measure for prediction over a period of years.

The *Stanford-Binet* and *Wechsler* tests require trained examiners and are relatively time-consuming. In the search for brief individual tests that can be administered by teachers without special training, the *Slosson Intelligence Test* seems to have greater validity than the *Peabody Picture Vocabulary Test* or the *Quick Test* (Jerrolds, Callaway, and Gwaltney, 1971; Buros, 1972, Vol. I, pp. 764–767). The *Slosson* is based largely on items from the *Stanford-Binet*. A recent report finds the PPVT and SIT to correlate equally well with the WISC for children with reading disabilities (Pikulski, 1973).

Group intelligence tests for the primary grades usually present questions in pictorial form, and so are not influenced directly by reading ability. Such tests as the *Pintner-Cunningham* and the *Kuhlmann-Anderson* have substantial but not high correlations with reading in the primary grades. From the fourth grade up, most group mental-ability tests present their questions in printed form which must be read and understood before they can be answered. One study found that children in the intermediate grades with reading grade scores below 4.0 were handicapped an average of ten IQ points on a typical group mental-ability test (Neville, 1965). Such tests are, therefore, of little value in differentiating between low reading ability and low mental ability.

Many children with reading disabilities have average or above-average general intelligence. In thirteen studies summarized by Belmont and Birch (1966), the average WISC IQ's for disabled readers ranged from 91.8 to 109.8. When they studied children who scored in the bottom 10 per cent in reading, those with IQ's below 90 were generally reading at a level commensurate with expectancy, while those with IQ's of 90 and above generally were a year or more below expectancy. However, even a mentally retarded child may be considered to have a reading disability if he has reached a level of mental maturity substantially above his reading level.

The WISC is the intelligence test most often used in the clinical examination of retarded readers, and opinions differ as to which of the three WISC IQ's (Verbal, Performance, or Full Scale) one should rely on as the best indicator of reading expectancy. Some researchers have used the Performance IQ (Doehring, 1968). Others suggest that one should use either the Verbal or the Performance IQ, whichever is higher. Since children with disparities of 10 or more points between Verbal and Performance IQ's are common and disparities of 30 or more points are sometimes found in children with reading disabilities, it makes quite a difference which IQ one uses. Using the highest IQ optimistically assumes that the child's abilities in the lower area of functioning can be substantially improved, an assumption that often is not borne out. Depending on which IQ one uses, the children one will identify as having disabilities will be somewhat different populations, and their common characteristics will vary accordingly. "The modality deficiencies, the cognitive defects, the aptitude weaknesses and the relation of verbal to performance abilities will vary according to the method of identifying the retarded reader" (Reed, 1970). At the present time it is probable that one will make fewer mistakes by relying on the Full Scale IQ rather than on the Performance IQ alone or the higher of the Verbal or Performance. If the *Stanford-Binet* is used, the S-B MA and IQ should take priority over other measures of intelligence.

Patterns of Abilities on the WISC

There have been many reports in which the scores of poor readers on specific subtests of the WISC have been compared to normal readers of equivalent IQ, looking for patterns of high and low scores. In many of these reports, poor readers are stated to have difficulty with the Arithmetic, Digit Span, Information and Vocabulary subtests, while reports vary regarding the Coding subtest (Belmont and Birch, 1966; Ackerman, Peters, and Dykman, 1971). In first graders, "no special cognitive characteristics were found to differentiate the normally achieving from the high-risk group as a whole" (Hagin, Silver, and Corwin, 1971). Performance IQ is more often higher than Verbal IQ, but the reverse is also found, as well as cases with approximately equal Verbal and Performance IQ's. In general, Verbal IQ predicts academic performance better than Performance IQ does, and this is more true in the upper grades than for school beginners. This is in line with the general finding that verbal abilities are more highly correlated with academic success than nonverbal abilities are (Vernon, 1965). When learning-disabled children were grouped according to activity level and neurological status, no characteristic WISC patterns were found (Ackerman, Peters, and Dykman, 1971). In general, one may conclude that there is no WISC pattern characteristic of all or most reading disabilities, but in individual cases the high and low scores may help a psychologist to understand a particular child's difficuties in reading.

Bannatyne (1971, pp. 591–592) recommended grouping WISC subtest scores into four groups: Conceptualizing Ability (Comprehension, Similarities, Vocabulary), Spatial Ability (Picture Completion, Block Design, Object Assembly), Sequencing Ability (Digit Span, Picture Arrangement, Coding), and Acquired Knowledge (Information, Arithmetic, Vocabulary). This seems logical, but no research evidence supports it as superior to other analytical schemes. More recently, he recommended replacing Picture Arrangement by Arithmetic in the Sequencing Ability group, so that Arithmetic is used in both the Sequencing and Acquired Knowledge groups (Bannatyne, 1974, pp. 272–273).

Intelligence and Progress in Remedial Reading

While in general there is a positive relationship between brightness as indicated by IQ and rate of improvement in remedial reading, the correlations reported are not high. One study found that younger remedial pupils tended to respond better than older pupils and that IQ was not a good predictor of progress (Chansky, 1963). Another study found low correlations (.35 and .37) between remedial gain and two group mental ability tests; if a minimum intelligence score had been required, some pupils who gained 1.5 years or more in one year of remedial reading would have been excluded (Frost, 1963). A follow-up study of reading clinic cases showed that WISC Verbal IQ had a significant correlation with reading scores in high school, while Performance IQ did not (Muehl and Forrell, 1973–74). These studies provide additional reason to use a measure of severity of disability in relation to expectancy, such as the Reading Expectancy Quotient. They call into question the widely used practice of setting a minimum IQ limit (usually 90) for eligibility for remedial help.

Many teachers who plan to select a small number of pupils for special attention in reading find it hard to resist the temptation to select the poorest readers, regardless of their intelligence. Some of them find it difficult to distinguish between slow learners and reading disability cases. Others recognize this distinction but argue that the dull child will become brighter as a result of the remedial teaching.

Cases do occur in which a marked change in IQ is found after remedial teaching. But in most of these cases the true reason for the change is the use of a group test which gave an untrue impression of mental retardation, or the presence of unrecognized handicaps which prevented the child from showing his ability at the time of the first testing. Unfortunately there is no factual basis for a belief in the efficacy of remedial reading as a cure for dullness. Moreover, if the dull child's reading ability is fully up to his mental age, relatively little return may be gained from remedial instruction.

While no radical changes in brightness should be expected, the effective functioning of a child may improve as his vocabulary enlarges, his range of knowledge expands, and his interest in schoolwork increases. These results, which may not show very much in intelligence test scores, are worthwhile in themselves.

III. LANGUAGE AND PSYCHOLINGUISTIC ABILITIES

Psycholinguistic Abilities

The *Illinois Test of Psycholinguistic Abilities* (ITPA), 1968 Revision, is a battery of twelve subtests that is widely used in the clinical study of children with problems in reading, speech, mental retardation, and neurological functioning. The original 1961 edition had nine subtests: two "decoding" tests, auditory and visual; two "association" tests, auditory-vocal and visual-motor; two "encoding" tests, vocal and motor; an "auditory-vocal automatic" test; and two "sequential" (rote memory) tests, auditory-vocal and visual-motor. In the 1968 edition there are three additional subtests: visual closure, auditory closure, and sound blending. The test is based on Osgood's model of communication and is intended to sample reception of information, central processing, and response, at rote and meaningful levels.

The *Seventh Mental Measurements Yearbook* (Buros, 1972, pp. 814–825) lists 261 references on the ITPA, an amazing total for only ten years, and contains detailed reviews by John B. Carroll and Clinton I. Chase. The following comments are based on those reviews. 1) Only about half of the subtests involve the use of language, and the rest of the subtests involve cognitive functions that are not linguistic or psycholinguistic. 2) The total score has substantial to high correlations with intelligence (r's in the .80's with the *Stanford-Binet* in some studies). 3) Factor analyses show expressive and receptive vocabulary factors, immediate memory span, and "auditory processing" (found in lower socioeconomic children and probably represents their inability to understand the examiner's speech). However, a recent factor-analysis study of six selected subtests found that they each seemed to measure mainly a unique factor (Hare, Hammill, and Bartel, 1973). 4) The norms are based on middle-class children, and there are no separate norms for disadvantaged or handicapped populations. 5) Several subtests penalize children who speak nonstandard dialects. 6) The test has good internal reliability but only fair retest reliability. 7) There is no particular pattern of high and low subtest scores that is characteristic of children with reading disabilities.

The ITPA, like other tests, is influenced by motivation. When a disruptive child was retested and given two cents for each right answer some of his subtest scores went up two to five years (Kubany and Sloggett, 1971).

The value of basing remedial efforts on ITPA profiles is debatable. In one study, two groups of third- and fourth-grade children who were reading below expectancy and showed specific ITPA deficits were chosen. One group was given remedial treatment intended to strengthen their weak abilities revealed by the ITPA. The other group was given remedial reading based on their reading skill deficits. Both groups continued with classroom reading instruction. After four months there were no significant differences in gain either on the ITPA or in reading (Lazerman, 1970). Kiniry (1972) studied thirty children from learning disability classes and found that the ITPA did not distinguish these children from regular elementary students or relate diagnostically to their reading skills; he questioned whether the time-consuming administration of the ITPA is merited in a reading diagnosis.

The ITPA is not a magical instrument which can solve most diagnostic problems. Used and interpreted with good judgment, it can be a useful part of a comprehensive diagnostic program. Many of its subtests measure functions that can also be measured with other tests. The ITPA has the advantage that the norms for its subtests, being based on the same population, allow somewhat more reliable identification of good and poor abilities than comparisons of tests normed on different populations.

Vocabulary

It has long been known that vocabulary knowledge is intimately related both to intelligence and to reading ability. The best individual intelligence tests include vocabulary subtests, and the vocabulary score usually correlates more highly with total score than any other subtest does. Although vocabulary obviously has to be learned, the vocabulary knowledge that a child acquires (other factors being equal) is a very important indicator of his general learning ability and particularly of his probable success in school.

Vocabulary is also tested in measuring reading performance. Nearly every silent reading test has a vocabulary subtest, and this is often given equal weight with comprehension in getting a total score. To do well on a printed vocabulary test a child must be able both to decode words and to select their appropriate meanings from the choices given; a low score in itself does not disclose whether the problem is mainly poor decoding, weak knowledge of word meanings, inefficient reasoning, or a combination.

The quality of a child's verbal concepts may be revealed in the way he usually defines or explains a word. To a preschool child, words are usually explained in terms of use or function—a ball is to throw. A primary-grade child is apt to add some description—a ball is a round thing and you play with it. An intelligent older child can usually state a category to which the item belongs, and then indicate one or more ways in which the item can be distinguished from other members of that category—a ball is a plaything and is usually round; it can be thrown, caught, hit, or kicked. In the administration of an oral vocabulary test such as that of the WISC or *Stanford-Binet*, such qualitative differences in conceptual maturity can be discerned. Immature verbal concepts, lack of knowledge of alternative meanings, as well as total unfamiliarity with some words, may be a real handicap to comprehension.

Comprehension of Syntactic Structure

In the early stages of reading, sentences are kept short and simple and few comprehension difficulties due to syntactic (grammatical) structure or sentence length are encountered by most children. From the third grade up, children encounter reading materials written in a variety of styles: formal textbook English, standard English of a less formal style in fiction, and dialect and archaic English in some stories. Linguists have pointed out that unfamiliarity with standard English such as is used by teachers and in school books may be a major source of comprehension difficulty for children who are not accustomed to that kind of syntactic structure.

De Stefano (1973, pp. 189–195) has developed the idea that there are not only many dialects of English, but also several styles, ranging from highly formal to highly informal and colloquial, which need to be mastered; these she calls *registers*. A register is a set of linguistic forms used in given circumstances, and has characteristic features of pronunciation, sentence structure, and vocabulary. Most school instruction is given in a quite formal style which she calls the *Language Instruction Register*. A less formal register is used by teachers in talking to their families and friends. De Stefano's results indicated that black children come to school with some familiarity with the Language Instruction Register and develop more as they continue in school; more than 50 per cent of first-graders' responses, more than 60 per cent of third-graders' responses, and more than 70 per cent of fifth-graders' responses were made in the Language Instruction Register. The extent to which lack of complete familiarity with the Language Instruction Register interferes with learning to read is still a debatable issue, although it seems probable that it may be an important factor for some children.

A child's performance on a listening-comprehension test may help to indicate the degree to which he is capable of understanding similar material in printed form. Low performance on such a test may be related to a variety of factors such as poor hearing or limited intelligence as well as unfamiliarity with the vocabulary and syntactic structure, or the dialect and register, of the material.

Recently developed procedures for assigning numerical values to the syntactic complexity of sentences (Botel and Granowsky, 1972; Botel, Dawkins, and Granowsky, 1973) may make it easier in the future to match the syntactic competence of children to the language used in reading materials.

Speech

There are many kinds of speech defects, among which stuttering, lisping, slurring, and generally indistinct speech are common. The two kinds of speech defects that the writers have noted most frequently in poor readers are indistinctness, with blurred consonant sounds and a generally "thick" quality, and a rapid, jerky, stumbling kind of speech which is sometimes called cluttering (Kelly, 1966). Any kind of speech defect may produce embarrassment in oral reading and a consequent dislike for reading if oral reading is stressed. Phonic analysis may also be very difficult for children with defective speech. They should usually be taught reading by methods which do not stress oral reading and phonics, and at the same time remedial speech work should be carried on.

Children who are slow in speech development during the preschool years are quite likely to develop reading disabilities later. In a longitudinal study to predict reading disability, de Hirsch, Jansky and Langford (1966b) found that three measures of language proficiency in kindergarten were among the tests which showed significant correlations with reading failure in first and second grades. Ingram (1969) has summarized several studies in Scotland which show that later reading disabilities are common among middle-class and upper-class children with retarded speech development before entering school. Lyle (1970) found that retarded early speech development and articulatory speech defects between the ages of 2.5 and 4 years showed a clear-cut relationship to later reading retardation. However, it would not be correct to turn the relationship around and assume that most children with reading disability also were delayed in speech development.

IV. SPECIFIC COGNITIVE FACTORS

Perception

Perception starts with the stimulation of sense organs such as the eyes and ears, but is far more than simple sensing. In perceiving the brain selects, groups, organizes, and sequences the sensory data so that people perceive meaningful experiences that can lead to appropriate responses. The perceptual aspects of reading are very complicated, because discriminations must be made not just on discrete stimuli but rather on a succession of stimulus conditions in which both spatial and temporal patterns must be distinguished. "Reading is a continuing cycle of excitation and reaction in which each moment of perception produces a feedback effect which sets the person for the following perception. In this rapidly repeating cycle the sequential perceptions are apprehended as forming linguistic sequences that convey large units of meaning" (A. J. Harris, 1961).

Among the important characteristics of perception, several seem to have particular relevance for reading.

1. Figure and Ground. Normally one major unit or group of units is perceived clearly against a background that is more vaguely perceived. The more "busy" or "noisy" the background is, the harder it is to perceive the foreground figure clearly.

2. Closure. There is a strong tendency to perceive wholes; when small parts are missing, one tends to fill them in. The abilities to get the correct meaning of a sentence in which not all the words are recognized, and to pronounce a word correctly when some letters are blotted out, are examples of closure. Auditory closure is shown in recognition of incompletely heard words, and in blending ability—the ability to hear or say a word that has been sounded in separate phonemes and to recognize the word.

3. Sequence. In listening, sequence is inherent in the sensory input; in reading, all the stimuli are on the page, and sequence is imposed by the reader. The left-to-right sequence is an arbitrary convention that every child has to learn.

4. Learning. Perceptions become meaningful units as they become

associated with learned concepts and their verbal labels. Particular perceptions become clearer and more distinct with practice.

5. *Set.* One's immediate mindset provides an anticipation of what is
likely to come that is helpful when the anticipation is correct, but leads to
errors when the anticipation is incorrect.

6. *Discrimination.* The development of perceptual skill as children
grow older is from vague perception of wholes, to reliance on prominent
details, toward mature perception in which the whole is perceived sharply
and the details within it are also clearly discerned. The abilities to analyze
a whole into its parts, and to synthesize the parts correctly into the whole,
are basic to success in visual and auditory discrimination of words (Vernon,
1971).

The problem often lies not so much in the perception or grasp of one
unit by itself, but rather in deficiencies in the capacity to associate visual
and linguistic sequences. Thus, there is likely to be difficulty in comparing
parts within wholes in visual or auditory perception or both, difficulty in
clearly distinguishing figure from background, difficulty in achieving closure (filling in missing parts), difficulty in grasping sequential arrangement, persistent directional difficulty with reversals in reading and writing,
difficulty in integrating (blending) parts into a recognizable whole, and
difficulty in establishing associations between sensory modalities—the
sound of a word or its component elements with its visual equivalent. In
short, the child with severe reading disability shows deficient ability to deal
with the Gestalt aspects of perception and cognition (A. J. Harris, 1961;
de Hirsch, 1962; Drew, 1965; Vernon, 1971).

Visual Perception. Since visual perception has been consistently significant in the measurement of reading readiness, it is not surprising that
persisting difficulties with visual perception are found in many children
with reading disabilities. Visual perception operates most strongly in the
early stages of learning to read (Gredler, 1972). The *Marianne Frostig
Developmental Test of Visual Perception* (DTVP) contains five subtests
called Eye-Motor Coordination, Figure Ground, Constancy of Shape, Position in Space, and Spatial Relationships, with norms to age 8. Factor-analysis
studies tend to show that the DTVP tests only one main factor, which may
be called *visual perception maturity* (P. Smith and Marx, 1972; Ward, 1970;
Olson and Johnson, 1970). The validity of two of the subtests, Figure Ground
and Position in Space, has been questioned (Olson, 1966b; Rosen and
Ohnmacht, 1968), and the usefulness of the DTVP in discriminating poor
readers has been challenged (Pederson, 1971). Some newer tests of visual

perception and still experimental (Rosner, 1973); Newcomer and Hammill, 1973; Rusch, 1970; Turaids, Wepman and Morency, 1972). School and clinical psychologists have for years used formboard and block-design tests to evaluate visual perception.

VISUAL-MOTOR PERFORMANCE. Psychologists have for many years used tests of the ability to copy visual designs as diagnostic tools. The *Bender Visual Motor Gestalt Test* presents a series of designs, one at a time, which the subject is asked to copy. While the products can be scored for age level, more important are such qualitative features as rotations, difficulty with diagonals, inability to place two parts in proper relation to each other, and distortions of the forms (Bender, 1938; Koppitz, 1964). In interpreting the *Bender* test the examiner cannot always be sure if a poor performance is due mainly to perceptual difficulty, to motor control, or to the linking of motor behavior to perception.

The use of the *Bender* test in the diagnosis of learning disabilities has been reviewed by its author (Bender, 1970) and by Keogh (1969). Numerous research studies have come out with somewhat conflicting results. Several recent studies have emphasized the overlapping between the scores of learning disability and normal groups, and have indicated poor differentiation when intelligence is partialled out (Ackerman, Peters, and Dykman, 1971; Henderson, Butler, and Goffeney, 1969; Giebink and Birch, 1970; Connor, 1968–1969). Although the *Bender* does correlate with reading, the relationship is too low to provide much improvement over chance in predicting the reading scores of individuals (Obrutz, Taylor, and Thweatt, 1972). On the other hand, poor readers of average-or-better intelligence have significant frequencies of rotations, distortions, perseveration, and poor integration (Hocker, 1970), and one study has found that the *Bender* can differentiate between "organics" (neurologically deviant) and other types of poor readers, among intelligent, advantaged boys (Stavrianos, 1970). A special adaptation of the *Bender* in which each figure was presented with an extraneous background is reported to differentiate between poor readers and satisfactory readers better than the regular Bender does (Sabatino and Ysseldyke, 1972).

The *Minnesota Percepto-Diagnostic Test* presents three of the *Bender* designs to be copied under three different conditions; the scoring is based on the degree to which the copies are rotated or slanted away from the vertical. Validity data supplied by the author indicate that the test should be helpful in distinguishing neurologically caused conditions from psychogenic emotional conditions and in distinguishing primary reading disability from secondary reading disability and brain damage (Fuller, 1969a, 1969b). Gredler (1968) found that both white and black disadvantaged children had mean scores on this test that fell within the pathological range, although the groups were not seriously retarded in reading and were rated average in emotional adjustment by their teachers. However, Krippner (1966) found a high agreement between scores on this test and an independent criterion. It is evident that the meaning of scores on this test is still uncertain.

Three recent tests utilize the recognition of *Bender* designs in a multiple-choice format as a way of determining whether a low *Bender* score is due more to perceptual or to motor difficulties (Beery, 1967; Fidel and Ray, 1972; Newcomer and Hammill, 1973).

The *Purdue Perceptual-Motor Survey* provides a test battery for aspects of functioning for which Kephart (1960) has provided remedial procedures. The *Oseretsky Motor Proficiency Tests* provide an age scale of development mainly in acts requiring small-muscle skill or finger dexterity.

Visual Memory

Poor memory for sequences of letters, numbers, or words may be found in children of otherwise normal mental ability. Usually it is a sign that the child is anxious or emotionally very tense while taking the test and suggests that anxiety interferes similarly with his efforts to read. More rarely it indicates a special type of intellectual deficiency which would tend to slow up the child's rate of learning even in a good remedial program. When this seems to be the case, one should look for other signs of a possible neurological deviation. Memory tests should usually not be attempted by teachers, but judgments can be formed on the basis of daily work.

A child's inability to remember what a word looks like may be the result of failure to perceive it clearly in the first place. Deficiencies in visual perception are common, if not universal, among children who have serious difficulty in building up a sight vocabulary. In most of these children, the poor visual perception cannot be explained in terms of defective visual acuity; the child can see well enough by vision tests, but he does not notice the finer points in the appearance of words or single letters. Sherlock Holmes's ability to notice and obtain meaning from clues that totally escaped Dr. Watson was not a matter of better eyes, but of a keener mind. Many of the children who have great difficulty in perceiving the details of words have no similar difficulty with tests involving perception of visual forms or numbers; other children show general vagueness in their perception of visual details.

Tests of visual memory are found in the *Monroe-Sherman Group Diagnostic Reading Test,* the *Detroit Tests of Learning Aptitude,* the ITPA, and the *Benton Visual Retention Test.* Poor scores on such tests can be interpreted as indicative of a memory difficulty only if a perceptual difficulty has been ruled out. One should also note that these are tests of short-term memory, while in reading, long-term visual memory is much more important.

Auditory Perception

The four aspects of auditory perception that are most significant for reading are discrimination of words, discrimination of particular phonemes (sounds) within words, auditory closure, and blending ability. The *Wepman Auditory Discrimination Test,* which has been widely used, requires a child to listen to pairs of words and respond as to whether each pair is alike or different; it has been shown that some retarded readers have considerable difficulty with this kind of simple discrimination (Christine and Christine, 1964). New norms have been proposed for the *Wepman* test (Snyder and Pope, 1970) and it was revised in 1973. In the *Goldman-Fristoe-Woodcock Test of Auditory Discrimination* a child selects one of four pictures that represents the word heard (*e.g., cap-cab-cat-catch*). The test material is recorded, there is a training procedure, and the words are presented with both a quiet background and a noisy background. The *Test of Non-Verbal Auditory Discrimination* includes subtests of pitch, loudness, rhythm, duration, and timbre; it is group-administered, seems culture-fair, and has good preliminary validity data (Buktenica, 1971). Oakland (1969) found that phonemic auditory discrimination tests correlated better with reading achievement than nonphonemic tests did.

Group tests that measure ability to determine which of several words begin or end with the same sound are included in several reading readiness tests (see p. 24). This kind of discrimination is probably more closely related to the way reading is usually taught today than deciding whether or not two spoken words are identical; it is also a more difficult kind of task.

It is well established that black inner-city children tend to do quite poorly on most phonemic auditory discrimination tests. An early explanation stressed such social factors as "tuning out" due to living in a noisy environment (C. Deutsch, 1964). Recent evidence indicates that this difficulty is largely due to pronunciation differences between black English and standard English (Elenbogen and Thompson, 1972; Gottesman, 1972).

Blending ability can be tested with the *Roswell-Chall Auditory Blending Test* (see Chall, Roswell, and Blumenthal, 1963), with a subtest of the *Gates-McKillop Reading Diagnostic Tests,* or with the ITPA. Before a child can learn to blend (combine separate sounds into the correct word), he has to be able to hear a spoken word as consisting of separate phonemes; lack of this ability may underlie an inability to blend or synthesize phonemes (Shankweiler and Liberman, 1972). The *Auditory Analysis Test* is a new test which requires a child to listen to a word, mentally subtract either the beginning phoneme or a final phoneme, and pronounce what is left; it seems to have good preliminary evidence of validity (Rosner and Simon, 1971).

Auditory Memory.   An apparent difficulty in auditory memory may be the result of an unrecognized defect in auditory acuity, an auditory perception problem, a failure to comprehend instructions, unfamiliarity with the language or with the dialect of the speaker, inattention, or strong anxiety, as well as occasionally a constitutional memory defect. Tests for both meaningful and rote auditory memory are included in the *Revised Stanford-Binet Intelligence Scale* and the *Detroit Tests of Learning Aptitude.* Rote memory tests are included in the WISC and the ITPA. These all test for short-term memory.

M. H. Neville (1968) found that auditory memory span improved during first grade and seemed to be influenced by the method of instruction; she also concluded that the low memory span found in some poor readers may be due to poor motivation and concentration. In another study, competent readers and retarded readers both improved substantially in memory span and accuracy in repeating directions when they were reinforced by the use of praise, knowledge of progress, and prospect of a reward (Rodgers, 1969). Thus it is clear that a low score on a memory test does not necessarily indicate a memory deficiency. Ability to recall the sequence in which auditory stimuli were heard is necessary for the production of correct responses.

Perception of Touch and Motion

Children in general can identify shapes and forms more readily by visual inspection than by touching and running their fingers over them blindfolded (Gaines and Raskin, 1970). When visual perception or visual memory is inadequate, however, reinforcement of the perceptual image by touching, feeling, or tracing may improve long-term retention of a learned perception.

Integration between Modalities

The importance of the ability to integrate—to fit things together—has been mentioned several times above. Visual closure and auditory blending are two very important kinds of integrative activity for reading. Reading also requires the building of associations between visual perception and auditory perception—between a grapheme and the phoneme it represents, between a written word and the spoken word it represents—and if the child fails at this level, higher reading skills cannot develop. In the early 1960's Birch and his co-workers explored the idea that the major difficulty for poor readers might lie in the ability to match corresponding auditory and visual patterns, such as identifying a visual pattern of dots as similar to a heard series of taps (Birch and Lefford, 1963; Birch and Belmont, 1964). This has been referred to as cross-modal perception or intersensory integration. Recent research indicates that audiovisual integration is significantly related to success in reading, but doesn't add much to prediction based on MA or IQ (Rodenborn, 1970–1971; J. P. Jones, 1970). It is also related to developmental level and economic background (Reilly, 1971). Some recent studies seem to show that cross-modal matching is more difficult than matching within the same modality, and matches involving a shift from sequential to spatial display are even more difficult (Bryden, 1972). Since reading involves matching a graphic pattern that is not sequential with a spoken word that is necessarily perceived sequentially, the task of word recognition should, according to these findings, be a difficult one.

However, not all studies find cross-modal integration to be more difficult than within-modal matching for poor readers. In a recent study, poor readers performed about equally poorly in auditory-auditory, visual-visual, and auditory-visual tasks (Van de Voort, Senf, and Benton, 1972). Deficiencies in attention and in formulating a verbal label for a perceived complex stimulus may be involved, as well as perception and associative learning (Blank and Bridger, 1966). The function of intersensory integration in the causation of reading disabilities is still not completely clear.

Attention

The ability to attend and concentrate is basic to efficiency in perception, learning, and memory. "A characteristic of recent psychological work is the rediscovery of attention. . . . In order to reduce incoming information to an amount that can be effectively handled it would seem . . . that something very like a 'filtering device' must be inserted in the sensory approaches to the brain" (Burt, 1968). Ability to attend and concentrate means that the person can maintain focus on particular stimuli and disregard or suppress other stimulation that reaches him at the same time, thus maintaining a stable figure in the focus of attention, against a noninterfering background.

Malmquist (1958) found that weaknesses in ability to concentrate and in persistence were among the personal characteristics that distinguished children with reading disability in the first grade. Strauss and Lehtinen (1947) stressed that inability to avoid responding to distracting stimuli was a major factor in the learning difficulties of brain-injured children. Cruikshank (1961) also emphasized the importance of reducing possible distractions to a minimum in the learning environment for brain-injured children. The attention problem for neurologically handicapped children is suppressing distracting external stimuli. When difficulties in attending are related to severe emotional disorders rather than to neurological problems, the distractions tend to be internal (thoughts and feelings) rather than external.

Recent studies have shown that children with reading disabilities are less able to sustain attention in a nonreading situation than normal readers (Noland and Schuldt, 1971; Anderson, Halcomb and Doyle, 1973). According to Estes (1970), individual differences in ability to focus attention may be more useful than differences in intelligence to explain variations in rate of learning. Kindergarten children selected as learning disabled by their teachers were observed spending significantly less time in task-oriented behaviors than their classmates; their attention did not stay on the task (Bryan and Wheeler, 1972). One point of view regards inability to pay attention, with accompanying distractibility and impulsiveness, as the central problem of disabled learners (Dykman, *et al.*, 1971).

Failure in any kind of test situation or learning situation may be due to inattention rather than to lack of the basic abilities required by the task. For this reason, diagnostic testing of children should be done individually so that the examiner can observe the child throughout and can evaluate the degree to which attention and concentration were adequate for the task.

Conceptualization

Several writers have expressed the point of view that the major interference with learning to read is not perceptual deficiency or poor memory, but rather confusion and a lack of understanding about the nature and purpose of reading (Vernon, 1957; Vygotsky, 1962; Reid, 1966; Downing, 1969). Vernon stated: "Thus the fundamental and basic characteristic of reading disability appears to be cognitive confusion and lack of system." Reid and Downing interviewed children who had had a few months of reading instruction and found that most of them had vague and inaccurate concepts for such terms as *word, letter,* and *sound,* and their ideas of what their parents do when they read were faulty.

Other lines of research suggest that in many cases reading disability is based more on difficulty with integrating or retrieving the verbal equivalents of perceptual input, than on perceptual deficiency. In a recent study reading disability cases and normal readers observed various kinds of stimuli for three-fifths of a second each, and were asked to reproduce and to read or name the items (Vellutino, Steger, and Kandel, 1972). There were no differences between the two groups on geometric designs or digits; little difference on scrambled letters and short words copied; but large differences on words read and spelled correctly. The authors concluded that the most basic difficulties of the poor readers were in verbal mediation and expression and in visual-verbal association, rather than in perception. Blank and Bridger (1966) had children match a simultaneous pattern of lights with a sequential pattern of lights. Both good and poor readers used verbal number labels as they viewed the stimuli, but the poor readers made many errors in the labels they assigned, and thus made more incorrect responses. Second-grade inner-city children with reading disabilities were able to learn the English equivalents of thirty Chinese characters and to read sentences written with those characters, leading the investigators to conclude that the children's difficulty was not with visual perception but rather an inability to cope with the abstract nature of phonemes (Rozin, Poritsky, and Sotsky, 1971). Seven-year-olds who did poorly on visual perception tests but did well on Piaget-type tasks were able to succeed in reading, showing that ability to do inferential reasoning can compensate in some cases for perceptual immaturity (Halpern, 1970).

In summarizing the recent evidence on conceptualization, it seems probable that lack of understanding of important terms used by teachers in reading instruction, confusion about the nature and purposes of reading, difficulty in grasping the idea of separable phonemes and their relation to graphemes, difficulty with labeling, and poor ability in inferential reasoning may all handicap a child in learning to read. These may be present with or without perceptual difficulties.

Cognitive Style

Cognitive style refers to the tendency to prefer certain ways of handling cognitive tasks to other ways. The preferred way may be a relatively strong aptitude, or a fairly consistent behavioral tendency. Some explorations of cognitive style seem relevant to the understanding of reading disabilities.

The *Children's Associative Responding Test* is a new test which measures the child's tendency to respond, in a verbal analogies test, with a common association rather than with the most logical response. Thus, in the item: *large* is to *small* as *good* is to (*night, bad, better, worse*), "night" is an incorrect common association while "bad" is the logical correct response. The test's author reports that for children with a high number of common associations this test has higher correlations with grades and achievement tests than intelligence tests such as the *Stanford-Binet* and *Otis*; for children with few common association responses, its correlations with achievement equal those of the intelligence tests (Achenbach, 1970).

According to Kagan (1965), the tendency to be impulsive or reflective is significantly related to the number of errors made in word recognition and connected reading by first- and second-grade children; the impulsive children tended to respond on the basis of the first letter of a word, or the first or last syllable in a longer word. Kagan suggested that such errors may be due more to an impulsive disposition than to a perceptual difficulty. In another study, boys with severe learning disabilities were found to be impulsive, and boys with either moderate or severe learning disabilities were found to be highly field dependent (Keogh and Donlon, 1972).

Marietta (1971–1972) tried to synthesize Guilford's model of   the dimensions of intellectual aptitudes with the personality dimensions developed by Witkin, Klein, and Gardner. He came out with four levels: 1) focal attention; 2) breadth of scanning—ability to detect patterns and ideas; 3) equivalence range—ability to sort and classify; and 4) leveling and sharpening—discriminating the relevant from the irrevelant, synthesizing, and sequencing. All of these would seem relevant to an understanding of reading problems, but no specific application of this conceptual scheme to reading has yet been made.

V. IDENTIFICATION OF SPECIFIC SUBGROUPS
OF READING DISABILITY

Although research studies continue to be published in which a group of children with reading disability (or sometimes a more broadly defined learning disability) is compared with a group of normal readers, the many important differences within the disabled population tend to be ignored or overlooked when emphasis is placed on a comparison of group averages. It would seem much more promising if the disabled population could be divided into subgroups, each with its own special characteristics. A number of attempts to do this have been made.

Rabinovitch (1959, 1962), a psychiatrist, proposed a classification of three main groups. Primary reading retardation includes cases with a basic disturbance in the pattern of neurological organization, without evidence of definite brain damage. Secondary reading retardation includes all cases in which the causation is not primarily within the nervous system, and thus covers such varied characteristics as impaired vision, emotional maladjustment, and environmental deprivation. His third category is brain damage with reading retardation. Rabinovitch's concept of primary reading retardation is quite similar to Critchley's (1970) concept of developmental dyslexia.

Bannatyne (1971) has proposed a classification of the causes and types of dyslexia (a term which he uses quite broadly, as the equivalent of reading disability) into four main categories. These are: 1) primary emotional communicative causes, such as parental rejection or neglect; 2) minimal neurological dysfunction, involving a disorder of one or more of visual-spatial, auditory, integrative, conceptual, or tactual and kinesthetic functioning; 3) social, cultural, or educational deprivation; and 4) genetic dyslexia, characterized by a strong tendency to run in families. Bannatyne differs from Rabinovitch in not attempting to distinguish brain damage from neurological dysfunction, and in setting "genetic dyslexia" apart from neurological dysfunction.

Wiener and Cromer (1967) postulated the existence of four different types of reading difficulty, each employing a different etiology and remediation: 1) *defect* attributable to some malfunction (*e.g.*, sensory-physiological factors) that prevents the learner from benefiting from his experience; 2) *deficiency* attributable to the absence of some function; 3) *disruption* which suggests something (*e.g.*, anxiety) is interfering with reading; and 4) *difference* in which there are differences or mismatches between the typical mode of response and that which is more appropriate.

Hermann (1959) concluded that there is a strong similarity between "congenital word blindness" and Gerstmann's Syndrome, an adult condition produced by cerebral damage in which the most prominent symptoms are right-left confusion, finger agnosia (inability to identify which finger has been touched), and difficulties with arithmetic (dyscalculia) and with handwriting (agraphia). Rabinovitch (1962) considered a Performance IQ higher than Verbal IQ to be one of the typical characteristics of primary reading disability. Recent research indicates that these two characteristics may identify specific subgroups of constitutional reading disability.

Ingram and Reid (1956; Ingram, 1969) studied children with reading disability who were healthy, intelligent, from good environments, and had disparities of 20 or more points between Verbal and Performance IQ's. They reported that those with higher Verbal IQ's more often showed visuospatial errors in reading and spelling, while those with higher Performance IQ's tended to have "audiophonic" difficulties (auditory discrimination, blending, letter-sound association.)

Kinbourne and Warrington (1966) standardized a test of finger identification on normal children and used it with reading disability cases showing large disparities between Verbal and Performance IQ's. Those with low Performance IQ's failed the finger differentiation test and had difficulties in arithmetic, while those with lower Verbal IQ's passed the finger differentiation test and were not disabled in addition and subtraction. They concluded that cerebral deficit may delay acquisition of reading and writing in different ways and that both the Gerstmann and the language-retardation types correspond to a syndrome of retarded cerebral development, however caused. Ingram (1969) has more recently reported evidence from a study of speech-retarded children that the more severe the reading disability, the greater the occurrence of both visuospatial and audiophonic symptoms in the same child. Thus finger identification and disparity between verbal and nonverbal intellectual performance may help to identify two relatively small subgroups within the total reading disability population.

Doehring (1968) reported a study in which a group of thirty-nine seriously disabled readers, age 10 to 14, was compared with a group of normal-reading boys and a group of normal-reading girls, matched with them for age and Performance IQ. A large battery of tests was used which provided 109 different scores. In addition, neurological examinations were given and case histories were obtained. The results were evaluated in several ways, including significance of differences on individual tests; blind analyses of neurological, case history, and selected test data; factor analyses; and case studies. Doehring interpreted his results as showing that deficiencies in sequential processing abilities, both visual and verbal, were intrinsically associated with reading disability. The most discriminating nonreading tests were measures that involved rhyming and rapid visual perception. He suggested that there are probably three types: a perceptual type, a language type, and a mixed type with both visual and verbal deficits. Thus he came to conclusions quite similar to those of Ingram and of Kinbourne and Warrington, despite marked differences in population and tests used.

Further careful research attempting to provide ways to differentiate between different subgroups of reading disability should help greatly in refining diagnostic procedures and providing a sounder basis for selecting remedial procedures.

This chapter has considered the nature of diagnosis, the question of single or pluralistic causation, and the significance of a variety of cognitive factors including intelligence, linguistic skills, visual perception and memory, auditory perception and memory, attention, conceptualization, and cognitive style in the causation of reading disabilities. The discussion of correlated factors continues in the next chapter.

SUGGESTED ADDITIONAL READING

BANNATYNE, ALEXANDER. *Language, reading, and learning disabilities: psychology, neuropsychology, diagnosis, and remediation.* Springfield, Ill.: Charles C Thomas, 1971. Chaps. 2, 3, 4, 7.

FISHBEIN, JUSTIN & EMANS, ROBERT. *A question of competence: language, intelligence, and learning to read.* Chicago: Science Research Associates, 1972.

FROSTIG, MARIANNE & MASLOW, PHYLLIS. *Learning problems in the classroom: prevention and remediation.* New York: Grune and Stratton, 1973. Chaps. 8, 13, 14.

KAVANAGH, JAMES F. & MATTINGLY, IGNATIUS. (Eds.), *Language by ear and eye: the relationships between speech and reading.* Cambridge, Mass.: MIT Press, 1972.

ROBECK, MILDRED C. & WILSON, JOHN A. R. *Psychology of reading: foundations of instruction.* New York: John Wiley and Sons, 1974. Chaps. 3, 4.

RUDDELL, ROBERT B. *Reading—language instruction: innovative practices.* Englewood Cliffs, N.J.: Prentice-Hall, 1974. Chaps. 2, 3, 4.

SEBESTA, SAM L. & WALLEN, CARL J. (Eds.). *The first R: readings on teaching reading.* Chicago: Science Research Associates, 1972. Pp. 86–128.

11

Correlates
of Reading Disabilities,
II: Physical and Physiological
Factors

In this chapter, the study of the correlates of reading disabilities continues. The main topics to be discussed are: neurological factors, lateral dominance, heredity, sensory defects, and other physical conditions.

I. NEUROLOGICAL FACTORS

Since reading is one of the most difficult, abstract, and symbolic human activities, it requires a brain that is functioning within normal limits. For a long time American psychologists and educators minimized the neurological aspects of reading disabilities. Since the pioneer work of Strauss and Lehtinen (1947), the diagnosis of learning disability based on minimal brain damage or minimal brain dysfunction has increased to the point where it is now probably used excessively. The brain is an incredibly complex organ, and knowledge of how it works in normal learning and in faulty learning is still meagre and inconclusive.

Neurological deviations of brain functioning that can interfere with learning to read can arise in five main ways:

1. The number of children who are brain-injured at birth and survive to grow up has increased greatly with improved medical care. Those who have obvious motor difficulties (cerebral palsy) are comparatively easy to identify. Gesell was one of the first to state that many cases of minimal birth injury to the brain show no obvious physical handicaps, but there is impairment of the ability to master language and reading (Gesell and Amatruda, 1941).

2. Brain tissue may be injured during childhood by diseases such as encephalitis. One of the writers' cases was a normal youngster until he lost his ability to speak following a high fever at age 2. All language functions developed slowly from then on, and learning to read required an unremitting effort for several years.

3. There are some rare cases of congenital and acquired brain defects of a specialized kind. For example, a teen-age nonreader of dull-normal intelligence was referred by one of the writers for neurological examination. Skull X-rays revealed a large undeveloped area in one part of his brain (porencephaly). Robb (1958) summarized evidence from the Montreal Neurological Institute, arriving at the conclusion that "minimal organic brain disease in the occipital region can be a cause of reading disabilities. Further, that the concomitant emotional and behavior disorders may not be the cause of the reading disability, but the result either of the brain injury, or secondary reaction to the reading problem."

4. There may be a pattern of growth in which the brain matures in an irregular pattern, with some functions developing normally and others much delayed. Bender's (1957) concept of developmental lag, Critchley's (1970) concept of dyslexia, and Rabinovitch's (1962) concept of primary reading disability emphasize delayed and irregular maturation. Rabinovitch described the common characteristics of these children (aside from their reading difficulties) as including lateness in learning to talk and somewhat immature speech patterns, vagueness and inaccuracy in visual and auditory perception, a directional confusion which involves not only difficulty with the left-right direction but also confusion about other kinds of space and time relationships, and a difficulty with part-whole relationships. He suggested that the more severe the reading disability, the more likely it is to be constitutional in origin.

5. There may be an inadequacy of brain functioning due to some biochemical peculiarity, without any structural defect in brain tissue. D. E. P. Smith and Carrigan (1959) attempted to explain all the different kinds of symptoms found in reading disabilities—the context reader, the word-caller, and others—in terms of two chemicals (acetylcholine and cholinesterase) which are probably involved in the conduction of nerve impulses in the brain. Using a special battery of tests, they differentiated five groups of cases and provided a physiological explanation of each. They

also tried, unsuccessfully, to demonstrate a relationship of these patterns to endocrine functioning.

Although the Smith-Carrigan research is open to criticism on many grounds and their explanations must be regarded as still in the realm of unproved hypotheses, they have opened up a new area for research which may prove fruitful in the future (A. J. Harris, 1960).

Symptoms that may lead a psychologist or teacher to suggest a neurological examination include the following: a history of difficult birth, with prolonged labor, instrumental delivery, marked deformity of the head, difficulty in getting breathing started, cyanosis, difficulty in sucking and swallowing, and so on; prematurity; poor equilibrium and general awkwardness; delayed speech development with otherwise normal mental ability; a history of convulsive seizures or lapses of consciousness; extreme restlessness and distractibility.

Diagnosis of a neurological problem calls for expert medical study, which at best is still beset with uncertainties. Birch (1964) has pointed out that the term "brain-damaged" is inadequate because there are many varieties of brain-damaged children, and the functional consequences may range from no discernible abnormality in functioning to complete paralysis and profound mental deficiency. The variety which is sometimes called the Strauss Syndrome has attracted the most attention. Such children are described as hyperactive and restless, emotionally very changeable, showing disorders of perception, impulsive, very distractible, and at times abnormally rigid and perseverative. Diagnosing a child as "brain-damaged" on the basis of such characteristics is drawing an inference from behavior, not stating a medically demonstrated conclusion.

One of the techniques used by neurologists is recording the electrical activity of the brain by taking an EEG (electroencephalogram). Although abnormal EEG's have been found in roughly half of several child populations diagnosed as having dyslexia or minimal brain dysfunction, similar "abnormal" records have been found in over 20 per cent of normal learners in control groups (Ayers and Torres, 1967; Muehl, Knott and Benton, 1965; Hughes, 1968, 1971). The EEG does not seem helpful in indicating specific areas of intellectual or academic impairment (Hartlage and Green, 1973). The value of including an EEG as part of the diagnostic study of children with learning disabilities has been questioned (Dyment, Lattin, and Herbertson, 1971; Freeman, 1971; Tymchuk, Knights and Hinton, 1970). Although new ways of interpreting the EEG through the use of computers may improve its accuracy (Conners, 1970; Ross, Childers, and Perry, 1973; Martinius and Hoovey, 1972; Shields, 1973), at present it is not particularly helpful to the psychologist or reading specialist to have the results of an EEG examination available.

With regard to the neurological examination of children, Kennedy and Ramirez (1964) concluded that in the majority of cases the question of the presence or absence of cerebral defect is left unanswered by X-rays of the skull or pneumoencephalography, and that the typical neurological examination does not reveal very much about the neurological basis of the higher mental processes. The diagnosis of "minimal cerebral dysfunction" is often made on the basis of "soft signs" which are of doubtful validity (Schain, 1972). Medical verdicts on the presence or absence of brain damage or dysfunction are not always made on the firmest of grounds, and the younger the child, the more difficult it is to distinguish between damage and simple immaturity which will be outgrown. The most severe reading disability can be present in a child who shows no neurological evidence of brain damage (Ingram, Mason, and Blackburn, 1970).[1]

Many clinical and school psychologists have in recent years interpreted certain kinds of performance on special psychological tests of perception, visual-motor functioning, and so on, as indicating "organicity" or "brain damage." Such interpretations should always be regarded as suggestive rather than conclusive. Even when evidence pointing to neurological irregularity is strong, psychological testing cannot as yet distinguish accurately between "minimal brain damage" and "delayed and irregular neurological development," or indicate the location and nature of brain damage if it exists (Rubino, 1972). This is in line with Birch's (1964) emphasis on the variety of symptoms that can be produced by brain damage, depending on its location, size, and type.

Hyperactivity

As we have seen, hyperactivity, distractibility, and difficulty in paying sustained attention are prominent among the characteristics that have been ascribed to severe reading disability, and are sometimes assumed to be indicators of cerebral dysfunction. Keogh (1971b), in reviewing the literature on hyperactivity in relation to learning disorders, concluded that the findings have been inconsistent and inconclusive. She proposed three main types of hyperactivity: 1) an accompaniment of cerebral dysfunction; 2) cases in which excessive activity disrupts attention and interferes with learning, without evidence of cerebral dysfunction; and 3) impulsiveness in making decisions, similar to Kagan's impulsive-reflective dimension of cognitive style. Keogh proposed that the first type be treated by medication

---

1. A very recent paper by two psychiatrists, J. Frank and H. N. Levinson (*Journal of Child Psychiatry*, 1974, *12*, 690), reports evidence of a cerebellar-vestibular dysfunction in 97 per cent of 115 dyslexic children. If confirmed, this could be a major breakthrough in the causal explanation of severe reading disability.

and the other two by behavioral management techniques. Marwit and Stenner (1972) pointed out that the term hyperactivity or hyperkinesis involves overactivity, impulsivity, low frustration tolerance, short attention span, distractibility, and excessive aggression. They attempted to provide criteria for distinguishing between cases that are neurologically based and those that are emotional in origin. It should be noted, also, that some psychiatrists differentiate between impulsivity, which is described as a kind of "driven" behavior that is internally determined and does not seem to be set off by particular stimuli, and the kind of hyperactivity and distractibility which involves excessive responsiveness to stimuli which most children can ignore; the former, often an aftereffect of encephalitis, is the more serious.

Despite some public outcry against drug treatment for hyperactive children, medical opinion seems to be quite favorable to the use of such drugs as Ritalin, thorazine, and dextro-amphetamine to control hyperactivity (Whitsell, Buckman, and Whitsell, 1970; Laufer, 1971; Oettinger, 1971). When a correct dosage is achieved, behavior often calms down and better learning is possible. Continuing medical supervision is necessary to check for possible undesirable side effects and to adjust dosage as necessary.

Prenatal Conditions and Prematurity

Kawi and Pasamanick (1958) compared the early medical histories of 205 boys of normal intelligence but retarded two or more years in reading, with a similar number of controls. In the reading disabled group, 16.6 per cent had been exposed during the prenatal period to two or more maternal complications such as preeclampsia, hypertensive disease, and bleeding; only 1.5 per cent of the controls had histories of this kind. Over 11 per cent of the disabled, and only 4.6 per cent of the normals, weighed less than 5.5 pounds at birth. The significance of these findings is that prematurity and the complications studied all can be associated with deficient oxygen for the fetus or newborn, and thus can induce brain damage. Poor readiness and poor early reading achievement for children born prematurely have also been reported by other investigators (de Hirsch, Jansky, and Langford, 1966a; Corrigan, *et al.*, 1967). Questions about early development are items to be included when taking a case history.

The Frequency of Neurological Patterns in Reading Disability

It would be quite helpful to know what proportion of disabled readers shows signs of neurological involvement, and particularly to have some idea of the prevalence of some of the patterns of symptoms that have been discussed above. Denckla (1972) attempted to classify 190 disabled readers seen in private practice, using an "extended neurological examination." Seventy per cent of the total group did not fit into any clear-cut group. The remaining 30 per cent fell into three syndromes, which we have met before. 1) Fifteen per cent had specific language disabilities, without perceptual deficits but with "poor visuomotor and audiovisual circuits." 2) Five per cent had specific visuo-spatial difficulties similar to the Gerstmann Syndrome, with left-right confusion, poor finger localization, poor visuo-spatial abilities, low Performance IQ, more difficulty with arithmetic and writing than with reading and oral spelling, and emotional problems. 3) Ten per cent fitted a "dyscontrol syndrome" and were characterized as impulsive, "sweet, silly, and sloppy"; one-third had a parent with similar characteristics and two-thirds had histories of possible brain injury at or near birth; and they tended to respond favorably to Ritalin or Dexedrine.

Denckla's results have been summarized in some detail for two reasons. First, they provide a tentative estimate of the frequency within the total reading disability population of some of the patterns that have been identified in recent research. Second, her estimate of 30 per cent with clear constitutional bases comes close to the estimate of 25 per cent which the senior author arrived at several years ago, on the basis of his own clinical experience. It seems probable that 70 to 80 per cent of disabled readers do not fall into the constitutional patterns described above.

Delayed and Irregular Neurological Development

As we have seen, there is a substantial body of medical opinion to the effect that severe reading disability is often the result of some delay in the maturing of the nervous system, slight enough to allow the development of normal general intelligence, but enough to slow down the development of abilities that are critical for learning to read. To do this, the delay or lag in development would affect only certain parts of the brain, with the rest developing normally (Bender, 1957; Rabinovitch, 1962: Critchley, 1970). Lags would not necessarily have to be all alike, so this idea allows for more than one pattern of deficits. A corollary is that as children with neurological lags get older some or all of the lagging abilities should improve sufficiently to allow improved reading.

Satz has added to this idea the theory that the kinds of abilities in which severely disabled readers are deficient change as the child gets older (Satz and Sparrow, 1970; Satz and van Nostrand, 1973). He hypothesized that young children with lags should be delayed in laterality, then in perceptual-spatial and cross-modal integration abilities, which would catch up to normal by the age of 10 or so; and that older disabled readers should be more delayed in language integration skills. His findings have been inconsistent, but give some support to his theory. Satz's analysis lumped all his reading disability cases together and did not attempt to distinguish subgroups; by depending only on a comparison of means, significant differences within his reading disability groups may have canceled one another out in the process of averaging.

Heredity

The fact that heredity has been considered an important factor in reading disability by some writers has already been noted. The monograph by Hallgren (1950) in which the families of 276 disabled readers were found to contain a large number of other individuals with reading disabilities and speech defects is often cited. When one of a pair of identical twins has a reading disability, nearly always the other twin has a similar problem, while this happens in only one-third of pairs of fraternal twins (Norrie, 1954; cited by Bannatyne, 1971). In the United States, Walker and Cole (1965) studied the families of boys with reading disabilities and found a large number of fathers and brothers with similar problems. An occasional family in which several members have reading disabilities comes to the attention of a clinic (Michal-Smith, et al., 1970). It would be difficult to deny that reading disability seems to run in certain families.

On the other hand, some studies of unselected populations have failed to find significant evidence of familial reading disability (Clark, 1970; de Hirsch, Jansky, and Langford, 1966b). Assuming that there are some families in which a constitutional predisposition toward reading disability is inherited, mainly by the males, the incidence of such families probably varies in different populations, and in some populations is too small to be statistically significant.

Bannatyne (1971) lists "genetic dyslexia" as one of the four main types of dyslexia and estimates that about one-third of all cases of dyslexia are of this type, comprising about 2 per cent of the general population. We believe that his estimate is substantially too high. Among the traits that he considers to be characteristic of genetic dyslexia are the following: poor auditory discrimination, particularly of vowels; poor memory for auditory sequences; poor blending ability; often, mild speech delay or defect; reasonably good to superior visuo-spatial ability; tendency to make reversals in reading and writing; difficulty learning to make left-to-right eye movements; difficulty in associating verbal labels with directional concepts; vulnerable to emotional disturbance; and tendency to have fathers in occupations in which spatial abilities are more important than verbal abilities (Bannatyne, 1971, pp. 402–405).

There is a strong resemblance between this list of characteristics, or most of them, and Rabinovitch's description of primary reading retardation; also with Ingram's group with "audiophonic" difficulties (see pp. 137, 260). A genetic basis for this constellation of characteristics has yet to be established, however, nor is it clear how many of these symptoms would have to be present to warrant classifying a child in such a pattern or syndrome, or which symptoms, if any, are minimum essentials for such a classification.

McGlannan (1968) reported a pilot study of sixty-five families having a child attending a school for disabled learners and hypothesized that there is a "vulnerable family syndrome" in which excessive and insufficient amounts of blood sugar and disturbances involving serotonin, histamine, and histadine are prevalent. As yet, no substantiating evidence has come to our attention and no relation between reading disability and either diabetes or allergic disturbances has been established.

One final note of caution seems necessary. When a boy grows up in a home with a father who has had trouble with reading, imitation and emulation can play an unknown part in the degree to which the son's behavior resembles that of his father. Even with twin studies, the possibility exists that one twin has learned a behavioral pattern from the other. Thus, while there is a strong presumption that inherited constitutional characteristics are involved in some families, the whole question of the relative importance of heredity and environment in the production of reading disabilities is far from being solved.

II. LATERAL DOMINANCE

One of the most puzzling and controversial issues in the whole field of reading is the significance of lateral dominance. By lateral dominance is meant the preferred use and superior functioning of one side of the body over the other. A person who uses his right hand in preference to the left and is more skillful with the right hand shows right-hand dominance. Similarly, the person who relies predominantly on his left hand shows left-hand dominance. Hand dominance has interested people for hundreds of years. The left-handed, because they are a minority, have often been regarded with suspicion. The word "sinister," which originally meant left, now means evil or ominous, and the word "dextrous," meaning skillful, comes from the Latin word meaning right-handed.

Many people are unaware of the fact that they also show a definite eye dominance, or preference for one eye in tasks such as aiming, looking into a microscope, and so on, which can be done with only one eye at a time.

The dominant (preferred) eye is usually but not always the eye with stronger acuity. In about one out of three people, it is on the opposite side of the body from the dominant hand. Foot dominance and ear dominance have been but little studied.

Dominance is said to be *crossed* when the dominant hand and dominant eye are on opposite sides of the body. *Mixed handedness* (or mixed hand dominance) means that the individual does not show a consistent preference for either hand or does not perform consistently better with the preferred hand; this includes ambidexterity and cases with a slight preference for one hand. *Mixed eyedness* means a lack of consistent preference, in sighting, for one eye. The term "mixed dominance" was used in former editions of this book to include both crossed dominance and mixed handedness or eyedness. Since recent research tends to show that mixed handedness is related to poor reading, while crossed dominance and mixed eyedness probably are not, the use of the term "mixed dominance" is no longer recommended. *Converted* hand dominance means that the person formerly preferred the other hand; usually it refers to the preferred use of the right hand by formerly left-handed individuals.

Sidedness and Brain Dominance

Neurologists regard the cerebral hemisphere that controls speech as the dominant or major hemisphere. It used to be thought (by Orton, for example) that the centers for speech are located in the left hemisphere in right-handed people and in the right hemisphere in left-handed people. Recent research indicates that the left hemisphere is dominant for speech in most left-handed people as well as in nearly all right-handed people.

The most dependable test of the dominant hemisphere for speech is the Wada test, in which sodium amytal (a barbiturate) is injected into the carotid artery on one side of the neck, producing a temporary aphasia (loss or disturbance of speech) if the dominant hemisphere for speech is on the same side as the injected artery. Using this test, Rossi and Rosadini (1967) found that 98.6 per cent of right-handed and 71.4 per cent of left-handed patients had speech dominance in the left hemisphere; they also found two cases of speech representation in both hemispheres, one of whom was right-handed and the other ambidextrous. In commenting on that report Milner (1967) stated that in 212 consecutive neurological patients of hers, there were 18 in whom some speech disturbance was found on both sides after injection, indicating that both hemispheres were involved in the control of speech. Of these, 17 were left-handed or ambidextrous and only one was right-handed.

The right hemisphere is dominant for handedness in left-handers, although not for speech in most of them. Recent evidence from a variety of kinds of studies have shown that people restricted to the use of the non-dominant hemisphere can recognize words, manage verbal associations, and make associations between visual, auditory, and tactile spheres. The nondominant hemisphere tends to be superior to the dominant hemisphere in visual constructional tasks and is involved in perception of and memory for melodies (Masland, 1967).

Dichotic Listening. Recently there has been considerable interest in the use of dichotic listening (sometimes called auditory rivalry) to identify the dominant ear, and therefore the hemisphere that is dominant for speech. In such a test the subject listens through earphones while a different set of stimuli is presented to each ear; for example, the right ear may be exposed to "one, three" while the left ear is simultaneously exposed to "five, eight." This is repeated with many pairs. The number of stimuli correctly reported is counted for each ear, and the ear with the higher score is considered to be the dominant ear (Kimura, 1961, 1967). This test has obvious advantages over the Wada test since no injection is required and there is not even a brief impairment of functioning; it is, however, less conclusive. Results are somewhat variable depending on details of technique, and the proportion of children showing a definite ear dominance increases between the ages of 7 and 10 with a significant difference between right-handers and left-handers not appearing until sixth grade (Bryden, 1964, 1970). The relation between dichotic listening and reading is not clear. Some studies have found a higher frequency of left-ear (right hemisphere) dominance in disabled readers (Sparrow, 1968; Bryden, 1970) while others have not (Zurif, and Carson, 1970).

Eye Dominance. Eye dominance is not represented in one hemisphere the way hand dominance and speech dominance usually are. Instead, the left half of the visual field of each eye has nerve connections to the right hemisphere, and the right half of each visual field connects with the left hemisphere. When one eye is dominant, both hemispheres are involved; and if the visual area in one hemisphere is injured, part of the visual field of each eye is lost. Thus the neurological significance of eye dominance is obscure (Mountcastle, 1962).

Theories of Lateral Dominance in Relation to Reading

Hundreds of investigations have been made on the relationships between different types of lateral dominance and the presence of many different kinds of defects, including not only reading, writing, and spelling difficulties but also speech defects, delinquency, and nervous disorders. Many investigators have concluded that reading disability is less common among children who show consistent right-sided dominance than among the consistently left-sided and those showing mixed or converted dominance. Many other studies have come out with negative results. There is a tendency for reports based on intensive clinical studies to find a relationship, while surveys of large numbers of school children tend to give negative findings. This difference may have two reasons: the use of more complete tests in the clinical studies, and the inclusion of a higher proportion of very severe cases of reading disability in the clinical studies than in the school surveys. The writers have become convinced that there is more than a chance relationship between lateral dominance and reading disability.

The most widely discussed theory relating dominance to reading is that of Samuel T. Orton, a neurologist. Orton assumed that the right-sided person develops memory traces for printed words in a part of the left hemisphere and also develops memory traces in the right hemisphere which are mirror images of those on the dominant side. In the consistently left-sided person, the right hemisphere is similarly dominant. When the person with clear dominance reads, only the memory traces on the dominant side are aroused. If, however, the individual fails to develop a consistent dominance of one side over the other, there will be confusion and conflict between the two sides of the brain; reversal errors will be prevalent, and the child will have great difficulty in learning to read and spell. Orton suggested the term "strephosymbolia" (twisted symbols) to describe what he called "*the* reading disability" and seemed uninterested in reading problems that could be explained on other grounds (Orton, 1937).

The Orton theory has been a controversial issue for over thirty-five years. Although recent neurological research has shown that there are a few people with speech centers in both sides of the brain, the presence of such a condition as a causal factor in reading disability has not been proved; and dominance has been found to be neurologically very complicated.

Another major theory is that of Dearborn (1933). Dearborn said that it is easier for the left-handed person to move his left hand from right to left than from left to right and easier for the left-eyed person to look from right to left than from left to right. Deviations from right-sidedness, then, would be expected to be accompanied by greater than average tendencies to move the eyes in the wrong direction in reading. With a lack of consistent preference for either side, confusion in the direction of eye movements in reading and reversals and other types of word recognition difficulties would be expected.

Zangwill (1962) has pointed out that although an excess of left-handedness among children with reading disability has been noted by some authors, by far the most frequent finding is that of weak, mixed, or inconsistent lateral preferences.

> On balance, the evidence suggests that an appreciable proportion of dyslexic children show poorly developed laterality and that in these there is commonly evidence of slow speech development. . . . If poorly developed laterality can be linked with incomplete cerebral dominance, it might be said that these patterns of disability reflect faulty establishment of asymmetrical (*i.e.*, normally lateralized) functions in the two hemispheres. (1962, p. 111)

Zangwill suggested three possible explanations: 1) both the reading disability and the poorly developed laterality are results of actual brain damage; 2) some with ill-defined laterality have a constitutional weakness in maturation which is possibly hereditary; and 3) children without strong lateral preferences may be particularly vulnerable to the effects of stress.

His point of view has received some experimental support from a study by Anthony (1968), who found that disabled readers with mixed dominance did more poorly on the *Bender, Benton Directionality,* and *Birch Audio-Visual Integration* tests than disabled readers with a dominant hand.

Kephart (1960) has emphasized the importance of laterality and directionality for learning. Laterality, in Kephart's sense, is awareness of the two sides of the body and ability to identify them as left and right. Directionality is the ability to project this correctly into the outside world, as in knowing which is the right hand of a person facing you.

Benton developed a test of laterality in terms of ability to identify the right and left sides correctly and found deviant responses in 30 per cent of 8- to 10-year-old reading disability cases. He concluded that "within the broad category of children with reading disability, there may be a special group characterized by confusion in handedness, impaired left-right discrimination, and other evidence of body-schema disturbance and neurologic abnormality and whose reading disability may reasonably be interpreted as the resultant of a global neurologic maldevelopment" (Benton, 1959, p. 57). A simiar emphasis was placed on left-right discrimination by Belmont and Birch (1965).

According to Rabinovitch, left-right problems are part of a larger conceptual deficiency in orientation, in which the child's ability to translate perceptions into symbols is poor. "Thus the child has no difficulty in telling which of two people is taller but he cannot define their heights in feet. Similarly he is well aware of the fact that school is closed in the hot weather but he cannot define that season as summer" (Rabinovitch, 1962, p. 77).

Measuring Lateral Dominance

Since perfect consistency in handedness, or in eye, ear, or foot dominance, is the exception rather than the rule, it is highly desirable to use a variety of tests. The *Harris Tests of Lateral Dominance* have been widely used. They include a brief test of ability to identify left and right; hand dominance measures including a test of ten hand preferences, simultaneous writing with both hands (to detect mirror writing with the dominant hand), and tests of relative speed and coordination in writing, tapping, and dealing cards with each hand. The eye-dominance tests include eye preferences in sighting with one eye, and the controlling eye when both eyes are open. There are two tests of foot dominance. The series is reasonably comprehensive and takes little time to administer (A. J. Harris, 1957). It is available in English, and also in French and Flemish translations.

Bannatyne has attempted to measure unlearned as distinguished from learned handedness. The "unlearned" tests include folding arms, clasping hands with fingers interlocked, and touching the left ear with a particular hand. The "learned" tests include speed of writing, piling up cards, and which hand is uppermost when clapping hands (Bannatyne and Wichiarajote, 1969). The rationale for his selection of tests is not completely convincing.

Silver and Hagin have strongly recommended the *Schilder Arm-Extension Test* as an indicator of deviant lateral dominance. In this test the subject stands with arms extended forward, eyes closed. The normal response is for the hand used in writing to be a little higher than the other hand. They reported that in a population of severely disabled readers from the Psychiatric Division of Bellevue Hospital, 94 per cent made atypical responses on this test (Silver and Hagin, 1964). However, in a recent study this test failed to differentiate between fifty satisfactory readers and fifty retarded readers at junior high school level (Bell, Lewis, and Bell, 1972). This does not rule out the possibility that the test may be useful at younger ages, but more evidence is needed.

The *D-K Scale of Lateral Dominance* is a 36-item scale covering handedness, footedness, eyedness, and ear dominance (Dusewicz and Kershner, 1969). Kershner (1970) found it expedient to combine use of the *Harris* tests for hand and eye dominance with the D-K tests for foot and ear dominance.

One of the reasons for the great variation in the results of research on lateral dominance is the variety of inadequate tests of laterality used in many of the studies. Handedness has been measured in such ways as simply questioning the child, his teacher, or his parent; noting the hand used in writing; or determining which hand is preferred more often in a specified list of activities. In general, tests that measure the speed and accuracy of doing certain tasks with each hand are more satisfactory than tests of pref-erences (Annett, 1970; Barnsley, 1971). Many investigators have ignored the category of ambidexterity or mixed handedness and have forced their in-between records into right or left, thus throwing out what is probably the most significant category. Some researchers have been interested only in the question of crossed dominance, hand and eye being on opposite sides; an issue that seems not very significant.

Recent Research on Lateral Dominance and Reading

Fairly recent reviews of the literature on reading and laterality have been prepared by Weintraub (1968), Zeman (1967), and Bφ (1972). Un-fortunately, the first two of these ignored the medical literature. Without attempting a comprehensive review here, it is pertinent to note that much of the research in this area has been faulty. Some of the reasons for negative or inconclusive results are as follows: 1) failure to use tests that are sensitive to mixed handedness and directional confusion; 2) failure to use large enough groups of disabled readers in making comparisons with school populations; 3) emphasis on crossed eye-hand dominance rather than on mixed handedness; 4) use of children age 10 or older, by which time most of the children with mixed-hand dominance and/or directional confusion have outgrown these symptoms; and 5) expectation by some researchers that disabled readers with atypical dominance should be poorer in reading than other disabled readers.

There is a preponderance of evidence that confusion in applying the labels "left" and "right" first to oneself and at a later age to others is sig-nificantly more common among disabled readers than among unselected children (A. J. Harris, 1957; Benton, 1959; Belmont and Birch, 1965; A. Cohen and Glass, 1968; Shearer, 1968; Ginsburg and Hartwick 1971; Croxen and Lytton, 1971).

Measures of handedness tend to show developmental changes with increasing age, with a decreasing percentage with mixed handedness, a marked increase in right-handedness, and a small increase in left-handedness (A. J. Harris, 1957; Shearer, 1968). All but about 7 per cent of unselected children have a definite handedness by age 7, while 30 per cent of disabled readers have mixed handedness at age 7, dropping to 6 per cent by age 9 (A. J. Harris, 1957). Mixed handedness is related to reading performance in the first grade, but the relationship has disappeared by the fourth grade (A. Cohen and Glass, 1968).

Eye dominance does not show developmental changes with age (A. J. Harris, 1957). Most recent studies show no relationship between crossed eye-hand dominance and reading disability (A. J. Harris, 1957; Boos, 1970;

Ginsburg and Hartwick, 1971; Helveston, Billips, and Weber, 1970; A. Cohen, 1969; opposed, Forness and Weil, 1970).

Hand dominance and ear dominance are strongly related. They are in agreement in nearly all right-handers. About two-thirds of left-handers show right-ear dominance and the rest show either left-ear dominance or no clear ear dominance. Neurological evidence indicates that speech representation in both hemispheres is found occasionally, and nearly always the person is left-handed or ambidextrous (see p. 270). As yet the connection between representation of speech in both hemispheres and reading disability is indirect. Newton (1970) compared the EEG's from the two hemispheres in disabled readers and found that they tend to show less than the normal amount of difference between the hemispheres in electrical activity. It may well be that further research in this area will furnish support for a modified version of the Orton theory.

Shimrat (1970) studied the relationship between the direction in which a language is written and children's handedness. She tested groups who were learning to write English only, to write Hebrew only (right-to-left, in Israel), and children who were being taught to write both languages at the same time. The right-handed were more proficient in writing in a left-to-right direction (English), while the left-handed were equally fast in both directions but made more errors in the left-to-right direction. Those taught both languages simultaneously showed less efficient writing and some directional confusion. This study gives some support to the Dearborn theory.

Despite the large amount of attention and the many researches done on lateral dominance, its true significance for reading is still somewhat uncertain.

Directional Confusion

The significant question probably is whether or not a person shows directional confusion, rather than what pattern of lateral dominance he has. Directional confusion is typically shown by the presence of reversals in reading. It may also show up in spelling and the writing of numbers, in typing, or in speech in the form of stuttering. In some cases there seems to be a related difficulty in distinguishing east from west or downtown from uptown.

Such directional confusion can be present with any pattern of lateral dominance, including complete right-sidedness, but it is most likely to occur in those with mixed hand dominance as measured by the *Harris* tests.

It seems probable that there is a physiological basis for the directional confusion in many cases. Many of the children showing severe reading disability with directional confusion are cases of delayed and irregular neurological maturation. Some of these children have birth histories that suggest minimal brain damage. In other cases inquiry into the development of the child's siblings and parents reveals that the pattern of delay in establishing dominance of one hand, a strong reversal tendency, some speech difficulty, and early difficulty in learning to read characterizes several members of the family, suggesting a familial growth pattern.

Conversion of a left-handed child to the use of the right hand can create a picture of mixed handedness accompanied by directional confusion, similar to that found in the cases of delayed maturation. After a year or two of practice, the right hand tends to establish definite superiority. If the transition period takes place before the child begins to read, it is not likely to produce directional confusion in reading. If the changeover takes place while the child is in the beginning stages of reading, or just before, a serious directional confusion may result. Once off to a poor start in reading, the child's reading difficulties may continue long after the directional confusion has cleared up. In some cases the right hand never establishes a consistent superiority, and directional confusion continues for many years to interfere with reading and other language activities.

In cases where there is a physiological basis for directional confusion, whether caused by neurological injury or defect, by a family growth pattern which includes slow and somewhat irregular neurological maturation, or by conversion from left to right, it is possibe that both the Orton and the Dearborn theories are correct in part. There may be an Orton type of rivalry between the two hemispheres of the brain and at the same time a conflict between left-to-right and right-to-left motor tendencies such as Dearborn emphasized.

Some directional confusion accompanied by reversal tendencies is so common among preschool children that it has to be considered a normal characteristic up to the age of 6. It is present in nearly one-fifth of unselected 7-year-olds. It is only when such a confusion persists after considerable instruction in the left-to-right direction in reading and writing that it requires careful consideration.

Barger (1953) reported some spectacular results in remedial reading with children showing strong reversal tendencies by having them read material by looking into a mirror, which causes the print to be seen upside down. He believed that this corrects a functional neurological peculiarity which causes these children to see normal print the way it looks to most people in the mirror, so that the mirror allows them to see the print normally; after a few weeks with the mirror they can read without it. An unpublished paper by Wayne Wrightstone delivered at the February 1960 meeting of the American Educational Research Association involved an experimental group taught by the Barger method and a control group taught by a conventional remedial technique by the same teachers; no significant difference was found between the results of the two methods.

The senior author has tried the Barger method on several children with marked reversal tendency and has confirmed their ability to read upside down as well as they do right side up; but no remedial miracles occurred. Since the procedure inverts the print vertically but not horizontally, and most reversals are left-to-right rather than vertical inversions, it is hard to understand why the method would or should help with left-to-right reversals.

There remains the probability that some cases of directional confusion are emotional in origin. The use of force, compulsion, or ridicule to make a left-handed child use his right hand quite often has harmful effects which may include the beginning of stuttering, assorted nervous habits, and emotional upset in addition to the directional confusion which otherwise might be quickly outgrown. Blau (1945) attempted to show that left-sidedness in general is a form of neurotic negativism or defiance; while as a general explanation of left-sidedness his theory seems farfetched, it may very well apply to a few cases. Park (1953) reported two cases in which a strong directional confusion in reading seemed to be a disguised form of negativism. In cases of this sort—and there are probably more of them—directional confusion can be found in a completely right-sided individual.

The point of view that directional confusion interferes with learning to read, and that directional confusion can in turn be the result of either physiological or psychological factors, makes it possible to explain why the results of the many research studies on lateral dominance and reading success are conflicting. One starts by assuming that the consistently right-sided child has an advantage over the left-sided child, or the child with crossed, mixed, or incomplete dominance, in learning to follow a consistent left-to-right direction. With appropriate instruction, however, most of these children who are not consistently right-sided do learn the left-to-right sequence and make progress in reading consistent with their abilities. But when an inconsistent lateral dominance pattern is complicated by neurological or emotional difficuties, a disabling directional confusion is likely to be established, and the usual classroom help is not sufficient to overcome it. Since these cases are a minority of all reading disability cases, and from this number those whose directional confusion is emotionally based would have to be subtracted, the remainder is really a small group. These woud be the cases where directional confusion is related to untypical lateral dominance as a sign of neurological immaturity or defect. Whether or not a particular investigator would find enough of them in his reading disability group to show some statistical relationship between reading disability and lateral dominance patterns would depend on the severity of disability in the group studied and the degree to which his tests were sensitive to directional confusion.

The Delacato Approach

Delacato (1959, 1963, 1966) has explained his theoretical basis and remedial procedures in three books. Obviously only a very sketchy summary can be given here. Very briefly, he believes that in some children a failure to achieve neurological integration below the cortical level of the brain is basic and must be corrected by such activities as sleeping in a particular position and learning to crawl and creep properly. When subcortical integration is present, he believes that the major cause of reading disability is lack of clear and consistent dominance of one cerebral hemisphere over the other. A variety of treatment procedures have the common purpose of strengthening the consistent use of the dominant hand and compelling the child to rely on the eye on the same side as the dominant hand. Among the procedures used are eliminating music, occluding one eye to force reliance on the other, and so on. Once neurological integration has been achieved, the child is said to learn to read by normal developmental teaching methods.

In his books Delacato has presented brief versions of fifteen studies, for several of which he did the statistical work on data supplied by others. A carefully analytical review of these studies has recently been made by Glass and Robbins, who analyzed each of the studies in detail, considering research design and statistical treatment. Their conclusions are summarized in the following quotation:

> Twelve experiments, which are purported to be evidence for the effectiveness of Delacato's therapy, are evaluated in light of the controls which were lacking in their execution and the shortcomings of the reported statistical analyses. Serious doubts about the validity of any of the twelve experiments are raised. . . . An analysis of correlational studies reported by Delacato reveals a conclusion quite contrary to the implications drawn by him from the data. Without exception, the empirical studies cited by Delacato as a "scientific appraisal" of his theory of neurological organization are shown to be of dubious value. (Glass and Robbins, 1967)

Recent research has cast doubt on the idea that crossed dominance—having the preferred eye on the opposite side from the preferred hand—has any relation to success in reading, although Delacato considers this sufficient evidence of neurological immaturity.

Independent studies bearing on the Delacato approach have not produced supporting evidence. Yarborough (1964) studied the value of the *Leavell Language-Development Service*, a procedure for strengthening the use of the eye on the same side as the preferred hand. Using a stereoscopic technique similar to one used by Delacato, she found no evidence of significant benefit in reading.

Robbins tried out Delacato procedures with second graders. Not only did he find no benefit in reading, but after the training to establish consistent sidedness there were two more children with crossed dominance than before the training (Robbins, 1966).

Anderson (1965) tried cross-pattern creeping and walking exercises with kindergarten children and found no significant improvement in readiness in the experimental as compared with a control group. He did a similar study with intermediate grade students and again found no significant differences for the total population, for lower IQ children, or for those with lower total initial reading ability. Kohlmorgen (1971) divided poor readers in the third, fourth and fifth grades into an experimental group given Delacato training for eight months and a control group given a "standard" remedial reading program; the experimental group showed no superiority in either reading or IQ gain.

In a scholarly review Whitsell (1967) summarized opinion and evidence on the Delacato approach and concluded that although it has had wide publicity, it has generally been rejected by the medical profession. "The theoretical basis and the major techniques of this method have not been validated and are not consistent with accepted neurological principles. This method may best be regarded as experimental, potentially harmful, and not to be recommended for general use at this time." Eight major medical and health associations issued a report which describes the theory underlying the Delacato approach as "without merit" and charges Delacato and his associates with making undocumented claims of cures (*New York Times*, May 8, 1968). Since then, reviews of the Delacato approach continue to be highly critical of it (Hartman and Hartman, 1973b; Birch, 1970).

It may turn out eventually that some of the Delacato procedures can be helpful with some cases of reading disability. Meanwhile it seems prudent not to use his procedures, but to encourage further research on them.

Two other approaches that somewhat resemble Delacato's warrant brief mention. Ayres (1968, 1972) advanced the point of view that poor neurological integration at the brain-stem level is at the root of many reading problems. She has devised a battery of tests and a training program to identify and remedy such problems. As yet, no independent validation of her theory or treatment program has come to our attention.

Heath and Bender (1971) reported that over half of the children seen for learning difficulties at the Purdue Achievement Center for Children show an immature persistence of the tonic neck reflex. The treatment described involves rocking on all fours against resistance, and creeping forward and backward. The IQ's and ages of the children were not given and a high percentage of severely mentally retarded children may have been included, since after treatment the children were said to be ready for pre-academic work.

III. SENSORY DEFECTS

Types of Visual Defects

There are many different kinds of visual defects, some of which seem to be more important in the causation of difficulties in reading than others.

The three defects which are best known to the layman are nearsightedness (myopia), farsightedness (hypermetropia), and astigmatism. These are all due usually to structural deviations from the normal shape of the eye. The myopic eye is too long from front to back, so that light focuses in front of the retina and tends to produce a blurred impression. The farsighted eye is too short from front to back, so that light, especially when coming from a source near the eye, focuses behind the retina. With moderate amounts of farsightedness, normal or better than normal vision for distant objects is often found; it is possible for the farsighted person to get near objects also into clear focus, but long-continued attention to near objects, as in reading, tends to produce eyestrain with accompanying fatigue and headaches. Astigmatism is usually the result of uneven curvature of the front part of the eye, so that light rays coming into the eye are not evenly distributed over the retina; the results are blurred or distorted images and eyestrain. All three of these conditions can be corrected with properly fitted glasses.

The eyes have to make four major types of adjustments for clear vision. There is an automatic reflex adjustment of the size of the pupillary opening to the amount of illumination (pupillary reflex); this permits a larger amount of light to enter in dim lighting and protects the eye against the dazzling effect of bright illumination. Second, there is an automatic reflex adjustment of the shape of the lens to the distance of the object being looked at; this is called the accommodation reflex and acts like the adjustment for distance in a camera. Third, there is an automatic reflex control of the degree to which the eyes turn in so both focus on the same spot (the convergence reflex); the eyes are almost parallel when viewing an object more than ten feet away, but turn in quite noticeably when aimed at a target a foot away. Fourth, the eyes must be aimed so that the objects we wish to see most clearly are in the center of the visual field, where acuity is greatest. This requires smooth, continuous movement when following a moving object, and quick, jerky movements (*saccadic movements*) with intervening pauses (*fixations*) when observing stationary objects. These movements are not easily seen on casual observation, but are easily noted in eye-movement photography or when making special observations of eye movements (see pp. 551–556).

There are some defects which cannot be detected when each eye is tested separately, but which appear when the eyes are used together. For normal two-eyed vision both eyes must be focused accurately on the same target. This allows a fusion in the brain of the slightly different images from the two eyes. Fusion difficulty is often the result of paralysis of an eye muscle. When there is no fusion the person sometimes sees double (as when under the influence of alcohol), but more commonly the image from one eye is ignored or suppressed in the same way that a person looking into a microscope or sighting a rifle ignores the other eye. Continued suppression of the vision of one eye for a period of years may eventually produce blindness in that eye, and the person will have to depend completely on the preferred eye. It is therefore very important to detect cases of visual suppression early. A one-eyed person is not bothered by his lack of fusion and may have clearer vision in the good eye than other people have with two eyes.

Partial or imperfect fusion is more apt to interfere with clear vision than a complete absence of fusion. When fusion is incomplete, a blurred image instead of a clear one is likely, even though the person may see clearly with either eye separately. Some people can fuse the images, but do it slowly. This may not be a handicap in the ordinary use of the eyes, but may interfere with clear vision when rapid, precise focusing is needed, as in reading.

Poor fusion is often associated with a lack of proper balance among the six pairs of muscles which turn the eyeballs. When the lack of balance is extreme, the condition is called *strabismus* ("cross-eyed" or "walleyed"). The person with strabismus usually ignores one eye completely and so has no interference with the vision of the other eye. Milder cases of poor muscle balance (*heterophoria*) occur in which one eye turns in too much (*esophoria*), turns out (*exophoria*), or focuses a little higher than the other (*hyperphoria*). Most people with these defects are able to obtain proper fusion when the eyes are not tired, but get blurred vision after extended reading or other close and exacting visual work. When the eyes are tired, they may get blurred images, may see a combination of the things each eye is looking at, or may see the two objects in reverse order. There also may be a complete suppression of one eye.

Color blindness of the usual type, which involves difficulty or inability in distinguishing reds from greens, is found in 4 to 8 per cent of boys and is quite rare in girls. There is no evidence to indicate that it has any effect on reading ability (Shearron, 1969). Weakness in the ability to perceive depth (called *astereopsis*) has been mentioned as possibly being involved in reading disability cases; it is related to poor fusion. A condition in which one eye forms a larger image of the object than the other eye (called *aniseikonia*) has been found to cause visual disturbances in some individuals; it would seem to be a reasonable cause for poor fusion in some cases.

As yet little is known about the possible importance for reading of the speed and precision with which the pupillary, accommodation, and convergence reflexes adapt the eyes to new targets or to a changing target. Vision tests currently in use do not attempt to measure these factors.

In addition to the conditions described above, there are very many ocular conditions, caused by injuries, disease, and so on, that may produce poor vision. The list above contains, however, about all the visual defects with which the schoolteacher or clinical psychologist needs to be acquainted.

The Significance of Visual Defects for Reading

Although there have been many studies on the relation of visual defects to reading ability, an exact statement of the degree to which poor reading is caused by poor vision cannot yet be made. One of the reasons for the discrepancies between different research studies is the fact that the subjects used and the vision tests employed are frequently not directly comparable. But there are more fundamental reasons why one cannot state exactly how much poor reading is caused by defective sight. A relatively slight visual defect may give one person acute discomfort, while another person with a more severe defect may not be bothered by it. People vary in their ability to adapt themselves to handicaps. For instance, a moderate degree of exophoria may cause one person no trouble because his ability to compensate for the tendency (that is, his duction power) is good, while a similar amount of exophoria may cause another person considerable difficulty in reading. And then, too, one must remember that poor vision is only one of many handicaps that may interfere with reading. If poor vision is a child's only handicap, he may be able to become a good reader in spite of it, while if he has several other handicaps as well the combination may be too much for him.

The research on this topic is already much too extensive to review here; those interested will find good summaries by H. M. Robinson (1946), Cleland (1953), and Rosen (1965).

An uncritical reading of the research reveals a lack of agreement. There is a fairly long list of researches in which little or no relation was found between vision test results and reading achievement. The present writers believe that positive findings outweigh negative findings and are inclined to trust the accumulated evidence of such investigators as Park and Burri (1943 a, b, c), Eames (1948), and H. M. Robinson and Huelsman (1953) all of whom found evidence of a relationship between certain types of visual defects and reading failures. It is very significant that these research studies placed most emphasis on such visual difficulties as poor near-point acuity and poor eye-muscle balance with accompanying deficiencies in fusion and depth perception—significant because these problems are usually not detected by the eye tests commonly used in schools. The Robinson and Huelsman study, probably the most intensive yet undertaken, studied the interrelationships among fifty-nine tests of vision and thirteen tests of reading, with first-grade, fourth-grade, and seventh-grade pupils. Reading success was correlated most highly with depth perception and near acuity; in addition, none of the sets of vision tests used in their study was found to be fully satisfactory.

In recent years there has been a tendency for ophthalmologists to minimize the significance of visual problems in the causation of reading disability (Lawson, 1968; Goldberg and Arnott, 1970; Martin, 1971; Norn, Rindziunski and Skydsgaard, 1970). Optometrists, however, tend to stress the importance of binocular vision, accommodation, convergence, and eye movements and to emphasize the value of orthoptic training in the remediation of reading disabilities (Wold, 1969; Flax, 1970; Friedman, 1972; Peiser, 1972; Swanson, 1972). "To succeed in the visual aspects of reading, the child has two choices. The first is to become monocular (only use one eye). The second is to develop an efficient binocular visual system. Anyone between the two extremes will have varying degrees of difficulty" (Wold, 1969, p. 29). Keogh (1974) made a comprehensive review of the literature and research on the effects of using vision training programs for developing scholastic readiness and for remediation of learning disabilities. She found that inadequacies of research methodology made the available evidence inconclusive about the value of such programs.

Although many children with reading disabilities have no visual defects, in a few cases undetected visual problems are highly significant.

> Tim was 10 years old and an almost total nonreader. He could recognize some words in isolation, but seemed unable to read even the simplest printed material. On a visual screening test he failed a test of vertical eye-muscle balance. When questioned, he said that pages in books "looked solid." It seemed probable that the lines of print he saw with one eye fitted between the lines he saw with the other eye, giving the "solid" appearance. Tim was referred for ophthalmological examination. After minor surgery to correct the eye-muscle problem Tim, who was quite bright, quickly learned to read with individual tutoring. His emotional and social problems were more persistent and required treatment for two additional years.

Calvert and Cromes (1966) reported that of the 20 percent of their remedial reading students not responding to help, over 90 per cent had fine oculo-motor spasms that could be seen in eye-movement photographs and that drug treatment for this condition both stopped the spasms and improved learning. Verification of this finding is needed.

The Detection of Visual Defects

In view of the great importance of conserving vision, it would be ideally desirable for every child to have a periodic examination by an eye specialist. Since the expense of such a practice is prohibitive for most schools, the common school practice is to give simple eye tests to select or screen out those whose eyes require careful examination. Even this limited program, however, is carried out inadequately.

The usual method of measuring vision in school makes use of the Snellen chart or a similar test. The child stands twenty feet away from a wall chart and tries to read letters of different sizes. Each eye is tested separately, the other eye being covered. A score of 20/20 is considered normal; 20/30, 20/40, and so on, mean defective acuity to the extent that the child can see at twenty feet letters large enough for the normal eye to see at thirty feet, forty feet, and the like. The assumption is sometimes made that the Snellen ratio represents a per cent of normal vision. That this is wrong can be clearly seen by inspecting Table 9; 20/30 acuity, which is usually considered to be borderline, represents an acuity only 8.5 per cent less than 20/20.

The Snellen-type vision test, if it is the only kind of vision test used, has many drawbacks. In addition to the fact that it is often administered in schools in such a way as to allow a child to cheat and simulate good vision by memorizing the chart, it fails to detect moderate degrees of farsightedness or astigmatism and fails completely to detect even severe cases of poor fusion and eye-muscle imbalance. The one defect that it readily discloses is nearsightedness. Eames (1942) reported that in the examination of one hundred children who had visual defects when given a thorough ophthal-

TABLE 9   *Percentage of visual loss for various acuity fractions[a]*

	Per cent	
	Efficiency	Loss
20/20	100.0	0.0
20/30	91.5	8.5
20/40	83.6	16.4
20/50	76.5	23.5
20/70	64.0	36.0
20/100	48.9	51.1
20/200	20.0	80.0

[a] *This table is reproduced from C. M. Louttit, Clinical Psychology (New York: Harper, 1947), p. 576. By permission of the publishers.*

mological examination, Snellen chart tests disclosed the présence of a defect in only forty-eight children.

There are several sets of vision screening tests which are considerably better than the Snellen chart for detecting children who should be referred for a thorough professional eye examination. Three sets of tests use stereoscopic slides in fairly expensive machines. The *Keystone Vision Screening Test* uses an instrument called the *Telebinocular*; it provides a brief series of tests to pick out those needing more careful screening and a longer series that includes tests of acuity, eye-muscle balance, and fusion for both distance vision and near vision, with additional tests of depth perception and color vision. The *Ortho-Rater* has an adult version for industrial use and a school model; it covers approximately the same functions as the *Keystone*. The *Titmus School Vision Tester* is very much like the *Ortho-Rater*. Despite the availability of these more comprehensive visual screening procedures, many school systems still rely on the inadequate Snellen test (Rosen, 1969).

With any of these tests one does not attempt to specify the kind of visual defect present, but simply to select or screen out those who should be referred to an eye specialist for examination. Unfortunately some ophthalmologists and optometrists stop when they have examined each eye separately and do not pay much attention in their examinations to those aspects of coordinated close binocular vision that are most likely to have a significant effect on reading. Sometimes it is not the fault of the visual screening test if a child who has done poorly on it is reported by the eye specialist to have normal vision.

For schools that want to improve their vision testing procedures but do not wish to purchase any of the screening tests described above, a number of suggestions can be made. First of all, the typical Snellen chart should be replaced, when testing poor readers, by an E chart, in which only the letter E is used, facing in different directions. Second, in order to detect the presence of significant amounts of farsightedness a plus 1.00 diopter spherical lens[1] should be obtained. After testing the eyes in the usual way, each eye should be retested looking through the lens. A farsighted child will see as well with the lens as without it, or even better; but those who have normal vision or are nearsighted will see less well with the lens. Third, near-point acuity can be tested with the *Good-Lite Near Point Card*.[2]

Appropriate questioning can sometimes reveal the probable presence of a visual difficulty that has not been detected by the school's eye tests. One can ask such questions as: Do you ever see double? Does a page sometimes get blurry while you are looking at it? Do you ever get a headache while reading?

1. Lenses and vision charts can be purchased through local opticians or optometrists, or directly from the American Optical Co., Southbridge, Mass. 01608.
2. Obtainable from the House of Vision, 135–7 N. Wabash Ave., Chicago, Illinois 60602.

The teacher should always be alert to detect signs of visual discomfort in the appearance or behavior of a child. Among the things to look for are bloodshot, swollen, teary, or discharging eyes; inflamed eyelids; complaints of sleepiness, fatigue, headache, nausea, dizziness; blurred, double, or distorted vision; and pain, or feelings of dryness, itching, burning, or grittiness in the eyes; strained and tense facial expression; rapid blinking or twitchings of the face; and such habits as holding a book very close or far away or holding the head on one side while reading.

No matter how complete the vision tests in a school may be, no teacher, nurse, or psychologist should attempt to prescribe treatment for eye defects. The school's function is to find those who are in need of expert attention; children who are found or suspected to have defective vision should be sent to an eye specialist.

Before leaving the subject of vision testing, mention should be made of two tests that have had some use in reading clinics. One of these is the *Keystone Tests of Binocular Skill*, an adaptation of the *Gray Standardized Oral Reading Check Tests* on stereoscopic slides, by which the relative efficiency of the two eyes in reading can be compared. The other is the *Spache Binocular Reading Test*, which uses stereoscopic slides in which some words are omitted from the left-eye selection and other words from the right-eye selection, to indicate whether either eye is failing to contribute its share.

Hearing

The degree to which poor hearing is a handicap in learning to read depends on the amount of emphasis given to oral instruction in reading. In a careful study Bond (1935) found significant differences in hearing between good and poor readers in the second and third grades and reported that partly deaf children were seriously handicapped in classes where oral-phonetic methods were stressed, but made normal progress in classes which stressed visual teaching materials and silent reading. This is another impressive bit of evidence to demonstrate that teaching methods must be adapted to the learning abilities and disabilities of the individual child. A recent British study found that even a relatively slight impairment of hearing frequently has marked effects on communication skills and verbal knowledge, and those with defects in both ears are more handicapped than those with defective hearing in one ear (Owrid, 1970). Embry (1971) found that children with mild hearing loss tended to be a half to a year retarded in achievement.

Testing Hearing

By far the most satisfactory way to measure hearing in the schools is to use an audiometer. For the purpose of singling out pupils who need careful medical examination of their hearing, audiometers are available that can be used to test as many as forty children at one time. In such a test each child listens through an earphone and writes down the numbers that he hears. The numbers, spoken with different degrees of loudness, are played on a special phonograph, and from the child's written answers the degree of hearing loss can be readily calculated. For individual testing, an audiometer that measures amount of hearing loss for pure tones of low, medium, and high pitches should be used.[3] A loss of over 25 decibels on an audiometer calibrated according to ANSI or ISO standards is almost certain to handicap a child in hearing in classroom situations and is usually accompanied by some indistinctness in speech. Because ear infections and other temporary conditions can cause a transitory hearing loss, California regulations require an audiometer retest two months after a failing performance (*Hearing Testing of School Children*, 1962).

As with defective vision, the handicapping effect of a partial hearing loss is much greater for some people than for others. Some make up for their sensory weaknesses by concentrating intently and getting the greatest possible meaning out of what they do hear; others, combining inattention or disregard for small differences with their sensory loss, seem greatly handicapped.

While the majority of children with somewhat impaired hearing show lessened acuity across the full range of pitch represented by the piano keyboard, there are others whose deficiency is concentrated in the higher frequencies. An example of high-frequency hearing loss is shown in Figure 11.1.

Raymond was a 10-year-old boy, barely able to read a primer. His *Stanford-Binet* IQ was 85, but his Performance IQ was 120, showing inferior verbal ability, but superior ability in nonverbal situations. His speech was marked by a lisp and general indistinctness in the pronunciation of *s, sh, z, th, f,* and *v* sounds; he also spoke very jerkily. His father, a mechanic, had exactly the same speech pattern. It seems probable that Raymond's inability to hear high-frequency sounds clearly (see Fig. 11.1) was responsible for his inability to pronounce them well and resulted in confusing him in reading because words that sounded alike to him had different letters in them and different meanings.

Some conditions that lead to progressively increasing deafness can be cured if treated early enough, and careful periodic tests of hearing should be part of the routine health procedure in every school. Teachers should watch for signs of poor hearing in a child's general behavior. Children with inflamed or running ears should of course be referred for medical treatment.

3. Good audiometers are marketed under the following names: Ambco, Audiovox, Beltone, Eckstein Brothers, Maico, and Zenith.

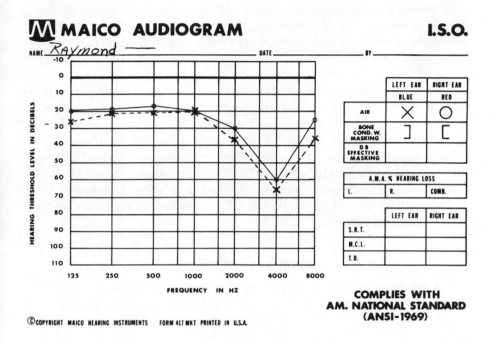

FIGURE 11.1 Chart of audiometer test results for a 10-year-old boy with a severe reading disability. The chart shows an impairment of acuity in the higher frequencies, in both ears, with the left ear slightly poorer than the right. Reproduced by permission of Maico Hearing Instruments.

Poor hearing should be suspected if a child asks to have statements repeated, cups a hand behind his ear, scowls, or otherwise shows intense effort in listening, confuses words of somewhat similar sounds, or has indistinct speech. Teachers sometimes mistakenly decide that a child is stupid because his face has a blank expression due to his inability to hear.

IV. OTHER PHYSICAL CONDITIONS

Illness

There is no evidence that surgical operations or the common infectious diseases of childhood are related to reading disability. Prolonged illness of any kind may influence reading ability if the child is out of school for a long period of time and misses important work. A history of a series of long absences in the first and second grades is found fairly often among children with severe reading handicaps. Many children show no lasting scholastic effects of such absences, either because they were ahead of the class or because their mothers and teachers give them special help to make up the lost ground. When neither of these conditions is present, the child may not catch up.

There are certain chronic conditions which lower a child's general vitality, so that he tires quickly and cannot put forth a normal amount of effort. Rheumatic fever is the major offender in this group, according to the writers' experience. Asthma, heart trouble, tuberculosis, sinus trouble, other chronic infections, and malnutrition are other conditions that cause intermittent absence and lower the child's energy output. Malnutrition may adversely affect brain development and behavior, producing reduced ability to learn (Food and Nutrition Board, 1973). Insufficient sleep is also common among poor readers.

Muscular Coordination

A considerable number of poor readers are generally clumsy. They are below average in athletic skill, are awkward in walking and running, and make poorly formed letters and numbers in writing. While there does not seem to be any direct causal connection between awkwardness and poor reading, in some cases they may both result from the same condition. Mild injuries to the brain, or delayed neurological maturation, may be responsible both for poor muscular coordination and for speech and reading disabilities.

The importance of general physical fitness and coordination has been stressed by some writers. Rosborough (1963) reported a high incidence of postural and skeletal difficulties among reading disability cases and recommends including an osteopath in the diagnostic team. Kephart (1960) emphasized the importance of basic motor skills and eye-hand coordination in slow learners and described a diagnostic and treatment program in these areas of functioning.

Glandular Disturbances

The endocrine or ductless glands are small organs which have tremendous influence on human growth and efficiency. Marked thyroid deficiency is usually accompanied by obesity and mental sluggishness; an overactive thyroid gland may cause loss of weight, fatiguability, and nervous irritability. Abnormalities of the pituitary gland may cause dwarfism and giganticism, obesity, and sexual immaturity. Each of the endocrine glands has important regulative functions, and medical authorities are still far from a complete understanding of them. Among the poor readers seen by the writers, the frequency of endocrine deviations has been greater than in normal child population. Most of these children have been overweight, with signs of either a thyroid deficiency or a general endocrine disturbance involving the thyroid, pituitary, and sex glands (Eames, 1960). Many of these children have shown marked improvement in mental alertness, effort, and learning ability after appropriate endocrine treatment. However, controlled experimentation has generally resulted in frustration when attempting to apply biochemical therapy to learning (Green and Perlman, 1971). No definite relationships have been established as yet between chromosome abnormalities and reading disabilities (Green and Perlman, 1971).

SUGGESTED ADDITIONAL READING

BANNATYNE, ALEXANDER. *Language, reading, and learning disabilities: psychology, neuropsychology, diagnosis and remediation.* Springfield, Ill.: Charles C Thomas. 1971. Chaps. 6, 7, 9.

BOND, GUY L. & TINKER, MILES A. *Reading difficulties: their diagnosis and correction* (3rd ed.). New York: Appleton-Century-Crofts, 1973. Chap. 5.

FROSTIG, MARIANNE & MASLOW, PHYLLIS. *Learning problems in the classroom.* New York: Grune and Stratton, 1973. Chap. 2.

FRY, EDWARD. *Reading instruction for classroom and clinic.* New York: McGraw-Hill, 1972. Chaps. 14, 15, 16, 18.

JOHNSON, DORIS J. & MYKLEBUST, HELMER R. *Learning disabilities: educational principles and practices.* New York: Grune and Stratton, 1967. Pp. 117–144, 162–334.

MONEY, JOHN (Ed.). *Reading disability: progress and research needs in dyslexia.* Baltimore: Johns Hopkins Press, 1962.

MYKLEBUST, HELMER R. (Ed.). *Progress in learning disabilities.* New York: Grune and Stratton, 1968, 1971. Vol. I, Chaps. 2, 6, 8; Vol. II, Chaps. 1, 2, 10.

NATCHEZ, GLADYS (Ed.). *Children with reading problems: classic and contemporary issues in reading disability.* New York: Basic Books, 1968. Pp. 89–158.

ROBECK, MILDRED C. & WILSON, JOHN A. R. *Psychology of reading: foundations of instruction.* New York: John Wiley and Sons, 1974. Chaps. 2, 6, 7, 8.

ROSWELL, FLORENCE G. & NATCHEZ, GLADYS. *Reading disability: diagnosis and treatment* (2nd ed.). New York: Basic Books, 1971. Chaps. 1, 3.

SCHELL, LEO M. & BURNS, PAUL C. (Eds.). *Remedial reading: classroom and clinic* (2nd ed.). Boston: Allyn and Bacon, 1972. Pp. 47–137.

THOMPSON, LLOYD, J. *Reading disability: developmental dyslexia.* Springfield, Ill.: Charles C Thomas, 1966. Chaps. 3, 4, 7.

ZINTZ, MILES V. *The reading process: the teacher and the learner.* Dubuque, Iowa: W. C. Brown, 1970. Chap. 20.

12

Correlates of
Reading Disability,
III: Cultural Factors

This chapter concludes our consideration of the factors that may be correlates of reading disability. The preceding two chapters have explored intellectual and physical factors. The present chapter discusses factors that are basically cultural in nature: educational factors, educational disadvantage and its sources, and personality factors. The chapter ends with a consideration of the interrelationships of factors as they may be found in an individual with a reading disability.

I. EDUCATIONAL FACTORS

Evidence from School Records

The child's cumulative school records usually provide evidence that is quite helpful in a reading diagnosis. From the records one should be able to determine how old the child was upon entering school; when his poor progress was first noted, and how severe it was thought to be; whether he has repeated, and if so, when; whether or not he has changed schools and teachers often.

His attendance record should be looked over for long absences that may have handicapped him and for frequent short absences that may indicate poor physical condition or possible truancy. If he has changed schools or classes frequently the reasons for the changes should be investigated. Failure to acquire good reading habits is sometimes the direct result of frequent changes of teachers in the primary grades, with consequent confusion of teaching methods. Ratings on conduct, effort, and personality traits may be highly significant. If scores on standardized tests of intelligence and achievement are on the record, they should, of course, be noted.

The health record may give valuable information about sensory or physical defects. Defects of vision and hearing are often not detected by the routine tests used in schools and may escape the notice of teachers, so a clear physical record should not be accepted at its face value. When possible it is desirable to have a thorough physical examination given to the child. Similarly it is desirable to test the child's intelligence even if an IQ or MA appears on the record.

Teachers who have had a child in their classes in previous terms should be consulted for information that is not placed on record cards. It is important to find out what methods of teaching reading have been used with the child, especially in the first grade. Such information can be obtained only from his former teachers. They also can often contribute valuable facts about the child's behavior and conduct in class, his attitude toward reading, and his home conditions.

Instructional History. Teacher effectiveness has a strong effect on how well children learn to read, particularly in the first grade (Bond and Dykstra, 1967). It seems reasonable to conclude that some children who have become disabled readers might have fared better with different teachers. On the other hand, if most members of a class make some progress and one child doesn't (which is usually true even with quite mediocre teaching), factors within the child which make it difficult for the child to respond probably have to be present also.

An accurate instructional history would often cast light on how a reading disability started and developed, but it is usually impossible to obtain. The child can seldom recall much detail about his early school experiences; and if a child had strong negative feelings about a teacher, he will often be unwilling to confide this information to a person he doesn't know very well. Parents can usually recall what they thought of the first-grade teacher, but they never really knew the details of what went on day by day in school. Even if the teacher should be available for interviewing, she probably never realized what she was doing that may have contributed to the child's learning problems. The child's instructional history can only rarely be obtained with enough accuracy and detail to clarify cause-effect relationships.

As yet, not much is known about the specific characteristics that differentiate superior reading instruction from mediocre reading instruction (A. J. Harris, 1969). Otto (1972) has proposed that, in view of the many unresolved problems in reading instruction, there is little reason to look beyond educational factors in seeking causes for reading disability. That is an extreme position with which we do not agree.

Yet it seems reasonable that teacher practices like the following must aggravate the learning problems of many children: 1) teaching a child with materials that are too difficult and frustrating for him; 2) instructing the child's group at a pace he cannot keep up with; 3) not noticing specific errors and correcting them before they become habitual; 4) often failing to notice and approve when the child does make a correct response; 5) giving the child the feeling that the teacher dislikes him, or at best tolerates him; 6) allowing other children to express disdain or derision for his efforts; 7) expecting a child to fail because older children in his family did poor work for that teacher. Glock (1972) has pointed out that a large proportion of preadolescents perceive teachers' behavior and feelings toward them as negative, and this has a marked effect on their self-concepts and school performance. When a child senses that he habitually fails to satisfy the teacher's standards, and he receives more disapproval than approval in reading situations, his attitude and effort are likely to deteriorate (Gever, 1970).

Arithmetic

Usually the child's school record card indicates whether or not his work in arithmetic has been satisfactory. For research purposes it is highly desirable to have an accurate measure of ability in arithmetic, but in practical remedial work such refinement is usually not necessary. Reading disability cases often do considerably better in arithmetic computation than in problem solving, in which their poor reading is more of a handicap. The child who is poor in problem solving should be asked to explain his attempts at solution step by step. It is then possible to determine if his errors are due to lack of understanding of the vocabulary, careless errors in reading, choice of the wrong operation, skipping of a necessary step, errors of computation, and so on. The diagnosis of difficulties in computation is too complicated to be discussed here.

Spelling

Poor reading is usually accompanied by poor spelling, and children are apt to make similar errors in word recognition and spelling. From the standpoint of diagnosing reading difficulties it is more important to get a clear idea of the kinds of errors a child makes in spelling than it is to get an exact grade score. Convenient short lists of spelling words are included in the *Monroe, Durrell* and *Gates-McKillop* diagnostic batteries. Standardized spelling tests such as those found in general achievement batteries often use multiple-choice questions, which are much less useful for diagnostic purposes than writing and spelling orally from dictation. For individual testing in both arithmetic computation and spelling, the *Wide Range Achievement Test* is convenient.

In analyzing spelling errors, part of the check list of oral reading errors given on page 208 may be used as a guide. Reversals, omissions, additions, substitutions, and ignorance of the alphabet are common mistakes of poor spellers. Other common sources of error in spelling are attempts to spell nonphonetic words phonetically (*nees* for *niece*), spelling which reflects mispronunciation (*liberry* for *library*), forgetting the end of a word while writing the first part, and lack of familiarity with the word or its meaning.

Handwriting

Poor penmanship occurs frequently in poor readers. Much of their difficulty is the result of failure to learn letter forms and inability to spell correctly. In order to test writing independently of spelling, it is advisable to provide a printed selection that may be copied. Since writing words is employed as one method of teaching them in both reading and spelling, it is highly desirable to improve legibility of penmanship as part of a remedial program. One should not overlook the possibility that poor penmanship in a reading disability case may be nothing more than a reflection of the child's dislike for reading and everything that goes with it. A history of previously better writing is significant in this regard. Poor penmanship may be a sign of an underlying visual-motor difficulty.

II. EDUCATIONAL DISADVANTAGE

The term "disadvantaged" has been defined as follows:

Typically included under this rubric are children who come from families of low socio-economic status (as measured by occupation of the breadwinner, educational attainment of the parents, income, place of residence, etc.) and children from minority groups (as determined by recent immigration of families from countries outside the United States or notable lack of acculturation of groups that may have been residents for generations) and minority racial status (in particular, Negroes and Indians who have been in a caste-like status in this country for generations). Also included in this population are children from rural areas which have been isolated from the mainstream of American culture. These definitions usually have in common the element of poverty or low income in relation to the median income of Americans. (Stodolsky and Lesser, 1967)

Disadvantage and Reading Achievement

There is ample evidence that these characteristics of disadvantage tend to be associated with low group attainment in school. The widely discussed Coleman Report found that the differential effect of schools on pupil achievement "appears to arise not principally from factors that the school system controls, but from factors outside the school proper" (Coleman, *et al.*, 1966). The factors outside the school were student-related and group-related characteristics, especially socioeconomic status and ethnic variables. Barton made a study of factors associated with reading achievement in 1,500 classrooms in the United States. His main conclusion was: "The gist of these findings is that the norm for upper middle-class children is a year ahead of 'grade level' from the end of first grade on; while the norm for lower working-class children (the poorer and more culturally deprived part of the working class) is to fall back until they are a year or more behind by the time they reach fourth and fifth grade" (Barton, 1963, p. 247).

Dyer (1968) has summarized several research studies which indicate that socioeconomic status of parents has the highest correlation with school achievement, but that other factors such as per-pupil expenditure, teacher experience, classroom atmosphere, and size of special staff also correlate significantly with achievement. In general, achievement in the North is ahead of achievement in the South, and urban achievement is ahead of rural achievement; this holds for both whites and blacks. The educational gap between the middle class and the disadvantaged tends to widen in terms of grade levels as children get older; often the disadvantaged have reading-grade averages two to three years below the norms by the time they reach secondary school age.

What this means can be shown somewhat more concretely with findings from two studies in which the senior author participated. One was a three-year study of the experiences and results of new teachers in a junior high school that was located in a slum-ghetto black section of New York City (Downing, *et al.*, 1965). At the beginning of the seventh grade the mean WISC Total IQ of the pupils was 89 and the mean reading-grade score was 4.8; 57 per cent were more than two years below grade level, and only 18 per cent were at or above grade level. Using the formula described in Chapter 7, the Reading Expectancy Quotient for the group mean was only 79, indicating that the majority were functioning well below their expectancy, at a reading disability level. This degree of reading retardation is typical for disadvantaged black adolescents in the northern cities; scores run still lower in the South.

The CRAFT Project was a three-year study of primary-grade reading instruction with about 2,000 disadvantaged black children in New York City. At the beginning of first grade the median reading-readiness score was at the 20th percentile of national norms; particular difficulty was shown in knowledge of word meanings (14th percentile) and auditory discrimination (first percentile). Reading tests were given in April, after seven months of each school year. For all teaching methods combined, mean reading-comprehension grades were 1.5 in first grade, 2.3 in second grade, and 3.4 in third grade. The third-grade average was nearly a half year higher than the corresponding average of the third grades in the same schools the year before. When the experiment was repeated with teachers who had been in the first study, the mean for first grade was again 1.5; the second-grade mean was 2.6, just one month below the norm. This study shows the severe readiness handicaps with which such children begin the first grade and also demonstrates that under experimental conditions of teacher training and motivation a close approximation to the norm can be achieved, at least in the primary grades (A. J. Harris, Morrison, Gold, and Serwer, 1968).

Family Influences

Recent evidence has shown that children from the same ethnic background, living in the same neighborhood and attending the same school, can vary widely in environmental characteristics that are correlated with success in reading. In a study of 489 elementary school children in England, social class was less closely related to reading than each of the following: a dominant parent–submissive child relationship, general deprivation, desire for education, intellectual enterprise, confidence, and parental support (G. Miller, 1970). First-grade children living with only their mother showed far more maladjustment in school than those living with both parents or with mother and grandmother (Kellam and Schiff, 1969). Callaway (1972) found that children with working fathers were better readers than children without working fathers; amount of reading material in the home was positively related to success in reading; and being in the lowest income group went with low reading scores, but being in the highest income group did not result in superior scores. In a very interesting study, a number of environmental variables were measured when a sample of Mexican-American children entered first grade, and these were correlated with the reading scores of the children at the end of the third grade (Henderson, 1972). The highest correlation with reading was for achievement press (.61). Significant correlations were also found for language models, academic guidance, activeness of family, range of social interaction, intellectuality in the home, identification with models, and perceived value of education. It seems noteworthy that parental pressure for their child's achievement predicted third-grade reading a little more accurately than most readiness and intelligence tests for first graders can.

Factors such as parental desire for their children to be educated, guidance without strict domination, emotional support, and parental intellectuality and interest in reading help to determine which children in a disadvantaged group will succeed in school and which will fail. Indeed, the blanket use of the term "disadvantaged" is open to question; some children in the studies cited above would seem to have been advantaged in many significant characteristics, and disadvantaged only in family income and social-class membership.

Language: Deficit or Difference?

Bernstein (1964), an influential British linguist, described lower-class language as less abstract, less flexible, and less subtle than middle-class language, and attributed the poor school progress of lower-class children to a lack of the linguistic tools needed for abstract thinking. This deficit theory, that lower-class and dialect-speaking children are deficient in language, has been challenged by many American linguists (for a useful review, see Adler, 1972). "There is no reason to believe that any nonstandard vernacular is in itself an obstacle to learning" (Labov, 1973, p. 43). Labov argued that it is teachers' interpretations that a child speaks an imperfect and inferior standard English, when he is actually speaking correctly in his dialect, that cause the teachers to underestimate the learning ability of the child and create barriers to learning.

The degree to which language differences may in themselves interfere with school learning is still a matter for debate (Weber, 1970). Teachers of bilingual children or children who speak a nonstandard dialect should be aware of the kinds of misunderstandings that can arise. Useful annotated bibliographies have been prepared by Ching (1969) on bilingual children and by Rosen and Ortega (1969) on Mexican-American children. An excellent collection of papers has been published by the International Reading Association (Laffey and Shuy, 1973). Illustrations of the kinds of language confusions experienced by Eskimo and Indian children have been given by Griese (1971).

Peer Influences

As we have seen, differences in parental characteristics and attitudes are significantly related to how well disadvantaged children learn to read, particularly in the lower grades. As children approach the age of 9 or 10, peer influences become increasingly important. If the child belongs to a gang or club, and the group's code is antagonistic to school and derogates school success, it becomes almost obligatory for a member to neglect learning.

> In our studies in South Central Harlem we have seen the reverse situation: the children who are rejected by the peer group are quite likely to succeed in school. In middle-class suburban areas, many children do fail in school because of their personal deficiencies; in ghetto areas, it is the healthy, vigorous popular child with normal intelligence who cannot read and fails all along the line. . . . Many children, particularly those who are not doing well in school, show a sudden down turn in the fourth or fifth grades. It is at the same age, at nine or ten years old, that the influence of the vernacular peer group becomes predominant. (Labov, 1973, p. 36)

It may be, as Labov suggests, that no school program will successfully counteract the tendency of such children to become increasingly retarded in reading as they grow older, until a way is found to bring the aims of the peer group and the aims of the school into harmony, or at least to neutralize peer-group antagonism to schooling. Labov's point of view is limited in its application, however. Within a gang, some learn to read well and others remain nonreaders, and if the gang influence were the only important factor, this would not happen.

Health Factors

In Chapter 11 health problems were discussed as they may be involved in reading disability. In general, health problems of many kinds tend to be more common among the poor, and when there is a health problem, it is more likely to be neglected or to receive poor attention and treatment. One might expect, for example, that poor maternal health during pregnancy, and the resulting possibility of neurological damage to the baby, would be more common among the poor than in the general population. In a study of 2,000 black children in Chicago, prematurity and maternal poor health during pregnancy were significantly related to school adjustment (Kellam and Schiff, 1969). Intensive clinical studies were made of 29 children chosen as the poorest readers at the end of first grade in a school with mainly black and Puerto Rican children, living in a low-income neighborhood. "A comparatively large proportion of the first-grade children in this study gave evidence of constitutional difficulties or developmental lag. The difficulties discovered were of several types and the etiology in most cases was not clear. Emotional and social factors compounded the difficulties in almost every case and complicated the diagnosis" (Fite and Schwartz, 1965). A multidisciplinary study of 306 disadvantaged children with learning disorders indicated that over half showed indications of neurological problems (Kappelman, Kaplan, and Ganter, 1969).

When a disadvantaged child functions in reading well below the norm for his peers as well as below his own expectancy, a search for persisting handicaps and inhibiting factors beyond those common to the group is important.

III. EMOTIONAL AND SOCIAL PROBLEMS

Children who fail in reading are usually studied a few years after their troubles have started, and because of the time that has passed and the difficulty of getting accurate information about the past, it is always difficult to determine what part emotional problems may have played in causing the reading difficulty. Usually there are evidences of other types of handicaps also, and the relative importance of the different handicaps is frequently impossible to determine. Estimates of the significance of emotional factors in the causation of reading disabilities vary widely. Most children with reading difficulties show signs of emotional maladjustment which may be mild or severe. The percentage of maladjustment reported by a particular investigator varies with the standards he uses, as well as with the kind of child population he has studied.

Some time ago Gates (1941) estimated that among cases of severe reading disabilities, about 75 per cent show personality maladjustment, and in about 25 per cent the emotional difficulty is a contributing cause of the reading failure. More recently, a study of 399 Swedish children resulted in the conclusion that nervous traits were probably contributing causes in 23 per cent (Malmquist, 1967), and in 306 disadvantaged children, 25 per cent were diagnosed as having emotional disturbances as predominating causes (Kappelman, Kaplan, and Ganter, 1969). Among several hundred reading disability cases seen in the Queens College Educational Clinic during a fifteen-year period, close to 100 per cent showed maladjustment of some kind, and the per cent in which the emotional difficulties were thought by the staff to have had a causal relationship to the reading problem ran over 50 per cent. The percentage varies according to the community from which the cases come and the bases used in making referrals.

Emotional Problems as Causes of Reading Difficulties

Attempts to find a type of personality or type of maladjustment characteristic of children with reading disabilities have failed completely.

Among children with reading problems one finds a few emotionally healthy children, some very inhibited "good" children, some children with definitely neurotic symptoms, some children whose misbehavior is conspicuous, some pre-delinquents, and some pre-psychotic and psychotic children. Reading disability is not a unique entity, but rather is found in combination with practically all other forms of child maladjustment. While case studies of children often reveal intimate connections between the child's emotional difficulties and his reading difficulties, research studies comparing the personalities of poor readers with good readers have failed to reveal any consistent group differences. This is probably due to the mistaken attempt to find a common personality type or problem in the reading disability cases (A. J. Harris, 1954a, 1954b, 1971b).

Teachers have come in recent years to blame reading problems on "emotional blocking." Unfortunately the term "emotional block" is a very vague one which is only the beginning of the description of what is wrong. There are different kinds of emotional blocking, and corrective procedures should differ according to the kind of blocking that has taken place. Even when an emotional problem has been identified and seems to have a causal relationship to the reading difficulty, one must remember that there are other children with similar emotional problems who read well. Often it is the combination of an emotional problem with an eye defect, a directional confusion, absence at crucial times for learning, or a particularly disliked or ineffectual teacher that centers the focus of the problem on reading.

Because reading is the first of the three R's to be systematically taught to children and is the one with which parents and teachers are most deeply concerned, it becomes quite naturally the first major educational issue around which problems of reluctance to grow up, resistance to going to school, or defiance of adult authority may be worked out. And because successful reading requires application and sustained concentration, emotional problems which prevent a child from concentrating and paying attention during reading lessons also prevent him from learning to read.

The attempt to describe carefully and accurately the different kinds of emotional problems that are contributory causes in reading disabilities is just in its early stages. Nevertheless, several different types can already be distinguished.

1. Conscious Refusal to Learn. The child feels real hostility to parents or teachers or both—hostility which is consciously realized and readily expressed—and rejects reading because it is identified with the adult or adults against whom these feelings are directed. This frequently occurs when there is a conflict between the cultural values of teacher and pupil; the child from a low socioeconomic background may not be willing to accept the goals which teachers approve. To do so might jeopardize his social standing in the gang and place him in danger of being considered a sissy. Or the child may be imitating an admired parent who frequently voices contempt for "book learning."

2. Overt Hostility. In some children, self-control is hard to maintain because the child has built up intense feelings of resentment, and his angry feelings are apt to break out with relatively little provocation. Such children are generally regarded as "bad," and school tends to become for them a continuing series of skirmishes and battles, interrupted by punishments. For the children of this kind, the teacher-pupil relationship is rarely of a type conducive to good conditions for learning.

3. Negative Conditioning to Reading. The child has built up a negative emotional response to reading (fear, anger, dislike) through the normal working of the principles of learning by association. Reading, having been present with someone or something already feared or disliked, becomes capable by itself of producing negative emotional reactions. As an example, a child had a first-grade teacher who walked around the room rapping knuckles with a ruler, and this teacher placed great stress on reading. The child's paniclike reaction to the teacher continued in response to reading lessons from other teachers in later years.

4. Displacement of Hostility. The child may be quite jealous of a favored brother or sister who is very good in reading, and his hostility becomes transferred to the act of reading which is the sibling's strong point. Another pattern is that of the child whose parent is an avid reader and who is unable to express hostility toward the parent in any open and direct fashion. The hostility may be expressed indirectly by failure in reading which is so important to the parent. Displaced hostility is rarely recognized as such by either parent or child.

5. Resistance to Pressure. It has been known for many years that mothers who are overanxious about a child's eating, and so try during early childhood to cram as much food as possible into the child, often find their children becoming feeding problems. Similarly the overambitious parent who wants Jimmy to be a genius can develop a resistance to pressure for intellectual attainment that may take the form of lack of interest in reading. Reading in such cases can become the main battleground on which the child fights for his rights.

6. Clinging to Dependency. The child who is overprotected and babied may, consciously or unconsciously, prefer to remain infantile and get attention through helplessness. Learning to read may mean growing up and becoming self-reliant, which the child is not yet ready to attempt. This is a common pattern among children who were only children for four or five years, the first brother or sister arriving while they were in kindergarten or first grade. Such children tend to interpret being sent to school as an attempt to get them out of the house so mother can give her full attention to the baby.

7. *Quick Discouragement.*   Some children start off with a desire to learn to read, but meet with some initial difficulty and quickly give up and stop trying. These children, as a rule, are boys and girls who come to school with marked feelings of inferiority and insecurity already well established. Their home life fails to provide them with security and affection. Often they come from broken homes or homes in which much quarreling goes on. Many of them have the feeling (justified or unjustified) that their parents do not care for them. In various ways their lives have failed to give them wholesome feelings of self-confidence and self-respect. Because of this, they are easily convinced that they are stupid and accept their inferior status in reading as natural when other, more self-confident children would exert extra effort.

8. *Success Is Dangerous.*   In some children with deep-lying emotional problems almost any successful form of self-expression may stir up feelings of intense anxiety and distress, related to unconscious fears of destruction or damage. For such a child success in reading may symbolize entering into an adult activity and therefore attempting to compete as a rival with a parent; such competition, in turn, implies the possibility of dreadful forms of retaliation. On an unconscious level such a child feels that safety lies in self-restriction and passivity. This type of reaction, based on deep-lying unconscious conflicts, tends to be quite resistive to remedial help unless psychotherapy is also provided.

9. *Extreme Distractibility or Restlessness.*   A high degree of tension in a child may build up an uncontrollable need for relief in the form of physical activity. The child who is unable to sit still is likely to fall behind in learning, and once he is aware of being behind, quick discouragement is likely to set in. Distractibility is often closely related to restlessness and complicates the picture, since the child's attention is pulled away from the reading task by almost any stimulus. In cases of neurological deviation, distractibility is one of the main problems to be overcome and often requires that the remedial work be completely individual, be conducted in a bare, distraction-free place, and be done calmly since high motivation may bring about disorganization.

10. Absorption in a Private World. Some children are absorbed in thoughts of their own to such an extent that they can give only intermittent attention to their environments and cannot devote to reading the sustained attention needed for good learning. Many of their daydreams and reveries are of a wish-fulfilling type, in which they hit home runs, score touchdowns, and fulfill other romantic ambitions. Sometimes their ruminations are of a morbid character. In either case, their inner preoccupation interferes with the attentive concentration that good reading requires. When retreat into fantasy is so severe as to interfere with progress in a good remedial situation, referral for study by a clinical psychologist or psychiatrist is desirable. Some of these children, who seem merely to be inattentive so far as the teacher is concerned, are found to have severe mental disturbances (obsessive-ruminative psychoneuroses or schizoid states) for which intensive psychotherapy is urgently needed. If the condition is severe (autism or childhood schizophrenia), residential care may be required. But some schizophrenic children can respond to remedial reading help on an out-patient basis (Levison, 1970).

In describing these ten types of emotional reactions found in reading problems, an attempt has been made to make them understandable to teachers. More technical descriptions have been given by Pearson (1952). One must not be surprised to find cases which do not fit neatly into any of these categories; Blanchard's published cases are excellent correctives for any misconception that reading cases fall into neatly separated types (1935, 1936, 1946). For the psychologist using projective tests, the *Rorschach* patterns described by Vorhaus (1952) and by Stavrianos and Landsman (1969), although not specific to children with reading problems, are worth careful study.

Irving Harris (1961) has reported in detail a comparison of 100 cases having learning difficulties with 100 cases not having difficulties, at the Institute for Juvenile Research in Chicago; all were boys. Particular significance was attributed to socioeconomic status, family disorganization, parental ambitiousness, birth order and expectations of maturity, and extremes of aggression and submission. The nonlearner group was more likely to be from a lower-class or lower-middle-class family. His family was likely to be disorganized by both marital incompatibility and a working mother, resulting in chronic anxiety as to whether the home would fall apart. His mother was likely to be overambitious for his success in school, despite his (usually) low average intelligence; he was likely to resist with dawdling and procrastination. He was less likely to be an oldest child and more likely to be a youngest child. If his parents tended to project blame onto scapegoats, he was likely to be highly aggressive; if they guiltily took on too much self-blame, the son was likely to be overly submissive and anxious to please. Poor readers were likely to be either aggressively hostile or extremely submissive. "One conclusion is clearly evident: namely, that since learning problems have several causes rather than just one, each case has to be understood in its own terms. . . . Any one of the factors discussed *may* predispose a boy to some difficulty in learning. The greater the number of factors existing simultaneously in one case, the greater is the likelihood that a learning problem will be present" (I. D. Harris, 1961, p. 143).

Effect of Reading Failure on Personality

Any child who finds himself outdistanced by the other children is apt to be disturbed by his lack of progress. At first he is likely to try harder. If his efforts are misdirected and fail to bring improvement, eventually he develops a strong feeling of frustration. He becomes convinced that he is "dumb" or stupid. When he is called upon to read, he is apt to become tense and emotionally upset, which makes his performance even worse. He generally builds up a strong dislike for reading and takes every opportunity to avoid it. In school, as he falls farther and farther behind, he loses interest in much of the classwork and becomes inattentive, at least during reading lessons. His parents are likely to show strong disappointment because of his poor report cards and may nag, threaten, or punish him. This in turn tends to intensify his emotional difficulties and increase his dislike for school. Thus a vicious cycle becomes established.

Disabled readers tend to be keenly aware that they are generally rated low in social acceptability by their classmates (Stevens, 1971). Many of them assume that their reading problems prove either that they are stupid, or that there is something special wrong with their brains. In a psychotherapy group for severely disabled readers from a vocational high school, much time had to be spent discussing their expressed hope that some kind of operation could fix their brains. It is no wonder that many disabled readers rate high in school-related anxiety (Neville, Pfost, and Dobbs, 1967), are low in self-esteem, and have poor self-concepts and marked feelings of inferiority (Athey, 1966; Martyn, 1972).

The child with a reading difficulty is very sensitive to the opinions of others and usually feels very keenly the criticism which teachers, classmates, and parents may express, even when the critical attitude is not stated plainly in words, but only implied in actions and facial expressions. If the teacher is lacking in sympathetic understanding of the child's problem, the child is likely to become bitterly resentful.

Different children react to feelings of failure in different ways. Some attempt to make themseves as inconspicuous as possible and develop a meek, timid attitude that seems to say that they hope nobody will notice them. These children often acquire the habit of daydreaming to excess. Nervous habits, such as twitching, nail biting, stuttering, and general fidgetiness, appear in reading disability cases who showed no signs of nervousness when they entered school. Some complain of headaches and dizziness or resort to vomiting spells in order to be sent home frequently. One youngster played hooky whenever he had a little money and would ride up and back on the subway until he was caught or hunger got the best of him. Fairly satisfactory compensations are achieved by some through becoming highly proficient in such school subjects as arithmetic and drawing, or by becoming outstanding in mechanical work or athletics. A few attempt to compensate for their shortcomings by boasting, bluffing, and exaggerating. One remedial case was described by his teacher as "a suitable prospect for the Tall Story Club." Still others adopt a truculent, defiant pose, as if to dare anyone—teacher included—to make fun of their weakness. The meaning of their behavior can be understood only by one who is willing to look for the reasons behind their behavior before taking disciplinary measures.

Even if a child is emotionally well adjusted when he enters school, continued failure in the most important part of schoolwork is practically certain to have unfavorable effects on his personality.

Parental Reactions

As we have noted, some children react negatively to reading in response to a home situation for which the parents are primarily responsible. Going beyond that, it is important to inquire how parents react to the discovery that their child is not learning to read.

In a follow-up study of over 200 cases, it was concluded that severe reading disabilities caused emotional problems in families more often than family emotional problems caused reading disabilities. The parents were especially hurt by three problems: 1) frustration in the attempt to find good diagnostic and treatment resources; 2) the ignorance, hostility, and defensiveness of some teachers and principals; and 3) actual cruelty to the child in the classroom (Kline and Kline, 1973).

Efforts to get accurate information from parents, and to convey diagnostic conclusions and recommendations to them, sometimes fail because the parents are unable to respond.

> Parental reactions of denial, projection, helplessness, and hopelessness are equally common and equally deterrents to adjustment. Denial is a basic form

of self-protection against painful realities. Some parents are unable to face the facts; they cannot "hear" the diagnostic interpretation; they "shop around" for magical cures; they acknowledge physical defects but are oblivious to mental disability. . . . The tendency of some parents to project blame elsewhere for the child's shortcomings is further symptomatic of stress. The obstetrician is blamed for inducing labor prematurely, the pediatrician is blamed for improper treatment of infection and injury, and sometimes parents blame each other. When the teacher is included as a target for blame, an effective partnership with the parent is difficult to achieve. In denial or projection, the child is the ultimate loser. (Begab, 1967)

Investigating Emotional and Social Conditions

Understanding of the child's emotional makeup comes best from learning his past history and from day-to-day contact with him. The first and perhaps the most important phase of remedial procedure is to get on terms of friendship with the child. After the teacher is accepted as a friend he can usually get the child to talk with some freedom about himself, his likes and dislikes, his fears and hopes, his hobbies and interests, his friends and enemies, his family—in fact, about nearly anything. Since many of these children regard themselves as friendless, the remedial teacher is in an ideal position to establish himself as a sympathetic listener.

Personality tests of the paper-pencil questionnaire type are often not very helpful with reading disability cases. Frequently it is necessary to read the questions to the child—a procedure that is time-consuming and probably less revealing than the information one could obtain by using the same time for informal talks. However, if the child can read well enough, tests like the *California Test of Personality* may give helpful information. There are some children who find it very difficult to talk about their feelings, but have less difficulty answering the more impersonal printed questions. An incomplete-sentence test like the one in Figure 18.2 (p. 527) may be very revealing.

The psychologist working in a clinic, who has only a limited time in which to try to understand the child, relies on interviews and observation of the child's behavior during testing, supplemented by case history material and by the use of projective tests of personality. The *Rorschach* is often used, supplemented by a picture interpretation test (the *Michigan Picture Test* seems more productive of material related to reading problems than the *Thematic Apperception Test* or the *Children's Apperception Test*) and interpretation of drawings and play activities.

The parents are important sources of information, and the opinions and information they can supply should be sought. With both children and parents it is important to seem understanding, sympathetic, and noncritical if true feelings are to be expressed. Even when a cordial relationship has been established, one must remember that self-protection and self-deception are both very prevalent trends, so that what one is told must be interpreted with discriminating judgment.

Among the questions one should try to answer are the following:

1] Who are the other people in the home? What are their ages? How much education have they had? Which ones work? What are their outstanding traits?

2] What is the social and economic status of the family? How large is the family income? What sort of house and what sort of neighborhood do they live in? Are they living at a poverty, marginal, adequate, comfortable, or luxurious level? Has the status of the family changed markedly since the child's birth?

3] How adequate is the physical care given the child? Is he provided with suitable food and clothing? Does he get proper attention when sick? Have his physical defects been corrected?

4] What intellectual stimulation is provided in the home? What language is spoken? How cultured are the parents and other members of the family? What newspapers, magazines, and books are available in the home? How much has the child been encouraged to read?

5] How is the child treated by his parents? Do they love him, or are there indications of rejection or of marked preference for other children? What disciplinary procedures do they use? Do they compare him unfavorably with other children or regard him as stupid? Are they greatly disappointed in him?

6] How is the child treated by his brothers and sisters? What do they think about him? Do they boss him or tease him about his poor ability?

7] How does the child feel about his family? Does he feel neglected or mistreated? Has he feelings of hatred or resentment against members of his family? Does he resort to undesirable behavior in order to get attention?

8] What efforts have been made to help him at home with his schoolwork? Who has worked with him? What methods have been used? How has the child responded to this help? What have the results been?

9] How does the child spend his spare time? What interests does he show? Does he have any hobbies? Does he show any special talent? What are his goals for the future?

10] Who are his friends, what are they like, and how does he get along with them? Does he play by himself? Does he prefer younger children? Is he a leader or a follower?

11] What signs of emotional maladjustment does he show? Has he any specific nervous habits? Is he a poor eater or poor sleeper? What variations from normal emotional behavior does he show?

12] How does he feel about himself? Has he resigned himself to being stupid? Does he give evidence of open feelings of inferiority and discouragement? If not, what substitute forms of behavior has he adopted?

When there seems to be evidence of a marked emotional disturbance the teacher should not try to analyze this himself, but should take the initiative to call the child to the attention of the person responsible for working with such problems in the school system; this may be the school guidance counselor, school psychologist, principal, visiting teacher, or school social worker. Intensive study in a child guidance clinic or examination by a clinical psychologist or psychiatrist is probably needed. Decisions on what kind of treatment should be started first, and whether or not to proceed with remedial teaching, should preferably be made by the specialist or the clinic. If, however, there will have to be a delay of several months before the special diagnostic study can be carried out, it is better to try remedial instruction than just to wait and do nothing.

Those who are interested in delving further into the relations between reading disability and social and emotional problems will find helpful integrative summaries and discussions, accompanied by useful bibliographies, by Sampson (1966), Connolly (1971), and A. J. Harris (1971b).

IV. INTERRELATIONSHIPS OF CAUSAL FACTORS

The diagnostic problem would be comparatively easy if one could expect to find only one important handicap in each reading disability problem. That would be, unfortunately, a mistaken expectation. Most children who develop severe disabilities labor under the burden of several different handicaps, any one of which could be an important drawback to progress in reading.

Mitchell was seven and a half years old and had just completed the second grade in a private school. His teacher did not think that his reading was very poor, but his mother was very much worried about it. During a morning of testing and interviewing, the following significant facts were discovered:

1) Mitchell had average or slightly above-average general intelligence, but showed definite inferiority in visual perception. 2) His speech was also somewhat indistinct, and a slight hearing loss was suspected. 3) He had entered the first grade in public school when only five and a half years old. His teacher rated him as immature and inattentive, and in addition he missed several weeks because of scarlet fever. He was transferred to a private school and entered the high first grade with zero reading ability. Lack of reading readiness because of too early a start was obvious. 4) Tests with the *Keystone Visual Survey* showed marked difficulty in binocular vision, with both vertical and horizontal eye-muscle imbalance. He had been taken to an eye specialist, who prescribed stereoscopic exercises to correct the condition, but Mitchell's mother had had difficulty in getting him to do the exercises and had discontinued them. 5) Mitchell showed marked right-hand dominance and equally definite left-eye dominance; he could not remember which was his right hand and which his left and could be considered a case of crossed lateral dominance with directional confusion. 6) The combination of inferiority in visual perception, indistinct speech, immaturity, inattentiveness, poor eye coordination, and directional confusion strongly suggests delayed and irregular neurological maturation. 7) He had been exposed to teaching that was undoubtedly ineffective and unsuited to his needs. Although the class was small, there was no individualization of work. The teacher used the now-outmoded story-memory method; one day the teacher would read a selection to the class, and the next day the pupils would take turns in oral reading of the same selection. Mitchell had good auditory memory, and by listening carefully he had been able to "read" well without paying much attention to the printed words. Actually he was unable to read primer material satisfactorily, but he had been trying to read first and second readers. No training in phonics or word analysis had been given. 8) There were several sources of emotional difficulty. Mitchell had been a nervous, overactive child since babyhood. His mother had taken him to a child guidance clinic when he was four years old, because she had had such trouble trying to get him to mind. He had one older sister whose good behavior and excellent schoolwork were frequently held up to him as examples. His father had been in the army for three years, stationed away from home. Since Mitchell was much more attached to his father than to his mother, this separation was undoubtedly a source of anxiety. 9) Mitchell had never shown evidence of a really strong desire to learn to read.

In this case, as in so many others, it was impossible to determine the relative contribution of each handicap to the total picture of failure. The number of different handicaps he showed is by no means unusual in severe reading disabilities. From a practical standpoint, the aim of a thorough diagnosis is not to fix the blame for the child's difficulties, but to discover each of the many conditions that may require correction. A person who develops an enthusiasm for any one theory of causation can frequently find evidence of the handicap he looks for, but is likely to overlook many other significant complications while doing so. An unbiased search for every possible handicap is needed for a really comprehensive and satisfactory diagnosis. This usually requires the combined efforts of professionals from several different professions.

It is satisfying to a diagnostician to be able to come out with a definite conclusion about causation in each case, but from a practical viewpoint this is unnecessary. The practical value of an intensive diagnostic study depends on the degree to which answers are provided to the following questions: 1) What persisting and present handicaps are likely to interfere with responsiveness to remedial instruction? 2) What can be done to eliminate these handicaps, or to lessen their impact? 3) Should remediation be started as soon as possible, or should it be delayed until other forms of treatment help the child to be more responsive to instruction?

Among the forms of non-educational treatment to be considered are correction or control of medical conditions, orthoptic training to improve visual efficiency, speech correction, drug treatment to control hyperactivity, and counseling or psychotherapy for the child, the parents or the family group. Aside from remedial instruction, educational recommendations may involve a change of school, of class, or of teacher, and may require providing information about the child to the school staff in a way that should improve their treatment of him.

SUGGESTED ADDITIONAL READING

BANNATYNE. ALEXANDER. *Language, reading and learning disability: psychology, neuropsychology, diagnosis, and remediation.* Springfield, Ill.: Charles C Thomas. 1971. Chaps. 5, 12, 13.

BOND, GUY L. & TINKER, MILES A. *Reading difficulties: their diagnosis and correction* (3rd ed.). New York: Appleton-Century-Crofts, 1973. Chap. 6.

FIGUREL, J. ALLEN (Ed.). *Reading goals for the disadvantaged.* Newark, Del.: International Reading Association, 1970.

HORN. THOMAS D. (Ed.). *Reading for the disadvantaged: problems of linguistically different learners.* New York: Harcourt, Brace and World, 1970.

LAFFEY, JAMES L. & SHUY, ROGER (Eds.). *Language differences: do they interfere?* Newark, Del.: International Reading Association, 1973.

NATCHEZ, GLADYS (Ed.). *Children with reading problems: classic and contemporary issues in reading disability.* New York: Basic Books, 1968. Pp. 23–89, 159–216.

OTTO, WAYNE; MC MENEMY, RICHARD A.; & SMITH, RICHARD J. *Corrective and remedial teaching* (2nd ed.). Boston: Houghton Mifflin, 1973. Chap. 4.

REID, JESSIE F. (Ed.). *Reading: problems and practices.* London, England: Ward Lock Educational, 1972. Pp. 45–124.

RUDDELL, ROBERT B. *Reading—language instruction: innovative practices.* Englewood Cliffs, N.J.: Prentice-Hall, 1974. Chap. 9.

RUSSELL, DAVID H. *The dynamics of reading.* Edited by Robert B. Ruddell. Waltham, Mass.: Ginn-Blaisdell, 1970. Chap. 5.

SCHELL, LEO M. & BURNS, PAUL (Eds.). *Remedial reading: classroom and clinic* (2nd ed.). Boston: Allyn and Bacon, 1972. Pp. 47–93; 130–137.

SEBESTA, SAM L. & WALLEN, CARL J. (Eds.). *The first R: readings on teaching reading.* Chicago: Science Research Associates, 1972. Pp. 361–419.

STRANG, RUTH. *Diagnostic teaching of reading* (2nd ed.). New York: McGraw-Hill, 1969. Chaps. 3, 5, 12, 13, 14.

ZINTZ, MILES V. *Corrective reading* (2nd ed.). Dubuque, Iowa: W. C. Brown, 1972. Chaps. 6, 7.

13

Basic Principles
of Remedial Reading

Remedial teaching is highly individualized teaching based on diagnostic study of the child's unique problems and needs. It is highly individualized also in the skills that are selected for emphasis, in the materials used, and in the varied approaches that help different children to achieve common basic skills.

In many ways remedial instruction resembles good classroom instruction. Both are aiming toward the same desired outcomes regarding reading skills and interests. Both try to apply or induce effective motivation. Both attempt to suit the nature and pace of instruction to learners. Both utilize many materials in common. Both involve applications of the same basic principles of learning.

The distinction between remedial teaching and classroom teaching has become less sharp as superior teachers have incorporated into their daily procedures the principles which are fundamental in good remedial work. In their classes, the level and type of instruction is based on an understanding of what the pupils need; drill is not an end in itself, but is employed when teacher and pupils recognize the need for it; work is related to vital pupil interests; and happy, busy children move on from one successful learning experience to another.

The problems involved in helping children with reading difficulties are much the same, whether the help is given in a regular classroom or in a special small group or individual teaching situation. For this reason, the term "remedial" is used in the rest of this chapter as applying both to corrective reading in classrooms and to remedial reading in an out-of-class situation.

I. GENERAL CHARACTERISTICS OF REMEDIAL TEACHING

Basing Remedial Instruction on Diagnosis

When a car is towed into a garage a good mechanic tries to find out exactly what has gone wrong with it—to locate the particular part that is defective or to discover what adjustment needs to be made. Effective remedial teaching is similarly based first of all on an attempt to find out what is wrong and in a similar way involves concentrated effort to improve the phases of performance which are deficient.

The slogan "Teach, test, reteach" has gained considerable popularity. It sums up very briefly a good deal of educational wisdom. It points out the need for accurate measurement of the success of pupils in mastering the subject matter to which they have been exposed and the desirability of emphasizing in review the particular phases of the work that escaped them the first time. The teacher who has acquired this point of view is applying the basic principle of remedial teaching in his everyday work.

When children are scheduled for remedial work, the slogan needs a little modification. It now should read, "Test, teach, retest." The pupils have failed to master the material when it was first taught to them, so the teacher starts with testing to determine what needs to be retaught. On the basis of his results he decides on an appropriate plan of teaching to overcome the difficulties which are apparent. After proceeding with this type of instruction for a while, it is necessary to test again to see whether the instruction has been effective. Sometimes the retest shows that the difficulties which were present at the beginning have been overcome, but that new difficulties have now become apparent. It then becomes necessary to plan another teaching program in the light of the new information and to continue in this way until achievement is generally satisfactory.

Starting from What the Pupil Knows

Laying a foundation before putting up a superstructure is as important in educational work as it is in building construction. In arithmetic it is accepted that a knowledge of number combinations is essential for progress in computation, that addition should be taught before multiplication, and so on. The sequence of instruction in reading is not as clearly established and stages of progress are not as clearly defined as in arithmetic, but the same principle of laying the necessary foundations before proceeding to a higher level holds good. If a 12-year-old has second-grade reading ability, his instruction should start at the second-grade level. If he has marked weaknesses in word recognition, those must be overcome before one can expect to get satisfactory results from instruction designed to increase comprehension.

Selecting Appropriate Material

The first important problem in the selection of materials is to find reading of the appropriate level of difficulty. The necessity of providing pupils with material which they can read without too much difficulty can hardly be overemphasized. The interest value of the reading is another very important problem, since pupils try hardest on materials that they like, and older boys and girls often express disdain for books written for younger children. An abundance of varied types of books and exercises should be available if a well-rounded program of reading is to be followed.

Securing Motivation

Perhaps the most important problems in remedial work are those which are concerned with arousing interest and maintaining effort. Without good motivation a remedial program is sure to be ineffective. Like a car with a dead battery, it cannot move along because it lacks the needed spark. Because motivation is so important, a separate section is devoted to it.

II. PRINCIPLES OF EFFECTIVE MOTIVATION[1]

The child whose initial efforts to read have been unsuccessful gets caught in a vicious cycle. Because his experiences in reading have been unpleasant, he has learned to dislike reading. Because he dislikes reading, he avoids it when he can. By doing a minimum of practice, he achieves a minimum of improvement. Meanwhile, those who enjoy reading keep on improving, and the poor reader's handicap keeps on increasing.

Without the will to learn, the child in need of help in reading rarely accomplishes very much. The term "remedial teaching" has tended to concentrate attention mainly on what the teacher does. It is time that we talk more about "remedial learning," since the heart of the problem is not what

1. Much of the material in this section is taken from A. J. Harris (1953, 1966a).

the teacher does but what the learner does. The teacher's main task is to arouse in the learner the motivation to do the necessary but not always easy or interesting jobs that must be accomplished in becoming a competent reader and to guide the learning situation in such a way that the motivation is sustained.

The poor reader feels his inadequacy not only in reading lessons but also in all other phases of schoolwork in which reading is done. One can accept a limited type of failure, such as being unable to sing in tune or write very legibly, without being hurt deeply or having one's self-estimate badly impaired. The stress placed on reading as a criterion of general competence in school, by teachers, by parents, and by fellow pupils, often causes the child who regards himself as a poor reader to feel that he is an intellectual pauper. Being a poor reader is far worse than being an inaccurate speller or a clumsy gymnast or an incompetent artist, because the poor reader so often concludes that he must be generally stupid.

From this standpoint, the central task in remedial reading is to help the learner to change his feelings about reading. A thorough program aimed at this goal has four main aspects. First, the poor reader should be helped to feel that he is liked, appreciated, and understood. Second, success experiences are needed to supply the basis for overcoming the negative aftereffects of frustration and failure. Third, active effort must be stimulated and sustained by use of both intrinsically interesting reading matter and extrinsic or somewhat artificial incentives. Finally, the learner should become involved as fully as possible in the analysis of his reading problem, the planning of his own reading activities, and the evaluation of his results.

The Remedial Teacher as a Person

The most important characteristic of a good remedial teacher is a real liking for children. The liking must be genuine; children quickly detect the difference between a warm, friendly person and one who puts on a show of friendliness without really feeling that way. Appearance, dress, age, speech, theoretical knowledge, experience—all these are less important than a genuine fondness for children as they are, complete with their faults and annoying habits.

Good remedial teachers convey a note of optimism and good cheer to the children. They may be full of contagious enthusiasm, or they may be quiet people who create a calm, relaxed atmosphere. In their contacts with children they try to avoid any display of vexation or irritation. They look for opportunities to praise and try to make all of their criticism kindly and constructive.

Good remedial teachers are also sensitive to the emotional needs of the children. They try to provide settings in which children can feel that they are appreciated and that their ideas and feelings are respected. They seek to build up their self-confidence and to restore their shaken feelings of personal worth. They encourage children to confide in them by accepting their confidences with friendly interest. They never force a child to do anything, but instead, arrange the situation so that the child will do willingly what the teacher wants.

A few people seem to be naturally endowed with warmth, tact, and sympathetic understanding. Such people usually get good results in remedial work even if the methods they employ are far from the best. A few others seem to be completely insensitive to children as people; these should avoid all branches of the teaching profession. The rest, comprising the majority, can improve their relationships with children greatly.

The teacher who succeeds with poor readers must be able to convey to them the feeling that they are liked, appreciated, and understood. Each teacher must do this in ways harmonious with his or her own personality. A quiet teacher who creates a calm, relaxed atmosphere, a vivacious teacher who stirs children up, and a strong teacher whose self-confidence conveys a feeling of security to children may all get fine results although their ways are different. Children know when they are liked and also have a keen sense for hypocrisy. The teacher who does not like a child usually cannot help him.

Acceptance, Approval, and Understanding

Some children are so deeply discouraged that they have given up trying and have resigned themselves to chronic failure. This attitude may pervade not only their response to school but also their general social relationships. Daydreaming may take the place of any attempt at real accomplishment. For such children it may be wise to delay a new start on reading until the child has found at least one other activity in which he feels successful and for which he has received merited approval and recognition.

Peter, a nonreader, was so withdrawn that a total break with reality was feared. Instead of starting immediately with reading, it was decided to work first on improving his social adjustment. With excellent cooperation from his classroom teacher, Peter was gradually drawn into activity with puppets. His first step was manipulating a puppet, out of sight behind the little stage. Performing at first for the teacher, then for a couple of classmates, he gradually worked up to larger audiences. This was the entering wedge. Gradually he became more communicative and began to enter more actively into social participation with his classmates. Remedial reading was successfully begun several months later.

Osburn (1951) strongly recommended starting the child with some easy-to-learn skill that is respected by other children and found magic tricks to be ideal for this purpose. It makes sense to attack total discouragement first by building success in an area in which good results can be obtained far more quickly than in reading.

The poor reader's needs go beyond being liked; he desperately wants to be understood. He often feels hurt or discouraged, or angry. The teacher who is sensitive to these feelings and can get across to the child the conviction that the teacher's kindly interest is not shaken by his awareness of these feelings actually can help the child greatly to get his emotions under control.

One of the feelings prevalent among poor readers is the notion that they are not like other children, that their troubles are strange and unusual. The teacher should, therefore, try to convey the ideas that one can be bright in many ways and still have trouble with reading, that many children have trouble learning to read, and that it is a difficulty which is neither unusual nor impossible to overcome.

During the course of a remedial program there are inevitable downs as well as ups. These are times when discouragement returns and effort slackens. These periods are sometimes induced by events outside the remedial program. A quarrel at home, a cold, insufficient sleep, or a sarcastic remark by another teacher may be the starting point of a slump. At these times the remedial teacher can provide invaluable support by slowing the pace and maintaining a steady faith in the child. Being a sympathetic listener for the child who wants to pour out his troubles also serves a useful purpose, provided the teacher remains a friendly teacher and does not trespass into psychotherapy.

Nothing Succeeds Like Success

Being understanding, sympathetic, and encouraging will not do much good if the child continues to experience frustration in his efforts at reading. It is essential at the beginning of a remedial program to start at a level easy enough so that a successful learning experience is virtually certain. The inexperienced remedial teacher often fails to recognize fully the extent of the child's deficiency and tends to overestimate the level at which he is able to experience success. Because of this, the invaluable lift that comes when hope is reinforced by real achievement may be forfeited.

One of the pitfalls for the unwary is relying too much on the grade scores obtained from standardized reading tests. These scores tend to show the level at which comprehension can be achieved with difficulty, rather than the level at which fluency and reasonable accuracy can be expected. Sometimes it is wise to begin one or two years below the level indicated by test scores. Informal tryouts of sample pages from books of different difficulty levels may provide a better indication of where to start than can be gained from test scores.

After a child has tasted the delightful flavor of an auspicious beginning, good judgment is needed in estimating how much to try to cover, how fast to go, and how soon to move to a higher level of difficulty. If the learner has developed real interest in his progress and is ready to go faster, he will often suggest a more rapid pace. The teacher who is patient and willing to proceed very slowly at first is often rewarded by accelerated progress later.

Dramatizing Progress

The principle of celebrating a child's success is essential in remedial teaching. Every sign of improvement in the child's work should be noted and praised. Since most poor readers are insecure and lack self-confidence, visible, concrete evidence of their improvement is more important than it is with normal readers.

Progress charts can be devised to record progress in any phase of reading. Different kinds of progress charts can be constructed for number of pages, stories, or books read; number of new words learned; decrease in number of errors in oral reading; number of word families or phonic principles learned; accuracy of comprehension; rate of reading; and so on. It is desirable to have a separate record for each goal that is being emphasized in the remedial program. At any one time, a remedial pupil should be keeping track of his improvement toward three or four different goals. After these goals have been achieved, new ones should be set up.

There are many different kinds of progress charts. With very young children, colored stars, paper bunnies, or pine trees that can be pasted onto a piece of stiff paper work very well. With older children, more sophisticated forms are usually desirable.

Some of the types of charts that have been used successfully are as follows:

1] The thermometer chart. This is useful for recording, a cumulative result, such as the number of pages read or number of words learned. A useful variant is a rocket ship chart (see Fig. 13.1).
2] The skyscraper chart. As the child finishes a unit, he fills in a window.
3] The race-track chart. Progress is recorded by moving a tiny auto or

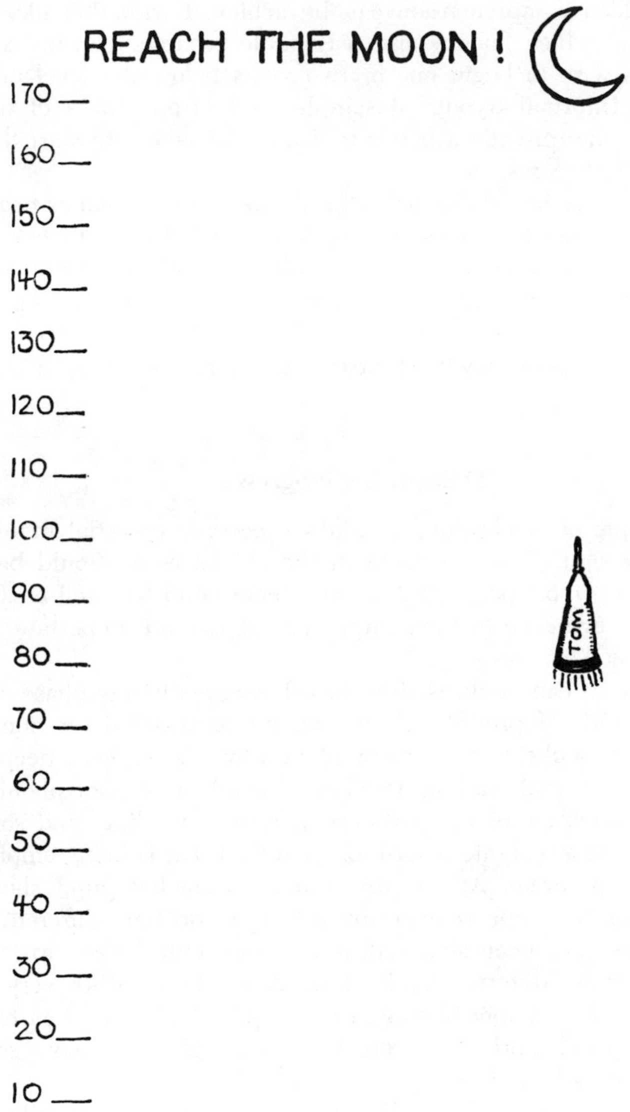

REACH THE MOON !

170 —

160 —

150 —

140 —

130 —

120 —

110 —

100 —

90 —

80 —

70 —

60 —

50 —

40 —

30 —

20 —

10 —

FIGURE 13.1   An individual progress chart that can be adapted to record number of words learned, exercises completed, pages read, rate of reading, etc. Can be used also with a small group, each child having his own rocket ship. Rocket ship is held in place with masking tape or with tape that is adhesive on both sides, and can be lifted off and replaced.

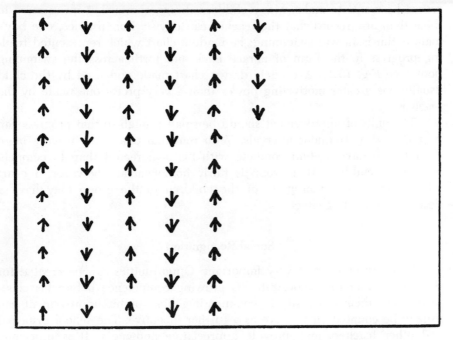

FIGURE 13.2   Progress chart in the form of 220-yard swimming race.
Each arrow represents two Dolch words learned. Credit
was given for all Dolch words known at the start. The pool
was colored blue.

horse around the track. A variant is a swimming pool, Figure 13.2.

4] The map chart. A trip by airplane across the country or to the North
Pole represents successive good lessons.

5] The bar graph. This can be used for the whole group. Each child
has a line and fills in another block as he completes each unit.

6] The bookcase chart. The child draws an empty bookcase and, as he
finishes each story or book, draws another book in the bookcase.
The books can be of various colors. See Figure 18.3.

7] The airplane or ship chart. Each child cuts an airplane or ship out of
colored paper, prints his name on it, and pastes it to a large piece
of stiff cardboard in such a way as to leave a little pocket. As he
finishes a story or book, he prints the name of it on a small slip of
paper and places it in his basket or ship. See Figure 18.4.

8] The line graph. This is best adapted for recording progress in speed
and accuracy of comprehension. See Figure 19.5.

Frequently it is advisable to let the child decide on the kind of progress record he wants to make. Many children design charts that mean more to them than any record that the teacher can devise. For instance, one boy's main enthusiasm was swimming; he made a chart which represented reading progress in the form of a race back and forth across the swimming pool (see Fig. 13.2). A crudely drawn chart made and used by the child usually has greater motivating power than a very pretty one made by the teacher.

The units of improvement should be small enough so that progress can be recorded at frequent intervals. With remedial cases it is usually more desirable to have a child compete with his own record than to compete with other children. If a group is fairly homogeneous, however, a chart which compares the progress of the children in the group may have a desirable motivating effect.

Social Recognition

Social recognition is very important. Opportunities can be created for the poor reader to demonstrate his growing competence before his classmates, and their generosity in commending him for his improvement can usually be counted on to serve as a further incentive. The school principal and other teachers may provide appreciative audiences. It is especially valuable to keep the parents well informed about the child's improvement. For many children the anxiety of the parents, shown in nagging, threats, punishment, and ineffectual attempts at tutoring, is one of the major deterrents to progress. When the parents begin to relax and discontinue these pressures at home, the child is able to function better.

The Interest Factor

The desirability of making reading interesting is not a controversial issue in theory. In practice it is often ignored, with teachers relying too much on drill and repetition.

To make reading interesting there are two main alternatives. One is to employ reading material that is intrinsically capable of attracting and holding the reader's interest. The other is to use the material available in ways that foster interest. The first places major reliance on finding or creating material, while the second emphasizes procedure. These are not alternatives in the sense that one has to choose one or the other, but rather two aspects which, when successfully combined, produce ideal results.

The teacher who has seen the magical effects obtainable when just the right book is placed in a child's hands cannot ever again disregard the importance of trying to match the book to the child. Some books have earned the honored place of being "starters"—books which over and over again have been a child's first captivating story book.

Two types of stories are particularly successful in this role. One type includes those which, like *Lentil* and *Mike Mulligan and His Steam Shovel,* employ the time-honored plot of the underdog who triumphs in the end. The other includes humorous stories, like *Mr. Popper's Penguin, Mary Poppins,* Bennett Cerf's *Book of Riddles,* and the absurd stories by Dr. Seuss, such as *The Cat in the Hat.* But no book has magic for all children. For one, animal stories; for another, cowboys and Indians; for a third, old-fashioned fairy tales; for a fourth, nothing will suit but solid scientific information. Mystery, adventure, sports, and hobbies provide spheres of interest for many. To find the right book, one must know both the child and the books. This problem is treated in detail in Chapter 18.

When unable to find material to fit the child's interest, the resourceful teacher is sometimes able to stimulate interest in material that is available. It is a mistake to assume that one must keep to the interests which a child already manifests. In attempting to sell a book in a new category it is well to use stories and books known to have wide appeal for many children.

Some children cannot read well enough for any book they are willing to try, and they will not accept "baby stuff." These children are usually trying to give the impression that they are grown up. Their inner insecurity makes it very difficult for them to acknowledge and accept the low level at which they actually can function in reading.

Creative writing can be both a way of building self-respect and an avenue to reading for these children. The emphasis placed by the late Grace Fernald (1943) on the use of stories created by the child was perhaps as great a contribution to remedial procedure as the kinesthetic procedures which she advocated.

This approach starts with conversation. The child is encouraged to talk about his recreational outlets—sports, pets, hobbies, or favorite radio and television programs. Careful note is made of anything about which he displays enthusiasm. Selecting one such topic, the teacher suggests that maybe he would like to make up a little story about it which the teacher will write down. With very inarticulate or inhibited children it is helpful to have pictures which can serve as the basis of brief descriptive statements. It is advisable to use the child's exact words, even if somewhat ungrammatical. As the child becomes more secure, he can select a favorite story for "editing" into correct spelling and usage. No effort should be made to simplify the vocabulary, since the child is using language that he understands and perhaps is quite proud of the long or unusual words he is able to employ. The early selections should be kept quite short.

Once dictated, the story is typed or printed in manuscript by the teacher, and then the child reads it. He is helped with the words when necessary. Several repetitions may bring the story to the point where it can be taken home and read to parents. The long and unusual words are likely to be identified quickly, while errors on common little words are apt to persist. Since the arousal of motivation is the most important goal of the early lessons, it is not wise to spend a large amount of time on word study. However, many children enjoy listing the new words they become able to recognize and are quite fussy about keeping the score accurately.

Essentially this procedure is very much the same as the language-experience approach which is widely used with beginning readers, and familiarity with that approach is necessary if one is to get the most out of it. It is important to avoid rote repetition without sufficient attention to the copy. Transfer of responsibility for writing the story to the child may be made as soon as he has enough of a writing vocabulary to feel like trying it; help with many words will continue to be needed. After a while the child will usually express a wish to start reading in a book, and a gradual transition to book reading can then be started.

The priceless ingredient of this approach is its ability to motivate many children who are resistive or antagonistic to easy printed materials. Its drawbacks are fairly obvious. It makes heavy demands on the teacher, who must prepare the reading matter and provide close supervision during the child's reading. It is also deficient in amount of reading and cannot provide the extensive reading practice necessary to develop fluency.

Fortunately, many poor readers are not so resistant to the use of easy and not too exciting books. For many, the experience of being able to read anything with ease and fluency more than makes up for the immature content; success itself generates and maintains interest. Some of these children are emotionally immature enough really to enjoy stories written for children several years their junior. Others can be given the incentive of preparing simple little stories to read to younger brothers and sisters or to a first-grade or kindergarten class. High-interest, low-vocabulary books are often acceptable to poor readers.

The Begin-Over Approach.   With older children the teacher may find it desirable to explain the reasons for going back to very easy books. The importance of learning the bothersome little first- and second-grade words can be pointed out. Then the fact that the child is much older and smarter than when he tried these books before can be emphasized. If the child is willing to start over again, things will come much more easily and quickly, and a foundation can be built for progressing to reading matter more appropriate for his age.

The "begin-over" approach is not successful with all poor readers. It seems to be most suitable to those who are willing to do almost anything if it will help them and for those who find the content of primary grade readers acceptable. For these children, the carefully controlled vocabularies and well-spaced repetition of good modern readers help greatly in building up fundamental reading skills. Of course, the child should be allowed to progress through the materials as rapidly as his learning allows, even skipping stories and exercises that are not needed.

Avoiding Monotony

Variety adds spice to the remedial program. Children, even if highly motivated to improve their reading, often get tired of doing the same thing again and again. Each lesson should be subdivided into at least three different kinds of reading activities; some tutors like to break an hour lesson into at least five or six different kinds of activity. When there are daily reading lessons, it is desirable to vary the plan from day to day. From time to time a surprise should be introduced.

Another reason for variety during a remedial lesson is the desirability of keeping *reactive inhibition* to a minimum. Reactive inhibition is a lessening of learning efficiency as the same learning task is continued. Otto (1966) has summarized research evidence which indicates that a tendency to accumulate reactive inhibition is likely to contribute to learning difficulties and that poor readers show more of it than good readers. As a poor reader continues uninterruptedly with the same learning task, the effect of more practice is increasingly canceled by more reactive inhibition, so that the net gain may be very little. Reactive inhibition can be held to a minimum by introducing short rest periods, or by shifting from one kind of learning task to another, spending just a few minutes on each. The duration of the task should be geared to the child; some children welcome frequent shifts of activity, others are bothered by them.

Transforming Drills into Games

There are many kinds of remedial activities, such as practice in word and phrase recognition, learning phonic skills, and workbook exercises to sharpen comprehension, that are not particularly enjoyable. The desire to improve will carry the learner through them, but is usually not enough to produce the intense concentration characteristic of highly effective learning. Such activities can often be more exciting by the appropriate use of incentives.

Many kinds of drill can be disguised as games, becoming play rather than distasteful work (Shankman, 1968; Wagner and Hosier, 1970). Adaptations of bingo are easily constructed or can be purchased ready-made. Card games such as rummy and poker are easily adapted to the use of word or phrase cards. A magnet on a string catches fish (word cards decorated with paper clips) from a pond (desk top). The rules of baseball, football, and basketball provide scoring systems for competitive scoring between two teams, which can be groups of learners, pupil against pupil, or pupil against teacher. A number of devices of this type are described on pages 359–393.

Most effective, if properly used, is the learner's competitive urge to improve his own previous record. This is what gives such motivating power to remedial activities in which the learner can keep his score in comparable units, lesson after lesson. The magic of the *G-score* keeps the McCall-Crabbs exercises popular after over thirty years of use (see p. 504). The graphing of rate and comprehension scores on successive practices can be a most effective device for speeding up slow readers. The immediate goal of trying to beat last time's score is a major part of the fascination of such popular forms of recreation as golf, bowling, and fishing. The same type of motivation can be successfully utilized in remedial learning. Failure to try to use it means neglecting one of the most effective types of incentives.

A related issue is the avoidance of fatigue. In general, activities that are easy and pleasurable can be carried on for long periods of time, while those that require self-discipline and concentrated effort soon tire the learner. Even when well motivated in game form, reading activities that demand a high level of effort should be brief and interspersed with less taxing activities.

Behavior Modification

Since 1965 there has been a tremendous upsurge of interest in the application of behavior modification techniques (sometimes called "classroom engineerng" or "precision teaching'") to remedial education. In essence, this approach has two main features: 1) arranging a series of learning experiences starting from what the child can already do and progressing by very small steps in which a predominance of success is assured; and 2) applying effective reinforcers (rewards) to motivate and sustain effort.

Behavior modification is based on operant conditioning, the learning theory on which Skinner developed teaching machines and programmed instructional material. Behavior can be changed by gradually decreasing the differences between stimuli to be discriminated, by modifying the program of reinforcement, or by requiring the behavior to be reinforced to become gradually more specific or elaborate. "All of these programs, whether they relate to reinforcers, behaviors, or discriminative stimuli, have in common that they start out with and accept the level the organism starts out with, and then gradually alter it, in steps to produce the level that the investigator desires" (Goldiamond and Dyrud, 1966, p. 99).

A general description of the steps to be taken includes the following:

1) Specify very carefully the behavior to be modified. 2) Collect data on the occurrence of this behavior (often by counting the number of occurrences in a given period of time). 3) Manipulate the environment, using stimulus change and reinforcement, so behavior will change in the desired direction. 4) Continue to collect data to show degree and direction of change. 5) If change is insufficient, modify the program (Knowles, 1970).

Very often a token system is used, in which one or more tokens are earned for a desired response or series of responses (chips, beans, pennies, checks on a record card); when enough tokens have been earned they can be exchanged for a prize (*e.g.*, candy, a toy, a privilege). The reinforcement schedule is changed as learning progresses. Near the start, every desired response may be reinforced. As the child improves, reinforcement is given for larger numbers of correct responses and intermittently; intermittent reinforcement seems to be more lasting than consistent reinforcement.

A list of procedures which seems applicable to use with many remedial and corrective groups is as follows:

1] Make explicit rules as to what is expected of children for every instructional period.
2] Communicate rules to children as clearly as possible.
3] Determine what are potent rewards for these children.
4] Use rewards which are as potent as feasible.
5] Reward behaviors which facilitate learning.
6] Administer rewards with minimum delay and make it clear to the child why he is being rewarded.
7] Determine the maximum initial delay between the token reward and the actual reward which the students can tolerate and increase this delay.
8] Ignore behaviors which interfere with learning or teaching.
9] Reward behaviors incompatible with those you wish to decrease.
10] Bring peer group pressure to bear on nonconformers by giving some rewards only when all members of the group are complying.
11] Make it clear to the students that they earn points and prizes according to an objective system which they are free to follow or ignore and not by pleasing the teacher (Wilson and Flugman, 1969).

Behavior modification has been used with reading behaviors as different as word recognition (Hauserman and McIntire, 1969) and outside reading (Mason, 1968). It has been used with beginning readers (Pikulski, 1971; Holt, 1971), disadvantaged third graders (Bernstein, 1971), disabled ninth graders (Glavach and Stoner, 1970), and juvenile offenders with reading disabilities (Halstead, 1970).

Reinforcement. Near the beginning of a program, and particularly with children who have received little reinforcement in their previous school experiences, the more frequent the reinforcement, the better (Heitzman, 1970). Among the effective reinforcers are tokens exchangeable for prizes, feedback on progress, social reinforcement (D. E. Smith, Brethower, and Cabot, 1969), and rewards based on behavior of the whole group (Graubard, 1969). Bannatyne (1972) has provided a helpful descriptive listing of reinforcers that are useful to remedial teachers.

The importance of social reinforcers has been stressed by Kuypers, Becker, and O'Leary (1968). They favor giving praise and privileges for improvement in behavior as well as for academic learnings. Children showing deviant behaviors should be ignored, unless someone is being hurt or prevented from learning, in which case the offender is simply removed temporarily. It is important to catch the child doing something that can be rewarded, such as being in his seat, not talking to his neighbor, having the right materials in front of him, paying attention, and working, even if little academic progress is taking place.

It is highly desirable for teachers interested in learning about behavior modification to read fairly detailed descriptions of specific programs, such as those by Staats, Minke, and Butts (1970), Curry (1970), Haring and Hauck (1969), and Camp (1973). Brief summaries of such papers cannot convey the same kind of understanding.

Some cautions about behavior modification have also been expressed. It has been pointed out that although token economies are successful while in operation, the continuance of gains afterward and the generalization of behavior gains to other learning situations often have not been checked (Kazdin and Bootzin, 1972). Unless token systems lead to more natural reinforcers, the lasting benefit is speculative (Macmillan and Forness, 1970). The concept of "classroom engineering" may lead to a coldly mechanical application of reinforcement, which can give children the feeling of being manipulated; this may incur resentment and distrust. Instead, the use of specific reinforcing rewards should take place in an atmosphere which focuses on trust, positive attitudes, and empathy with the child (Griffiths, 1970–1971).

It is evident that reinforcement theory provides one kind of theoretical explanation for the strong emphasis that good remedial teachers were placing on motivation long before the concepts of behavioral modification were developed. They emphasized starting low enough and with small enough steps to insure success. They made the work interesting with games and carefully chosen materials. They provided frequent feedback on successful tries ("That's fine!", "OK!", "Terrific!", "Very good!"), and provided encouragement and praise for effort when the going was harder. They arranged for social reinforcement through praise from classroom teachers, parents, class-mates, the principal, and so on. They used progress charts and records to make progress vividly visible. The one thing that is new is the use of tokens exchangeable for prizes or privileges, and high motivation can be achieved without tokens.

Cooperation between Teacher and Learner

One of the vital ingredients of a well-motivated remedial approach is the learner's feeling that the program is his program, not something imposed on him by somebody else. This can be achieved if the reading problem is approached as something on which teacher and pupil can work together. For this to succeed, there must be a teacher-learner relationship in which the learner trusts the teacher's good intentions and wants to help himself. Under these conditions the learner can take an active part in discussing his problems in reading, in trying to select the particular weaknesses that are most urgently in need of attention, in the selection of materials to be used, and in evaluating progress. This is particularly true with adolescents.

The degree of insight some children possess into their own difficulties is amazing. Sometimes they not only can pick out the major weak points in their reading skills but also have intelligent ideas about how they came to be poor readers. Such children can often be given wide latitude in selecting their own materials. They delight in devising ways of checking their work and in constructing charts to record their progress.

This does not mean that the teacher adopts a passive role. On the contrary, the teacher is responsible for the entire process. He encourages the learner to make suggestions, but is obligated to point out important issues the learner may have overlooked, to correct erroneous interpretations and proposals, and to provide helpful guidance at every stage. Encouraging the learner to help in planning does not mean abdication of responsibility, but rather creating an atmosphere of truly cooperative work.

Occasionally one finds a pupil who resents the implication that anything is wrong with his reading. "Why pick on me? I can read all right," is a familiar complaint, particularly to junior high school teachers. In a way, many of these boys and girls are right. They can read enough to plow through a passable portion of the assigned reading. But their reading is likely to be laborious, halting, slow, full of minor inaccuracies and misunderstood words, and only partially understood. On standardized tests these pupils usually rate two or more years below grade placement. They are aware that they are not particularly good readers, but usually do not realize how faulty their reading actually is.

Bob, an eighth grader, was resentful about having been singled out of his class for special help in reading. "Maybe you are right," said the teacher. "You can take a reading test if you want to, and we can score it together. After that you can decide whether or not you want to work on your reading." Bob took the *Iowa Silent Reading Test, Elementary* (1943 Edition), on which his subtest grade scores ranged from 3.3 in Rate to 7.6 in Use of Index. A bright boy of 13, he was quite shocked at his poor showing. But he had checked the scoring himself, and soon he and the teacher were discussing possible reasons why his reading was so slow and listing some of the things he could do to increase his rate.

Learning exactly where one stands is not a good stimulus for some poor readers. To a sensitive, easily discouraged child it may be disheartening. It is also inadvisable for those whose reading is on a par with their general intellectual development and who are already reading about up to capacity. For them, emphasizing their retardation may be a form of needless cruelty. For pupils like Bob, however, the opportunity to learn just where they stand on objective standardized tests may be exactly what is needed to break through the crust of real or assumed indifference. One of the potential values of standardized tests often overlooked in schools is the function of helping the pupil, as well as the teacher, to appraise progress and become aware of needs.

Children sometimes develop the notion that the main reason for learning to read is to please the teacher. The teacher shows pleasure when one reads well and shows or implies displeasure when one reads poorly. If the child wants to retaliate against the teacher, it may seem logical to get even by not reading or by reading poorly.

Such an attitude is usually a transfer to the classroom of attitudes learned at home. Many children eat, not because they are hungry, but to please mother. Such children can often beat their mothers in a contest of wills by refusing to eat. If a child who has learned this technique has a mother who is quite concerned over his reading, he is likely to experiment to find out if rejecting reading can be used in the same way as rejecting food. Often the experiment is successful. Not progressing in reading can become a way of keeping mother's attention centered on the child, and this may be more important to the child than the satisfactions of successful learning. Since for young children teachers are to a large extent substitute parents, by not trying to read the child may be attempting to capture a larger share of the teacher's attention.

If the child is refusing to read because he thinks that he can control his mother and teacher that way, obviously the first step is to demonstrate to him that it will not work. Mother and teacher must both switch over to the attitude that they are not going to try to make Johnny read—if he does not learn, he is the one who will be hurt—and must maintain this attitude steadily for a period long enough to convince him. This is a plan that requires perseverance and should not be attempted unless there is good reason to believe that it will be carried through without faltering. In class, the teacher must be able to put across the idea that Johnny doesn't have to read if he doesn't want to and that while she likes him and would like to see him succeed, Johnny himself is the only one who loses out if he doesn't learn to read.

Underlying such a problem is the fact that the child has learned an undesirable way of getting attention, probably because he was not getting enough attention to satisfy him before. Since the underlying need for attention will persist, a really satisfactory solution must involve providing the child with better ways of getting the attention and affection that he craves. Approval must be given for many things he does which deserve commendation if he is to give up less praiseworthy means of attracting notice. When resistance to reading arises out of the fundamental emotional needs of the child, more than a change in teaching technique is required.

Remedial Reading and Psychotherapy

Good remedial teaching has some of the characteristics of good psychotherapy. It is based on the development of a friendly, warm, comfortable relationship between teacher and pupil, for which the term "rapport" is used. It employs suggestion and reassurance, sometimes used in psychotherapy, to encourage the child and express the faith of the teacher in his ability to learn and improve. It provides the child with the security of feeling that the adult knows what he is doing and can be relied on, while at the same time the child is offered some choice in the selection of activities. It requires that the teacher be clear about what kinds and degrees of freedom the child may be allowed and that he be pleasantly firm in maintaining the particular limits he feels it necessary to employ. It requires sufficient objectivity on the teacher's part to see the child clearly and to avoid becoming involved as a partisan in the child's struggles with his parents or complaints about his teachers. It is intended to strengthen the child's self-respect and to build his confidence so that he becomes able to attack his problems with courage, energy, and persistence.

There are, however, some important differences. A remedial situation must have a definite structure of planned activities, and the freedom allowed is to choose among approved learning activities, whereas in psychotherapy a much wider freedom of action is usually permitted. The major difference, though, is in regard to interpretation. One of the major goals of psychotherapy is the development of insight and self-understanding through the therapist's interpretations of remarks and actions. The remedial teacher should in general avoid interpreting to the child what he thinks the true significance of his remarks or conduct may be or giving advice outside the field of reading.

If a child in remediation wants to spend some of his time talking about problems or pleasant experiences, it is usually advisable to allow this. "If the child chooses to do so, the tutor should listen respectfully and make natural comments, expressing sympathy, understanding, happiness for the child's triumphs, or whatever would be appropriate between any two people who respect one another and have something in common" (Dahlberg, Roswell, and Chall, 1952). When in doubt, the safest procedure is to say, "You think that . . ." or "You feel that . . . ," and to complete the sentence by restating the gist of the child's statement to you. This is one way of using the technique called "reflection of feeling" by Carl Rogers (1942), whose nondirective methods of handling interview material can be very useful to remedial teachers.

Many remedial pupils do not accept their remedial teachers at face value, but test them again and again to try to find out what they are really like. As a guarded, conforming, polite child begins to be less suspicious of the teacher, he may let a bit of hostility show and later may become critical or argumentative. It is important for the teacher to recognize this for what it is: a venture in the direction of self-assertion and the overcoming of shackling inhibitions. It is important for the child to feel that he can be liked even when he wants to do objectionable things, and this helps to set the teacher's objectives, which should be to accept and show liking for the child, while drawing the line firmly against unacceptable behavior. Expressions of jealousy of other pupils point to a need for reassurance about the teacher's interest in the jealous one. Attempts to prolong lessons beyond their time limits should be understood as efforts to get a larger share of the teacher's attention. In various ways, children also try to discover whether the teacher is really stable and dependable or is unpredictable or capable of being manipulated. The setting of reasonable limits in a kindly but firm and consistent manner is in itself a therapeutic process, which provides for some children a basic feeling of security and safety they have lacked in their relationships with other adults (Bixler, 1949).

Some psychologists have explored the possibilities of a therapeutically oriented remedial setting in which the teacher is quite permissive and the child may choose freely among reading and play activities and is encouraged to explore and express his feelings about reading, schoolwork, or his family. A skillful psychotherapist may be able to get very good results with such a combined approach. The writers' limited observations of such efforts lead them to believe that results in both reading improvement and better adjustment come faster when remediation and psychotherapy are carried on concurrently by different people and are coordinated.

There have been relatively few controlled research studies on the value of counseling or psychotherapy with disabled readers, and most of them are limited in applicability because of small groups, the difficulty of matching groups on variables significant for responsiveness to psychotherapy, and the difficulty of trying to control the quality of treatment. Pumphrey and Elliott (1970) reviewed the evidence on the value of psychotherapy for disabled readers and concluded that unequivocal proof of the effects on adjustment and reading skills had not been shown. Printed case reports describe varied ways to combine remedial instruction with psychotherapy or counseling (Cases 1, 5, 6, 7, and 14 in A. J. Harris, 1970a; Edelstein, 1970; Krasnow, 1971–1972; Wright and McKenzie, 1970), and provide persuasive evidence of the value of such combined approaches in specific cases.

Hypnosis. The use of hypnosis has been recommended as an aid in improving study habits, improving concentration, reducing test anxiety, increasing motivation, and facilitating learning (Krippner, 1970, 1971). Self-hypnosis can be taught to highly susceptible subjects and can be used to improve rate and comprehension (Willis, 1972). However, not all people are hypnotizable; the value of hypnosis in treating cases of severe disability has not been explored sufficiently; and even if further results should be favorable, properly trained hypnotists are scarce.

Enlisting the Cooperation of the Family

The importance of home conditions as causes of unfavorable emotional reactions to reading has been discussed in the preceding chapter. Naturally, the remedial teacher should keep track of how the child is treated at home during the remedial work. With the best of intentions, parents can sometimes defeat the work of the teacher.

William (IQ 105) was a difficult problem when he entered grade 3 after repeating the preceding grade. He was totally uninterested and created disorder by bothering the children around him. His teacher devoted a great deal of attention to him and succeeded in getting him to work hard at his reading and other studies. After a few weeks she noticed that his work was growing worse again and that he was getting increasingly nervous and restless. The mother was invited to come to school. She told the teacher that she and her husband were trying their best to help. She kept William in the house studying every afternoon, and his father quizzed him every night and beat him when he did not know his lessons.

William's parents were not unusual, but reacted in the way that many parents do when they try to help in remedial work. They are so anxious for success that they lack the patience to allow the child to learn at his own rate of speed. In consequence, they become easily discouraged and emotionally tense and sometimes resort to severe punishment in an attempt to spur the child on to better work.

In talking with the parents of a child who has a reading disability, it is advisable first to inquire about their ideas concerning the causes of his difficulty. Sometimes they bring out many complaints about the child: he is lazy, he will not work, he must be stupid. Very often their attitude is defensive, and they attempt to prove that his poor work is not their fault. After the parents have made their suggestions, one can try to correct their misconceptions. In general, an attempt should be made to restore the parents' confidence in the child and to convey the impression that neither the parents nor the child should be blamed for his failure.

Most children with reading disabilities have already had a great deal of "help" at home from parents or from a brother or sister. If this had succeeded, we would not be concerned about them now; so it is a fairly safe assumption that the family efforts were not helpful. Parents are usually unskilled at teaching, and their procedures (about phonics, for instance) are often at variance with what the school is teaching and therefore confusing. They expect too much and lose patience quickly. Often these sessions end with the parent angry and the child crying. Many parents nag, scold, punish, and exhort the poor reader to be more like a scholastically more successful brother or sister. Siblings often make things worse by sarcastic comments and uncomplimentary remarks ("You're a dope, dunce, dummy, dimwit," etc.). The problem of how to discuss these issues with parents without antagonizing them requires more understanding than could be imparted in a sentence or two here (Lieben, 1958). Perhaps the main idea to remember is that the parents have been trying to do the right thing.

On the positive side, parents should be given encouragement to believe that there are important things they can do to help the remedial program. Particularly with younger children, the importance of continuing (or resuming) the reading and telling of stories to the child can be stressed. Many parents do not realize the value of conversation, visits to places of interest, and trips in helping the child to enrich his ideas, expand his vocabulary, and provide a base for improved comprehension. Sharing these and other activities with the child may improve the parent-child relationship.

Many overanxious parents are unable to stop their attempts to teach the child to read, even when they have agreed to do so. When this seems likely, it is often better to give them a very limited job to do than to ask them to step out of the reading instruction entirely. When this is tried the job should be one which can be completed in five to ten minutes and consists more of review than of new learning. The exact procedure the parent is expected to use must be explained in detail and demonstrated in a sample lesson.

As the child progresses in his remedial work, it is desirable to send notes home at frequent intervals (once a week is not too often) praising his effort and mentioning some of his new achievements. Cooperative parents welcome opportunities to discuss the child's other adjustment problems, and often very desirable changes in the total home situation can be brought about.

Group counseling sessions for parents can be quite helpful. Parents learn that their child's problem is not unique, can give vent to feelings of hostility toward school, teachers, and others, and can begin to explore with other parents the ways in which they can become more helpful (Bricklin, 1970).

III. MANAGEMENT PROBLEMS IN REMEDIAL READING

Selecting Pupils for Remedial Programs

Objective definition of the severity of a reading disability in terms of the Reading Expectancy Quotient and Reading Quotient has been described in detail in Chapter 7 (see pp. 145–158). When there are many more children nominated for a remedial reading program than can be accommodated in it, their R Exp Q's may be computed and the children placed in rank order. Vacancies can then be filled from the bottom of the order upward. However, such an impersonal, numerical procedure should usually be tempered by giving consideration to age, grade placement, and the recommendations by teachers and other members of the professional staff.

It is not desirable to set a minimum IQ for the remedial reading program. The chances that the measured IQ of a child is inaccurate are far greater for a retarded reader than for a normal achiever. In addition, correlations between IQ and rate of gain in remedial reading are positive but not high, with some children whose intelligence test scores are low making surprising gains in reading.

Mild degrees of reading disability and retardation can usually be taken care of by giving corrective help in the regular classroom. The children who are not making progress despite the classroom teacher's efforts should be given priority for the remedial program. Often the reading specialist can advise the classroom teacher on materials and methods to use, and the teacher can then proceed successfully.

Schiffman (1970) found the chances of a satisfactory outcome to be strongly related to the grade placement of the child when remediation was begun. As shown in Table 10, the earlier the problem was detected and remediation started, the more likely it was that the child would be reading at grade level after two years of remediation. For example, whereas 82 per cent of those who began receiving remediation in second grade were reading at grade level two years later, only 8 per cent of those who began receiving remediation in ninth grade were able to make such gains. Table 10 also indi-

TABLE 10   *Percentage of pupils reading at grade level after having, or not having, received two years of remediation (Schiffman, 1970).*

	Per cent reading at grade level	
Grade in which remediation began	With remediation	Without remediation
2	82	1
3	46	6
4	42	6
5	18	3
6	8	1
7	10	0.5
8	11	0.25
9	8	0.25

cates that the likelihood for improved reading ability is greatly increased when remediation is provided.

Many remedial programs now admit some children from the first and second grades. The earlier the child enters such a program, the shorter the distance he has to go. Also, his experience of failure has been for a shorter period of time, and emotional defenses and resistances have usually not become crystallized as yet. Successful remedial teaching should bring a child in these grades to a satisfactory reading performance in considerably less time than is required for upper-grade children and thus involve a substantial economy of teacher time.

When a remedial program is first started it is probably desirable to take the most serious cases first, regardless of grade level. As the program progresses, the usual entering time should be as soon as the child's need is evident. In the elementary school, quotas will have to be reserved for children who have started remediation and still need more help, for newcomers to the school, and for children whose problems have become more acute without remedial help. In junior high school, the seventh grade is the place to concentrate most remedial time; in a four-year senior high school, the ninth grade; and in college, the freshman year.

Remedial Groups

A special remedial teacher in a school generally gets best results working with small groups, ranging from two to six children. The saving as compared to teaching one child at a time is obvious. The small group not only is economical but also has definite psychological advantages. The group is small enough for each child to receive individual attention, yet retains many of the desirable features of a classroom situation. It is usually good for a child to know that he is not the only one who has a handicap, and he may take courage and inspiration from the progress of other members of his group. In many exercises and drills the children can work in pairs or can take turns at testing each other, thus relieving the teacher of some routine tasks and giving more time for planning, testing, and other necessary work. Games can be introduced in which all the children in a group can take part.

Not all children need the same intensity of treatment. Some groups can make good progress meeting twice a week; some do much better with three periods; and some children seem to need to see the remedial teacher every school day, or their forgetting almost keeps pace with their learning. One or two children may not be able to adjust to even a small group and need the teacher's exclusive attention; if possible, they should be started with individual help and worked into a group as soon as they are ready.

Arranging a Remedial Schedule

The time of day has relatively little effect on the learning ability of children, so special remedial reading periods may be scheduled for any time that is convenient. The teacher giving special coaching to one or two pupils may meet them before or after school, during assembly periods, or at any other time when the necessary minutes can be found. A regularly assigned remedial teacher usually meets several different groups of children during the day and must schedule them for regular periods. It is desirable to arrange the groups so that the children in one group are at about the same level of reading ability, although it is not essential. It is also desirable to avoid as far as possible any encroachment on the time required for other necessary activities. The best time to give a child a remedial lesson is the period when the rest of his class is having reading or literature. One should try to avoid interference with lessons in other basic subjects such as arithmetic. It is also inadvisable to schedule remedial reading at the expense of vocational or physical education, as those may be the only parts of the school day that the disabled readers really enjoy. It is often possible to reduce conflicts to a minimum by conferring with the classroom teachers. When conflicts cannot be avoided, one should remember that the remedial work is for the time being the child's most important school activity and should take precedence over other subjects.

Like any other form of systematic teaching, remedial reading should be scheduled at regular, frequent intervals. One cannot usually expect to get good results if one sees a child only once a week. The length of the period, in most cases, should be about 45 minutes. Periods shorter than that are not as effective because too large a proportion of the time is spent in getting started and in clearing up. Children whose attention is flighty or who tire easily may be kept occupied through the period by having a variety of things to do.

Individual Remedial Teaching

There are many children who need more help and attention than they can be given under most classroom conditions. Many schools are so organized that the teachers are not encouraged to individualize their teaching or provided with the materials which individualized methods require. Even when small-group instruction or individualized attention is given in the classroom, there are usually some children who are so far behind or whose difficulties are so different from those of the other children that they do not seem to profit from teaching which is highly beneficial to the others in the low reading groups.

Most of these children respond well to special remedial group instruction of the type described above. However, there are always a few (usually less than 10 per cent) who do not make progress even under that kind of arrangement. For these few, thorough diagnostic examinations should be provided and completely individual tutoring arranged if necessary.

Very few schools at present have on their staffs special remedial teachers who devote part of their time to completely individual tutoring. Some schools expect their regular teachers to give individual coaching to pupils who need it and set aside special periods for that purpose. If the kindergarten and first-grade children attend school for only part of the school day, their teachers are sometimes assigned to give individual help to upper-grade pupils during the remaining time. Such teachers should have remedial training. Sometimes assembly and gymnasium periods are arranged so as to free one or two teachers for remedial teaching. In entirely too many schools no provisions at all are made, and help is available to the child who needs it only because a devoted teacher finds time to work with him in private, before or after school.

Outside of the schools, some individual teaching of reading is done by the personnel of clinics and by private tutors who specialize in remedial work. The number of people who are qualified and available for this work is still small, and the cost of their services is high. When, however, such highly skilled help salvages children who would otherwise remain total failures, the monetary cost is small if balanced against the alternative of ruined lives.

The Reading Specialist as Diagnostician

In some school systems the reading specialist's role is primarily to provide diagnostic information about individual children, after carrying out a somewhat limited diagnostic study. The reading specialist or consultant then outlines specific skills to be taught and recommends materials to be used, and the child's regular classroom teacher is responsible for carrying out the recommendations. Such a program depends very strongly on the abilities of the teachers to provide effective individualized help within the structure of classroom instruction. It tends to work comparatively well with underachievers and mildly disabled readers, and is usually not very successful in meeting the needs of the more severe cases.

Tutoring by Partially Trained Personnel

A substantial number of recent papers have described successful programs in which adult volunteers, college students, paraprofessional teacher aides, high school students, and even elementary school students have been used as tutors. After a short period of training they are assigned to children, usually on an individual basis.

Most adult volunteers have been educated women whose children no longer need them to be at home constantly, and who want something interesting and useful to do. A representative program reported by Pollack (1969) provided individual tutoring for several hundred elementary school children, with most of them showing "dramatic improvement." The tutors were given a short training course and were supervised by a professional staff.

Undergraduate teacher-education students in some colleges have done tutoring in reading as part of their work in methods of teaching (Klosterman, 1970; Guszak and Mills, 1973). A major problem is that the course instructor usually cannot devote enough time to supervision to meet the tutors' needs.

The use of paraprofessional teacher aides as tutors has been increasing. One of the promising developments is programmed tutoring, in which teacher aides, chosen usually from the same disadvantaged groups as the pupils, and usually with no more than a high school education, are given a carefully planned, step-by-step procedure to follow (Ellson, *et al.*, 1965; Ellson, P. Harris, and Barber, 1968; McCleary, 1971). According to another report, tutors from disadvantaged backgrounds can be taught to manage remedial groups of five children (Hill and Tolman, 1970).

Using older children (fifth grade and up) to tutor younger children has been tried successfully in several places (Niedermeyer and Ellis, 1971;

Willis, Morris, and Crowder, 1972; Snapp, Oakland, and Williams, 1972). Sometimes underachieving older children are used as tutors, with reading gains for the tutors as well as for the tutees (Frager and Stern, 1970; Mohan, 1971). Minority-group college students with reading problems have also been used as tutors for primary-grade children with benefit to both groups (McWhorter and Levy, 1971).

A comprehensive plan using five different tutorial reading programs was developed in New Haven (Criscuolo, 1971). This included: 1) community tutors, who were inner-city residents paid to give individual help to intermediate-grade children; 2) Youth Serving Youth, 50 high school students who tutored third graders after school; 3) student teachers from a local college who taught after-school reading; 4) Junior Assistants Corps— sixth graders tutoring first graders; and 5) School Volunteers, a group of 135 women recruited by the Junior League.

Regardless of who the tutors are, a substantial investment of professional time has to go into preliminary training and continuing supervision if good results are to be achieved.

Homework

In learning to read, as in the learning of any other complex skill, the more practice the better. Children who are good readers often read more outside of school than in school, and this voluntary reading is a very important factor in their continued improvement. If the poor reader can be induced to read extensively between lessons, his progress will be that much greater.

One should not, however, impose reading homework on poor readers. At the start of a remedial program it is advisable not to suggest any home reading. One should wait until the child shows that he is gaining confidence in his reading and finds that he can get some pleasure from it. Then one can suggest that perhaps he would like to do some reading between lessons. The importance of doing as much reading as possible can be discussed, and a progress chart for voluntary reading can be started. Books or stories for home reading should be short at first and should be at the child's independent reading level. Reports on this outside reading should at first be oral, and a page or so of the material read can be used for an oral reading check. If this procedure is handled successfully, the child may soon be reading as much as a book a week in his free time.

Exercises of the workbook type are less interesting than story material and should usually not be assigned for home reading unless the child shows that he enjoys them. The same principle, that the child should want extra practice, should govern decisions about homework with other types of drill material.

Keeping Records

The remedial teacher should have a separate Manila folder or envelope for the records of each child. In this should be kept the results of all tests and other diagnostic studies, a preliminary analysis of the child's instructional and other needs, an outline of the teaching plan to be followed, and records of the progress of the work. Since record keeping can become a very time-consuming burden, thought should be given to setting up a record system that will be reasonably comprehensive and, at the same time, require comparatively little writing.

The process of bringing together all the information about a child in a comprehensive case study is discussed in the next section. Unless a formal report is to be prepared, much of the content of the case study is not written down on paper. However, it is highly advisable to have a concise summary of the most important information. A three-page diagnostic summary form is shown in Figure 13.4. If many copies are needed, this form, or something like it, can be mimeographed.

If a teacher is working individually with only one or two children, it is frequently worthwhile to keep a day-by-day diary that contains notations about the child's emotional behavior as well as his reading. This is especially true if the teacher is new to remedial work and wishes to discuss his procedures with a supervisor or instructor. For an experienced and busy remedial teacher such a detailed record is impractical. However, it is desirable to keep a memorandum pad handy and to jot down a brief note, dated, about any unusual behavior or any significant change in the child. These notes are placed in the child's folder. From time to time the brief anecdotal records can be reread, giving the teacher a better perspective on the child's progress.

One should keep a record of the assignments given to each child, notations about when they were finished, and comments about how well they were accomplished. A convenient form for such an assignment record is shown in Figure 13.3. This form can be left with the child, so that when he finishes one job he knows what to do next. Each child should have a notebook in which he can do his written work and a large Manila envelope in which he can keep his notebook, assignment sheet, progress charts, and other reading materials. Many other kinds of record-keeping forms have been devised for use in reading clinics.

Types of Remedial Reading Organization

The years 1965–1970 saw a veritable explosion of remedial reading programs of many kinds, financed mainly under Titles I and III of the Elementary and Secondary Act of 1965. The haste with which many of these were planned, and the lack of time to obtain properly trained personnel or

READING ASSIGNMENT SHEET

Name ——

Date Assigned	Assignment	Date Completed	Comments

FIGURE 13.3   A form that can be used for individual reading assignments.

to develop them through in-service programs, led to disappointing results
in many instances. Whether results were good or indifferent, many of these
projects ended abruptly in 1969 or 1970 with the nonrenewal of federal
funding.

The American Institutes for Research in the Behavioral Sciences were
commissioned by the U.S. Office of Education to select remedial reading
programs with superior results that might serve as models. The descriptive
reports they issued are available through the ERIC system in microfiche or
hard copy (photocopy), and in the brief mentions that follow, their ERIC
order numbers are given instead of the usual type of citation. The model
programs chosen were of many kinds and included the following: programmed tutoring of disadvantaged first graders by paraprofessional tutors,
individually, a few minutes a day (ED 053 883); a Reading Center for each

elementary school in a large district, which provided both small-group remedial instruction for children and in-service training and consultation for teachers (ED 053 885); Intensive Reading Centers providing concentrated instruction for disadvantaged first graders in groups of 10 or 11, for a full morning each day for 10 weeks (ED 053 866); a remedial reading program for Spanish-American children in grades 2–4, 30 minutes a day in small groups (ED 053 890); summer sessions providing individualized and small-group instruction, elementary (ED 053 884) and junior high (ED 053 882); a county reading-learning center to which children were bused for one-hour lessons four days a week, and in which classroom teachers were trained as reading specialists (ED 053 887); a multilevel program including a diagnostic clinic, small-group remedial reading instruction in the schools, and in-service teacher training (ED 053 776); and a high school program including a reading clinic, a reading laboratory open to good readers as well as poor readers, and a program of individually prescribed study (ED 053 881). Other innovative programs have included the use of fully equipped reading clinics or laboratories in busses that travel from school to school; programs to train and use volunteers, high school pupils, or paraprofessional teacher aides as reading tutors; after-school study centers, some of them located in out-of-school places like churches or empty stories; and the like.

Reading Clinics, Centers, and Laboratories.   Children with severe reading disabilities and those who fail to respond to remedial efforts in their schools should, when possible, be referred for more intensive and complete diagnosis to a reading clinic, center, or laboratory. The differences among these terms are based more on preferences in choosing a name than on actual differences in organization and program. There are now several hundred such units. Many are run by universities and colleges and combine training of graduate students as reading specialists with research and service to undergraduate and public school clients. Some are outpatient clinics located in the neurological, psychiatric, or pediatric services of a hospital. Some are organized within the pupil personnel services of a school system. A few are privately operated. Many children with reading disabilities are also seen in child guidance clinics, in which a psychiatric orientation usually predominates.

In addition to a director and one or more reading specialists, such a clinic or center should have on its staff representatives of professions such as clinical psychology, psychiatry, neurology, pediatrics, social work, opthalmology or optometry, and speech correction, or should have the connections to refer to such specialists for examinations or consultations that seem desirable. After the clinical findings have been interpreted and integrated, recommendations are made both about the treatment of handicaps that interfere with learning, and about the kind of remedial instruction the child needs. Treatment is often provided in the same clinic.

Information about reading clinic procedures and management can be found in several sources (A. J. Harris, 1965; *Manual for Reading Clinic Teachers*, 1965; Cohn and Cohn, 1967; Adams, 1970). A partial listing of university and college clinics made several years ago may still be helpful (Helms, 1967), a partial listing is published annually in *Academic Therapy*, and a few local directories have been compiled (*e.g.*, Junior League of New York City).

Remedial Schools. A few full-time schools take children with very severe reading disabilities. Some of them are sponsored by universities, while others are under private auspices, usually on a nonprofit basis. There are also schools for children who need special education which include learning disabilities among the groups served. Unless a remedial school is heavily endowed, tuition is necessarily quite high.

The Reading Resource Room. Some schools have found it efficient to combine remedial reading with enrichment for normal readers in one setting, which is sometimes called a reading resource room or a reading laboratory. In an interesting example from a middle school (grades 6 to 8) each of two reading labs is staffed by a reading specialist and a corps of student volunteer aides. The lab offers three kinds of programs: a remedial program for those who need it; mini-courses in specific reading and study skills, for average and above-average readers; and a recreational reading program, open to all students (Crawford and Conley, 1971). This kind of program deserves emulation.

Providing Support in Other Curricular Areas

Sometimes a child makes good progress in a remedial program and gains confidence as he experiences successful learning, only to be crushed when, at the end of the year, he fails in other subjects and is required to repeat. The remedial teacher should try to prevent this from happening. Conferring with the child's teacher or teachers may make it possible for him to receive shorter and simpler homework assignments. Arrangements can be made to have his assignments read to him, by a student volunteer, by a member of his family, or by providing him with a taped recording of the textbook. Tests can be given and answered orally. When the reading tasks required are well above a child's frustration level, it seems reasonable to give him the same opportunities to learn that one would give a child with severely defective vision (Murphy, 1972–1973). Further suggestions about content subject instruction for disabled readers may be found on pages 495–496.

Long-term Effects of Remediation

The most common way to measure the effectiveness of remedial reading instruction is to give tests at the beginning and end of the remedial program and compare the rate of gain with the rate of previous progress in reading (Ekwall, 1972). It should be noted, however, that unless a child's Reading Expectancy Quotient increases, he is not closing the gap between his reading level and that of the average child of his age. It is also important to note what happens after remedial help is stopped.

It is well established that many bright children who were given high-quality remedial help long enough so that they became able to handle school reading assignments have been able to complete high school, college, and even graduate programs (H. M. Robinson and H. K. Smith, 1962; Rawson, 1968). They are likely to concentrate in areas that do not require extensive reading, and they often have residual problems of slow reading and uncertain spelling.

H. C. M. Carroll (1972) has summarized the results of several follow-up studies in Great Britain. In these, the general result has been a slowing down of reading gain after remedial help was discontinued, and in some studies this was so marked that eventually the gains from the program were washed away. Carroll pointed out some reasons for this disappointing result. One of them is the continuation, for many children, of the same environmental conditions that were causal initially. Another is the failure of schools to make good provisions for a child who improves up to a just-marginal level of reading ability. Still another is the probability that the remediation given to some children did not fully meet their needs.

A longitudinal study by Balow and Blomquist (1965) cast some light on the reasons why the good effects of remediation sometimes do not last. They followed up children who had been helped in a university reading clinic. Those given remedial help for long periods of time (two to three years) tended to continue to improve, while those given short-term remedial programs, such as in a summer reading clinic, tended to stop improving. Those whose remediation tapered off gradually, with opportunities to return to see the remedial teacher about once a month, were more likely to continue improving than those whose remediation ended abruptly.

There are two main criteria by which one can judge if a child is ready to continue to improve in reading on his own. The first is, Has he reached a level where he can cope successfully with school reading assignments in content fields? The second is, Has he made a substantial start in reading independently for pleasure? If the answer to these questions is no, one can expect that the child will stop improving in reading when remedial help is discontinued. If the remedial teacher cannot continue to offer less intensive supportive help, the alternative is a close working relationship with the classroom teacher who takes over the responsibility for helping the child continue to make progress.

IV. HOW TO MAKE A ·CASE STUDY

After a child has been selected for intensive study, the teacher should spend the first remedial period or two getting acquainted with him and leading him into the proper frame of mind for the diagnostic and remedial work. The school records should naturally be consulted as soon as possible. Testing may be started as soon as the child seems ready to cooperate. One should be careful not to give too many tests at once; the testing program can be spread over several periods, and some of the tests can be given after remedial work has been started. It may take weeks before one has an adequate picture of the child's emotional makeup and home background. It is advisable to begin the remedial work as soon as possible, even though the remedial procedures may have to be changed as soon as a more complete diagnosis has been made. When the diagnostic evidence has been collected, it is necessary to consider the complete picture and arrive at conclusions about what the child's major difficulties in reading are, what seem to be the most reasonable explanations of how these difficulties have come about, what persisting handicaps may impede progress, and what remedial procedures should be employed to overcome them. After the remedial work is under way one should check up periodically with informal and standardized tests to determine the effectiveness of the procedures that are being used and to find out if a shift in methods should be instituted. Before finishing work with a case, one should, of course, retest to find out how much progress the pupil has made.

All the factors that need to be considered in the diagnostic phase of a case study have been discussed in the six chapters preceding this one. The selection of appropriate remedial methods and materials will be considered in the chapters that follow. The task of the person making a case study, after the separate data have been obtained, is to get an overall picture of the child and his needs. This task, never easy, is simplified somewhat if all the relevant information is briefly summarized in such a way that the interrelations can be seen. Such a summary form is shown in Figure 13.4.

If a formal case report is to be submitted, it is desirable to follow a definite outline. This is fairly good insurance against omitting important information, as well as an aid to a person reading the report. The outline

SUMMARY OF READING DIAGNOSIS

Name _____ Date of Birth _____ CA _____ Grade, Class _____

Teacher _____ School _____ Examiner _____

Date of Summary _____

Instructional Reading Level _____ Oral _____ Silent _____

Independent Level _____ Frustration Level _____

Reading Expectancy Quotient _____ Reading Quotient _____

Classification: Normal _____ Disabled _____ Severely Disabled _____

Underachiever _____ Slow Learner _____

Test Results

Reading Test   Form   Date   RG   RA   Other Score

_____

_____

_____

_____

Intelligence Test Form   Date   MA   IQ   Subscores

_____

_____

_____

Other Test   Form   Date   Results

_____

_____

_____

Comments on tests results: _____

_____

_____

FIGURE 13.4 A three-page record form for summarizing briefly the results of a reading disability case study.

Reading Skill Strengths and Weaknesses

Word recognition _____

_____

Decoding _____

_____

Vocabulary _____

_____

Comprehension _____

_____

Rate _____

_____

Oral Reading _____

_____

Silent Reading _____

_____

Health: Vision _____

Hearing _____

Present physical condition _____

Health history _____

Home Background: Cultural _____

Socio-economic _____

Family _____

Siblings _____

Treatment of child _____

_____

Personality: Personality traits (temperament, mood)

Self-esteem _____

Interests _____

Emotionality _____

Attitude toward reading _____

Relationships w/adults _____

Relationships w/peers _____

Remarks _____

School History: Grade Progress _____

Attendance _____

Marks in reading _____

Methods of reading instruction _____

Marks in other subjects _____

Conduct & behavior _____

Possible Contributing/Causal Factors: _____

_____

Recommendations

Reading _____

_____

_____

_____

School adjustment _____

_____

Advice to parents _____

_____

Other exams or treatment _____

_____

on the next two pages can be useful to teachers as a guide in writing up remedial reading cases. The amount of space given to a heading does not indicate its comparative importance; headings G, H, and I should be much more important in a case report than the space allocated to them in the outline would seem to suggest.

A. Objective Data
   1. Child's name
   2. Date of birth and age at beginning of study
   3. School grade at beginning of study
   4. Intelligence test data, including name of test and form, date of administration, MA, and IQ
   5. Silent reading test scores, including name of test and form, date of administration, reading age, and reading grade
      When separate norms are available for parts of the test, the scores on the parts should be listed as well as the total score
   6. Oral reading test scores, including name of test and form, date, and reading grade
   7. Results of standardized tests in other school subjects if such tests have been given
   8. Results of informal testing
B. Health Data
   1. Results of vision tests and other evidence about vision
   2. Results of hearing tests and other evidence about hearing
   3. Summary of child's present health status
   4. Summary of child's health history
   5. Laterality
C. Home Background
      The questions listed on pp. 308–309 may be used as a guide in summarizing information about home background
D. Child's Personality
   1. Statement of outstanding personality traits, with illustrations
   2. Child's interests in reading, school, and play
   3. Child's attitudes toward teachers, playmates, and family
E. School History
   1. Record of progress through the grades
   2. Marks in reading and other subjects
   3. Attendance record
   4. Notations about conduct and general behavior
   5. Methods of teaching reading used by former teachers
F. Interpretation of Reading Results
   1. Interpretation of silent reading performance
   2. Interpretation of oral reading performance

G. Summary of Diagnosis
  1. Summary of outstanding strengths and difficulties in reading
  2. Summary of factors related to the child's difficulties
H. Recommendations for Remedial Treatment
  1. Recommendations concerning reading instruction
  2. Other recommendations for school adjustment
  3. Recommendations to the parents
  4. Recommendations for medical examination or treatment
  5. Other recommendations
I. Description of Remedial Treatment
  The description of treatment should be given in detail. Preferably a chronological order should be followed, describing procedures used at the beginning and explaining changes made in procedure as the remedial work progressed. Methods should be described in sufficient detail to allow others to reproduce them. Materials used should be indicated.
J. Evaluation of Results
  1. Tabular summary of initial test scores and retest scores
  2. Evaluation of progress shown by formal and informal tests
  3. Evidence of change shown in the child's general schoolwork
  4. Evidence of change shown in the child's personality and behavior

Rigid adherence to an outline such as that given above is not absolutely necessary, but a systematic procedure should be followed. Some cases are more complex than others and need to be described in greater detail.

SUGGESTED ADDITIONAL READING

BOND, GUY L. & TINKER, MILES A. *Reading difficulties: their diagnosis and correction* (3rd ed.). New York: Appleton-Century-Crofts, 1973. Chap. 10.

GATES, ARTHUR I. *The improvement of reading* (3rd ed.). New York: Macmillan, 1947. Chap. 15.

GOLDIAMOND, ISRAEL & DYRUD, JARL E. *Reading as operant behavior.* In John Money (Ed.). *The disabled reader.* Baltimore: Johns Hopkins Press, 1966. Chap. 7.

GUSZAK, FRANK J. *Diagnostic reading instruction in the elementary school.* New York: Harper & Row, 1972. Chap. 14.

HARRIS, ALBERT J. & SIPAY, EDWARD R. (Eds.). *Readings on reading instruction* (2nd ed.). New York: McKay, 1972. Chap. 16.

LA PRAY, MARGARET. *Teaching children to become independent readers.* New York: Center for Applied Research in Education, 1972. Chap. 9.

NATCHEZ, GLADYS (Ed.). *Children with reading problems: classic and contemporary issues in reading disability.* New York: Basic Books, 1968. Pp. 307–331.

OTTO, WAYNE & SMITH, RICHARD J. *Administering the reading program.* Boston: Houghton Mifflin, 1970. Chap. 7.

OTTO, WAYNE; MC MENEMY, RICHARD A.; & SMITH, RICHARD J. *Corrective and remedial teaching* (2nd ed.). Boston: Houghton Mifflin, 1973. Chap. 3.

ROBECK, MILDRED C. & WILSON, JOHN A. R. *Psychology of reading: foundations of instruction.* New York: John Wiley and Sons, 1974. Chap. 5.

ROSWELL, FLORENCE G. & NATCHEZ, GLADYS. *Reading disability: diagnosis and treatment* (2nd ed.). New York: Basic Books, 1971. Chap. 4.

THORESON, CARL E. (Ed.). *Behavior modification in education,* 75th Yearbook of the National Society for the Study of Education, Part I. Chicago: University of Chicago Press, 1972. Chaps. 1, 3, 6, 10, 11, 12, 13, 14.

WILSON, ROBERT M. & HALL, MARYANNE. *Reading and the elementary school child: theory and practice for teachers.* New York: Van Nostrand, 1972. Chap 11.

ZINTZ, MILES V. *Corrective reading* (2nd ed.). Dubuque, Iowa: W. C. Brown, 1972. Chaps. 3, 4.

14

Developing
Word-Identification Skills

To identify or recognize a written or printed word means to say aloud the spoken word it represents, to have an auditory image of the word while reading silently (to "hear" the word in "inner speech"), or, in very rapid silent reading, to become aware of the meaning of the word without necessarily having an auditory image of it. The developmental teaching of word identification is treated in this chapter. Remedial instruction in word identification is discussed in Chapter 15, and the teaching of word meanings is dealt with in Chapter 16.

Effective reading requires both that most words be identified immediately at sight and that the reader can, when necessary, decode unfamiliar words.

Word recognition provides a necessary foundation for reading comprehension. At first- and second-grade levels the correlation between word recognition and comprehension tests runs high. This should not be surprising, since nearly all the words used in beginning reading material are within the listening vocabularies of most children, and most sentence patterns used are simple. At upper-grade levels the correlation between word recognition and comprehension is lower, as meaningful vocabulary, complexity of sentence structure, demands on abstract reasoning ability, and so on become more important influences on the ability to understand. At any level, however, inability to recognize most of the words can effectively block comprehension.

It is, of course, essential that the meaning of words being taught should be known to the reader. In the first and second grades, in which the major word-recognition skills are developed, most of the words which occur in reading matter have meanings well known to most kindergarten children. While some word meanings need to be taught in those grades, major emphasis in the teaching of words can be placed on recognition skills. As the child progresses in school, the emphasis shifts to the teaching of word meanings.

I. DEVELOPMENT OF SIGHT-RECOGNITION VOCABULARY

As we have seen in Chapter 3, current basal reader series differ greatly in the relative emphasis placed on sight recognition as compared to decoding. Traditional eclectic basal readers begin with sight vocabulary and introduce decoding skills gradually. Some basal readers combine decoding with sight recognition from the beginning. Phonic and linguistic series place beginning emphasis almost exclusively on decoding. But all series have to provide children both with expanding sight vocabularies and with skill in decoding. Even in decoding-emphasis programs, words with quite irregular phoneme-grapheme relationships have to be learned as sight words.

Methods of Teaching Sight Words

Children are helped to learn sight words in various ways. Usually the word is introduced by the teacher in a spoken sentence or story, and if the meaning is unfamiliar that is developed first. The sentence can be presented on the chalkboard, and the word can be underlined, framed with the hands, or set off by pointers. The children are encouraged to look carefully at it while saying it; this is a whole-word or visual method. Phrases consisting of the new word with one or two familiar words may then be presented and read. The word may then be presented by itself on a card, and various types of practice employed, such as selecting from several cards the one which the teacher says, matching the word card with the word in the sentence or phrase, or rearranging word cards to form new sentences. Reading of connected material which contains the new words should follow immediately, providing additional repetition and opportunity to recognize the word in a meaningful context. This may be followed by workbook exercises in which the word is to be matched with a picture, written into an incomplete sentence, or used in comprehension questions.

A second commonly used procedure is to present the new word in connection with a picture, which lends vividness of meaning. The child looks at the picture and is told the word or guesses what the word must be. If he forgets the word, he looks back at the picture again. Some workbooks present new words by means of pictures. Published sets of picture-word cards are available and can be used to good advantage. Picture dictionaries can be placed on the library table, and the children can be taught how to look up a new word in the dictionary. Children can also construct their own picture dictionaries, drawing the illustrations or cutting them out from magazines, and refer to them when they forget a word.

Children are also encouraged to infer from the context. They study the illustration on the page to find out what new character, object, or action is portrayed. They read the rest of the sentence and try to decide what the missing word must be. As with other techniques, the use of context is valuable, but can become a handicap if the child learns to rely on it too heavily.

When a child forgets a word that has recently been introduced, many teachers encourage him to look back and find the word in a previous sentence. By reading that sentence again, he can often remember what the word says.

Although practice with flash cards has been a widely used method of providing drill on new words, such cards sometimes encourage dependence on the wrong kinds of cues. "The one with the dirty thumb mark on it is 'baby.' I always know it by that, else I'd swear it was 'lady.' . . . 'Saw' and 'was' are easy too. 'Saw' is the one with the corner torn off" (McCullough, 1955).

Flash cards can be used to build sentences, to test new words after they have been taught, and to develop speed of recognition after the words are known. When used for first teaching they not only encourage dependence on accidental cues but also may develop disappointingly little carryover to the recognition of the word in connected meaningful context.

Configuration Clues. Children can be helped to observe salient characteristics of words as an aid to recalling them. Most children have no difficulty with the word *grandmother*, even at the pre-primer level, because it is a long word and looks distinctively different from all the other words. Another word that is learned almost at once is *elephant*, which not only is long but also has a distinctive shape, with a unique pattern of ascending and descending letters. The tail at the end of the word *monkey* makes that a very easy word for the beginning reader. In contrast, words that are similar in size and general appearance are easily confused with one another. Words like *went* and *want, and* and *said, no* and *on* are troublesome to many children long after they should have been well learned. Noticing and calling attention to the distinctive characteristics of words and sequence of letters within these words are very helpful to children. However, when the child has to distinguish between *grandfather* and *grandmother*, or between *donkey* and *monkey*, such cues as size, general shape, and a tall letter in the middle or a "tail" at the end no longer suffice and must be supplemented by more systematic methods of decoding.

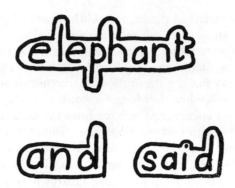

FIGURE 14.1   A unique word shape and two shapes frequently confused
by beginning readers.

Some recent studies have concluded that configuration is an ineffective and seldom-used cue to word identification (Timko, 1970; Williams, Blumberg, and Williams, 1970). Since these studies used only words of equal length, they cannot be generalized to normal reading in which word length is a major factor in configuration. Nevertheless, it seems advisable not to teach children to rely much on the shape or length of words as cues.

Repetition and Reinforcement

Many teachers are amazed that children can misread words which they have seen hundreds of times. They remember the "law of exercise" as one of the most important principles of learning; they believe that "practice makes perfect"; and they have relied on repetition and drill as the cure of imperfect learning. Mere repetition, however, was never considered a sufficient basis for learning, and the weakness of relying on it is more clearly recognized today than it used to be. "The 'law of exercise' does not guarantee that mere countless repetitions of any given reaction will serve to fix it, although the erroneous belief that it does has led in some schools to the institution of drill methods diametrically opposed to the principles of effective learning" (Skinner, 1945). In the modern psychology of learning, less emphasis than formerly is placed on repetition, and much more attention is given to readiness, motivation, the attainment of insight, and reinforcement. As it relates to the learning of word recognition, insight means attaining a clear and accurate perception of the printed word. If a child has never really seen the word clearly, endless repetition of a faulty perception may only increase the tendency to perceive the word in the same faulty way.

While repetition is now considered to play a subordinate role in the learning process, it is still important. Children differ greatly in their quickness in learning to recognize a word, as they do in all other abilities. Some fortunate children can remember a word easily when they have seen it only once or twice before. Mentally slow children may need several times as much repetition as children of average mental ability. To be effective, this repetition should not be monotonous drill, but should be presented in such a way as to maintain the child's interest at a high level and encourage accuracy of perception. Modern sets of primary-grade readers attempt to make the child's task easier by carefully controlling the rate at which new words are introduced and by providing systematic repetition of each new word a large number of times in differing contexts. The use of correlated workbooks provides additional repetition.

The principle of reinforcement is to the effect that a response is more likely to be repeated in similar situations if it has been followed by satisfaction or reward. The reward can be of many kinds: a bit of food or candy, a symbolic token such as a colored star, a privilege, social approval, or just the knowledge of having been right. Programmed instruction relies heavily on the reinforcement effect of finding out after each response whether it was correct or not.

Supplementary Word-Recognition Procedures

One of the most important aspects of reading readiness is the ability to perceive similarities and differences in word forms. If the teacher finds, after she has started a group of children on book reading, that several of them are still weak in this ability, she can introduce special supplementary practice exercises in visual discrimination of letters and words of the sort to be found in reading-readiness workbooks.

There are some children whose ability to remember the appearance of words after purely visual study remains very poor. These children may be very inferior in visual imagery. They often make surprisingly good progress if the teacher helps them to acquire methods of word study that are easier for them than the look-and-say procedure. Many of them can be helped by the use of a visual-motor method of word study; others are benefited greatly by early, intensive training in phonics; a few may require a systematic kinesthetic procedure.

Tracing Procedures. For some children look-and-say does not work very well because when they look their visual perception of the word is vague and insufficiently clear to provide a basis for effective discrimination from other somewhat similar words, or for recall after an interval of time. For such children additional sensory cues are often quite helpful. Tracing a large copy of the word letter by letter while pronouncing the word is the heart of the kinesthetic method developed by Fernald (see pp. 393–396) and has aided many children who had trouble building a sight vocabulary.

Although a recent study found that poor readers tended to learn more words when visual and auditory cues were stressed than when tracing cues were emphasized (Vandever and Neville, 1972–1973), this does not negate the value of tracing for those who do not profit from visual and auditory emphases. Some workbooks now provide large copies of the words with directions for tracing, as part of their regular learning procedure. This is usually called the VAKT method (visual-auditory-kinesthetic-tactual).

Visual-Motor Word Study. Many children do not need extensive practice in tracing, but are helped a great deal by a method which combines visual observation while saying the word with writing the word from memory (VAK). As used with a slow group, the procedure can be about as follows:

1] The teacher selects for teaching a small number of new words that are to be met in the next connected reading.

2] Each word is introduced in meaningful context, and meanings are checked or taught.

3] The new word is presented on the board in a sentence and framed or otherwise emphasized, as in the visual method.

4] The teacher holds up a card with the word printed on it and pronounces it. The children look at it and pronounce it softly, and then a few times to themselves. They should be cautioned *not* to spell letter by letter.

5] Each child shuts his eyes and tries to "make a picture" (visual image) of the word; he then opens them and compares his mental image with the original.

6] The card is covered, and each child attempts to print (or write) the word *from memory.*

7] The word is exposed again, and each child compares his reproduction with the original, paying particular attention to any parts not reproduced accurately.

8] The process of looking at the word, saying it, and attempting to reproduce it from memory is repeated until the child can reproduce the word correctly.

9] The other words are taught the same way.

10] The word cards are shuffled and reviewed for speedier sight recognition.

11] The children proceed to read a selection in which the new words are met in meaningful context.

After using the VAK (visual-auditory-kinesthetic) method for a month or two, children usually discover that they no longer need to write the word in order to be able to remember it. They then shift to the visual method.

Gradually, also, they begin to utilize their developing phonic knowledge in combination with study of the word as a whole.

According to Fernald, who originated the VAK procedure, the method is a modified kinesthetic approach in which the motor imagery of the movements involved in writing the word reinforces the auditory-visual association between the sound of the word and its printed form. It seems probable that the kinesthetic elements are of minor importance. Instead, it seems likely that writing helps the child to remember the word because he must perceive the word correctly in all its details in order to reproduce it accurately. The method seems to work just as well whether the child prints the word, writes it, or reproduces it on a typewriter. Whatever the true explanation may turn out to be, it is a fact that many children whose visual memory is very inexact and who show no aptitude for phonics find that they can learn and remember words when they use the visual-motor procedure.

Materials for Building Sight Vocabulary

Word cards that can be used for independent study and self-teaching can be made by teacher or pupils. Index cards cut into thirds provide a good size. The card must be opaque; if the material on the back can be seen through the card, the purpose is defeated. The word is printed on one side, and an illustrative picture with the word below it is placed on the back (see Fig. 14.2). Clipping one corner makes it easier to keep the cards right side up. The child studies each word, using the side with the picture. After doing this with a few cards he turns the cards over and tests himself, checking the correctness of each response by looking again at the picture.

Nouns are easiest to depict. Action words (*run, jump*) and direction words (*to, from, over*) are also relatively easy to represent, using stick figures, arrows, and so forth. Often the child can devise a drawing that represents the word to him, although others may not see the connection. Function words (conjunctions, prepositions, auxiliaries) are difficult to picture, and usually one must resort to a phrase or sentence in which context is the main cue to the underlined word.

A commercial set of illustrated word cards that has been widely used is the *Dolch Picture-Word Cards* (Garrard), presenting 95 nouns that are very common in primary-grade reading.

Word cards without picture cues are also widely used. The *Dolch Basic Sight Vocabulary Cards* (Garrard) present the 220 words selected by Dolch (1936) as being the most common English words exclusive of nouns. Printed word cards based on the vocabulary of the first-grade readers are available from the publishers of most basal reading series. Handmade word cards can be prepared by a teacher to provide practice on any list of words that need special attention; when using them, the teacher or a helper must provide the cues, saying each word as it is exposed.

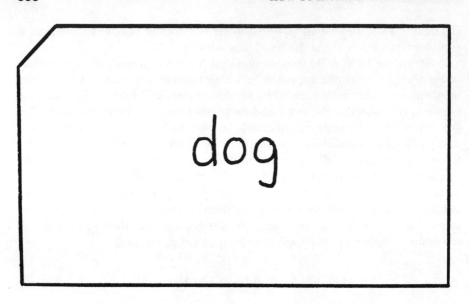

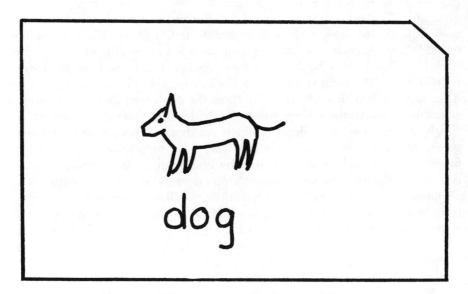

FIGURE 14.2   A teacher-made picture-word card.

Auditory cues can also be provided by special machines. The *Language Master* (Bell & Howell), the *e f i Audio Flashcard Reader* (Educational Futures, Inc.), and the *Audio-Q-Motivator* (Teaching Technology Corp.), the *Skill Master Audio Card Player* (Educators Publishing), and the *Mast Electronic Card Reader* (Mast) employ large cards on which strips of magnetic tape are mounted. The child can look at the card, attempt to identify the word, then place it on the machine and listen as a recorded voice pronounces the word. The child's response can also be recorded and played back, if desired. Both printed, prerecorded cards and blank cards can be purchased for these machines.

Even when a linguistic or phonic beginning method is used, some very common words need to be learned as sight words because they do not follow the most common phoneme-grapheme correspondences. With these methods, repeated encounters with the same printed words gradually lessen the need to utilize phonic and spelling cues, and more and more words become known at sight, as in basal reader methods.

For most children, recognition of known words becomes almost instantaneous as a result of sufficient practice in normal reading. If slowness in word recognition persists and becomes a real handicap, a child may need special training to speed up word perception. This is discussed on pages 417–418.

What Sight Words Should be Taught?

Ever since E. L. Thorndike (1921) compiled the first reading vocabulary list, new lists have appeared from time to time. Recently three comprehensive listings of reading vocabulary have appeared, one based on textbooks for grades one through 6 (A. J. Harris and Jacobson, 1972), one based on a wide variety of educational materials for grades 3 through 9 (Carroll, Davies, and Richman, 1971), and one based on adult reading materials (Kučera and Francis, 1967). Each of these made use of computerized techniques for analyzing the very large number of words found. Many shorter lists have also been developed for specific purposes. For descriptions and comparisons of many current word lists see A. J. Harris and Jacobson (1973–1974) and Hillerich (1974).

In beginning reading and in remedial teaching, teachers can make good use of a list of words that occur frequently in easy reading material. The *Dolch Basic Sight Vocabulary*, which contains 220 words exclusive of nouns, have been found to make up over 50 per cent of the running words in samples of reading material from pre-primer to sixth grade. While most of these words are of first-grade level, about 15 per cent are second reader level and a few are third reader level. In setting up an instructional sequence it may be helpful to use the *Harris-Jacobson Core Words* for pre-

CORE PREPRIMER LIST

a	daddy *	green	look	ride	want
and	did	have	make	said	we
are	do	he	me	see	what
at	dog *	help	mother *	something *	with
ball *	down	here	my	stop	work
big	for	I	no	that	you
blue	fun *	in	not	the	
call	funny	is	play	this	
can	get	it	ran	to	
come	go	little	red	up	

CORE PRIMER LIST

about	car *	home *	of	show	tree *
all	eat	house *	on	sit	two
around	fast	into	one	so	us
ask	father *	jump	out	some	went
away	fish *	know	paint *	soon	word *
bike *	from	let	pet *	take	yellow
birthday *	goat *	like	put	thank	yes
boat *	good	man *	run	then	your
book *	has	may	saw	they	
but	him	new	say	too	
cake *	his	now	she	train *	

CORE FIRST READER

after	cat *	girl *	live	prize *	think
again	catch *	give	long	rabbit *	those
airplane *	children *	gone *	lost *	race *	three
along *	coat *	good-by *	made	rain *	time *
am	cold	got	many	read	told *
an	color *	grass *	maybe *	ready *	tomorrow
animal *	could	guess *	men *	right	took *
another *	cow *	had	met *	road *	town *
any	cry *	hair *	miss *	rocket *	toy *
as	cut	hand *	money *	sang *	truck *
baby *	dark *	happy *	more *	sat *	try
back *	day *	hard *	morning *	school *	turtle *
bag *	didn't *	hat *	must *	seen *	TV *
balloon *	does	head *	name *	shoe *	under
bark *	don't	hear *	never	should *	very
barn *	dress *	hello *	next *	sing	wagon *
be	drop *	hen *	night *	sister *	walk
bear *	duck *	her	nothing *	sleep	was
bed *	fall	hill *	off	sound *	water *
bee *	far	hold	oh *	stay	way *
before	farm *	hop *	old	step *	were
began *	fat *	horse *	or	still *	wet *
behind *	feet *	how	other *	stopped *	when
better	fight *	hurry *	our	store *	where
bird *	find	I'll *	over	story *	which
black	fire *	ice *	own	street *	white
box *	first	if	pan *	sun *	why
boy *	five	it's *	party *	surprise *	window *
bring	fly	just	peanut *	talk *	wish
brown	food *	kind	penny *	tell	won't *
build *	found	kitten *	picnic *	than *	would
bus *	four	last *	picture *	their	zoo *
by	fox *	laugh	pig *	them	
cage *	friend *	leg *	please	there	
came	game *	letter *	pocket *	these	
can't *	gave	light	pony *	thing *	

FIGURE 14.3   Harris-Jacobson Core Words for first grade, quoted from Albert J. Harris and Milton D. Jacobson, *Basic elementary reading vocabularies.* New York: Macmillan Publishing Co., 1972, pp. 60-62, by permission of authors and publisher. Words that are not also in the Dolch Basic Word List are marked with asterisks.

primer, primer, and first reader levels. These are shown in Figure 14.3. These 332 words include most of the *Dolch* words and show the levels at which they are commonly introduced in basal readers. To this list can be added the 41 *Dolch* words that have Harris-Jacobson ratings of second reader or third reader level (see Fig. 14.4).

always	eight	once	start
ate	every	only	ten
because	full	open	today
been	goes *	pick	together
best	grow	pretty	upon * *
both	hot	pull	use
buy	hurt	round	warm
carry	its *	seven	wash
clean	keep	shall	well
draw * *	much	six	write
drink	myself	small	

FIGURE 14.4 Dolch Basic Words that are not in the Harris-Jacobson Core Words for the first grade. Words marked with one asterisk are inflected forms of H-J first grade words. Words marked with two asterisks are H-J third grade words. The remaining words are H-J second grade words.

In preparing children to read a new selection in graded reading material, pre-teaching of the "new" words is desirable in both developmental and remedial instruction. In reviewing, however, it is desirable to concentrate on the words that will be met again and again, while words needed just for this particular story can safely be ignored. Practice on high-frequency words that are not yet coming up in the selections to be read soon is more relevant to remedial than to developmental teaching.

When teachers use a language-experience approach there are two points of view about vocabulary selection. In experience stories dictated or written by pupils, all words employed by the children are utilized. However, some of the words are high-utility words that are worth teaching carefully, while others are specific to the story and are unlikely to be met again for quite a while. Use of a basic word list can help the teacher to decide which words are worth teaching and reviewing for long-term retention.

The opposite point of view is that certain "key" words carry high emotional charges for individual children, and these are the words that the children are most interested in learning and can learn most easily. The development of a so-called organic reading vocabulary of words with strong emotional appeal was first advocated by Ashton-Warner (1959) and has recently been systematically developed (Veatch, *et al.*, 1973). The limited research related to this issue seems to show that the interest loading of words is unrelated to rate of learning them among low socioeconomic children (L. A. Harris, 1969).

II. A MODERN PROGRAM OF DECODING

Beginners taught exclusively by a look-and-say method become confused and resort to guessing when they meet with words that are quite similar in length, shape, and conspicuous letters—words such as *look* and *like,* or *this* and *them.* At that point the teacher can help them by pointing out the specific features by which the two words can be distinguished. But that is not enough to produce good readers, since it leaves the child dependent on someone to tell him what each new word is. A child must become able to decode unknown words and to work out their pronunciations and meanings, in order to be self-reliant and independent in reading. How best to accomplish this aim has been the subject of violent arguments for many years and is still a problem to which many different answers are given. Most of the arguments have revolved around the subject of *phonics:* when, how, and how much phonics to teach.

During the past few years all popular sets of basal readers have had systematic, sequentially developed programs for developing independence in word recognition as an integral part of the method of teaching described in their manuals for teachers. These programs vary considerably in the order in which particular items are introduced, exact study and presentation methods suggested, amount of practice recommended, and so on. They may be eclectic, teaching a variety of decoding skills, or they may be phonic or linguistic in emphasis (see Chapter 3).

The eclectic series have certain principles in common. None of them relies mainly on phonic sounding and blending, as the older phonic systems did. Instead they attempt to provide comprehensive, varied word-attack skills which include attention to meaning, configuration clues, morphemic analysis,[1] and phonics. Such an approach assumes that a word needs to be attacked analytically only when it cannot be recognized as a whole and that a good reader is not dependent on any one way of decoding words, but has several techniques and makes use of the one that best fits the situation.

The recent evidence on the place of phonics in beginning reading has been discussed earlier (see Chapter 3). The third edition of this book recommended a somewhat earlier and more intensive teaching of phonic principles than was to be found in the most popular basal readers at that time. Since then a trend in that direction is discernible. If a basal reader system seems to have a weak or thin program for teaching decoding skills, if the teachers using it seem to neglect the recommended teaching of these skills, or if some children seem to need more intensive phonics, the use of an inde-

1. Linguists define a *morpheme* as a language element that conveys a meaning. Morphemes may be free (whole words) or bound (found only as parts of words, such as prefixes and suffixes). Morphemic analysis is the analysis of words into their morphemic units: roots, prefixes, suffixes, inflectional endings. Reading specialists have used the term *structural analysis* for what is here called morphemic analysis.

pendent set of phonics materials along with the readers may be helpful in the first grade. Materials that can be used in this way are described on pages 426–432.

Decoding Skills

Some of the ways in which a good reader can decode an unknown word are the following:

Use of Meaning Cues

1] He infers from context, the rest of the sentence suggesting what the missing word probably is. *Example:* Jerry went into the store to _____ some candy. Use of language clues suggests the missing word is almost certainly to be a verb. (He needn't know this term, but his past experience with oral language suggests the type of word needed to make sense.)

2] He then can reduce the uncertainty as to what the verb is by using as many additional cues as necessary. Configuration clues would lead to the rejection of such possibilities as "purchase." Or perhaps the initial consonant alone, or in combination with the word's configuration, may be sufficient. Although "buy" and "big" have the same configuration; the latter would be rejected because it doesn't make sense.

Use of Phonic Cues

3] Consonant or vowel substitution. He notes that the word is similar to a word he knows except for one or two letters, the sounds of which he knows. *Examples:* "mast": Knowing "fast" and *m*, he mentally substitutes the sound of *m* for the *f* to get "mast." "track": Knowing "back" and *tr*, he substitutes the sound of *tr* for *b* to get "track."

4] He applies phonic rules, such as the effect of final *e* on preceding vowel. *Examples:* "cane": Knowing the rule, he gives the *a* its long sound. "decent": Knowing that *c* is usually soft before *e, i,* or *y*, he uses the sound of *s* instead of the sound of *k*.

5] He uses syllabication, dividing into syllables and sounding the syllables phonically.
Examples: "unfortunate" *un for tu nate*
         "permitting" *per mit ting*

6] He thinks of a "word family" or "spelling pattern" to which the word belongs. *Example:* "fright": He recognizes it as belonging to the *ight* family along with "night," "right," and "fight."

7] He sounds the word out by groups of letters and blends the sounds together.
   Examples: "treaty" *tr eat y* or *tr ea ty* or *trea ty*
   "back" *ba ck* or *b ack*
8] He sounds the word letter by letter and then blends the sounds together.
   Examples: "pant"   *p-a-n-t*
   "triangle"   *t-r-i-a-n-g-l*

Use of Morphemic or Structural Cues
9] He divides the word into large parts which he already knows as units. *Examples:* "Postmaster" divides into *post* and *master;* "rainfall" divides into *rain* and *fall;* "superimposition," *super im position.*
10] He notes that the word consists of a familiar root and an ending.
   Examples: "playing"   *play* and *ing*
   "started"   *start* and *ed*
11] He looks for familiar little words within longer words (often unhelpful).
   Example: "candidate" *can did ate*
12] He analyzes words into known prefixes, roots, and endings.
   Examples: "reporter" *re port er*
   "independence" *in depend ence*

Use of Reference Cues
13] He looks the word up in the dictionary and uses the dictionary's syllable divisions, accent marks, and diacritical marks or phonetic respelling to get the correct pronunciation.

With all these techniques, the good reader is constantly aware of the meaning of the sentence in which the word is found. Thus, he can only decide whether to give the *i* in *live* a long or short sound, or whether to place the accent in *desert* on the first or second syllable, when he grasps the significance of the word in the total sentence. The old-fashioned phonic methods, with their emphasis on sounding words in lists, failed to emphasize this need for meaning.

Flexibility in word attack is also important. A child coming to the new word *everyone* will have no trouble if he sees it immediately as consisting of two known words, *every* and *one.* But if he picks out *very* and *on* as his known parts, and adds the *e* at both ends, the result will be a nonsense word that should stimulate him to try to solve the word in a different way. Application of the rule of the final silent *e* making the preceding vowel long will cause the word to rhyme with *bone.* Application of the rule that a vowel followed by a single consonant and another vowel generally has the long sound certainly will not help in this case. English is a sufficiently irregular language from the phonic standpoint to make it unwise to follow the rules blindly. Teachers must lead children to expect exceptions and to use intelligent trial and error when the first attempt to solve the word does not make sense. As Sister Caroline (1960) suggested, the child should ask himself, "Does it sound like a word I know? Does it make sense in this sentence?"

III. METHODS OF TEACHING PHONICS

Readiness for Phonics

A research study by Dolch and Bloomster (1937) had a great effect on phonics instruction. They gave to first-grade and second-grade pupils a test of recognition of uncommon one-syllable words, requiring the application of phonic principles without the aid of meaningful context. They found a substantial correlation between phonic ability, as measured by that test, and mental age. The children whose mental ages were below 7 years were able to do little or nothing on the phonics test. Dolch and Bloomster concluded that the ability to learn and apply phonic principles requires a higher type of mental maturity than is needed for learning sight words and recommended that the major part of phonics instruction should be placed in the second and third grades because the majority of first-grade pupils are not ready to profit from such instruction.

Most widely used basal readers for many years followed these recommendations and introduced relatively few phonic principles in the first grade (usually the single initial consonants and a few consonant digraphs such as *ch, sh,* and *th*), leaving the vowels and most consonant combinations for later levels. The Dolch-Bloomster phonics test presented the children with a more difficult task than they face in connected, meaningful reading, and it seems probable that their findings consequently underestimated the phonic readiness of first graders.

Auditory Discrimination. If a child listens to the words *mud* and *sand* and answers "Yes" when asked if they rhyme, or if he listens to *send, sit, soap, mat,* and *sun* and cannot pick out the one that starts differently from the others, he is obviously lacking in auditory discrimination skills and therefore in readiness for phonic instruction. Many teachers who have struggled unsuccessfully to impart phonic knowledge to certain children are not aware that the child's ability to perceive similarities and differences in the sounds of words must be developed if phonic teaching is to be effective.

Auditory discrimination for word sounds can be weak and faulty in children whose hearing, as measured by acuity tests, is excellent. It is not a matter of sensory acuity, but rather one of hearing selectively the beginning, or end, or middle of the word and comparing it with the sound of the corresponding parts of other words, thus having the basis for comparisons and the recognition of both similarities and differences.

Poor auditory discrimination is often accompanied by inaccurate or indistinct pronunciation. The child who says *wiv* for *with* is likely not to notice any difference between a *v* sound and a *th* sound within a word, and children who confuse *m* with *n* in reading often mumble the sound in their own speech so as to produce something between /m/ and /n/ for either. A child who says *mudder, fadder,* and *brudder* cannot easily learn the *th* symbol-sound association for reading. It is hard for many children to discriminate the short vowels: *pin* and *pen, men* and *man,* sound just alike to them. It is particularly difficult for children to learn to make a discrimination that does not occur in the dialect they speak.

Developing Readiness for Phonics

According to the results of Durrell and Murphy (1953), training in auditory discrimination speeded up the rate of learning new words and resulted in significantly higher reading scores than those obtained in control groups. When combined with training in visual discrimination, the results were still better. The order of increasing difficulty for children was found to be initial consonant sounds, final consonant sounds, long vowel sounds, and short vowel sounds, but the relative difficulty of specific letter sounds could not be established. Auditory training of this type was enhanced by the use of visual aids such as lantern slides. Ear training was especially valuable to those whose initial auditory discrimination scores were low and of little help to those whose initial scores were high. Ear training also tended to eliminate sex differences in learning rate in the first grade.

The important aspects of phonic readiness are as follows: 1) The child should be able to hear that there is a difference between words that sound somewhat alike, such as *cap* and *cup,* or *had* and *hat.* 2) He should be able to detect whether two words begin with the same sound or not. To test this ability, one can ask the child to pick out the one word that begins differently in a spoken list such as *moon, many, soon, make, mother.* He should also be able to listen to a word and supply two or three other words that begin with the same sound. 3) He should be sensitive to rhymes, should be able to pick out words that rhyme, and should be able to supply words to rhyme with a given word. This ability is fundamental to the construction of "word families." 4) He should be able to hear similarities and differences in word endings. 5) He should be able to hear similarities and differences in middle vowels; for example, he should be able to tell whether *rub* and *rob,* or *hill*

FIGURE **14.5**   A workbook page to develop auditory perception for the initial phoneme represented by *s*. Reproduced from *Teacher's Edition of Finding Out: A Discovery Book to Accompany Opening Books, A Magic Box, Things You See* (pre-primers), p. 27. Copyright by Macmillan Publishing Co., 1974. Reproduced by permission of the publishers; reduced in size. The directions read: "Have *Said* and *said* read and the first letters traced. Have objects in the first row named. (Repeat for each row.) (To pupils) 'Draw a line around the things that begin like *said*.'"

and *pit,* have the same middle sound. 6) He should be able to listen to the pronunciation of a word sound by sound and fuse or blend the sounds mentally so as to be able to recognize the word intended.

These six aspects of phonic readinesss have been listed roughly in order of increasing difficulty. Stage 6 is the hardest. While some children find it easy to blend sounds when they enter the first grade, other children go through school without ever becoming skillful at phonic blending. All these abilities, however, can be improved somewhat by special practice.

The most effective time to teach any phase of phonic readiness is just before the corresponding discrimination is to be made in printed words. However, certain general phases of phonic readiness, such as speaking distinctly and correctly, and listening to and reciting rhymes and poetry, can be started in the preschool period.

In developing auditory discrimination, a variety of devices can be used. In general, the technique is to provide a list of spoken words containing the element to be taught, get the children to focus attention on the particular sound in the words, get them to compare words which contain the sound with words which do not, and encourage them to think of additional words which contain the sound. For example, in teaching *f* as an initial consonant, some of the usable techniques are:

1] Ask the children to listen to a short list of words and tell you how they are alike. Pronounce such words as *fun, fox,* and *field.* Have the children explain how they are the same.

2] Play listening games in which the children signal, by raising a hand, clapping, or standing whenever you pronounce a word that begins with the same sound as the two words you pronounce first. After giving the stimuli (*e.g., fat, fur*), use lists such as *fun, fan, make, fence, toy.* Then reverse by having them signal when they do not hear a word begin like *fat* and *fur,* using lists in which about half the words do not begin with *f.*

3] Ask the children to suggest words that begin like *fat* and *fur.* To make this more challenging, it may be done by categories: names, animals, things, or games to play.

4] Give incomplete oral sentences or riddles which the children are to finish by adding a word that begins like *fat* and *fur.* For example:
   Playing ball is lots of (fun)
   What game do boys like to play in the fall? (football)

5] After two or more sounds have been taught, practice should be given in discriminating between and among them.

Instruction in sound-symbol associations (hearing a sound and associating a letter with it) may follow, or be given concurrently with, auditory-discrimination training. Pronounce a list of words beginning with the same sound, then on the board print the letter that represents that sound giving its name and the sound in isolation. For instance, pronounce *fig, farm*, and *food*. Print *f* on the board, explaining that all the words begin with the letter *f*, which makes the sound /f/.[2]

Once sufficient instruction has been given, the children can be asked to respond to a list of words by holding up a card with the letter on it, or write or say that letter, whenever they hear a word that begins with the sound represented by that letter. Learning to discriminate between and among sounds and making sound-symbol associations should facilitate the acquisition of symbol-sound associations (seeing the letter and determining what sound it represents).

Types of Phonic Analysis

Many different phonic methods have been evolved. In general they can be divided into two broad types: those which involve sounding the separate parts of a word and then blending them together, and those which avoid the separate sounding of word parts.

Sounding and Blending. Procedures involving sounding and blending have been of three major types. Each of these has certain advantages and also definite limitations.

1. Probably the oldest of these is letter-by-letter sounding, as *c-a-t*, *p-i-ck*. This method teaches a systematic left-to-right sequence in decoding the word and requires the teaching of a relatively small number of phonic elements. It has two main disadvantages: 1) extraneous sounds may distort the sounding, particularly the addition of an *uh* sound to consonants, as *cuh-a-tuh, puh-i-kuh;* and 2) blending its comparatively difficult, even when extra sounds are minimized.

2. The initial consonant is sounded and the rest of the word is sounded as a phonogram unit or spelling pattern of two or more letters, as *c-at, p-ick*. Words with the same final phonogram are taught as families, such as *at, bat, cat, fat, hat*. Because there are many one-syllable words that belong to such word families, this had been a popular procedure. Since there are only two parts to be blended together, blending is easier than with letter-by-letter sounding. The following sources of difficulty can be anticipated: 1) the child

2. There has been disagreement as to whether only letter names or only letter sounds should be used in such exercises. Common sense suggests that letter names and sounds should be introduced at the same time. Because many children can identify most letters by name before starting to read, it is important to make clear to them the distinction between letter names and the sounds they represent. There is also some evidence that teaching letter names and sounds concurrently facilitates the learning of reading skills (Nevins, 1973).

is encouraged to cultivate the habit of looking at the word ending before the beginning, developing improper eye movements; 2) there is a widely prevalent tendency, among teachers as well as children, to add an extra *schwa* or *uh* sound to the initial consonant, as *cuh-at,* which makes correct blending difficult; 3) practice on word families in list form may have little carryover to the recognition of the words in printed context; and 4) the phonograms which are taught in this way, like *-ap, -end, -ist, -ong,* and *-ock,* are infrequent in words of more than one syllable.

3. The initial consonant and following vowel are sounded as a unit, and the final consonant is added, as *ca-t, pi-ck.* The advantages claimed for this method are that it avoids extraneous sounds, makes blending comparatively easy, and prepares the way for syllabication of longer words (Cordts, 1955). Critics have pointed out that 1) the number of consonant-vowel combinations that have to be taught is very large; 2) it is difficult, when sounding in this way, to know whether to give the vowel its long or short sound because that depends on what follows the vowel; and 3) if followed exclusively, the method prevents the teaching of such phonograms as *ight* and *ound,* which are best learned as units.

Since a good reader needs flexibility in his attack on words, exclusive devotion to any of these three procedures is probably less desirable than a varied approach.

There are a few important matters of technique that have a great influence over the success or failure of instruction in sounding and blending. 1) In order to achieve good progress, considerable attention should be given to the development of auditory and visual discrimination for words. 2) In helping a child to sound out words, the teacher must be very careful to avoid extraneous sounds. 3) Words should be sounded continuously, with the sound of one letter running into the sound of the next letter. If it is necessary to pronounce the sound separately, the time interval between sounds should be as small as possible. 4) When a child is having difficulty in blending a word, the teacher should pronounce the whole word, then pronounce it successively more slowly until the individual sounds are given separately. Then the process is reversed, starting with separate sounds and speeding up gradually, so that the relation between the separate sounds and the usual pronunciation of the word as a whole can be more clearly appreciated. 5) Phonic analysis is very fatiguing to children who are learning the process, and therefore lessons of this type should be short, preferably not more than ten minutes. 6) If the skills developed in phonics lessons are to function in connected reading, abundant practice should be provided in which the child reads interesting material, recognizing most of the words at sight and falling back on decoding only when he meets a word he cannot recognize immediately.

Recent research has shown that the physical sound waves for a phoneme such as the one represented by the letter *d* are quite different depending on the letter's position in the word, and the vowel phoneme that follows it. The phoneme is really a concept representing recognition of a common property of somewhat different physical stimuli (Liberman, Cooper, Shankweiler, and Studdert-Kennedy, 1967; Shankweiler and Liberman, 1972). In criticizing sounding and blending procedure, the ability of normal readers to recognize a spoken word when it is pronounced by segments, even with distorted consonant phonemes, tends to be overlooked. Inability to achieve such closure seems to be a major reason why some children can "learn their sounds" but cannot seem to use them in decoding new words.

It has been suggested that this inability to combine phonemes is a conceptual difficulty rather than a perceptual one. Before one can put together some sounds and recognize the equivalent of a specific spoken word one must grasp the concept that a spoken word, which is heard as an unbroken, continuous pattern, can be segmented into phonemes. Some writers have recently advocated teaching initially by syllables rather than by phonemes, on the ground that the syllable is a unit more easily discerned within the spoken word (Gleitman and Rozin, 1973). Such an approach may be better for children who cannot blend well than single-phoneme phonics, but its limitations can be glimpsed just by comparing *famous* with *family*.

Whole-Word Phonics

Because so many children taught to sound and blend words either became slow, laborious word-by-word readers or remained unsuccessful in their attempts at blending, phonic techniques were worked out which attempt to avoid the separate sounding of word parts. The basic principle is to help the child become aware of the contribution of letters and phonogram units to the sound of the word by comparing and contrasting whole words, rather than by separate sounding of the parts.

The basic technique is that of letter substitution (or phonogram substitution). The child, when he comes to an unknown word, is encouraged to think of words that begin and end like the unknown word. For example, if the child comes to a new word, *mast*, he may think: "It begins like *man*, and ends like *last*, so it must be *mast*." He must be able mentally to drop off the ending of *man* and carry over the beginning while he thinks of the ending of *last*, so this is really a kind of quick mental blending.

Another variant of the method teaches initial consonants by means of cue words; if the child has difficulty remembering the sound of *m* he thinks of the cue word, which might be *milk*. The child is taught four steps: 1) think of a known word that resembles this new word; 2) drop off the part that is different; 3) think the sound of the new part, or think of a cue word that gives the sound of the new part; 4) without sounding the two parts

bags   truck

_____

_____

Draw a ring around the right line.

The cat is on the truck.

The cat is on the clown's back.

The cat is on the bags.

_____

sand   truck

Draw a ring around the right line.

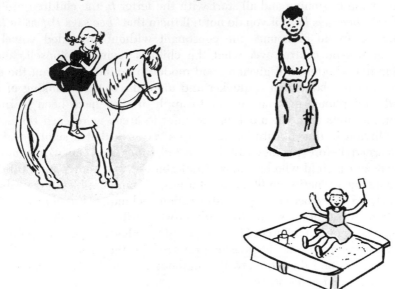

Tom is on the pony's back.

Tom is in the sack.

Tom is playing in the sand.

FIGURE **14.6** Page illustrating the use of picture and word cues in developing skill in the use of initial consonant-vowel combinations and consonant endings. From Anna D. Cordts *Functional Phonetics*, Book 1, p. 15. Chicago: Benefic Press, 1961, reproduced by permission of the publisher, and reduced in size.

separately, say the new word. Using the same example above, in which *mast* is unknown and *last* is known, the child would think: *last, ast, milk* (cue word for *m*), *mast*. As the consonant sounds become securely learned and skill in the method grows, the second and third steps drop out, and the new part is immediately substituted, so that the child thinks: *last, mast*. The same technique of thinking of a familiar word and making the necessary substitutions can be used also for final consonants (*meat, meal*), and for vowels (*spin, spun*).

Although some proponents of whole-word phonics are vehemently opposed to ever mentioning the phoneme represented by a letter or phonogram as a separate entity, the wisdom of such a prohibition is decidedly questionable. If you point out to children that *baby, book, boat*, and *bunny* all sound alike at the beginning and all start with the letter *b*, the children are going to think "*bee* says *buh*" if you do not tell them that "*bee* says /b/ as in *baby*," being careful to pronounce the consonant without an added vowel. The teacher has no control over what the child is saying to himself, and the children are better off if given a good model to imitate. Thinking the sound of a letter or phonogram is quicker and more direct than thinking of a cue word, and phonic units are easier to apply if they have been learned as separable units than when one has to refer to a cue word each time.

Obviously the substitution technique requires that a sight vocabulary be learned before phonics can be started, since the cue words must be known. For a child who has poor visual abilities, but shows an aptitude for learning by primarily auditory techniques, a sounding-blending technique is likely to work better than a substitution technique. For the majority of children, substitution seems to work satisfactorily. Although experimental comparisons of the different kinds of phonic methods are not available, substitution techniques are at present preferred by the majority of authors of basal readers and therefore are the methods by which most of today's children are trained in decoding.

Syllabication and Accent

A syllable is an uninterrupted unit of speech containing one vowel phoneme, forming either a whole word or part of a word; also the grapheme or graphemes which represent the spoken syllable. A syllable may consist of a vowel only; a vowel preceded by one or more consonants; a vowel followed by one or more consonants; or a vowel both preceded and followed by consonants.

By the third grade, many of the printed words that a child meets are words of more than one syllable. Many words of more than one syllable have already been learned as sight words. By second grade, one can begin to call children's attention to the fact that words are made up of syllables and can begin to develop skill in noting the number of syllables in a word.

Children can learn a word which has been divided into syllables for them by pronouncing it syllable by syllable long before they can make independent use of rules of syllabication. For children who have trouble with blending single phonemes together, the blending of syllables to make a spoken word is often much easier. It is not necessary, therefore, to wait until rules are taught before using syllabication as an aid in word recognition.

Syllabication is employed in spelling as well as in reading. Most spelling systems teach the pronunciation of words by syllables as one phase of a multisense approach in learning to spell. In this area reading instruction and spelling instruction should be mutually helpful.

Only the syllabication generalizations which have wide application and relatively few exceptions should be taught. They should be worded as simply as possible, and their application rather than recitation should be stressed.

The following generalizations may be useful in decoding unknown disyllabic and polysyllabic words:

1] Divide between words that form a compound word; other divisions may take place in either or both parts.
2] Usually divide between two consonants that are not a digraph or a blend.[3]
3] Usually divide between the root word and affixes; other divisions may take place within the root word.
4] A single consonant between two single vowels may go with either syllable.
5] Final *le* and the consonant preceding it usually form the final syllable.
6] If the root word ends with *t* or *d,* the final *ed* usually is a separate syllable.

Although there has been criticism of teaching syllabication generalizations (Groff, 1971), the fact remains that if properly taught and utilized they do provide the learner with some guidelines for dividing polysyllabic words into some units to which he can apply any necessary phonic skills. A point often overlooked is that syllabication often provides cues to vowel sounds. For example, if the syllable ends with a consonant (a closed syllable) he

3. The qualifier in this generalization is more applicable to digraphs than blends, because many words are divided between letters that commonly form blends. Some programs teach two generalizations, one involving unlike consonants, the other, double consonants. At least one program suggests dividing *after* double consonants.

Divide the words below according to Rule 3 or Rule 4. Be sure to try to divide the word **before** the middle consonant **first.** Most words will divide this way.

1. l a d y	9. s p i d e r
2. o v e r	10. g r a v y
3. t r u l y	11. F r i d a y
4. e v e r	12. o m i t
5. f e v e r	13. c l o s e t
6. r e m i t	14. i r i s
7. v a l o r	15. c l e v e r
8. l i l a c	16. e v i l

FIGURE **14.7**   Part of an exercise on syllabication. Rule 3 states that a word with a single consonant between 2 vowels may be divided after the consonant, and the vowel is short; Rule 4, that the word may be divided after the first vowel, and the vowel is long. From Lida G. Helson, *A First Course in Phonic Reading,* Revised Edition, p. 66. Cambridge, Mass.: Educators Publishing Service, 1971. Reproduced by permission of the publisher; reduced in size.

should first try the short sound represented by the single vowel letter. If it ends with a single vowel (open syllable) he should try the long vowel sound first. In conjunction with teaching generalization 4 above, the child should be informed that if he decides that consonant goes with the preceding syllable, he should try the short vowel first. If that doesn't result in a word he knows, he should try the long sound and begin the next syllable with the consonant. As for generalization 6, the child may be taught that *ed* is sometimes pronounced as a separate syllable. There is less need to inform children that at other times the *ed* may represent /t/ or /d/ because if the word is in their speaking vocabulary, they will automatically provide the correct word.

Accent.   Accent or stress is the prominence given to a syllable in a word (or to a word in a sentence) that makes it stand out in comparison to adjacent syllables (or words). In words of two syllables, one syllable is usually accented; it may be either the first or the second syllable. In words of three or more syllables, one syllable has a primary accent ($'$); there is sometimes a secondary accent ($'$) on another syllable. Rules of accent are not very helpful to children in working out the pronunciation of unfamiliar words. About the only accenting generalizations worth mentioning are: 1) usually accent the first syllable in two-syllable words; and 2) affixes are usually not accented. The resourceful reader tends to try accenting one syllable to see if the result is a word that he knows and that fits the meaning of the sentence; if not, he tries accenting another syllable.

Vowel Phonemes in Syllables. The sound values represented by vowel letters in syllables are affected both by the content of the syllable and by the placement of accent in the word. A few principles that seem useful are as follows:

1] When an accented syllable ends with a single vowel letter, that vowel is usually long.
2] When an accented syllable ends with a consonant (other than r) the vowel is usually short.
3] When an unaccented syllable ends with a vowel, that vowel sometimes has a long vowel sound but is reduced in duration (mu·si'cian) and sometimes tends toward a short sound (re·duce').
4] In many unaccented syllables the vowels are diminished to the point where their distinctive characteristics are almost lost and they can be represented by the schwa (∂).

The relationship between vowel sounds and accent implies that a resourceful reader should try varying the vowel phonemes as well as the accented syllable when working out an unfamiliar word.

IV. MORPHEMIC ANALYSIS

When a child compares *runs* with *run* and observes that the former is *run* with an *s* added, he is using the simplest form of morphemic analysis. During the first grade, children generally are helped to recognize words with variant endings such as *s, es, ed, er,* and *ing*.

A second form of morphemic analysis that is started early is the discovery that some words are compounds made up of smaller familiar words, like *into* and *something*. This technique should be limited to words that naturally separate into known words; children should not be encouraged to look for little words in the interior of bigger words, because that fosters confused eye movements, and often the little word is not a natural unit *examples*

1 number _____ *num´-ber* _____   3 nation _____ *na´-tion* _____

2 table _____ *ta´-ble* _____   4 remain _____ *re-main´* _____

practice

1 devote _____   4 cowboy _____

2 dinner _____   5 agent _____

3 teacher _____   6 about _____

test

1 review _____   6 cheated _____

2 bandit _____   7 baseball _____

3 station _____   8 bottle _____

4 firmly _____   9 able _____

5 above _____   10 freshest _____

FIGURE 14.8   An exercise on syllabication and accent. The concept of stressed syllables and guides for determining which syllables are to be stressed are introduced via a cassette. The pupil has to divide the words into syllables and place an accent mark on the stressed syllable. From Henry A. Bamman, Robert P. Hilder, and Maurice Poe, *Target Blue*: Structural Analysis Kit, p. 38. Copyright © 1972 by Field Educational Publications, Inc. Reproduced by permission of the publisher; reduced in size.

of the larger word. For instance, the *in* in *final* both provides the wrong vowel sound and prevents the proper division of the word into two syllables; the *at* and *on* in *nation* similarly do more harm than good.

A third form of morphemic analysis that becomes important when polysyllabic words are met with some frequency is the technique of looking for familiar prefixes, root words, and suffixes. This is an effective method with words like *in depend ence* and *en courage ment*, provided the parts can be recognized or decoded. Training in the recognition and meaning of common prefixes and suffixes is useful in the middle grades and secondary school and can be started even earlier.

Combining Morphemic Analysis, Phonics, and Context Clues

If the goal is recognizing the word as quickly and economically as possible, the less the child has to do, the better. Thus instantaneous recognition of the word as a whole is quickest and most satisfactory. When the first quick look does not disclose the identity of the word, the combination of an intelligent anticipation based on context with whatever familiar part or parts are immediately discernible is often enough.

Usually the earliest aid to independence in word recognition that is taught is the use of context. The child is asked to look at the illustration (if it is helpful), to think of what the whole sentence is saying, and to infer what the missing word might be.

As soon as children have begun to make use of initial consonants, they can be helped to combine this with use of the context. For instance, a sentence in a first reader might be: "Jim rode on the horse." The child sees the letter *h* and thinks that the word might be either *house* or *horse*. But a boy could not ride on a *house*, so the word is probably *horse*. This procedure of combining the anticipation of a certain meaning with the cue supplied by the first letter or so of the word is one which is usually learned in the first grade and continues to be serviceable to expert adult readers. In the sentence, "We like to watch our television set," either the *tel* at the beginning or the *vision* at the end would be sufficient cue for many children, in combination with context, to determine that the unknown word is *television*. Usually the beginning of the word is more helpful than the ending in this kind of solution.

When context and one familiar part do not suffice, a more systematic attack is necessary. Morphemic analysis may be sufficient when all, or most, of the parts of the word are already known at sight. For the most part, however, morphemic analysis is used in combination with phonics and context. The unknown word is divided into reasonable parts, the parts are sounded and blended together, and the result is tried to see if it makes sense in the sentence. At this point the child's listening and speaking vocabularies become important. If the word is one which the child understands, uses, and can pronounce correctly, an approximate or partial sounding is often sufficient for recognition. If the word is completely new to the child, he has to guess at both the pronunciation and the meaning, and neither can help him with the other. Thus a fourth-grade child, attacking a word like *incognito*, may divide it neatly into syllables and sound each in a reasonable way, but may accent the wrong syllable or give long vowel sounds where they should be short and so on, because the word is entirely unfamiliar to him.

Look at the first sentence. One word is missing. The missing word is one of the three words under the sentence. Find the right word. Draw a line under it. Do all the other sentences this same way.

1. Everybody likes to watch the _____.

   <u>baboon</u>   balance   between

2. The hot pan _____ Ann's hand.

   buttoned   blurred   <u>burned</u>

3. Our cat left a_____ mouse on the steps.

   <u>dead</u>   decide   desk

7. Let's have cheese _____ for lunch.

   steps   sleeves   <u>sandwiches</u>

8. Has Ann _____ your cookies?

   trapped   <u>tasted</u>   tooted

9. Use a green pencil for _____ your papers.

   <u>marking</u>   making   melting

FIGURE **14.9**   Part of an exercise on using context clues to distinguish between words of similar appearance. From William K. Durr, Jean M. LePere, and Bess Niehaus, *Workbook for Rewards*, Teacher's Annotated Edition, p. 28. Boston: Houghton Mifflin Co., 1971. Reproduced by permission of the publisher; reduced in size.

Skill in the combined use of context, phonics, and morphemic analysis can be developed by the use of practice material which demands both attention to the meaning and careful attention to the details of words. One form of practice material useful for this purpose is shown in Figure 14.9. This kind of exercise, in its many variations, is very useful for enforcing accuracy in word recognition and noting the details of words while reading for meaning. The child has to understand the sentence as a whole in order to know what word to expect; then he has to choose correctly among words that look very much alike in order to complete the sentence correctly.

Phonic Generalizations

Some phonic systems rely heavily on the teaching and application of rules concerning grapheme-phoneme relationships. One system, for example, taught 82 rules ("keys") in the first grade. There has been a considerable research interest recently in the utility of phonic generalizations or rules (Clymer, 1963; Bailey, 1967; Burmeister, 1968, 1969; Emans, 1967; Gibson, 1972). Some of the most commonly taught rules have so many exceptions that their utility is limited. Most rules about long and short vowels need to be qualified when the vowel is followed by *r;* and to be more accurate, rules should specify whether they apply to one-syllable words, accented syllables, or unaccented syllables. Among the rules considered limited in application because of many exceptions are the one on vowel digraphs (first vowel is long, second is silent) and the one on magic *e* (makes the preceding vowel say its name). The per cent of exceptions can be reduced by making each rule more specific; but that makes each rule harder to learn, increases greatly the number of rules, and decreases the number of words to which each of the new rules would apply.

When second- and fifth-grade children were given a list of unfamiliar words to decode, they made practically no use of phonic rules; instead, they relied mainly on "a letter clustering approach associated with sounds" (Glass and Burton, 1973). Considering the many exceptions to phonic rules and the lack of evidence that children find such rules very helpful, a heavy emphasis on phonic rules does not seem to be justified.

It seems best (especially with average and below-average pupils, whose ability to understand and apply generalizations is limited) to teach the phoneme most commonly represented by a letter or letter combination first, and to call attention to alternative phonemic values as they come up in reading material. Children should learn and practice the strategy of trying one sound, checking to see if the word makes sense in the sentence, and if necessary trying alternative sounds. This strategy makes the memorization and application of a large number of highly specific rules unnecessary.

V. SCOPE AND SEQUENCE IN TEACHING DECODING

Many different sequences for introducing phonic learnings have been devised. Most authors of basal readers provide for the introduction of initial consonants first, followed by some word families and simple endings, in the first-grade manuals. Two-consonant blends and short and long vowels are usually taught at second reader level, and less common phonic elements are brought in at third reader level. Syllabication, prefixes, and suffixes are usually started at third reader level and developed further in the middle grades.

Some of the special phonics materials which have been designed for independent use as supplements to a basal reading program follow other sequences. One, for example, introduces all short vowels before the consonants. Another begins with long vowels. This runs contrary to the available research on phonic readiness and to the practical experience of most teachers, which indicates that vowels are more difficult than consonants for most children and that consonants are more essential in word recognition than vowels, but it is not an impossible sequence.

In attempting to determine a sensible sequence for phonic units, the major guiding principles are to introduce early those elements which are frequently met in primary-grade words and those which are most readily learned. If one adheres to these common-sense ideas reasonably well, many different sequences can be used with satisfactory results.

It is probably true that the ideal time to introduce a new phonic principle or unit is when the children have need for it and are ready for it. This is what the basal reader systems attempt to do, since usually a new phonic idea is introduced at a point where several words exemplifying it have been learned as sight words, and the new idea can be developed from these known words. A good teacher should not hesitate to teach a word-attack skill or a new sound when there seems to be a suitable occasion, even if that means deviating from a previously planned sequence.

The contents of Table 11 indicate what, in our judgment, should

TABLE 11.　*Desirable word-identification outcomes by reading levels*

Readiness
　　Developing an awareness of phoneme-grapheme relationships
　　Hearing similarities and differences in initial phonemes
　　Hearing the phonemes for selected initial consonant phonemes
　　Hearing and supplying rhyming words
Preprimer
　　Associating grapheme with phoneme for most consonants: *b, c* (hard), *d, f,*
　　　g (hard), *h, j, l, m, n, p, r, s, t, v, w, y*
　　Using initial consonants with context to identify new words
　　Using some final consonants to help in identifying new words
　　Substituting initial and final consonants in known words
　　Morphemes: inflectional endings *s* and *ed*
Primer
　　Associating grapheme with phoneme
　　　single consonants *k, z*
　　　consonant digraphs *ch, sh, th*
　　　consonant blends *pl, st, tr*

short vowels *a, e, i, o, u*

vowel digraph *ea* (each)

spelling patterns: *er, or, ur, ar, ow, et, an, ight, at, ay, all*

Substitution: using known grapheme-phoneme relationships with known words to identify new words

Using terms vowel and consonant

Morphemes: inflectional endings *'s, ed, d, er*

suffix *er* (farmer)

Dictionary: learning to use a simple picture dictionary

First Reader (1²)

Associating grapheme with phoneme

Consonants *x, q(qu)*

Consonant digraphs, *wh, ck*

Consonant blends *br, cr, dr, fr, gr, bl, cl, fl, ld, nd, sc, tw*

Silent consonants *kn, wr, ll*

Long vowels *a, e, i, o, u, y*

Rule: *Y* a consonant at beginning of a word, vowel at end of word

When there are two vowels one of which is final *e*, the *e* is silent and the first vowel is usually long.

Vowel digraph *ie*

Rule: Two vowel letters together usually represent one sound

Vowel diphthongs *ow (cow), oi, oy*

Spelling patterns: *ook, old, en, ad, eat, ite, ame, nd, ew, eigh*

Morphemes: Contractions with *'t*

Inflectional endings *ing, est*

Separating compound words into known words

Grade 2 (2¹ and 2²)

Associating grapheme with phoneme

Consonants: hard and soft sounds for *c, g*

Consonant digraph *ph*

Consonant blends *fl, gl, nk, pr, qu, sk, sl, sm, st, sw, str, squ, thr*

Silent consonants *ch, gh, mb*

Vowels: *Y* at end of a one-syllable word usually long; at end of a two-syllable word, usually short

Vowel digraphs *oa, ay, ai* (tail, certain), *aw, ei* (eight, receive), *ey* honey), *oo* (foot, room), *ow* (blow), *ou* (through, could, country, though), *ue* (true)

Vowel diphthong *ou* (shout)

Schwa: *a* as an initial letter (again)

R-controlled vowels: *ar, er, ir, or, ur, ear* (year, search, bear), *our* (hour, fourth)

Syllabication: counting the number of vowel sounds in a word as a clue to the number of syllables

Morphemes: Prefix *un*

Suffixes *ful, fully, ish, less, ly, en, er, est, n, ness, self, y*

Spelling changes when adding or subtracting suffixes (subtracting or adding final *e*; changing *y* to *i* or *vice versa*; doubling consonant which follows a short vowel)

Grade 3 (3¹, 3²)
    Associating grapheme with phoneme
    Consonant blends *ng, nt, spl, spr*
    Phonic rules: A single vowel followed by a consonant (other than *r*) in a
               one-syllable word or an accented syllable is usually short.
               When a vowel ends a one-syllable word or an accented syl-
               lable, the vowel is usually long.
               Rules for final *e* and vowel digraphs extended to accented
               syllables.
    Schwa: A vowel in an unaccented syllable often represents the schwa
        sound.
    Diacritical marking: use of macron (⁻) to indicate long vowel sound
    Syllabication: Hearing and marking syllable divisions
               Learning to syllabicate two-syllable and three-syllable words
               Using cues for syllabication
               prefixes and suffixes
               double consonants and two consonants together
               consonant digraphs and blends treated as one consonant
    Accent: Hearing and marking accented syllables
        Prefixes and suffixes not accented
        Noting effect of accent on vowel sounds
    Morphemes: Prefixes *im, in, dis, super, re*
             Suffixes *le, or* (agent), *ous, tion, sion, ion, ation, self, ment,*
             ship, ward, teen, ty
    Dictionary: Learning to use a glossary or simple dictionary
             Learning to use diacritical markings and pronunciation spell-
             ings

---

usually have been covered in word-attack skills by the time reading at a
given level of difficulty has been completed. At a particular difficulty level
no attempt has been made to indicate a sequence in which the items should
be taught. This table is intended to provide a list of objectives and a check
list to see what needs to be reviewed or first taught, rather than an instructional sequence. It can be taken for granted that many children will not
master a particular phonic skill the first time it is introduced, and therefore
review at higher levels of instruction is a necessity. No attempt has been
made to indicate specific readiness activities at the different levels, since the
general principle should be that listening for sounds within words and
looking for the corresponding visual symbols is part of all phonic instruction.

    The levels at which particular skills are listed in Table 11 tend in general
to be lower than is customary in many basal reader systems. For example,
short vowels are listed at primer level and long vowels at first reader level,
while many series introduce both short and long vowels at second-grade
level. Experience and recent research confirm that vowels can successfully

be taught to first graders. The contents of Table 11 correspond closely to the skills placement employed in the Harris-Clark (Macmillan) readers.

VI. SPELLING AND WORD IDENTIFICATION

The close relationship between success in reading and success in spelling has already been mentioned in this book several times. Good readers are sometimes poor spellers, but readers who are poor in word recognition are rarely if ever good spellers. In reading, one sees the visual symbols and has to think of the corresponding sounds; in spelling, one hears the word and has to think of the corresponding symbols. Learning for recognition in reading does not require the complete mastery needed for correct recall in spelling.

Effective spelling instruction utilizes much the same type of procedure that has been described in this chapter. A typical classroom method of teaching spelling proceeds about as follows: The word is first spoken by the teacher in a sentence, then by itself, and written or printed on the board. The meaning is brought out through use in sentences. The word is then analyzed into component parts, with syllables separated by vertical lines, underlying, or some other device. Attention is called to difficult parts by underlining or using colored chalk. Many types of sensory reinforcement are employed, such as pronouncing the word, spelling it in concert, visualizing the word followed by recall of the visual image with the eyes closed, writing the word in the air while spelling it aloud, and finally writing the word from memory and checking against the correct form. It is evident that good spelling is based first of all on correct perception of the word, followed by repetition and sensory reinforcement to bring about permanent retention in memory.

Many of the devices used in spelling instruction, such as dividing the word into syllables, pointing out and emphasizing the difficult parts, and using a varied sense appeal, are also effective aids in word recognition. When a word is learned so that it can be spelled from memory, it is usually recognized without difficulty in reading. An efficient classroom teacher can use the spelling period for practice on many of the abilities that are necessary for good word recognition.

Dangers of Rote Spelling

Many children whose spelling is poor are victims of an inefficient method of word study. They memorize a word by reciting the sequence of the letters over and over, without paying attention to syllable divisions, without trying to visualize the word, and without trying to note the specific features of the word that may be confusing. Since this type of practice is comparatively uninteresting and devoid of meaning, it is less effective for most children than the kind of procedure described in the preceding paragraphs.

Many children who have difficulty in acquiring a sight-reading vocabulary try to learn and recall their reading words by spelling them letter by letter. This is a very inefficient method of word recognition, and in order to make real progress the child has to give it up in favor of more effective procedures. Rote spelling as an avenue to reading has the following defects: 1) it is a slow procedure and results in halting, word-by-word reading; 2) it usually fails on words of more than five or six letters; 3) the children who resort to spelling as an aid in word recognition are usually poor spellers also; 4) the spelling procedure interferes with the use of more adequate methods of word study; and 5) it prevents the perception of the word as a whole, since the child's attention is not on a word form containing distinctive parts, but on a string of letters possessing no form quality that can be remembered.

In getting a child to discontinue letter-by-letter spelling in his reading, the first step should be an explanation of the weaknesses of the procedure and encouragement to try a different method. As he studies a word, he should be encouraged to pronounce it as a whole, by syllables, or by phonic elements, but not to recite the names of the individual letters.

This chapter has surveyed the methods used in developmental reading instruction for teaching word-recognition skills. Attention has been given to building sight vocabulary, providing varied and flexibly used decoding techniques, methods of teaching phonics, morphemic analysis, the scope and sequence of a decoding program in primary grades, and the relation between word recognition and spelling. Understanding the developmental word-recognition program is a necessary basis for remedial teaching to overcome difficulties in word identification, which is covered in Chapter 15.

SUGGESTED ADDITIONAL READING

DAWSON, MILDRED A. (Ed.). *Teaching word recognition skills.* Newark, Del.: International Reading Association, 1971.

DUFFY, GERALD G.; SHERMAN, GEORGE B.; ALLINGTON, RICHARD L.; MC ELWEE, MICHAEL R.; & ROEHLER, LAURA R. *How to teach reading systematically.* New York: Harper & Row, 1973. Modules 11, 12, 13, 14.

FROSTIG, MARIANNE & MASLOW, PHYLLIS. *Learning problems in the classroom.* New York: Grune and Stratton, 1973. Chaps. 5, 6.

HARRIS, ALBERT J. & SIPAY, EDWARD R. (Eds.). *Readings on reading instruction* (2nd ed.). New York: McKay, 1972. Chap. 8.

HARRIS, LARRY A. & SMITH, CARL B. *Reading instruction through diagnostic teaching.* New York: Holt, Rinehart and Winston, 1972. Chaps. 8, 9, 10.

HEILMAN, ARTHUR W. *Phonics in proper perspective* (2nd ed.). Columbus: Charles E. Merrill, 1972. Chap. 7.

————. *Principles and practices of teaching reading* (3rd ed.). Columbus: Charles E. Merrill, 1972. Chap. 7.

RUDDELL, ROBERT B. *Reading—language instruction: innovative practices.* Englewood Cliffs, N.J.: Prentice-Hall, 1974. Chap. 10.

SCHELL, ROBERT E. *Letters and sounds: a manual for reading instruction.* Englewood Cliffs, N.J.: Prentice-Hall, 1972.

WALLEN, CARL J. *Word attack skills in reading.* Columbus: Charles E. Merrill, 1969.

15

Remedial Procedures for Deficiencies in Word-Identification Skills

In most reading disabilities, deficiencies in recognizing, decoding, and recalling printed words are central to the remedial picture. This is true not only of the very severe cases, but also of many milder cases who are able to cope with reading material above primary-grade levels despite carelessness and inaccuracy in word recognition and the lack of an adequate independent method for identifying unfamiliar words.

I. BASIC STRATEGY IN CHOICE OF METHOD

Children who enter remedial reading programs with word-recognition skills at a first- or second-grade level have been exposed to developmental reading programs of various kinds. Some have failed with typical basal readers; some, with linguistic or phonic readers; some, with i/t/a; some, in language experience or individualized programs. It can be taken for granted that these children were quite deficient in one or more of the important aspects of reading readiness when they entered first grade and that their failure to learn at that time was more probably due to these readiness lacks than to poor instruction.

By the time such children are accepted into a remedial program their readiness patterns are greatly varied. Some have outgrown their immaturities and have the ability to learn to recognize words as normal first graders do. Others have persisting deficits in visual and/or auditory perception, in visual and/or auditory memory, in ability to make visual-auditory associations, in directional confusion, in persisting sensory or health defects, in motivation or emotional blocking, which must be taken into account if the remedial program is to succeed.

Strategy in the Selection of Remedial Emphasis

Broadly speaking, there are three possible basic strategies for using diagnostic knowledge about strengths and weaknesses of the learner. 1) Base teaching on known strengths, by-passing or minimizing the need to utilize weak abilities. 2) Emphasize known strengths in teaching new material while strengthening the deficient abilities through readiness activities, and teach skills requiring these abilities when they have become adequate. 3) Concentrate on building up the deficient abilities, and delay reading instruction until a satisfactory level of readiness has been achieved.

The first of these three strategies has obvious limitations. Successful learning can occur, but the skills developed tend to be restricted in scope and relatively inflexible. Thus a child whose teaching program is exclusively phonic may remain a slow, plodding, word-by-word reader; or a child with weak auditory abilities may develop a sight vocabulary, but remain with no method of attack on new words. Furthermore, the deficient abilities probably handicap the child in other activities, and his pattern of abilities may be more uneven after remedial help than before.

The second strategy is the one advocated by most authorities on remedial reading. A start on word recognition can begin immediately, using whatever method the child is able to employ with some success. Meanwhile, part of the remedial time is used for developing deficient abilities that are needed for a varied, flexible word attack. To the extent possible, readiness activities are closely related to reading activities. Thus, visual-discrimination practice can emphasize the noting of similarities and differences in letters, letter groups, and words, rather than geometric shapes or pictures of objects. Auditory-discrimination practice can stress phonemes and spoken words; the transfer value to reading of listening to and comparing musical sounds or sequences of taps is questionable. There seems to be fairly general agreement among proponents of this strategy that the major part of available remedial time should be spent in reading and a minor part in training designed to build up deficient perceptual or other abilities.

The third strategy, stressing readiness, is a quite recent one. It has been clearly stated by Silver, Hagin, and Hersh (1965, 1967), Wiseman (1970),

Keogh (1971a), and Frostig (1972b). Frostig (1972a), in another article, had advocated simultaneously teaching specific reading skills according to whatever abilities the child can use, and presenting activities to strengthen weaker abilities.

> Our initial concept had been that compensation was a basic principle, *i.e.*: after assessing perceptual assets and deficits, we should train in the areas of greater perceptual strength, via the most intact modalities. Results of the follow-up studies, however, suggest that this technique does not appear to enhance perception or to effect lasting improvement in reading. Efforts now are directed to the stimulation of the defective perceptual areas. This is almost a complete reversal of our earlier approach. Our purpose now is really to enhance cerebral maturation, to bring neurological functioning to the point where it is physiologically capable of learning to read. (Silver, Hagin, and Hersh, 1965)

In a shorter published version of the same paper they said:

> The results so far suggest that where perceptual defects are first trained out, reading instruction at intermodal and verbal levels will have a better chance of success. This is particularly true of the more severe language disabilities, those with defects in multiple modalities and those in whom "soft" neurological signs may be found. (Silver, Hagin, and Hersh, 1967)

This point of view has been opposed on theoretical grounds by Mann (1970) who regards perceptual-motor training as an educational fad, and by S. A. Cohen (1969) who concluded that it is not necessary to teach perceptual-motor behaviors in order to teach disadvantaged underachievers to read.

A substantial number of research studies related to this issue have appeared, and several critical reviews of this research have been written (H. M. Robinson, 1972a; Hammill, Goodman, and Wiederholt, 1974; Klesius, 1972; Balow, 1971). None of these reviewers found that emphasis on perceptual or perceptual-motor or motor training had any advantage over direct remedial teaching of needed reading skills.

> To conclude, the results of attempts to implement the Frostig-Horne materials and Kephart-Getman techniques in the schools have for the most part been unrewarding. The readiness skills of children were improved in only a few instances. The effect of training on intelligence and academic achievement was not clearly demonstrated. Particularly disappointing were the findings which pertained to the effects of such training on perceptual-motor performance itself. For if the training is not successful in this area, can the

positive results of such instruction reported by a few authors be anything other than spurious? (Hammill, Goodman, and Wiederholt, 1974)

II. WORD-IDENTIFICATION METHODS FOR SEVERE DISABILITIES

Perception, Imagery, and Recall

When a child is unable to remember words after painstaking teaching efforts, the teacher is apt to wonder what is wrong with the child's memory. Sometimes the problem is one of difficulty in recall, particularly in cases where anxiety is strong and emotional blocking is severe. But often the main problem is not one of poor memory, but rather of failure to develop a mental image of the word which can be recalled at a later time. If there is no initial registration of the word, there will be nothing to remember.

The first step must necessarily be reasonably good perception of the word. Testing with brief exposures discloses that many severe reading disability cases perceive a word at first glance in very incomplete and hazy fashion, and additional looks at the word do little to amplify and improve this first impression. If perception has been unsatisfactory, the mental image of the word which the child forms cannot be any better.

It is also possible for initial perception to be fairly good, but upon closing his eyes and trying to "see" the word mentally the child has little or no visual image. Difficulty in forming mental images may be present not only for word forms but also for places or things.

The methods which have generally succeeded with severe cases all involve the development of clearer perception of words and the provision of additional cues which lend vividness to the memory image so that it can be retained in memory. This is done either by tying in sensory and perceptual cues from other senses, as in the kinesthetic and phonic methods, or by systematic efforts to improve visual perception and imagery, as in the predominantly visual techniques.

The Kinesthetic Method

In 1921, Grace M. Fernald and Helen B. Keller described a method for teaching nonreaders which emphasizes tracing and writing as basic procedures. The following description of the method is based on the account given in Fernald's book (1943).

In the early stages, no printed material is used. At first the child is asked to tell the teacher a few words he would like to learn. These are taught one by one. As soon as he has learned a few words, he is encouraged to compose a little story and is taught any words in the story that he does not already know. The compositions are at first dictated to the teacher and later written by the child. After the story has been read in written form, it is typed out so that he can read it the next day in type. The child's own compositions are the only materials used until a fairly large sight vocabulary has been learned.

The method of teaching words changes as the child's ability to learn words improves. Four stages are distinguished.

Stage 1. *Tracing.* The word is written for the child on a strip of paper about 4 inches by 10 inches, preferably in large cursive writing (manuscript printing can also be used). The child traces the word with his finger in contact with the paper, saying each syllable of the word as he traces it. This is repeated until he can reproduce the motions of writing the word from memory. He writes it on scrap paper and then in his story. Later the story is typed and read in typed form. Each new word that is learned is placed by the child in an alphabetical file. The following points of technique are stressed: 1) Finger contact is important; tracing in the air or with a pencil is less useful. 2) The child should never copy a word, but always writes from memory. 3) The word should always be written as a unit. 4) The child must say each syllable of the word either to himself or out loud as he traces it and writes it. 5) Whatever he writes must be typed and read before too long an interval; this provides transfer from the written to the printed form.

Stage 2. *Writing without Tracing.* After a while (days in some cases, weeks in others) the child does not need to trace most new words. He looks at the word in script, says it to himself several times, tries to "see" the word with his eyes shut, and writes it from memory. If he makes an error he compares his result with the model, paying particular attention to the part or parts he missed. This is repeated until he can write the word correctly from memory. Index cards with the words in both script and print form are substituted for the large word strips and are filed alphabetically. Essentially this is the same procedure as the VAK method described on page 358.

Stage 3. *Recognition in Print.* It becomes unnecessary to write each new word on a card. The child looks at the word in print, is told what it says, pronounces it once or twice, and writes it from memory. Reading in books is usually started about the time that this stage is reached.

Stage 4. *Word Analysis.* The child begins to identify new words by noting their resemblance to words he already knows, and it is no longer necessary to teach him each new word. Although phonic sounding of single letters is not taught, skill in word analysis gradually develops through noticing grapheme-phoneme correspondences that are met repeatedly.

Total nonreaders are started at Stage 1. Children with partial disabilities are often started at Stage 2. No special techniques are used to overcome such difficulties as reversals or omissions; these are said to drop out without special attention, since the tracing-writing process enforces a consistent left-to-right direction and requires correct reproduction of the entire word.

Unique features in Fernald's method are the great emphasis on tracing and writing, the teaching of difficult as well as easy words from the very beginning, the use of the child's own compositions as the only reading material in the early stages, and the beginning of book reading on a fairly difficult level.

Kinesthetic reinforcement is recommended as a supplementary procedure both by those who place major reliance on visual word-study methods and by those who rely primarily on a systematic phonic method.

The kinesthetic method has produced very successful results with many severe disability cases. In addition to the many cases in Fernald's book, recent cases using the Fernald approach have been described by Kress and Johnson (1970), Berres and Eyer (1970), Enstrom (1970), and Coterell (1972). The approach has several desirable features: 1) It enforces careful and systematic observation and study of words. 2) It makes necessary a consistent left-to-right direction in reading. 3) It provides adequate repetition. 4) Errors are immediately noted and corrected. 5) Progress can be noted by the child at practically every lesson. 6) The sensory impressions from tracing, writing, and saying the words reinforce the visual impressions and seem to be of definite value to children whose visual memory is very poor.

There are, however, several objections to the use of the kinesthetic method as outlined by Fernald. 1) The teacher has to direct and check every step in the child's work and teach him every new word until he has progressed far along the road to good reading. During the early stages, the child is unable to do any independent reading. The method is well suited to use in a special clinic school such as the one supervised by Fernald, in which the children were with the remedial teacher for a full school day five days a week, but is not so well adapted to a remedial setup in which the child has only a small number of remedial periods each week. 2) The majority of nonreaders can learn to recognize words by methods that are faster than the rather cumbersome tracing-writing procedure. The VAK method of word study (Fernald's Stage 2) is, however, very often helpful. 3) We see no advantage in avoiding the use of easy books in the early stages of remedial work unless the child has a strong resistance to them. It is desirable to start reading in books as early as possible, even if pre-primers must be used, provided that the child's cooperation can be obtained, and the words are pre-taught.

It has become customary to call tracing methods VAKT (visual-auditory-kinesthetic-tactual) methods (M. S. Johnson, 1966). Actually the child's experience includes the following: 1) see teacher write the word; 2) hear teacher say the word; 3) say the word; 4) hear himself say the word; 5) feel the movements he makes as he traces the word; 6) feel the surface with his fingertips as he traces; 7) see his hand move as he traces; and 8) say and hear himself say the word (or syllables) as he traces.

In the VAK method (look, hear, say, visualize, write from memory) the child's experience includes looking at the word, hearing the teacher say it, saying it, hearing himself say it, trying to visualize it, attempting to write it, feeling and seeing the movements involved in writing and saying, and hearing himself say it as he writes it. This is essentially Fernald's Stage 2. A step-by-step description of a VAK method with a group has been given on page 358.

Roberts and Coleman (1958) found that children who were failures in reading tended to be inefficient in learning words by visual cues only and were aided by adding kinesthetic cues, but poor readers who had normal visual perception scores were not aided by kinesthetic cues. Berres (1967) found that motoric reinforcement did not help disadvantaged retarded readers in speed of learning, but did improve their long-time retention; tracing and writing helped more than writing without tracing, and both promoted retention over visual study without motor reinforcement. Ofman and Schaevitz (1963) compared two tracing methods with look-and-say in learning nonsense syllables. Tracing with the eye was as effective as tracing with the finger; both were superior to look-and-say. They speculated that enforced attention to details in sequence rather than tactual -kinesthetic sensation is the significant aid to learning. This would seem to explain the success of VAK for many children; it does not rule out the need for VAKT by a few.

A new and as yet unresearched variation is to trace three-dimensional letters, keeping the eyes closed (Blau and Blau, 1968). The rationale offered is that this allows development of clear kinesthetic perception, imagery, and memory, without interference from deficient or distorted visual perception. Another reason why such a procedure might work in some cases is that it may avoid neurological overloading, such as may happen in an immature or damaged brain when several sensory avenues are stimulated simultaneously. Of course, after the "feel" of the word has been learned, it will still be necessary to build a visual-kinesthetic association. This proposal deserves further study, particularly in very severe cases in which progress with VAKT or with phonics is extremely slow. A "blind writing" procedure has been recommended by Frostig (1965) for use with children who have inferior visual perception.

Methods Based on Sounding and Blending

Synthetic phonic methods based on learning the phonemes represented by letters, sounding them and blending the sounds together, and supplemented by some use of kinesthetic procedures, have been advocated by many remedial specialists, particularly by those influenced by the late Dr.

Samuel T. Orton. A clear and relatively brief summary of the Orton point of view has been given by Mrs. Orton (1966). A lengthy and detailed manual of procedure by Gillingham and Stillman (1966) has been the main training textbook for followers of the Orton school. A detailed manual adapting the approach for classroom use by primary-grade teachers has been prepared by Slingerland (1971). Somewhat briefer manuals have been prepared by Mrs. Orton (1964) and by Cox (1967). A guide for teaching spelling in a way consistent with Orton procedures has been written by Childs and Childs (1963). Several workbooks designed to give practice in sounding and blending are listed on page 429.

The basic common features of the approach used by followers of Orton have been briefly summarized by Mrs. Orton as follows:

> Their common conceptual background can usually be seen in their introduction of the kinesthetic element to reinforce the visual-auditory language associations and to establish left-to-right habits of progression. Their phonetic approach is generally the same: teaching the phonic units in isolation but giving special training in blending; introducing the consonants and the short sounds of the vowels first and building three-letter words with them for reading and spelling; programming the material in easy, orderly, cumulative steps. (1966, p. 144)

According to Gillingham, the method requires five lessons a week for a minimum of two years. Drill on letter sounds and blending is the main activity for many weeks. The first group of letters taught includes *a, b, f, h, i, j, k, m, p, t*. After these have been learned (usually not more than one new letter a day) and used in blending and spelling short words, simple sentences using only words containing these letters may be introduced. One way of teaching blending has been described earlier in a sample lesson procedure (see p. 230). Gillingham preferred to sound the initial consonant and vowel together, then add the final consonant (*ba-t*). She emphasized the importance of simultaneous oral spelling (saying the sounds in sequence, then saying the letter names in sequence while writing them). Kinesthetic procedures were used to teach words with irregular grapheme-phoneme relationships. Other points stressed by Gillingham included: 1) parents were advised to read all homework to the pupil until he became able not only to read but to read with reasonable fluency; 2) teachers were asked to excuse the child from written tests and to test him orally; and 3) independent reading was not allowed until the major part of the phonics program had been covered.

If on the basis of diagnostic testing and sample lesson tryouts it seems likely that a child may make more rapid progress with a systematic phonic approach than with a predominantly visual or kinesthetic approach, there are many different phonic systems that may be used with success. The con-

umbrella
u

FIGURE 15.1   A card providing picture and word cues for the short
u sound. From *Teacher's Phonic Skill Builders*: Key Cards
for *Building Reading Skills* Series. Cincinnati: McCormick-
Mathers Publishing Co., © 1965. Reproduced by permission of the publishers; reduced in size.

siderations that apply when phonics is used for remedial work are no different from those that apply in developmental instruction. At this point, therefore, it is desirable to review pages 367–376. Ear training is vitally important. Rigid adherence to any one method of sounding will inevitably produce difficulties, due to the irregularity of the phonic structure of the language. As much as possible, practice should be given in applying phonic skills in meaningful context, rather than concentrating on drill with isolated words. As soon as it is feasible, words which originally have to be sounded out should be practiced for immediate sight recognition.

Gates has criticized the phonic approach on the following grounds: 1) It is a "definite, rigid, hard-drill program." 2) It forfeits interest in the initial stages because real reading is not attempted. 3) It delays the reading of meaningful material much longer than the visual method does. 4) It is apt to produce slow, labored reading, with excessive amounts of lip movement (Gates, 1947, p. 496).

These criticisms can be answered in the following ways: 1) Interest and motivation are created by evidence of successful progress. 2) When the child is introduced to genuine reading he has acquired a basis which insures successful accomplishment. 3) Fluency and comprehension can be built up when a thorough basis in word recognition has been established. 4) The method works, as Gates has acknowledged, in some cases where the visual approach does not succeed.

For the majority of reading disability cases, phonic instruction is more effective when used in combination with other procedures than when it is made the major method of attack in learning words. There are some children, however, whose previously disappointing progress becomes very rapid when they are changed to a systematic phonic method. In this issue, as in others, what is inadvisable for most children may be just the right thing for a few.

Methods Stressing Visual Analysis and Visualizing

In addition to the kinesthetic and phonic approaches that have just been described, there is a third basic method which emphasizes visual analysis and visualizing. Such a procedure has been described and advocated by Gates (1947). Words are taught as wholes, to be recognized at first on the basis of general shape or configuration. Pictures and illustrations are used freely as ways of introducing and giving clues to words. Workbook exercises are used to present new words and to give practice in word recognition and comprehension. The pupil is encouraged to close his eyes and visualize words, first part by part in left-to-right order and then as a whole. Later he is asked to pronounce the word softly part by part while writing it; this is essentially the VAK procedure. Phonic work and writing are used as supplementary devices when pupils seem not to be progressing satisfactorily without them. Familiarity with word elements is developed through finding similarities and differences in words that have already been learned.

Essentially this program is similar to that used for teaching normal beginners with most basal readers. It differs mainly in that the pupil's learning is more carefully supervised and more attention is devoted to making sure that new words are really learned than is the case in most classroom teaching. It is a program which assumes that the child has the capacity to learn as normal readers do, but has been handicapped by some such factors as immaturity when first exposed to reading instruction, inefficient teaching, or something else which does not affect the child's present learning ability.

Gates said that the purely visual method is successful in most cases, as are the phonic and kinesthetic approaches. However, he had come to believe that "better results are obtained in a program which is broader and includes all the helpful aids" (Gates, 1947, p. 498).

A Combination Method

The majority of cases of reading disability do not have special types of mental or neurological defects, but result from such causes as lack of reading readiness when first exposed to reading instruction, uncorrected sensory defects, discouragement, emotional disturbance, and poor teaching which is sometimes aggravated by linguistic and cultural mismatches between teachers and pupils. If that is so, the remedial work with those cases should not have to be radically different from the general methods used with primary grade children.

The majority of severe cases of reading disability (nonreaders or those with less than second-grade reading ability) show inattention to details in visual perception, have very poor phonic aptitude, and are slow and clumsy in handling pencil or chalk. Such children can be started at the beginning of the easiest pre-primer in an unfamiliar set of readers and the accompanying workbook using the "begin-over" explanation to make the easy materials acceptable. If resistance to beginning basal materials is strong, a language-experience procedure is used for a while.

These children need to be carefully pre-taught the new words that they will meet in the next few pages of connected reading. Each new word is printed on a card. It is studied by a look-and-say visual method or by the VAK method, whichever seems to suit the child better. After a few words have been taught, the cards are shuffled and reviewed. Then the child reads the connected material in which the new words appear and reviews his new word cards again. The workbook provides practice in matching the few words in the pre-primer vocabulary with pictures, and between the repetition in the workbook and that in the pre-primer, the child learns the words by being prompted every time he stumbles or forgets. The number of repetitions needed to learn new words gradually lessens. The cards are reviewed in the next few lessons. When the child recognizes a word without prompting, a little check mark is made on the back of the card. Three checks, on different days, indicate that the word has been learned.

Rather than depend exclusively or primarily on visual word study, phonics is taught early and systematically. However, the majority of these children require a good deal of phonic readiness work before they can begin to apply phonics in word recognition. By the time the child has completed reading one or two pre-primers he has usually become sound-conscious and pays attention to initial consonants. Ear training is continued throughout the phonics program. Systematic teaching of phonics accompanies the use of a primer and first and second readers, with adaptations for individual differences. Some children catch on to blending and can be given a systematic covering of vowel sounds with the letter-by-letter sounding technique. Others never become proficient at blending and are taught vowel phonics through the use of a large number of word families or by initial consonant-vowel combinations.

On the other hand, some children seem, right from the start, to have poor visual perception but excellent phonic aptitude. With such children it seems sensible to follow a synthetic phonic procedure with emphasis on the teaching of letter sounds and blending. Nonphonetic words have to be learned by these children also, and many of them need the VAK method because of their lack of success with a pure visual method. With some of these children, a hard part of the remedial job is in persuading them to give up the practice of spelling the words letter by letter, in favor of a sounding procedure.

Sample lessons such as those described in pages 228–233 are helpful in deciding which teaching approach to use with a child in the first stage of the remedial program. As lessons proceed, the child's responsiveness, both in rate of learning and in emotional acceptance or resistance, should guide the teacher in modifying the plan.

Few of the children seen by us have seemed to need tracing of the sort emphasized by Fernald. The VAK method of word study has, however, been very helpful to many, and supplementary practice in writing words from dictation on paper and at the blackboard has been used considerably.

When resistance to the use of first- and second-grade readers is strong, it is advisable to give up the use of books entirely for the time being, using instead a combination of experience stories and teacher-devised material. In such cases much time can be spent in the early stages playing games with word and sound cards. If a typewriter is available, the opportunity to use it is welcomed by most of these children. Fairly soon the child will be ready for first-grade books.

Use of Newer Materials and Methods

Linguistic basal reader programs stress regularity of spelling patterns and avoid the use of words with irregular grapheme-phoneme relationships in beginning reading material (see pp. 62–63). Such materials can be used with retarded readers, with emphasis on spelling patterns in whole words. They can also be employed as supplementary reading in a synthetic phonics program. As yet little on the value of linguistic readers in remedial reading has appeared in print, but it is known that many reading clinics have been trying them out.

Their possible value in the initial stages of instruction lies in the consistency of the symbol-sound association in the words employed, particularly the vowels. The child does not have to decide which of its possible sounds a letter represents, and massive practice on the associations is provided. Contrary to their use in developmental reading, many remedial teachers provide direct instruction in symbol-sound association *before* the element is met in the program. The disadvantages are: 1) some children are confused by the repetitiveness of only short-vowel words, 2) the language structure and story content are restricted and often artificial, and 3) no set for diversity is established.

A "massive oral decoding technique" makes simultaneous use of several series of linguistic readers (R. J. Johnson, Johnson, and Kerfoot, 1972). After a spelling pattern has been introduced with one series, the pages emphasizing the same pattern in several other series are read before introducing a new pattern. The teacher guides oral reading of selection after selection, providing reinforcement of correct decoding responses. No phonic generalizations are taught and no comprehension questions are asked. The procedure is said to have proved effective across a considerable range of retarded readers.

Material printed in i/t/a has also been used in remedial reading. Gardner (1966), who started to use i/t/a in remediation in 1961, reported that it worked better with disabled readers with at least average intelligence than with mentally slower children. Apparently Gardner liked to use i/t/a if the child has failed with the conventional alphabet and prefers the conventional alphabet if the child has failed with i/t/a. Mazurkiewicz (co-author of an i/t/a basal series) recommended the use of i/t/a in remedial reading, but has presented very little evidence in support of his claims (1966). It should be noted that i/t/a basal readers used in Great Britain employ an eclectic methodology similar to that of most basal readers, while those used by Mazurkiewicz employ a synthetic phonic procedure. The problems that arise when disabled readers learn to read in i/t/a and then must transfer to the conventional alphabet have not yet been sufficiently studied.

Two systems which use color as a mediator between a phoneme and the graphemes which may at times represent that phoneme have been described and advocated for use as remedial materials by their originators (Bannatyne, 1966; Gattegno and Hinman, 1966). In methodology these color systems seem to belong to the synthetic phonic approach. The prohibitive cost of multicolor printing makes it seem probable that if color should prove a helpful cue in remedial reading, it will have to be used with language-experience content created by teacher and pupils, and a transition to an uncolored alphabet will have to be made before book reading is introduced. There is as yet no well-controlled research on the value of these color systems in remedial teaching.

Programmed instruction would seem to have considerable promise in remedial reading, particularly in providing self-correcting work that the pupil can do while the teacher is working with another child or group. The principle is attractive, but the remedial value of any particular set of programmed materials still needs to be verified. Programmed tutoring, shown to be effective with slow first graders when provided by paraprofessionals (Ellson, P. Harris and Barber, 1968), can be helpful when volunteers or aides can be trained to employ it.

For many years, remedial teachers have used part of their time for reading interesting stories to the child, encouraging the child to look at the printed page while he listens and to chime in when he can. This read-along procedure, usually employed as a pleasant breather during the remedial period, has recently been raised to the dignity of special methodology with an impressive-sounding name, The Neurological Impress Remedial Technique. The simultaneous seeing of the printed word and hearing the spoken word is said to produce a neurological memory trace easily and painlessly (Heckelman, 1966). An adaptation of this procedure has been made for group use, having the pupils listen to a tape-recorded story through earphones while looking at the book (Jordan, 1967). A read-along procedure would seem to be a useful kind of activity for a child or reading group while the teacher is busy elsewhere. It is hard to see how it could help to overcome perceptual and directional difficulties. Since the teacher can neither control nor observe where the child's eyes are focused, the child may or may not be looking at the right word, on the right line, as he hears the spoken word. For these reasons, reading along would seem to have more promise as a supplementary procedure than as a main remedial approach.

The Choice of Method

It is not always possible to tell, in advance of actual tutoring, what procedure will work best with a child. Sometimes deficiencies of visual perception, auditory perception, or motor control are so obvious that their bearing on the choice of methods is clear. With many children, it is helpful to try brief sample lessons with each of several word recognition procedures (see pp. 228–233). In some cases, one finds the best procedure only by trying one method after another.

The remedial teacher must be resourceful. If the pupil has not made adequate progress after a fair attempt to utilize one method, the teacher must be willing to try something else. Adaptability to the pupil's needs is far more important than devotion to a particular plan of procedure. For example, Russell's teacher found that he was practically a nonreader and decided to use a systematic phonic-blending method with him. He found that the boy had had quite a bit of phonic work in his first year and disliked it heartily. Russell said, "It's too hard; I can't do it." Thereupon the teacher switched to a whole-word method, and Russell began to make progress.

Three different strategies in the choice of remedial method were described at the beginning of this chapter. For most cases the second strategy is preferable, using a method that employs the child's relatively strong abilities and minimizes use of his weak ones, and at the same time providing readiness training to develop the weak abilities without postponing reading.

It seems likely that any remedial program in word recognition that provides good motivation, insures careful observation of words and word parts, and enforces consistent left-to-right habits in reading will succeed with most cases. The specific details of the method are less important than the fact that the major objectives are attained in one way or another.

III. CORRECTING SPECIFIC FAULTS IN WORD IDENTIFICATION

Most children who need remedial help in word recognition show a small number of specific weaknesses. One such child may need daily training to overcome a reversal tendency; a second may make mistakes only on vowel sounds; a third may concentrate on neglecting or mispronouncing word endings. These children have made some progress in decoding, but have developed faulty habits or have failed to learn some important elements of word recognition. Their remedial work should be aimed directly at the specific faults that are evident in their reading.

A study by Tovey (1972) suggests that a major reason for gaps in pupils' phonic knowledge may be mismatches between the phonics instruction for which they are ready, and the phonics instruction they receive. Twenty first-grade classes near the end of the year were given a phonics mastery test and the results were compared with the phonics instruction the children were receiving. There was little relationship between the phonics instructional patterns employed by teachers and the phonic knowledge of

FIGURE **15.2** Exercise requiring discrimination among *b*, *d*, and *p*. Answers are underlined. From Teacher's Annotated Edition, *Speedboat Book*, Level 1, *Building Reading Skills* Series. Cincinnati: McCormick-Mathers Publishing Co., p. 72. © 1970. Reproduced by permission of the publisher; reduced in size.

the children. In general, children in high academic schools were receiving phonics instruction that was too easy for them and children in average and low academic schools tended to receive phonics instruction that was too advanced for them. Only 8 per cent of the children were receiving phonics instruction that matched their scores.

Teaching Phonic Units

A great many children who need corrective or remedial help in reading have only a partial knowledge of the sound equivalents of phonic units. They may know the majority of single consonants, but have trouble with consonant blends. Ignorance of short vowel symbol-sound associations is very prevalent. Many children confuse letter names with letter sounds. Knowledge of phonograms of two, three, or four letters is likely to be uneven, and syllabication is often completely unknown territory. Some of these gaps represent deficiencies in previous instruction, but many of them are aftereffects of teaching for which the child was not yet ready. It is desirable to find out by preliminary testing and observation which associations are known and which need to be taught, and those that seem to be most urgently needed should be given priority in the teaching sequence.

Training in Visual and Auditory Discrimination. Teaching a phoneme and its usual grapheme in corrective or remedial work need not be essentially different from the methods advised for developmental instruction. One should start with practice in listening for the sound within known words (see p. 368). Then several known words containing the phonic elements are printed in column form, and the common element is underlined or circled as the words are pronounced. Additional words containing the sound are suggested by pupil or teacher, pronounced, printed, and marked. Comparisons are made with words that sound somewhat similar, but do not contain the element, and with words that look somewhat similar, but do not contain it.

Vivid Cues. For children who have difficulty in remembering sounds it is important to provide vivid associations which the child can use to recall the sound. Picture cards representing cue words are often helpful. If a child comes to the word *bunny* and has difficulty remembering the short *u* sound, he can look at the umbrella in Figure 15.1 and, saying "umbrella" to himself, can remind himself of the sound. Cue cards like this can be mounted above the chalkboard for reference, or each child can have a personal set. Sometimes cue cards which the children make themselves are more effective than those which are commercially available.

It is sometimes quite effective to dramatize sounds. Each sound can be associated with a situation in which the sound is made, as /s/—the hissing of a steam radiator; /t/—the tick of a clock; /ō/—what we say when we are surprised; and so on.[1] Tracing and writing the letter may be used for reinforcement. Clara Schmitt (1918) in a very early article, advocated teaching letter sounds in this way. She employed a continued story, in which bells rang /l/, dogs barked /r/, and cows mooed /m/, one new sound being added each day. This was followed by practice in which the teacher pronounced words sound by sound ((/r-un/ to me; /f-old/ your hands), as a preliminary to training in blending.

Monroe (1932) pointed out that many children who confuse letters do not hear the differences between letters clearly. She therefore advocated preliminary training in auditory discrimination. To teach an initial consonant sound, she started by presenting pictures of several objects, some of whose names begin with the letter. The child was taught to discriminate letters in the following way: As the child looks at the pictures he says, "/S/—soap, yes, *soap* sounds like /s/; /s/—man, no, *man* doesn't sound like /s/," and so on. If the child had difficulty in pronunciation with such sounds as /d/, /t/, and /th/; /s/ and /sh/; /r/, /l/, and /w/; or /f/ and /v/, he was taught the differences in the lip, tongue, and throat movements involved in making the sounds. After the phonemes could be correctly distinguished and pronounced, they were associated with the printed letter forms.

Research indicates that rather than rely on repetition alone to build recognition of a letter, it is desirable to point out to the learner the specific feature or features that distinguish that letter from other letters (Guralnick, 1972; Samuels, 1973a).

A persistent tendency to confuse two letters can be treated by following a sequence of five steps:

1] Teach each of the letters in the way suggested above.
2] Present a printed list of words all of which have the first letter to be taught in a prominent place. For consonants, use words beginning with the letter; for vowels, use one-syllable words with the vowel in the middle. Present a similar list for the other letter. Have the child read each list; help him when necessary.
3] Use the principle of minimal variation to present pairs of words which are alike except that one contains the first letter while the other contains the second letter, as *hill, till; can, cat; hat, hit.*
4] Give the child silent reading exercises of a multiple-choice or completion type, as, The cat ran after the (*house, mouse*); The cat ran after the __ouse.

1. Letters within slashes stand for phonemes; letters in italics represent graphemes.

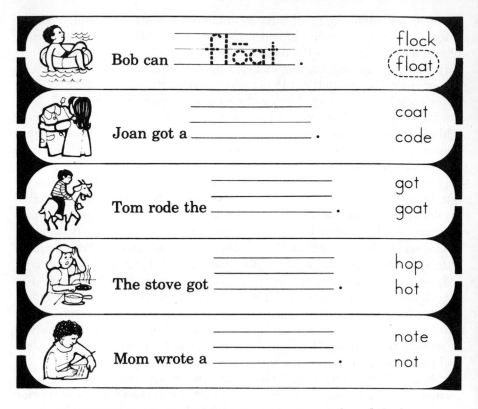

Bob can _____float_____ .   flock
                                  (float)

Joan got a _____ .   coat
                                  code

Tom rode the _____ .   got
                                  goat

The stove got _____ .   hop
                                  hot

Mom wrote a _____ .   note
                                  not

FIGURE 15.3   Part of an exercise using context, vowel, and final consonant cues to complete sentences. From Arthur W. Heilman, *Phonics We Use*, Book C, p. 36. Chicago: Rand
McNally and Co., 1972. Reproduced by permission of the
publisher; reduced in size.

5] Give the child sentences to read orally which contain many words
in which the two letters are used.

This same procedure can be used when there is a tendency to confuse two-
or three-letter combinations, such as *th* and *wh*, *scr* and *str*.

As an example of this procedure, assume that a child confuses *m* and
n. The letter *m* is presented, and the fact that it has two humps (like some
camels) is pointed out. Then *n* is presented, and the fact that it has only one
hump is noted. The two letters are sounded and written. The fact that /m/
is pronounced with lips closed and /n/ with lips open is demonstrated. Next
a list of words such as *mat, milk, make,* and *melt* is presented and read, fol-

lowed by a list such as *neat, not, nip,* and *nut.* Then pairs of words are introduced such as *map* and *nap, mail* and *nail.* Sentences are then employed such as: A boy grows into a (*man, nan*); We get light from the (*moon, noon*) and the (*sum, sun*); A __ouse ran across the roo__. Finally, oral reading of such sentences as: Many men went miles to see the sun and moon both shining at noon; or, Men and women need good manners.

Bryant (1965) suggested a method for use with a child who has extreme difficulty learning symbol-sound associations; particular vowels. First, one association is taught to the point of overlearning, then a second association is taught similarly. This is followed by mixed practice with words containing these two associations. Next, a third association is taught, followed by mixed practice, and so on.

Errors on Beginnings, Middles, and Endings of Words

There are many poor readers who observe carefully only the beginning of a word they cannot recognize at sight and guess at the rest. This kind of error is common in context readers and is also found in children who get little or no help from the context. In either case, such errors tend to destroy the meaning of a passage when there are several unknown words. Some of these children are so generally poor that they need a thorough, basic training in word recognition of the kind described in Section II above. Others can profit greatly from training directed specifically at this particular kind of error.

The kind of training that is most directly beneficial in these cases is based on the teaching of common spelling patterns/phonograms which combine with initial consonants to form many different words. The procedure in teaching phonograms is similar to that described for teaching letters except that the phonogram is taught as a unit, rather than as a group of individual letters.

Let us assume that a child has said *bent* for *band, make* for *main,* and *shine* for *shore.* There are six phonograms to be taught: *ent, and, ake, ain, ine, ore.* One may start by teaching each of these phonograms separately and combining each with different initial consonants. Starting with *and,* the phonogram is presented in printed form, pronounced by the teacher and then by the pupil, and written a few times. Then such words as *hand, sand, land* and *band* are presented and their similarity pointed out. The same procedure is followed with the other five phonograms. Preferably only one new phonogram is introduced in a remedial period. Pairs of words starting with the same letter but ending in different phonograms may next be presented, such as *sent* and *sand, rake* and *rain, mine* and *more.*

After practice has been given on reading separate words involving the

2 | Short *a*

Reading Sentences

Read the sentences. Which ones are true?
Draw a line under *yes* or *no* for each one. The
sight words are in slanted type. Do not sound
them out.

Yes	No	**1**	*Are* rafts flat?
Yes	No	**2**	*Are all* cats fat?
Yes	No	**3**	Can *you* trap rats?
Yes	No	**4**	Can a tramp grab a ham?
Yes	No	**5**	*Do you* add bags and bats?
Yes	No	**6**	Can a man hand *you* a bat?
Yes	No	**7**	*Are all* cans *always* flat?
Yes	No	**8**	*Does* a lad *always* act sad?

FIGURE 15.4   Part of an exercise to provide decoding practice using the
symbol-sound association for short *a*. From William
Kottmeyer, *Reading Booster Code Book*, p. 9. New York:
Webster Division, McGraw-Hill Book Co., 1972. Reproduced by permission of the publisher; reduced in size.

phonograms, the words should be presented in context in such a way as to
compel the child to pay careful attention to the total word. For this purpose
multiple-choice sentences are again useful, as: The man put his money in
the (*benk, bank, band*). Unless practice on isolated words is followed by
the reading of the same words in context, the amount of carryover of the
training to connected reading may be disappointingly small. It is also possible that children who respond correctly only to the initial elements in
words cannot make the necessary symbol-sound associations for the vowels
following the initial consonants. If follow-up testing so indicates, the necessary associations should be taught, followed by guided practice in their
utilization.

Some of the errors on word endings consist of failure to note or discriminate endings as *-s, -es, -ed, -ly, -est, -er, -ness*. Usually specific practice
is sufficient to overcome these errors. After pointing out how the ending
changes the meaning of a word, sentences can be used for practice such as:
There are many (*horse, horses*) in the barn; I can run (*fast, faster, fastest*)
than you. In other cases, the errors either indicate the child cannot recognize the element as a unit or does not possess the necessary skills to decode

it. In some cases, the omission or "mispronounciation" merely reflects the reader's dialect.

The most common divergences from standard English of the oral reading of black nonstandard-speaking children are elisions of four common inflected forms: *-s* and *-es* marking noun plurals and third person singular verbs, *'s* marking possessive nouns, and *-d* and *-ed* marking a past tense of a verb (Rosen and Ames, 1972). Rather than treat such a pronunciation automatically as an error, the teacher should question to find out whether or not the grammatical significance of the inflected ending was understood. A correct interpretation rendered in black English should be accepted as correct reading.

Medial errors usually involve inability to make some vowel symbol-sound associations, and therefore these associations need to be taught. If the errors are not numerous, the general procedure is similar to the methods already described. One should give practice on lists of words which are alike except for the medial vowel, such as *hit, hat, hot* and *hut,* and also practice on words which are different except for the same medial vowel, such as *man, rat, pack,* and *glad.* Again, local pronunciations should be respected. In some parts of the United States, *set* and *sit* sound alike; in others, *man* and *men* are indistinguishable. A New York City youngster who successfully sounded and blended *cod* thought it was a piece of string (*cord*) or something to play with (*card*). Words that rhyme according to the dictionary do not rhyme in certain regions.

Printing or writing the vowels being studied in a color can help some children in learning the associations. Allington (1973) found that use of color, which was gradually reduced, enhanced the learning of tasks involving visual discrimination, visual memory, and paired-associate learning, apparently as a result of improved attention to the distinctive features of the stimuli. Color coding has been recommended by Frostig (1965, 1972b).

A form of error on word middles that is found in individuals of fairly advanced reading level is the confusion of words of several syllables that have similar beginnings and endings, such as *commission* and *communion,* or *precision* and *procession.* In these cases the person must be trained to make use of the context and to attack such words systematically, syllable by syllable. It is often helpful to insert vertical lines between the syllables, or to emphasize the part omitted or misread by underlining it.

Errors on the beginnings of words are usually found associated with reversal tendencies or as one phase of serious general weakness in word recognition. When that is the case, the correction of the other errors will tend to eliminate the errors on word beginnings. In cases where the beginnings of words seem to present special difficulty, procedures similar to those used for errors on endings should be employed, except that emphasis is placed on noticing the beginning of the word rather than the ending. Exercises in alphabetizing and the use of dictionaries are also helpful, as they call attention to the beginning of the word.

Reversal Errors

The term "reversal" is used to describe a variety of different kinds of errors, including: 1) confusion of single letters such as *b*, *d*, *p*, and *q*; *n* and *u*; *m* and *w*; 2) complete reversals of words such as *on* and *no*, *saw* and *was*, and *tap* and *pat*; 3) partial reversals of words such as *ram* for *arm*, *ate* for *tea*, and *never* for *even*; and 4) reversals of the order of words in a sentence, as "The dog saw a boy" for "The boy saw a dog." Reversals are not the commonest types of error in word recognition, as they are prominent among the errors of about one reading disability case out of ten. When they persist, however, they are very significant and deserve careful analysis and treatment.

Reversals are very prevalent in young children beginning to read. Apparently young children tend to think that the difference in position of letters such as *b* and *p*, or of the order of letters in words like *rat* and *tar*, is not important. They take the same attitude as they do toward a picture of a man, which they can recognize about as well when it is sideways or upside down as when it is right side up (Jackson, 1972).

Some recent studies have found that reversals of the letter-orientation type are uncorrelated with letter-sequence errors, suggesting that the two types may have different causes (Liberman et al., 1971; Lyle, 1968). Bannatyne (1972) distinguished four types of reversals: mirror images (*b-d*), inversions (*u-n*), rotation (*b-p*), and word reversals; the first three are subdivisions of letter-orientation reversals.

According to Orton, reversals were the prime symptom of "*the* reading disability," which he named *strephosymbolia* (twisted symbols) and were due to failure to develop a clear dominance of one cerebral hemisphere over the other, in which mirror images of the memory traces in the more dominant hemisphere had been formed in the less dominant hemisphere; when the less dominant hemisphere took over sporadically, reversals occurred (S. T. Orton, 1937; J. Orton, 1966). Delay in the establishment of dominance of the left hemisphere has been recently emphasized by Satz as a major factor in the causation of reading disability (Satz and van Nostrand, 1973).

Other factors besides immaturity may cause reversal errors. Failure to develop consistent left-to-right eye movements in reading is in many cases the reason for frequent reversals. Due to regressive movements, the parts of a word may be inspected in the wrong order, or words may be seen in the wrong order, and reversal errors are the result. Other major causes of reversals are difficulty with fusion and eye coordination, directional confusion, and mixed hand dominance.

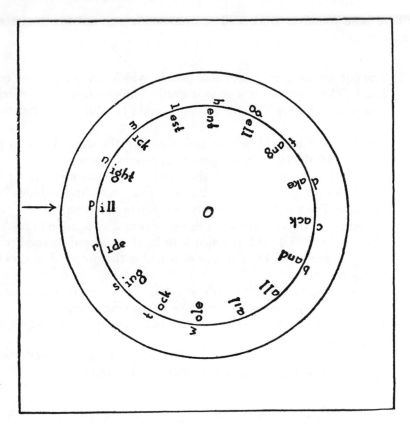

FIGURE **15.5** "Lucky Wheel" for phonic practice; both outer and inner circles can be rotated.

Of all letter confusions, the one involving *b, d, p,* and *q* is probably the most common. These four letters are different orientations of the same form. Other letter confusions that are vertical reversals are *m* and *w,* and *u* and *n.* The general principles described in this chapter for overcoming letter confusions will usually suffice to remove these tendencies to reverse letters. The need for tracing and writing is greater for children who reverse letters than it is for those who make other types of letter errors, and more intensive drill is usually necessary before the confusion is eliminated.

Reversals of words, parts of words, and the order of words in sentences usually indicate that the child needs training to develop a consistent left-to-right sequence in reading. The need for such a consistent direction should first be explained to him, with illustrations of how the words and meanings are changed when the correct order is not maintained. Then various methods may be employed to build up proper directional habits. Among the devices that have been found to work well in overcoming reversal tendencies are the following:

1] Tracing, writing, and sounding words which are frequently confused. These procedures automatically enforce using the correct sequence of letters. Cursive writing is more helpful than manuscript writing.

2] Covering a word with a card and removing the card slowly to the right so that the letters are exposed in proper sequence.

3] Underlining the first letter in the word. Sometimes underlining the first letter in green and the last letter in red—"traffic lights"—is effective. The child is told to start on green and stop on red.

4] Encouraging the child to use a finger or pencil as a guide in reading along a line. While this practice is to be discouraged in good readers, it is very helpful as a means of teaching the proper direction for eye movements.

5] Exposing a line of print a little at a time by means of a card, or by means of an opening cut in a card, or by opening a zipper.

6] Drawing an arrow pointing to the right under words which are frequently reversed.

7] Allowing the child to use a typewriter. This has favorable effects on spelling and composition as well as on word recognition.

Fernald (1943, p. 89) stated that reversals quickly disappeared when children were taught by the kinesthetic method, making sure that they started to write at the left edge of the paper. Monroe (1932, p. 127) found that systematic letter-by-letter phonic training, combined with tracing, had a similarly beneficial effect on the reversal tendency.

When a child has persistent difficulty in remembering which hand is left or right, it is helpful to provide a simple cue such as a ring to be worn on a finger of the left hand. This can also be useful in clearing up a *b-d* confusion; the ring in the *d* is on the same side as the ring on the finger. Training to improve laterality and directionality of the kind advocated by Kephart (1960) may be worthwhile. Daniels (1967) reported that a simple teaching technique, used for one twenty-minute lesson with preschool children, was effective in preventing reversals two years later. He used paired form boards in which the two cutout figures were mirror images of each other. The child was shown how to fit each shape into its proper place and then practiced it, with about a dozen pairs. It may reasonably be doubted that a real directional confusion can be prevented or cured by such a simple procedure, but the idea certainly deserves to be investigated further.

Omissions, Additions, and Substitutions

Omissions and additions of letters or syllables are rarely found unaccompanied by other types of errors. They are commonly associated with errors on word endings and middles. As systematic training in overcoming the other errors is given, the omissions and additions usually disappear. About the only kind of special attention that these errors require is to have the child reread the word on which he made the mistake and to point out the difference between what he said and what the word really is. Such errors are often noticed by the child and corrected immediately. They represent mainly a form of carelessness and call for somewhat slower and more careful reading until the tendency is overcome. This last statement is true also of most additions and omissions of whole words.

When a child substitutes a completely different word for the word in print, he is almost always guessing or trying to make use of the context. If the substitutions he makes are reasonable ones which do not alter the meaning, such as *castle* for *palace*, or *boy* for *lad*, and are not very frequent, one can usually ignore them without doing any great harm. If, however, a large number of his substitutions are such as to spoil the meaning of the passage, the fault needs to be remedied. Such meaningless substitutions, as "The boy called for a house" for "The man caught a horse," indicate that the child needs thorough basic training in word-recognition skills. As he learns how to recognize words the substitutions will disappear. When meaningless substitutions occur in the reading of poor readers at the secondary school or college level, they may indicate reading that is too rapid and careless, or material beyond the reader's level of comprehension.

Difficulties with Long Words

Above the third-grade level, difficulties in word recognition are more apt to involve long words than short words. The word-recognition habits that have been successful in learning such words as *went*, *their*, and *across* do not seem to work when employed on such words as *migration*, *provocative*, *theoretical*, and *constitutionally*. In fact, difficulties in word recognition may arise during the upper grades in children who have previously had little difficulty with reading.

Many of these children have little or no background in phonics. They were either not taught phonics or were exposed to phonics teaching when they were not yet ready for it and so did not profit from it. They developed satisfactory sight vocabularies as long as the new words were taught to them, and their sight vocabularies, aided by guessing from the context, keep them going fairly well. Their lack of decoding knowledge, however, makes it impossible for them to work out the correct pronunciation of the separate

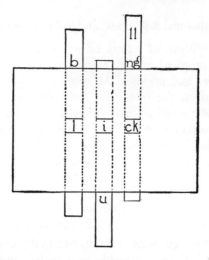

FIGURE 15.6   A phonic card, showing how strip inserts can be used to form a variety of words.

syllables in a long, unfamiliar word. They soon form the habit of guessing from the context, aided by the general appearance of the word, with perhaps a more careful inspection of the word beginning. Sometimes they form the habit of skipping the long words altogether, filling in during oral reading with a vague mumble. These children, whose difficulties with the longer words is largely the result of an omission in their previous instruction, are often helped greatly in their attack on unknown words by teaching of the phonic skills usually covered in the second and third grades.

The main requirements in teaching an adequate method of decoding long words are a systematic procedure of dividing a long word into recognizable groups of letters, figuring out a reasonable pronunciation for each letter group, and combining them in left-to-right order to get the whole word. The teaching of syllabication generalizations is not really necessary. If the pupil shows difficulty in learning these more or less arbitrary rules, he should be encouraged to look for letter groups that seem to him to form natural units. Skill in dividing words into prefixes, word roots, and endings should be developed, and in general the combination of morphemic analysis skills with phonic sounding in combination with the meaningful context should be the aim. Remedial help along these lines need not differ essentially from good first teaching.

Inability to Make Use of the Context

Because it has been emphasized that pupils who rely greatly on the context may develop habits of carelessness in word recognition or may fail to develop other important techniques, there may be a temptation to assume that pupils who need training in word recognition should be discouraged from attempting to utilize the context at all. Nothing is farther from the truth. Pupils who have failed to acquire other methods of attack in recognizing words need to be taught the other methods but should not be discouraged from utilizing the context. All good readers make use of context clues, so there is no reason to discourage poor readers from doing the same, except as a temporary measure while other techniques are being learned.

There are also many children—word-by-word readers—who have not learned how to employ the context as a way of figuring out a new word. They should be taught first of all how to infer the meaning of the word by reading the rest of the sentence. In the sentence, "The man has a ＿＿＿＿ with two doors," the child should be asked what the missing word could be. If he says car, he should be shown that there are other possibilities, such as house and garage. He should then be given the same sentence with the first letter of the missing word supplied and be shown that if the letter is *h*, the missing word is probably *house*; if *c*, *car*; if *g*, *garage*; or if *s*, *store*. Sentences such as Cows give m＿＿＿; dogs like to eat b＿＿＿; and boys like to play b＿＿＿, can be used for practice. Exercises like the ones in Figures 14.9, 15.1, and 15.4 can be used. After the pupil has grasped the idea, he will enjoy reading paragraphs in which a few words have been blotted out.

Slowness in Word Recognition

Children who have been given intensive phonic training often develop the habit of reading painstakingly and very slowly. They try to sound out most words, and this keeps their speed far below what it would be if they could recognize the words at a glance. Readers of fairly advanced levels are sometimes slow because they have to sound out all long words, although they have no difficulty with short ones. When it is evident that because of a letter-by-letter or syllable-by-syllable attack a reader's rate is being kept unnecessarily low, practice should be given to increase speed of word recognition.

The most helpful procedure for increasing speed of word recognition is to use flash cards or tachistoscopic exposure. One should start with one-syllable words, printed one on a card. The card can be exposed in a simple tachistoscope (see p. 219) or by covering the card with a blank one which is withdrawn and quickly replaced with a flick of the wrist. The time of exposure should be less than half a second, so as to prevent more than one look at the word. At first the words should be short and of different shapes, such as *pill, here, pony,* and *cart*. As skill in quick recognition is gradually acquired, words of the same general configuration may be used in groups, such as *hall, bill, kill,* and *tell*. Longer and longer words can then be intro-

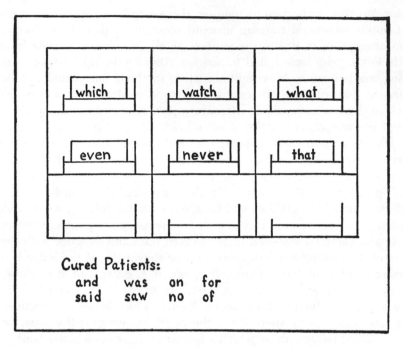

FIGURE 15.7   A "hospital" for "sick" words. A word with which the
child has persistent difficulty is printed on a small card
and is put to bed (inserted in the slit corresponding to the
mattress of the bed). When a sick word is cured, its
name is entered at the bottom of the chart.

duced, until the reader has developed to the point where he can recognize
immediately words like *opposite* and *superiority*. Similar short-exposure
practice should also be given in the reading of short phrases, such as *to me,
in the house,* and *from the store.*

Since the very common short words make up more than half of the
running words of most reading material, speeding up recognition of those
words often helps both to increase rate and to improve concentration; the
attention previously spent on decoding can be shifted to attaining meaning.
The emphasis in quick-exposure drills should be on changing "two-look
words" to "one-look words."

Repetitions

The oral reading of some children is marred by frequent repetitions.
These may be repetitions of part of a word, of a whole word, of a phrase, or

of the entire sentence to that point. For example, a child may read "The boy went for a walk with his spotted dog," as follows: "The boy—the boy want for—the boy went for a—a walk—with his stop—spotted dog."

Some repetitions are due to slowness in word recognition; the child repeats a preceding word or two, or part of a word, to have more time for decoding. These repetitions will drop out as greater skill in word identification is achieved. Another cause of repetitions is realization that the first reading didn't make sense; two examples of this type, involving *want* for *went* and *stop* for *spotted*, are in the example above. Sometimes a child loses the trend of thought of the sentence and goes back in order to pick up the thread of meaning again. As comprehension improves, the need for repetitions of this sort lessens.

Many children repeat because of nervousness or self-consciousness in oral reading. They need to have their confidence built up, and then their hesitations and repetitions will diminish. These children should be given opportunities to rehearse easy selections carefully and then to read the selections before children who are unfamiliar with the story. They also need large doses of encouragement and praise. Regressive eye movements accompany repetitions, but usually the need to repeat causes the regressive movements rather than vice versa.

Refusal to Attempt Words

A common type of error in oral reading is reluctance by the child to try to read a word. He may stop and wait to be prompted, may try to skip it without the omission's being noticed, or may simply say that he does not know that word. The majority of refusals are caused by inadequate word-recognition techniques; they diminish in frequency as skill in word recognition improves.

There are some children, however, who do not try words even when they have the skills to decode the word. This is nearly always due to the fact that the child has not yet built up confidence in his own ability. He has developed the habit of giving up quickly as the result of a long period of frustrated effort. He needs to be encouraged and gently prodded by remarks like, "I'm sure you can get that word if you try it." When this is insufficient, he may be given hints such as, "What would the word be if the first letter were *c* instead of *t*?" If it becomes evident that he cannot solve the word, he should be told what it is and allowed to continue. He should be praised for successful efforts and should be reminded of previous successes if he shows an inclination to get discouraged. Refusals may be problems of motivation rather than skill.

IV. MATERIALS FOR IMPROVING WORD-RECOGNITION AND DECODING SKILLS

Manipulative Devices and Games

A great many manipulative devices and games can be used to add variety and interest to word-recognition and decoding programs. They serve very well to break the monotony which may otherwise cause a pupil's effort to slacken. A few of the popular ones are described below. Depending on the task set for the learner and the nature of the stimuli, most can be used for either teaching or reinforcing sight vocabulary or decoding skills.

1] *Lucky Wheel.* Two circles, one smaller than the other, are fastened together by a nail, brass pin, or buttonhook through their centers so that each can be rotated freely without disturbing the other. Initial consonants are printed around the outer circle and phonograms around the edge of the inner circle so that different words can be formed. By rotating the outer circle, different initial consonants can be combined with the same phonogram, and by rotating the inner circle the same initial consonant can be combined with different phonograms. Many variations of this general idea have been devised. Such a wheel can be used as a basis for competitive games. Commercial materials of this type include the *New Webster Word Wheels* (Webster) (sixty-three wheels for use at grade 3 and above), and the *Phonetic Word Analyzer* (Milton Bradley) (a wheel with interchangeable disks). Some, such as *Vowel Wheels* (Milton Bradley), are designed only for particular phonic elements.

2] *Phonic Strips.* Three horizontal slits, close together and in line, are made across a 4 x 6 index card. Three other slits are made directly below them. A number of thin strips are prepared (by cutting up another index card) of a proper width so that they can be threaded through the slits in such a way as to expose only a small part of the strip. On one strip a number of initial consonants can be printed, one below the other, on a second strip middle vowels, on a third common word endings, and so on. By inserting the strips and moving them up and down, a large number of different words can be formed. This device can be adapted for practice on beginnings, middles, or endings and can be used with phonograms as well as single letters.

An interesting variation of phonic strips is the *Sort and Sound Making Cards* (ETA). The cards are cut into strips which contain a picture and a three-or-four-letter word. In assembling the picture, the corresponding word is formed automatically.

3] *Rhyme Making.* Lines from several verses are printed on separate strips. The child is to pick out all the lines which end in the same sound and assemble them into a little poem. High poetic standards are not necessary. A sample verse:

> The Indians on the hill,
> Led by Big Chief Bill,
> Are standing very still,
> For they are out to kill.

4] *Darts.* A cheap dart-and-target set is used. Small cards with one phonogram on each are pasted to the target, and an initial consonant is pasted on each dart. If the child reads correctly the word formed when his dart hits a phonogram, he scores a point. A bean-bag toss game may be substituted for the dart set.

5] *Word-O.* Cards can be made modeled after bingo or lotto, with words instead of numbers, and the usual rules for such games can be used or modified. To teach words, the leader says the word as he holds up the card; the children look for the word on their cards and cover it if they find it; to review, the word is said but not shown. The first child who covers five words in a row or column and can identify them correctly wins.

Commercial materials of this type include the *Group Word Teaching Game*, the *Consonant Lotto*, the *Vowel Lotto* and the *Group Sounding Game* (Garrard) designed by Dolch, *Phonetic Quizmo* (Milton Bradley), *Wingo Wordo* (EPS), and *Primary Phonics* (SVE).

6] *Anagrams.* An inexpensive anagram set can be purchased, or letters can be printed on small squares of pasteboard. Word-building games of several kinds can be played. The *Ruled Letter Cards* (Kenworthy) and *Word Builders* (Kenworthy) are commercial sets that include both capital and small letters and are quite inexpensive. The phonic elements are color coded (*e.g.*, consonants on white cards, vowels on blue) in the *Rainbow Word Builders* (Kenworthy). Plastic letters that can be linked together are found in *Link Letters* (Milton Bradley), *Unilock Plastic Word Making Letters* (ETA), and *Interlocking Word Builders* (Dick Blick).

7] *Spin the Pointer.* Words are arranged around the outside of a circle, and the child tries to read the word at which the pointer stops. Failures and successes can be scored according to the rules of different games such as baseball and football. In baseball scoring a success is a hit and a failure is an out, and score is kept in terms of

e

e

	Write the missing vowel.	Write the word.
	Trace the word.	Underline the vowel.

bed

b_d
×

hen

h_n
×

ten

t_n
×

sled

sl_d
×

FIGURE 15.8 A page intended for use following first teaching of the
sound of short *e*. The combination of picture clues, tracing,
writing, and underlining provides several kinds of reinforcement. From Ruth B. Montgomery and Selma Cough-
lan, *Sound, Spell, Read: The Phonovisual Vowel Book*,
Revised Edition, p. 18. Phonovisual Products, 1972. Reproduced by permission of the publisher and reduced in
size.

runs. By making slits into which word cards may be inserted, the
same circle and pointer can be used indefinitely.

8] *Fishing.* One word, phrase, or sentence is printed on each of a number of cardboard cutouts in the shape of fish, to which paper clips
are attached. The child picks up a fish by means of a horseshoe

magnet on a string and keeps it if he can read it correctly. Similar games can be devised involving pulling leaves off a tree, and so on.

9] *Racing.* A large race track is drawn and divided into boxes, in each of which a word is placed. Each child has a cutout auto of a different color. When a child's turn comes, he spins a pointer which indicates a move of one, two, three, or four boxes. If he can read the word he advances his auto that many spaces; if not, he has to wait for his next turn.

10] *Word Hospital.* Words that cause persistent difficulty are called "sick" words, and the child, as doctor, puts them to bed in a word hospital until he cures them (see Fig. 15.7).

11] *This to That.* Starting with one word, one of the letters in the word is changed each time, making a series of words, as: *his, him, ham, ram, ran, run.* The game can also be played with changing of two-letter combinations allowed, as: *sheep, sheet, shoot, shook, spook, spoke, broke.* Reading such a sequence is a welcome change from the monotony of word families and provides an interesting form of review.

12] It is possible to buy packs of playing card blanks, with decorative backs but no printing on the face side, from some playing card manufacturers. By printing the same word on four cards it is possible to make a "rummy" deck containing thirteen words or to adapt the deck to the rules of other simple card games, such as casino. Oak tag cut into rectangles of appropriate size can also be used. Commercially available sets of cards which can be used to teach sight vocabulary or decoding skills include the following:

Basic Sight Vocabulary Cards, by E. W. Dolch. 220 common "service words" on individual cards. The same words on slightly larger cards are available as *Popper Words,* Set 1 and Set 2, each containing 110 words (Garrard).

High Frequency Words, by Alden Moe. The 100 *High Frequency Words* account for 53 per cent of the over 100,000 words found in 110 widely used trade books in grades one and 2; the 100 *High Frequency Nouns* account for approximately 45 per cent of all the nouns used in the same books (Ambassador).

Picture Word Builder. Pictures of 36 familiar objects on cards die cut so only the correct word can be inserted to complete the word-picture matching (Milton Bradley). *Phonic Couplets* is a similar set of materials containing 20 cards (ETA). In such exercises, it is important for the child to associate the printed word with the correct name of the picture and not just rely on the die cut for matching.

Word Demons, a card game similar to the classic game of

Authors; contains many common nonphonemic words that must be learned as sight words (EPS).

Build It, a challenging word-recognition game that requires quick visual perception of the similarities and differences within words. Four decks, 2 with short vowels (#1 with single consonants, #2 with blends) and 2 with long vowels (#3 with single consonant, #4 with blends) (Kingsbury).

Same or Different Word Cards. Each card has a pair of words that are the same, or differ only slightly. In Set 1 only one letter differs; in Set 2, the letter order differs (DLM).

Big Deal, by Helen Grush and Pauline Fennel. Six basic card games (*Concentration, War, Sourpuss, Go Fish, Rummy,* and *I Doubt It*) can be played using sets of words at 10 levels of spelling complexity (EPS).

Picture Word Cards, by Dolch. Cards with a picture and word on one side and the word only on the back, including 95 common nouns (Garrard).

Take, a Dolch card game involving matching the sounds of the beginnings, the middles, or the endings of words (Garrard).

The Syllable Game, by Dolch, designed to be used to teach syllabication in the middle and upper grades (Garrard).

Go Fish, an interesting card game well liked by remedial pupils, for reinforcing phonic learnings; one deck for initial consonants, another for initial blends (Kingsbury).

Vowel Dominoes, played something like dominoes but involving the matching of short vowel sounds (Kingsbury).

Phonic Rummy, a game involving matching phonic elements and using the rules of rummy; each set has two packs of 60 cards each (Kenworthy).

Junior Phonic Rummy, a matching game using 110 frequently occurring words with short vowels (Kenworthy).

ABC Game, a matching game similar to Old Maid played with cards each of which has a letter, a cue word, and a picture for the cue word (Kenworthy).

Doghouse Game, containing 12 cards each with 35 word-ending spelling patterns, to which initial consonants and blends are added (Kenworthy).

Fun with Words, by Richard A. Boning. Six boxes of small cards, each presenting three riddles with phonic and meaning cues, many of which are in rhyme (Dexter and Westbrook, Ltd.).

Phonics We Use Learning Games Kit, a carton containing 10 packaged games, with a manual (Lyons).

Reading Laboratory 1: Word Games, a large carton containing

44 word games, a Phonics Survey, a pupil workbook, teacher's handbook, and check tests (SRA).

Many other games and devices for teaching word-recognition and word-analysis skills which can be made by teachers can be found in Russell and Karp (1961), Wagner and Hosier (1970), Herr (1970), Dorsey (1972), Mattleman (1973), and Thompson (1973).

13] *Crossword Puzzles.* Crossword puzzles can be constructed to provide practice in either word recognition or word analysis, or to develop vocabulary. Published crossword puzzles include *Phonic Crossword Puzzles* (McCormick-Mathers), *Crossword Puzzles* (Ideal) which are reusable, *Crossword Puzzles for Phonics* (Continental) and *Word Puzzles and Games* (Scholastic) which are suitable for older students reading at the fourth- to sixth-grade level.

14] *Letter/Word Cubes.* Letters, phonograms, word parts, or words may be attached to or printed on the side of one-inch or larger cubes. The cubes are cast like dice, with the learner's task being to form as many words or sentences as he can. Difficulty of the task can be controlled by limiting or increasing the possible number of responses. For example, if practice with only three initial consonants is desired, each consonant letter would appear twice on the cube, thus limiting the number of words that can be formed when added to the vowel-consonant phonogram(s) on the other block(s). Among the activities for which the cubes can be used are: 1) single letter and/or multiple letters (blends, digraphs, diphthongs) on all the cubes, to form as many words as the player can think of; 2) single consonants and/or consonant clusters in some blocks, and vowel-consonant and/or consonant-vowel phonograms on the others, to practice substituting initial and final consonants to form words; 3) root words on some blocks, affixes on the others, to practice use of prefixes and suffixes (this can be made into a vocabulary exericse by having the learner define the words he constructs); and 4) words on all the cubes, to practice word recognition, "sentence sense," or comprehension. Commercially prepared cubes under various trade names are available from Scott Foresman, McCormick-Mathers, Educational Teaching Aids, and Lakeshore.

15] *Flip cards.* Cards that have flip folds can be used for practice in substituting word beginnings and endings or to aid morphenic analysis. One part of the card can be folded over to form a new word. Examples of published flip-fold cards are *Phonetic Drill Cards* (Milton Bradley) which substitutes initial consonants and blends, *Phonetic Word Drill Cards* (ETA) that use initial conso-

FIGURE 15.9   Part of a self-correcting exercise on discriminating between
short vowels. Answers are marked with a special marker; if
correct, the box shows diagonal lines when filled in, if
incorrect the box looks solid. From Margaret M. Bishop,
Phonics with Write and See, Book A, p. 78. New York:
New Century, © 1968 by Meredith Corporation. Reproduced by permission of the publisher; reduced in size.

nants with 60 word families, and *Word Prefixes* and *Word Suffixes*
(Kenworthy) which also present the meanings of the affixes.

Workbooks

The workbooks that accompany basal readers have many pages of practice material on decoding skills, and for many children supplementary material of this type is not necessary. Independent workbook material can be
quite helpful in remedial and corrective work and in teaching children who
seem to need a more systematic phonic procedure than the reader method
provides. It should be clearly understood, however, that simply having a
learner complete workbook pages or exercises does not constitute teaching.
If the child can complete the task successfully, he probably has whatever
skills are required in performing that task. If he cannot perform the task, the
teacher must seek to determine *why* he cannot. Even when the student can
demonstrate his skills in workbook or other exercises, the teacher cannot be
assured that he will apply or utilize his "new found" skills in the actual

reading act. Opportunities for doing so must be provided, and periodic checks made to determine if the skills are being employed. The same is also true of teaching vocabulary, comprehension, and study skills. Some good independent materials are:

Building Reading Skills, 1971 edition, by Rowena Hargrave (McCormick). A series of six workbooks developing word-analysis skills sequentially with emphasis on meaningful content and considerable practice in writing. There is a separate *Teachers' Annotated Edition* and a box of large *Phonics Skill Builder Cards.*

Eye and Ear Fun, second edition, by Clarence R. Stone (Webster). A series of five workbooks with emphasis on exercises that combine meaning, picture, phonic, and structural cues.

New Phonics We Use, 1972 edition, by Arthur Heilman, *et al.* (Lyons). A series of seven workbooks very much like *Eye and Ear Fun* in method; somewhat more gradual in pace and more modern in appearance.

Phonovisual Method, 1972 revision, by Lucile D. Schoolfield and Josephine B. Timberlake (Phonovisual). Consists of a large Consonant Chart, a large Vowel Chart, smaller reproduction of the two charts for individual pupil use, several workbooks, a phonograph record, duplication masters, games, and accompanying manuals.

Breaking the Sound Barrier, by Sister Mary Caroline (Macmillan). A hard-cover pupil's book and separate teacher's edition, emphasizing a thinking approach in the application of phonics.

The output of phonics workbooks and boxed sets of phonics practice materials has been so great in recent years that a comprehensive listing would run on for pages. Each of those listed below has some reasonable claim for the attention of remedial teachers.

Macmillan Reading Spectrum: Word Analysis, revised 1973, by Joel S. Weinberg (Macmillan). A series of six programmed, self-checking workbooks for use in the middle grades or secondary remedial programs.

Speech-to-Print Phonics, by Donald D. Durrell and Helen A. Murphy (Harcourt). A box for classroom use, with cards for presentation by the teacher and response cards for the pupils; requires combined use of phonics and word meaning, but uses no printed context.

Durrell-Murphy Phonics Practice Program, by Donald D. Durrell and Helen A. Murphy (Harcourt). Carton contains a large number of cards each providing self-directing and self-checking seatwork.

Time for Phonics, by Louise B. Scott and Virginia A. Pavelko (Web-

FIGURE 15.10 Part of an exercise on distinguishing words that are alike
except for final consonants. From Barbara W. Makar,
Primary Phonics, Workbook One, p. 21. Cambridge, Mass.:
Educators Publishing Service, Inc., 1969. Reproduced by
permission of the publisher; reduced in size.

ster). Books R, A, B, C, readiness—Grade 3. Workbooks teaching
phonics with use of picture and context cues. Content more suitable for
primary children than for older remedial pupils.

Read Clues, by Louise B. Scott (Webster). A workbook for grades
4–6 that uses the same techniques for building decoding skills as *Time
for Phonics.*

Conquests in Reading, by William Kottmeyer (Webster). A remedial
workbook for grades 4–9 that presents opportunities for utilizing the
introduced phonic and structural-analysis skills in context.

Reading Essentials Series, 1973 edition, by Ullin W. Leavell and
others (Steck-Vaughn). Series of eight graded workbooks and one
workbook for fifth–seventh graders reading at third to fourth reader
level. Stress placed on phonic and structural analysis skills, but opportunities presented for reading in context.

Merrill Phonics Skilltexts, 1973 edition, by Josephine B. Wolfe, *et al.*
(Merrill). A series of six workbooks (Books A–F) for developing

phonic, structural, and contextual skills. Program provides for a great deal of review. Skill tapes available for audio-tutorial use.

Functional Phonetics, by Anna D. Cordts (Beckley-Cardy). A manual for ear and eye training, followed by three hard-cover phonic practice books. Emphasizes initial consonant-vowel combinations. Provides considerable ear training and some practice in meaningful context.

Reading with Phonics, revised, by Julie Hay and Charles E. Wingo (Lippincott). A hard-cover book for the pupil accompanied by a 128-page teacher's manual and three workbooks. Nearly all of the practice, both in ear training and in sounding, is on isolated words. Initial consonant-vowel combinations are stressed, and red and black inks are used to make phonic units stand out.

Phonics with Write and See, by Margaret M. Bishop (New Century). A series of four workbooks with a self-checking feature: when the answer is marked with a special pencil, the appearance of the line (interrupted or solid) shows whether the answer is correct or not.

There are also practice materials intended for use in synthetic (sounding and blending) phonic teaching programs.

Several of these are published by Educators Publishing Service, including: *First Phonics*, by Mary H. Burnet; *Primary Phonics*, by Barbara W. Makar; *My First Letters*, by M. B. Miles and R. W. Simmons; *A First* and *A Second Course in Phonic Reading*, by Lida G. Helson; *Improving Word Skills*, by Margaret L. Smith, *Recipe for Reading*, by Nina Traub and Frances Bloom, and *Situation Reading*, by Aylett R. Cox.

It is a pity that so many schools lack funds for the purchase of work books and other individualized teaching materials. The cost per pupil is so little when compared to the cost of failure that the penny-wise, pound-foolish policy followed in so many places cannot readily be justified. Nevertheless, even if prevented by lack of funds from purchasing perishable workbooks, the resourceful teacher is still not entirely prevented from making some use of them. From single copies, which are generally quite inexpensive, the teacher can get ideas which can be incorporated into blackboard work or developed in duplicated work sheets of his own construction. However, while imitation is permissible, outright copying is plagiarism and is a violation of the law.

Many successful remedial teachers have developed files of useful practice exercises. They order two copies of each of a number of workbooks and cut them up (since pages are printed on both sides, two copies are needed).

The pig ran away. Which word says "pig"?

Try again. Find "pig."

Look at the funny pig! The first letter in "pig" is _____.

No. "Pig" is in the box. Find the first letter in "pig."

FIGURE 15.11 A four-frame review sequence for the initial consonant *p* using multi-media *System80®*. As the first frame appears on the screen, a voice speaks the words shown beneath the frame (these words do not appear on the screen).

If the student responds correctly, he skips the second frame and goes to the third. If he responds correctly to the third frame, he goes to the first frame of the next review sequence.

If the student does not respond correctly to the first frame, he is advanced to the second frame. If he responds incorrectly again, he is advanced to the fourth frame. Here, the message repeats until he answers correctly.

Reprinted, with permission, from *Learning Letter Sounds.* © Copyright 1972 Borg-Warner Corporation. System80® Registered Trademark of Borg-Warner Corporation.

Each page is mounted on heavy paper or oak tag and can be shellacked or covered with transparent plastic for permanency. Large plastic envelopes and markers are available from Ideal and Imperial. By assembling pages from several workbooks, a comprehensive series of exercises can be built up. Exercises constructed by the teacher can be inserted into the series at any time. A grocery carton can be used as a file drawer. The exercises should be classified by type and numbered within each type. Care in classifying and numbering the exercises will make it possible for a bright pupil, acting as librarian, to keep the collection in order and to select for each pupil the exercises assigned by the teacher. A separate file of answer keys, corresponding to the exercises, makes it possible for the teacher to correct written work very quickly, or for the pupils to correct their own work.

Programs and Kits

There are programs, which although primarily designed for developmental reading, contain material and procedures that may be used in corrective or remedial work. It should be realized, however, that the pace suggested by the manuals may be inappropriate, or the materials may provide too little or too much skill practice. Unless the student is very deficient, it is more efficient to work on only the skills in which he is weak, rather than take him through an entire program.

A few of the more useful programs are:

New Structural Reading Series, by Catherine Stern, *et al.* (Singer). A phonic-linguistic program in eight work texts emphasizing discovery, insight, and application in meaningful context. Contains many interesting exercises and six readers.

Sullivan Reading Program, by M. W. Sullivan (Behavioral). *Programmed Reading,* by Sullivan Associates, Cynthia Dee Buchanan, Program Director (McGraw-Hill). These two essentially similar programmed series are advertised for both developmental and remedial reading; they begin with letters and short, regular words, with self-checking after each answer.

Phoenix Reading Series, by Marion Gartler and Marcella Benditt (Prentice-Hall). A three-level program developed primarily to "reteach" symbol-sound associations to intermediate-grade children. Use of photographs, a short, simple writing style, and contemporary themes should make the materials appealing to "turned-off" readers.

Among the phonic programs that might be used with children who need or might profit from a decoding-emphasis approach are *Phonetic Keys to Reading,* 1973 edition (Economy) which also stresses comprehension, *Distar* (SRA) a highly-structured program, and *Basic Reading* (Lippincott).

Linguistic programs include the *Palo Alto Program* (Harcourt), the *SRA Reading Program* (SRA), the *Merrill Linguistic Readers* (Merrill), *Let's Read* (Barnhart), and the *Miami Linguistic Readers* (Heath). Although in these programs there is almost complete one-to-one correspondence (a given letter only signals one sound), there is rarely any direct teaching of symbol-sound associations. While some children may generalize on their own from the constant spelling patterns, most children who are deficient in decoding need direct instruction in grapheme-phoneme relationships.

Although most kits contain materials for developing a variety of reading skills, some are designed primarily for developing decoding skills. Among these are:

+4 Reading Booster, by William Kottmeyer (Webster). Kit contains workbooks, cassettes, word cards, phonic wheels, reading cards, oral reading tests, library books, and a teacher's manual; emphasis is also given to developing comprehension.

Stott Programmed Reading Kits, by L. M. Stott (Scott, Foresman). Kits contain games and exercises for teaching decoding skills.

Diagnostic/Prescriptive Program for Word Analysis, by Elizabeth C. Adamson (Bobbs-Merrill). Kit contains brief "diagnostic" tests, and materials for developing 51 word-analysis skills.

Multimedia Materials

An increasing number of programs use two or more media. Most of these combine recordings on tape or records with one or more forms of reading material. They are listed in approximate order of increasing cost, excluding hardware.

Listen and Learn with Phonics (Career Institute). Includes three records, five word books, a game set, and a word box. A correlated set of transparencies is also available.

Learning with Amos and His Friends and *Learning the Consonant Blends with Amos and His Friends* (Imperial Productions, Inc.). Each set includes one tape, a set of picture charts, a manual, and a set of spirit duplicator masters.

Consonant Sounds and *Vowel Sounds/A Self Instructional Modalities Approach* (Milton Bradley). Each program consists of a number of lessons on cassettes, accompanying response sheet, and student manipulatives.

Mast Programed Instructor (Mast Keystone). Hardware for use with linear programs on 35 mm. strip film cartridges. Programs may be purchased from Mast or they will film one you construct. In using the equipment, the student pushes a button to advance a frame, reads the material on the screen, writes his answer on the response tape, presses the answer button, and can compare his response with the one on the screen.

Basic Reading Vocabulary and *Basic Sight Words* (Psychotechnics). The first program has 2 levels (119 and 149 words) covered by 20 films, workbooks, flash cards, wall charts, and teacher's manual. The second program has 2 sets of words, common nouns and service words, each having 30 films and accompanying materials.

Target (Field). Two self-instructional kits (*Yellow* for phonics, *Blue* for structural analysis), each containing duplicating masters to accompany the cassettes each of which is based on a single behavioral objective, pretests, and a teacher's manual.

Listen-Look-Learn (Ideal). Six sets of recorded phonic lessons with accompanying duplicator workbooks or Mark-on-Wipe-off lesson cards.

Hoffman Language Arts Reading System (Hoffman). Audiovisual instructional programs for grades 1–6. Consists of a self-contained viewer and accompanying stories and exercises on film slides and records that operate synchronously. Printed materials and teacher manuals are included.

Phonics Program and *Word-Picture Program* (Bell and Howell). Sets of prerecorded magnetic cards for use with the *Language Master*.

Patterns in Phonics (Educational Futures, Inc.). Sets of prerecorded cards for use in the *efi Audio Flashcard System*.

Directional Phonics (Teaching Technology Corp.). A synthetic phonics program that includes filmstrips, tapes, records, magnetic cards, and student and teacher manuals, for use with the *TTC Magnetic Card Reader*.

Systems 80 (Borg Warner). Machine administered and scored pretesting. Each program has specific objectives. Each lesson, which employs modified branching programming (see Fig. 15.11) has 80 frames with corresponding audio messages. The student evaluates his own program. There are spaced reviews and tests. Available programs include: Learning Letter Names, Learning Letter Sounds, Reading Words in Context, and Improving Reading Skills (a literacy program). The hardware may be purchased or rented.

Reading and Writing with Phonics (PDL). Program on films or loops with accompanying tapes and teacher's manual. Stress symbol-sound associations, but also includes some sight words and reading of sentences.

CAI Remedial Reading (Harcourt). Computer Assisted Instruction programs (decoding, vocabulary, syntax, comprehension) provide individualized daily lessons for junior high students and above; pre- and posttests, daily and weekly summary reports.

New multimedia learning packages will unquestionably continue to be placed on the market faster than their usefulness can be determined. Since the costs of such materials tend to run high, it is desirable to arrange for a careful local evaluation and, if possible, for a trial use on approval, before investing in such programs. However, when trained remedial personnel is scarce, materials that amplify the teacher and allow him to give remedial help to more children by providing self-directing and self-checking learning experiences may justify their cost.

SUGGESTED ADDITIONAL READING

BANNATYNE, ALEXANDER. *Language, reading, and learning disabilities: psychology, neuropsychology, diagnosis, and remediation.* Springfield, Ill.: Charles C Thomas, 1971. Chap. 15.

BOND, GUY L. & TINKER, MILES A. *Reading difficulties: their diagnosis and correction* (3rd ed.). New York: Appleton-Century-Crofts, 1973. Chaps. 11, 12.

CARTER, HOMER L. J. & MC GINNIS, DOROTHY J. *Diagnosis and treatment of the disabled reader.* Macmillan, 1970. Chap. 11.

DUFFY, GERALD G. & SHERMAN, GEORGE B. *Systematic reading instruction.* New York: Harper and Row, 1972. Chap. 4.

ELKONIN, D. B. USSR. In John Downing (Ed.). *Comparative reading: cross-national studies of behavior and processes in reading and writing.* New York: Macmillan, 1973. Chap. 24.

FROSTIG, MARIANNE & MASLOW, PHYLLIS. *Learning problems in the classroom.* New York: Grune and Stratton, 1973. Chap. 18.

GATES, ARTHUR I. *The improvement of reading* (3rd ed.). New York: Macmillan, 1947. Chap. 16.

JOHNSON, DORIS J. & MYKLEBUST, HELMER R. *Learning disabilities: educational principles and practices.* New York: Grune and Stratton, 1967. Chap. 5.

MONEY, JOHN (Ed.). *The disabled reader.* Baltimore: Johns Hopkins Press, 1966. Chaps. 7–14.

NATCHEZ, GLADYS (Ed.). *Children with reading problems: classic and contemporary issues in reading disability.* New York: Basic Books, 1968. Pp. 341–346, 397–412.

OTTO, WAYNE; MC MENEMY, RICHARD A.; & SMITH, RICHARD J. *Corrective and remedial teaching* (2nd ed.). Boston: Houghton Mifflin, 1973. Chap. 7.

ROSWELL, FLORENCE G. & NATCHEZ, GLADYS. *Reading disability: diagnosis and treatment* (2nd ed.). New York: Basic Books, 1971. Chaps. 5, 6.

16

Improving Reading
Comprehension, I

Reading has been defined earlier in this book as "the meaningful interpretation of written or printed verbal symbols." The heart of the act of reading is obtaining appropriate meanings. Word recognition, which has been considered in the preceding two chapters, is a necessary prerequisite for reading comprehension, but recognition without understanding is worth very little.

There is a close relationship between listening comprehension and reading comprehension (Reeves, 1968; Butler, 1970). Before one can understand, he must have sufficient mastery of the language to meet ordinary conversational needs. If the material is of a technical or specialized character, a certain amount of specialized information and vocabulary may be necessary. The possession of a level of mental ability adequate to follow the reasoning presented is needed for both listening and reading comprehension. Active attention is necessary in both if the train of thought is to be followed.

Reading, however, imposes additional tasks which are absent when one listens. For one thing, the words must be recognized if their meaning is to be appreciated. A second difference is that, in reading, one must organize the material into meaningful phrases and thought units, while in listening this is to a large extent done for the listener by the phrasing and expression, the intonation and stress patterns, of the speaker. A third point of difference

435

is that in listening, the rate of presentation is set by the speaker, while in reading one has to learn to govern one's rate of reading so as to go fast enough to catch the flow of ideas, but not so fast as to miss too many of the details. Reading is similar to listening in many ways, but involves the need for additional skills.

In this chapter attention will be devoted to gaining meaning from words and from thought units of phrase, clause, and sentence size. Chapter 17 will take up specific comprehension skills, the essential study skills, and the nature of remedial work in comprehension.

I. VOCABULARY DEVELOPMENT

In our highly verbal culture an accurate understanding of the meanings of words is a necessary prerequisite for reading with meaning. Vocabulary is so closely related to comprehension and reasoning that a good vocabulary test can serve effectively as a measure of general intelligence, and most good intelligence tests contain many vocabulary items. A minimum essential for comprehension in reading is an understanding of the words used by the author. The development of a reading vocabulary that is both extensive and accurate is a necessary phase of good comprehension.

Types of Vocabulary

The first type of vocabulary knowledge that a person acquires is a listening vocabulary. Most babies show that they can respond correctly to spoken words before they are able to use those words in their own speech. Listening vocabulary develops earlier than speaking vocabulary, and throughout life the number of words to which a person can react appropriately when he hears them remains larger than the number he can employ correctly in his own speech or writing. When children start to read, they begin to acquire a reading vocabulary: words they both recognize and understand. Gradually they begin to learn the meanings of words that occur in their reading but have not been in their previous vocabularies; they begin to acquire new meaningful vocabulary in reading. They also learn, through composition and spelling, to use a large number of words in their writing; these words, which are nearly always fewer in number than the speaking, hearing, or reading vocabularies, can be called writing vocabulary. A child's total meaningful vocabulary is the sum of all the words which he can understand or use correctly, whether in listening, speaking, reading, or writing.

In the writing of materials for beginners in reading, great care is usually taken to use only words whose meanings are already familiar to the children or can be easily explained to them. The task of learning to recognize the words is hard enough without the added burden of having to learn new meanings at the same time. Because of this, the child's reading vocabulary is at first composed entirely of words which should already be part of his meaningful vocabulary. As the child progresses in reading, new words and ideas are introduced.

Size of Meaningful Vocabulary

Until the 1940's, the majority of studies of the size of children's vocabularies seemed to indicate that the average child entered the first grade with a knowledge of the meanings of about 2,500 words and increased his vocabulary at a rate of about 1,000 words a year in the primary and middle elementary grades, and 2,000 words a year in grades 7 to 9, so that his vocabulary would be about 8,500 words in the sixth grade and about 15,000 words in the ninth grade (Seegers, 1939). Wide individual differences were known to be present at every age. These older studies were based on samplings taken from word lists like the Thorndike *Teacher's Word Book*, or from small dictionaries, or on counts of words used by children in their speaking and writing.

Seashore (1948) constructed a vocabulary test based on a sampling of the Funk and Wagnalls *New Standard Dictionary* (unabridged). Using this test, he estimated the basic vocabulary of the average college undergraduate as about 58,000 words; if derivatives, rare words, and compound words were included, the average rose to about 155,000 words. M. K. Smith (1941), using Seashore's test with children in grades one through 12, found a fairly steady increase in basic vocabulary from an average of nearly 17,000 words in the first grade to 32,000 in the sixth grade and 47,000 in the twelfth grade.

Lorge and Chall (1963) made a careful analysis of Seashore's method of selecting words for his test and concluded that the test was unintentionally loaded with too many easy words, making his estimates of vocabulary size much too high. They concluded that the truth lies closer to the old estimates than to those of Seashore and his followers.

Dale (1965), an authority on vocabulary research, summarized the best available evidence as follows: "If we assume that children finish the first grade with an average vocabulary of 3,000 words, it is likely that they will add about 1,000 a year from then on. The average high school senior will know about 14,000 to 15,000 words, the college senior 18,000 to 20,000."

Anything approaching an exact answer to this question is impossible for the present because of uncertainty concerning the exact meaning of "a word" and lack of exact criteria on what is meant by "knowing" a word. Many English words have a variety of meanings and can be used with different syntactical functions; they also have a variety of inflectional endings. Is a word with thirty dictionary definitions to be counted as one word? Is being able to identify one meaning sufficient for "knowing," or must one be able to use the word correctly in the majority of its listed meanings? Most vocabulary studies consider a word "known" if one meaning is correctly identified on a multiple-choice test; hardly a complete measure.

Roellse (1969) found that three dimensions of vocabulary were significantly related to comprehension. Extensiveness (number of words for which the child can select a synonym) was most important; intensiveness (number of meanings known per word) was next; and flexibility (selection of the particular meaning which fits a given context) was third. In these terms, most tests of reading vocabulary are tests of extensiveness only.

Another significant dimension of vocabulary is the degree to which the concept represented by a word is abstract or concrete. Children who are bright and good readers tend to give abstract or generalized definitions of words, while children who are slow and poor readers tend to define words in terms of use or function.

Words and Concepts

A word is a verbal label that represents a concept or idea. As children mature, the concept represented by the word gradually becomes more refined and accurate. The concept represented by *dog*, for example, is usually vague and overgeneralized by tots beginning to talk, who may apply it to any four-footed animal. The child learns to exclude large animals like horses and cattle; then develops criteria (wags tail, barks, etc.) which include dogs of various sizes and exclude cats and other animals whose sizes overlap the range of dog sizes. Rentel (1971) recommended the following principles for the teaching of concepts: 1) establishing the proper word label for the concept or attribute; 2) placing emphasis on significant differentiating characteristics; 3) providing examples and instances of a concept in an appropriate sequence; 4) encouraging and guiding student discovery of the essence of the concept; and 5) providing for application of the concept. Providing children with experiences from which a concept can be developed may not be enough. The teacher can help children to extract the generalized characteristic, clarify it, and codify it (Frazier, 1970).

Concepts representing things (nouns) or actions (verbs) or observable qualities (adjectives, adverbs) are comparatively easy to develop, while concepts representing relationships (function words such as conjunctions and prepositions) are more difficult. According to Stoodt (1972), the most frequently used conjunctions through the fourth grade are: *and, as, because, but, either, for, if, how, now, either, or, since, so, than, that, though, where, when, while, why,* and *yet.* The best understood were *and, how, for,* and *as.* The following were comparatively difficult: *when, so, but, or, where, while, how, that,* and *if.* Robertson (1968) found that sentences containing clauses

FIGURE 16.1 A page from a dictionary for first and second grades. Features include: a thumb index; presentation of inflected forms with the root word; use of both picture and sentence cues; decoding help by presenting words in syllables and providing phonic cues from words previously introduced. Reproduced from Mae Knight Clark, *My Word-Clue Dictionary*. The Macmillan Reading Program, Primary Grades, Revised. New York: Macmillan Publishing Co., 1974. Reproduced by permission of the publisher. Reduced in size; original in color.

introduced by *however, thus, which, although,* and *yet* were difficult for children in grades 4–6; understanding of these connectives was related to intelligence and listening comprehension and closely correlated to reading comprehension (.83).

Causes of Deficiencies in Meaningful Vocabulary

When a child has a small meaningful vocabulary, the first possible cause to investigate is intelligence. Low general intelligence shows itself clearly in retarded language development and difficulty in understanding and acquiring the meanings of words. The most important test in the *Stanford-Binet Intelligence Scale* is one designed to measure the richness and accuracy of speaking vocabulary. One of the outstanding characteristics of the mentally retarded is their difficulty in understanding words of a general or abstract nature.

Lack of intellectual stimulation and practice in the use of language are also important causes of vocabulary weakness. Words have meaning to a child only when they are related to things he has experienced or knows about. A child who has had a very restricted life is ignorant of many things that are commonplace to the average child and so has not the basis for understanding words which refer to those things. Children whose parents mainly speak a foreign language in the home are handicapped in their language development because they do not receive enough practice in hearing and speaking English. Speech defects and defective hearing also interfere with the acquisition of a rich vocabulary because they cut off many conversational opportunities.

A child who likes to read enriches his vocabulary continually with words and ideas that he gains from his reading. When a child has made a poor start in reading he usually dislikes to read and thus gives up one of the best opportunities to expand his vocabulary. A vicious cycle is set up in which limited reading restricts the opportunity to learn new words, and failure to build up vocabulary prevents improvement in reading.

The factors that have just been described as hindrances to the development of meaningful vocabulary are the same ones that were described in Chapter 2 in relation to the language aspects of reading readiness. Causes that handicap a child in making a proper start in reading continue to interfere with his later progress if they are not corrected. The same general objectives that are involved in developing readiness for reading are also important for later training in the acquisition of vocabulary.

When, in reading, a child comes across a word and says that he does not know it, there are three possible explanations: 1) he may be able to pronounce it, but he has no understanding of what it signifies; 2) he may know the meaning of the word if presented orally, but be unable to recognize it; and 3) he may be both unable to pronounce it and ignorant of its meaning. If a child has difficulties of the first type, he needs to have his meaningful vocabulary built up. If his difficulties are of the second type, he needs training in word recognition. If he is weak in both word recognition and meaningful vocabulary, both kinds of training need to be given simultaneously.

Providing a Background of Experience

The first essential in a program of vocabulary development is to provide children with a background of meaningful experience. Vivid firsthand sensory experience is the best basis for the development of accurate concepts. For this reason trips and excursions, when intelligently planned, are excellent for broadening children's horizons. The main difficulty with them is that in most schools they occur too infrequently to make a real dent in the problem. Also, when a trip is made the teacher often feels that he has done well if he gets the children back safely. The opportunities for developing meaningful concepts and vocabulary are too frequently neglected. When firsthand experience is not available, visual teaching materials, such as moving pictures, filmstrips, slides, pictures, and charts, are the best substitutes. Storytelling and oral reading by the teacher are also valuable ways of imparting experience, especially in the lower grades. Practice in the use of language is highly important. Natural opportunities for intelligent listening and speaking arise in discussions, reports, informal conversation, and dramatics.

Developing Vocabulary through Wide Reading

E. L. Thorndike (1936–1937) concluded that "of the 60,000 or more different words that would be found in books recommended for reading by pupils in grade eight or below, the majority would occur only rarely, probably not oftener than once in three million words, or fifty books of the average size for juveniles." Because of the impossibility of teaching all or most of the words that a child will meet in his reading, Thorndike recommended, as the best solution to the problem of vocabulary building, providing pupils with a wide variety of interesting books that are easy enough so that the new words and ideas can be learned from the context.

It is not so easy, however, for children to derive correct meanings from the context of unfamiliar words. H. A. Robinson (1963) found that fourth-grade pupils were not very good at gaining the meaning of a word from context, since correct answers varied between 61 per cent and only 10 per cent. Rankin and Overholser (1969) reported that overall accuracy in using context clues ranged from 43 per cent in fourth grade to 62 per cent in sixth

Unit No. 3

The thirteenth floor is missing in many hotels. Floor numbers jump from twelve to fourteen. Many people think (1) .... thirteen is unlucky. They would (2) .... to take a room on the thirteenth floor.

1. (a) **letter**   (b) **number**   (c) **color**   (d) **lady**
2. (a) **fight**   (b) **forget**   (c) **refuse**   (d) **try**

Some boys and girls make money by raising and selling frogs. Frogs are easy to raise. They require little (3) .... Owners of meat and fish markets are willing to (4) .... about four dollars a dozen.

3. (a) **shoes**   (b) **music**   (c) **care**   (d) **wagons**
4. (a) **buy**   (b) **pay**   (c) **steal**   (d) **light**

A mechanical nose has been invented. The "sniffer" is placed deep beneath the deck of large cargo ships. When the gadget smells smoke, an alarm is rung. Water is then (5) .... on the (6) ....

5. (a) **tasted**   (b) **eaten**   (c) **rested**   (d) **sprayed**
6. (a) **feet**   (b) **dishes**   (c) **blaze**   (d) **chairs**

FIGURE 16.2   Part of an exercise to develop ability to use context clues. From Richard A. Boning, *Using the Context*, Book D, *Specific Skills Series*. Barnell Loft, 1962. Reprinted by permission of the publishers.

grade. Some types of clues were easier to use than others, and reading ability was significantly related to success in using context clues.

For the child who easily infers meanings from context and reads widely, an extensive vocabulary is pleasantly acquired in this way. But those who most need vocabulary enrichment—the dull child, the verbally insensitive child, the slow reader, the child who does not enjoy reading—are not so likely to be reached in this way.

The poorer the child's reading ability, the harder it is to find easy, interesting books to fit his needs. The word-by-word reader has difficulty in using the context and finds reading a slow process at best. Normal readers usually benefit from direct vocabulary instruction, especially with regard to the special vocabularies of content fields; poor readers need such instruction even more (Petty, Herold, and Stoll, 1968).

It is probable that children in general would learn words more easily if writers would make definite provisions to help them to do so (Deighton, 1959). Several ways in which the meaning of a word can be presented in context have been described. Among the most helpful are the following:

1] The new word is set off by italics, quotation marks, or boldface type, to call attention to it.
2] A brief explanation or definition of the word is given in parentheses or in a footnote.
3] A clause or phrase which explains the meaning of the word is inserted in the sentence.
4] A synonym or substitute phrase is used to indicate the meaning (for example, "a typhoon or terrific storm").
5] Similes and metaphors can be used.
6] The meaning of the word can be shown in a pictorial illustration.
7] A direct explanation of the word can be presented in a full sentence.
8] The sentence can be written so that there is only one meaning that the new word could possibly have.

The greater use of these eight procedures by writers would make it easier for children to absorb new vocabulary directly from their reading.

What Word Meanings Should Be Taught?

There are too many different words in reading matter written for children to allow the direct teaching of the meanings of even the majority. How to select the important words that are worth teaching carefully is a real problem.

Teachers who are successful in providing reading material of appropriate difficulty for their pupils avoid much of this problem. When the reading material is easy enough, most of the new words can be taught directly without consuming too much time in word study.

When a choice has to be made of which words to teach, the first consideration is to select the words whose meanings must be understood if the selection is to be comprehended. Some words are essential to the meaning of a passage; others can be skipped without interfering too much with comprehension. With experience, a teacher can become skillful at picking out the key words in a selection.

Children are often confused more by a familiar word used in an unfamiliar sense than by a word which is totally new to them (Saeman, 1970). A child who knows the word *strike* as meaning "to hit" may need help in understanding the use of the word in such expressions as *to strike it lucky, to go on strike, to strike a camp,* and so on. The learning of new meanings for old words is an important phase of vocabulary development.

There are a great many words which children should know eventually, but may or may not be needed at a particular grade level. It would be helpful if there were a specific grade-by-grade list of words which should be definitely taught. Although many attempts have been made to establish such a list, the task is essentially impossible, since any such list is based on books of the past and will always lag behind the latest trends in interest and content. Children today, for example, are familiar with many terms relating to space flight that are not to be found in any lists compiled before 1960. Nevertheless, there is a common core which makes up perhaps as much as 90 per cent of the running words in ordinary reading matter and can be identified by means of consulting available word lists such as the Harris-Jacobson Core List (see below). Some of the more useful word lists to those interested in reading vocabulary, as distinguished from writing vocabulary, are the following:

Harris-Jacobson *Basic Elementary Reading Vocabularies* (A. J. Harris and Jacobson, 1972). Based on a computerized analysis of all words in six series of basal readers and eight series of content textbooks for grades 1–6. Contains a graded Core List of 5,167 words appearing in three or more of the basal reader series, an Additional List of 1,699 words, also graded, Technical Lists in four content areas, and a Total Alphabetical List. Inflected forms are represented by their root words. The first- and second-grade words are used in the Harris-Jacobson Readability Formula and can be found in Appendix D (see pp. 658–675).

The *Dale List of 3,000 Words* (Dale and Chall, 1948) contains 2,946 words in one alphabetical order, which were checked as "known" by at least 80 per cent of fourth graders. It is used in the Dale-Chall Readability Formula.

The *Dale-Eichholz List* (Dale and Eichholz, 1960) extends the *Dale List of 3,000 Words* by adding words known by at least 50 per cent of pupils in grades 4, 6, 8, 10, and 12; arranged alphabetically by levels.

The *American Heritage List* (J. B. Carroll, Davies, and Richman, 1971) is based on 1,045 samples taken from a wide variety of reading materials for grades 3–9. Contains 86,741 entries including every unique item that was identified by computer as separated from preceding and following items by spaces; includes real words, formulas, initials, numerals, nonsense items, etc.; about 35,000 items occurred only once. Arranged alphabetically and in descending order of frequency.

The *Kučera-Francis List* (Kučera and Francis, 1967) is based on 500 samples drawn from a wide variety of adult reading materials. Contains 50,406 items, using criteria similar to those for the *American Heritage List*; about 23,000 occurred only once and about 7,000 occurred only twice. Arranged alphabetically and in descending order of frequency.

The *Thorndike-Lorge List* (E. L. Thorndike and Lorge, 1944) extended the Thorndike lists of 10,000 words and 20,000 words to 30,000 by adding more words from adult sources; based on both child and adult materials. Words are arranged alphabetically and in descending order of frequency. This has been the most widely used of all reading vocabulary lists.

The primary-grade word lists that have been described on pages 359–362 are also useful sources of words whose meanings should be known.

The Vocabulary Burden in Textbooks

Many studies have shown that entirely too many textbooks are loaded with unnecessary rare and technical words. This has been shown over and over again in studies of textbooks used in the teaching of science, the social studies, and arithmetic (Dale and Razik, 1973; Petty, Herold, and Stoll, 1968).

The vocabulary problem is more acute in the textbooks of the content subjects than it is in general reading material. Many of the books used as texts in the elementary and secondary schools are written by specialists who have little understanding of the reading limitations of the children who are expected to use them. Serra (1953) found that the concept burden of social studies material is excessive and that difficult or unusual concepts are not repeated sufficiently often in social studies textbooks.

Each of the content subjects has a vocabulary of its own that must be learned. One cannot expect a pupil to understand without assistance technical terms such as *dividend, factor,* and *decimal* in arithmetic, *longitude* and *latitude* in geography, and similar technical terms in other subjects. Whenever an important new concept is introduced, there is need for a detailed explanation.

It is not safe to allow pupils to pick out the words that they need to study. Even at the college level, it has been found that "the pupils most in need of vocabulary enlargement are too often the students least likely to realize their need or to appraise their limitations correctly" (Bear and Odbert, 1941). This is even more true at lower scholastic levels.

Methods of Teaching Vocabulary

A recent critical survey of vocabulary instruction classifies vocabulary teaching procedures as either direct or context (Petty, Herold, and Stoll, 1968). Direct study methods include 1) study of word lists—usually a list is assigned to be looked up in a dictionary and used in sentences; 2) study of word parts—English roots, prefixes, and suffixes, particularly those of Latin or Greek origin, are studied and applied; 3) additional direct methods include teaching the use of the dictionary; vocabulary notebooks; study of word origins; synonyms, antonyms, and homonyms; workbooks; programed materials; and audiovisual aids. Context methods include: 1) direct instruction in how to use the context; 2) reliance on incidental learning from wide reading; 3) a variety of related procedures including discussion of connotation and denotation, idioms, multiple meanings, and word origins. The authors note that teachers reporting on favorite techniques usually begin with discussion of how student interest in word study was stimulated, while research reports often ignore motivation. They conclude that most of the research comparing the effectiveness of different methods of teaching vocabulary is inconclusive, partly because of limitations of research design and partly because methods employed in many of the research studies do not seem representative of good classroom practice.

Explanation and Discussion

The conventional method of teaching new words is about as follows: The teacher looks through the selection in advance and picks out a few words that may need explanation. Before the children read the selection, the teacher writes the new words on the board, explaining the meaning of each, using it in one or more sentences, and showing appropriate illustrative material if any is available. The children are asked to suggest other sentences in which the word can be used. The words are taken up in turn, and then the selection is read.

One difficulty with this procedure is the danger of relying on superficial verbalizations. Meanings that are clear to the teacher may be quite hazy to the child. Many of the classical boners are due to superficial and inadequate grasp of word meanings. It is not sufficient to tell a child that *frantic* means *wild*, or that *athletic* means *strong*; he may try to pick frantic flowers, or pour athletic vinegar into a salad dressing.

The other main difficulty with this procedure is the danger of spending too much time on word study. This can be avoided if the reading material is not overloaded with new words.

Some teachers prefer to have a group of pupils read the selection first and then ask them at the end what new words caused them trouble. These

EXERCISE

A. Find the meaning under **B** that matches each use of *get* under **A**.

A		B
1. get away	_____	**a.** to do well
2. get along	_____	**b.** to make clear
3. get across	_____	**c.** to reach the end
4. get over	_____	**d.** to forget
5. get through	_____	**e.** to rise
6. get up	_____	**f.** to leave

B. Read the following sentences. Match the ordinary meanings of *get* to the special meanings in Column **B** above.

1. We get up late on Sunday morning. _____
2. Will we ever get through washing
these dishes? _____
3. Jane couldn't get over the way Mark
spoke. _____

4. Julie gets along well at school. _____
5. Dad couldn't get away from the office
on time. _____
6. Bill doesn't get across his ideas
very well. _____
7. It took Connie two weeks to get over
her disappointment. _____

FIGURE 16.3 Part of a programmed lesson on the special meanings of verb phrases. From Lee C. Deighton, *Vocabulary Development*, Level 1, p. 51. The Macmillan Publishing Co., 1973. Reprinted by permission of the publisher; reduced in size.

words can then be explained in the usual way. Two advantages are claimed for this procedure: that the number of words pupils will ask about is nearly always less than the number that the teacher would have selected for preliminary teaching, and that the teaching arises from a need felt by the pupils and therefore is more apt to be well motivated and to produce effective learning. This procedure can work well with children who are good readers; poor readers fail to ask about many of the words they do not know.

The Use of the Dictionary

As soon as possible, children should be taught to help themselves to acquire new meanings independently by making use of glossaries and dictionaries. Picture dictionaries can be used as early as the first grade and are helpful additions to the library table through the primary grades and in upper-grade remedial work (see Fig. 16.1).

The use of a simple glossary can be introduced as early as the third grade. From the fourth grade up, regular dictionaries can be introduced. The main drawback about stressing the use of dictionaries in the past was the poor type of dictionary that formerly was available for school use. School dictionaries published recently have overcome the former difficulties to a very large extent. Clear type, simple vocabulary in definitions and explanations, illustrative sentences, simplified guides to pronunciation, and abundant illustrations make them attractive for child use.

Most present-day teachers learned to use a dictionary by trial and error. Many have never learned how to find what they want quickly and easily and so refer to a dictionary only as a last resort. A dictionary is a complex work, and in order to get children to use it willingly, it is advisable to prepare a planned sequence of lessons to teach elementary dictionary skills. The following outline lists the major dictionary skills. The simplest ones can be started in first grade; the more difficult ones can be made the objective of planned lessons in the fourth, fifth, and six grades.

1] Location of words in alphabetical order
   a) Learning the sequence of the alphabet
   b) Practice in determining which letter comes before and which letter comes after a given letter
   c) Arrangement of a list of words in alphabetical order according to first letter
   d) Arrangement of words having same first letter in alphabetical order according to second, third, and fourth letters
   e) Practice in opening the dictionary at a point near the word
   f) Practice in the use of a thumb index
   g) Learning how to use the guide at the top of a page

2] Finding out the pronunciation of words
   a) Practice in reading words by syllables
   b) Interpretation and use of the accent mark
   c) Understanding of phonetic respelling
   d) Understanding and use of diacritical marks
   e) Location and use of the guide to pronunciation
3] Finding out the meaning of words
   a) Ability to interpret typical dictionary definitions
   b) Ability to select from several meanings listed in the dictionary the one which fits the present context
   c) Ability to find synonyms for a word
   d) Ability to relate derived forms of a word to the basic form
   e) Ability to distinguish current usage from obsolete or slang usage

A good definition usually has two elements: it states a class or category to which the concept belongs, and it gives one or more descriptive characteristics which distinguish this concept from other members of the category. A dictionary definition of a *fanatic* says: "a person with an extreme and unreasoning enthusiasm or zeal, especially in religious matters." The category is "person"; the rest tells how fanatics differ from other persons. Children can be helped to analyze definitions, to construct their own definitions for familiar words, and to compare theirs with the definitions in the dictionary.

Synonyms are often given as definitions. This is fine when the synonym is already understood or is clearly and understandably defined. Learning synonyms is one good way of enlarging one's vocabulary, especially when the dictionary explains fine distinctions, as among *ancient, antique, antiquated,* and *old-fashioned.* Fortunately, circular definitions (fantasy—hallucination; hallucination—a form of fantasy) are very rare in today's dictionaries.

Practice exercises in the use of the dictionary can be found in a number of reading workbooks for the middle and upper grades. Good dictionaries for elementary school use are published by G. and C. Merriam Co.; The Macmillan Co.; Scott, Foresman and Co.; Holt, Rinehart and Winston. Some elementary dictionaries have teachers' editions with specific lesson plans for teaching use of the dictionary.

Individualized Word Study

Pupils must be stimulated to take advantage of the opportunities for self-help that dictionaries offer (E. F. Miller, 1962). Vocabulary notebooks are effective in encouraging the use of dictionaries. When such notebooks are used a pupil is expected to enter in his notebook new words that he meets in his reading, together with a brief description or explanation of each

Write *letter* of correct definition before *number* of word to be defined.

EXERCISE 2

Words	*Definitions*

NOUNS

........1. **bulwark**
........2. **cataract**
........3. **dialect**
........4. **enmity**
........5. **multitude**
........6. **nuisance**
........7. **tantrum**

A. fit of bad temper or ill humor
B. large number
C. art of logical discussion
D. form of speech of a particular region
E. bother; annoyance
F. harmony; complete accord
G. defense; protection
H. ill will; hatred
I. steep waterfall
J. agreement between two parties

MODIFIERS

........8. **allegedly**
........9. **ferociously**
......10. **jovial**
......11. **lithe**
......12. **martial**
......13. **skeptical**
......14. **sublime**

A. supremely beautiful; majestic
B. good-humored and merry
C. gaunt; haggard
D. doubting; distrustful
E. pertaining to war; military
F. supposedly; assertedly
G. positively; without doubt
H. limber; flexible
I. pertaining to marriage
J. savagely; fiercely

VERBS

......15. **baffle**
......16. **bolster**
......17. **corrode**
......18. **incur**
......19. **stifle**
......20. **stress**

A. keep back; suppress
B. make evil or wicked
C. emphasize
D. strengthen; support
E. eat away gradually
F. come up again; repeat
G. puzzle; mystify
H. bring about; bring on oneself

Score 5 for each correct answer.   My score: . . . . .

FIGURE 16.4   A vocabulary exercise involving matching words with brief definitions. Material is of secondary level. From *Grow in Word Power*, Word Games and Exercises Selected from *Reader's Digest Educational Edition*. Compiled and Edited by Natalie Moreda. Reader's Digest Services, Inc., © 1967. Reproduced by permission of the publishers.

and one or two sentences illustrating its use. Very important new words should be looked up immediately. Others can be allowed to accumulate until the pupil has fifteen or twenty new words, and then these can be looked up at one time. This procedure reduces the irritation many pupils feel if they have to interrupt their reading frequently to consult a dictionary.

The use of index cards of the usual 3 x 5-inch size is preferred to the use of notebooks by many teachers. The word is written on one side, and the pronunciation, definition, and one or more illustrations of the use of the word can be put on the back. An inexpensive filing box and set of alphabet guide cards can be used to give excellent practice in filing and locating in alphabetical order. Children can easily test themselves on their own cards, or they can work in pairs, each testing the other.

Motivation is a big problem in keeping up an interest in vocabulary study. Teachers should not hesitate to talk about the importance of words as the bricks from which ideas are built and should find varied ways of impressing on their pupils the importance of using the right word to fit each idea. In order to prevent an initial enthusiasm for word study from waning, the teacher should check on the progress of each pupil and make it clear that the learning of new vocabulary is an important aspect of the work in English. Sometimes enthusiasm can be whipped up by staging a contest; for example, the class can appoint themselves "word detectives," and prizes can be awarded for the largest number of "missing" words located during a week or month (Bougere, 1968; Lake, 1967, 1971).

Study of Verbal Relationships

Many kinds of exercises and games can be used to give training in word meanings through practice in various kinds of relationships between words. They can be adapted for either oral or silent work. In the latter case it is necessary to prepare mimeographed sheets or to write the questions on the board and use answer sheets. Many useful vocabulary exercises can be found in published workbooks. Some samples of different kinds of word-meaning exercises now follow:

Synonyms
1] What word means the same as: good? attractiveness? uncivil?
2] Underline the word that means the same as *quiet*: pretty, still, steady.
3] A tactful remark is: a) rude b) courteous c) deceitful d) intact.
4] List all the words you can think of that mean about the same as *happy*.

Opposites

1] What word means the opposite of: big? warlike? pretentious?
2] Underline the word that means the opposite of *curved*: twisted, bumpy, round, straight.
3] A *compulsory* act is not: a) optional b) contagious c) necessary d) repulsive.
4] Animated—lethargic. Same   Opposite (Underline one.)

Classification

1] What are the parts of: an automobile? a plant? a city government?
2] A *wing* is a part of: a) an animal b) a bird c) a fish d) a plant.
3] Make one list of the fruits and another list of the vegetables in the words: orange, potato, pineapple, spinich, lettuce, pear, pea, grape, bean, lemon, squash, cucumber, strawberry, peach.
4] Make a list of all the kinds of clothing you can think of (or jobs, colors, animals, vehicles, and so on).

Analogies

1] Foot is to hand as shoe is to _____.
2] Good is to bad as light is to: bright, naughty, dark, happy.
3] Governor: state: mayor: a) city b) town c) country d) president

The major purpose of the kinds of exercises just illustrated is to clarify the meanings of words through bringing out important relationships between ideas. As the child comes to grasp these relationships his understanding of the words becomes more accurate, and he is therefore able to use and interpret them more effectively. When in going over the answers to exercises like these it is found that some of the words are unfamiliar, the teacher can take the opportunity to teach the meaning of the words and also to add them to the child's reading vocabulary. Vocabulary tests can also be employed deliberately to afford opportunities for introducing and teaching new words.

Study of Prefixes, Suffixes, and Roots

A large number of English words start with prefixes. These little word parts have fairly constant meanings, and a person who knows the meanings of the more common prefixes can frequently make a fairly close guess as to the meaning of a new word, particularly when it is met in a meaningful context. Stauffer (1942) found that 24 per cent of the first 20,000 words in the Thorndike list have prefixes. While the total number of prefixes is large, many of them are used but seldom, and fifteen prefixes account for 82 per cent of all the words in which prefixes appear. A recommended list is as follows:

ab (from)	abnormal, abuse
ad, ap, at (to)	admit, appear, attract
be (by)	beside, behind
con, com, col (with)	conductor, commercial, collection
de (from)	deduct, defense
dis (apart, not)	disappear, disarm, disrupt
en, em (in)	engage, enjoy, embrace
ex (out)	exit, export
in, im (in, into)	income, impose
in, im (not)	incorrect, impure
ob, of, op (against, away, from)	obstruct, offend, oppose
pre, pro (before, in front of)	prepare, predict, projectile, promote
re (back)	refer, remodel
post (behind)	postpone
super (over, above)	superior, supervisor
trans (across)	transportation
sub (under)	submarine, subject
un (not)	unarmed, unbroken

The rarer prefixes are also worth knowing, but probably should be left for individual study or left for incidental consideration in connection with the learning of particular words that contain them.

A knowledge of the meanings of some of the more common Latin roots which are found in many English words is unquestionably helpful in attacking unknown words at a mature level. Roots like *port*, meaning to carry, *fac* or *fic*, meaning to make, and a few others can be easily learned by mature pupils. It is probable that nearly all the help in learning new English words that is claimed as one of the benefits accruing from the teaching of Latin can be just as well secured from a few hours spent in consideration of the commonest Latin roots and prefixes. From one of the roots it is possible to build up a family of words, helping in the clarification of the meanings of those words, the root that is common to all of them, and the different shades of meaning created by their different prefixes and suffixes. Such a family might be *porter, import, export, deport, report, reporter, transport, portable*, and so on.

According to one study, 82 Latin roots and 6 Greek roots occur 10 or more times each in children's vocabulary. The most common Latin roots are the following (Breen, 1960):

fac, fact, fic (to make or do)	factory, fact, fiction
sta, stat (to stand)	static, station
pos, pon (to place, put)	post, opponent, position
fer (to bear, carry)	transfer, ferry, infer
mis, mit (to send)	submit, admission
tend, tens (to stretch)	tendon, tension, extend
vid, vis (to see)	vision, provide
mov, mot (to move)	move, motion
spect, spic (to look, see)	inspection, conspicuous
ven, vent (to come)	convention, event
par (to get ready)	prepare, repair
port (to carry)	export, transport

There are many suffixes in English, and the majority of them have more than one meaning, so that teaching only the most common meaning may create some confusion. Those which are both fairly common and have a reasonably constant meaning include:

er, or, ist, ian (performer of)	teacher, sailor, dentist, physician
tion, sion (act of)	temptation, decision
ry, ty, ity (condition of)	finery, safety, purity
al (pertaining to)	formal, musical
ble, able, ible (capable of being)	adaptable, forcible
ment (result of, act of)	judgment, management
ful (full of)	careful, wonderful
man (one who)	policeman
ic (pertaining to)	comic, terrific
ous, ious, eous (like, full of)	joyous, laborious, nauseous
ence, ance (state of)	repentance, persistence
ly, y (in the manner of)	truly, windy

It takes a fairly high level of mental ability to understand a generalized meaning and to apply it correctly in particular situations, so as to be able to utilize a knowledge of word roots, prefixes, and suffixes effectively in attacking the meaning of unknown words. Such a level is probably not reached by the average student below the ninth- or tenth-grade level. In the elementary grades, only the brightest pupils are likely to be able to profit from such instruction.

Learning Fine Shades of Meaning

There are fads in the use of words, as in clothing styles. One year, every-thing commendable is "super"; a year or two later, everything is "cool,"

▪ CHANGING MEANINGS WITH SUFFIXES ▪

In your study in various subjects, you will meet many words whose meanings have been changed by adding suffixes. It will help you in your reading if you know how suffixes change meanings.

Some of the meanings of five suffixes are given on this page. Suffixes often have several meanings. Only a few of the most common ones are given.

In working with these suffixes, you will see how they change meanings. The suffixed words with which you will work appear frequently in your social studies, science, and mathematics books.

Common Meanings of Some Suffixes

er: one who does   *en:* made of, to become   *ful:* full of
ly: like in appearance or manner   *ness:* quality or state of

Write one of the above suffixes in the blank space at the right of each word below. Use a suffix that will make the word mean the same thing as the phrase to the right of the word. The first one is done for you.

1. wonder *ful* : full of wonder   6. spoon _____: a full spoon

2. hard _____: to become hard   7. buy _____: one who buys

3. man _____: like a man   8. earth _____: made of earth

4. dark _____: state of being dark   9. brother _____: like a brother

5. sing _____: one who sings   10. own _____: one who owns

Below are some words to which suffixes have been added. Think about the meaning of the suffix at the end of each word, then write the meaning of the word as a whole. The first one has been done for you.

1. worker: *one who works*   9. fatherly: _____

2. queenly: _____   10. fighter: _____

3. thickness: _____   11. kindness: _____

4. sisterly: _____   12. rancher: _____

5. teacher: _____   13. leader: _____

6. powerful: _____   14. friendly: _____

7. wooden: _____   15. darkness: _____

8. planter: _____   16. strengthen: _____

FIGURE **16.5**   Exercise on common English suffixes. From Nila Banton Smith, *Be a Better Reader,* Foundations A, p. 139. Prentice-Hall, Inc., 1968. Reproduced by permission of the publishers; reduced in size.

"sharp," or "dynamite." Many children fall victim to the insidious habit of using a small number of stock adjectives and adverbs and fail to develop a command of a vocabulary that can express fine shades of meaning. In the upper grades, it pays to devote some attention to the comparison of words which express somewhat similar meanings. If a boy describes a party as a "lousy" time, instead of scolding him for the use of an inelegant word, it is more profitable to ask him to try to describe more exactly the way in which the party was "lousy." Were the people infested with lice? Was it boring, dull, dreary, disappointing? Were the refreshments insufficient, unappetizing? Discussions of this sort form one of the very best ways of awakening children to the desirability of stating their meanings with precision, rather than relying on a few stock words whose overgeneralized meanings are worked to death. At the secondary school level, it is worth while to take time to acquaint students with the organization of a good thesaurus, such as Roget's *Thesaurus in Dictionary Form.* An elementary-level thesaurus, *In Other Words,* is published by Scott, Foresman.

Learning to Recognize Implied Meanings

Much of the delicacy of expression in spoken and written language comes from the suggestion of ideas by indirect means. Figurative language may lend grace and charm to linguistic expression. It also frequently obscures the intended meaning.

To some extent ability to interpret ideas when they are presented through analogies, similes, metaphors, euphemisms, and circumlocutions grows from meeting such forms of expression again and again in settings which make their meaning clear. It does not take a young man long to realize that the plea of a headache, used to break a date, is usually a polite evasion. Few people are deceived by the "great regret" with which a public official's resignation is received by his superior.

Sensitivity to implied meanings also requires a fairly high level of verbal intelligence. The person who easily recognizes analogies and readily notes similarities and differences in concepts is likely to enjoy discovering the implied meanings in what he reads. The person who lacks facility in understanding verbal relationships is likely to grasp only the obvious stated meanings.

Probably the best way to develop a real understanding of figurative or indirect language is through practice in paraphrasing. The attempt to restate another's thoughts in clear, unambiguous language of one's own is a crucial test of whether the thought has really been understood. Erroneous interpretations can be discovered and the correct interpretation can be explained.

Using Context to Make Sense

You test your skill in using context clues when you try to unlock the meaning of a word you have never met before. In the pairs of sentences that follow, the underlined words are used in stories that you have not yet read in *The Magic Word*. At least one, and sometimes both, of the meanings will be new to you; but you can unlock the meaning of both words *if you use the context clues*.

Two correct definitions, (a) and (b), are given for each underlined word. Put a check mark (✔) by the letter of the definition that fits the sentence. Then draw a box around the word or words in the sentence that gave you clues to the meaning of the underlined word.

bluff (a) to fool or try to fool someone by acting very sure of yourself

   (b) a high, steep bank or cliff

1. Don't try to bluff if you don't know the answer to each question.

   Bluff means (a)__✔__ (b)_____

2. The boy stood on the windy bluff and looked straight down at the river far below.

   Bluff means (a)_____ (b)__✔__

dash (a) to smash or to strike roughly

   (b) a short, fast run or race

3. Johnny made a dash for the ball as it flew past him, far out into the field.

   Dash means (a)_____ (b)__✔__

4. Everyone was shocked to see Tom dash the bottle against the wall and break it to pieces.

   Dash means (a)__✔__ (b)_____

hide (a) to put something away or keep it out of sight

   (b) the skin of an animal

7. Joe was planning to hide the rabbit skin so that his mother wouldn't see it.

   Hide means (a)__✔__ (b)_____

8. He wanted to use the rabbit hide to make his mother a purse.

   Hide means (a)_____ (b)__✔__

quiver (a) to shake with quick, little, trembling movements

   (b) a case for holding arrows

9. The Indian drew an arrow out of his quiver and fitted it to his bow.

   Quiver means (a)_____ (b)__✔__

10. The wind in the trees made all the leaves quiver as though they were frightened.

   Quiver means (a)__✔__ (b)_____

FIGURE 16.6 Part of an exercise that uses context to teach new words that have two meanings. From *Extension activities to accompany The Magic Word*, Teacher's Edition, by Albert J. Harris, Marion Gartler and Caryl Roman, p. 35. Copyright © 1974 by Macmillan Publishing Co. and reproduced by permission of the publisher.

Materials for Vocabulary Development

Many vocabulary-building activities are provided in workbooks that are correlated with basal readers and also in independent workbooks that cover a variety of comprehension skills (see pp. 503–509).

Workbook-like Materials

DEIGHTON, LEE C. *Vocabulary Development*, The Macmillan Reading Spectrum, Rev. Ed. (Macmillan, 1973). A series of 6 programmed workbooks for grades 4–6. Allows individualized practice.

HARDWICK, H. C. *Words are Important* (Webster). A series of 6 thin workbooks and alternate editions, junior high school and up, teaching some of the less common words in the Thorndike-Lorge *Teacher's Word Book* in lessons averaging 18 words each. A review after every third lesson is a good feature.

HODKINSON, KENNETH & ORNATO, JOSEPH G. *Wordly Wise*, Books 1–9 for grades 4–12 (Educators, 1971). Each book contains 30 lessons. Books 1–6 teach about 12 words per lesson, and Books 7–9 about 15 words. There are several kinds of exercises in each lesson.

WORKS, AUSTIN M. *A Vocabulary Builder*, Books 1–7, rev. ed. (Educators, 1964). A series of vocabulary workbooks for secondary school use. Emphasizes teaching of prefixes, roots, and suffixes and use of these in learning a basic vocabulary of difficult words.

Grow in Word Power, Compiled and Edited by Natalie Moreda (Reader's Digest Services, 1967). A compilation of exercises from the high school edition of the *Reader's Digest.*

Word Clues (EDL, 1962). A series of 7 programmed vocabulary workbooks emphasizing use of context in dealing with multiple word meanings. Self-administering and self-checking for grades 7–13. A related set of recordings is optional.

STANFORD, GENE. *Stanford/McGraw-Hill Vocabulary* (Webster, 1971). A 6-book series for grades 7–12. Each short lesson introduces two new words; build-in systematic review.

DIEDERICK, PAUL, *et al. Vocabulary for College* (Harcourt). Series of workbooks at 4 levels designed to help high school students to master the 976 word meanings most frequently missed by college freshmen.

Scope/Visuals (Scholastic). A series of spirit masters and matching acetate transparencies for use with junior and senior high students reading at a fourth- to sixth-grade level. *Vocabulary Building* covers homonyms and words describing people, actions, and things; *Word Power* contains 4 lessons each on homonyms and vocabulary building and dictionary skills; *Word Meaning through Context* has 7 lessons, each focusing on a single word and its multiple meanings; and *Figurative Language* contains 8 lessons on differences between literal and figurative language, comparisons, exaggerations, similes, etc.

Picto-Cabulary Series (Barnell Loft). *Basic Word Sets* include 36 illustrated booklets that cover 720 words for beginning readers; *Words to Eat, Words to Wear,* and *Words to Meet* each contain 6 different titles covering vocabulary from a range of topics; suitable for grades 5–9.

What's in a Name? and *Podunk and Such Places* (Barnell Loft). Each set contains 6 different titles, the first set focusing on people's names, the latter on names of places; useful as an introduction to etymology.

Vocabulab III (SRA). Kit, for use in grades 7–9, contains 150 exercises and 20 root and affixes word wheels. The material spans 6 reader levels and is taken from 10 interest areas.

Multi-media

Wordcraft Vocabulary Programs (Communacad). Has programs at four levels (grades 4–6, 6–8, 8–10, and 8–13) which also may be used in remedial work because of their adult format.

Target Green (Field). For grades 4–6, has lessons on word classification, use of context clues, homonyms, homographs, synonyms, antonyms, roots and affixes. *Target Orange,* for grades 7–9, emphasizes use of context clues, derivatives, figurative language and connotations.

Games

Fun with Words (Dexter and Westbrook). Series of gamelike aids at 6 levels for generating interest in word meanings.

Synonimbles and *Phantonyms* (Curriculum Associates). Games for intermediate-grade children. In the first, students must relate 2 given synonyms to an unknown third; 125 puzzles with clues at 5 levels. In the latter, the players must find a mystery word (antonym) concealed in the clue sentence; 110 puzzles at 5 levels.

Homonym Cards, Antonym Cards, Homophone Cards (DLM). Three games in which the basic task is to match pairs of pictured words, other tasks also may be required of the players in order to score points. Similar cards are published by Milton Bradley.

Press and Check Bingo Games (Milton Bradley). Four games, *Prefixes and Suffixes, Homonyms, Synonyms and Antonyms,* and *Abbreviations and Contractions.* In response to questions, the players push the tab above a possible answer and are able to see the answer-question relationship.

A variety of vocabulary games and exercises may be found in Platts (1970), Dale and O'Rourke (1971), and Wagner, Hosier, and Cesinger (1972).

II. READING IN THOUGHT UNITS

In first-grade material each line of print usually presents a sentence, or complete unit of thought. When sentences become too long to go on one line, the authors are careful always to break the sentence as a division between phrases, and the fact that the two lines form a sentence is shown by indentation. This kind of typographical arrangement encourages the children to expect a line of words to convey a unified meaning. Even at the pre-primer level, however, the sentence is not a complete, self-sufficient unit; from the beginning, each sentence is part of a sequence that tells a little story. The word has meaning as part of a phrase; the phrase, as part of a sentence; the sentence, as part of a paragraph; the paragraph, as part of a story.

Sentence Meaning

Long ago, Huey (1908) wrote: "Language begins with the sentence and this is the unit of language everywhere." Although children in beginning reading programs have already developed substantial competence in understanding and in speaking, they are usually not aware of the semantic rules that they follow. Some of them do not even realize that a sentence consists of separate words (Francis, 1973). For example, "How are you?" may be spoken and perceived as one undivided word: "Howaryuh?" Grasping the idea that sentences are composed of separate words which can be arranged in a great variety of sequences to express different ideas is an essential concept for the beginning reader.

Modern linguists stress the idea that every sentence has a surface structure and a deep structure (Jacobs and Rosenbaum, 1968). The sentence is understood when the meaning of the deep structure is grasped. Understanding of a sentence can be checked in a variety of ways. One of them involves choosing the two sentences that mean the same (have the same deep structure) from a set like the following:

a. He painted the house red.
b. He painted the red house.
c. He painted the house that was red. (Simons, 1971, p. 359)

Here *b* and *c* have the same deep structure and therefore the same meaning, while *a* and *b* have the same surface structure but different meanings.

What Makes a Sentence Difficult?

There is a complex interplay between word identification and interpretation, in which the first words of a sentence set up anticipations which influence both the word identifications and the comprehension of the rest of the sentence. If the rest of the sentence fits this anticipation the reader continues and usually is unaware that he has erred; if there is a misfit, he is likely to reread to get a reading that makes sense. The reader is not clearly aware of this complicated process.

Research on readability has shown again and again that two kinds of measures, combined in the correct proportion, provide most of the essential information needed for the measurement of the difficulty of reading materials (Chall, 1957; Klare, 1963; Bormuth, 1968). The first, and more important, is difficulty of vocabulary, which is usually measured by counting the percent of words that fall outside a particular list of common words. The second is the average number of words per sentence, or average sentence length. These two variables are the ones used in the Lorge Formula (1959), the Dale-Chall Formula (1948), the Spache Formula (1953, 1974), and the new Harris-Jacobson Readability Formulas for which directions are given in Appendix D (see pp. 658–675).

Long sentences are likely to be more difficult to understand than short sentences because they contain dependent clauses, embedded phrases and clauses, clauses introduced by the less common connectives, plural subjects or predicates, changes from the normal word order, and other constructions that complicate the reader's job of understanding. Direct measures of sentence complexity or depth have been devised (Allen, 1966; Yngve, 1962; Botel and Granowsky, 1972). Yet it seems that sentence length, which is so much more easily determined, does as good a job of indicating the reading difficulty of a selection as these more sophisticated measures (MacGinitie and Tretiak, 1971). Of course, this applies to whole selections and not to individual sentences.

One of the factors underlying comprehension difficulties in reading sentences is the fact that printed material tends to use a much more formal "register" or style of English than children are accustomed to in conversation. Children who have had much experience in listening to stories read to them before they enter school have become accustomed to such language and are not bothered much by it. At second-grade level a program in which the teacher regularly read stories to the children and discussed the stories with them seems to have had beneficial effects on comprehension (D. Cohen, 1971).

Development of Phrase Reading

As good readers proceed they organize the material into meaningful units such as phrases. Some poor readers do not do this, and as a result their comprehension is poor even when they have been pre-taught every word in the selection (Oakan, Wiener, and Cromer, 1971). Specific training in reading by phrases may not be needed by the good reader, but it can be very helpful to those who do not spontaneously read by phrases.

Oral reading provides a natural setting for the development of ability

When you watch / a ball game, / you like / a front seat. / You even try / to help / the team / by cheering them. / You think along / with the players / in every play. / In this way / you actually / take part / in the game./ Then you feel / that you helped / win it. / You can do / the same thing / when you read. / Come close / to the scene / of the story / and feel that / you are seeing / the incidents happen. / Think about / what you are / reading / or be one / of the characters. / You will then find / enjoyment / in reading, / and your ability / to read will / grow and grow.

FIGURE **16.7**   Part of a workbook exercise intended to develop efficient phrase reading and to diminish frequency of regressions. From Ullin W. Leavell and Betty D. Via, *Pathways to Build*, p. 116. The Reading Essentials Series, copyright © 1973 by Steck-Vaughn Co. Reprinted by permission of the publisher, Steck-Vaughn Co.

to read phrases as meaningful units. The alert teacher notices whether the child habitually groups his words or tends to read in word-by-word fashion. It is important to distinguish whether hesitations between words are caused by slowness in recognizing the words or by the habit of paying attention to only one word at a time. If a child departs from reading in a connected, meaningful way only when difficulties with particular words slow him down, the problem is primarily a word recognition difficulty rather than a phrasing problem. By encouraging children to read as if they were telling a story, the teacher trains the child to read with natural expression.

Many primary teachers prefer to present new words, not in isolation, but in phrases or sentences. For practice in word recognition they use phrase cards instead of word cards. Such phrase cards can be used in various ways: as flash cards for quick recognition, in following-directions games, in assembling sentences on a wall chart, in answering questions by selecting the proper phrase card, and so on. They should be aware, however, that most primary grade children cannot really perceive a phrase as a unit and therefore depend mainly on the first word and perhaps same distinctive feature of the card when phrase cards are used.

Comprehension questions can be used to direct attention to phrases. Oral questioning during a group reading lesson can emphasize phrase answers. For example, the following sentence occurs in a basal reader: "They got four windows and a door at the lumberyard." The teacher could ask, "Where did they get what they needed?" The correct answer necessarily requires reading "at the lumberyard" as a meaningful unit. Comprehension questions in written form, based on silent reading, can also require answers in phrase form. For example, on the same sentence, written answers could be requested to such questions as:

The boys got what they needed ———.
Underline the best answer:
The boys got what they needed
    at the store.   in the woods.
    at the lumberyard.   from their father.

The child whose progress in reading is normal does not need much special practice in reading phrases. Reading words in meaningful groups develops as part of the total pattern of reading skills, without having to be singled out for special attention.

Amble (1967) investigated the value of training in phrase reading for fifth- and sixth-grade pupils and for remedial reading pupils. He found that phrase reading can be improved with training, that it is independent of reading vocabulary, and that improvement in phrase reading is durable. Thus there is some justification for a moderate amount of specific practice in phrase reading.

Remedial Work in Phrase Reading

The child who reads word by word has difficulty in getting the meaning of a larger unit of thought such as a phrase, clause, sentence, or paragraph. He is unable to see the forest because of the trees. Because he is not anticipating meanings, he fails to utilize context clues and so makes unnecessary errors in word recognition. After he has read the words, he often has to go back and reread for meaning and even then may find it difficult to understand the material.

There are two main ways in which the habit of word-by-word reading develops. Word-by-word reading is frequently a secondary result of slowness and inaccuracy in word recognition. The child has to concentrate most of his attention on recognizing or figuring out the words and has little attention left for the meaning. After the word-recognition difficulty has been overcome, word-by-word reading frequently persists as a habit.

Word-by-word reading can also develop as a result of much practice in oral reading of the mechanical reading-in-turn type, when there is little or no discussion of the meaning. If the teacher does not seem to be concerned with the meaning, many children are satisfied to disregard it. Sometimes they read orally with some expression and apparent attention to the thought, but questioning discloses that they have not been attending to the meaning and have made no effort to remember what they were reading. Such

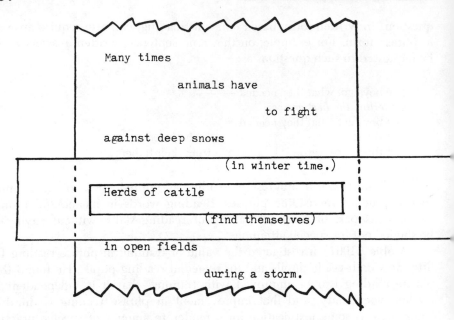

FIGURE 16.8   One type of practice material for reading in phrases. A strip of paper with one phrase typed per line is placed flat on the reading surface and a strip of stiff paper with a rectangular opening is moved steadily down the page, exposing one phrase at a time. Phrases in parentheses are concealed by the strip.

mechanical, thoughtless reading is often called "word-calling." Children whose reading is of this sort frequently draw a distinction between "just reading" and reading in order to be able to remember and answers questions. It is important to note that a child who reads with perceptible pauses between each two words may actually be understanding the material very well, while other children who sound as if they are reading fluently get little or nothing of the meaning.

Many different procedures can be helpful in overcoming word-by-word reading and faulty phrasing. Among the most helpful are the following:

1] In order to allow the child to concentrate on the phrasing and meaning, reading matter which is used for practice in phrasing should present few or no difficulties in word recognition and word meaning.

2] It is helpful to provide a good model for the pupils to imitate. The teacher can read a sentence orally with somewhat exaggerated phrasing and then have the children imitate her reading of the sentence. Reading of alternate sentences by teacher and pupils is also helpful. Some children gain considerable benefit from reading in unison with the teacher.

3] Practice can be given in reading printed material in which the phrases have been marked off by the teacher. A vertical line can be made in pencil between each two phrases, or each phrase can be underlined. The following sentence is shown with the phrases marked off in three different ways:

> The boy|is going|to the store|for some milk.
> The boy is going to the store for some milk.
> The boy is going to the store for some milk.

4] When special material is typed, mimeographed, or printed by hand, perhaps the best way to set off phrases is to leave additional space between them. For example:

> The boy   is going   to the store   for some milk.

5] After the pupil has developed some skill in the use of marked reading material, he can be given an unmarked selection to mark off the phrases. His ability to group words properly can be quickly evaluated, and faulty grouping can be corrected.

6] Practice can be given in the recognition of phrases as units during brief exposures. This can be done in a variety of ways.

   a) Phrases can be printed or typed on flash cards for practice in quick recognition. For use with a group, large cards with clear, black printing can be made. For individual practice, index cards of 3 x 5-inch or 4 x 6-inch size can be used. A cover card is lifted up and then replaced, using a flick of the wrist, as rapidly as possible; it is not possible to flash a card by hand too quickly for a reader to recognize a short, simple phrase.

   b) Phrase cards can be prepared and presented in a simple home-made tachistoscope (see p. 219).

   c) Both small, hand-held tachistoscopes and projection tachistoscopes are commercially available (see p. 563). Most makes of tachistoscopes also have phrase practice material to go with them.

   d) Material can be typed with one phrase on a line, as in Figure 16.8. A piece of stiff paper or cardboard with an opening the length of a full line is moved at a steady rate down the page, exposing one phrase at a time. Some remedial teachers prefer to keep the opening stationary and pull the page up. In the latter case, it is usually necessary to paste several pages together so as to form a continuous strip.

It is important for the child to try to use his new phrasing skills in his everyday reading. Unless the results of special drills are carried over into general reading, the time spent on them is wasted.

A word of caution is needed concerning the feasibility of getting slow, word-by-word readers to perceive phrases of two or three words in one glance. A college student who is well above average in reading ability generally perceives a line of about ten words in about four or five quick looks or fixations. An average high school student will require about ten fixations. To be able to average two words to each fixation is to be a very good reader. Obviously when a child is still somewhat slow and hesitant in recognizing single words, he should not be told to try immediately to see long phrases in one quick glance. The ability to set up goals which are within the child's reach in the near future is one of the marks of the expert teacher. If too high a goal is set at the beginning, discouragement will probably result.

Teaching the Use of Punctuation Marks

Some children become confused in reading connected material because they do not make use of the clues provided by punctuation. They have not learned to recognize a capital letter as a sign of the beginning of a sentence, a period or question mark as the end of a sentence, or a comma as a "partial stop" separating parts of a sentence. Children of somewhat higher reading ability may need assistance in the interpretation of semicolons, colons, and dashes. Simple explanation and supervised practice in noticing punctuation marks will usually overcome difficulties of this sort. If errors persist, coloring the first letter of a sentence in green, commas in yellow, and periods in red is an effective way to emphasize the punctuation.

As a follow-up after the teaching of punctuation, one can employ unpunctuated material. The pupil is given a selection that has been prepared with all punctuation omitted and is asked to insert the necessary symbols. If he has difficulty, he should be asked to read the passage orally. He may need to repeat considerably before he is able to decide where the punctuation marks belong. If he makes errors, they should be corrected and the reasons for the correct insertions should be explained.

Improving Ability to Read Sentences

As a child improves his word recognition, enlarges his vocabulary, learns to read in phrases, and develops an appreciation of punctuation, his ability to read sentences improves. Little else is usually required other than to give him practice in reading sentences and answering questions on them designed to test his comprehension.

When it is evident that weaknesses in reading sentences are prominent

EXERCISE 7

This exercise will show you how much meaning you can get by concentrating on important words. In the selection below, only the important words are given. Skim quickly over the selection. Work for speed.

Directions: Number your paper 1–8. Write the word or words that complete each of the sentences on page 168. Do not write in this book.

_____ coyote _____ always _____ considered _____ villain _____ western plains. _____ recent years, _____ moved east _____ become _____ problem _____ Adirondacks _____ New York State. No one _____ sure_____ _____ coyote _____ travel _____ far _____, but hunters, cattlemen _____ poultry keepers _____ hate _____ animal as _____ westerners _____.

_____ coyote _____ larger _____ fox _____ more crafty. _____ eat _____ anything _____ sheep, calves, chickens _____ mice. _____ everything _____ available. _____ will eat berries, grasshoppers _____ June bugs. _____ hard _____ trap _____ will not rush _____ bait. _____ Conservation Department _____ worried _____ coyotes _____ increasing _____ number.

_____ no one _____ reported _____ coyote _____ harmed _____ human _____. Perhaps _____ coward, or perhaps _____ too smart _____ close _____ man. _____ places, _____ bounty _____ $25 _____ paid _____ killing _____ coyote.

1. The coyote is described as a ___?___.
2. ___?___ is now troubled by coyotes.
3. Men who deal with ___?___ hate the coyotes.
4. A reward of ___?___ is often paid for killing a coyote.
5. A coyote will eat ___?___.
6. In this article he is compared to the ___?___.
7. The ___?___ Department is worried about the increasing number of coyotes.
8. Coyotes are not known to attack ___?___.

FIGURE 16.9 An exercise giving practice in gaining meaning using only the more important words in a selection. From Joseph C. Gainsburg, *Advanced Skills in Reading*, Book 1, pp. 167, 168. The Macmillan Co., 1967. Reprinted by permission of the publishers.

features of a pupil's comprehension, practice should be given in reading sentences, with a specific question asked about each sentence. The essential ideas of most sentences can be tested by questions asking *who, what, where, when, how,* or *why.* Some sample types of sentences and questions are as follows:

1] A horse can run fast.
   What can a horse do? _____
2] Honest men can be trusted not to steal. True   False
3] Do most automobiles have more than four wheels? Yes   No[1]
4] We were awakened by one of the servants who seemed alarmed.
   How did the servant feel? _____
   afraid   happy   angry   disappointed
5] Although they had to endure many hardships, the soldiers at Valley Forge remained confident that they would win the war because of their faith in their leader.
   Check one: ___ The soldiers were afraid that they would lose.
   ___ The soldiers trusted their general to bring victory.
   ___ The soldiers had an easy time resting at Valley Forge.

Help in locating the subject, verb, and object can be given by asking questions such as: Who did something? What happened? To whom (or to what) did it happen?

Difficulty in understanding sentences is related to the complexity of sentence structure. Simple sentences are usually understood without difficulty, provided that the pupil knows the vocabulary. Compound sentences with clauses joined by *and* or *but* are also generally easy. Complex sentences which contain subordinate clauses tend to be more confusing. When a pupil has difficulty in unraveling complicated sentences, guidance in sentence analysis is needed. Asking the pupil who did something, what did he do, to what did he do it, and so on, and showing him the answers when he cannot find them, is a serviceable procedure. The use of formal grammatical terms such as "prepositional clause" may confuse the pupil more than it helps.

The understanding of dependent or subordinate clauses depends to a considerable extent on familiarity with the meanings of the words that are used to introduce them. For effective reading above the lower grades it is necessary to understand the shades of meaning indicated by the commonly

1. While most children will answer, "No," a few will correctly argue that a spare wheel in the trunk makes "Yes" correct. This is, therefore, a faulty item. Formulating true-false or multiple-choice items for which only one answer is correct is not as easy as it may seem.

used connectives. For reading of any degree of complexity, acquaintance with the following list is essential:

Who, which, what, that, from, whom, to which
How, like, so as, so that, in order to
Because, since, as, thus
Until, as soon as, before, while, as, after, following
If, unless, provided that, whether, should
As well as, all but, hardly, except, without, although
However, moreover, therefore, nevertheless

One of the main reasons why these words may cause trouble is the fact that many pupils are not accustomed to speech and conversation which makes use of them to any extent. Practice in the construction of sentences employing these connectives is one good way to clarify their meanings so that they can be understood when they are met in reading. Paraphrasing or expressing the same idea in different words is another valuable form of exercise for this purpose.

This chapter has been concerned with the comprehension of words, phrases, and sentences. Understanding of these units of meaning is a basic necessity if the reader is to make sense out of longer selections. However, a mastery of the parts does not necessarily bring with it mastery of the whole; it is possible to read each word, phrase, and sentence correctly and yet not gain a comprehensive grasp of a connected selection. When the unit of reading matter is longer than a single sentence, as it usually is, higher-level comprehension skills are involved. These are considered in the next chapter.

SUGGESTED ADDITIONAL READING

BAMMAN, HENRY A.; DAWSON, MILDRED A.; & MC GOVERN, JAMES J. *Fundamentals of basic reading instruction* (3rd ed.). New York: McKay, 1973. Chap. 11.

BOND, GUY L. & WAGNER, EVA BOND. *Teaching the child to read* (4th ed.). New York: Macmillan, 1966. Chap. 9.

DALE, EDGAR & O'ROURKE, JOSEPH. *Techniques of teaching vocabulary.* Palo Alto, Calif.: Field Educational, 1971.

DURKIN, DOLORES. *Teaching them to read* (2nd ed.). Boston: Allyn and Bacon, 1974. Chap. 13.

GATES, ARTHUR I. *The improvement of reading* (3rd ed.). New York: Macmillan, 1947. Chap. 11.

HAFNER, LAWRENCE E. *Improving reading in middle and secondary schools* (2nd ed.). New York: Macmillan, 1974. Sect. 10.

HARRIS, ALBERT J. & SIPAY, EDWARD R. *Effective teaching of reading* (2nd ed.). New York: McKay, 1971. Chap. 10.

————. *Readings on reading instruction* (2nd ed.). New York: McKay, 1972. Chap. 9.

LAPRAY, MARGARET. *Teaching children to become independent readers.* New York: Center for Applied Research in Education, 1972. Chap. 8.

ROSWELL, FLORENCE G. & NATCHEZ, GLADYS. *Reading disability: diagnosis and treatment* (2nd ed.). New York: Basic Books, 1971. Chap. 7.

TINKER, MILES A. & MCCULLOUGH, CONSTANCE M. *Teaching elementary reading* (3rd ed.). New York: Appleton-Century-Crofts, 1968. Chap. 7.

17

Improving Reading
Comprehension, II

This chapter continues the discussion of reading comprehension. It begins with consideration of the nature of comprehension. It continues with methods for enhancing a number of specific comprehension skills, discusses the development of study skills and habits, outlines procedures for remedial work in comprehension, and concludes with a section on materials for comprehension development.

I. THE NATURE OF READING COMPREHENSION

In his pioneering report on reading comprehension, E. L. Thorndike (1917) concluded that "reading is a very elaborate procedure, involving the weighing of many elements in a sentence, their organization in the proper relations one to another, the selection of certain of their connotations and the rejection of others, and the cooperation of many forces to determine final response . . . the act of answering simple questions about a simple paragraph . . . includes all the features characteristic of typical reasonings." Simons (1971, 1972) reviewed seven approaches to the understanding of reading comprehension and concluded that not a great deal of progress has been made since Thorndike. Since much is still unknown about reading comprehension, both the instructional procedures used and the materials employed are based more upon the intuitions and accumulated experience of reading teachers than on research evidence.

Simons suggested that a more promising approach to the understanding of comprehension might lie in the application of linguistic principles. But linguists have only recently begun to develop a theoretical analysis of language that might provide a base for a theory of comprehension. This has not yet been refined to the point where it can be translated into teaching methods and materials. Thus it is easy to state that comprehending a sentence requires a grasp of its deep structure, but ways of helping children to become more capable at discovering deep structure have not yet been developed and tested.

However, the broad principles of transfer of training apply to reading as they do to other areas of learning. Maximum transfer is possible when the training tasks resemble as closely as possible the situations in which the trained skill is to be used. Opportunities to employ a learned skill are most likely to be realized when the learning situation has been set up with generalization and transfer in mind.

An example of results that fit transfer theory is a study (Kennedy and Weener, 1973) in which equated groups of below-average readers in third grade were given training in filling in missing words (cloze procedure). The group that practiced listening to the selections and supplying the missing words made a higher mean score on the *Durrell Listening Comprehension Test*, while the group that read the selections silently and supplied missing words scored higher on the *Durrell Reading Comprehension Test*. Although there were only five practice sessions, both experimental groups did better than control groups on listening, but only the reading experimental group was significantly ahead in reading comprehension. These results suggest that time spent in reading comprehension practice will give more payoff than time spent in listening practice, if better reading comprehension is the goal.

Statistical Analysis of Reading Comprehension

A series of factor-analysis studies of reading comprehension, begun by F. B. Davis (1944), has come out with varying conclusions as to whether reading comprehension contains a number of separable subskills or must be considered a fairly unitary ability. F. B. Davis (1968, 1971) presented evidence that at senior high school level the following subskills are identifiable: recalling word meanings, drawing inferences about a word from context, getting the literal sense meaning of details and weaving together ideas in the content, drawing inferences from the content, and recognizing an author's purpose, attitude, tone, mood, and techniques. R. L. Thorndike (1973–74) reanalyzed Davis's data and concluded they showed the presence of a separate word knowledge factor, but that none of the other skills was separately distinguishable and they could all be described as "reasoning in reading." A third analysis of Davis's data using new factor-analysis techniques (Spearritt, 1972)resulted in the conclusion that four skills are distinguishable (recalling word meanings, drawing inferences from the content, following the structure of a passage, and recognizing a writer's purpose, attitude, tone, and mood). Spearritt concluded, however, that aside from word knowledge, which accounted for most of the variance, other types of comprehension tests are so highly intercorrelated that they largely measure "reasoning in reading." F. B. Davis (1972) essentially agreed with Spearritt when he pointed out that word knowledge and reasoning in reading accounted for about 89 per cent of the variance, leaving only 5 per cent for the other comprehension subskills. Davis also suggested that the following abilities might be highly important in determining comprehension: decoding skill, listening vocabulary, memory for ideas heard, and ability to weave ideas together.

Chapman (1969), using statistical arguments, presented a hierarchical skills theory of comprehension, which states that comprehension is made up of separate but correlated skills and that these differ in complexity because the more complex skills include all or parts of the simpler or more basic skills. Her view is consistent with Davis's results and is corroborated by her findings that training in sentence comprehension also improves paragraph comprehension, but training in paragraph comprehension does not improve sentence comprehension (Chapman, 1971). It is also supported by Cromer's (1968) study of the effects of using material grouped in phrases. Poor comprehenders who were good in word recognition benefited from the phrasing practice, while poor comprehenders who were poor in word recognition did not benefit.

Logical Analysis of Reading Comprehension

The *Taxonomy of Educational Objectives: Cognitive Domain* (Bloom, *et al.*, 1956) is a classification of objectives designed to systematize the desired intellectual outcomes of education in a comprehensive and logically sound hierarchical arrangement. Barrett adapted the Bloom taxonomy to produce a classification of reading objectives (see Clymer, 1968). Barrett used five main headings (literal comprehension, reorganization, inferential comprehension, evaluation, and appreciation), each of which had subheadings and finer subdivisions. For example, literal comprehension had two main subheadings (recognition, recall), and each of these is further divided into details, main ideas, sequence, comparison, cause and effect, and character traits. Similar subdivisions are used for inferential comprehension.

Another widely used classification employs four main headings: 1) literal comprehension, the skill of getting the primary, literal meaning; 2) interpretation, the probing for greater depths of meaning; 3) critical reading, the evaluating and passing of personal judgment; and 4) creative reading, which starts with an inquiry and goes beyond implications derived from the text (N. B. Smith, 1972). Still another classification identifies three levels of comprehension: literal, interpretive, and applied—students read to find out what the author said, what the author meant, and how to use the ideas (Herber, 1970). It is evident that inferential comprehension means the same as interpretation, evaluative and critical are synonyms, and creative reading and application are somewhat alike but not identical.

Granted that the correlations among reading comprehension tests are high and that there is not complete agreement as to how to classify the skills involved, it still makes sense to provide practice in answering many different kinds of questions. When this is done, students can improve their ability to reason while reading many kinds of materials with a variety of specific purposes. They can also learn what questions to ask themselves while reading different kinds of material.

Teacher's Questions and Objectives

Literal comprehension is the simplest level of comprehension and the one that makes the least demands on reasoning. Research indicates that questions calling for the literal meaning are the kinds most frequently asked by elementary school teachers. Such questions usually call for an answer directly in the words of the book, or a paraphrase. Guszak (1966, 1967) classified teachers' questions under six categories and found the following percentages: recognition, 13.5; recall, 56.9; translation, 0.6; conjecture, 6.5; explanation, 7.2; and evaluation, 15.3. The emphasis on recognition and recall (literal comprehension) was higher in the primary grades than in grades 4–6. The highest-scoring teachers not only asked more inferential and evaluation questions, but also gauged their questions so as to elicit a low percentage of incorrect responses, and were less likely to allow an incorrect or irrelevant response to pass unchallenged. High reading groups were more likely to be asked questions calling for evaluation, explanation, or conjecture, while low reading groups were asked mainly recall and recognition questions. Thus the children most in need of improvement in reasoning while reading were given the fewest opportunities to practice higher comprehension skills.

Another study compared the objectives stated by primary teachers with the questions they asked (Bartolome, 1969). The most frequently stated objectives involved analysis and application. The most frequently asked questions pertained to memory (47.5 per cent), while few questions involved application (2.3 per cent) and evaluation (2.6 per cent). Thus there was quite a contrast between the stated objectives of the teachers and the questions they actually asked. In addition, many of the objectives as stated by the teachers were quite vague.

Guiding the Development of Reading Comprehension

Since most elementary teachers use basal readers, the lesson plans in the teachers' guides largely determine the kinds of comprehension practice the pupils will receive. Guided silent and oral reading is usually preceded by a question which alerts the children to look for a main idea. After they have read the selection and their answers to that question have been discussed, a detailed rereading is guided by a sequence of questions. The degree to which these questions emphasize literal comprehension and recall or making inferences and judgments varies greatly from one series to another. Some teachers prefer to formulate their own questions and ignore the guide. Some rely largely on the comprehension exercises in the related workbook or stencil, which also differ in skills emphasized from series to series. In a language-experience or individualized reading program the teacher usually improvises questions calling for comprehension or recall.

Training can improve teachers' abilities to use a variety of types of questions. When student teachers were required to practice writing questions to fit objectives based on the Bloom taxonomy, the proportion of memory questions dropped from 74.3 per cent to 45.6 per cent, with a corresponding increase in questions calling for translation, interpretation, application, analysis, synthesis, and evaluation (Galloway and Mickelson, 1973). It must be remembered that if higher comprehension skills are built upon lower ones, literal comprehension is a necessary prerequisite for inferential and evaluative comprehension and needs to be checked. Devoting 50 or 60 per cent of questions to literal comprehension of various kinds seems reasonable.

Stauffer (1969) advocates a type of lesson plan which he calls a "directed reading-thinking activity." In this, pupils preview a selection to identify purposes for reading it, are encouraged at several points to conjectures about how the story will develop, and verify their anticipations by reading. Group discussion is encouraged. "Thus, the role of the teacher becomes one of organizer, moderator, and intellectual agitator while the students become active participants in the group process" (Petre, 1972). Petre reported that fourth graders taught with a directed reading-thinking strategy showed more quantity, higher quality, and greater variety of responses than those taught with a typical basal reader lesson plan.

II. DEVELOPING SPECIFIC COMPREHENSION SKILLS

Although some doubt exists about the statistical independence of types of comprehension, as we have seen above, there is evidence that specific practice tends to produce improved performance in the skill practiced. For example, fourth graders given systematic practice in following printed directions made more improvement in following printed directions than a control group given regular basal reader instruction (Calder and Zalatimo, 1970).

Such special practice will not work, however, if the material is so difficult that decoding the words, phrases, and sentences is a challenging or frustrating task. If a reader lacks a background of information and concepts in a particular area, he may be unable to apply his paragraph comprehension skills to material which takes that background for granted (Levine, 1970). This is especially true in content subjects. In one study, all of the eighth-grade texts analyzed were too difficult for a majority of the eighth-grade pupils (Janz and E. H. Smith, 1972). For the development of comprehension skills it is essential to use materials which are within the pupil's instructional level.

There is not enough space in this chapter to discuss all of the specific comprehension skills. A few of them are considered below.

Reading for Main Ideas

Reading for the Central Thought. One of the most valuable of comprehension skills is the ability to find the main idea or central thought in what one reads. To be able to select the most important thought from a mass of words calls for an ability to distinguish between essentials and nonessentials, between the most important idea and subordinate details or illustrations. It is a form of reasoning which involves comparison and selection. It is not strange, therefore, that children of below-average intelligence often have more trouble with this type of comprehension than they do in reading and understanding details.

Several different kinds of practice can be given to develop this type of comprehension.

1] In story reading, comprehension of the significance of an incident can frequently be tested by asking what feeling or emotion was felt by the main character during or after the incident.
2] Another form of question appropriate for story material is a request for a one-sentence summary of the incident.
3] In formational material, one can ask the pupils to select the main idea in each paragraph. The questions can take the form of multiple-

choice items in which the most adequate statement of the main idea is to be selected from other statements, or they can call for oral or written answers in sentence form.

Learning to find key sentences is helpful. In the upper grades and secondary school, children can be taught to look for a topic sentence which states the most important or most inclusive idea in the paragraph. Usually this is the first sentence, sometimes the last sentence. Sometimes it is within the paragraph. Not every paragraph has a topic sentence; in some, the main idea has to be generalized from the entire paragraph.

4] After skill has been attained in finding the central thought in single paragraphs, similar practice questions can be used, based on a short selection of a few paragraphs.

5] An excellent way of helping children to develop skill in finding and expressing main ideas is to have them practice writing headlines for selections, as though they were preparing the selections for a newspaper.

6] Another variation is to provide practice in making up a title for a selection, or in choosing the most satisfactory of several proposed titles. This can be done for both single paragraphs and longer selections.

7] Many authors provide headings, subheadings, marginal notes, introductory statements, final summaries, or other ways of emphasizing what they consider to be the most important ideas. Discussion of the use of these aids is helpful to the pupils, who otherwise might fail to use them.

8] Similarly, readers should learn to pay special attention to introductory and concluding paragraphs.

Skimming to Get a Total Impression. A very useful reading skill is skimming, which involves very superficial, rapid reading to get a general overall impression. Some of the situations in which skimming is useful are as follows:

1] Looking over a chapter in a textbook, prior to serious study, in order to get an idea of the general scope of the chapter.

2] Sampling a few pages of a novel or other type of work to form an opinion as to whether it is worth reading.

3] Going quickly through an article on a controversial issue to find out the author's point of view, without bothering to note his specific arguments.

4] Looking through reading material to judge if it is likely to contain the kind of information one is seeking.

5] Examining reading material to decide if it is comprehensible or too difficult.

In this type of skimming, the reader must have a specific purpose. The teacher may suggest reading activities as the following:

"John, look this book over and let me know if you think you would enjoy reading it." "Phyllis, look over these three books and decide which one will help you most in your selection of an Indian legend that the class could make into a play." "Harold, look through the section on mining in this book to see if it is too hard for you to read." As with other reading skills, improved efficiency in this type of reading comes gradually with motivated practice. Skimming can be successfully taught to sixth-grade pupils (Harrington, 1970). One useful skimming technique involves reading only the first sentence of each paragraph, while reading the introduction and conclusion or summary more carefully.

Reading to Note and Recall Details

There are many reading situations in which it is just as important to note and remember significant details as it is to understand the main ideas. This is especially true in the type of functional reading called *study*, in which the purpose is to assimilate as thoroughly as possible the material presented by the author. Some pupils who are expert, rapid readers in fiction and who get the main thoughts easily in factual material seem to have little or no interest in details, do not notice them as they read, and cannot remember them later. Balanced training in reading should include practice in reading for details.

It is probable that in American education too much attention has been paid to details as such, standing alone and unrelated to the situations in which they have significance. This tendency is sometimes encouraged by teachers who make up tests consisting mainly of questions on minor points. A general fondness and esteem for the ability to recall isolated, unrelated bits of information is glorified in many of the radio and television quiz programs which have large audiences. There are too many questions that ask who, what, where, and when, and too few questions that call for meaning, significance, or analysis of relationships.

Ideally, children should be taught to see details in their relation to the major ideas which they support. Details have many functions in expository material: they provide concrete illustrations which make a generalization more meaningful; they provide evidence in support of a conclusion; or they show ways in which an idea can be applied. What is needed is not so much a disparagement of attention to details as encouragement of the ability to relate the details to the major ideas.

16. Clever Workmen

The American Indians knew how to do a surprising number of things. The men made scrapers, hammers, axes, and chisels of stone, and smaller tools of wood and bone. Their arrows, tipped with stone or bone, were powerful weapons. Fish were caught with hooks made of bone, with spears, or with nets woven from the fibers of tree bark. Wooden traps were set for small animals on land.

Indian women were excellent weavers. They wove fine mats of rushes and grasses for the walls of their houses, and baskets in which to store food. Some tribes could weave baskets so tight they would hold water. Indian women also knew how to shape jars and bowls of clay and bake them in a hot fire.

Probably the two most important things the Indians made for their own use were snowshoes and birchbark canoes. Snowshoes enabled them to travel quickly over the frozen crust of snow when hunting game. The birchbark canoes, being light and easy to paddle, carried them quickly across lakes and along streams.

1. Indian hammers, axes, and chisels were made of
   a. bone   b. stone   c. wood   d. clay
2. Mats for the inside of the house were made by
   a. sewing   b. baking   c. weaving   d. stitching
3. The fibers of tree bark were used to make
   a. fishhooks   b. jars   c. pipes   d. nets
4. Indian women shaped jars and bowls of
   a. clay   b. bone   c. grasses   d. wood
5. Indians were able to travel over snow with
   a. birchbark canoes   b. spears   c. snowshoes

FIGURE 17.1   Exercise to develop ability to read for details. Reprinted with the permission of the publisher from Arthur I. Gates and Celeste C. Peardon, *Gates-Peardon Reading Exercises,* Intermediate-RD. Teachers College Press, © 1963.

Some of the kinds of practice in noting and recalling details in reading are as follows:

1] In informal discussion after oral or silent reading, the main thought should first be discussed. Then attention can be called to the details by such questions as:
   What are the ways in which this is shown?
   What evidence of the truth of this statement is presented?
   What applications of this idea are given?
   What are the places where this holds true?
2] An incomplete outline of a selection can be presented, with the main ideas filled in and blank spaces left for the details. After reading, the pupils complete the outline. See Figure 17.4.
3] Straightforward questions about details also have their uses. Questions can be put in multiple-choice, completion, or short-answer form. The multiple-choice type is quicker to mark, but the other forms encourage a more attentive attitude while reading because they require recall rather than simple recognition.

Ability to Find Answers to Specific Questions

There are many reading situations in which the reader has a specific question in mind and reads to find an answer to that question. Sometimes the question is one which requires careful reading and analytical reasoning; for example, reading to find out why oxygen is essential for combustion to take place. In such reading the question provides point, purpose, and a way for the reader to determine if his reading was satisfactory: Does he have an answer? Children who have not had practice in reading to find answers to definite questions are likely to have difficulty in selecting the relevant from the irrelevant; even superior readers in the middle grades have difficulty in distinguishing between paragraphs that are helpful in providing information on a specific question and paragraphs that are somewhat related, but provide no information on that question. At times, therefore, questions should precede reading, and the reading should be for the purpose of answering those particular questions. Written or oral answers, followed by discussion, provide a means for judging success and correcting errors.

Scanning.   One of the most important types of comprehension skills is the ability to skim rapidly over reading material. Two kinds of skimming can be distinguished (Fleming, 1968). One kind involves rapid reading to find the answer to a very specific question, such as a name, a date, a telephone number, and so on. This is often called *scanning*.

Practice in learning how to scan for a specific item of information can be best provided through use of the kinds of material that are normally scanned in functional reading. Some of the kinds of question to which answers are found by scanning are as follows:

On what date did a certain event take place?
What is the Mason-Dixon Line?
Who was the American commander at the Battle of Saratoga?
What is the largest wheat-producing state?
What are the leading industries in Boston?
What is an Indian tent called?
What is Mr. John X. Smith's telephone number?
At what theater is a particular moving picture playing?

To give practice in scanning, the teacher can prepare in advance a list of questions based on the reading matter to be used. The questions should be presented to the pupils before they read the selection, and they should be encouraged to find the answers as quickly as possible and write them. After the pupils have finished, there can be discussion of the answers, with oral reading of the sentences which contain the answers, or the written answers can be collected and scored as a test. Material of many different sorts can be used. There is no reason why schools should not make greater use of such reading materials as daily newspapers for practice in skimming. Textbooks in the various content subjects can also be used to good effect.

The expert at scanning for specific information has developed a distinctive skill which is quite different from other types of reading. As he runs his eyes rapidly over the material, he does not absorb the meaning, but merely notices that what he is looking for is not there. When he comes to the desired item, it seems to stand out as if in boldface type. Some people are able to achieve almost incredible speed in scanning.

Reading to Follow a Sequence of Events

An essential part of the understanding of narrative material, whether fictional or historical, is the ability to note the order or sequence of events, to grasp the cause-effect relationships involved, and to anticipate the rest of the story. Practice in this type of comprehension can be given in many ways, of which the following are examples:

1] The most effective and most natural procedure is to ask for a retelling of the story. Omissions of significant events, changes in the order of events, and misunderstandings can easily be noted and corrected through discussion and rereading.
2] As a group or class exercise following silent reading, the major

CAN YOU SCAN?

You look down a list of names to see if yours is on it. You glance at a newspaper article to see if the person or team you rooted for won. You pick up the movie listings to learn what is playing at the Diamond Theater. When you do these things, you are *scanning* the material.

Scanning means letting your eyes pass quickly over some lines of print until you come to the part you want. You do not read anything until you find that part. *Then you read*—learning just what you want and no more.

Scanning can save you time if you use it wisely. When you want to answer a question that calls for a specific fact, you should scan. Of course, before you scan, you must know what information to look for.

Scan the following article to find the answer to this question: How old was Chico when he left school? _____

> Chico Hinojosa, 28, still cannot believe he is a store manager. Ten years ago, he was making $26 a week as a grocery helper in a small store in Kingsville, Texas. As the oldest son in a large family, Chico had left school to work at the age of 16.
>
> Life was hard for his family, with nine children. His father, a railroad worker, could never count on more than six months of work each year. So Chico got a job at the grocery store, where he mopped floors, trimmed vegetables, stocked shelves, checked out groceries, and packed them.

You should not have read anything else in the article besides the information asked for. If you did, you were not letting your eyes move quickly enough. You should try to scan very quickly, until you come to the information you want.

FIGURE 17.2   Exercise to develop scanning skills. Reprinted by permission from *Sprint* by Beryl Goldsweig, © 1970 by Scholastic Magazines, Inc., reduced in size.

events described in the selection can be listed in scrambled order on the board or in mimeographed form, and the pupils can be asked to number them in the order in which they happened, or to rewrite the list in correct order.

3] The habit of thinking ahead while reading, and trying to anticipate the story, can be developed by presenting brief unfinished stories and asking the pupils to make up a suitable ending for each, or to select the most plausible of several suggested endings. In a longer story, the teacher can stop at a critical point and ask the pupils what they think will happen next.

Following Printed Directions

One of the most important uses for reading in everyday life is to find out how to do things. In former times, children learned mainly by watching and imitating their elders. In modern life, people must rely more and more on printed directions and manuals of procedure. The housewife with her cookbook, the auto mechanic with his printed specifications for different makes and models, the surgeon reading an account of a new type of operation, the worker filling out a social security application—all need to be able to read carefully and accurately and to follow a series of directions precisely and in correct order. During World War II, the armed forces were able to train millions of men to become hundreds of different kinds of specialists largely because the men could teach themselves by following directions in printed manuals.

Practice in reading and following directions is best provided in relation to activities which children wish to carry out or skills which they want to learn. In many subjects, textbooks contain directions which can be used for reading practice. This is particularly true in arithmetic and science. Directions for handwork activities can also be used to good effect. If the task is one easily corrected or repeated, the children can attempt to carry it out with no preliminary discussion, and the teacher can judge by the results whether the directions were properly read. If the task is a long one or involves expensive materials, it is desirable first to discuss the directions and clarify any misconceptions through rereading and further discussion.

Many different sources of material can be used. Children like to work on directions from the *Scout Handbook*, magazines like *Popular Mechanics*, books such as *How to Make Toys*, directions for performing scientific experiments, and so on. Or they can be interested in cooking recipes, directions for sewing, knitting, making marionettes, and the like. When additional practice in following directions seems to be needed, workbook exercises can be employed.

Grasping the Author's Plan

Good writing is organized writing, in which the author starts with something he wants to say, thinks out the order, sequence, relative importance, and interrelatedness of the specific ideas he intends to convey, and plans his exposition accordingly. In fiction there are characters to be introduced, a setting to be described, and a line of action which, if well planned, leads up to a climax. In informational or factual writing there are usually an introduction, a body, and a conclusion or summary. There are differences between exposition and argument, between writing intended to inform and writing intended to persuade. The particular pattern a writer uses can vary greatly, but in well-written material the pattern should be discernible.

In books written for children, many types of clues are provided which can be used to discover the author's plan. A chapter may start with an overview and end with summary and questions for application. In between there are headings, subheadings, material in bold type, marginal notes, and so on, which help the reader to determine what a particular section is about. Although the utility of these devices seems obvious and the purpose clear, many children need specific guidance in how to use these aids.

Development of Critical Reading Ability

Nearly all reading tests now in use attempt to measure the success of the reader in understanding what the author has to say. Comparatively few have tried to find out how well the reader can evaluate what he reads.

An important type of critical reading involves comparison of two or more sources of information. Children are usually amazed when for the first time they find two authorities contradicting each other. An experience like that can serve as a preliminary to discussion of such questions as the reputation and prestige of each author, his impartiality or bias, the comparative recency of the two sources, and so on. Reading experiences of this sort develop naturally when children do wide reading to find data on a problem. The teacher should be alert to make use of such occasions as steppingstones toward a more mature attitude on the credibility of reading matter. In the study of current events, comparison of the treatment of an event by two newspapers or magazines of opposing points of view can form an effective point of departure.

A second type of critical reading involves considering new ideas or information in the light of one's previous knowledge and beliefs. The thoughtful reader asks himself: Is it reasonable? Is it possible? He does not, of course, automatically reject the unfamiliar idea or challenging conclusion. But he becomes doubly alert when he finds disagreements with what he has previously accepted as true.

One of the most important aspects of critical reading is the ability to detect and resist the influences of undesirable propaganda. In recent years, the molding of public opinion has become tremendously important in political and social affairs. While the term "propaganda" has sometimes been defined to include all activities which are intended to influence people in a given direction, concern has been centered mainly on the kinds that attempt to persuade people to believe or act in a biased fashion.

There is reason to believe that teachers do influence the degree to which children read critically, by the kinds of discussions they lead. Davidson (1967) found significant gains in the critical reading of elementary school children when he trained teachers to encourage critical thinking by giving them the results of an interaction analysis of their tape-recorded lessons and having them listen to their own lessons. Listening to the lessons without the interaction feedback was ineffective.

It is not easy, however, for teachers to change their established personal habits of questioning. Some teachers in a large-scale study of critical

7 REVIEW

The preceding three lessons introduced and gave practice on the *shifty word,* the *false authority,* and the *either-or fallacies.* In this lesson you are to identify these fallacies when they occur. Be careful, for some items may not contain any of these fallacies.

Directions: On your answer sheet write *SW* for the *shifty word, FA* for the *false authority,* and *EO* for the *either-or* fallacy; otherwise write *NF.*

1. The President was much distressed at the reception Congress gave a literacy education bill. Since it is our duty to help those in distress we should write our congressmen and ask that they support the bill.

2. Research conducted by the British Government Laboratories reveals that cigarette smokers are more likely to get lung cancer than non-smokers.

3. While it is important that we consider the findings of scientists concerning the link between cigarette smoking and cancer, we cannot ignore the opinion of the millions who smoke. There are more of them then there are of the scientists. In a democracy the opinion of a majority should be accepted.

4. Wives and children are dependents, and persons who are dependent upon others are unable to take care of themselves; so wives should be treated like children and not permitted to vote.

5. When some of the students in a class complained that the classroom was too hot, others said it was too cold. Since it must have been one or the other, the teacher thought that the students were complaining in order to waste time.

6. The Declaration of Independence states that man has the right to over-throw his government, so it is really illegal for the government to prosecute a man for advocating revolution.

7. The average person often uses the false authority, shifty word, and either-or fallacies without being aware of these errors. This indicates that the average man is likely to reason fallaciously at times.

8. Everyone knows that people are different. Human nature tells us that differences between peoples should be respected.

9. John is a scholar, and to speak of him as an athlete is silly. He can't be both!

FIGURE 17.3 A review exercise of three aspects of critical reading. Advanced secondary or college level. Reprinted with the permission of the publisher from William A. McCall, Edwin H. Smith, *Test Lessons in Reading-Reasoning.* Teachers College Press, © 1964.

reading continued to favor factual and application (noncritical) questions, despite participation in a special workshop and the availability of carefully planned units with illustrative question models (Wolf, King, and Huck, 1968).

Remembering What One Has Read

Many people, children and adults alike, complain that they understand what they read when they read it, but cannot remember it later. This is a serious complaint and one which deserves careful consideration.

There are, of course, large individual differences both in speed of assimilation and in permanence of retention. Some people have naturally better memories than others. However, the correct application of known and generally accepted principles of learning would enable most of these complainers to remember what they read far better than they do at present.

The principles listed below are not original, but can be found in almost every textbook of educational psychology.

1] Material is easy to remember in proportion as it is meaningful. It is very difficult to recall ideas that have been only partially understood.

2] Material that is well organized in the reader's mind is easier to remember than material which is unorganized. The efficient reader tries to grasp the author's plan and to understand the relationships between ideas and the relations between the major ideas and the facts or details which give them definite meaning.

3] Many people are aided in remembering what they read by outlining, summarizing, or taking notes as they read. Others obtain similar benefits from underlining significant points or writing comments in the margin.

4] An active intention to remember is an aid to recall. When one is determined to remember, one's attention seems better concentrated and one tends to read more effectively.

5] Recall should be selective. One cannot hope to remember everything that one reads. The points that one really wants to remember should be singled out for special attention.

6] A single reading is rarely enough. Most people have to do some reviewing and rereading if they want to remember for any length of time.

7] After reading, one should try to recall the points worth remembering and recite them to oneself. If there is time, it is desirable to check one's recall by rereading and then reciting again. At least half of the time spent (after the first reading) in trying to fix the material in memory should be spent in active recitation. Omission of this procedure is one of the most frequent errors of those who complain about their poor memories.

8] What we learn but never review or use is gradually forgotten. What we really want to remember must be refreshed by review from time to time.

Poor memory for what one has read, then, results from unselective, passive reading in the first place, followed by an overoptimistic failure to review and recite to oneself the points one wishes to remember. Both of these major faults are correctible.

Some teachers encourage reading without the intent to recall by the kinds of reading practice they give and the kinds of questions they ask. In most workbook exercises, the child is free to look back into the material if he cannot remember the answer. Unless some practice is given in answering questions with the book closed or the page covered, the child may become excessively dependent on rereading. He may also learn to read the questions first and then read for the answers, a desirable procedure in many situations, but not suitable when one is trying to stimulate the ability to recall. Excessive reliance on multiple-choice or true-false questions may also be harmful to recall, since such questions require only recognition of the correct answer, and pupils may become quite skillful at recognizing what they cannot remember. It is therefore important to ask recall questions and to provide at least some practice in reading with the intent to reproduce the gist of the material.

Encouraging Creativity in Reading

Creative reading may be described as going beyond understanding of reading matter to arrive at new ideas or conclusions. The encouragement of creativity has been a major goal for some psychologists and educators in recent years. They contrast convergent thinking (arriving at a specific correct answer) with divergent thinking (in which the individual can develop alternative answers, none of which is incorrect); divergent thinking is a synonym for creative thinking.

Reading teachers can encourage creative reading by a number of procedures. Some of them are as follows:

1] Stop the children at a given point in the story and ask each one to think of an ending for the story. Compare the endings developed with each other and with the one provided by the author.

2] After finishing a story, ask children to devise endings for it that are different from the author's ending. Let each child devise as many different endings as he can.

3] Ask children to use the plot of a given story, but to change the setting to a different time and place. What changes will have to be made?

4] Stop a story at a given point and change a specific event (*e.g.*, a character finds money instead of losing it). How will this change the rest of the story?

Procedures such as the ones just described can enliven the reading period and provide needed practice in applying creative thinking to reading.

III. THE DEVELOPMENT OF STUDY SKILLS

Functional reading, which means using reading skills for the purpose of getting information, is sometimes called work-study skills or just study skills. The outline of objectives on pages 7–10 lists four main subheads under functional reading: ability to locate needed material, comprehending information material, selecting the material needed, and organizing and summarizing the information gained. Another look at that list of objectives and their finer subdivisions is suggested at this point. A brief discussion of some of the main issues in study skills is presented below; for more complete treatments, see the references at the end of this chapter.

Learning to Locate Information

The most widely used tool in finding information is the index, a great timesaver to those who know how to use it. As soon as textbooks contain indexes, definite lessons in the use of an index should be provided. Teachers in higher grades can profitably devote time to the development of this study skill, if their pupils show the need of it.

In an introductory lesson on the use of an index, one should start with a problem to which an answer is desired; preferably one that can be found in an available textbook. Pupils can be asked to suggest headings under which the information might be classified. For instance, information on the number of cattle raised in Colorado might be sought in a social studies book under several headings: Cattle, production of; Colorado, cattle raising in; Production, of cattle; Meat, sources of; Livestock; and so on. After the most probable heading has been chosen in discussion, the group looks for that heading in the index. The other headings suggested can also be checked. When page references have been found, the group turns to the page indicated and skims to find the specific information desired. Skill in locating items in an alphabetical order should already have been developed through dictionary work. After the general procedure has been learned, the teacher can make up a series of questions to be answered by use of the index.

When the technique of using a book index has been fairly well mastered, the pupils should be encouraged to try their ability on the indexes of encyclopedias, almanacs, or atlases. The use of the card index in a library should also be taught. The skills required for locating entries to encyclopedias and bibliographic sources like the *Readers Guide to Periodical Literature* are similar in the main to those involved in using a book index. A suitable teaching sequence should include 1) knowledge of the kinds of information that can be found in the different types of reference works; 2) practice in thinking up several relevant headings or entries under which the information might be found; 3) in works of several volumes, how to choose the correct volume; and 4) the interpretation of abbreviations commonly employed.

The use of the table of contents of a book is usually introduced early in the primary grades. When one wants to find a particular story or section in a book one can turn to the table of contents and find out the page on which the selection begins. One can also locate a specific item within a section by finding the section and skimming through it. However, for those who know how to use an index, that is the faster way to locate specific details.

Comprehending Informational Material

Technical Vocabulary. As we have seen, knowledge of word meanings is a very important factor in reading comprehension. Every special field of knowledge has its own technical vocabulary. Successful teachers take pains to introduce new concepts and the verbal labels which represent them with meaningful illustrations and examples, guide the formulation of a statement of what the term means, and then check carefully to see if the concept has been really understood. Technical vocabulary is of two main kinds: words that are specific to that content field, like *divisor* and *longitude,* and words that have a specific technical meaning in addition to more general meanings, such as *bank interest* as contrasted with interest in art or interesting conversation. The teacher of each content field has the responsibility of making sure that the really important terms used in that field are understood.

Reading Maps, Graphs, Charts, and Tables. It is often possible for an author to present a large amount of material concisely in visual form by means of a map, a graph, a chart, or a table. Teaching children how to interpret these efficient aids to understanding is the responsibility of the teacher in each subject field in which they are used. Entirely too many students today have the habit of skipping past anything of this sort with the briefest glance. Teachers-in-training at the college sophomore and junior level are frequently unable to interpret the visual reading matter in their education textbooks. It is worth the time it takes to develop in each subject an understanding of these types of nonverbal reading materials.

Graphical representations of various types are being increasingly used, and more definite provisions are being made for teaching the interpretation of common types of graphical representations. For example, a series of arithmetic texts devotes twenty-six pages at the seventh-grade level to the explanation of different types of graphs and charts. Map reading has always been an important phase of geographical study. As new types of graphical reading matter become more widely used, teachers should provide practice in their interpretation.

Outlining and Summarizing

No skill is more essential to the student of today than the ability to write an effective summary of what he reads. When all of one's study is from a single textbook, written notes are not absolutely essential. But when one's study involves consulting a variety of sources, most of which are in a library and cannot easily be taken out again when one wants to review, a satisfactory summary is indispensable.

In addition to its value for review, note taking performs a useful function in enforcing selective, thoughtful reading. In taking good notes one must try to select the major from the minor points, decide what is worth recording, consider the relation of one idea to another, and rephrase the author's idea into a condensed but accurate restatement in one's own words. Passive, thoughtless reading is impossible when one is taking good notes.

In modern elementary schools, summarizing is a natural activity from the first grade on. Each experience story used in beginning reading is a little summary. In the planning of units or projects, the results of class discussions are summarized and organized in terms of main headings, and the questions or topics to be investigated are listed under their appropriate headings. As committee or individual reports are made, their important points are inserted in the unit outline. When they reach the higher grades, these children have a background of familiarity with the concept of an organized summary which makes it a comparatively simple task to teach them to apply the idea in their reading.

In teaching a group of children to outline, one should use material of a factual or textbook nature which is well organized and has a definite structure that is easy to detect. Material from scientific or social studies text-

books is generally most suitable. There should, of course, be some preliminary discussion of the importance of being able to outline what one reads.
The teacher can point out that an outline shows the relative importance of
each idea or fact, its relation to the other facts and ideas, and its place in
the whole selection; that it is, in effect, the skeleton or framework of ideas
which the writer has dressed up by expressing it in well-written sentences
and paragraphs. The skilled reader easily finds the framework, while ap-
preciating the decoration; the unskillful reader fails to discover the pattern
of the author's thinking, which is expressed by the outline of what he has
written.

Once motivation has been established, the task of the teacher is to present a series of graded practice exercises in outlining, in which the pupils
are given a great deal of help at first and proceed gradually to do more
and more of the outline by themselves. For the first two or three practices,
the teacher should place on the blackboard a complete outline of the
selection. After the pupils read the selection, the outline is discussed. In
this meaningful setting it is easy to explain the system of progressive indentation and the sequence of Roman numeral, capital letter, Arabic
numeral, small letter, and so on. When the group has learned the plan of
a formal outline, the second stage is to assign an outline in which the complete skeleton is shown, but only a few of the headings are filled in. After
reading, each pupil completes the outline, and discussion follows. In some
of these, the main headings are given and the details are to be filled in.
In others, the details are provided and the headings have to be inserted.
Figure 17.4 shows the kind of help given at this stage. In a third stage, the
structure of the outline is given, but no headings are filled in by the teacher.
In stage four, only the number of main headings is given, and in the final
stage the pupils write a complete outline without assistance.

In a teaching sequence of this sort, learning how to condense a sentence
into a few words can be achieved naturally through discussion of the most
satisfactory way to state a given point in the outline. Different statements
can be compared as to clarity and conciseness, and the best ones selected.
The writing of acceptable incomplete sentences, the leaving out of unnecessary words, and the writing of what is sometimes called "telegram style"
can be taught naturally in this way.

It is desirable to teach the use of the formal outline before taking up the
use of informal reading notes. The essential difference between good reading notes and a formal outline is the absence of the number-and-letter
scheme. Learning to make a formal outline, is, then, desirable as a preliminary. Once one has learned to think in outline terms, the trappings can be
discarded without losing the ability to reduce what one reads to its essential
structure. The writing of a précis, or paragraph-type summary, lacks the

HOW CLOTH IS MADE

I.   The history of weaving

   A. Hand looms

      1. _____

      2. _____

      3. _____

   B. Development of power looms

      1. _____

      2. _____

II. How cloth is made today

   A. A modern textile mill

      1. _____

      2. _____

   B. Modern fabrics

      1. _____

      2. _____

FIGURE **17.4**   Example of the kind of partially completed outline used
in the second stage of teaching outlining.

organizational structure which is so important and therefore seems to be a
less valuable technique than outlining, although desirable in summarizing
certain types of narrative material.

Learning to take efficient reading notes is not easy. Many students leave
out so much detail that the notes are ineffective because they cannot be
substituted for rereading the material. Other students take voluminous
notes, quoting verbatim at length, and get lost in the details; they often
miss important relationships. The correction of these faults has to start with
the erroneous reading habits reflected in the unsatisfactory notes. Then

some critical analysis and discussion with the student can help him to see how his note taking can be improved.

Assimilative Study

A systematic study procedure developed by Francis P. Robinson (1962), called the SQ3R system, has been very widely used. This system involves five steps: 1) survey—make a quick overview of the material; 2) question—turn each heading and subheading into a question; 3) read—to find answers to the questions; 4) recite—state the answers and evidence found to yourself, subvocally, orally, or in the form of written notes; and 5) review—at appropriate intervals for permanent retention. This system seems to be well grounded in the experimental psychology of learning, but has not been subjected to much experimentation.

Survey involves reading the table of contents, looking over the section headings and making a preliminary outline, reading the first and last paragraphs, and studying pictorial aids. Reading should be active; one should turn headings into questions, read to answer the questions, and check understanding by expressing the author's ideas in one's own words. Note taking involves organizing, restating the author's ideas, and underlying key words. Remembering involves spending a large amount of time in reciting to oneself, stressing key terms, distributing practice, and learning for the future.

One report indicates that the SQ3R system can be successfully taught to pupils in the seventh grade (Sister Mary Donald, 1967). Two comparable classes were taught social studies with the same materials; one class was taught the SQ3R plan and guided in applying it in studying the textbook, while the other class was given no special guidance in how to study their assignments. The experimental class finished the year significantly ahead on teacher-made tests, although there were no significant differences on standardized social studies tests. Although this was a small-scale study and lacked some desirable experimental controls, it does show that the SQ3R plan can be successfully taught as early as the seventh grade.

A number of minor modifications of the SQ3R formula have been developed. For example, "survey" is sometimes called "previewing." There has not been any experimental comparison to show any of these study pattern formulas to be superior to the others. Actually any study pattern which involves careful reading with good comprehension, followed by appropriate review, seems to work well for many students. Some students who do extremely well in college rely mainly on taking good notes while reading the material once quite carefully, and then reviewing the notes thoroughly before each test. Others are very successful with a pattern of a single quite careful reading involving the underlying of important sentences and phrases, with rereading concentrated on the underlined material shortly before each test (Carver, 1971b).

Research Reading

Although problem-centered or project-centered reading has been employed in schools to some extent since the beginning of the Progressive Education movement (A. J. Harris, 1964) very little research has been done on this important kind of reading. Over thirty years ago Gans (1940) studied the ability of superior readers in grades 4 through 6 to distinguish between paragraphs that are helpful in providing information on a specific question and paragraphs that are somewhat related, but provide no information on that question. Although these children scored well on standardized tests, they had considerable difficulty in selecting the relevant paragraphs. It seems probable that unless specific skills of research reading are taught, many children will not acquire them.

A necessary preliminary to the formulation of sound research in this area is a satisfactory classification of the behaviors involved in research reading. H. Alan Robinson (1965) has developed such a classification, based on the use of interviews, introspection, and written reports on the procedures used by bright fourth-grade pupils. The resulting categories include seven types of location skills and eight types of comprehension skills and closely resemble the classifications to be found in several textbooks on how to teach reading. The comprehension headings he used are: using experience and/or knowledge; defining the problem; grasping main ideas; reading for details; making inferences; drawing conclusions; comparing ideas; and understanding vocabulary.

This area of research-type reading is one in which considerable new research is needed.

Reading and Study Patterns for Specific Content Areas

Some curriculum areas require special adaptations of general reading skills. The responsibility for teaching these adaptations should lie with the teacher of that subject. If a remedial teacher finds that a child is failing in a subject and that the subject teacher has not provided guidance in how to read the subject matter, it is obviously desirable to provide the help needed.

Mathematics is an area in which reading has to be slow and thorough. A five-step reading pattern for reading arithmetical or other mathematical problems is as follows: 1) Read to visualize or grasp the situation presented. 2) Reread to note the specific facts given. 3) Note any difficult concepts or terminology and get help if needed. 4) Reread to select the operations to be used and to plan the solution. 5) After finding an answer, reread again to check the process chosen and the reasonableness of the solution (Earp, 1970).

Science is another area in which exactingly slow, careful reading and rereading is necessary. A science teacher who takes the trouble to guide his students in how to read a science textbook recommends the following:

> The reader first quickly looks over the material to be read to get the general idea; then he reads the material. I suggest that my students read only a few paragraphs at a time, attempt to grasp the ideas presented, and remember specific points, terms, or other data presented. Then, when the students are satisfied that they understand the paragraphs, they may proceed. After completion of the reading, they go through the material again, this time concentrating on individual words to be learned, data to be memorized, and the like. Finally they are asked to check themselves for comprehension by using the questions at the end of each section. (Ferguson, 1969)

Each curriculum area has some specialized types of reading material that require modified reading and study patterns. The interpretation of special types of illustrations such as maps, diagrams, graphs, and tables needs to be guided in each subject in which they form part of the reading material. Books providing detailed consideration of reading needs in particular curriculum areas will be found in the reference list at the end of this chapter.

Content Subject Instruction for Disabled Readers

Some teachers, particularly subject-matter specialists, feel that there is little that can be done to assist the student to learn if he cannot read the on-grade texts. Thus disabled readers, and at times even average readers, are left to flounder and fail because they cannot cope with the reading assignments. Contrary to such beliefs, things can be done to assist disabled readers to develop the concepts and attitudes called for by the curriculum.

Although by no means the only possible program change that can be made, material more appropriate for learner's level of reading ability might be obtained. Granted that material on exactly the same topic as in the on-grade text may not always be available, an increasing amount of material is becoming available for use in the content areas with students reading below grade level. For example, in the physical sciences Globe has published a series of twelve texts, *Pathways in Science,* for junior and senior high school students who are reading at the fifth–sixth grade level. There are three books for each earth science, chemistry, physics, and biology. Other reading materials that might be used include the Reader's Digest *Science Readers* whose reading levels go from the third to the sixth grade. Some of the materials found in the series listed in Appendix B may be appropriate.

For those who might benefit more from a "discovery" science program than a standard text, *Science/Search* (Scholastic) has four books, each of which has seventeen to nineteen investigations for junior and senior high school students to do.

In the social sciences, there are similar programs such as *American Adventures* (Scholastic), *American Studies* and *World Studies* (Globe), and *Civics, World History,* and *American History* (Follett). These materials are intended for use with junior-senior high students who are reading at the fourth- to eighth-grade level. The *Reading Range Plus* (Macmillan) is an adaptation of their on-grade social studies series for use with elementary school children who have reading problems. Other books written at a low level, but with high interest, are those in series such as *How They Lived* and *Living in Today's World* (Garrard). Both written at the fourth reader level, the former deals with documentaries of America's growth and heritage, the latter with people of other cultures.

Similarly, there are programs in English such as *Pathways to the World of English* (Globe), *Activity-Concept English* (Scott, Foresman), and *Learning Your Language* (Follett). In the literature area, either other books or paperbacks can be substituted for those called for by the curriculum, or adapted classics may be read.

Materials are much less available in the field of mathematics. However, it is possible to rewrite written problems to a lower reading level by using more familiar words and shorter and less complex sentences.

It is highly advantageous for disabled readers to receive information through media other than print. Texts may be read to the student at home, or by a volunteer during study periods, or lessons may be recorded. If learning is to be primarily auditory, lessons in listening comprehension should be built into the child's program. If "learning through listening" programs were initiated early enough, disabled readers could have more academic success when they finally learn to read because they would have the conceptual background necessary to understand the texts.

Whatever the adjustments made for disabled readers, it is important to allow the learner to display his knowledge. For some severely disabled readers it is advisable to administer tests orally. If he cannot read the test, the student cannot demonstrate his knowledge—a situation that can be quite frustrating and kill motivation to learn.

Study Habits

Individual students develop habits about the amount of time they spend in studying, the promptness or dallying with which they get to work, the physical conditions in which they do their studying, their degree of concentration, and so forth. Many students who fail or marginally pass despite satisfactory scores on reading tests have problems in the area of study habits rather than reading or study skills. A remedial approach for study habit problems is described in the next section.

IV. OVERCOMING DEFICIENCIES IN COMPREHENSION

As with other faults in reading, poor comprehension can result from a variety of causes, and the nature of the remedial work to be employed depends on a diagnostic analysis. Sometimes inability to comprehend well is a secondary result of a more basic difficulty, such as low intelligence, poor word recognition, or a deficient vocabulary, which has to be the starting point of planning. In other cases imperfect comprehension seems to be a primary difficulty and should be attacked directly. In the following discussion, each of a number of factors that sometimes interfere with comprehension will be discussed, and the nature of the remedial work needed will be indicated. Where several factors are present, a number of different types of remedial activities may need to be carried on at the same time.

Intellectual Limitations

The significance of intelligence as an indication of the level of difficulty at which a child can reasonably be expected to understand reading material has been discussed in previous chapters. Verbal intelligence is highly correlated with scores on reading tests like the *Stanford,* which perhaps should be called tests of reasoning in reading. The dull child tends to understand only the directly stated, literal meanings of what he reads; implications, subtleties, and abstractions are particularly hard for him to grasp. When working with the mentally limited, it is necessary to adjust not only the difficulty of the material to their abilities but also the types of questions one asks.

Word-Identification Difficulties

Poor comprehension is sometimes the direct result of the fact that the child cannot read the words. In these cases, specific work on developing a sight vocabulary, overcoming confusions between words, and teaching a method of independent attack on words results directly in improved comprehension.

One should not rely heavily on test scores for an analysis of the relation between word recognition and comprehension. For example, a dull 14-year-old boy made the following grade scores on reading tests:

	Grade
Stanford Primary Reading Test, Form D	*Equivalent*
Paragraph Meaning	2.4
Word Meaning	3.0
Gray Oral Reading	1.9
Gates Word Pronunciation Test	3.1

One might be tempted to assume, because his vocabulary and word-recognition scores were higher than his paragraph comprehension and connected oral reading, that the immediate remedial problem is primarily one of comprehension with the word problem less important. Actually, this boy's recognition of words was a painfully slow phonic attack. For instance, he solved the word *peach* by saying under his breath *ch, each, peach.* On the word-recognition tests, of which one is untimed and the other has a generous time limit, this slowness did not prevent him from working out a considerable number of correct answers. In connected reading, however, he had to stop so often to puzzle over words that he lost the flow of language and thought in any but the simplest reading matter. Only by listening to him read orally could one find out what was the major difficulty in his reading. In the early stages of remedial work with this boy, major emphasis had to be placed on clearing up his word-recognition difficulties before he could be considered ready for stress on comprehension.

Poor Comprehension Resulting from Inappropriate Rate

Comprehension may suffer when the rate of reading is either too fast or too slow. Some inaccurate readers need to be temporarily slowed down until they reach a satisfactory standard of accuracy; when that result has been attained, they can gradually speed up again while maintaining the newly achieved precision. Some very slow readers do poorly in comprehension because their many repetitions and hesitations break up the continuity of thought. The relation between rate and comprehension, and the procedures that are effective in coordinating them, are treated in detail in Chapter 19. For practice materials, timed reading exercises with thorough comprehension checks are usually desirable.

Vocabulary Weakness

The importance of knowledge of the meanings of the words used by an author will become strikingly evident to anyone who takes the trouble to try to read an article in a scientific journal in a field in which he has not specialized. To the pupil with a weak general vocabulary but adequate decoding skills, a similar inability to comprehend develops when he tries to read material that is above his instructional level. The importance of reading vocabulary and methods for teaching it have been discussed in Chapter 16. It should be noted, however, that progress in building up a limited meaningful vocabulary is usually much slower than progress in most other areas of reading skills.

Poor Concentration

Unquestionably, inability to concentrate one's attention on the meaning of what one is reading is a very important reason for poor comprehension. But lack of ability to concentrate is itself a result of causes, a name for the fact that the individual is unable to adjust to the requirements of the reading situation. Inability to concentrate is not in itself an explanation. Before one can take practical measures, one should try to find out what the reasons are that make it difficult for the person to concentrate. The causes will usually be found in the answers to one or more of the following questions:

1] Does the person suffer from eyestrain? Eyestrain resulting from farsightedness, astigmatism, poor eye-muscle balance, and so on is a frequent and often unsuspected cause of concentration difficulties. Examination by an eye specialist is a desirable routine procedure. People who wear glasses may need a changed prescription.

2] Is he physically below par? There are many physical conditions that lower vitality and impair the ability to exert effort. Among poor readers, one should pay special attention to undernourishment, insufficient sleep, and thyroid dysfunction as possible causes of difficulty.

3] Is he generally overworked? Accumulating fatigue resulting from an effort to carry too heavy a load may bring on a decline in ability to concentrate.

4] Is the material he is trying to read much too difficult for him? The children who can maintain good effort and concentration when working on very difficult material usually do not become remedial problems.

5] Is he interested in what he is trying to read? A marked improvement in concentration sometimes occurs when more interesting material is provided.

6] Does he read in suitable physical conditions? For most efficient reading, one should sit upright or bending slightly forward in a straight-backed chair, with good, glareless lighting, in surroundings free from distracting sights and sounds. While some people can read very well in unfavorable surroundings, the poor reader should give himself the benefit of good working conditions.

7] Do other thoughts keep running through his mind? One's attention can be focused well on only one thing at a time. To read well, one must be able to exclude other thoughts for the time being. When questioning discloses that the reader's mind runs off on other things when he is supposed to be reading, one has to try to determine whether this is a superficial habit which can be broken or a symptom of a deep-lying emotional difficulty which needs expert treatment.

Some children who are musically inclined find tunes "running through their heads" while they read. Once they become convinced that this inner musical accompaniment interferes with their reading efficiency, they can usually by a voluntary effort at least reduce its interfering effect.

A regrettably large number of students deliberately invite trouble by attempting to do their reading and studying with the radio or television set going. It can be done, but not with top efficiency.

The tendency to slide away into daydreams when reading is an insidious one and is not easy to overcome. Easy, interesting reading matter helps. A very specific goal—so many pages to be finished within a time limit—also helps. The child who is interested in improving his concentration sometimes benefits by making a tally mark every time he finds his thoughts wandering and recording on a progress chart the declining number of tallies.

In some cases, there seems to be a real obsessive trend. The child is bothered by ideas that are persistent and unwelcome, which seem to have a strong existence of their own and seem to resist all efforts to banish them from his mind. These thoughts may involve ideas of fear, shame or guilt, morbid speculations about sex, family relationships, death, horror scenes from movies, and so on. The treatment of a condition like this is best left to a psychotherapist.

In helping a child to develop better concentration, it is sometimes desirable to start with very small units. Two or three minutes of intensive silent reading are followed by discussion of the meaning of the material, and then a brief period of relaxation, before another practice exercise is tried. For work of this type, exercises such as one found in the *New Practice Readers* (Webster) and *Standard Test Lessons in Reading* (Teachers) can be used to very good advantage. When proficiency is attained in handling brief assignments of this type, longer selections can be gradually introduced.

Difficulties in Specific Types of Comprehension

In the first section of this chapter, several different kinds of comprehension skills were described, and the procedures that are useful for developing these skills in normal developmental reading lessons were discussed. If a teacher finds that a whole class is weaker in one or two of these skills than

⟶ *27* ⟵

How do you know when your goldfish are hungry?

A man once taught his goldfish to ring a little bell when they wanted food. He began by letting them go hungry for a few days. Their food was tied to one end of a string and a little bell to the other. The food was then dropped into the water. When the fish nibbled, the bell outside the bowl rang loudly. For several days they were fed in this way. Then the string without food was put into the bowl and the fish bit at the end just the same. When the bell rang the man threw in some water fleas for the goldfish to eat. After several days of such training they learned to ring the bell whenever they were hungry.

1. The string was tied to the (a) food (b) fish (c) pebbles (d) bowl

2. The bell was (a) in the water (b) on the man (c) outside the bowl (d) on the fish

3. The man fed the fish with (a) flies (b) gold (c) string (d) water fleas

4. The fish were not fed for (a) several weeks (b) a month (c) a few days (d) eight days

5. The bell rang when the fish (a) swam (b) pulled the string (c) were hungry (d) drank

6. The fish were taught to (a) swim (b) nibble food (c) ring a bell (d) catch flies

7. To train the fish required (a) several days (b) two weeks (c) four weeks (d) one day

8. The fish pulled the string when they wanted to (a) sleep (b) eat (c) swim (d) play

9. This story tells you how to (a) feed fish (b) catch fish (c) cook fish (d) train fish

10. Choose the best title for this story: (a) Hungry Goldfish (b) Fish Frolics (c) Nibble the Bait (d) The Goldfish Dinner Bell

FIGURE 17.5 An exercise to increase rate of comprehension. A time limit of three minutes is allowed for reading and answering questions. Reprinted with the permission of the publisher from William A. McCall and Lelah M. Crabbs, *Standard Test Lessons in Reading*, Book B. Teachers College Press, © 1961.

in the others, he will naturally try to provide corrective practice to develop the weaker skill. The same principle applies if the weakness is found in only a few pupils, or in a single pupil. With differentiated teaching methods it should, for example, be possible to give one group extra practice in reading for details and another group extra practice in getting a balanced comprehension program.

In general, remedial work for a specific comprehension skill can be of the same types as are used to develop that skill in normal readers. The use of published practice material in workbook form often reduces the teacher's burden and allows the assignment of special types of reading practice that otherwise would be impracticable if the teacher had to rely entirely on practice material of his own construction. A file of comprehension exercises, classified by level of difficulty and by type as selecting main idea, reading for details, following directions, and the like, allows individualized teaching of comprehension skills and the assignment of extra practice in any kind of comprehension skill in which a pupil may be weak. Such a file can also include exercises made up by the teacher to supply types of practice that are not provided adequately in available workbooks.

Many of the shortcomings in comprehension that are discovered in the upper grades are caused, not by any particular difficulty in learning, but by the absence of any previous instruction to develop the missing skills. What is frequently called remedial work in comprehension turns out, in these cases, to be nothing but delayed first teaching.

Sometimes the problem cannot be solved by providing first teaching or more practice. It may be necessary to break the skill down into simple components and lead the learner through them one by one. If the problem is inability to select the main idea of a paragraph, for example, it may be necessary to go through the paragraph one sentence at a time. Check for decoding errors, erroneous word meanings, and misunderstood phrases and clauses. Ask the child to restate the sentence in his own words. When the sentence is understood, ask if that could be the main-idea sentence. After all sentences have been gone through, ask the pupil which has the main idea and why he thinks so. If there is difficulty in grasping a sequence of events, have the child read once to find out what happened first. Then let him reread to find out what happened second; etc. Ask for reasons for wrong answers so that misunderstandings can be corrected.

Improving Study Habits

Before one can modify study habits one should know what they are. A class or group can be asked to keep individual detailed logs of their use of time for a week, from getting up to bedtime. An individual pupil can be asked to tell orally what he did yesterday (and last weekend) from the time he got up until he went to bed. Periods of time that are wasted or could be put to better use often show up clearly in such a time log.

It is desirable to use behavioral modification techniques when attempting to change study habits. For example, if dawdling is a problem, the pupil can award himself a token each time he settles down to work in less than five minutes; reduce it later to three minutes, to two minutes, and finally to immediately. When he has accumulated an agreed-on number of tokens he can exchange them for a privilege or prize; the conditions for earning tokens, the number required, and the nature of the desired reward should be agreed on in advance. If the problem is insufficient total study time, a token can be earned for each ten minutes of study above the total for the corresponding day last week, until a desired amount of total time is reached; then tokens can be earned by maintaining that amount of time. In all token systems, the amount to be done to earn a token is gradually increased and the use of the tokens is gradually faded out.

V. MATERIALS FOR DEVELOPING COMPREHENSION

In addition to the workbooks which are correlated with specific programs, there are many useful practice materials of different types for the fostering and sharpening of comprehension skills. Some of them require the answers to be written in, so that a new copy must be supplied to each pupil. Others are arranged for repeated use, with the answers to questions written by the pupil on separate paper. The teacher who wants to become acquainted with workbooks and what they have to offer should order one copy of each workbook that seems possibly suited to his needs and inspect the contents carefully to get a clear idea of what it has to offer. Even if he decides not to use it, he may get suggestions from it concerning types of practice exercises that he can devise for use in his class.

An increasing number of independent workbooks is available for use in the elementary school.

STONE, CLARENCE R. & GROVER, CHARLES C. *et al. New Practice Readers* (Webster, 1962). Books A to G, grade 2 to 8 in difficulty. Each consists of short selections with vocabulary introductions and 6 varied comprehension and vocabulary questions.

GATES, ARTHUR I. & PEARDON, CELESTE C. *Gates-Peardon Reading Exercises,* rev. ed. (Teachers College Press, 1965). Contains short selections, with 3 types of questions: getting the main idea, following directions, reading for details. Introductory, Levels A and B (grade 2) and Preparatory, Levels A and B (grade 3) have the 3 types of questions following each selection. At the Elementary (grade 4), Intermediate (grade 5), and Advanced (grade 6) levels there are separate booklets for main idea, directions, and details.

BONING, RICHARD A. *Specific Skills Series* (Barnell Loft, 1962–1973). Separate series of workbooks for Getting the Main Idea, Getting the Facts, Drawing Conclusions, Following Directions, Locating the Answer, Detecting the Sequence, and Using the Context. There are 6 workbooks in each series, of primary- and intermediate-grade difficulty.

New Reading Skill Builder Series (Reader's Digest, 1966–1973). Reading levels 1 to 9, two or three booklets at each grade level. Contain stories based on articles in *Reader's Digest* adapted to low reading levels, each followed by varied comprehension questions. Mature appearance and content make these attractive to disabled readers.

SANFORD, ADRIAN B. *et al. Reading Comprehension*, Macmillan Reading Spectrum, rev. ed. (Macmillan, 1973). A series of 6 programmed workbooks, grades 3 to 8 in difficulty, for use in intermediate grades or remedial secondary programs, to develop comprehension skills.

HUTCHINSON, MARY MC C. & BRANDON, PAULINE R. *Gaining Independence in Reading* (Charles E. Merrill). Three hard-cover textbooks, grades 4 and up, containing a wide variety of exercises; mature content suitable for secondary corrective and remedial programs.

JOHNSON, ELEANOR M. (Ed.). *New Diagnostic Reading Workbooks* (Charles E. Merrill). A series of workbooks from kindergarten through sixth grade. Each exercise consists of a selection followed by questions of several kinds: main ideas, details, implications, directions, word recognition, vocabulary, and so on.

Merrill Skilltexts (Charles E. Merrill). Separate workbooks for grades 1 to 6. Each lesson has a selection followed by a variety of questions. Content of primary levels better suited to developmental than to remedial use.

MC CALL, W. A. & CRABBS, L. M. *Standard Test Lessons in Reading*, rev. ed. (Teachers College Press, 1961). Books A, B, C, D, and E, about third- to seventh-grade difficulty. Each booklet contains 78 one-page exercises, consisting of a short selection followed by multiple-choice questions, to be administered with a 3-minute time limit. Rough grade norms are supplied which are useful as a basis for progress charts. May be used for speed of comprehension exercises.

LEAVELL, U. W., *et al. Steps to Take*, Reading Essentials Series (Steck-Vaughn). A workbook of about grade 3 to 4 difficulty intended for remedial use above the fourth grade. Contains a variety of exercises on word analysis, vocabulary, and aspects of comprehension.

BONING, RICHARD A. *Supportive Reading Skills* (Dexter and Westbrook, 1973). Separate series of workbooks for Understanding Questions, Understanding Word Groups, and Predicting Paragraph Content. There are 5 or 6 workbooks in each series for grades 1 to 5 or 6.

Instructional Aid Kits (Dexter and Westbrook). Series of kits, each containing 50 cards and an answer key. Sentence comprehension kits for the first-grade level are One Too Many and We Read Sentences. Pronoun Parade (practice in understanding function of referral words) has kits for grades 1 to 6.

LIDDLE, WILLIAM (Ed.) *Reading for Concepts* (Webster). Series of 8 workbooks (reading levels 1.9 to 6.4) each containing 72 or 80 stories taken from 13 academic disciplines, particularly social studies and science. Eight different comprehension skills are checked. May be used to develop content subject concepts for poor readers.

Read-Study-Think. Weekly Reader. Series of 5 workbooks for grades 2–6. Designed to develop critical and creative reading.

At the secondary school level many of the workbooks listed above will be suitable for corrective or remedial work. In addition there are some designed specifically for junior high school use.

OLSON, JIM. *Step up Your Reading Power* (Webster Division, McGraw-Hill, 1966–1967). A series of 5 workbooks designed to be used with remedial students. The selections are very short in the first workbook and become progressively longer. There are 6 fact questions and 2 thought questions after each selection. Also available on individual cards.

SCHACHTER, NORMAN & WHELAN, JOHN K. *Activities for Reading Improvement*, Just for Fun Series, Books 1, 2, 3 (grades 7–9), rev. ed. (Steck-Vaughn, 1971). Each contains exercises grouped in four units: comprehension, skimming, vocabulary, reading for enjoyment (timed).

SMITH, NILA B. *Be a Better Reader*, Books 1–6 (grades 7–12) (Prentice-Hall, 1969–1973). Each contains a variety of exercises on word recognition, comprehension, basic study skills, and special study skills in content fields.

MILLER, LYLE L. *Developing Reading Efficiency* (Burgess, 1972). A workbook for junior high, containing exercises on word recognition, phrase and sentence reading, and timed reading of longer selections.

GAINSBURG, JOSEPH C. *Advanced Skills in Reading*, Books 1, 2, 3 (Macmillan, 1967). Hard-cover books for developmental or corrective use in junior or senior high school. Combine explanations of reading techniques with graded practice exercises in word meaning, sentence reading, paragraph analysis, a variety of comprehension skills, and study skills.

GUILER, W. S.; COLEMAN, J. H.; & JUNGEBLATT, A. *Reading for Meaning,* Books 4–12 (Lippincott, 1955–1965). Workbooks for grades 4 to 12. Each exercise contains questions on word meanings in context and several types of comprehension questions.

MONROE, M.; ARTLEY, A. S.; & ROBINSON, H. M. *Basic Reading Skills* (Scott, Foresman). Program for grades 7 and 8 encompasses a workbook, correlated tapes, and overhead visuals. Workbook covers word analysis, comprehension, and study skills.

NILES, OLIVE S., *et al. Tactics in Reading* and *Reading Skills for Young Adults* (Scott, Foresman). Series of five paperbacks for intensive work on reading skills for seventh to twelfth-grade students with reading problems. Emphasis is on reading for understanding.

Scope Skills: Wide World, Dimensions, Spotlight (Scholastic). Three paperbacks written at the fourth- to sixth-reader level, but geared to junior-senior high school interests. Various types of comprehension skills included.

Since the first *SRA Reading Laboratory* appeared, there has been considerable interest in the use of multilevel individual practice units. Those now available include:

PARKER, DON H. *SRA Reading Laboratories* (SRA). There are 10 different laboratories, for use from primary grades to college, with the range of readability in any one kit being from 2 to 8 grade levels. Each consists of a large carton containing materials for a classroom. Exercise units called "Power Builders" consist of short selections followed by questions on word study, vocabulary, and comprehension; there is a set of these at each of several levels of difficulty. A series of "Rate Builders" is also included in the higher-level laboratories. Listening exercises and notetaking exercises are given in the teacher's manual. Each pupil needs a record book. A set of scoring keys is included.

Study Skills Library (Educational Developmental Laboratories, Inc.). A set of multilevel kits for secondary school use, one in each of several content areas, providing practice in applying reading and study skills in that subject area.

BOARD OF EDUCATION OF THE CITY OF NEW YORK. *Building Reading Power: The Programmed Course for Improving Reading Techniques* (Charles E. Merrill). Intended for corrective use in secondary school. Each kit contains separate booklets on context clues, structural analysis, and comprehension; exercises are self-administering and self-correcting.

Reading Improvement Skill File, for Junior and Senior High Schools (The Reading Laboratory, Inc.). Contains 20 selections on each of 9 levels of difficulty, from 5 subject areas; each is timed and followed by comprehension questions. Also a variety of supplementary exercises and a "Cal-Q-Rater" to determine rate of reading.

SACK, ALLAN & YOURMAN, JACK. *100 Passages to Develop Reading Comprehension* (College Skills Center). Mature content at secondary level for refinement of comprehension skills.

Reading Practice Program (Harcourt Brace Jovanovich). Organized by skill areas (decoding, vocabulary, comprehension), the program has over 230 self-explanatory lessons and pre- and post-criterion-referenced tests. For reading levels 3 to 9.

Reading Development (Addison-Wesley). Three kits, each with a series of lesson cards covering word-analysis, vocabulary, and comprehension skills. Kit A is written at the second to fourth reader levels, Kit B at the fifth and sixth reader levels, and Kit C at seventh to tenth reader levels. The subject matter is taken from five content areas and should be of interest to older readers.

Specific Reading Skills (Jones-Kenilworth). A flexible program whose components may be useful for individualizing instruction or in a junior high remedial reading program. Each level concentrates on 3 skill areas: word building, comprehension, and critical and creative reading. Of the 3 sections at each grade level (each may be purchased separately in softback) the first 2 are written below grade level. Reading levels for the eight books range from one to 8.

Reading for Understanding (SRA). Series of 3 multilevel kits (grades 5 through college, 3–8, and 8–12), each containing 400 exercise cards containing short selections designed to help develop reading comprehension, analyze ideas, and draw conclusions.

Materials for Reading in the Content Subjects

Some materials directed at improving comprehension focus on reading in the content subjects. Among them are:

SMITH, NILA B. *Be a Better Reader* (Prentice-Hall, 1968–1973). Books A–C for reading levels 4 to 6, Books 1–6 for grades 7–12. Each contains a variety of exercises on word recognition, vocabulary, comprehension, basic study skills, and special study skills in four content fields.

REITER, IRENE M. *Reading Line* (Polaski, 1973). Separate workbooks for each of 6 content areas including Business and Vocational-Technical. Within each book are 10 reading selections which contain passages written at varying levels of difficulty. For high school use.

REITER, IRENE M. *Why Can't They Read It?* (Polaski). An accompanying text designed to assist content subject teachers in helping students to overcome reading and study difficulties.

Reading Improvement Skill File for Junior and Senior High School (The Reading Laboratory). Contains 20 selections on each of 9 levels of difficulty, from 5 subject areas; each is timed and followed by comprehension questions. Also a variety of supplementary exercises and a "Cal-Q-Rater" to determine rate of reading.

HERBER, HAROLD. *Scholastic Go* (Scholastic). Reading program in the content areas for students reading below grade level in grades 4 to 8. In each text, which is organized in 4 content areas, the reading level begins below grade level and gradually progresses to grade level.

PAUK, WALTER & WILSON, JOSEPHINE. *How to Read Factual Literature* (SRA). Three books for grades 7–8, 9–10, and 11–12 designed to meet specific problems of those who can read but need to develop careful comprehension and retention of expository material. *How to Read Creative Literature* is a single text for high school use that provides practice in reading for a given purpose and under given circumstances. Six questions per selection involve basic literature analysis.

STAUFFER, RUSSELL & BERG, JEAN H. *Communication Through Effective Reading* (grades 7–9) and *Rapid Comprehension through Effective Reading* (grades 10–12) (Learn). Designed to accomplish transfer of skills to content subjects by using the student's texts for reinforcement. Reading levels stair-stepped in each of 7 skill areas.

ERVIN, JANE. *Reading Comprehension in Varied Subject Matter* (Educators, 1971). Eight workbooks for grades 3–10 each composed of 31 selections followed by various types of comprehension and vocabulary questions. Each book covers a variety of subject areas.

Earth's Atmosphere, Weather and Climate, Solar System, Biography (SRA). Four separate science kits, each of which presents a series of "Big Ideas" in booklets written at reading levels 3 to 7.

Locational and Study Skills Materials

Among the materials available for developing study skills are:

Learning to Use the Library (Xerox Educational). Series of 4 books for grades 3–6: Book A covers the parts of a book; Book B, finding a particular book; Book C, locating periodicals; and Book D, using key reference books.

Study Skills for Information Retrieval Series (Allyn and Bacon, 1970). Three workbooks for use in the fourth grade and above. Exercises on locating, organizing and summarizing information.

Study Skills Library (EDL). Set of multilevel kits for grades 3–9, one in each of several content areas, providing practice in applying reading and study skills in that subject area.

Organizing and Reporting Skills Kit (SRA). Kit for use in grades 4–6; deals with effective reporting, note taking, and outlining.

Thirty Lessons in Outlining (Curriculum Associates). Two series, elementary and advanced, each having 5 lesson books covering a variety of subskills needed for outlining.

Children Writing Research Reports (Curriculum Associates). An intermediate-grade program containing two units; one on intensive, detailed, in-depth research and reporting; the other stresses the ability to generalize from research.

PRESTON, RALPH & BOTEL, MORTON. *How to Study* (SRA). A workbook designed to improve study skills and habits; for use in grades 9–14.

How to Be a Better Student (SRA). Text on how to use study time effectively; for junior high.

Better Work Habits (Scott, Foresman). Workbook for grades 7–8 containing 55 problems, each contributing to mastery of a study skill.

Table and Graph Skills (Xerox Educational). Series of 4 workbooks for grades 3–6; begins with simple tables and graphs and builds to the more complex.

Map Skills for Today (Xerox Educational). Series of 5 workbooks for grades 2–6; deals with map terminology, symbols, and different types of maps.

Graph and Picture Study Skills Kit (SRA). Kit for use in grades 4–6; deals with interpreting illustrative materials such as editorial cartoons, graphic data, charts, and diagrams.

Map and Globe Skills Kit (SRA). Kit for use in grades 4–8; covers various types of maps and globe reading skills.

Newslab (SRA). Kit for use in grades 4–6; deals with how to read and interpret 12 sections of a newspaper.

SUGGESTED ADDITIONAL READING

BURMEISTER, LOU E. *Reading strategies for secondary school teachers.* Reading, Mass.: Addison-Wesley, 1974. Chaps. 2, 7, 8, 9.

DECHANT, EMERALD V. *Improving the teaching of reading* (2nd ed.). Englewood Cliffs, N.J.: Prentice-Hall, 1970. Chap. 13.

FRY, EDWARD. *Reading instruction for classroom and clinic.* New York: McGraw-Hill, 1972. Chaps. 8, 9, 10.

HARRIS, ALBERT, J. & SIPAY, EDWARD R. *Effective teaching of reading* (2nd ed.). New York: McKay, 1971. Chaps. 11, 12.

———. *Readings on reading instruction* (2nd ed.). New York: McKay, 1972. Chaps. 10, 11.

HEILMAN, ARTHUR W. *Principles and practices of teaching reading* (3rd ed.). Columbus: Charles E. Merrill, 1972. Chaps. 13, 14, 15.

HERBER, HAROLD L. *Teaching reading in content areas.* Englewood Cliffs, N.J.: Prentice-Hall, 1970.

HUNKINS, FRANCIS P. *Questioning strategies and techniques.* Boston: Allyn and Bacon, 1972.

LUNDSTEEN, SARA W. *Listening: its impact on reading and the other language arts.* Urbana, Ill.: National Council of Teachers of English, 1971. Chaps. 1, 2, 3.

ROBINSON, H. ALAN & THOMAS, ELLEN L. (Eds.). *Fusing reading skills and content.* Newark, Del.: International Reading Association, 1969.

RUDDELL, ROBERT B. *Reading-language instruction: innovative practices.* Englewood Cliffs, N.J.: Prentice-Hall, 1974. Chaps. 11, 12.

SHEPHERD, DAVID L. *Comprehensive high school reading programs.* Columbus: Charles E. Merrill, 1973. Chaps. 8–12.

SMITH, NILA B. *Reading instruction for today's children.* Englewood Cliffs, N.J.: Prentice-Hall, 1963. Chaps. 22, 23.

THOMAS, ELLEN L. & ROBINSON, H. ALAN. *Improving reading in every class: a sourcebook for teachers.* Boston: Allyn and Bacon, 1972. Chaps. 5, 6, 7.

THORNDIKE, ROBERT L. *Reading comprehension education in fifteen countries: an empirical study.* New York: John Wiley & Sons, 1973.

TINKER, MILES A. & MCCULLOUGH, CONSTANCE M. *Teaching elementary reading* (3rd ed.). New York: Appleton-Century-Crofts, 1968. Chaps. 9, 10, 13.

18

Fostering Reading
Interests and Tastes

Of what value is it to develop skillful readers, if the skill is used to little purpose in adulthood? Enormous amounts of time, effort, and money are expended in teaching children how to read, yet as indicated in Chapter 1, we apparently have produced what Huck (1971) referred to as a nation of "illiterate literates." A successful reading program must not only develop children who *can* read, but also children who *do* read. Two major objectives of any total reading program should be to build a lasting interest in reading and improve reading tastes. A good reading program must create the desire to read and help the individual to find pleasurable recreation in reading. It also should foster the desire to read for personal development, to learn more about the world, and to gain increasing understanding of people and society.

The following statement by the Joint Committee on Reading Development deserves wide attention:

> At all times and with every means at her command, the teacher must learn how best to counteract the attitude that reading is for school only; that reading is a second-hand and, therefore, an inferior form of experience. Reading must be understood and interpreted as a tool of invention, relevance, and creativity, as a sort of depth-perception device that gives dimension to first-hand experience; and as a principal means by which the intellectual inheritance is tested and developed. (Dietrich and Mathews, 1968)

I. READING INTERESTS[1]

It is difficult to make definitive statements regarding the reading interests of children and young adults for a variety of reasons. The term "interest" is often not defined or is often used differently. In addition, marked differences among studies as to the methods through which interests were determined and in the populations studied make it difficult to compare research findings. In reading the following section, it should be remembered that group studies only suggest topics that about half the students prefer (H. M. Robinson and Weintraub, 1973).

Interest Categories by Age Levels

The limited research dealing with the reading interests of preschool children is inconclusive. It is quite possible that interests are fleeting and do not stabilize until children can read on their own. Illustrations have as much or more appeal than story content, but very young children like repetition and repeatedly ask to hear familiar stories.

Prior to the past decade, the interests of primary-grade children were generally listed as short stories involving animals (real and fanciful), fairy tales, children of other lands and at home, and nature stories. Within the past decade, investigations continue to show strong interests in animals, make-believe, and some interest in children's activities. Middle-class first graders prefer the pranks theme over the pollyanna theme, peer interaction over child-parent interactions, and activities dealing with their own sex (Rose, Zimet, and Blom, 1972). Interest in the fanciful usually increases until the age of 8 or 9 and then gradually declines. Most preschool and primary-grade children seem to prefer humorous poems, followed by poems about animals and poems related to their own experiences.

Intermediate-grade children have a greater variety of interests than their younger schoolmates. By the age of 9 or 10, however, definite sex differences are apparent. Boys become absorbed in adventure and mystery tales. They also read fictionalized history and biography, and many of them read extensively on mechanics, science, invention, and material related to hobbies. Girls enjoy sentimental stories of home and school life and usually develop an interest in romantic fiction between the ages of 11 and 14. They share the boys' liking for mystery and adventure, but usually do not care for reading related to science and invention. Boys, on the other hand, tend to ignore the human interest stories which are feminine favorites and in general avoid anything that seems definitely feminine. Intermediate-grade chil-

1. Much of this section is based upon the summary by H. M. Robinson and Weintraub (1973).

dren tend to like stories in which the characters have to struggle with problems similar to the ones they face in their own lives (Worley, 1967). Most children enjoy the "comics," both in newspapers and in comic-book form. They also read magazines and newspapers. There are frequently marked differences between what children want to read and what teachers and librarians recommend; many books that have been selected by adult committees as the best children's book of the year have been ignored by children (Terman and Lima, 1937; Vandament and Thalman, 1956; Taylor and Schneider, 1957).

A study of children in grades 4 through 6 in Texas found that reading competed with sports as the two favorite hobbies. Fifty-four per cent of the children received books from a book club subscription. More than half had been stimulated to read a book by seeing the story in a movie or on TV. Over 90 per cent had read at least one book a second time. Children's magazines were read regularly by 71 per cent; comic books, by 77 per cent; newspapers, by 89 per cent. Adult magazines such as *Reader's Digest* were popular (A. Miller, 1967). If these children could be taken as representative of the country as a whole, much of the alarmist fear about the future of reading would seem unjustified; but the representativeness of the group cannot be taken for granted.

The fact that poetry is not very popular with children has been well documented (W. S. Gray, 1960). For intermediate-grade children, the most popular poems tend to be those related to children's experiences, those with humor, and those having strong rhythm and rhyme (Bridges, 1967).

At the junior and senior high school levels, studies have shown a continuing trend toward individual differentiation, with the range of interests becoming so varied that they defy generalization. Nevertheless, rough categories for boys include: action and adventure, sports, crime and war, historical novels, and mystery. Girls' interests include: books about people and social relationships, romance, humor, and mystery without violence. And although few fundamental changes have occurred in adolescents' reading interests, the interest in reading books has steadily declined in the past five decades (Mott, 1970). Young people dislike many of the titles considered classics by their English teachers, even more so in recent years (Norvell, 1958, 1972).

Voluntary reading usually increases in amount until the age of 12 or 13. In some schools there is a marked decline in voluntary book reading which coincides in time with both increasing homework and the teaching of literature. In other schools, teachers are successful in maintaining the amount of voluntary reading and in helping adolescents toward mature tastes. Although book reading may decline, magazine and newspaper reading increases thereafter.

Norvell (1966) explored the popularity of magazines with 6,000 children. He found marked differences between the preferences of boys and girls, except for *National Geographic*, which was popular with both. Children showed a liking for adult magazines quite early. Seven of the ten magazines most popular with children in grades 4 through 6 were adult magazines. One may wonder to what extent the presence of adult magazines in homes, and absence of children's magazines, may have contributed to that result. Boys read more magazines than girls below grade 7, but girls read more from grade 7 up. On the whole, interest in magazine reading was somewhat lower in the 1960's than it had been in the 1930's.

Probably the most important finding about reading interests, however, is the tremendous range of individual differences both in amount of voluntary reading and in the specific interests that are expressed. Even in a group of children who are similar in intelligence, age, and cultural background, the range of individual preferences is tremendous. While a knowledge of the general trends is helpful to teachers in allowing them to anticipate the interests of pupils, it does not relieve them of the responsibility of trying to discover the particular interests of each pupil.

Personal and Institutional Factors
Influencing Reading Interests

A number of factors seem to influence reading interests. None of these factors appears to operate in isolation, but their interrelationships have not been clearly established. As with much research, it is difficult to separate which variables are operative and to what extent they interact. Furthermore, there is some question as to the reliability of the instruments and techniques used to determine reading preferences (McNinch, 1970–1971; H. M. Robinson and Weintraub, 1973). The following summary is based primarily on the research review by Purves and Beach (1972) who categorized the factors influencing reading interests under two main headings—personal and institutional determinants.

Personal Determinants. Personal factors that may influence reading interests are age, sex, intelligence, reading ability, attitudes, and psychological needs. It should be noted that these factors are not mutually exclusive.

Reading interests of elementary school children show a definite development by grade level. Students of all ages maintain an interest in stories that have characters of their own age. Although it is difficult to generalize at the early age, there is an identification with fantasy figures (usually animals) who represent childlike experiences. Older elementary school students prefer more realistic stories that portray peers undergoing suspenseful adventures. There is some evidence that the reading interests of children two years or so below or above grade level are more influenced by reading age than chronological age (Geeslin and Wilson, 1972).

Changing interest patterns appear at the junior and senior high school levels. Seventh and eighth graders display a wider range of interests than younger children, but by the last two years of high school, the interests narrow. At about the eighth and ninth grades, adult interests seem to begin and the motivation for reading shifts from reading for entertainment to reading for self-understanding. After age 16, interests do not change considerably, unless drastically affected by education or employment.

The most important determinant of reading interest is the sex of the reader. Generally, girls read more and mature earlier in reading ability. Cultural influences and sexual maturation rather than intelligence seem to account for such differences. Sex differences are found in reading preferences during the primary grades, but they are not very strong. Martin (1972) found that the expressed reading interests of sixth graders were greatly affected by sex and race, less so by IQ, reading achievement, and socioeconomic status, and not at all by chronological age. Sex was also the predominant factor in determining the reading interests of intermediate-grade children (Klein, 1970; Bouchard, 1971; C. Brown, 1971). Sex difference in reading interests are most pronounced in junior high school, lessen during the senior high years, and are not as relevant in adult readers.

The relationship between intelligence and reading interests has not been clearly established. Generally, bright children read much more than the average child, have a wider range of reading interests, and are usually a year or two ahead of the average child in interest maturity. The mentally slow child reads less and usually has preferences which are slightly immature for his age, but more mature than those of younger children of his mental level (Lazar, 1937; R. L. Thorndike, 1941; Lewis and McGehee, 1940). At the secondary school level, however, little relationship was found between IQ level and liking for specific selections (Norvell, 1973).

Although reading ability is related to sophistication of interests, it does not correlate directly with reading interests. Interest as a factor in comprehension is significantly more important for those reading at or below grade level than for better readers. For the former, low interest has a negative effect on comprehension. Poor readers and high school students of below-average intelligence tend to give higher ratings to material in which it would be easy for them to identify emotionally with the central character (Emans and Patyk, 1967). The same principle probably applies to younger poor readers also.

Only a small number of studies have been done on the influence of attitudes on reading interests. On the basis of his study with sixth-grade children, Sauls (1971) concluded that there were significant relationships between the number of books read and the pupil's attitude toward reading, the pupil's reading ability, and home and teacher encouragement. Attitudes do not necessarily entail interest, but interest does involve an attitude. If reading fulfills a need, positive attitudes toward reading usually develop, but a positive attitude toward books does not necessarily lead to an active reading of these books. Attitudes vary with the reader's level of reading ability, background, efforts, and peer influences. They are unique, personal, and highly unpredictable. Perhaps with the advent of scales to measure reading attitudes (Estes, 1971; Rowell, 1972), more research will be done in this area.

One of the major determinants of reading interests is the satisfying of psychological needs. Needs and interests are not synonomous, because the same need may find expression in different interests. Among the needs are the need to develop self-concept, intellectual needs, emotional needs, social needs, and aesthetic needs. Whether or not elementary school children read to satisfy their developmental needs remains an unanswered question. For example, the reading interests of children do not appear to correspond very closely to their felt needs. They frequently turn to sources of information other than reading when they need information, and regard reading primarily as a recreational activity (Rudman, 1955). Satisfying both entertainment and social adjustment needs seems to be operating for secondary school students. However, individual differences vary so considerably that it is impossible to generalize about the relationship of needs and interests. Whether needs are fulfilled through reading is partially determined by the student's reading ability, the time available for reading, and cost. Students may turn to other media to satisfy their needs if the expectations of reward from reading are not high.

Institutional Determinants. Purves and Beach (1972) listed the following factors as institutional determinants of reading interests: availability of books; socioeconomic status and ethnic background; peer, parent, and teacher influences; and TV and movies.

Much of the research regarding reading interests has been biased in that reading choices have been limited in one way or another. If more choices were available, other results might have been obtained. Research has indicated that students are highly self-dependent. As availability affects interests, there is a difference between directed availability and free-option availability. Books borrowed from public libraries are more often completed than those taken from school libraries, as are books read during "free time" as opposed to those read during school library periods. Students also prefer to read books from a library or book club to those given to them in class.

Accessibility and availability have a strong influence on children's choices. Study after study has shown that the amount and kind of reading matter in a child's home have a marked relation to his reading habits. The use of a public library by children is directly related to the distance of the library from the child's home and school. Increasing recognition of the importance of accessibility has been one of the major factors in the building up of library collections in schools. Each classroom in a well-equipped school today has a library collection of its own. Many elementary schools, as well as most secondary schools, have a central library collection, and the number of positions for librarians in schools has increased. Interest in reading is highest when there are both classroom and school libraries (Schulte, 1969). Traveling libraries have been created to provide better library service to rural schools. In cities and towns, loan systems have become common by which a teacher can borrow a large assortment of books from a public library and replace it with different books from time to time.

Most research has concluded that socioeconomic status factors do not significantly affect interests. Although differences in amount and range of reading apparently due to such factors as intelligence and reading ability do occur, low-, middle-, and upper-class students have similar reading interests. Among the possible explanations for their lack of differences are: 1) most studies employed white subjects who were exposed to middle-class-oriented literature; 2) interests usually were inferred from titles known or available to the subjects, thus actual interests may not really have been indicated; 3) until recently, titles on check lists or questionnaires have not included works of ethnic or minority writers; and 4) the response required of the subjects may be biased toward verbal ability. There appears to be little difference in the reading interests of rural, suburban, and metropolitan students.

Most studies have shown significant differences between ethnic groups at all age levels, with the widest differences occurring in the intermediate grades. The influence of ethnicity on reading interests may begin early. Lewis (1970) found that black kindergarteners in Texas strongly favored books about children in ghetto areas, whereas white children disliked such books. It is impossible to state what other factors may have influenced these choices, however. Lickteig (1972) found that although there were some similarities between inner-city and suburban children, such as preference for science fiction at both fourth and sixth grade, inner-city children tended to prefer black fiction more than did suburban children, while white suburban children preferred horse stories more than did inner-city children.

On the other hand, Bouchard (1971) did not find any significant differences among the reading interests of blacks, whites, and Spanish speakers in the intermediate grades. Johns (1973) reported that, contrary to the prevailing belief, the intermediate-grade inner-city children in his study, most of whom were black, preferred to read stories or books containing middle-class settings, characters with positive self-concepts, and characters in positive group interactions. In studying the expressed reading interests of Anglo, Negro, American Indian, and Mexican-American fifth graders, Barchas (1971) found that in most general reading interests, the four ethnic groups were more alike than different, expressing high interest in mystery-adventure, animal stories, humor, and languages. When reading content provided opportunity for minority-group ethnic identification, however, their expressed interests were more different than alike. Minority-group children expressed a high degree of interest in topics related to their own ethnic group and immediate environment, but generally low interest in topics related to other minority groups. Within each minority-culture title collection, certain titles were of high interest to all groups, particularly fiction stories combining minority culture with suspense and adventure, folk tales, and certain biographies, sports books, and cookbooks. While the sex groups shared many common interests (mystery-adventure, humor, animal stories, and child's immediate environment) sports and science topics were of more interest to boys. As with general populations, a wide range of individual interests was found within each ethnic and sex group, with much overlapping of interests among all groups.

Peers, friends, parents and teachers influence reading interests directly through recommended or assigned reading, and indirectly by serving as models. Friends and peers play an important role in why fifth graders selected certain books to read, whereas TV and movies did not (Lawson, 1972). Next to peer recommendations, teachers' enthusiasm can be an important factor in developing interests, although many studies have indicated that teachers often misjudge student interest. In general, the research suggests that students should be consulted about their reading interests more frequently than is usually the case. For example, the most frequently cited reason for selecting a book was that it dealt with a particular interest of the child (Bouchard, 1971).

The effect of other media on reading interests is very complex. Only the short-term effects of TV on interests have been studied; we do not know what the long-range effects may be.

Witty (Witty and Melis, 1965; Witty, 1966) has summarized his annual surveys of the television habits of children. In the mid-1960's, elementary school children viewed TV an average of 20 hours a week; slightly less for the primary grades, slightly more for grades 4 through 6. Currently, TV viewing averages about 20–28 hours per week for children, whereas only 7 hours is spent weekly in reading outside of school (Feeley, 1973). Yet the general lack of significant correlations between hours of TV viewing and hours of voluntary reading tends to support the contention that individual differences preclude any generalization about the effects of TV watching (Purves and Beach, 1972).

As TV viewing has increased, time spent reading comics and pulp magazines seems to have permanently decreased. Over the long run, books, newspapers, and better magazines appear to hold their own as leisure-time activities. Although there is some evidence that TV may influence reading choices (Hamilton, 1973), whether or not watching TV influences reading tastes is still an open question (Feeley, 1973). For the most part, average and superior readers who use one or more media widely also tend to spend more time reading. Children who are inadequate readers have less of an interest in reading than in other media (H. M. Robinson and Weintraub, 1973).

Witty (1965, 1966) also inquired about movies, radio, and voluntary reading. The majority of children went to the movies biweekly; about one-third went every week. Radio listening (mainly popular music) averaged about 7 hours a week in elementary school and 12 to 14 hours a week in high school. Children in the 1960's were doing a little more voluntary reading than in the 1930's, even though the hours per day for reading were only one-third of the time spent watching TV. Comparable data are not available for the 1970's.

Witty's data, gathered mainly in Evanston, Illinois, are probably more representative of suburban and middle-class children than of disadvantaged children. The trends he reported are quite interesting and remained quite stable over several years.

The attraction of TV was beautifully expressed by a youngster quoted by Shayon: " 'It gives you stories like a book, pictures like movies, voices like radio, and adventure like a comic. Television has action while you stay in one spot' " (Shayon, 1951 p. 29). As Witty and Shayon have both pointed out, television is filling otherwise unmet needs in a somewhat satisfactory fashion. Regulating the amount of time spent in watching is highly desirable, but does not solve the problem completely. A comprehensive approach would require working with parents to develop more active and creative forms of recreation in the home, helping children to develop and apply criteria for evaluating and selecting TV programs, and using television for motivating and enriching reading (McDonald, 1959). Suggestions for using TV viewing to stimulate reading interests may be found in Becker (1973).

Before the advent of television, the failure of many children to read at home was blamed on radio, the movies, and comic books. The comics will be discussed below. Both movies and radio now take up less of children's time than they did before TV. The fact is that if a child does not like to read he will find other things to do with his spare time, and if he loves to read he will find time for reading no matter what competing attractions there are. If a child finds reading to be easy, interesting, and accessible, we shall not need to blame the mass media for capturing and holding his attention.

Other Factors Influencing Reading Interests

Three other factors may influence reading interests of preferences: illustrations, the reading of comics, and the difficulty of the material itself.

Illustrations.   Marked changes in the illustrations used in books have taken place over the past forty years. Colorful covers have become general. Boxed-in small pictures have given way to pictures without definite margins, which sometimes spread across two pages. Line drawings with flat, primary colors have been supplanted by pictures employing shading and a wide range of attractive tints. Illustrations occupy a greater proportion of the total page space and are more carefully integrated with the story. Amsden (1960) found that preschool children generally preferred illustrations with more colors, and light tints and dark shades over bright saturated colors. Whereas 3-year-olds preferred modified realistic drawings, 5-year-olds chose realistic drawings. Fourth-grade children prefer illustrations that have a definite center of interest, are colored, and depict action (Whipple, 1953). Children prefer realistic pictures in color, but will choose a realistic black-and-white picture over a less realistic colored one (Rudisill, 1952). There is some evidence that illustrations appear important in children's selection of books only insofar as they serve the purpose of clarifying the content of the book (C. Brown, 1971).

Reading the Comics.   Many teachers are concerned over the great interest shown by children in the so-called comic books, most of which contain adventure tales or portray the exploits of a superhuman character. It is futile, even if it were possible, to try to prevent children from reading the comics. Instead, one should attempt to help them to discriminate between the better and poorer types and to use their comic-book reading as a springboard toward the reading of stories and books that will satisfy the same interests at a higher level. The inclusion of freedom to criticize and compare comic books during a book club meeting provides a basis for developing a group opinion which almost inevitably will frown on the worst specimens. In the upper grades, a skillful teacher can lead the more voracious readers of comics into reading books of the *Tom Swift* and *Tarzan* varieties and later to Jules Verne, H. Rider Haggard, and H. G. Wells. Anything to which children respond as enthusiastically as they do to comic books must have educational values that can be developed.

The effect on children of being exposed to repeated acts of violence and killing in the mass media has been a debated question for over thirty years. Some have asserted that watching such acts creates a callous acceptance of violence and a tendency to imitate it. Others, including some child psychiatrists, have expressed the opinion that watching or reading about violence gives children some vicarious expression for their aggressive and hostile impulses, with more benefit than harm (Bender and Lowrie, 1941). Berkowitz (1968) summarized recent research relating to this question. "The first series indicates that even so small a matter as the casual sight of a gun can sometimes stimulate aggressive behavior. The second suggests that, contrary to what the so-called catharsis theory predicts, the sight of violence can increase the chance that a viewer will express aggression himself." Thus it would seem that parental and teacher concern over this issue is to some extent justified.

Interest and Difficulty. Few people, whether children or adults, can really enjoy reading a book that taxes their skill. One of the reasons why so many children place reading low on the list of their leisure time activities is that, for the most part, the books which they have been given to read have been too difficult to allow easy and enjoyable reading.

Many a teacher finds that he has been given books to use as texts and readers which seem to be much too difficult for his pupils. When that happens the teacher must do the best he can with inadequate materials. Such a situation is all too prevalent in public schools and is probably one of the reasons why normal development of reading skills is not more commonly achieved. The need for adequate reading materials is even more important for a remedial teacher. To handicap him with improperly chosen materials is to saddle him with a burden that he can carry only by the unnecessary expenditure of a great deal of effort.

In general, disabled readers should be given reading material which is not more difficult than the grade level at which they can read successfully. At the beginning of remedial treatment it is often desirable to give them materials which are at their independent reading level rather than at their instructional reading level. This insures successful reading from the beginning of the remedial work and thus tends to stimulate effort. It also gives opportunity for fluent reading and for paying attention to thought getting —something which is overshadowed when much attention has to be devoted to the mastery of new vocabulary.

Despite the pressure from teachers for simpler instructional materials, textbooks in the content fields continue to be difficult reading matter for the majority of children in the grades for which they are intended. Even when the vocabulary is not excessively difficult, the tendency to try to cram in as many facts as possible creates a "concept density" which makes for difficult reading (Serra, 1953; Mallinson, Sturm, and Mallinson, 1950).

There is, of course, a tendency for interesting material to be understood better than uninteresting material. This would be true because it is hard to keep one's mind on dull content, if for no other reason. Schnayer had sixth-grade pupils read a number of stories that were two grades above the pupils' reading level. The children rated the stories for interest and answered questions about them. There were three main findings: 1) interest in a selection may allow students of average ability to read and comprehend material that is above their measured reading level; 2) low interest has a negative effect on comprehension; and 3) the comprehension of high-ability students is less affected by interest than that of average or low-ability students (Schnayer, 1967).

This should not lead to the assumption that if a selection is sufficiently interesting, its difficulty does not matter. In a corrective or remedial program satisfactory comprehension is only one of the desired outcomes. If a selection contains a large number of words that are new to a particular child, he is unlikely to learn and remember them, even if he can grasp the meaning of the selection.

Estimating the Difficulty of Reading Material

Several different methods are employed in estimating the reading difficulty of books. A classroom teacher who has had experience in several grades can usually form a rough estimate of the difficulty of a book by looking through it and studying a few pages carefully. Difficulty of ideas and complexity of sentence structure should be considered, as well as vocabulary. In evaluating basal readers he will find the page-by-page lists of new words given in many recently published books to be helpful. The teacher should, however, check his personal impression by consulting published studies of the difficulty of books. Such references are found in the next section.

In choosing a book for an individual child, the teacher can estimate its difficulty by having the child read a few sample selections from the book orally. A book intended to provide practice in fluent reading of easy material should not have an average of more than two or three words in a hundred running words that are unknown to the child. Work-type materials may be satisfactory if not more than five out of one hundred running words are unfamiliar.

Among the criteria used in the readability formulas developed prior to the last decade, the most frequently used are the number of words that do not appear on the word list accompanying the formula, and average sentence length. Recent research has indicated that vocabulary level (Linville, 1969) and sentence length (MacGinitie and Tretiak, 1971; Glazer, 1974) are valid measures of readability. Guthrie (1972) found that word difficulty and sentence length were better measures of learnability (the extent to which new learning results from reading a passage) than were linguistic measures.

Among the mostly widely used formulas are the Spache Readability Formula (Spache, 1953, 1974) for the primary grades, and the Dale-Chall Formula (Dale and Chall, 1948; it also appears in Hunnicutt and Iverson, 1958) for the middle and upper grades. A table for the rapid determination of Dale-Chall scores has been developed by R. T. Williams (1972).

Two new formulas have been developed recently. The Harris-Jacobson Readability Formulas (see Appendix D) are easier to apply than the Spache and Dale-Chall Formulas. Fry's Readability Graph (Fry, 1968, 1972) is based on the number of syllables and sentences in a 100-word sample, and also should be easy to apply.

Use of noun-frequency counts (Elley, 1969) and syntactic complexity (von Glaserfeld, 1970–1971; Botel and Granowsky, 1972) also have been considered as factors in readability. For comprehensive treatments of readability see Chall (1957), Klare (1963), Bormuth (1968b), and for an annotated bibliography see Seels and Dale (1971).

Since Taylor (1953) first introduced the cloze procedure (in which the reader is asked to write in words which have been deleted from the passage) as a measure of readability, it has received increasing attention. Bormuth (1968a) reported that when a student's correct response to the deletions fall between 44 and 57 per cent, the material is at the child's instructional level. Materials on which the score is above 57 per cent is at the independent level. However, at least two studies (Sauer, 1969; Hodges, 1972) appear to indicate that cloze test scores do not closely approximate functional reading levels as determined by other measures.

The usefulness of the cloze procedure in assessing readability continues to be a debated issue; however, research does not suggest that the cloze procedure is an effective teaching technique (Jongsma, 1971). Those interested in learning more about the cloze technique may refer to Bickley, Ellington, and Bickley (1970) and R. D. Robinson (1972).

Both readability formulas and the cloze procedure have limitations. For example, one is likely to get somewhat different results depending upon the readability formulas used. They do not necessarily yield similar reading levels when applied to the same material (Jongsma, 1972). Just because a word appears on a list does not assure that its particular meaning in a given context will be understood by the reader. Neither do readability formulas consider the concept load or interest of the materials, two factors that often affect the difficulty of material. As for the cloze procedure, deleted content words (nouns, main verbs, and adjectives) may be more difficult to produce as cloze items than structure words, thus affecting the test results (Hittleman, 1973). Jefferson (1969) concluded that although the cloze was a strong research tool, it was not a highly valid measure of reading comprehension or of passage difficulty. Another study (Byrne, Feldhusen, and Kane, 1971) found that associational fluency has a significant influence on cloze results.

II. METHODS OF DETERMINING READING INTERESTS

Many elaborate techniques have been used in research studies on reading interests. Circulation data for newspapers and magazines have been compiled, the popularity of books has been studied by counting the number of times each was withdrawn from a library, and elaborate questionnaires have been employed. Most of these methods are too complicated and time-consuming to be practical for the classroom teacher. Simpler methods are needed for general application.

One of the simplest and most effective ways of finding out a child's interests is to watch his daily behavior for indications that could be followed up in reading. In schools in which children are encouraged to be spontaneous, they display their preferences in many ways: in conversation, in play, in drawing, and in other activities that encourage self-expression. Donald's absorption in aviation shows in his drawings and in the many airplane models that he builds. Lillian's love for playing nurse can lead to reading a biography of Clara Barton. Tommy's devoted care of the class's rabbits suggests the reading of books of animal stories. The alert teacher can find many leads concerning possible reading interests by observing his children.

A second useful procedure is to arrange for a "hobby club" period, or a period in which each child has a chance to tell about the things he likes to do in his spare time. This not only informs the teacher about the leisure-time activities enjoyed by the pupils but also helps to popularize certain interests. An enthusiastic report about stamp collecting, a home aquarium, or some other hobby may start several other children on the same activity. Groups with similar hobbies can be established, and special reading matter supplied for each group.

A third useful procedure is to arrange for a quiet interview with each child. During the interview the teacher can encourage the child to talk about his likes and dislikes in games, movies, TV programs, the books he has read, what he wants to be when he grows up, and so on. Naturally the teacher must be liked and trusted by the children if he wants them to confide in him. The preparation of a mimeographed record form helps to keep such interviews fairly uniform in terms of the questions asked and provides a convenient way of recording information. With large classes, it is often impractical to attempt to interview all the pupils.

Another possible technique is the use of a check list such as the one developed by Eberwein (1973) for use in junior high school. As shown in

Reading Interest Inventory

Directions: Below are the titles of some books that you might like to read or use during the next year. If you think you would like to read or use the book, make a √ mark on the line in front of the title. If you are fairly sure that you would not like to read or use the book, or if you do not know if you would like to read or use the book, leave the line blank. Please be sure to read all the titles and decide if you would, would not, or do not know if you would like to read or use each book during the next year.

_____ 1. Bionics, The Science of Living Machines 001.5

_____ 2. Reference Books, a Brief Guide for Students 016

_____ 3. Books for the Teen-Age 028.52

_____ 4. How to Use the Library 028.7

_____ 5. The World Book Encyclopedia 031

_____ 6. Readers' Guide to Periodical Literature 051

_____ 7. Museum, The Story of America's Treasure Houses 069

_____ 8. Behind the Headlines, The Story of Newspapers 070

_____ 9. Witches 133.4

_____10. How to be a Successful Teen-Ager 155.5

_____11. The Tree of Life, Selections from the Literature of the World's Religions 208

_____12. The Story of the Dead Sea Scrolls 221.4

_____13. Jesus of Israel 232.9

_____14. Prayers for Young People 242

_____15. Religions in America 280

_____16. Heroes, Gods and Monsters of Greek Myths 292

_____17. Questions Teen-Agers Ask 301.43

_____18. Black Pride, A People's Struggle 301.451

_____19. Information Please Almanac 317.3

_____20. Petticoat Politics, How American Women Won the Right to Vote 324.73

_____27. How to Study Better & Get Higher Marks 371.3

_____28. For Good Measure, The Story of Modern Measurement 389

_____29. Fashion as a Career 391.069

_____30. Manners Made Easy 395

_____31. King Arthur and His Knights of the Round Table 398.2

_____32. All About Language 400

_____33. Egyptian Hieroglyphs for Everyone 411

_____34. Webster's Third New International Dictionary of the English Language 423

_____35. The New Cassell's German Dictionary 433

_____36. Mansion's Shorter French and English Dictionary 443

_____37. Cassell's Spanish Dictionary 463

_____38. Cassell's New Latin Dictionary 473

_____39. The Russian Alphabet Book 491.7

_____40. 700 Science Experiments for Everyone 507.2

_____41. The Wonderful World of Mathematics 510.9

_____42. Exploring Mars 523.4

_____43. The Riddle of Time 529

_____44. Push and Pull, The Story of Energy 531

_____45. Inside the Atom 539.7

_____46. The A B C's of Chemistry 540.3

_____47. World Beneath the Oceans 551.4

_____48. Instant Weather Forecasting 551.59

_____54. The Wildlife of South America 591.98

_____55. Field Book of Insects of the United States and Canada 595.7

_____56. The Birds of America 598

_____57. The World of the Opossum 599

_____58. The Young Inventors' Guide 608

_____59. The Wonderful Story of You, Your Body— Your Mind—Your Feelings 612

_____60. Human Growth, The Story of How Life Begins and Goes on 612.6

_____61. Drugs, Facts on Their Use and Abuse 613.8

_____62. Here is Your Hobby, Amateur Radio 621.3841

_____63. Motors and Engines and How They Work 621.4

_____64. Your Future as a Pilot 629.13

_____65. How to Build Hot Rods and Race Them 629.22

_____66. Walk in Space, The Story of Project Gemini 629.45

_____67. The Book of Horses 636.1

_____68. Young America's Cook Book 641.5

_____69. Strictly for Secretaries 651

_____70. The Story of Glass 666

_____71. Cloth from Fiber to Fabric 677

_____72. Model Making 688

_____73. Careers in the Building Trades 690.69

_____74. The World of Art 709

_____75. Old Cities and New Towns, The Changing Face of the Nation 711

FIGURE 18.1 Part of a *Reading Interest Inventory* for use in the junior high school. From Lowell Eberwein, "What do book choices indicate?" *Journal of Reading*, December 1973, 17, 186-191. Reproduced by permission of the author and the International Reading Association. Approximately two-thirds of the items are shown.

Figure 18.1, the student is asked to read a number of book titles and to check these he would like to read or use.

The Incomplete Sentence Projective Test reproduced in Figure 18.2 can be used over a wide range of ages. If it is used as a group test, the children write the answers, but the teacher can read the items to them and help them with spelling if necessary. Used individually, it can be given to non-readers. It is often very revealing of the child's true feelings, especially about reading. The question "I'd read more if . . ." has brought such answers as "I liked to read," "books weren't so hard," "I could read better," and so on. In answer to "I'd rather read than . . .," Ruth wrote, "I wrath get bet by a snake." Positive ideas and feelings come out just as freely. When the children trust the teacher, a device like this can help the teacher greatly in the effort to understand (Boning and Boning, 1957). However, it should be realized that responses may be contaminated by attitudes only indirectly related to reading (H. M. Robinson and Weintraub, 1973).

III. CREATING AND ENRICHING READING INTERESTS

One of the most crucial tasks in a reading program is the transformation of children's attitudes toward reading from indifference or active dislike into avid reading. As long as progress depends entirely on what the children read under the eyes of the teacher, it is likely to remain slow. Spectacular gains in reading ability often result when the children begin to read a book or two a week, aside from class lessons. The most carefully planned lessons may bring disappointing results unless the teacher is able to ignite a tiny spark of interest and then nurture it carefully into a clear flame of enthusiasm for reading.

Creating Interest in Reading

The basic principles of successful work in developing reading interests have been admirably summarized as consisting of "a lure and a ladder" (Committee of the Upper Grades Study Council, 1943). The lure may be any of a variety of ways of enticing children to begin pleasurable reading. The ladder involves providing suitable reading matter which will intensify the child's interest in reading and in which he can gradually progress to reading material of superior quality.

The first essential is to provide physical surroundings in the classroom that will create an atmosphere favorable to reading. There should be a "reading corner" in every classroom. Its furnishings do not have to be elaborate. A table or two, a few chairs, and book shelves are the essentials.

1. Today I feel ....
2. When I have to read, I ....
3. I get angry when ....
4. To be grown up ....
5. My idea of a good time is ....
6. I wish my parents knew ....
7. School is ....
8. I can't understand why ....
9. I feel bad when ....
10. I wish teachers ....
11. I wish my mother ....
12. Going to college ....
13. To me, books ....
14. People think I ....
15. I like to read about ....
16. On weekends I ....
17. I'd rather read than ....
18. To me, homework ....
19. I hope I'll never ....
20. I wish people wouldn't ....
21. When I finish high school ....
22. I'm afraid ....
23. Comic books ....
24. When I take my report card home ....
25. I am at my best when ....
26. Most brothers and sisters ....
27. I don't know how ....
28. When I read math ....
29. I feel proud when ....
30. The future looks ....
31. I wish my father ....
32. I like to read when ....
33. I would like to be ....
34. For me, studying ....
35. I often worry about ....
36. I wish I could ....
37. Reading science ....
38. I look forward to ....
39. I wish ....
40. I'd read more if ....
41. When I read out loud ....
42. My only regret ....

FIGURE **18.2** Incomplete Sentence Projective Technique. From Thomas Boning and Richard Boning, "I'd Rather Read Than . . ." *The Reading Teacher*, 1957, *10*, p. 197. Reproduced by permission. The items are adapted from an earlier version by Ruth Strang.

Interest can be stimulated if, at the beginning of the term, the children build or paint the bookcases (sometimes improvised from orange crates), make and hang curtains, place colorful jackets on the books, and so on.

A good class library should contain at least fifty books. They should range in difficulty from some easy and interesting enough for the poorest readers in the class to others which will appeal to the most advanced readers. There should, of course, be a special collection of books of varied difficulty relating to the activity unit which is currently engaging the attention of the class. In addition, there should be fairy tales and legends, animal stories, adventure tales, stories with foreign settings, humor and nonsense, nature study and science, and at least some poetry. Current and back issues of the good children's magazines should find a place also.

A simple classification scheme makes it easier for the children to select books. The books can be arranged under a few simple headings: "make-believe," "real-life stories," "animals," "people and places," and so on. Some teachers use colored tabs, a different color for each reading group in the class, to help the children find the books of appropriate difficulty for them. Of course, the daily class schedule must provide some free time for browsing and for independent silent reading if the reading corner is to function properly.

A teacher who makes it a regular practice to read fascinating stories to his class usually has no trouble arousing interest in reading. Children of any age through high school love to listen to a lively tale. A good book or story which the teacher has read to the class will find many readers when it is placed in the library collection. Teachers who take the trouble to study the art of telling and reading stories to children reap dividends in improved attention, listening comprehension, and interest in reading (Martin, 1968; Thornley, 1968). Stories prerecorded by the teacher on tape can also be used, with the child or group either listening or following in the book while listening.

Children often show great interest in stories which are too difficult for them to read independently. After hearing the story, however, they can often read it with pleasure, since they have become acquainted with the author's style and have learned the meanings of the unfamiliar concepts and vocabulary that would otherwise be stumbling blocks.

Audience reading can be used to very good effect to foster independent reading. The nature of audience reading has been described on page 81. The desire to find and prepare a suitable selection to read to the class is a powerful incentive for many children and creates a natural motive for reading with a critical and evaluative attitude. Through the short selections that are presented in an audience reading period, the listeners are exposed to samples from many different sources and may have their interests awakened in books and stories that they might otherwise have overlooked.

Many teachers have made excellent use of a book club. Membership is open to the entire class. The usual requirements include possessing a library card and being ready to report on one book. The club elects officers, ordinarily a president and secretary, with sometimes a treasurer. Meetings may be held weekly, on Friday afternoons. At each meeting a few members are given the privilege of reporting on books they have read, telling whether or not they recommend the book and, if they like, reading to the club some especially delightful portion. Greatly increased liking for book reading and marked improvement in critical ability and taste are the normal results of a well-run club.

Some book clubs decide to have dues, which may be as little as a cent a week. The funds are used by a purchasing committee to buy materials for the class library collection. The judgment shown by a pupil committee in selecting materials to buy with club funds is often amazingly good, and the experience the children gain in visiting bookstores and inspecting books for possible purchase is invaluable. The handling of the funds also provides a real situation for the use of functional arithmetic. At the end of the year the purchases can be distributed to the members of the club, or left behind for the next class.

Use of paperbacks in the schools has been steadily increasing over the past decade. These inexpensive books have been employed successfully to stimulate interest in a variety of classroom organizations (J. Davis, 1970) and even in a reform school (Fader and McNeil, 1966). There is also a voluntary national program, Reading Is Fun-Damental (RIF), that in seven years has distributed more than 3 million free paperbacks which children are allowed to choose freely and to keep. Most trade book publishers produce paperbacks, some of which are aimed at the reluctant reader, and among the paperback book clubs are those of Scholastic, Weekly Reader, and Xerox Education. A helpful reference found in many libraries is *Paperback Books for Children* (Simmons, 1972) which annotates more than 700 books arranged by subject area with suggested grade levels.

The Child Who Dislikes Reading

The procedures just described are usually successful in creating a classroom atmosphere favorable to recreational reading and work well with the majority of children. With children who have a confirmed dislike for reading, special procedures may be necessary.

The first step in introducing such a child to pleasurable, voluntary reading is to locate a book that is easy and brief and will attract and hold his interest. For this purpose it is desirable to try a book that has many pictures, few lines to a page, and comparatively few pages. The thinner the book, the better. Naturally, content should be chosen in relation to what is known about the child's interests. Humorous books usually make an excellent start. Few children who can read them can resist the fun in *The Cat in the Hat*, Bennett Cerf's *Book of Riddles*, *Curious George*, or *Mr. Popper's Penguin*. After a successful first taste, the child is likely to want several more books of the same general type before venturing into a different sort of content.

In introducing such a book, it is desirable to show the book, turn a few pages to show the illustrations, and then read enough of the story aloud to arouse a desire to know the rest of it. Then the child can be asked if he would like to continue reading by himself. It may be desirable to suggest that he read ahead five or ten pages. If by the next lesson he has read more than the suggested amount, the teacher knows that the procedure has been successful. From then on, the problem is mainly one of keeping the child supplied with a succession of suitable books.

Sometimes older children are reluctant to take books home because they are afraid that other children will notice the "baby books" and make fun of them. Supplying a large Manila envelope in which books can be carried minimizes this difficulty.

After the child has made a good start in voluntary reading, he should be introduced to the public library (or to the school library, if there is one). If possible, the teacher should accompany him on his first visit, help him through the formalities of getting a library card, and show him where to look for books and how to take them out. For quite a while, he may need the assistance of a specific list of four or five suggested books to take with him; otherwise the long rows of books may be bewildering, and if his first few attempts at selecting his own books turn out poorly, he may become discouraged.

One should try to select reading material in accordance with a child's known likes until the habit of voluntary reading is well established. Some children want nothing but fairy tales; others disdain anything that is not true; narrow preferences confined to animals or airplanes or blood and thunder should be respected as far as is possible. Schulte (1972) suggested starting with the student's current interests such as poverty, war, and drug addiction and provided a bibliography for use in doing so.

A good children's librarian can be of invaluable help to both teacher and child in suggesting suitable books. A teacher of reading should, however, regard a continually enlarging acquaintance with children's books as an essential part of his own professional equipment. Aids to the location of reading matter of various kinds are discussed in the last part of this chapter.

Although primary motivation in voluntary reading comes from enjoyment of the reading itself, progress charts help here, as in other phases of reading improvement. A type of individual progress chart that appeals to all ages is shown in Figure 18.3, consisting of a bookcase, with books filled

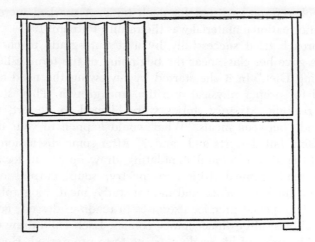

FIGURE 18.3   A bookcase chart for recording independent reading. As the child finishes a book, he draws another book in his bookcase. If the bookcase is made about 6 x 9 in., the books will be large enough to allow printing the author and title on each, and the date completed. Coloring the books in crayon adds to the attractiveness of the chart.

in as they are completed. Coloring the books with crayons adds to the attractiveness of such a chart. A popular kind of class record for voluntary reading is shown in Figure 18.4.

Expanding and Improving Reading Interests

While it is vitally important to help children to find reading matter that is closely related to their present interests, teachers should also try to broaden children's reading horizons. Children's attitudes are not fixed; they change as children get older and are susceptible to many environmental influences, not the least of which is the influence of the teacher. There are many good ways in which children's reading interests can be improved and enriched. The worst way is to attempt compulsion through required assignments and detailed book reports.

An ingenious teacher can find many ways of suggesting new fields of reading and awakening curiosity about new books. One teacher reported excellent results from displays of the colorful jackets of books that were added to the class library (Colburn, 1944). Another teacher found that her pupils were reading nothing but fiction. To stimulate interest in nonfiction, she asked them to write on slips of paper the topics or questions about which they would like to find information. A card index of topics was set up, with book references listed for each topic. A marked increase in the reading of informational material was the result (Putnam, 1941).

An approach tried successfully by a seventh-grade teacher is worth relating. She gave her class, near the beginning of the term, a little talk on "Your Reading Diet." In it she started by reviewing the need of a proper diet of food for proper physical nutrition and growth. Then she drew an analogy to reading. Mystery stories were likened to dessert, and comic books to candy between meals. "What would happen to your digestion if you ate nothing but desserts and candy?" After some discussion, the class, which found the idea novel and stimulating, drew up a plan for a balanced eight-course reading meal: fruit cup, poetry; soup, current events; fish course ("brain food"), science and nature study; meat, biography and history; vegetables, special practice exercises in reading; dessert, fiction; milk, sports and hobbies; after-dinner mints, comics. Each child drew up a menu and filled in the titles of his reading as the term progressed. He could take as many helpings as he wished of the courses he liked best, provided that he ate at least one dish of every kind.

An intelligent interest in current events should be one of the outcomes of education. Some schools develop interest in news events gradually, through the regular reading and discussion of one of the weekly papers that are prepared for school. Such papers as the series of weekly papers published by Scholastic Magazines and *My Weekly Reader* published by Xerox Education Publications, make it possible to introduce reading about current happenings as early as the first grade and to continue it with reading matter appropriate to each grade through the elementary and secondary school years. There is even a magazine *Kids* (Kids Publishers) written by children; *World Traveler* (Open Court), which is a monthly written at the primary-grade level using material from *National Geographic*, should interest elementary and junior high school children.

Another procedure that can be used at the upper levels is to devote some of the social studies time to current events periods, in which each child is expected to present a brief oral report about some interesting development in the news of the preceding week. This combines motivated independent reading in newspapers and news magazines, critical comparison of possible selections, practice in organizing a summary, and effective oral English work.

Among the other ways for stimulating interests in books and voluntary reading suggested by W. Johnson (1972) and Roeder and Lee (1973) are: 1) having the students advertise and sell books, each trying to prove that the book they read is the best; 2) displaying colorful posters to advertise a specific monthly topic; 3) having a read-in: the child selects a partner and time is set aside for them to read to each other; 4) teacher reading to the students, stopping at an exciting point, then providing several copies of the

FIGURE 18.4 Wall chart for recording independent book reading. When a pupil has finished a book and has made a satisfactory report, the teacher prints the name of the book on a colored slip of paper and places it in the child's plane.

book for them to read. Even book reports need not be deadly dull. Decker (1969) offers many imaginative ideas for using them to stimulate student involvement in and enjoyment of reading. Yet another way of interesting some students to read books is to allow free use of kits such as the *Pilot Library Series* (SRA) that contain short excerpts from books, and then to provide the books in which they express an interest.

The quality and quantity of children's voluntary reading also can be improved through a planned literature program of daily oral reading by the teacher (Sirota, 1971) and establishment of a free reading period (Sperling,

1970). One of the most important ingredients in stimulating interest is free —free time during which the children are allowed to read materials of their own choice and to discuss what they have read. If we do not demonstrate that reading is a worthwhile activity by providing school time, how can we expect children to value reading?

Poetry has become somewhat neglected in reading programs in recent years. The amount of space devoted to poetry in readers has decreased markedly, and the tendency to substitute wide individualized reading for uniform class study of specific selections has lessened the amount of attention devoted to poetry in the upper grades. There many ways in which the modern teacher can awaken and develop an appreciation of poetry. One of the most important is the reading of well-chosen poems to the class by the teacher. A teacher who loves poetry and can read it well can make poems come alive for children (Jacobs, 1959). A second useful procedure is choral reading and speaking. Poems that the children enjoy can be prepared for group presentation. Choral reading is a comparatively new practice, which is ideally suited to the development of an appreciation of poetry. At a simple level, the whole class can read the poem in unison. As the children become more expert, delightful contrast effects can be achieved through a balancing of solo parts and choral effects. A third way in which interest in poetry can be developed is through encouraging children to prepare poems for presentation in audience reading periods. Other suggestions may be found in Harp (1972) and Hopkins (1972).

With a little planning and effort, the summer can be an ideal time for recreational reading. Aasen (1959) planned a real sales campaign. She worked on two fourth-grade classes, promoting the idea of summer reading, letting each child know what his reading test scores were, bringing in the librarian, providing a recommended list of books, arranging for Bookmobile service, and setting up a system of recording one's reading. In September these two classes showed a gain of .7 years in reading grade, while a control class not given this program showed no change. This program deserves to be widely imitated.

IV. VALUES OF READING: AFFECTIVE GROWTH

As H. M. Robinson and Weintraub (1973) pointed out, few would disagree that reading may change attitudes and behaviors since reading offers an opportunity to identify with a character or to solve a problem. Yet most of this "conventional wisdom" is based on opinion. The few studies conducted in this area neither support nor refute these possible values of reading. Therefore a number of possibilities exist: 1) readers do not have access to material that answers their questions adequately; 2) the problems facing the student are so demanding that many sources of information about possible solutions are necessary, and there also may be cumulative effects of reading many selections; 3) what readers acquire from a given selection may be an indivdual matter influenced by their own needs and problems; and 4) reading by itself is not sufficient to evoke change, and must be supplemented by other forms of communication. Perhaps as Huus (1973) believes, attitudes are changed more often through reading followed by discussion, than by reading alone. It is presently difficult to assess attitudinal or behavioral changes because of the apparent complexity of the behaviors themselves and the inadequacies of available instruments to measure change.

One of the possible values of reading is therapeutic. Bibliotherapy is the attempt to promote mental and emotional health by using reading materials to fulfill needs, relieve pressure, or help an individual in his development as a person (Hoagland, 1972). Basically the process involves three steps: identification, catharsis, and insight. As for its effectiveness, some studies have shown that bibliotherapy may be useful in group therapy, but the results of classroom studies are mixed (Purves and Beach, 1972). Those who wish to learn more about bibliotherapy may refer to Riggs (1971), Schultheis (1972), and *Bibliotherapy: Methods and Materials* (Association of Hospital and Institution Libraries, 1971). Books may be used to promote sensitivity and empathy through techniques such as those suggested by Greer (1972) or through using ideas suggested in publications like *Reading Ladders for Human Relations* (V. Reid, 1972).

V. LOCATING READING MATERIALS

There is such a wealth of reading matter for children today that the task of selection is by no means easy. The purpose of this section is to acquaint the reader with sources in which he can look up recommended books and materials to meet all sorts of reading needs. The references are grouped in four categories: for elementary school children, for secondary school, for retarded or reluctant readers, and for special purposes.

Book Lists for Elementary School Children

The references that follow are useful primarily for selecting books for children who are average or above-average readers, or for locating books to read to children. The age or grade designations which they give are usually quite broad, covering three or four years, and are more likely to underestimate than to overestimate the level of reading skill required to read the books independently.

Children's Catalog, 12th ed. (H. W. Wilson, 1971). Annual supplements. A very comprehensive listing containing 5,119 titles recommended for libraries, with reviews and a system of cross indexing by author, title, subject matter, and grade level. Especially recommended books are starred. Kept up to date by annual supplements until the next edition appears.

Best Books for Children (Bowker, 1974). Revised annually. Over 4,000 books for preschool to high school ages arranged by topics and levels, with author, title, and series indexes. Paperback.

Good Books for Children, 3d ed. A Selection of Outstanding Children's Books Published 1950–1965 (University of Chicago Press, 1966). Compiled by Mary K. Eakin. Contains 1,391 titles arranged alphabetically by author, with subject and title indexes, and reviews from the *Bulletin of the Center for Children's Books*.

Books for Children, Preschool through Junior High School, 1968–1969, as Selected and Reviewed by *The Booklist and Subscription Books Bulletin* (American Library Association, 1970). Annual supplements, 1969–1970, 1970–1971, 1971–1972. Gives a one-paragraph review of over 3,000 titles; indicates broad grade levels and if primarily for boys or girls; gives classification number.

Adventuring with Books, 2nd ed. (Citation Press, 1973). Prepared by Shelton L. Root, Jr. An annotated list of 2,400 titles for pre-kindergarten to grade 8 with suggested interest and difficulty levels by category.

Bibliography of Books for Children, 1971 rev. (Association for Childhood Educational International). About 1,800 books arranged informally by subject; particularly good for preschool and primary levels.

Most teachers will find much help in any of the book lists described above or in the sources annotated by Ladley (1970). Those who want reviews of the most recent books for children can find them in such publications as *Horn Book*, *Junior Libraries*, *Elementary English*, the *Bulletin of the Center for Children's Books* (University of Chicago), and the *Booklist* and *Subscription Books Bulletin* of the American Library Association.

Book Lists for the Secondary School

There are several book lists useful in finding books for junior and senior high students. The following are representative:

Junior High School Library Catalog, 2nd ed. (H. W. Wilson, 1970). A selected catalog of over 3,400 books with brief reviews, classified by topic, author, and title. Annual supplements between editions.

Senior High School Library Catalog, 10th ed. (H. W. Wilson, 1972).

A selected catalog of over 4,750 titles with brief reviews, classified by topic, author, and title. Annual supplements between editions.

WALTER, ELINOR (Comp.). *Book Bait*: Detailed notes on adult books popular with young people, 2nd ed. (American Library Association, 1969). Annotations of 100 adult titles that have immediate and strong appeals to 13- to 16-year-olds; specifies appealing qualities in terms of audience.

Books for Secondary School Libraries: A Basic List. Compiled by the Library Committee of the Independent Schools Education Board. (R. R. Bowker, 1971). A relatively mature list of 4,000 titles containing books of college level as well as secondary.

CARLSEN, G. ROBERT. *Books and the Teen-Age Reader* (Bantam Books, 1971). Discusses different types of reading material in separate chapters, with recommended lists in each chapter.

WILSON, JEAN A. (Ed.). *Books for You*, 1971 rev. (National Council of Teachers of English). Annotated list of over 2,000 titles in 45 subject categories.

Books Lists for Disabled and Reluctant Readers

The following references are helpful in selecting materials for disabled and reluctant readers:

SPACHE, GEORGE D. *Good Reading for Poor Readers*, rev. 1974 (Garrard). Discusses principles of choosing books, contains listings on: trade books useful with poor readers; adapted and simplified materials; text-books, workbooks, and games; magazines and newspapers; series books; book clubs, indexes and reading lists; programmed materials; and visual perception. Appendix gives directions for Spache readability formula. Author and title indexes.

ROSWELL, FLORENCE G., *et al. Selected Reading Materials*, rev. 1970 (City College Reading Center, School of Education, The City College). Lists useful books, workbooks, games, and so on, indicating difficulty and interest levels.

SISTER MARY JULITTA & SISTER MICHAELLA. "A List of Books for Disabled Readers," *Elementary English*, 1968, 45, 472–477. Lists books of first- through third-grade difficulty based on experience at the Reading Clinic of Cardinal Stritch College; Spache readability score also given, and interest level.

STRANG, RUTH; PHELPS, ETHLYENE; & WITHROW, DOROTHY, *Gateways to Readable Books*. An Annotated Graded List of Books in Many Fields for Adolescents Who Find Reading Difficult, 4th ed. (H. W. Wilson,

1966). Classifies books under nearly thirty headings. Particularly helpful in locating books for disabled readers in high school.

WHITE, MARIAN E. (Ed.) *High Interest–Easy Reading for Junior and Senior High School Students*, 2nd ed. (Citation Press, 1972). An annotated list of hundreds of easy to read books for use by reluctant, not disabled readers, listed by 18 subject categories; broad range of reading levels indicated.

LEIBERT, ROBERT E. (Ed.). *A Place to Start* (University of Kansas Reading Center, 1971). Computerized list of over 7,000 titles arranged by increasing level of reading difficulty according to topics; interest level also indicated.

CRAMER, WARD & DORSEY, SUZANNE. *Read-Ability Books for Junior and Senior High Students* (Walch, 1970). Briefly annotated list of 1850 books grouped by reading levels (grades 1–8); interest levels also indicated (grades 1–12).

Books Written Especially for Disabled Readers. It is much easier to find material that is both easy enough and interesting to disabled readers than it used to be. For those reading at or below second-grade level, the easier books in such series as *Cowboy Sam, Butternut Bill, Dan Frontier, Jim Forest, Moonbeam,* and *Sailor Jack* (see Appendix B) are generally more palatable than primary grade readers, while employing a reasonably well-controlled vocabulary. Other series that have worked well with retarded readers include the *American Adventure Series,* the *Morgan Bay Mysteries,* the *Modern Adventure Series,* and *Deep Sea Adventures.* A list of such series is given in Appendix B. Increasingly more materials, especially paperbacks, are becoming available for use with older students who have reading problems.

There are also very many simplified and shortened versions of famous books that are frequently used at secondary school level. Some of these are well done; others are quite poor. They range in difficulty all the way from third-grade level to eighth-grade level so the fact that a book is a simplified version gives no indication of its actual difficulty. Stevenson's *Treasure Island,* for example, is available in four different simplified versions ranging from fourth- to eighth-grade level in difficulty. The most valuable of these are the collections of short stories, such as Kottmeyer's adaptations of *Tales from Sherlock Holmes* and *The Gold Bug and Other Stories* (Webster) and Moderow's *Six Great Stories* (Scott, Foresman). A listing of about 250 books of this type, with difficulty levels estimated, has been given by Spache (1974). Some series of adapted classics are included in Appendix B.

Materials Written by Teachers and Pupils. It is often necessary, as has been pointed out before, to use stories written especially to appeal to a particular child. The first step is naturally to find out what the child would like to talk about. It is easy to get the child's cooperation in such an undertaking, and he is usually very proud to dictate a story to the teacher and later read it in his own words. In addition to their interest value, such stories have an important advantage in that all the words used are from the child's own speaking vocabulary and therefore easy for him to understand; training in word recognition is therefore not hampered by comprehension difficulties. Stories written by one child are often enjoyed by other children. Scrapbooks of stories written by the children themselves have great appeal as supplementary reading in remedial classes. The stories should be typewritten or printed.

A remedial teacher may also find it advisable because of a scarcity of suitable books to rely largely on material prepared by himself. Sometimes stories and selections from advanced books can be rewritten so as to be readable by disabled pupils. Unless a teacher has considerable originality, he will ordinarily be more successful in adapting the writings of others than in attempting to write completely original material.

In planning story-type or informational material for disabled readers it is a good idea to make each unit short enough so that it can be finished in one remedial period. A brief introductory statement may be used to give the pupil suggestions about the way in which the selection should be read. At the end of the selection specific questions should be included which may be answered in writing or may serve as a basis for oral discussion.

Materials written for remedial pupils should be couched in a simple and straightforward style and at a level of complexity within the grasp of the pupil. Compound and complex sentences may be used in moderation, provided that they do not contain many inversions of normal word order or other involved constructions. During the writing one should naturally try to use an easy word in place of a more difficult synonym whenever possible. After the material has been written, its vocabulary may be checked against one or more of the standard word lists to make sure that it does not contain an unreasonable number of unusual or difficult words. The best test of the suitability of the story, however, is the ease with which the pupil can read it.

Since writing special materials is very time-consuming, remedial reading teachers should make every effort to utilize the materials that are available in printed form.

Ethnic Materials

Although research does not clearly indicate whether or not minority-group students prefer to read pertaining to their own cultural or ethnic backgrounds, an increasing amount of such material (particularly for blacks) has been published in the past decade. There is also some question as to how closely the stories should approximate reality in order to be effective or interesting, and there are dangers in attempting to make literature relevant to minority youngsters (Elkind, 1972). However, it is probable that many children do like to read about their own kind and perhaps about those who are different, so that ethnic materials may be of interest to both minority- and majority-group children. Literature may be used as a vehicle to enculturate the reader (Cianciolo, 1971). A useful source in attempting to extent sensitivity toward others is *Reading Ladders for Human Relations* (V. Reid, 1972) which annotates 1300 books and offers suggestions for their use.

According to Bachner (1969) a review of the literature revealed that literature for minority-group adolescents should deal with contemporary problems, employ a writing style that is informal and forceful, and have characters with whom the students can identify. Beauchamp (1970) studied the reading interests of ninth graders who were three to five years retarded in reading ability. Among his findings were: 1) their reading interests did not vary substantially from those of other children of their age, but they did develop at a later date; 2) these students could and did read books that "ought to be too difficult" for them *if* the books had extremely high interest; 3) they preferred books with fewer characters, but without a clear preference for characters similar to themselves; 4) they tended to reject love and romance themes, preferring those of perseverence, physical strength, triumph over adversity and obstacles, and detective stories; and 5) adapted classics were successful provided description was minimized and action and suspense maximized.

Among the materials published for and about minority groups are:

Open Door Books (Children's Press). Thirty-six books that contain realistic autobiographies of minority men and women who have faced modern society and won. Reading level about fifth grade; interest level, grades 5–12.

Stories of the Inner City (Globe). Twenty-seven contemporary short stories written at the fourth or fifth reader level for junior and senior high school students.

Toward Freedom (Garrard). History and heritage of black Americans, written from the black man's point of view; highlights important contributions they made to America. Reading level about 6, interest level, 5–9.

Target Today Series (Benefic). One hundred short story lessons in each book deal with contemporary urban-life episodes. Reading level 2–6, interest level 3–9.

Americans All (Garrard). Biographies of great Americans of all races, creeds, and national origins; emphasis on character and personal determination. Reading level about 4, interest level 3–6.

Living City Adventure Series (Globe). Three collections of short stories that focus on the problems and dreams of multi-ethnic young people of today. Written at the fourth or fifth reader level, these stories should be of interest to those in grades 7–12.

We Are Black (SRA). Selections of from 300–900 words taken from books and periodicals. A reading skill program accompanies the materials. Reading levels 2–6, interest levels 4–8.

Multi-Ethnic Reading Library (Scholastic). Three paperback collections that children at various grade-level ranges should be able to read and enjoy.

Selections from the Black (Jamestown). A 3-book college-level developmental reading series containing 90 selections by black writers. Reading levels: Olive 6–8, Brown 9–11, Purple 12–college.

Voices from the Bottom (Jamestown). Same as above, but the selections are by and about Indians, Chicanos, and Puerto Ricans.

Our Native Americans Book (Benefic). Customs, lives, ceremonies, and games of various Indian and Eskimo tribes and Hawaiians. Reading level 2–3, interest level 2–5.

Indians (Garrard). Factually accurate biographies of Indian men and women, honest and unstereotyped; American history from the Indian's viewpoint. Reading level about 3, interest levels 2–5.

Indian Culture Series (Montana). Authentic, interesting books depicting the true life of the Indians before the coming of the white man, and present-day life. Reading levels 3–5, interest level 4–12.

Folk Tales and Legends (Montana). Eleven different titles of the authentic tales and legends from different Indian tribes. Written at reader levels 1–4, the books should interest elementary and junior high school children.

Books of interest to and about minority-group children have been listed by Hopkins (1969), Griffin (1970), Spache (1974), Archer (1972), Weber (1972) and Strickland (1973b). An annotated bibliography of literature by and about American Indians has been prepared by Stensland (1973), and the needs in literature of minority groups have been discussed by Tanyzer and Karl (1972).

Parents and Children's Reading

The impact of the home on the child's readiness for reading and the relationship between home conditions and the development of reading disabilities have been discussed earlier in this book. Obviously the emotional attitudes of the older members of the family toward books and reading have a real impact on young children.

A professional man consulted the senior author about his son's lack of interest in reading. It was ascertained that the boy emulated and admired his father, who spent most evenings watching television or playing cards with friends. The suggestion was made that the father should keep the TV set in the living room off for a week, get a book he might enjoy, and sit in the living room and read during the usual TV hours. It worked; by the time the week was up, father and son were sitting in the living room, each enjoying a book.

Most parents need guidance concerning their role in relation to their children's reading. Some excellent books for parents are now available, among which the following are outstanding:

> LARRICK, NANCY. *A Parent's Guide to Children's Reading,* 3rd ed., rev. and enlarged (Doubleday, 1969). Also available in a Pocket Books Edition. Sponsored by the National Book Committee and with consultants from eighteen national organizations. Discusses the prereading periods, explains modern reading instruction and the parents' role in it, and recommends specific books for parents to read to children and get for them.
>
> *Let's Read Together: Books for Family Enjoyment,* 3rd ed. (American Library Association, 1969). Guide for selecting children's books; describes more than 500 books; interest and age levels indicated.

This chapter has stressed the importance of finding "the right book for the right child" as a way of increasing children's interest in reading for pleasure and providing a basis for the gradudal maturing and refining of taste and critical standards. The child who reads extensively will make his own comparisons and will, in the long run, prefer sound writing and get to dislike trash. Even if he does not, an omnivorous reading diet is far superior to none at all. In the face of the competition from mass media, such as television, it takes both superior materials and clever salesmanship by teachers to develop the reading habit; without this habit, much of reading instruction is wasted. For the disabled reader, fluency and ease in reading can develop only through much reading of interesting, easy material.

SUGGESTED ADDITIONAL READING

BOND, GUY L. & TINKER, MILES A. *Reading difficulties: their diagnosis and correction* (3rd ed.). New York: Appleton-Century-Crofts, 1973. Chap. 17.

CATTERSON, JANE H. (Ed.). *Children and literature.* Newark, Del.: International Reading Association, 1970.

HARRIS, ALBERT J. & SIPAY, EDWARD R. (Eds.). *Readings on reading instruction* (2nd ed.). New York: McKay, 1972. Chap. 12.

HUCK, CHARLOTTE S. *Get children excited about books.* Glenview, Ill.: Scott, Foresman, 1971.

LARRICK, NANCY. *A teacher's guide to children's books.* Columbus: Charles E. Merrill, 1963.

PAINTER, HELEN W. (Ed.). *Reaching children and young people through literature.* Newark, Del.: International Reading Association, 1971.

PURVES, ALAN C. & BEACH, RICHARD. *Literature and the reader: research in response to literature, reading interests, and the teaching of literature.* Urbana, Ill.: National Council of Teachers of English, 1972.

SEBESTA, SAM L. & WALLEN, CARL J. (Eds.). *The first R: readings on teaching reading.* Chicago: Science Research Associates, 1972. Pp. 7–38, 68–147.

SMITH, NILA B. *Reading instruction for today's children.* Englewood Cliffs, N.J.: Prentice-Hall, 1963. Chaps. 12, 13, 14.

TINKER, MILES A. & MCCULLOUGH, CONSTANCE M. *Teaching elementary reading* (3rd ed.). New York: Appleton-Century-Crofts, 1968. Chap. 15.

ZINTZ, MILES V. *The reading process: the teacher and the learner.* Dubuque, Iowa: W. C. Brown, 1970. Chap. 12.

19

Increasing Rate of Reading

There is so much to read today that the ability to read quickly has become an important asset. A century ago, an average adult's personal library may have consisted of little more than the Bible, an almanac, and a few treasured books read over and over again. There was plenty of time not only to read but also to memorize poems and favored quotations.

A literate adult in today's hectic world goes through more reading material in a week than his great-grandfather probably covered in a year. The college student who has to take six hours for what his instructor considers a three-hour assignment, the business executive who wishes he could get through his reports and mail in two hours instead of three or four, the physician who cannot keep up with his professional journals—these are typical of the people who have made "speed reading" courses popular.

The average reader wastes a great deal of useful time in unnecessarily slow reading. There is abundant evidence that the typical high school or college student can increase his rate of reading by 25 to 50 per cent without any decline in accuracy of comprehension. The very slow reader can sometimes achieve an increase of 50 to 100 per cent in rate in a comparatively short time. If we assume, rather conservatively, that a typical pupil in the upper grades or secondary school spends two hours a day in reading, including recreational and study-type reading, an increase of 25 per cent in rate would release about three hours of his time each week for additional reading or for other activities.

Recognizing that to read rapidly is an advantage, it is important to keep always in mind that to go through material, without understanding it and without being able to remember what it said, is a waste of time no matter what the speed at which this may be accomplished.

I. RELATION OF RATE TO COMPREHENSION

The question of how fast readers compare with slow readers in comprehension was one of the early questions that reading researchers tackled, and by 1950 a large number of studies had been completed. The results favored neither those who expected fast readers to be careless and inaccurate, nor those who expected the good reader to be both fast and accurate in comprehension.

The degree of relationship between rate and comprehension varies with the age of the readers, the kinds of material used, and the methods used in measuring the two factors. In the primary grades one would expect to find a fairly high relationship, because slow reading at that level is usually caused by difficulty in word recognition which impairs comprehension also. At higher levels, the many research studies show great variations in results. At the secondary and college level most of the correlations tended to be positive but quite low, around .30 (Tinker, 1939). Among bright pupils fast readers tended to comprehend better than slow readers, while at lower intelligence levels there was some evidence that the slower readers tended to comprehend better (Shores and Husbands, 1950). In mathematics and science the correlations tended to be low and negative; with many exceptions, the faster the pupil read, the less he tended to understand (Blommers and Lindquist, 1944).

There is no one rate of reading that is appropriate in all situations; rather, the efficient reader varies his rate according to his purposes and the requirements of the material. Yoakam (1955) distinguished four major rates of reading and indicated some of the kinds of reading situations in which they are appropriate:

Reading Rates Appropriate for Different Purposes

1] Skimming Rate
   Work-type reading: to find a reference; to locate new material; to answer a specific question; to get the general idea of a selection
   Recreational reading: to go through a book or magazine to get a general idea of the contents; to review a familiar story
2] Rapid Reading
   Work-type: to review familiar material; to get the main idea or central thought; to get information for temporary use

Recreational: to read narrative material primarily for the plot; to read informational material for pleasure or relaxation; to reread familiar material

3] Normal Rate

Work-type: to find answers to specific questions; to note details; to solve a problem; to grasp relation of details to main ideas; to read material of average difficulty

Recreational: to appreciate beauty of literary style; to keep up with current events; to read with the intention of later retelling the story

4] Careful Rate

Work-type: to master content including details; to evaluate material; to get details in sequence, as in following directions; to outline, summarize, or paraphrase; to analyze author's presentation; to solve a problem

Recreational: to read material with unusual vocabulary or style; to read poetry; to read with the intent of memorizing; to judge literary values

The choice of an inappropriate rate of reading is sometimes an important factor in comprehension difficulties. Some children, given a reading diet that consists almost entirely of light, easy fiction, become rapid, fluent readers. Later, when they are expected to read materials that require careful study, they try to employ the same reading habits that are effective in their recreational reading. Then their tendency to read rapidly and superficially produces sad results. Other children are drilled carefully for accuracy from the very beginning. They find it easy to note details in their reading, but may experience difficulty in discovering the central thought of a selection or in following a sequence of events.

Flexibility in Reading

Out of recognition of the complexity of the relationship between rate and comprehension grew the point of view that pupils should learn to vary their rates of reading according to their purposes for reading and the nature of the reading material. Research findings indicate, however, that most readers are rigid rather than flexible in their rate of reading. McDonald (1960, 1965), for example, studied over 6,000 readers at elementary, secondary, college, and adult levels and found that more than 90 per cent of them tended to maintain a characteristic approach and a relatively invariant rate with all of the types of reading tested, despite instructions for differentiation of purpose and in spite of variations in difficulty, style, and content of the materials.

To some extent this individually characteristic and relatively invariant rate of reading may be constitutional; Buswell (1951) found that there is a substantial correlation between rate of reading and rate of thinking on nonreading tasks. H. Brown (1970) tested the reaction time and movement time of seventh-grade boys and found that both correlated significantly with oral and silent reading rate. It may be that quickness or slowness is a characteristic common to reading and many other categories of human responses.

To some extent this inflexibility is learned; many professional men complain that the habit of slow, careful reading that they employ in their occupational reading carries over into their recreational reading. Lack of flexibility in rate may simply be the result of lack of appropriate training. Although lip service in favor of flexibility has been given for many years, not much effective teaching to develop flexibility has taken place.

T. L. Harris (1965) has shown that significant improvement in flexibility can be achieved by fourth graders given specific instruction to produce this result. Braam (1963) trained high school seniors on five types of content and found that their average difference between highest and lowest rate increased from 19 to 159 words per minute. In such a program the initially faster readers usually gain more than the initially slow readers, so it is possible for constitutionally based differences to be present even when there is a favorable response to training.

Readers also can show some flexibility in modifying rate according to the kind of answer they are reading for and the difficulty of the material. Intermediate-grade children tend to read faster for details than for main ideas, and faster for main ideas than for sequence (Otto, Barrett, and T. L. Harris, 1968). Rankin (1970–1971) found that college students vary their rates within a selection, slowing down for difficult portions and reading faster when the material is easier. Rate, then, is related to the kind of "idea collecting" that the task demands (Stone, 1962).

In regard to speed and comprehension, an individual may show one of three unsatisfactory patterns: 1) he may be retarded in both rate and comprehension; 2) he may have a satisfactory rate but poor comprehension; or 3) he may have satisfactory comprehension but be excessively slow.

When a pupil is poor in both speed and comprehension, the major efforts of the remedial teacher should be expended on the improvement of comprehension. Speed should not be emphasized at all until there is an adequate basis for reading with understanding. Many of the factors which interfere with comprehension also retard speed. As a pupil develops more effective word-recognition habits, acquires a more extensive vocabulary, and learns to read in thought units, his speed will increase even though no attention is specifically devoted to it. This principle of stressing comprehension rather than speed when both are weak should be adhered to in all cases except those in which it is felt that excessively low speed is a major factor in preventing better comprehension.

Pupils who read at a rapid rate but whose understanding is poor likewise need training which emphasizes comprehension. Many of this group are context readers, whose difficulty is due in part to inadequate word-recognition techniques. When that is true, emphasis should be devoted first of all to the improvement of word recognition. In other cases, the trouble may simply be due to an attempt to employ a rapid or skimming rate on material which requires careful reading. The first step in overcoming this difficulty is to explain to the child that he is underestimating the difficulty of the material and is not reading carefully enough. The second and major step is to check for comprehension everything that he reads. Many different kinds of reading matter and varied types of comprehension checks should be employed.

It is not advisable to place much stress on slowing down the rate of reading, since it is desirable to retain as much speed as is consistent with adequate comprehension. As the pupil learns through experience the degree of accuracy that is necessary in different kinds of reading, he will develop ability to adjust his rate to the requirements of his task.

When comprehension is satisfactory but rate is below normal, the remedial teacher can concentrate his energies directly on the problem of increasing speed. This is the easiest of all remedial problems and one in which considerable improvement can be expected.

What Is a Normal Rate of Reading?

One of the questions most frequently asked of the teacher of reading is, "How fast should I be able to read?" It should be obvious from the preceding discussion that there can be no one answer to this question; the reader's rate should vary according to the kind of material he is reading and the thoroughness with which he wants to read it. Because of this, one can suggest a typical or normal rate for a specific kind of material, but should not encourage the mistaken belief that all kinds of material should be read at one standard rate. Norms or averages are good only for the kind of reading matter that was used in obtaining them. For this reason, the typical reading rates found by different investigators show marked differences.

Further light on this question is cast by the rates shown in Table 12. This table shows the median rate of reading for each grade from 2 to 9 and for grade 12, as given in the norms of several standardized silent reading tests. There is a steady upward trend from grade 2 to grade 9. The top figure at each grade is not the rate of the fastest reader, but the median rate determined by the test which has the highest median. Similarly the lowest rates shown are not the rates of the slowest readers, but the median rate reported for one of the tests. The median for grade 12 is no higher than that for grade 9. One may take the rate of 250 words per minute as a rough estimate of the normal rate of reading for high school students and adults, for material of average difficulty.

Results of the most extensive normative study of eye-movement photographs yet conducted are given in Table 13. These norms are based on students who scored 70 per cent or better in comprehension when reading material of average difficulty for the grade. The Rate with Comprehension norms show steady gains through the primary grades, a very slow rate of improvement from fifth grade on, and (allowing for many dropouts) little or no gain from tenth grade on. The slowing down of progress in rate seems to run parallel with decline in the time and attention devoted to developmental reading..

Norms for rate of reading tend to be misleading, because results vary so much according to the nature of the material used and the type of comprehension checks employed (Carlson, 1951). As yet no one has attempted to set up rate norms for the four different kinds of rates described above.

An efficient reader should vary his rate of reading over a wide range. In reading light fiction or easy nonfiction, a rapid rate is highly advantageous. A superior adult reader should be able to go through material of this sort at a rate of at least 400 words per minute; rates of more than 5,000 words per minute have been reported. A person's normal reading rate, for somewhat more careful reading, may be only two thirds as fast as his most rapid reading. In very careful reading, it may be sometimes desirable to slow down to less than one third of one's rapid rate.

Individual differences in rate of reading are great, and it is futile to hope to bring all slow readers up to the average. Furthermore, when practice for improving speed of reading is given, those who are originally fast readers usually gain more than the slower readers.

For example, a few years ago the senior author conducted a little experiment in improving rate of reading with about fifty college students in edu-

TABLE 12. *Median rates of reading for different grades as determined by several standardized reading tests*

| | | | | | Grade | | | | |
	II	III	IV	V	VI	VII	VIII	IX	XII
Highest test	118	138	170	195	230	246	267	260	295
Median test	86	116	155	177	206	215	237	252	251
Lowest test	35	75	120	145	171	176	188	199	216

NOTE: *The number of tests included in the table is 7 for grades 2 and 3; 8 for grades 4, 5, 6, and 7; 6 for grades 8 and 9; and 3 for grade 12.*

cational psychology. The fastest reader improved from 450 to 700 words per minute; the slowest, from 175 to 250 words per minute. Each gain was important and valuable to the student who made it, although the difference between the two students was greater at the end of the experiment than at the beginning.

To some extent, rate of reading is related to rate of thinking. It does no good to try to read faster than one can assimilate ideas. Of two readers whose rate is 175 words per minute, one may be able to improve tremendously, while the other may already be close to his maximum rate of effective thinking.

One can test a person's rate on a standardized rate of reading test and let him compare his rate with the averages for different groups. However, the correct answer to the question, "How fast should I read?" is nearly always, "Considerably faster than you read at present."

II. EYE MOVEMENTS

In 1878 a French physician named Javal published the first account of systematic observations of the movements of the eyes during reading. His work stimulated others to work on similar problems, and when Huey (1908) published the first important book on the psychology of reading, a considerable store of information had been gathered. The early investigators were handicapped by clumsy and sometimes painful apparatus. After Dodge invented a camera for photographing eye movements, many important studies were made, notably by Buswell (1922). A portable eye-movement camera called The Reading Eye is in production.[1] For special research studies, more precise cameras which record eye movements electronically have been built.

The way eye movements are represented on a photograph is illustrated in Figure 19.1. The camera contains a roll of moving picture film which unrolls at a steady speed. A thin beam of light shines on each eyeball and is reflected onto the film. When the eye moves sideways between fixations, the turning of the eyeball shifts the beam of light so as to record an almost horizontal line on the film; and when the eye is motionless during a fixation, the unrolling of the film causes a vertical line to be made. The movements of both eyes are photographed simultaneously on the film, and their parallel movements give a sort of descending staircase effect. The duration of each fixation is shown by the length of the vertical line, and the amount of print taken in during a fixation is indicated by the length of the horizontal line representing the movement between fixations. A regression is shown by a

1. Manufactured by Educational Developmental Laboratories.

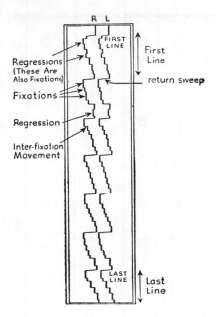

FIGURE 19.1 Diagram showing how eye-movement characteristics are represented in a photograph. Reproduced by courtesy of American Optical Corporation.

short horizontal movement to the left, and a return sweep from the end of one line to the beginning of the next line is shown by a long horizontal movement to the left.

When a person reads, his eyes progress in a series of alternating pauses and quick jerky movements called *saccadic* movements. The pauses, which are called *fixations*, last only a fraction of a second each. The eyes see in reading only during the fixations. When one comes to the end of the line there is a smooth continuous movement back to the beginning of the next line. This is called a *return sweep*.

The efficient reader usually sees one or two words at each fixation. The amount a reader can see at one fixation is called his *recognition span*. The more he can see at one fixation, the fewer fixations are made. Sometimes the eyes move backwards to get a second look at something that was not clearly seen. Such a backward movement is called a *regression*. Good reading is characterized by a wide recognition span, a small number of fixations per line, and a small number of regressions. Norms for these characteristics are shown in Table 13. Increased rate is accompanied by decreasing number of fixations and regressions and by increasing recognition span. Duration of fixations changes very little.

TABLE 13. *Eye-movement norms**

Grade	1	2	3	4	5	6	7	8	9	10	11	12	Col
Fixations per 100 words (including regressions)	224	174	155	139	129	120	114	109	105	101	96	94	90
Regressions per 100 words	52	40	35	31	28	25	23	21	20	19	18	17	15
Average Span of Recognition (in words)	.45	.57	.65	.72	.78	.83	.88	.92	.95	.99	1.04	1.06	1.11
Average Duration of Fixations (in seconds)	.33	.30	.28	.27	.27	.27	.27	.27	.27	.26	.26	.25	.24
Rate with Comprehension (words per minute)	80	115	138	158	173	185	195	204	214	224	237	250	280

* Sanford E. Taylor, Helen Frackenpohl, and James L. Pettee, Grade Level Norms for the Components of the Fundamental Reading Skill, Research Information Bulletin, No. 3. Huntington, N.Y.: Educational Developmental Laboratories, Inc., a Division of McGraw-Hill Book Company, 1960. p. 12. Reproduced with permission.

The Value of Eye-Movement Photographs

Eye-movement photographs show such data as the average number of fixations per line, words per fixation, duration of fixations, frequency of regressions, rate of reading, skill in going from one line to the next, and so on. In some cases, the photographs detect difficulties in eye coordination, shown when the lines representing the two eyes do not remain parallel (Ahrendt and Mosedale, 1971; Charlton, 1971).

When selections of sufficient length are used, eye-movement photography gives reliable and valid measures of reading performance (Tinker, 1946). However, the expense of the apparatus and the necessity of having a trained technician to run the machine, develop the photographs, and interpret the results make the eye-movement camera a luxury that has seemed impractical for most school and clinical situations.

Calvert and Cromes (1966) reported an unusual diagnostic use of eye-movement photographs. They inspected the photographs from children who were not responding well to remedial reading instruction and found evidence of fine tremors or spasms occurring at intervals of about 18 seconds. Treatment of a few of these children with the drug Primidone both stopped the tremors permanently and was followed by improved learning. If this is verified by other investigators, it will provide a very powerful argument for the routine use of eye-movement photography in the diagnosis of reading disabilities.

Informal Measurement of Eye Movements

Two procedures are in common use for observing eye movements. One of them is the *mirror* method. The child is seated at a table on which he rests the book in reading position. The examiner sits slightly behind and to one side of him, also facing the table. A rectangular mirror, of the sort that can be purchased cheaply at variety stores, is placed on the table fairly close to the book and held by the examiner at such an angle that by looking at it he can observe the child's eyes.

The other method is called the Miles Peep-Hole Method (Miles and Segel, 1929). An appropriate reading selection is mounted on a sheet of pasteboard. A small opening about one-quarter of an inch square is made near the middle of the page between two lines. The examiner holds the sheet against his face so that he can look through the opening, and the child faces him and reads the selection. If the examiner is taller than the child, he should be seated and the child should stand, to make it unnecessary for the child to look up while reading.

The mirror method is the more flexible of these two, as any reading material can be used without special preparation. The peep-hole method, on the other hand, gives a somewhat clearer vision of the eye movements. These methods are not as objective and accurate as photography, but are good enough to provide most of the information that is sought.

In a third procedure, which we prefer, the reader sits and holds a book on a level with his eyes as he reads, while the observer sits across the table and watches his eyes across the top of the book. This procedure can be used only for the top half of each page, as the reader's eyes are obscured by his eyelashes when he nears the bottom of the page.

It is advisable to practice on a few normal readers before attempting to observe the eye movements of a reading disability case. One should not attempt to watch more than one phase of eye movements at a time. The first three lines or so should be used to get settled. Then count the number of fixations in each of the next ten lines. The recognition span may be roughly estimated by dividing the average number of words per line by the average number of fixations per line. Next count the regressions in the following ten lines. Do not count the top or bottom lines of a page, or lines which begin or end a paragraph. If there are so many fixations and regressions that they cannot be counted, the tester should not be disappointed, as that fact in itself is highly significant. Norms for eye movements will be found in Table 13.

A third set of about ten lines of reading should be used to watch for any other significant facts. Some children have difficulty in making a return sweep at the end of a line and so drop down to the end of the next line and follow it back to the beginning before starting to read it. This is obviously a wasteful procedure that interferes greatly with speed. Many children have difficulty in finding the beginning of a line and make extra fixations there. Other peculiarities may be found occasionally, such as a tendency to move the head rather than the eyes.

The Significance of Eye Movements

Photography or informal observation of eye movements discloses *what* the eyes do while the person reads; it does not provide an explanation of *why* they move as they do. Reading, like walking, is controlled by the brain. One cannot walk without legs, but the speed and direction of a person's walking are controlled by his central nervous system. In reading, similarly, the eyes are the servants of the brain. Regressive movements, for example, may be the result of many different causes. Among very poor readers, the most common cause of regression is failure to recognize a word, necessitating additional inspection of the word. Some other causes of regressions are failure to recognize the basic meaning of a word; failure to select the correct meaning of a word in its present context; inappropriate phrasing, spoiling the meaning and making rereading necessary; overlooking punctuation

THE MATURATION OF READING PERFORMANCE

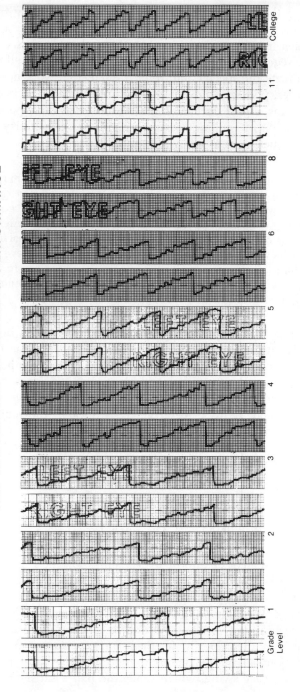

FIGURE 19.2 Samples of eye-movement photographs, showing development through the school years and in college. From a photograph supplied by Educational Developmental Laboratories and used with their permission.

marks, confusing the meaning; inadequate perception resulting from an eye movement which overreaches the reader's span of perception; and external distraction which interrupts the reader's train of thought. Discovering that there are many regressions in a person's reading does not in itself explain the difficulty or indicate the specific nature of the remedial work needed.

In most cases, poor eye movements are not the cause of poor reading; they are symptoms of the fact that the reader is reading poorly. Tinker studied the question of training eye movements for over thirty years and summarized his conclusions as follows:

> Actually, there is no evidence to support the view that eye movements determine reading proficiency. . . . All experimental evidence derived from well-designed studies shows that oculomotor reactions are exceedingly flexible and quickly reflect any change in reading skill and any change in perception and comprehension. . . . Real progress in programs of teaching reading would be achieved if the term and concept of rhythmical eye movements were abandoned, if eye-movement photography were confined to the research laboratory, and if the use of gadgets and other techniques to train eye movements were discarded. (Tinker, 1965, pp. 111–112)

The good reader is not aware of what his eyes do when he reads any more than he is aware of what his stomach does when he is digesting a tasty meal. If he tries deliberately to control his eyes while he reads, his concentration on the meaning suffers and his reading efficiency deteriorates. If a reader's comprehension and rate are satisfactory, his eye movements can be safely ignored. If his eye movements are poor, the remedial work should usually stress the basic elements of good comprehension: accurate word recognition, knowledge of word meanings, phrasing, good concentration, and so on. There are some who need training to overcome specific bad eye-movement habits, but they are definitely in the minority.

III. ELIMINATION OF FAULTY HABITS

Experienced teachers of almost every skill know how important it is for the learner to perform smoothly and correctly before trying for speed. The music teacher knows how ruinous it is to allow a child to increase tempo too quickly. The swimming coach keeps his pupils swimming slowly up and down, ironing out the flaws in their technique, until he is satisfied with their form; only then does he let them compete against time. The golf professional cautions his pupils against trying to hit the ball hard. What he wants is a smooth, easy swing, which sends the ball a satisfactory distance without disrupting coordination. In these and in other complex skills, the basis of a highly expert performance is not the expenditure of a great deal of effort, but rather the attainment of a smooth, graceful, easy, relaxed, well-coordinated performance.

Reading is no exception to the principle that the attempt to develop speed should be postponed until good form has been achieved. Before trying to accelerate the reading of a child or adult, one should try to establish fluent reading first. There are many faulty habits which interfere with fluency in reading. These should be eliminated, or at least reduced in severity, before any pressure is exerted for greater speed in reading.

Excessive Word Analysis

Occasionally one finds a child whose reading is extremely slow because he inspects each word syllable by syllable or even letter by letter. Such cases were much more common in the days when phonics was overemphasized. Today they are less frequent, but still do occur.

A good example of this condition is Mervin. When first seen, Mervin was twelve years old, had an IQ of 82, and was able to read at third-grade level but with first-grade speed. Sections of two photographic records of his reading are shown in Figure 19.3. These photographs were taken one week apart. In the earlier record, it is practically impossible to distinguish one fixation from another. His eyes went across the line letter by letter or, at the most, two letters at a time. His rate of reading in this record was 53 words per minute. Between the two records he received six lessons, in which major attention was devoted to practice in the rapid recognition of words as wholes and to phrasing. The second record shows a very marked change. He was now seeing words as words, not by single letters. His rate of 150 words per minute was still slow, but was an improvement of nearly 200 per cent in rate. The fixations were of excessively long duration, and there were several other faults in the total record, of which only a part is shown here.

Slowness in Word Recognition

When it is found that words are perceived as units but that the child's reaction time is slow, speed of recognition can be gradually increased by direct practice in recognizing words which are exposed for only a brief duration. The use of flash cards has been discussed on page 417, and a simple easy-to-make hand tachistoscope is illustrated in Figure 9.3. The use of tachistoscopic exposure for speeding up perception and increasing the span of recognition is discussed below.

Word-by-Word Reading

The harmful effect of reading each word as a separate unit has already been discussed in relation to its interference with good comprehension. Obviously, reading in which there is a pause between each two words is unnecessarily slow reading. The usual treatment for this habit is practice in phrasing, as described on pages 463–466.

Lip Movements and Subvocal Reading

Nearly all children learn to read by associating printed symbols with previously acquired listening and speaking skills. When asked to read to himself the beginner continues to mouth the words, but barely audibly. Silent reading soon becomes inaudible, but lip movements may continue in silent reading for many years. For children whose auditory imagery is strong—they "hear" an inner voice pronounce each word as they read silently—accompanying movements of the lips, tongue and larynx representing the words are not as important as for children whose auditory imagery is relatively weak. For the latter group, early suppression of lip movements may interfere with reading comprehension and retard growth in reading competence.

In silent reading, even superior adult readers show tiny changes in the electrical activity of the muscles involved in speech (Edfeld, 1960). These changes are similar to the ones that occur during overt speech, but at a miniature level, requiring sensitive electrodes to detect them. Thus nearly all people when reading silently go through the motions of speaking the words, but without any externally observable movement or sound. This covert or unobservable behavior is accompanied by "inner speech" which is often termed *subvocal reading* or *silent speech*. The person reports that he "hears" the words as though spoken by an inner voice, similar to the inner speech that occurs during thinking.

The attainment of true silent reading involves a gradual process of the type described as *cue reduction* (Woodworth, 1929). This is the process by which a smaller and smaller part of a total stimulus situation becomes adequate to bring about a response that was originally made only to the total situation. Similarly, an original response involving action of the entire body may gradually be reduced until its significance is conveyed by a slight movement of one part of the body; the lifting of one eyebrow, for example, may convey the meaning of a paragraph of comment. In reading, both types of cue reduction take place. While the beginner must inspect each word carefully and often has to look at the separate letters, the expert recognizes most words in an almost instantaneous glance and frequently sees a phrase as a unit. On the response side, the beginner has to read aloud to obtain

FIGURE **19.3** Photographs of Mervin's eye movements in reading. Left, taken June 17, shows practically a letter-by-letter inspection, with the separate words indistinguishable. Right, taken June 25, shows clearly the improvement in perceiving words as units, although the fixation time on some words is very long.

meaning. Gradually he reduces the response to mumbling, to silent lip movement, to subvocal reading with tiny movements that cannot easily be detected, to a "hearing" of the words (in other words, having an auditory image without any detectable motor accompaniment), and finally, in a comparatively few exceptionally fast readers, to an instantaneous flash of meaning that seems to have no special motor or sensory accompaniment.

It seems probable that as rate of reading rises significantly above a comfortable rate of speaking (for pupils making normal progress, around fifth- or sixth-grade level), subvocal reading diminishes but does not disappear. The reader still has inner speech and accompanying tiny muscle changes, but not for every word. A kind of "telegram style" pattern develops in which key words represent phrases. By the dropping out of the less important words inner speech becomes compressed and silent reading at a rate two or more times oral reading rate becomes possible.

The research on subvocal reading suggests that a natural decrease in subvocalization should take place without teacher intervention in a learning environment which provides ample experience in reading at independent and instructional levels, avoiding frustration (Pomerantz, 1971). Subvocal activity may provide needed reinforcement and be beneficial to comprehension. Teachers should regard this as a natural part of the reading act and should not try to suppress it. There is no need to make pupils conscious of such activity. Even lip movements may be needed by the pupil who continues to make them, and attempts to get pupils to stop them should be made only with a cautious appraisal of the probable effects on comprehension. The persistent use of a "crutch" often means that the child still needs it, and premature efforts to stop its use may be harmful (Davies, 1972).

Finger Pointing and Head Movement

Two habits about which teachers are often too much concerned are pointing with the finger and moving the head while reading. Pointing with the finger is a crutch which some children need. It is an aid to children who tend to lose the place and to those with reversal tendencies, and it may help to develop progressive reading for those who make too many regressions (Hanf, 1970). Teachers are on the whole too anxious to have this habit stopped and sometimes make a child stop pointing when he still has need of it. Pointing by itself does not interfere with rate of reading or comprehension, but it is often an accompaniment of excessive word analysis and word-by-word reading. As those faults are overcome, the pointing is usually discontinued by the child without the need of any pressure from the teacher. A card held under the line of print as a marker serves as a good intermediate step in doing away with pointing. Those children who have difficulty managing a marker should be allowed to continue to point with a finger.

Moving the head from side to side is another habit which is not necessary for most individuals, but also not really harmful. There is no advantage in moving the head, except possibly for children who have mild difficulties in binocular coordination. Most head-waggers can give up the habit very quickly without ill effects.

Difficulty with the Return Sweep

Some children have difficulty in making a return sweep from the end of one line to the beginning of the next line. This is shown in the observation of eye movements by the fact that one or two extra fixations are made at the beginning of each line. There are a few children who, after reading a line, look back along the line and then drop vertically to the beginning of the next line. This habit results in taking nearly twice as long to read the line as is necessary. When difficulty in making the return sweep is discovered, one should look for evidence of eye-muscle difficulty or slow fusion, which at reading distance sometimes is a result of uncorrected farsightedness.

To develop greater skill in making the return sweep, which should be a single quick diagonal movement, one can use widely spaced lines, with diagonal lines connecting the end of each line with the beginning of the

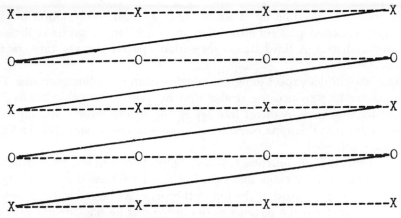

FIGURE **19.4** Several lines of a cross-line exercise prepared on a typewriter, triple spaced.

next line. The child is instructed to try to look along the diagonal when
going from line to line. There is very little prepared material of this sort
available, and usually it is necessary to make up special material on the
typewriter, starting with triple spacing and reducing to double spacing as
the child improves. Often only a few days of practice are needed.

Regressions

The type of remedial work needed to reduce the frequency of regressive movements depends on the causes, which have been listed on page 412.
Regressions are the eye-movement equivalents of repetitions in oral reading. When they are due to deficiencies or inaccuracies in word recognition
or word meaning, attempting to train the eye movements will obviously be
of little or no value. Any reader, no matter how skillful, will make a large
number of regressions when reading material which is heavily loaded with
unfamiliar words, peculiar or highly involved sentence structure, or very
difficult ideas. If a tendency to excessive regressions persists as a lingering
bad habit in a reader whose word recognition and comprehension are at a
high level, however, specific exercises to overcome the regressions may be
advisable.

A type of practice that is sometimes helpful in the reduction of unnecessary regressions is the use of *cross-line exercises*. In the beginning one uses
a page prepared on the typewriter as shown in Figure 19.4. The instructions
are to go across the top line, taking one look at each letter, then follow the
diagonal to the second line, and so on down the page. At the beginning of
each remedial practice period the reader goes over this page three to five

times, gradually speeding up. After the reader has become skillful in using this page, a second page is introduced in which single words replace the meaningless letters. A third stage uses widely spaced phrases, three or four to a line.

One should not expect too great benefits from cross-line exercises. They serve mainly to convince the reader that he can go smoothly across lines without looking back. A direct transfer of the steady, evenly spaced movements, built up in this type of exercise, to connected, meaningful reading is not usually achieved.

A second type of practice which is helpful for reducing regressions is to use a cover card. A blank index card of the 4 x 6-inch size is convenient. The reader starts the card at the top of the page. As he reads, he moves the card gradually down the page so as to cover what he has already read and in that way prevents regressions. The card should be slanted slightly with the left corner a little lower than the right, so as to cover the beginning of each line before the end of the line. This type of practice, which can be used by the reader himself with any kind of printed reading matter, should have a greater transfer to normal reading than the cross-line type of exercise, because it utilizes a normal reading situation to which only a slight addition has been made.

The elimination of regressions is also one of the purposes of the several kinds of controlled reading practice which are described in the next section.

IV. INCREASING RATE BY DIRECT PRACTICE

Once the slow reader has reached satisfactory levels in word recognition and comprehension and has begun to eliminate specific interfering habits of the types described in the preceding section, he is ready for practice aimed directly at speeding up his reading. There are five main types of practice for increasing rate of reading: tachistoscopic training, controlled reading, timed reading, the so-called dynamics method, and extensive reading without specific emphasis on speed.

The Use of the Tachistoscope

A tachistoscope is a device that allows the presentation of visual material for brief intervals of time. It can range in complexity from a simple handmade cardboard device (see Fig. 9.3) to a complex laboratory instrument controlling the exposure time with great accuracy. Some inexpensive small tachistoscopes for individual practice, which are powered by simple springs or levers, include:

Pocket-Tac (Reading Institute of Boston). A very small and convenient hand-held tachistoscope for flashed exposures of words or phrases, with related rolls of material.

Tach-X (Educational Developmental Laboratories). A round, hand-held tachistoscope with related word and phrase material.

Phrase-Flasher (The Reading Laboratory, Inc.). A tachistoscopic device for flashing phrases.

AVR Eye-Span Trainer, Model 10 (Audio-Visual Research). A hand-operated small tachistoscope for flashing digits, words, or phrases.

Projection tachistoscopes generally have two parts: a slide or filmstrip projector, and a tachistoscope device like an enlarged camera shutter which can be set for different speeds of exposure. These range from inexpensive one-speed devices to fairly expensive ones.

Flash-Meter (Keystone View Co.). A large shutter, of metal and glass, with variable control of illumination and speeds ranging from one to 1/100th second. Used with a Keystone Daylight Overhead Projectors, the combination is a *Keystone Tachistoscope*. Masks permit exposure of any material from a single word to an entire 3 x 4-in. slide. Usable with commercial or homemade slides.

SVE Speed-i-o-Scope (Society for Visual Education). A metal and glass tachistoscopic shutter very much like the *Flash-Meter*, with variable exposure times from "time" to 1/100th second and control of intensity of illumination.

Flash-X (Educational Developmental Laboratories). A tachistoscopic shutter used with a projector, with special filmstrips. Speeds controlled up to 1/150th second.

Perceptoscope Mark III (Perceptual Development Laboratories). A versatile projector that can be used as a tachistoscope, a filmstrip projector, a motion picture projector, or a pacing projector. Expensive.

T-Matic 150 Tachistoscopic Projector (Psychotechnics, Inc.). Provides exposure speeds from 4 seconds to 1/100th second. Uses 35 mm. filmstrips.

Tachist-O-Flasher (Learning through Seeing). May be used with most projectors; hand-operated shutter; speed up to 1/40th second. An electronic version, *Protach*, with variable speeds is available.

Tac-Ette (Keystone View). Electronically operated individual tachistoscope into which cards are inserted. Stroboscopic flash exposure at speeds from one to 1/100th second.

TT-30 Flash Reader (Teaching Technology). Self-contained 35 mm. filmstrip projector with flash-timing mechanism for speeds from one to 1/50th second.

The All-Purpose Tachistoscope Attachment (Lafayette). An attachment for converting projectors into tachistoscopes; shutter speeds from 1 second to 1/100th second.

Tachistoscopes proved valuable during World War II in training observers to recognize types of military planes rapidly and accurately. Soon afterward they were widely used to speed up recognition of words and phrases. Research at that time showed that transfer of such training to ordinary reading was quite disappointing (Cleland, 1950; Manolakes, 1952).

As we have seen, the average duration of fixations for college and superior adult readers is approximately ¼ second. Learning to respond to words or phrases exposed for much briefer periods (1/25th of a second or even less) is irrelevant to continuous reading because most of the fixation time in connected reading is required for the brain to process the incoming visual information.

Kleinberg (1970) compared the effect of pseudo-tachistoscopic training with tachistoscopic training for fourth-grade classes. The genuine tachistoscopic group was trained at an exposure time of 1/10th second, short enough to prevent a second fixation, while the pseudo group was trained with an exposure time of 1½ seconds, long enough for four to six fixations. The pseudo group's training was as effective as that of the true tachistoscopic group in increasing reading speed and accuracy; there was no effect on reading vocabulary and comprehension in either group. This suggests that the value of tachistoscopic training lies mainly in its effects on motivation and attention rather than on speed of perception, for most pupils.

For readers who wish to learn more about the details, a clear step-by-step exposition of tachistoscopic procedures for reading improvement has been given by Barnette (1951).

Controlled Reading

The *Metron-O-Scope*, a device which used reading material printed on specially prepared continuous rolls and had a three-shutter arrangement by which one third of a line at a time could be exposed, allowed the presentation of reading material at a rate which was selected by the instructor and could be increased at each practice session. It came in two sizes, one for individual and one for group use. Widely publicized during the 1930's, it is now only of historical interest.

Motion picture films which presented one phrase at a time brilliantly lit against a fainter background of the rest of the page were the second venture in the creation of reading material that would control the phrasing and the rate of reading during practice. The original Harvard films, planned by

Dearborn, were replaced by the *Harvard University Reading Films, Second Series* (Harvard University Press), a series of sixteen films suitable for college-level work, with the speed of projection increasing from less than 300 words per minute to about 500 words per minute. These have been successfully used in many college and adult reading programs. The *Iowa High School Training Films* (Iowa State University) is a quite similar series of fourteen films with somewhat simpler material appropriate for high schools.

Specialized projectors have been developed which can project material from filmstrips or special slides at varying speeds, a line at a time or a part of a line at a time. These have the advantage that the materials to be projected are far less expensive than motion picture films and can provide essentially the same kind of reading practice.

The Controlled Reader (Educational Developmental Laboratories). A filmstrip projector equipped with a variable-speed automatic drive. Special filmstrips are used to project connected material one line at a time. A moving slot travels from left to right, uncovering words and covering them again at a rate set by the instructor. For group use. *Controlled Reader Jr.* is for individual practice.

Tachomatic 500 Filmstrip Projector (Psychotechnics, Inc.). Projects connected reading material from special filmstrips at speeds from 100 to 1,200 words per minute, a third of a line, a half line, or a full line at a time. For group use.

Cenco Overhead Projection Reader Pacer (Cenco Educational Aids). A device that fits over the projection table of an overhead projector, with speeds from 50 to 800 words per minute. Spring-powered. Uses special materials printed on rolls of transparent Mylar. For group use.

Craig Reader (Craig Corporation). A projector for individual use, with material projected on a built-in screen like the face of a TV tube. Employs special rigid slides that feed through automatically at rates from 80 to 600 words per minute. Also may be used as a tachistoscope and pacer.

Perceptoscope. See entry above, under tachistoscopes.

Projection Reader (Singer Graflex). Similar to the *Controlled Reader*; speeds adjustable from 60 through 1,000 words per minute. Taschistoscopic attachment available.

Reader Mate (Singer Graflex). Portable unit for individual use, with filmstrip material projected on small built-in screen. Speeds adjustable from 80 to 840 words per minute.

These methods try to compel the reader to move his eyes in a set pattern and to fixate each word or phrase for a predetermined time interval.

They make it impossible for the reader to slow down when he meets with difficulty, or to reread. For that reason they are regarded with some suspicion by those who view eye movements as symptoms rather than as causes of poor reading. The machinery is intriguing, effective motivation is provided for most pupils to try to speed up their reading, and comprehension questions follow the reading so that attention to meaning cannot be neglected.

Reading Pacers. A method for controlling reading rate without imposing a set pattern of phrasing or a uniform rate of speed was worked out by Buswell (1939), involving the simple principle of a shutter which gradually covers a page from top to bottom at a speed which can be regulated. Several devices using the Buswell principle and designed for individual practice are now available.

AVR Reading Rateometer (Audio-Visual Research). Uses a horizontal plastic bar as a shutter which descends over the page at a rate controlled by an electric motor; wide range of speeds; built-in rate calculator; comparatively inexpensive. Models A, B, and C, with different ranges of speed.

SRA Reading Accelerator (Science Research Associates). *Models III* (metal), *IV* (plastic). Uses an opaque shutter and a nonelectrical motor; wide range of speeds. Lightweight, can be held by hand over the material.

Shadowscope Reading Pacer (Psychotechics, Inc.). Employs a horizontal beam of light reflected by a turning mirror so as to move steadily down the page; the intensity of the illumination can be reduced at will until the beam is barely perceptible, thereby producing an almost natural reading situation; speed controlled by an electric motor.

Prep-Pacer (The Reading Laboratory). Provides a wide range of rates; electric motor.

These machines are widely used in high school, college, and adult reading programs. They provide individualized practice in which the learner can set his own rate at each practice session, and when the practice is followed by adequate questioning on comprehension, they provide what seems to be a well-motivated procedure for guiding the learner toward gradually increased rate without loss in understanding.

The problem with these, as with all somewhat artificial methods of practice, is that the amount of carryover to natural reading situations is sometimes disappointingly small. How much of the favorable effect is the result of controlling the rate and how much is motivation which could be secured by nonmechanical procedures is impossible to estimate at present.

Increasing Rate through Motivated Reading

In contrast to the point of view that favors controlled reading is one that puts major emphasis on increased motivation in natural reading situations. The major causes of slow reading are considered to be lack of enough practice in reading easy, interesting material and lack of motivation to improve speed.

From this point of view, a program for increasing rate of reading should have three major components. The first consists of overcoming specific interfering habits, as described in Section III of this chapter. The second involves motivating the reader to do a large amount of easy reading. This provides the abundant practice needed to develop fluency. The absence of vocabulary and comprehension difficulties in such material allows the reader to read easily, without the need to hesitate and reread that is created by difficult reading matter. If the subject matter is sufficiently interesting, the desire to find out what comes next provides natural motivation to read quickly, while the absence of pressure to read at a rate set by someone else eliminates strain and tension. Methods for developing greater interest in voluntary reading have been discussed in Chapter 18.

The third phase of the program involves a series of timed silent reading exercises with comprehension checks. For these, one can use either published workbook selections or general reading matter of a comparatively easy nature. The timed exercises strengthen motivation to keep the rate going up, provide a definite record of progress, and at the same time insure that comprehension does not suffer in the process.

There are several workbooks that can be used for timed reading in the upper grades and secondary school. The McCall, Crabbs *Standard Test Lessons in Reading* have been used successfully in many programs. Each page consists of a brief selection, followed by several multiple-choice questions. Three minutes are allowed for reading the selection and answering the questions. If the reader goes too slowly, he cannot answer enough of the questions; if he reads carelessly or too rapidly, he gets too many answers wrong. In successive exercises he learns to read so as to increase his scores. Approximate grade scores are given for each exercise. These grade scores are a powerful incentive, as practically every reader strives to raise his grade scores. Provided that one is willing to count or estimate the number of words, almost any suitable selection for which a good method of checking comprehension can be devised can be adapted for use as a timed reading exercise. Green (1971) trained ninth graders on McCall, Crabbs, and similar materials and found a greatly improved balance between rate and comprehension as well as an improvement in total reading scores.

The senior author has successfully used a series of practices for improving rate of reading as a laboratory exercise in educational psychology (Goldstein and Justman, 1942). After a preliminary discussion of the purposes of the experiment and its potential value to the student, each student is asked to bring in an interesting nonfiction selection of about one thousand words, selected from current magazines or pamphlets. Each student mounts his selection in a folder, counts the number of words and writes the number at the end of the selection, and prepares a set of short-answer questions. The questions are mounted in the folder in such a way that they cannot be seen while the selection is being read. The correct answers are placed on the back of the question sheet. The instructor examines all selections and questions for suitability before they are used and replaces any that are unsuitable. Each folder is numbered.

At the beginning of each practice session, the folders are shuffled and distributed, care being taken that each student gets a folder which he has not used before. At a signal, all start to read. The instructor holds up a set of cards numbered in sequence, changing the number each ten seconds. As each student finishes reading, he jots down the number being displayed. He then answers the questions and marks his answers by means of the key. Then he computes his rate in terms of words per minute.[2] Finally he enters his rate and comprehension scores on a progress chart similar to that shown in Figure 19.5. Such practice periods usually take between ten and fifteen minutes.

Repetition of this experiment with several classes has shown that substantial improvement is the rule. In Figure 19.5 the median results from one class of twenty-nine students are shown. The median improvement was 96 words per minute, an improvement of 39 per cent over the beginning rate of 247 words per minute. Accuracy scores varied somewhat, but ended up about as high as they were at the beginning. In the second and fifteenth practice sessions, approximately equivalent textbook selections were used. The total time spent was about three and a half hours, divided among the sixteen practice sessions. The rate of improvement obtained, considering the time spent, compares favorably with the results of any of the methods of controlled reading. Similar results have been obtained with several other classes.

No individual diagnosis was done in this class. Instead, a volunteer committee looked up the causes of slow reading and reported their findings to the class. While many reported that they were helped by suggestions about the desirability of reading in phrases and so on, this procedure did not meet the needs of all. Two students showed practically no improvement; for them, and for some whose gains were comparatively small, a better outcome might have been attained if the causes of their slowness had been

---

2. To get a student's rate, multiply the number of words in the selection by 6 and divide by the number jotted down.

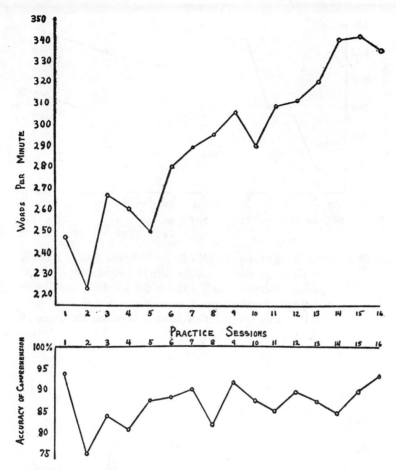

FIGURE 19.5   Median rate and accuracy scores of 29 students in educational psychology who took part in 16 practice sessions for increasing rate of reading.

investigated and special types of exercises had been provided as needed.

A similar procedure can be employed for practice in timed reading at any grade level from the fifth or sixth grade up. In the elementary school, the teacher would probably have to take responsibility for the selection and preparation of the selections to be used, but the rest of the procedure could be employed without change.

As compared with controlled reading in groups, this procedure has two major advantages: normal reading matter is used, and each student, although reading in a group, governs his own rate of reading and competes with his own past performances.

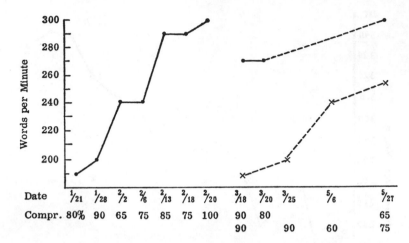

FIGURE **19.6** Bobby's results on the SRA *Better Reading Books,* 1 and 2.
Dots represent exercises done with the *Rateometer,* crosses
represent exercises done without the machine. Solid lines
indicate consecutive practice sessions; dotted lines indicate that there were other lessons between the ones on
the graph.

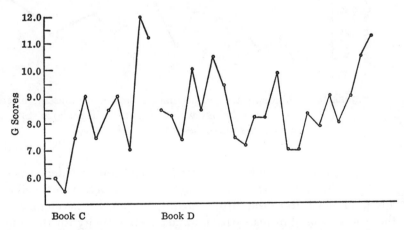

FIGURE **19.7** Bobby's results on the McCall, Crabbs *Standard Test Lessons in Reading,* Books C and D. The G scores are crude
grade equivalents. Sometimes two exercises were done in
one lesson. The wide fluctuations are fairly typical;
because of this, it is desirable to average each three
exercises and record the averages on a graph like this.

A Combination Method

It is possible to combine a limited use of machine practice with other activities in an effective program. The following case illustrates one way of doing this.

Bobby, an eighth-grade boy, was doing quite poorly in the first part of the year although at the end of the seventh grade he had scored at or above the 90th percentile on all parts of the *Iowa Tests of Basic Skills*. His oral reading was good, scoring above the ninth-grade norms on the *Gilmore*. A slow rate of reading, coupled with a lack of interest in studying, seemed to explain his poor marks. Arrangements were made for two remedial lessons a week.

Stress was placed at the beginning on arousing interest. The desirability of improving his rate was discussed, and he was shown how to operate a *Rateometer* (see p. 566) and use it with exercises in the *SRA Better Reading Book 1*. He was quite intrigued with the machine and enjoyed setting it for a given rate, scoring his own answers, and computing his own rate. One exercise was done at each of the first seven lessons, with results shown on the left side of Figure 19.6, a gain from 190 to 300 words per minute, with no loss in comprehension. Meanwhile, Book C of the McCall, Crabbs *Standard Test Lessons in Reading* was also used, with results shown on the left side of Figure 19.7: improvement from sixth to eleventh grade in the G scores.

At that point the difficulty of the practice material was increased. In the *SRA Better Reading Book 2* he started at 270 words per minute with good comprehension, but when given another exercise without the machine on the same day his rate was only 197 words per minute. From then on most of his practice was done without the machine, and rate without the machine went up to 255 words per minute, but comprehension fell a little. At the same time he started the next harder level of the McCall, Crabbs, with results shown on the right side of Figure 19.7.

While this practice was going on, Bobby was introduced to *Teen Age Tales* and other easy, interesting books and began to do some voluntary reading at home. He was also given training in study skills, using his regular textbooks. He was encouraged to try to apply his new reading procedures to all of his reading. His confidence in his ability to do well increased, and he achieved passing marks in English and Citizenship, in which he had received grades of 60 and 50 in November. At the close of the remedial work his rate was still not on a par with his level of comprehension, but had improved enough to make quite a difference to him. More important, his attitudes toward reading and schoolwork in general had improved greatly.

This case is not a perfect example by any means; it illustrates an error of technique that is very common. Bobby was moved into harder materials as soon as he achieved a couple of high scores; that this was premature and interfered somewhat with his progress is suggested by the lower results obtained after the change was made. It is also probable that specific help was discontinued before the new habits of faster reading with better concentration had become solidified by enough practice.

The ease with which Bobby increased his rate when reading with the machine and the difficulty he had in transferring the higher rate to other reading is perhaps the most instructive feature of this case. Unless such transfer is made a primary objective of the program, the results are liable to be disappointing.

The "Dynamics" Method

A method widely advertised by a commercial organization has never been revealed to educators in detail, so the description here is necessarily sketchy. The "dynamics" method attempts to replace the usual reading pattern of reading across each line in a series of fixations by a pattern in which the reader's eyes follow his finger down the page, presumably with one fixation per line. Advertising claims of rates as high as 25,000 words per minute have been made. The technique also involves spending several minutes in an overview of the material, which is not included in the rate computation. It is not known how much of the resulting comprehension is due to the overview and how much to the "reading." Considerable skepticism about the value of this method was expressed in an article based on student experiences with it (Alexander, 1967).

It is debatable whether such a procedure should be considered genuine reading or a special form of skimming. Spache (1962) pointed out that while rates of several thousand words per minute can be attained by rapid skimming or scanning in which large portions of the printed matter are not perceived, genuine reading in which most of the printed words are perceived cannot proceed faster than 800 to 900 words per minute. Tinker (1958) also concluded that 800 words per minute is about the fastest rate possible for genuine reading and that rates faster than that are based on skimming. These calculations are based on the assumption that ten-word lines are read with an average of three fixations per line, of approximately one-quarter of a second each, plus the very brief times required for moving the eyes from one fixation to the next and from the end of one line to the beginning of the next line. This would be truly superior reading, for average college students read at 280 words per minute with nine fixations for a ten-word line (see Table 13). Thus, genuine reading is possible at a rate about three times the rate used by average college students. It is open to serious question whether turning pages at rates of over a thousand words per minute is really reading or a form of skimming.

Spache (1962) also reported eye-movement studies of some graduates of one of the commercial speed-reading organizations. In reading test selections for the eye-movement camera their rates tended to fall between 400 and 600 words per minute, with about 70 per cent comprehension; these are representative results for superior readers at the college level. In reading a book in the way they had been taught, group average rates ranged from 1,800 to 2,400 words per minute, with about 50 per cent comprehension. While there are some reading situations in which 50 per cent comprehension may satisfy the reader's purpose, such a low comprehension score can hardly be recommended as satisfactory in typical reading situations.

Liddle (1965), in a doctoral thesis, compared twenty-five college students taught by the Wood Reading Dynamics Method with a control group. The experimental group increased their rates of reading tremendously, 6.1 times in fiction and 5.6 times in nonfiction. However, the experimental group after training did not do as well on comprehension tests either as they themselves had done before training or as the control group did. This study reinforces the conclusion that present techniques for achieving extremely high reading rates are not compatible with high comprehension. For the already highly competent reader, development of a rapid skimming method of reading can save a great deal of time on material that does not require careful reading.

Reinforced Reading. Schale (1964) described a procedure she called the "2R-OR-ALERT method." The symbols stand for: Reinforced Reading; Overview, Read rapidly, Answer questions, Locate mistakes, Examine mistakes, Reread at the same rate (if comprehension unsatisfactory), and Transfer adjustment of comprehension to rate to another article. Emphasis is placed on using "inclusive skimming" (reading only the first sentence of each paragraph horizontally, and skimming the rest vertically for key words). She reported a gain of one group of 24 students from a pretest mean of 506 words per minute to a posttest mean of 2,313 words per minute. This group obviously had very superior rate on the pretest. In a later paper (Schale, 1972) she reported two girls who reached speeds of over 50,000 words per minute after training in Reinforced Reading; one was able to read vertically, taking in two columns at a time! We have not found reports by other investigators on this procedure, which deserves careful independent evaluation.

Effect of Rate Improvement on Comprehension

Reports of fairly conventional programs to increase rate of reading generally state that comprehension averaged near 70 per cent at the beginning of the program. Gains of 20 to 50 per cent in average rate are usual, with no significant change up or down in comprehension (A. J. Harris, 1968c).

At the elementary school level there is some evidence that practices designed primarily to stress rate do not produce as much growth in comprehension as developmental reading programs in which rate is not stressed. For example, Skarbeck (1965) compared the effects of an experimental program designed to improve rate of comprehension with a control conventional developmental reading program, using pupils in the sixth grade. The experimental group made greater gains in rate, but the control group made greater gains in the comprehension of study-type exercises. Witham (1966) compared the gains made by eighth-grade students in three programs: a group using a machine which required them to read at a given rate; a materials group using the same content as the controlled reader group, but in normal printed format without the machine presentation; and a control group following the regular curriculum in English language arts, with little or no attention to reading skills. Both experimental groups gained more in reading than the control group. The machine group made slightly greater gains in rate than the materials group, while the materials group made slightly greater gains in comprehension. Pauk (1965) reported that a college course of only six hours that concentrated on study skills and ignored rate resulted in more improvement in grades than a fourteen-hour course that gave attention both to rate and to study skills. One is tempted to repeat the old generalization that we learn what we practice: when greater stress is on rate, that is the area of greater gain; and when greater stress is on comprehension, greater gains are made in comprehension.

Comparison of Methods

At the primary-grade levels, it seems extremely doubtful that any direct efforts should be made to develop speed in reading. A good developmental reading program, which creates fluent, intelligent reading through balanced attention to word recognition and comprehension, oral and silent reading, careful directed reading and extensive independent reading, should result in adequate rate of reading as a by-product.

In the third, fourth, and fifth grades, there is also some doubt about the advisability of aiming at greater speed through specific practice. Cason (1943), working with matched groups at the third-grade level, found that free library reading brought about as good an improvement in rate as either controlled reading with the *Metron-O-Scope* or timed silent reading practice. Bridges (1941) compared several methods with pupils in the fourth, fifth, and sixth grades. She concluded that "training that emphasized comprehension and took no account of speed was more effective in developing both speed and comprehension than was training that emphasized speed and minimized comprehension. Undirected daily practice in reading was also more effective at this level than training in rapid reading." These conclusions held good for the average and below-average pupils, but not for those whose reading was above sixth-grade level.

At present, there is no reason to consider controlled reading superior to the procedure described above as motivated, timed reading for increasing rate. The methods which do not require any special type of apparatus seem at present to give as good results as those which require elaborate equipment. When the equipment is available, our preference would be for a procedure which includes some tachistoscope practice and some use of individual pacers, but puts major emphasis on well-motivated practice sessions stressing both rate and comprehension.

Definitive research on the "dynamics" approach and other superspeed techniques such as Schale's is lacking. It is possible that conservative reading specialists are ignoring a real breakthrough to rates previously considered to be impossible. Good research in this area should have high priority.

In the light of present evidence, training for improved speed of reading should come in as a definite part of a developmental reading program at and above the sixth grade. Individual pupils may, of course, need remedial help at lower grade levels because of extremely slow reading; but for the majority, rate can be expected to develop as a by-product of a good reading program until the sixth grade. From then on, specific provisions for speeding up reading seem desirable through high school and at least the first year in college.

SUGGESTED ADDITIONAL READING

BOND, GUY L. & TINKER, MILES A. *Reading difficulties: their diagnosis and correction* (3rd ed.). New York: Appleton-Century-Crofts, 1973. Chap. 16.

BURMEISTER, LOU E. *Reading strategies for secondary school teachers.* Reading, Mass.: Addison-Wesley, 1974. Chap. 10.

DALLMAN, MARTHA; ROUCH, ROGER L.; CHANG, LYNETTE Y. C.; & DEBOER, JOHN J. *The teaching of reading* (4th ed.). New York: Holt, Rinehart and Winston, 1974. Chaps. 7A, 7B.

GATES, ARTHUR I. *The improvement of reading* (3rd ed.). New York: Macmillan, 1947. Chap. 14.

KARLIN, ROBERT. *Teaching reading in high school* (2nd ed.). Indianapolis: Bobbs-Merrill, 1972. Chap. 9.

SPACHE, GEORGE D. *Toward better reading.* Champaign, Ill.: Garrard, 1963. Chaps. 14, 15.

THOMAS, ELLEN L. & ROBINSON H. ALAN. *Improving reading in every class: a sourcebook for teachers.* Boston: Allyn and Bacon, 1972. Chap. 4.

TINKER, MILES A. *Bases for effective reading.* Minneapolis: University of Minnesota Press, 1965. Chaps. 5–9.

Bibliography

AARON, IRA E. Learning of basal reading skills by mentally and nonmentally handicapped children. In Helen K. Smith (Ed.), *Meeting individual needs in reading.* Newark, Del.: International Reading Association, 1971. Pp. 85–93.

AASEN, HELEN B. A summer's growth in reading. *Elementary School Journal,* 1959, *40,* 70–74.

ABRAMS, ALFRED L. Delayed and irregular maturation versus minimal brain injury: recommendations for a change in current nomenclature. *Clinical Pediatrics,* 1968, 7, No. 6, 344–349.

ABRAMS, JULES C. An interdisciplinary approach to learning disabilities. *Journal of Learning Disabilities,* November 1969, *2,* 575–578.

ACHENBACH, THOMAS M. The Children's Associative Responding Test. A possible alternative to group IQ tests. *Journal of Educational Psychology,* 1970, *61,* 340–348.

ACKERMAN, PEGGY T.; PETERS, JOHN E.; & DYKMAN, ROSCOE A. Children with specific learning disabilities: WISC profiles. *Journal of Learning Disabilities,* March 1971, *4,* 150–166.

ADAMS, ANNE H. *The reading clinic.* New York: Macmillan, 1970.

ADAMS, RICHARD B. Dyslexia: a discussion of its definition. *Journal of Learning Disabilities,* December 1969, *2,* 616–633.

ADELMAN, H. S. The not so specific learning disability population. *Exceptional Children,* March 1971, *37,* 528–533.

ADLER, SOL. Dialectal differences and learning disorders. *Journal of Learning Disabilities.* June–July 1972, *5,* 344–350.

ADLER, SOL. Data gathering: the reliability and validity of test data from culturally different children. *Journal of Learning Disabilities,* August–September 1973, *6,* 429–434.

AHRENDT, KENNETH M. & MOSEDALE, DONALD S. Eye-movement photography and the reading process. *Journal of the Reading Specialist,* March 1971, *10,* 149–158.

ALEXANDER, JEFFREY C. Evelyn Wood: most just waste the money. *Harvard Crimson,* May 3, 1967. Pp. 3, 5, 6.

ALLEN, JAMES E. The right to read—target for the 70's. *Elementary English,* April 1970, *47,* 487–492.

ALLEN, M. Relationship between Kuhlmann-Anderson Intelligence Tests and academic achievement in grade IV. *Journal of Educational Psychology,* 1944, *44,* 229–239.

ALLEN, R. L. *The verb of present day American English.* The Hague: Morton, 1966.

ALLEN, ROBERT L. *The structure of the English sentence.* New York: Noble and Noble, 1968.

ALLINGTON, RICHARD. An evaluation of the effects of the use of color cues to focus attention in discrimination and paired associate learning. Unpublished doctoral dissertation, Michigan State University, 1973.

ALMY, MILLIE. *Children's experiences prior to first grade and success in beginning reading.* Contributions to Education, No. 954. New York: Bureau of Publications, Teachers College, Columbia University, 1949.

AMBLE, BRUCE R. Reading by phrases. *California Journal of Educational Research,* 1967, *18,* 116–124.

AMES, LOUISE BATES. Learning disabilities: the developmental point of view. In Helmer R. Myklebust (Ed.), *Progress in Learning Disabilities,* Vol. 1. New York: Grune & Stratton, 1968. Pp. 39–74.

AMSDEN, RUTH H. Children's preferences in picture story book variables. *Journal of Educational Research,* April 1960, *53,* 309–312.

ANDERSON, ROBERT H. & RITSHER, CYNTHIA. Pupil progress. In Robert L. Ebel (Ed.), *Encyclopedia of Educational Research* (4th ed.). New York: Macmillan, 1969. Pp. 1050–1062.

ANDERSON, ROBERT P.; HALCOMB, CHARLES G., & DOYLE, ROBERT B. The measurement of attentional defects. *Exceptional Children,* April 1973, *39,* 534–538.

ANDERSON, RUSSELL W. Effects of neuro-psychological techniques on reading achievement. Unpublished doctoral dissertation, Colorado State College, 1965.

ANGOFF, WILLIAM H. Scales, norms, and equivalent scores. In Robert L. Thorndike (Ed.), *Educational Measurement* (2nd ed.). Washington, D.C.: American Council on Education, 1971. Pp. 508–600.

ANNETT, M. A classification of hand preference by association analysis. *British Journal of Psychology,* 1970, *3,* 303–321.

ANTHONY, GEORGE A. Cerebral dominance as an etiological factor in dyslexia (severe reading disability). Unpublished doctoral dissertation, New York University, 1968.

ARCHER, MARGUERITE P. Minorities in easy reading through third grade. *Elementary English,* May 1972, *49,* 746–749.

ARTLEY, A. STERL. Are secondary developmental reading programs feasible? In Howard A. Klein (Ed.), *The quest for competency in teaching reading.* Newark, Del.: International Reading Association, 1972. Pp. 74–83.

ASHTON-WARNER, SYLVIA. *Spinster.* New York: Simon and Schuster, 1959.

ASKOV, WARREN; OTTO, WAYNE; & SMITH, RICHARD. Assessment of the de Hirsch Predictive Index tests of reading failure. In Robert C. Aukerman (Ed.), *Some persistent questions in beginning reading.* Newark, Del.: International Reading Association, 1972. Pp. 33–42.

ASSOCIATION OF HOSPITAL AND INSTITUTION LIBRARIES. *Bibliotherapy: methods and materials.* Chicago: American Library Association, 1971.

ATHEY, IRENE. Personality factors and the development of successful readers. In G. B. Schick & M. M. May (Eds.), *New frontiers in college-adult reading,* Yearbook of the National Reading Conference. 1966, *15,* 133–139.

ATHEY, IRENE. Language models and reading. *Reading Research Quarterly,* Fall 1971, *7,* 16–110.

ATKINSON, RICHARD C. & FLETCHER, JOHN D. Teaching children to read with a computer. *The Reading Teacher,* January 1972, *25,* 319–327.

AUKERMAN, ROBERT C. *Approaches to beginning reading.* New York: John Wiley & Sons, 1971.

AYERS, FLOYD W. & TORRES, FERNANDO. The incidence of EEG abnormalties in a dyslexic and a control group. *Journal of Clinical Psychology,* 1967, *32,* 334–336.

AYRER, JAMES E. & MC NAMARA, THOMAS C. Survey testing on an out-of-level basis. *Journal of Educational Measurement,* Summer 1973, *10,* 79–84.

AYRES, A. JEAN. Reading—a product of sensory integrative process. In Helen K. Smith (Ed.), *Perception and reading.* Newark, Del.: International Reading Association, 1968. Pp. 77–82.

AYRES, A. JEAN. *Sensory integration and learning disorders.* Los Angeles: Western Psychological Services, 1972.

BACHNER, SAUL. Teaching literature to the disadvantaged. Unpublished doctoral dissertation, Wayne State University, 1969.

BAILEY, MILDRED H. The utility of phonic generalizations in grades one through six. *The Reading Teacher,* February 1967, *20,* 413–418.

BAKWIN, HARRY. Reading disability in twins. *Developmental Medicine and Child Neurology,* 1973, *15,* 184–187.

BALOW, BRUCE. Perceptual-motor activities in the treatment of severe reading disability. *The Reading Teacher,* March 1971, *24,* 513–525.

BALOW, BRUCE & BLOMQUIST, M. Young adults ten to fifteen years after severe reading disability. *Elementary School Journal,* 1965, *66,* 44–48.

BANKS, ENID M. The identification of children with potential learning disabilities. *Slow Learning Child: The Australian Journal on the Education of Backward Children,* 1970, *17,* 27–38.

BANNATYNE, ALEXANDER D. The color phonics system. In John Money (Ed.), *The disabled reader.* Baltimore: Johns Hopkins Press, 1966. Pp. 193–214.

BANNATYNE, ALEXANDER D. *Language, reading and learning disabilities: psychology, neuropsychology, diagnosis and remediation.* Springfield, Ill.: Charles C Thomas, 1971.

BANNATYNE, ALEXANDER D. Choosing the best reinforcers. *Academic Therapy,* Summer 1972, *7,* 483–486.

BANNATYNE, ALEXANDER D. Mirror-images and reversals. *Academic Therapy,* Fall 1972, *8,* 87–92.

BANNATYNE, ALEXANDER D. *Reading: an auditory vocal process.* San Rafael, Calif.: Academic Therapy Publications, 1973.

BANNATYNE, ALEXANDER D. Programs, materials, and techniques. *Journal of Learning Disabilities,* May 1974, *7,* 272–273.

BANNATYNE, ALEXANDER D. & WICHIARAJOTE, P. Hemispheric dominance, handedness, mirror imaging, and auditory sequencing. *Exceptional Children*, September 1969, *36*, 27–36.

BARATZ, JOAN C. Beginning readers for speakers of divergent dialects. In J. Allen Figurel (Ed.), *Reading goals for the disadvantaged.* Newark, Del.: International Reading Association, 1970. Pp. 77–83.

BARATZ, JOAN C. & SHUY, ROGER W. *Teaching black children to read.* Washington, D.C.: Center for Applied Linguistics, 1969.

BARCHAS, SARAH E. Expressed reading interests of children of differing ethnic groups. Unpublished doctoral dissertation, University of Arizona, 1971.

BARGER, WILLIAM C. An experimental approach to aphasic and to non-reading children. *American Journal of Orthopsychiatry*, 1953, *23*, 158–170.

BARNETTE, GASPAR C. *Learning through seeing with tachistoscopic teaching techniques.* Dubuque, Iowa: William C. Brown, 1951.

BARNSLEY, ROGER H. Handedness and related behavior. Unpublished doctoral dissertation, McGill University, 1971.

BARRETT, THOMAS C. The relationship between measures of pre-reading visual discrimination and first-grade reading achievement: a review of the literature. *Reading Research Quarterly*, Fall 1965, *1*, 51–76.

BARSCH, RAYMOND H. *A movigenic curriculum.* Bulletin No. 25. Madison, Wisc.: Bureau for Handicapped Children, Wisconsin Department of Public Instruction, 1965.

BARTOLOME, PAZ I. Teachers' objectives and questions in primary reading. *The Reading Teacher*, October 1969, *23*, 27–33.

BARTON, ALLEN H. Reading research and its communication: the Columbia-Carnegie project. In J. Allen Figurel (Ed.), *Reading as an intellectual activity.* Newark, Del.: International Reading Association, 1963. P. 247.

BATEMAN, BARBARA. The efficacy of an auditory and a visual method on first-grade reading instruction with auditory and visual learning. In Helen K. Smith (Ed.), *Perception and reading.* Newark, Del.: International Reading Association, 1968. Pp. 105–112.

BEAUCHAMP, ROBERT F. Selection of books for the culturally disadvantaged ninth grade student. Unpublished doctoral dissertation, Wayne State University, 1970.

BEAR, R. & ODBERT, H. Insight of older pupils into their knowledge of word meaning. *School Review*, 1941, *49*, 754–760.

BECK, ISABEL L. & BOLVIN, JOHN O. A model for non-gradedness: the reading program for individually prescribed instruction. *Elementary English*, February 1969, *46*, 130–135.

BECK, ISABEL L. & MITROFF, DONNA D. *The rationale and design of a primary grade reading system for an individualized classroom.* Pittsburgh: Learning Research & Development Center, University of Pittsburgh, 1972.

BECKER, GEORGE J. *Television and the classroom reading program.* Newark, Del.: International Reading Association, 1973.

BEERY, K. E. *Developmental Test of Visual-Motor Integration.* Chicago: Follett Educational Corp., 1967.

BEGAB, MICHAEL J. Childhood learning disabilities and family stress. In John I. Arena (Ed.), *Management of the child with learning disabilities: an interdisciplinary challenge.* San Rafael, Calif.: Academic Therapy Publications, 1967. Pp. 81–87.

BELL, ANNE E. & AFTANAS, M. S. Some correlates of reading retardation. *Perceptual & Motor Skills*, October 1972, *35*, 659–667.

BELL, D. BRUCE; LEWIS, FRANKLIN D.; & BELL, BEVERLY W. Is the Schilder hand test really an adequate measure of cerebral dominance? *Academic Therapy,* Spring 1972, 7, 339–347.

BELMONT, LILLIAN & BIRCH, HERBERT G. Lateral dominance, lateral awareness, and reading disability. *Child Development,* 1965, 34, 57–71.

BELMONT, LILLIAN & BIRCH, HERBERT G. The intellective profile of retarded readers. *Perceptual & Motor Skills,* 1966, 22, 787–816.

BENDER, LAURETTA. *A visual-motor gestalt test and its clinical use.* Research Monograph No. 3. New York: American Orthopsychiatric Association, 1938.

BENDER, LAURETTA. Specific reading disability as a maturational lag. *Bulletin of the Orton Society,* 1957, 7, 9–18.

BENDER, LAURETTA. Use of the visual motor gestalt test in the diagnosis of learning disabilities. *Journal of Special Education,* Winter 1970, 4, 29–39.

BENDER, LAURETTA & LOWRIE, R. S. The effect of comic books on the ideology of children. *American Journal of Orthopsychiatry,* 1941, 11, 540.

BENGER, KATHLYN. The relationships of perception, personality, intelligence, and grade one reading achievement. In Helen K. Smith (Ed.), *Perception and reading.* Newark, Del.: International Reading Association, 1968. Pp. 112–123.

BENTON, ARTHUR L. *Right-left discrimination and finger localization.* New York: Hoeber, 1959.

BERG, PAUL C. Evaluating reading abilities. In Walter M. MacGinitie (Ed.), *Assessment problems in reading.* Newark, Del.: International Reading Association, 1973. Pp. 27–34.

BERKOWITZ, LEONARD. Impulse, aggression, and the gun. *Psychology Today,* September, 1968, 2, 19.

BERNSTEIN, BASIL. Elaborated and restricted codes: their social origins and some consequences. *American Anthropologist,* 1964, 66, 56.

BERNSTEIN, MELVIN A. *Modification of the reading process by behavioral activities.* Final Report. ED053905. National Center for Educational Research and Development, Washington, D.C., January 1971.

BERRES, FRANCES B. The effects of varying amounts of motoric involvement on the learning of nonsense syllables by male culturally disadvantaged retarded readers. Unpublished doctoral dissertation, University of California at Los Angeles, 1967.

BERRES, FRANCES & EYER, JOYCE T. John. In Albert J. Harris (Ed.), *Casebook on reading disability.* New York: McKay, 1970. Pp. 25–47.

BETTS, EMMETT A. *Foundations of Reading Instruction.* New York: American Book, 1946. Chap. 21.

BICKLEY, A. C.; ELLINGTON, BILLIE J.; & BICKLEY, RACHEL T. The cloze procedure: a conspectus. *Journal of Reading Behavior,* Summer 1970, 2, 232–249.

BIRCH, HERBERT G. Research issues in child health: some philosophic and methodological issues. *Pediatrics,* 1970, 45, 874–883.

BIRCH, HERBERT G. (Ed.) *Brain damage in children: the biological and social aspects.* Baltimore: Williams and Wilkins, 1964. Pp. 3–11.

BIRCH, HERBERT G. & BELMONT, LILLIAN. Auditory visual integration in normal and retarded readers. *American Journal of Orthopsychiatry,* October 1964, 34, 852–861.

BIRCH, HERBERT G. & LEFFORD, A. Intersensory development in children. *Monographs of the Society for Child Development,* 1963, 28, 1–47.

BISHOP, CAROL. Transfer of word and letter training in reading. Unpublished masters' thesis, Cornell University, 1962.

BIXLER, RAY H. Limits are therapy. *Journal of Consulting Psychology,* 1949, *13,* 1–11.

BLAKELY, W. PAUL & MC KAY, BEVERLY. Individualized reading as part of an eclectic reading program. *Elementary English,* March 1966, *43,* 214–219.

BLANCHARD, PHYLLIS. Psychogenic factors in some cases of reading disability. *American Journal of Orthopsychiatry,* 1935, *5,* 361–374.

RLANCHARD, PHYLLIS. Reading disabilities in relation to difficulties of personality and emotional development. *Mental Hygiene,* 1936, *20,* 384–413.

BLANCHARD, PHYLLIS. Psychoanalytic contributions to the problem of reading disabilities. *Psychoanalytic Study of the Child,* 1946, *2,* 163–188.

BLANK, MARION & BRIDGER, WAGNER H. Deficiencies in verbal labeling in retarded readers. *American Journal of Orthopsychiatry,* 1966, *36,* 840–847.

BLANTON, WILLIAM; FARR, ROGER; & TUINMAN, J. JAAP (Eds.). *Reading tests for the secondary grades: a review and evaluation.* Newark, Del.: International Reading Association, 1972.

BLAU, ABRAM. *The master hand.* Monograph Series, No. 5. New York: American Orthopsychiatric Association, 1945.

BLAU, HAROLD & BLAU, HARRIET. A theory of learning to read. *The Reading Teacher,* November 1968, *22,* 126–129, 144.

BLIESMER, EMERY P. A comparison of results of various capacity tests used with retarded readers. *Elementary School Journal,* May 1956, *56,* 400–402.

BLIESMER, EMERY P. Informal teacher testing in reading. *The Reading Teacher,* December 1972, *26,* 268–272.

BLOMMERS, PAUL J. & LINDQUIST, E. F. Rate of comprehension of reading: its measurement and its relationship to comprehension. *Journal of Educational Psychology,* November 1944, *34,* 449–473.

BLOOM, BENJAMIN S., *et al. Taxonomy of educational objectives, handbook I, cognitive domain.* New York: David McKay, 1956.

BLOOMFIELD, LEONARD & BARNHART, CLARENCE L. *Let's read: a linguistic approach.* Detroit: Wayne State University Press, 1961.

BØ, OLA O. The extent of the connection between cerebral dominance of speech functions (auditory and vocal), hand dominance, and dyslexia. *Scandinavian Journal of Educational Research,* 1972, *16,* 61–88.

BOND, GUY L. *Auditory and Speech Characteristics of Poor Readers.* Contributions to Education, No. 657. New York: Bureau of Publications, Teachers College, Columbia University, 1935.

BOND, GUY L. & DYKSTRA, ROBERT. The cooperative research program in first-grade reading instruction. *Reading Research Quarterly,* Summer 1967, *2,* 5–142.

BOND, GUY L. & TINKER, MILES A. *Reading difficulties: their diagnosis and correction* (3rd ed.). New York: Appleton-Century-Crofts, 1973. Pp. 99–105.

BONING, THOMAS & BONING, RICHARD. I'd rather read than. . . . *The Reading Teacher,* 1957, *10,* 196–200.

BOOS, R. W. Dominance and control: relationship to reading achievement. *Journal of Educational Research,* 1970, *63,* 466–470.

BORMUTH, JOHN R. The cloze readability procedure. In John R. Bormuth (Ed.), *Readability in 1968, a research bulletin prepared by a committee of the National Conference on Research in English.* Champaign: National Council of Teachers of English, 1968. Pp. 40–47. (a)

BORMUTH, JOHN R. (Ed.). *Readability in 1968, a research bulletin prepared by a committee of the National Conference on Research in English.* Champaign: National Council of Teachers of English, 1968. (b)

BOTEL, MORTON. A comparative study of the validity of the Botel Reading Inventory and selected standardized tests. In J. Allen Figurel (Ed.), *Reading and realism.* Newark, Del.: International Reading Association, 1969. Pp. 721–727.

BOTEL, MORTON. Dyslexia: Is there such a thing? In Nila Banton Smith (Ed.), *Current issues in reading.* Newark, Del.: International Reading Association, 1969. Pp. 357–371.

BOTEL, MORTON; DAWKINS, JOHN; & GRANOWSKY, ALVIN. A syntactic complexity formula. In Walter H. MacGinitie (Ed.), *Assessment problems in reading.* Newark, Del.: International Reading Association, 1973. Pp. 77–95.

BOTEL, MORTON & GRANOWSKY, ALVIN. A formula for measuring syntactic complexity. *Elementary English,* April 1972, *49,* 513–516.

BOUCHARD, LOUISA-MAY D. A comparative analysis of children's independent reading interests and the content of stories in selected basal reading texts, grades 4–6. Unpublished doctoral dissertation, Marquette University, 1971.

BOUGERE, MARGUERITE B. Vocabulary development in the primary grades. In Albert J. Harris and Edward R. Sipay (Eds.), *Readings on reading instruction.* New York: David McKay, 1972. Pp. 244–248. Reprinted from J. Allen Figurel (Ed.), *Forging ahead in reading.* Newark, Del.: International Reading Association, 1968. Pp. 75–78.

BRAAM, LEONARD. Developing and measuring flexibility in reading. *The Reading Teacher,* January 1963, *16,* 247–254.

BRAUN, FREDERICK G. Individualization: making it happen. *The Reading Teacher,* January 1972, *25,* 316–318.

BREEN, L. C. Vocabulary development by teaching prefixes, suffixes, and root derivations. *The Reading Teacher,* November 1960, *14,* 93–97.

BREKKE, GERALD. Actual and recommended allotments of time for reading. *The Reading Teacher,* 1963, *16,* 234–237.

BRICKLIN, PATRICIA M. Counseling parents of children with learning disabilities. *The Reading Teacher,* January 1970, *23,* 331–338.

BRIDGES, ETHEL B. Using children's choices of and reactions to poetry as determinants in enriching literary experience in the middle grades. *Dissertation Abstracts,* 1967, *27,* 3749A.

BRIDGES, L. H. Speed versus comprehension in elementary reading. *Journal of Educational Psychology,* 1941, *32,* 314–320.

BRONNER, AUGUSTA F. *Psychology of special abilities and disabilities.* Boston: Little, Brown, 1917.

BROWN, CAROL L. A study of procedures for determining fifth grade children's book choices. Unpublished doctoral dissertation, Ohio State University, 1971.

BROWN, FLORA M. Becoming a reading teacher on short notice. *Journal of Reading,* January 1972, *15,* 286–291.

BROWN, HARRY J. Reaction and movement time as related to oral and silent reading rate in disabled readers. Unpublished doctoral dissertation, University of Minnesota, 1970.

BROWN, VIRGINIA & BOTEL, MORTON. *Dyslexia: definition or treatment?* Bloomington, Ind.: ERIC/CRIER, Reading Review Series, 1972.

BRUININKS, ROBERT H. Relationship of auditory and visual perceptual strengths to methods of teaching word recognition among disadvantaged negro boys. Unpublished doctoral dissertation, George Peabody College for Teachers, 1968.

BRUININKS, ROBERT H.; GLAMAN, GERTRUDE M.; & CLARK, CHARLOTTE R. Issues in determining prevalence of reading retardation. *The Reading Teacher,* November 1973, *27*, 177–185.

BRUMBAUGH, F. Reading expectancy. *Elementary English Review*, 1940, *17*, 153–155.

BRUTON, RONALD W. Individualizing a basal reader. *The Reading Teacher*, October 1972, *26*, 59–63.

BRYAN, TANIS S. & WHEELER, ROSLYN. Perception of learning disabled children: the eye of the observer. *Journal of Learning Disabilities*, October 1972, *5*, 484–488.

BRYANT, N. DALE. Some principles of remedial instruction for dyslexia. *The Reading Teacher*, April 1965, *18*, 567–572.

BRYDEN, M. P. The manipulation of strategies and reports in dichotic listening. *Canadian Journal of Psychology*, 1964, *18*, 126–137.

BRYDEN, M. P. Laterality effects in dichotic listening: relations with handedness and reading ability in children. *Neuropsychologia*, November 1970, *8*, 443–450.

BRYDEN, M. P. Auditory-visual and sequential-spatial matching in relation to reading ability. *Child Development*, September 1972, *43*, 824–832.

BRZEINSKI, JOSEPH E. & ELLEDGE, GERALD E. Early reading. In Robert C. Aukerman (Ed.), *Some persistent questions on beginning reading*. Newark, Del.: International Reading Association, 1972. Pp. 65–76.

BUCHANAN, DOUGLAS. Development of cortical localization. In Arthur H. Keeney and Virginia T. Keeney (Eds.), *Dyslexia: diagnosis and treatment of reading disorders*. St. Louis: C. V. Mosby, 1968. Pp. 11–16.

BUKTENICA, NORMAN A. Auditory discrimination: a new assessment procedure. *Exceptional Children*, November 1971, *38*, 237–240.

BURGE, PAUL D. A comparison of selected methods for determining reading expectancy. Unpublished doctoral dissertation, University of Missouri-Columbia, 1971.

BURMEISTER, LOU E. Usefulness of phonic generalizations. *The Reading Teacher*, January 1968, *21*, 349–356.

BURMEISTER, LOU E. The effect of syllabic posistion and accent on the phonemic behavior of single vowel graphemes. In J. Allen Figurel (Ed.), *Reading and realism*. Newark, Del.: International Reading Association, 1969. Pp. 645–649.

BUROS, OSCAR K. (Ed.). *Reading: tests and reviews*. New Brunswick, N.J.: Gryphon Press, 1968.

BUROS, OSCAR K. (Ed.). *The seventh mental measurements yearbook*, Vols. I & II. New Brunswick, N.J.: Gryphon Press, 1972.

BURT, CYRIL. Counterblast to dyslexia. *AEP News Letter*, No. 5, March 1966, 2–6.

BURT, CYRIL. Review of J. P. Guilford, *The nature of human intelligence*. *Contemporary Psychology*, 1968, *13*, 546.

BUSWELL, GUY T. *Fundamental reading habits: a study of their development*. Supplementary Education Monographs, No. 21. Chicago: Department of Education, University of Chicago, 1922.

BUSWELL, GUY T. *Remedial reading at the college and adult levels*. Supplementary Education Monographs, No. 50. Chicago: University of Chicago, 1939.

BUSWELL, GUY T. Relationship between rate of thinking and rate of reading. *School Review*, September 1951, *49*, 339–346.

BUSWELL, GUY T. An experimental study of eye-voice span in reading. *Supplementary Educational Monograph*, No. 17, 1920.

BUTLER, JOSEPH. Comparison of listening abilities, categorized as good and poor, of inner-city children in the sixth grade. Unpublished doctoral dissertation, Indiana University, 1970.

BYRNE, MARY A.; FELDHUSEN, JOHN F.; & KANE, ROBERT B. The relationships among two cloze measurement procedures and divergent thinking abilities. *Reading Research Quarterly*, Spring 1971, *6*, 378–393.

CALDER, C. R. & ZALATIMO, S. D. Improving children's ability to follow directions. *The Reading Teacher*, December 1970, *24*, 227–231.

CALLAWAY, BYRON. Pupil and family characteristics related to reading achievement. *Education*, February-March 1972, *92*, 71–75.

CALVERT, JAMES C. & CROMES, GEORGE F. Oculomotor spasms in handicapped readers. *The Reading Teacher*, 1966, *20*, 231–236, 241.

CAMP, BONNIE W. Learning rate and retention in retarded readers. *Journal of Learning Disabilities*, February 1973, *6*, 65–71.

CANE, B. & SMITHERS, JANE. *The roots of reading*. Slough: National Foundation for Educational Research in England & Wales, 1971.

CARLSON, THORSTEN R. Effect of certain test factors in measurement of speed of reading. *Journal of Educational Research*, 1951, *44*, 543–549.

CARNER, RICHARD L. Reading forum. *Reading News*, August 1973, *2*, 1.

CAROLINE, SISTER MARY. *Breaking the sound barrier: a phonics handbook*. New York: Macmillan, 1960.

CARROLL, H. C. M. The remedial teaching of reading: an evaluation. *Remedial Education*, February 1972, *7*, 10–15.

CARROLL, JOHN B. Review of the *Illinois Test of Psycholinguistic Abilities*. In Oscar K. Buros (Ed.), *Seventh mental measurements yearbook*, Vol. I. Highland Park, N.J.: Gryphon Press, 1972. Pp. 819–823.

CARROLL, JOHN B.; DAVIES, PETER; & RICHMAN, BARRY. *American Heritage word frequency book*. Boston: Houghton Mifflin, 1971.

CARVER, RONALD P. A computer model of reading and its implications for measurement and research. *Reading Research Quarterly*, Summer 1971, *6*, 449–471. (a)

CARVER, RONALD P. *Sense and nonsense in speed reading*. Silver Spring, Md.: Revrac Publications, 1971. (b)

CASON, ELOISE B. *Mechanical methods for increasing the speed of reading*. Contributions to Education, No. 878. New York: Bureau of Publications, Teachers College, Columbia University, 1943.

CASWELL, HOLLIS L. Non-promotion in the elementary school. *Elementary School Journal*, 1933, *33*, 644–647.

CEGELKA, PATRICIA A. & CEGELKA, WALTER J. A review of the research: reading and the educable mentally retarded. *Exceptional Children*, November 1970, *37*, 187–200.

CHALL, JEANNE S. Ask him to try on the book for fit. *The Reading Teacher*, December 1953, *7*, 83–88.

CHALL, JEANNE S. *Readability: an appraisal of research and application*. Bureau of Educational Research Monographs, No. 34. Columbus: Ohio State University, 1957.

CHALL, JEANNE S. *Learning to read: the great debate. An inquiry into the science, art, and ideology of old and new methods of teaching children to read 1910–1965*. New York: McGraw-Hill, 1967.

CHALL, JEANNE S.; ROSWELL, FLORENCE G.; & BLUMENTHAL, SUSAN H. Auditory blending ability: a factor in success in beginning reading. *The Reading Teacher*, 1963, *17*, 113–118.

CHANSKY, NORMAN M. Age, IQ, and improvement in reading. *Journal of Educational Research*, 1963, *56*, 439.

CHAPMAN, CARITA A. An analysis of three theories of the relationships among reading-comprehension skills. Symposium on psycholinguistics and reading, International Reading Association, May 1969 (unpublished).

CHAPMAN, CARITA A. A test of a hierarchical theory of reading comprehension. Unpublished doctoral dissertation, University of Chicago, 1971.

CHARLTON, BETTY. Seeing is believing. *The Reading Teacher*, November 1971, *25*, 162–164.

CHASE, CLINTON I. Review of the *Illinois Test of Psycholinguistic Abilities*. In Oscar K. Buros (Ed.), *Seventh mental measurements Yearbook*, Vol. 1. Highland Park, N.J. Gryphon Press, 1972. Pp. 823–825.

CHILDS, SALLY B. & CHILDS, RALPH DE S. *Sound spelling.* Cambridge, Mass.: Educators Publishing Service, 1968.

CHING, DORIS C. Reading, language development and the bilingual child. *Elementary English*, May 1969, *46*, 622–628.

CHOMSKY, NOAM. Phonology and reading. In Harry Levin & Joanna P. Williams (Eds.), *Basic studies on reading*. New York: Basic Books, 1970. Pp. 3–18.

CHRISTINE, DOROTHY & CHRISTINE, CHARLES. The relationship of auditory discrimination to articulatory defects and reading retardation. *Elementary School Journal*, 1964, *65*, 97–100.

CIANCIOLO, PATRICIA JEAN. A recommended reading diet for children and youth of different cultures. *Elementary English*, November 1971, *48*, 779–787.

CLARK, MARGARET M. *Reading difficulties in schools.* Baltimore: Penguin Books, 1970.

CLARK, MARGARET M. Symposium on reading disability: III. Severe reading difficulty: a community study. *British Journal of Educational Psychology*, February 1971, *41*, 14–18.

CLAY, MARIE M. & IMLACH, ROBERT H. Juncture, pitch, and stress as reading behavior variables. *Journal of Verbal Learning & Verbal Behavior*, April 1971, *10*, 133–139.

CLELAND, DONALD L. An experimental study of tachistoscopic training as it relates to speed and comprehension in reading. Unpublished doctoral dissertation, University of Pittsburgh, 1950.

CLELAND, DONALD L. Seeing and reading. *American Journal of Optometry*, 1953, *80*, 467–481.

CLELAND, DONALD L. Clinical materials for appraising disabilities in reading. *The Reading Teacher*, March 1964, *17*, 428.

CLEMENTS, SAM D. *Minimal brain dysfunction in children: terminology and identification.* National Institute of Neurological Diseases Monograph, No. 3, Public Health Service Publication No. 1415, 1966. Washington, D.C.: Government Printing Office, 1966.

CLYMER, THEODORE. The utility of phonic generalizations in the primary grades. *The Reading Teacher*, January 1963, *16*, 252–258.

CLYMER, THEODORE. Research in corrective reading: findings, problems, and observations. In Marjorie S. Johnson and Roy A. Kress (Eds.), *Corrective reading in the elementary classroom*. Newark, Del.: International Reading Association, 1967. Pp. 1–10.

CLYMER, THEODORE. What is reading? Some current concepts. In Helen M. Robinson (Ed.), *Innovation and change in reading instruction*. Sixty-seventh yearbook of the National Society for the Study of Education, Part II. Chicago: University of Chicago Press, 1968. Pp. 7–29.

COHEN, ALICE. Relationship between factors of dominance and reading ability. In

George D. Spache (Ed.), *Reading disability and perception.* Newark, Del.: International Reading Association, 1969. Pp. 38–45.

COHEN, ALICE & GLASS, GERALD G. Lateral dominance and reading ability. *The Reading Teacher,* January 1968, *21,* 343–348.

COHEN, DOROTHY H. Word meaning and the literary experience in early childhood. *Elementary English,* November 1971, *46,* 914–925.

COHEN, S. ALAN. Studies in visual perception and reading in disadvantaged children. *Journal of Learning Disabilities,* October 1969, *2,* 498–507.

COHN, STELLA M. & COHN, JACK. *Teaching the retarded reader.* New York: Odyssey, 1967.

COLBURN, EVANGELINE. A device for stimulating reading interests. *Elementary School Journal,* 1944, *44,* 539–541.

COLEMAN, JAMES S., et al. *Equality of educational opportunity.* Washington, D.C.: Government Printing Office, 1966. P. 17.

COMMITTEE OF THE UPPER GRADES STUDY COUNCIL, CINCINNATI. Developing the reading interests of children. *Elementary English Review,* 1943, *20,* 279–286.

CONGREVE, WILLARD J. & RINEHART, GEORGE J. (Eds.). *Flexibility in school programs.* Worthington, Ohio: Charles A. Jones, 1972.

CONNOLLY, CHRISTOPHER. Social and emotional factors in learning disabilities. In Helmer R. Myklebust (Ed.), *Progress in learning disabilities,* Vol. II. New York: Grune & Stratton, 1971. Pp. 151–178.

CONNOR, JAMES P. Bender Gestalt Test performance as a predictor of differential reading performance. *Journal of School Psychology,* 1968–1969, *7,* 41–44.

CONNORS, C. KEITH. Cortical visual evoked response in children with learning disorders. *Psychophysiology,* November 1970, *7,* 418–428.

COOPER, J. LOUIS. The effect of adjustment of basal reading materials on reading achievement. Unpublished doctoral dissertation, Boston University, 1952.

CORDTS, ANNA D. And it's all called phonics. *Elementary English,* 1955, *32,* 376–378.

CORRIGAN, FRANCIS C.; BERGER, STANLEY I.; DIENSTIBER, R. A.; & STROK, E. S. The influence of prematurity on school performance. *American Journal of Mental Deficiency,* 1967, *71,* 533–535.

COTERELL, GILL. A case of severe learning disability. *Remedial Education,* February 1972, *7,* 5–9.

COX, AYLETT R. *Remedial language training for alphabetic phonics.* Cambridge, Mass.: Educators Publishing Service, 1967.

CRAMER, R. L. Dialectology—a case for language experience. *The Reading Teacher,* October 1971, *25,* 33–39.

CRAWFORD, GAIL & CONLEY, DICK. Meet you in reading lab! *Journal of Reading,* October 1971, *15,* 16–21.

CRISCUOLO, NICHOLAS P. Training tutors effectively. *The Reading Teacher,* November 1971, *25,* 157–159.

CRITCHLEY, MACDONALD. *The dyslexic child.* Springfield, Ill.: Charles C Thomas, 1970.

CROMER, WARD. The effects of "pre-organizing" reading material on two levels of poor readers. Unpublished doctoral dissertation, Clark University, 1968.

CRONNELL, BRUCE. Designing a reading program based on research findings in orthography. *Elementary English,* January 1973, *50,* 27–34.

CROWLEY, HARRY L. & ELLIS, BESSIE. Cross validation of a method for selecting children requiring special services in reading. *The Reading Teacher,* January 1971, *24,* 312–319.

CROXEN, MARY E. & LYTTON, HUGH. Reading disability and difficulties in finger localization and right-left discrimination. *Developmental Psychology,* September 1971, 5, 256–262.

CRUIKSHANK, WILLIAM M., *et al. A teaching method for brain-injured and hyperactive children.* Syracuse: Syracuse University Press, 1961.

CURRY, DALE R. Case studies in behavior modification. *Psychology in the schools,* 1970, 7, 330–335.

CUSHENBERY, DONALD C. The Joplin plan and cross grade grouping. In Wallace Z. Ramsey (Ed.), *Organizing for individual differences.* Perspectives in Reading, No. 6. Newark, Del.: International Reading Association, 1967. Pp. 33–46.

DAHLBERG, CHARLES C.; ROSWELL, FLORENCE G.; & CHALL, JEANNE S. Psychotherapeutic principles as applied to remedial reading. *Elementary School Journal,* 1952, 52, 211–217.

DAINES, DELVA & MASON, LYNNE G. A comparison of placement tests and readability graphs. *Journal of Reading,* May 1972, 15, 597–603.

DALE, EDGAR. Vocabulary measurement: techniques and major findings. *Elementary English,* 1965, 42, 895–901, 948.

DALE, EDGAR & CHALL, JEANNE S. A formula for predicting readability. *Educational Research Bulletin,* Ohio State University, 1948, 27, 11–20; 28, 37–54.

DALE, EDGAR & EICHHOLZ, GERHARD. *Children's knowledge of words: an interim report.* Columbus: Bureau of Educational Research and Service, Ohio State University, 1960.

DALE, EDGAR & O'ROURKE, JOSEPH. *Techniques of teaching vocabulary.* Palo Alto, Calif.: Field Educational Publications, 1971.

DALE, EDGAR & RAZIK, TAHER, *Bibliography of vocabulary studies* (5th ed.). Columbus, Ohio: Ohio State University Press, 1973.

DANIELS, J. C. Children with reading difficulties. *Slow Learning Child,* 1967, 13, 138–143.

DAVIDSON, HELEN P. An experimental study of bright, average, and dull children at the four-year mental level. *Genetic Psychology Monographs,* 1931, 9, Nos. 3, 4.

DAVIDSON, ROSCOE L. The effects of an interaction analysis system on the development of critical reading in elementary school children. Unpublished doctoral dissertation, University of Denver, 1967.

DAVIES, WILLIAM C. Implicit speech—some conclusions drawn from research. In Robert C. Aukerman (Ed.), *Some persistent questions on beginning reading.* Newark, Del.: International Reading Association, 1972. Pp. 171–177.

DAVINO, ANTOINETTE C. Reading program for the Afro-American. In Helen K. Smith (Ed.), *Meeting individual needs in reading.* Newark, Del.: International Reading Association, 1971. Pp. 94–100.

DAVIS, FREDERICK B. Fundamental factors of comprehension in reading. *Psychometrica,* 1944, 9, 185–197.

DAVIS, FREDERICK B. Research in comprehension in reading. *Reading Research Quarterly,* Summer 1968, 3, 499–545.

DAVIS, FREDERICK B. *Psychometric research on comprehension in reading.* Graduate School of Education, Rutgers University, New Brunswick, N.J., 1971.

DAVIS, FREDERICK B. Psychometric research on comprehension in reading. *Reading Research Quarterly,* Summer 1972, 7, 628–678.

DAVIS, JOANNE W. Teaching reading with paperbacks in an elementary school:

three models for classroom organization. *Elementary English,* December 1970, *47,* 1114–1120.

DAVIS, O. L., JR. & PERSONKE, CARL R., JR. Effects of administering the Metropolitan Readiness Test in English and Spanish to Spanish-speaking school entrants. *Journal of Educational Measurement,* 1968, *5,* 231–234.

DAVIS, OLGA; GLADNEY, MILDRED; & LEAVERTON, LLOYD. *The psycholinguistic reading series: a bi-dialectal approach* (experimental ed.). Chicago: Board of Education of the City of Chicago, 1969.

DEARBORN, WALTER F. Structural factors which condition special disability in reading. *Proceedings of the American Association for Mental Deficiency,* 1933, *38,* 266–283.

DECKER, ISABELLE M. *100 novel ways with book reports.* New York: Citation Press, 1969.

DE HIRSCH, KATRINA. Psychological correlates in the reading process. In J. Allen Figurel (Ed.), *Challenge and experiment in reading.* Newark, Del.: International Reading Association, 1962. Pp. 218–226.

DE HIRSCH, KATRINA; JANSKY, JEANNETTE; & LANGFORD, WILLIAM S. Comparisons between prematurely and maturely born children at three age levels. *American Journal of Orthopsychiatry,* 1966, *36,* 616–628. (a)

DE HIRSCH, KATRINA; JANSKY, JEANNETTE J.; & LANGFORD, WILLIAM S. *Predicting reading failure: a preliminary study.* New York: Harper & Row, 1966. (b)

DEIGHTON, LEE C. Vocabulary development in the classroom. In Albert J. Harris & Edward R. Sipay (Eds.), *Readings on reading instruction.* New York: David McKay, 1972. Pp. 254–257. Reprinted from Lee C. Deighton. *Vocabulary development in the classroom.* New York: Teachers College Press, 1959. Pp. 2–6, 15–16.

DELACATO, CARL H. *Treatment and prevention of reading problems.* Springfield, Ill.: Charles C Thomas, 1959.

DELACATO, CARL H. *The diagnosis and treatment of speech and reading problems.* Springfield, Ill.: Charles C Thomas, 1963.

DELACATO, CARL H. *Neurological organization and reading.* Springfield, Ill.: Charles C Thomas, 1966.

DELLA-PIANA, GABRIEL & HOGBEN, MICHAEL. Research strategies for maximizing the effectiveness of programmed reading. Unpublished paper presented at Association for Programmed Learning, Glasgow, Scotland, April 1968. Salt Lake City; Granite School District Exemplary Center for Reading Instruction.

DENCKLA, MARTHA B. Clinical syndromes in learning disabilities: the case for "splitting" vs. "lumping." *Journal of Learning Disabilities,* August–September 1972, *5,* 401–406.

DENHOFF, ERIC; HAINSWORTH, PETER K.; & SIQUELAND, MARIAN L. The measurement of psychoneurological factors contributing to learning efficiency. *Journal of Learning Disabilities,* November 1968, *1,* 636–644.

DE QUIROS, BERNALDO & DELLA CELLA, M. La dislexia como sindrome: estudio estadistico sobre la dislexia infantil en la Ciudad de Rosario-Santa Fe, *Acta Neuropsiquiatrica Argentina,* 1959, *5,* 178–193.

DE STEFANO, JOHANNA S. (Ed.). *Language, society, and education: a profile of Black English.* Worthington, Ohio: Charles A. Jones, 1973. (a)

DE STEFANO, JOHANNA S. Register: a concept to combat negative teacher attitudes toward black English. In Johanna S. De Stefano (Ed.), *Language, society, and education: a profile of Black English.* Worthington, Ohio: Charles A. Jones, 1973. Pp. 189–195. (b)

DEUTSCH, CYNTHIA P. Auditory discrimination and learning: social factors. *Merrill-Palmer Quarterly of Behavior and Development,* 1964, *10,* 277–296.

DIETRICH, DOROTHY M. & MATHEWS, VIRGINIA H. (Eds.), *Development of lifetime reading habits.* Joint Committee on Reading Development of the American Book Publishers and the International Reading Association. Newark, Del.: International Reading Association, 1968. P. 2.

DI LORENZO, LOUIS T. & SALTER, RUTH. Co-operative research on the nongraded primary. *Elementary School Journal,* 1965, *65,* 269–277.

DOEHRING, DONALD G. *Patterns of impairment in specific reading disability: a neuropsychological investigation.* Bloomington: Indiana University Press, 1968.

DOLCH, E. W. A basic sight vocabulary. *Elementary School Journal,* 1936, *36,* 456–460; *37,* 268–272.

DOLCH, E. W. How to diagnose children's reading difficulties by informal classroom techniques. *The Reading Teacher,* January 1953, *6,* 10–14.

DOLCH, E. W. & BLOOMSTER, M. Phonic readiness. *Elementary School Journal.* 1937, *38,* 201–205.

DONALD, SISTER MARY. The SQ3R method in grade seven. *Journal of Reading,* October 1967, *11,* 33–35, 43.

DORSEY, MARY E. *Reading games and activities.* Belmonte, Calif: Fearon, 1972.

DOWNING, GERTRUDE L.; EDGAR, ROBERT W.; HARRIS, ALBERT J.; KORNBERG, LEONARD; & STOREN, HELEN F. *The preparation of teachers for schools in culturally deprived neighborhoods* (The Bridge Project). Cooperative Research Project No. 935. Flushing, N.Y.: Queens College, 1965. Available through university microfilm library services.

DOWNING, JOHN. *The initial teaching alphabet explained and illustrated.* London: Cassell, and New York: Macmillan, 1964.

DOWNING, JOHN. How children think about reading. *The Reading Teacher,* December 1969, *23,* 217–230.

DOWNING, JOHN. A psycholinguistic theory for i.t.a. *Elementary English,* November 1970, *47,* 952–961.

DOWNING, J. A gap has two sides. *The Reading Teacher,* April 1972, *25,* 634–638.

DOWNING, JOHN. *Comparative reading: cross-national studies of behavior and processes in reading and writing.* New York: Macmillan, 1973.

DOWNING, JOHN, et al. *The i.t.a. symposium: research report on the British experiment with i.t.a.* London: National Foundation for Educational Research in England and Wales, 1967.

DREW, A. L. A neurological appraisal of familial congenital word-blindness. *Brain,* 1956, *79,* 440–460.

DUKER, SAM. *Individualized reading: an annotated bibliography.* Metuchen, N.J.: Scarecrow Press, 1968. P. 25.

DUNKELD, COHN G. M. The validity of the informal reading inventory for the designation of instructional reading levels: a study of the relationships between children's gains in reading achievement and the difficulty of instructional materials. Unpublished doctoral dissertation, University of Illinois at Urbana-Champaign, 1970.

DUNN, LLOYD M. Minimal brain dysfunction: a dilemma for educators. In H. Carl Haywood (Ed.), *Brain damage in school age children.* Washington, D.C.: Council for Exceptional Children, 1968. Pp. 161–181.

DUNN, LLOYD M., et al. *The effectiveness of three reading approaches and an oral language stimulation program with disadvantaged children in the primary*

grades: an interim report after one year of the cooperative reading project.
IMRID Behavioral Science Monograph No. 7. Nashville: Institute on Mental
Retardation and Intellectual Development, George Peabody College for
Teachers, 1967.

DUNN, LLOYD M.; POCHANART, PRAYOT; PFOST, PHILIP; & BRUININKS, ROBERT H. *The
effectiveness of the Peabody Language Development Kits and the Initial
Teaching Alphabet with disadvantaged children in the primary grades: a
report after the third grade of the Cooperative Language Development Project.* IMRID Behavioral Science Monograph No. 9. Nashville: George Peabody
College for Teachers, 1968.

DUNNING, JACK D. & KEPHART, NEWELL C. Motor generalizations in space and time.
In Jerome Hellmuth (Ed.), *Learning Disorders,* Vol. 1. Seattle: Special Child
Publications, 1965. Pp. 77–121.

DURKIN, DOLORES. *Children who read early.* New York: Teachers College Press,
1966.

DURRELL, DONALD D. *Improvement of basic reading abilities.* Yonkers, N.Y.: World
Book, 1940.

DURRELL, DONALD D. *Improving reading instruction.* New York: Harcourt, Brace,
and World, 1956. Pp. 367–392.

DURRELL, DONALD D. (Ed.). Adapting instruction to the learning needs of children
in the intermediate grades. *Journal of Education,* December 1959, *142,* 1–78.

DURRELL, DONALD D. & HAYES, MARY T. *Durrell Listening-Reading Series: Manual
for listening and reading tests, primary level, Form OE.* New York: Harcourt
Brace Jovanovich, 1969.

DURRELL, DONALD D. & MURPHY, HELEN A. The auditory discrimination factor in
reading readiness and reading disability. *Education,* 1953, *73,* 556–560.

DUSEWICZ, RUSSELL A. & KERSHNER, KEITH M. The D-K Scale of Lateral Dominance.
Perceptual & Motor Skills, 1969, *29,* 282.

DYER, HENRY S. Research issues on equality of educational opportunity: school
factors. *Harvard Education Review,* 1968, *38,* 38–56.

DYKMAN, ROSCOE A.; ACKERMAN, PEGGY T.; CLEMENTS, SAM D.; & PETERS, JOHN E.
Specific learning disabilities: an attentional deficit syndrome. In Helmer R.
Myklebust (Ed.), *Progress in learning disabilities,* Vol. II. New York: Grune &
Stratton, 1971. Pp. 56–93.

DYKSTRA, ROBERT. Auditory discrimination abilities and beginning reading achievement. *Reading Research Quarterly,* Spring, 1966, *1,* 5–34.

DYKSTRA, ROBERT. *Continuation of the coordinating center for first-grade reading
instruction programs.* Final Report, Project No. 6-1651. Minneapolis: University of Minnesota Press, 1967.

DYKSTRA, ROBERT. Summary of the second-grade phase of the cooperative research
program in primary reading instruction. *Reading Research Quarterly,* Fall
1968, *4,* 49–70. (a)

DYKSTRA, ROBERT. The effectiveness of code- and meaning-emphasis beginning
reading programs. *The Reading Teacher,* October 1968, *22,* 17–23. (b)

DYMENT, PAUL G.; LATTIN, JOHN E.; & HERBERTSON, LEON M. The value of the
electroencephalogram in evaluating children with minimal cerebral dysfunction. *Journal of School Health,* January 1971, *41,* 9–11.

EAMES, THOMAS H. The effect of correction of refractive errors on the distant and
near vision of school children. *Journal of Educational Research,* 1942, *36,*
272–279.

EAMES, THOMAS H. Comparison of eye conditions among 1000 reading failures, 500 ophthalmic patients, and 150 unselected children. *American Journal of Ophthalmology*, 1948, *31*, 713–717.

EAMES, THOMAS H. Some neurological and glandular bases of learning. *Journal of Education*, April 1960, *142*, 1–35.

EARP, N. W. Procedures for teaching reading in mathematics. *Arithmetic Teacher*, 1970, *17*, 575–579.

EAST, ROBERT C. A study of the effectiveness of specific language disability techniques on reading ability of potentially retarded readers. *Bulletin of the Orton Society*, 1969, *19*, 95–99.

EBERSOLE, MARYLOU; KEPHART, NEWELL C.; & EBERSOLE, JAMES B. *Steps to achievement for the slow learner.* Columbus: Charles E. Merrill, 1968.

EBERWEIN, LOWELL. A comparsion of a flexible grouping plan with a three-way achievement plan in fourth grade reading instruction. *Journal of Educational Research*, December 1972, *66*, 169–174.

EBERWEIN, LOWELL. What do book choices indicate? *Journal of Reading*, December 1973, *17*, 186–191.

ED 053 881 Model programs: reading. Bloom Township high school reading program, Chicago Heights, Ill., 1971.

ED 053 882 Model programs: reading. Summer junior high schools, New York, N.Y., 1971.

ED 053 883 Model programs: reading. Programmed tutorial reading project, Indianapolis, Ind., 1971.

ED 053 884 Model programs: reading. Summer remedial and enrichment program, Thomasville, Ga., 1971.

ED 053 885 Model programs: reading. Elementary reading centers, Milwaukee, Wisc., 1971.

ED 053 886 Model programs: reading. Intensive reading instructional teams, Hartford, Conn., 1971.

ED 053 887 Model programs: reading. Yuba County reading-learning center, Marysville, Calif., 1971.

ED 053 888 Model programs: reading. The Topeka reading clinic, centers, and services, Topeka, Kan., 1971.

ED 053 889 Model programs: reading. School-within-a-school, Keokuk, Iowa, 1971.

ED 053 890 Model programs: reading. Remedial reading program, Pojoaque, N.M., 1971.

EDELSTEIN, RUTH R. Use of group processes in teaching retarded readers. *The Reading Teacher*, January 1970, *23*, 318–324.

EDFELDT, AKE W. *Silent speech and silent reading.* Chicago: University of Chicago Press, 1960.

EDWARDS, THOMAS J. The progressive choice reading method. In John Money (Ed.), *The disabled reader.* Baltimore: Johns Hopkins Press, 1966. Pp. 215–228.

EKWALL, ELDON E. Measuring gains in remedial reading. *The Reading Teacher*, November 1972, *26*, 138–141.

ELENBOGEN, ELAINE M. & THOMPSON, G. R. A comparison of social class effects in two tests of auditory discrimination. *Journal of Learning Disabilities*, April 1972, *5*, 209–212.

ELKIND, DAVID. Ethnicity and reading: three avoidable dangers. In Harold Tanyzer & Jean Karl (Eds.), *Reading, children's books, and our pluralistic society.* Newark, Del.: International Reading Association, 1972. Pp. 4–8.

ELLER, WILLIAM & ATTEA, MARY. Three diagnostic tests: some comparisons. In J.

Allen Figurel (Ed.), *Vistas in reading.* Newark, Del.: International Reading Association, 1966. Pp 562–566.

ELLEY, WARWICK B. The assessment of readability by noun frequency counts. *Reading Research Quarterly,* Spring 1969, *4*, 411–427.

ELLEY, WARWICK B. & TOLLEY, CYRIL W. *Children's reading interests, a Wellington survey.* Wellington, New Zealand: New Zealand Council for Educational Research, 1972.

ELLSON, DOUGLAS G. Report of results of tutorial reading project. Indianapolis Public Schools. Indiana University: Mimeographed, August 22, 1969.

ELLSON, DOUGLAS G.; BARBER, LARRY; ENGLE, T. L.; & KAMPWERTH, LEONARD. Programed tutoring: a teaching aid and a research tool. *Reading Research Quarterly,* Fall 1965, *1*, 77–127.

ELLSON, DOUGLAS G.; HARRIS, PHILLIP; & BARBER, LARRY. A field test of programed and directed tutoring. *Reading Research Quarterly,* Spring 1968, *3*, 307–368.

EMANS, ROBERT. Teacher evaluations of reading skills and individualized reading. *Elementary English,* March 1965, *42*, 258–269.

EMANS, ROBERT. When two vowels go walking and other such things. *The Reading Teacher,* December 1967, *21*, 262–269.

EMANS, ROBERT & PATYK, GLORIA. Why do high school students read? *Journal of of Reading,* February 1967, *10*, 300–304.

EMBREY, JAMES E. A study of the effects of mild hearing loss on educational achievement. Unpublished doctoral dissertation, University of Tulsa, 1971.

ENSTROM, E. A. A key to learning. *Academic Therapy,* Summer 1970, *5*, 295–297.

ERICKSON, FREDERICK D. F'get you honky!: a new look at black dialect and the school. *Elementary English,* April 1969, *46*, 495–499, 517.

ESPOSITO, DOMINICK. Homogeneous and heterogeneous ability grouping: principal findings and implications for evaluating and designing more effective educational environments. *Review of Educational Research,* Spring 1973, *43*, 163–179.

ESTES, THOMAS H. A scale to measure attitudes toward reading. *Journal of Reading,* November 1971, *15*, 135–138.

ESTES, WILLIAM H. *Learning theory and mental development.* New York: Academic Press, 1970.

EVERTTS, ELDONNA. Review of learning to read: the great debate. *Elementary English,* May 1968, *45*, 652–656.

FADER, DANIEL N. & MC NEIL, ELTON B. *Hooked on books.* New York: Berkley, 1966.

FARR, ROGER. *Reading: what can be measured?* Newark, Del.: International Reading Association, 1969.

FARR, ROGER & ANASTASIOW, NICHOLAS. *Tests of reading readiness and achievement: a review and evaluation.* Newark, Del.: International Reading Association, 1969.

FEELEY, JOAN T. Television and children's reading. *Elementary English,* January 1973, *50*, 141–150.

FELDHUSEN, HAZEL J.; LAMB, POSE; & FELDHUSEN, JOHN. Prediction of reading achievement under programmed and traditional instruction. *The Reading Teacher,* February 1970, *23*, 446–454.

FERGUSON, JERRY. Teaching the reading of biology. In H. Alan Robinson & Ellen L. Thomas (Eds.), *Fusing reading skills and content.* Newark, Del.: International Reading Association, 1969. Pp. 114–119.

FERNALD, GRACE M. *Remedial techniques in basic school subjects.* New York: McGraw-Hill, 1943.

FERNALD, GRACE M. & KELLER, HELEN. The effect of kinesthetic factors in development of word recognition in the case of non-readers. *Journal of Educational Research,* 1921, *4,* 357–377.

FIDEL, EDWARD A. & RAY, JOSEPH B. The validity of the Revised Objective Perceptual Test in differentiating among nonorganic, minimally organic, and grossly organic children. *Journal of Special Education,* 1972, *6,* 279–284.

FIGUREL, J. ALLEN (Ed.). *Reading goals for the disadvantaged.* Newark, Del.: International Reading Association, 1970.

FITE, JUNE H. & SCHWARTZ, LOUISE A. Screening culturally disadvantaged first grade children for potential reading difficulties due to constitutional factors. Abstract. *American Journal of Orthopsychiatry,* 1965, *35,* 359–360.

FLANAGAN, JOHN C. The PLAN system for individualizing education. *NCME Measurement in Education,* January 1971, *2,* 1–8.

FLAX, NATHAN. The contribution of visual problems to learning disability. *Journal of the American Optometric Association,* October 1970, *41,* 841–845.

FLEMING, JAMES T. Skimming: neglected in research and teaching. *Journal of Reading,* December 1968, *12,* 211–214, 218.

FLESCH, RUDOLPH. *Why Johnny can't read.* New York: Harper & Row, 1955. P. 23.

FOOD AND NUTRITION BOARD. *The relationship of nutrition to brain development and behavior.* National Academy of Sciences, National Research Council, Washington, D.C., 1973.

FORNESS, STEVEN R. & WEIL, MARVIN C. Laterality in retarded readers with brain dysfunction. *Exceptional Children,* May 1970, *36,* 684–695.

FRAGER, STANLEY & STERN, CAROLYN. Learning by teaching. *The Reading Teacher,* February 1970, *23,* 403–405, 417.

FRANCIS, HAZEL. Children's experience of reading and notions of units in language. *British Journal of Educational Psychology,* February 1973, *43,* 17–23.

FRANCIS, W. NELSON. Linguistics and reading: a commentary on chapters 1 to 3. In Harry Levin & Joanna P. Williams (Eds.), *Basic studies of reading.* New York: Basic Books, 1970. Pp. 43–56.

FRAZIER, ALEXANDER. Developing a vocabulary of the senses. *Elementary English,* February 1970, *47,* 176–184.

FREEMAN, ROGER D. Review of medicine in special education No. 3.: medical-behavioral pseudorelationships. *Journal of Special Education,* Winter/Spring 1971, *5,* 93–99.

FREER, FRANK J. Visual and auditory perceptual modality difference as related to success in first grade reading word recognition. Unpublished doctoral dissertation, Rutgers University, 1971.

FREMER, JOHN. Criterion-referenced interpretation of survey achievement tests. Princeton, N.J.: Educational Testing Service, Test Development Memorandum TDM-72-1, January 1972.

FREMER, JOHN. Services in the area of criterion-referenced and objectives referenced measurement. What, why, and where next? Paper presented at the Michigan School Testing Conference, Ann Arbor, Michigan, March 14, 1973.

FRIEDMAN, NATHAN. Specific visual fixation stress and motor-learning difficulty: II. *Journal of the American Optometric Association,* February 1972, *43,* 165–173.

FROST, BARRY P. The role of intelligence "C" in the selection of children for remedial reading. *Alberta Journal of Educational Research,* 1963, *9,* 73–78.

FROSTIG, MARIANNE. Corrective reading in the classroom. *The Reading Teacher,* April 1965, *18,* 573–580.

FROSTIG, MARIANNE. Disabilities and remediation in reading. *Academic Therapy,* Summer 1972, 7, 373–391. (a)

FROSTIG, MARIANNE. Visual perception, integrative functions and academic learning. *Journal of Learning Disabilities,* January 1972, 5, 1–15. (b)

FROSTIG, MARIANNE & HORNE, D. *The Frostig program for the development of visual perception.* Chicago: Follett, 1964.

FROSTIG, MARIANNE & MASLOW, PHYLLIS. Reading developmental abilities and the problem of the match. *Journal of Learning Disabilities,* November 1969, 2, 571–574.

FRY, EDWARD. *Comparison of three methods of reading instruction (ITA, DMS, TO): results at the end of third grade.* Final report, Project No. 3050. New Brunswick: Rutgers, The State University, 1967.

FRY, EDWARD. A readability formula that saves time. *Journal of Reading,* April 1968, *11,* 513–516.

FRY, EDWARD. *Reading instruction for classroom and clinic.* New York: McGraw-Hill, 1972.

FULLER, GERALD B. The Minnesota Percepto-Diagnostic Test (revised). *Journal of Clinical Psychology,* Monograph Supplement No. 28, 1969. (a)

FULLER, GERALD B. Perceptual behaviors and reading disabilities: emphasis on the neurological impaired. *Learning Disability.* Arlington, Va.: Council for Exceptional Children, 1969. Pp. 40–50. (b)

FUSARO, JOSEPH. Eye-voice span and linguistic constraints in elementary school children. Unpublished doctoral dissertation, State University of New York at Albany, 1974.

GADWAY, CHARLES J. *National assessment of educational progress. Reading: summary.* Preliminary Report 02-R-00. Denver, Colorado: Education Commission of the States, May 1972.

GAINES, BEVERLY J. & RASKIN, LARRY M. Comparison of cross-modal and intramodal form recognition in children with learning disabilities. *Journal of Learning Disabilities,* May 1970, 3, 243–246.

GALLAGHER, J. ROSWELL. Specific language disability: dyslexia. *Bulletin of the Orton Society,* 1960, *10,* 5–10.

GALLOWAY, CHARLES G. & MICKELSON, NORMA I. Improve teachers' questions. *Elementary School Journal,* December 1973, *74,* 145–148.

GANS, ROMA. *A study of critical reading comprehension in the intermediate grades.* Contribution to Education, No. 811. New York: Bureau of Publications, Teachers College, Columbia University, 1940.

GARDNER, KEITH. The initial teaching alphabet (i.t.a.) and remedial reading programme. *Slow Learning Child,* 1966, *13,* 67–71.

GATES, ARTHUR I. *The improvement of reading: a program of diagnostic and remedial methods.* New York: Macmillan, 1927; 2nd ed., 1935; 3rd ed., 1947.

GATES, ARTHUR I. The necessary mental age for beginning reading. *Elementary School Journal,* 1937, 37, 497–508.

GATES, ARTHUR I. The role of personality maladjustment in reading disability. *Journal of Genetic Psychology,* 1941, 59, 77–83.

GATES, ARTHUR I. Character and purposes of the yearbook. In Nelson B. Henry (Ed.), *Reading in the elementary school.* 48th Yearbook of the National Society for the Study of Education, Part II. Chicago: University of Chicago Press, 1949. Chap. 1.

GATTEGNO, CALEB & HINMAN, DOROTHY. The color phonics system. In John Money

(Ed), *The disabled reader*. Baltimore: Johns Hopkins Press, 1966. Pp. 175–192.

GEESLIN, DORINE H. & WILSON, RICHARD C. Effect of reading age on reading interests. *Elementary English*, May 1972, *49*, 750–756.

GESELL, ARNOLD & AMATRUDA, CATHERINE S. *Developmental diagnosis: normal and abnormal child development*. New York: Hoeber, 1941. Pp. 238–239.

GETMAN, GERALD N. The visuomotor complex in the acquisition of learning skills. In Jerome Hellmuth (Ed.), *Learning Disorders*, Vol. 1. Seattle, Wash.: Special Child Publications, 1965. Pp. 49–76.

GEVER, BENSON E. Failure and learning disability. *The Reading Teacher*, January 1970, *23*, 311–317.

GEYER, JOHN J. Perceptual systems in reading: the prediction of a temporal eye-voice span. In Helen K. Smith (Ed.), *Perception and reading*. Newark, Del.: International Reading Association, 1968. Pp. 44–52.

GEYER, JOHN J. Comprehensive and partial models related to the reading process. *Reading Research Quarterly*, Summer 1972, *7*, 541–587.

GIBSON, ELEANOR J. Reading for some purpose. In James F. Kavanagh & Ignatius G. Mattingly (Eds.), *Language by ear and eye*. Cambridge, Mass.: MIT Press, 1972. Pp. 3–19.

GIEBINK, JOHN W. & BIRCH, ROBERT. The Bender Gestalt Test as an ineffective predicator of reading achievement. *Journal of Clinical Psychology*, October 1970, *26*, 484–485.

GILLINGHAM, ANNA & STILLMAN, BESSIE W. *Remedial training for children with specific difficulty in reading, spelling, and penmanship* (7th ed.). Cambridge, Mass.: Educators Publishing Service, 1966.

GINSBURG, G. P. & HARTWICK, ANN. Directional confusion as a sign of dyslexia. *Perceptual & Motor Skills*, April 1971, *32*, 535–543.

GLASER, ROBERT. Adapting the elementary school curriculum to individual performances. *Proceedings of the 1967 Invitational Conference on Teaching problems*. Princeton, N.J.: Educational Testing Service, 1968.

GLASER, ROBERT & NITKO, ANTHONY J. Measurement in learning and instruction. In R. L. Thorndike (Ed.), *Educational Measurement*. Washington, D.C.: American Council on Education, 1971.

GLASS, GENE V. & ROBBINS, MELVYN P. A critique of experiments on the role of neurological organization in reading performance. *Reading Research Quarterly*, Fall 1967, *3*, 5–52.

GLASS, GERALD G. & BURTON, ELIZABETH H. How do they decode? verbalizations and observed behaviors of successful decoders. *The Reading Teacher*, March 1973, *26*, 645.

GLAVACH, MATT & STONER, DONOVAN. Breaking the failure pattern. *Journal of Learning Disabilities*, February 1970, *3*, 103–105.

GLAZER, SUSAN M. Is sentence length a valid measure of difficulty in readability formulas? *The Reading Teacher*, February 1974, *27*, 464–468.

GLEITMAN, LELA R. & ROZIN, PAUL. Teaching reading by means of a syllabary. *Reading Research Quarterly*, Summer 1973, *8*, 447–483.

GLENN, HUGH W. The effect of silent and oral reading on literal comprehension and oral reading performance. Unpublished doctoral dissertation, University of Southern California, 1971.

GLOCK, MARVIN D. Is there a Pygmalion in the classroom? *The Reading Teacher*, February 1972, *25*, 405–408.

GLOGAU, LILLIAN & FESSELL, MURRAY. *The nongraded primary school: a case study*. West Nyack, N.Y.: Parker, 1967.

GOINS, JEAN T. *Visual perceptual abilities and early reading progress.* Supplementary Educational Monograph, No. 87. Chicago: University of Chicago Press, February 1958.

GOLDBERG, HERMAN K. & ARNOTT, WILLIAM. Ocular motility in learning disabilities. *Journal of Learning Disabilities,* March 1970, 3, 160–162.

GOLDBERG, MIRIAM L. & TAYLOR, MARION S. Working with the urban disadvantaged: beginning reading project. In J. Allen Figurel (Ed.), *Reading goals for the disadvantaged.* Newark, Del.: International Reading Association, 1970. Pp. 91–113.

GOLDIAMOND, ISRAEL & DYRUD, JARL E. Reading as operant behavior. In John Money (Ed.), *The disabled reader: education of the dyslexic child.* Baltimore: Johns Hopkins Press, 1966. Pp. 93–115.

GOLDSTEIN, HARRY & JUSTMAN, JOSEPH. A classroom approach to the improvement of reading rate of college students. *Journal of Educational Psychology,* 1942, 33, 506–546.

GOMEZ, MANUEL R. Specific learning disorders in childhood. *Psychiatric Annals,* May 1972, 2, 49–65.

GOODLAD, JOHN I. & ANDERSON, ROBERT H. *The nongraded elementary school.* New York: Harcourt, Brace, and World, 1959.

GOODMAN, KENNETH S. Dialect barries to reading comprehension. *Elementary English.* December 1965, 42, 853–860.

GOODMAN, KENNETH S. Reading: a psycholinguistic guessing game. *Journal of the Reading Specialist,* May 1967, 6, 126–135.

GOODMAN, KENNETH S. Analysis of reading miscues: applied psycholinguistics. *Reading Research Quarterly,* Fall 1969, 5, 9–30.

GOODMAN, KENNETH S. Orthography in a theory of reading instruction. *Elementary English,* December 1972, 49, 1254–1261.

GOODMAN, YETTA M. & BURKE, CAROLYN L. *Reading miscue inventory.* New York: Macmillan, 1972.

GOOLSBY, T. M. & FRARY, R. B. Effect of massive intervention on achievement of first grade students. *Journal of Experimental Education.* 1970, 39, 46–52.

GOTTESMAN, RUTH L. Auditory discrimination ability in Negro dialect-speaking children. *Journal of Learning Disabilities,* February 1972, 5, 94–101.

GRASSI, JOSEPH R. Prevention of learning disabilities by the Scoptec method. *Academy News* (Gable Academy, Miami, Fla.), Summer 1973, 4, 2–5.

GRAUBARD, PAUL S. Utilizing the group in teaching disturbed delinquents to learn. *Exceptional Children,* 1969, 36, 267–272.

GRAY, CLARENCE T. *Deficiencies in reading ability: their diagnosis and remedies.* Boston: D. C. Heath, 1922.

GRAY, WILLIAM S. *Remedial cases in reading: their diagnosis and treatment.* Supplementary Educational Monographs, No. 22. Chicago: University of Chicago Press, 1922.

GRAY, WILLIAM S. A modern program of reading instruction for the grades and high school. In Guy M. Whipple (Ed.), *Report of the national committee on reading.* 24th Yearbook of the National Society for the Study of Education, Part I. Bloomington, Ill.: Public School Publishing Co., 1925. Pp. 21–74.

GRAY, WILLIAM S. Reading. In Chester W. Harris (Ed.), *Encyclopedia of educational research* (3rd ed.). New York: Macmillan, 1960. P. 1106.

GREDLER, GILBERT R. Performance on a perceptual test in children from a culturally disadvantaged background. In Helen K. Smith (Ed.), *Perception and reading.* Proceedings of the 12th Annual Convention, Vol. 12, Part 4. Newark, Del.: International Reading Association, 1968. Pp. 86–91.

GREDLER, G. R. Severe reading disability: some important correlates. In J. H. Reid (Ed.), *Reading: problems and practices*. London: Ward Lock Educational, 1972. Pp. 142–160.

GREEN, ORVILLE C. & PERLMAN, SUZANNE M. Endocrinology and disorders of learning. In Helmer R. Myklebust (Ed.), *Progress in learning disabilities*, Vol. II. New York: Grune & Stratton, 1971. Pp. 1–17.

GREEN, RICHARD T. Evaluation of materials designed to improve the balance in reading between comprehension and rate. Unpublished doctoral dissertation, Boston University, 1971.

GREER, MARGARET. Affective growth through reading. *The Reading Teacher*, January 1972, *25*, 336–341.

GRIESE, ARNOLD A. Focusing on students of different cultural backgrounds—the Eskimo and Indian pupil—special problems in reading comprehension. *Elementary English*, April 1971, *48*, 229–234.

GRIFFEN, LOUISE (Comp.). *Multi-ethnic books for young children: annotated bibliography for parents and teachers*. Washington, D.C.: National Association for the Education of Young Children, 1970.

GRIFFIN, MARGARET; HIBBARD, LOUISE; & MULDOON, KATHLEEN. *Guide to clinical evaluation instruments in reading*. Bloomington: Indiana University, ERIC Clearinghouse on Retrieval of Information and Evaluation on Reading, 1972.

GRIFFITHS, ANITA N. Self-concept in remedial work with dyslexic children. *Academic Therapy*, Winter 1970–1971, *6*, 125–133.

GROFF, PATRICK. *The syllable: its nature and pedogogical usefulness*. Portland, Ore.: Northwest Regional Educational Laboratory, April 1971.

GRONLAND, NORMAN E. *Stating behavioral objectives for classroom instruction*. New York: Macmillan, 1970.

GRONLAND, NORMAN E. *Preparing criterion-referenced tests for classroom instruction*. New York: Macmillan, 1973.

GURALNICK, MICHAEL J. Alphabet discrimination and distinctive features: Research review and educational implications. *Journal of Learning Disabilities*, August 1972, *5*, 427–434.

GUSZAK, FRANK J. Relations between teacher practice and knowledge of reading techniques in selected grade school classes. Madison: University of Wisconsin, School of Education, BR5-8402, 1966. ED 010 191.

GUSZAK, FRANK J. Teacher questioning and reading. *The Reading Teacher*, December 1967, *21*, 227–234.

GUSZAK, FRANK J. & MILLS, WALLACE R. Preparation of a reading teacher: a program metamorphosis. *Journal of Reading*, March 1973, *16*, 444–448.

GUTHRIE, JOHN T. Learnability versus readability of texts. *Journal of Educational Research*, February 1972, *65*, 273–280.

HAGIN, ROSA A.; SILVER, ARCHIE A; & CORWIN, CAROL G. Clinical-diagnostic use of the WPPSI in predicting learning disabilities in grade 1. *Journal of Special Education*, Fall 1971, *5*, 221–232.

HALL, MARYANNE. *Teaching reading as a language experience*. Columbus, Ohio: Charles E. Merrill, 1970.

HALL, MARYANNE. *The language experience approach for the culturally disadvantaged*. Newark, Del.: International Reading Association, 1972.

HALL, NANCY A. *Rescue*. Stevensville, Mich.: Educational Services, 1969.

HALL, VERNON C.; TURNER, RALPH R.; & RUSSELL, WILLIAM. Ability of children from four subcultures and two grade levels to imitate and comprehend crucial aspects of standard English: a test of the different language explanation. *Journal of Educational Psychology*, April 1973, *64*, 147–158.

HALLAHAN, DANIEL P. & CRUICKSHANK, WILLIAM M. *Psychoeducational foundations of learning disabilities.* Englewood Cliffs, N.J.: Prentice-Hall, 1973.

HALLGREN, BERTIL. Specific Dyslexia. *Acta Psychiatrica Neurologica*, Supplement No. 65, 1950. Pp. 1–287.

HALPERN, ESTHER. Reading success by children with visual-perceptual immaturity: explorations within Piaget's theory. *American Journal of Orthopsychiatry*, March 1970, *40*, 311–312.

HALSTEAD, LESTER M. A new approach to teaching retarded children to read. *Corrective Psychiatry & Journal of Social Therapy*, 1970, *16*, 59–62.

HAMILTON, HARLAN. New heroes for old? In M. Jerry Weiss, Joseph Brenner, & Warren Heiss (Eds.), *New perspectives in paperbacks.* York, Pa.: Strine, 1973. Pp. 43–50.

HAMMILL, DONALD D.; COLARUSSO, R. P.; & WIEDERHOLT, J. L. Diagnostic value of the Frostig Test: a factor analytic approach. *Journal of Special Education*, 1970, *4*, 279–282.

HAMMILL, DONALD; GOODMAN, LIBBY; & WIEDERHOLT, J. LEE. Visual-motor processes: can we train them? *The Reading Teacher*, February 1974, *27*, 469–478.

HAMMILL, DONALD & MATTLEMAN, MARCIENE. An evaluation of a programmed reading approach in primary grades. *Elementary English*, March 1969, *46*, 310–312.

HANF, MARILYN B. The use of the hand as a pacer in reading. *Elementary English*, November 1970, *47*, 986–987.

HARDY, MADELINE; SMYTHE, P. C.; STENNETT, R. G.; & WILSON H. R. Developmental patterns in elemental reading skills: phoneme-grapheme and grapheme-phoneme correspondence. *Journal of Educational Psychology*, October 1972, *63*, 433–436.

HARE, BETTY A.; HAMMILL, DONALD D.; & BARTEL, NETTIE R. Construct validity of selected subtests of the ITPA. *Exceptional Children*, September 1973, *40*, 13–20.

HARING, NORRIS G. & HAUCK, MARY A. Improved learning conditions in the establishment of reading skills with disabled readers. *Exceptional Children*, January 1969, *35*, 341–352.

HARKER, W. J. An evaluative summary of models of reading comprehension. *Journal of Reading Behavior*, Winter 1972–1973, *5*, 26–34.

HAROOTUNIAN, BERJ. Intellectual abilities and reading achievement. *Elementary School Journal*, 1966, *66*, 386–392.

HARP, M. WILLIAM. Poetry in the primary grades. *Elementary English*, December 1972, *49*, 1171–1176.

HARRINGTON, NANCY D. The development of twenty lessons to teach skimming to sixth grade pupils. Unpublished doctorial dissertation, Boston University, 1970.

HARRIS, ALBERT J. Motivating the poor reader. *Education*, 1953, *73*, 566–574.

HARRIS, ALBERT J. Egoistic learning. *American Journal of Orthopsychiatry*, 1954, *24*, 781–784. (a)

HARRIS, ALBERT J. Unsolved problems in reading, II. *Elementary English*, 1954, *31*, 416–418. (b)

HARRIS, ALBERT J. Lateral dominance, directional confusion, and reading disability. *Journal of Psychology*, 1957, *44*, 283–294.

HARRIS, ALBERT J. A critical reaction to *The nature of reading disability. Journal of Developmental Reading*, 1960, *3*, 238–249.

HARRIS, ALBERT J. Perceptual difficulties in reading disability. In J. Allen Figurel,

(Ed.), *Changing concepts of reading instruction*. Newark, Del.: International Reading Association Conference Proceedings, Vol. 6, 1961. Pp. 281–290.

HARRIS, ALBERT J. Progressive education and reading instruction. *The Reading Teacher*, November 1964, *18*, 128–138.

HARRIS, ALBERT J. (Ed.). *Some administrative problems of reading clinics*. Institute Highlights, No. 3. Newark, Del.: International Reading Association, 1965.

HARRIS, ALBERT J. Improving the teaching of remedial reading. *Education*, 1966, 87, 236–240. (a)

HARRIS, ALBERT J. *The Macmillan Reading Readiness Test, manual for administering, scoring, and interpreting*. New York: Macmillan, 1966. (b)

HARRIS, ALBERT J. Diagnosis and remedial instruction in reading. In Helen M. Robinson, (Ed.), *Innovation and change in reading instruction*, 67th Yearbook of the National Society for the Study of Education, Part II. Chicago: University of Chicago Press, 1968, Chapt. 5. (a)

HARRIS, ALBERT J. Five decades of remedial reading. In J. Allen Figurel, *Forging ahead in reading*. Proceedings of the Twelfth Annual Convention. Newark, Del.: International Reading Association, 1968, 12, Part 1. Pp. 25–34. (b)

HARRIS, ALBERT J. Research on some aspects of comprehension: rate, flexibility, and study skills. *Journal of Reading*, 1968, *12*, 205–210. 258. (c)

HARRIS, ALBERT J. The effective teacher of reading. *The Reading Teacher*, December 1969, *23*, 195–204.

HARRIS, ALBERT J. (Ed.). *Casebook on reading disability*. New York: David McKay, 1970. (a)

HARRIS, ALBERT J. A comparison of formulas for measuring degree of reading disability. In Robert E. Liebert (Ed.), *Diagnostic viewpoints in reading*. Newark, Del.: International Reading Association. 1971, Pp. 113–120. (a)

HARRIS, ALBERT J. Psychological and motivational problems. In Dorothy K. Bracken & Eve Malmquist (Eds.), *Improving reading ability around the world*. Proceedings of the third IRA World Congress on Reading, Sydney, Australia. Newark, Del.: International Reading Association, 1971. Pp. 97–103. (b)

HARRIS, ALBERT J. New dimensions in basal readers. *The Reading Teacher*, January 1972, *25*, 310–315. Also in Howard A. Klein (Ed.), *The quest for competency in teaching reading*. Newark, Del.: International Reading Association, 1972. Pp. 124–130. (a)

HARRIS, ALBERT J. To what extent are skills centered developmental reading programs necessary? In Howard A. Klein (Ed.), *The quest for competency in teaching reading*. Newark, Del.: International Reading Association, 1972. Pp. 106–118. (b)

HARRIS, ALBERT J. & JACOBSON, MILTON D. *Basic elementary reading vocabularies*. New York: Macmillan, 1972.

HARRIS, ALBERT J. & JACOBSON, MILTON D. Basic vocabulary for beginning reading. *The Reading Teacher*, January 1973, *26*, 392–395.

HARRIS, ALBERT J. & JACOBSON, MILTON D. Some comparisons between the Basic Elementary Reading Vocabularies and other word lists. *Reading Research Quarterly*, 1973–74, 9, No. 1, 87–109.

HARRIS, ALBERT J.; MORRISON, COLEMAN; SERWER, BLANCHE L.; & GOLD, LAWRENCE. *A continuation of the CRAFT Project: comparing reading approaches with disadvantaged urban negro children in primary grades*. Final Report, U.S.O.E. Project No. 5-0570-2-12-1. New York: Selected Academic Readings, 1968.

HARRIS, ALBERT J. & ROSWELL, FLORENCE G. Clinical diagnosis of reading disability. *Journal of Psychology*, 1953, 63, 323–340.

HARRIS, ALBERT J. & SERWER, BLANCHE L. *Comparison of reading approaches in first-grade teaching with disadvantaged children* (The CRAFT Project). Final Report, Cooperative Research Project No. 2677. New York: Division of Teacher Education, The City University of New York, 1966 (a)

HARRIS, ALBERT J. & SERWER, BLANCHE L. The CRAFT Project: instructional time in reading research. *Reading Research Quarterly*, Fall 1966, 2, 27–56. (b)

HARRIS, ALBERT J. & SIPAY, EDWARD R. *The Macmillan Reading Readiness Test, RE: manual for administering, scoring, and interpreting.* New York: Macmillan, 1970.

HARRIS, IRVING D. *Emotional blocks to learning.* New York: Free Press, 1961.

HARRIS, LARRY A. Interest and the initial acquisition of words. *The Reading Teacher*, January 1969, 22, 312–314, 362.

HARRIS, LOUIS, & ASSOCIATES. Survival literacy study. *Congressional Record*, November 18, 1970. Pp. E9719–E9723.

HARRIS, THEODORE L. *Experimental development of variability in reading rate in grades four, five and six.* USOE Cooperative Research Project, No. 1775. Madison: University of Wisconsin, 1965.

HARTLAGE, LAWRENCE C. & GREEN, JOSEPH B. The EEG as a predictor of intellective and academic performance. *Journal of Learning Disabilities*, April 1973, 6, 239–242.

HARTMAN, NANCY C. & HARTMAN, ROBERT K. Perceptual handicap or reading disability? *The Reading Teacher*, April 1973, 26, 684–695. (a)

HARTMAN, NANCY C. & HARTMAN, ROBERT K. The theory of neurological organization in historical perspective. *Journal of Reading Behavior*, Summer 1973, 5, 177–185. (b)

HAUSERMAN, NORMA & MCINTIRE, ROGER. Training elementary reading skills through reinforcement and fading techniques. *Proceedings of the 77th Annual Convention of the American Psychological Association*, 1969, 4, Part 2, 669–670.

HAYES, ROBERT B. & WUEST, RICHARD C. *Factors affecting learning to read*, Final Report, Project No. 6-1752. Harrisburg, Pa.: State Education Department, 1967.

HAYWARD, PRISCILLA. *Diagnostic tests in reading: an annotated bibliography.* Albany, N.Y.: Bureau of Pupil Testing and Advisory Services, New York State Education Department, 1968. Mimeographed.

Hearing testing of school children and guide for hearing conservation programs. Berkeley, Calif.: California State Department of Public Health, 1962.

HEATH, EARL J. & BENDER, MIRIAM L. Motor and reflex evaluation: some new insights. *Academic Therapy*, Summer 1971, 6, 413–416.

HECKELMAN, R. G. Using the neurological impress remedial technique. *Academic Therapy Quarterly*, 1966, 1, 235–239.

HEITZMAN, ANDREW J. Effects of a token reinforcement system on the reading and arithmetic skills learning of migrant primary school pupils. *Journal of Educational Research*, July 1970, 63, 455–458.

HELMS, WALTER E. *A directory of college and university reading clinics/centers in the United States.* Jackson, Tenn.: Lambuth College, 1967.

HELVESTON, EUGENE M.; BILLIPS, WILLIAM C.; & WEBER, JANET C. Controlling eye–dominant hemisphere relationship as factor in reading ability. *American Journal of Ophthalmology*, July 1970, 70, 96–100.

HENDERSON, NORMAN B.; BUTLER, BRUCE V.; & GOFFENEY, BARBARA. Effectiveness of the WISC and Bender-Gestalt Test in predicting arithmetic and reading achievement for white and nonwhite children. *Journal of Clinical Psychology*, 1969, *25*, 268–271.

HENDERSON, RONALD W. Environmental predictors of academic performance of disadvantaged Mexican-American children. *Journal of Consulting and Clinical Psychology*, April 1972, *38*, 297.

HERBER, HAROLD L. *Teaching reading in content areas.* Englewood Cliffs, N.J.: Prentice-Hall, 1970.

HERMANN, KNUD. *Reading disability: a medical study of word-blindness and related handicaps.* Springfield, Ill.: Charles C Thomas, 1959.

HERMANN, KNUD. Specific reading disability. *Danish Medical Bulletin*, 1964, *11*, 34–40.

HERR, SELMA E. *Learning activities for reading* (2nd ed.). Dubuque, Iowa: William C. Brown, 1970.

HEYDENBERK, WARREN R. A comparison of four methods of estimating reading potential. Unpublished doctoral dissertation, University of Northern Colorado, 1971.

HILL, C. H. & TOLMAN, R. Tutoring: an inexpensive alternative. *Journal of Reading Specialist*, 1970, *10*, 19–23.

HILL, FRANK G. A comparison of the effectiveness of Words in Color with the basic reading program used in the Washington Elementary School District. Unpublished doctoral dissertation, Arizona State University, 1967.

HILLERICH, ROBERT L. Pre-reading skills in kindergarten: a second report. *Elementary School Journal*, 1965, *65*, 312–317.

HILLERICH, ROBERT L. Word lists—getting it all together. *The Reading Teacher*, January 1974, *27*, 353–360.

HINSHELWOOD, JAMES. *Congenital word-blindness.* London: H. K. Lewis, 1917.

HITTLEMAN, DANIEL R. Seeking a psycholinguistic definition of readability. *The Reading Teacher*, May 1973, *26*, 783–789.

HOAGLAND, JOAN. Bibliotherapy: aiding children in personality development. *Elementary English*, March 1972, *49*, 390–394.

HOCKER, MARY E. M. Visual motor characteristics of retarded readers and the relationship to their classroom behavior. Unpublished doctoral dissertation, University of Virginia, 1970.

HOCKMAN, CAROL M. Black dialect reading tests in the urban elementary school. *The Reading Teacher*, March 1973, *26*, 581–583.

HODGES, ELAINE J. A comparison of the functional reading levels of selected third grade students of varying reading abilities. Unpublished doctoral dissertation, University of Northern Colorado, 1972.

HOFFMAN, M. S. Early indications of learning problems. *Academic Therapy*, Fall 1971, *7*, 23–35.

HOLLOWAY, RUTH L. The worldwide right to read. In Robert Karlin (Ed.), *Reading for all.* Newark, Del.: International Reading Association, 1973. Pp. 27–33.

HOLT, GARY L. Effect of reinforcement contingencies in increasing programmed reading and mathematics behaviors in first-grade children. *Journal of Experimental Child Psychology*, December 1971, *12*, 362–369.

HONEL, MILTON F. The effectiveness of reading expectancy formulas for identifying underachievers. Unpublished doctoral dissertation, Northern Illinois University, 1973.

HOPKINS, LEE BENNETT. *Let them be themselves.* New York: Citation Press, 1969.

HOPKINS, LEE BENNETT. *Pass the poetry, please!* New York: Citation Press, 1972.

HORN, ERNEST. Spelling. *Encyclopedia of Educational Research* (3rd ed.). New York: Macmillan, 1960. P. 1338.

HORN, THOMAS D. (Ed.). *Reading for the disadvantaged: problems of linguistically different learners.* New York: Harcourt Brace Jovanovich, 1970.

HUCK, CHARLOTTE S. Strategies for improving interest and appreciation in literature. In Helen W. Painter (Ed.), *Reaching children and young people through literature.* Newark, Del.: International Reading Association, 1971. Pp. 37–45.

HUEY, EDMUND B. *The psychology and pedagogy of reading.* New York: Macmillan, 1908. Reprinted by MIT Press, Cambridge, Mass., 1968.

HUGHES, JOHN R. Electroencephalography and learning. In Helmer R. Myklebust, (Ed.), *Progress in learning disabilities,* Vol. I. New York: Grune & Stratton, 1968. Pp. 113–146.

HUGHES, JOHN R. Electroencephalography and learning disabilities. In Helmer R. Myklebust (Ed.), *Progress in learning disabilities,* Vol. II. New York: Grune & Stratton, 1971. Pp. 18–55.

HUMPHREY, JACK W. & REDDEN, SANDRA R. Encouraging young authors. *The Reading Teacher,* April 1972, *25,* 643–651.

HUNNICUTT, C. W. & IVERSON, WILLIAM J. *Research in the three R's.* New York: Harper & Row, 1958. Pp. 194–212.

HUTCHINSON, JUNE O'SHIELDS. Reading tests and nonstandard language. *The Reading Teacher,* February 1972, *25,* 430–437.

HUUS, HELEN. The effects of reading on children and youth. In Robert Karlin (Ed.), *Reading for all.* Newark, Del.: International Reading Association, 1973. Pp. 132–141.

ILG, FRANCIS L. & AMES, LOUISE B. *School readiness: behavior tests used at the Gesell Institute.* New York: Harper & Row, 1964.

INGRAM, T. T. S. The nature of dyslexia. *Bulletin of the Orton Society,* 1969, *19,* 18–50.

INGRAM, T. T. S. Symposium on reading disability: II. specific learning difficulties in childhood: a medical point of view. *British Journal of Educational Psychology,* February 1971, *41,* 6–13.

INGRAM, T. T. S.; MASON, A. W.; & BLACKBURN, I. A retrospective study of 82 children with reading disability. *Developmental Medicine & Child Neurology,* June 1970, *12,* 271–281.

INGRAM, T. T. S. & REID, JESSIE F. Developmental aphasia observed in a department of child psychiatry. *Archives of Diseases of Childhood,* 1956, *31,* 131.

INTERNATIONAL READING ASSOCIATION. Causes of reading disability. *The Reading Teacher,* December 1972, *26,* 341.

JACKSON, MERRILL S. Modes of adaptation to the first confrontation with English orthography in the visual modality. *Journal of Learning Disabilities,* January 1972, *5,* 25–30.

JACKSON, REX. Developing criterion-referenced tests. TM Report, No. 1. Princeton, N.J.: ERIC Clearinghouse on Tests, Measurement & Evaluation, June 1970.

JACOBS, LELAND. Individualized reading is not a thing. In Alice Miel (Ed.), *Individualizing reading practices.* Practical Suggestions for Teaching, No. 14. New York: Bureau of Publications, Teachers College, Columbia University, 1958. Pp. 1–17.

JACOBS, LELAND. Poetry books for poetry reading. *The Reading Teacher*, 1959, *13*, 45–48.

JACOBS, R. & ROSENBAUM, P. *English transformational grammar*. Waltham, Mass.: Blaisdell, 1968.

JAEGER, RICHARD M. The national test-equating study in reading (the Anchor Test study). *NCME measurement in education*, Fall 1973, *4*, No. 4.

JANSKY, JEANETTE & DE HIRSCH, KATRINA. *Preventing reading failure: prediction, diagnosis, intervention*. New York: Harper & Row, 1972.

JANZ, MARGARET L. & SMITH, EDWIN M. Students' reading ability and the readability of secondary school subjects. *Elementary English*, April 1972, *49*, 622–624.

JASON, MARTIN H. & DUBNOW, BEATRICE. The relationship between self-perceptions of reading abilities and reading achievement. In Walter H. MacGinitie (Ed.), *Assessment problems in reading*. Newark, Del.: International Reading Association, 1973. Pp. 96–100.

JEFFARES, DOLORES J. & COSENS, GRACE V. Effect of socio-economic status and auditory discrimination training on first-grade reading achievement and auditory discrimination. *Alberta Journal of Educational Research*, 1970, *16*, 165–178.

JEFFERSON, GEORGE L., JR. Lexical and structural items as predictors of readability for high and low ability readers. Unpublished doctoral dissertation, University of Georgia, 1969.

JENNINGS, FRANK G. *This is reading*. New York: Teachers College, Columbia University, 1965.

JERROLDS, BOB W.; CALLAWAY, BYRON; & GWALTNEY, WAYNE. A comparative study of three tests of intellectual potential, three tests of reading achievement, and the discrepancy scores between potential and achievement. *Journal of Educational Research*, December 1971, *65*, 168–172.

JOHNS, JERRY L. What do inner city children prefer to read? *The Reading Teacher*, February 1973, *26*, 462–467.

JOHNSON, DORIS J. & MYKLEBUST, HELMER R. *Learning disabilities: educational principles and practices*. New York: Grune & Stratton, 1967. Pp. 7–10.

JOHNSON, MARJORIE S. Tracing and kinesthetic techniques. In John Money (Ed.), *The disabled reader*. Baltimore: Johns Hopkins Press, 1966. Pp. 147–160.

JOHNSON, RONALD J.; JOHNSON, KAREN L.; & KERFOOT, JAMES F. A massive decoding technique. *The Reading Teacher*, February 1972, *25*, 421–423.

JOHNSON, WILLIAM. Books for sale. *Elementary English*, February 1972, *49*, 233–234.

JONES, J. KENNETH. *Colour story reading*. London, England: Thomas Nelson and Sons, 1967.

JONES, J. KENNETH. Comparing i.t.a. with colour story reading. *Educational Research*, June 1968, *10*, 226–234.

JONES, JOHN P. A study of the relationships among intersensory transfer, intersensory perceptual shifting, modal preference and reading achievement at the third grade level. Unpublished doctoral dissertation, University of Georgia, 1970.

JONES, JOHN P. *Intersensory transfer, perceptual shifting, modal preference, and reading*. Newark, Del.: International Reading Association, 1972.

JONGSMA, EUGENE. *The cloze procedure as a teaching technique*. Newark, Del.: International Reading Association, 1971.

JONGSMA, EUGENE A. The difficulty of children's books: librarians' judgments versus formula estimates. *Elementary English*, January 1972, *49*, 20–25.

JORDAN, WILLIAM C. Prime-o-tec: the new reading method. *Academic Therapy Quarterly*, Summer 1967, *2*, 248–250.

JUSTMAN, JOSEPH. Reading and class homogeneity. *The Reading Teacher*, January 1968, *21*, 314–316.

JUSTUS, HOPE. Status report on reading. *American Education*, August–September 1972, *8*, 9–13.

KAGAN, JEROME. Reflection-Impulsivity and reading abilities in primary grade children. *Child Development*, 1965, *36*, 609–628.

KAPPELMAN, MURRAY M.; KAPLAN, EUGENE; & GANTER, ROBERT L. A study of learning disorders among disadvantaged children. *Journal of Learning Disabilities*, May 1969, *2*, 262–268.

KASDON, LAWRENCE M. Diagnosing learning disabilities: a positive view. *Journal of the Reading Specialist*, October 1971, *11*, 43–50.

KASS, CORRINE E.; HALL, ROBERT E., & SIMCHES, RAPHAEL F. Legislation. In Norris G. Harding (Ed.), *Minimal brain dysfunction in children*. Washington, D.C. Public Health Service Publication, No. 2015, 1969.

KASS, CORRINE E. & MYKLEBUST, HELMER R. Learning disability: an educational definition. *Journal of Learning Disabilities*, July 1969, *2*, 377–379.

KATZ, MARTIN. Selecting an achievement test: principles and procedures. Princeton, N.J.: Educational Testing Service, 1973.

KAWI, A. A. & PASAMANICK, B. Association of factors of pregnancy with reading disorders of childhood. *Journal of the American Medical Association*, 1958, *166*, 1420–1423.

KAZDIN, ALAN E. & BOOTZIN, RICHARD R. The token economy: an evaluative review, *Journal of Applied Behavior Analysis*, Fall 1972, 5, 343-372.

KELLAM, SHEPPARD G. & SCHIFF, SHELDON K. Effects of family life on children's adaptation to first grade. *American Journal of Orthopsychiatry*, March 1969, *39*, 276–278.

KELLY, EDWARD. A measurement of the extent of the relationship between articulatory defects and reading disability. Unpublished doctoral dissertation, University of Oregon, 1966.

KENNEDY, CHARLES & RAMIREZ, LOURDES S. Brain damage as a cause of behavior disturbance in children. In Herbert G. Birch (Ed.), *Brain damage in children*. Baltimore: Williams & Wilkins, 1964. Pp. 13–23.

KENNEDY, DELORES K. & WEENER, PAUL. Visual and auditory training with the cloze procedure to improve reading and listening comprehension. *Reading Research Quarterly*, Summer 1973, *8*, 524–541.

KEOGH, BARBARA K. The Bender Gestalt with children: research implications. *Journal of Special Education*, 1969, *3*, 15–22.

KEOGH, BARBARA K. A compensatory model for psychoeducational evaluation of children with learning disorders. *Journal of Learning Disabilities*, December 1971, *4*, 544–548. (a)

KEOGH, BARBARA K. Hyperactivity and learning problems: implications for teachers. *Academic Therapy*, Fall 1971, *7*, 47–50. (b)

KEOGH, BARBARA K. Optometric vision training programs for children with learning disabilities: review of issues and research. *Journal of Learning Disabilities*, April 1974, *7*, 219–231.

KEOGH, BARBARA K. & DONLON, GENEVIEVE M. Field dependence, impulsivity, and learning disabilities. *Journal of Learning Disabilities*, June 1972, 5, 331–336.

KEPHART, NEWELL C. *The slow learner in the classroom*. Columbus, Ohio: Charles

E. Merrill, 1960.

KEPHART, NEWELL C. Perceptual-motor aspects of learning disabilities. *Exceptional Children*, December 1964, *31*, 204–206.

KERSHNER, JOHN R. Children's spatial representations and horizontal directionality. *Journal of Genetic Psychology*, 1970, *116*, 177–189.

KIMURA, D. Cerebral dominance and the perception of visual stimuli. *Canadian Journal of Psychology*, 1961, *15*, 166–171.

KIMURA, D. Functional assymetry of the brain in dichotic listening. *Cortex*, 1967, *3*, 163–178.

KINBOURNE, MARCEL & WARRINGTON, ELIZABETH K. Developmental factors in reading and writing backwardness. In John Money (Ed.), *The disabled reader*. Baltimore: Johns Hopkins Press, 1966. Pp. 59–71.

KINGSLEY, HOWARD L. *The nature and conditions of learning*. New York: Prentice-Hall, 1946.

KINIRY, MARTHA S. M. Differentiating elementary children with learning disabilities using the Illinois Test of Psycholinguistic Abilities. Unpublished doctoral dissertation, East Texas State University, 1972.

KIRK, SAMUEL A. & BATEMAN, BARBARA. Diagnosis and remediation of learning disabilities. *Exceptional Children*, October 1962, *29*, 73.

KIRK, SAMUEL A. & KIRK, WINIFRED D. *Psycholinguistic learning disabilities: diagnois and remediation*. Urbana, Ill.: University of Illinois Press, 1971.

KLARE, GEORGE R. *The measurement of readability*. Ames, Iowa: Iowa State University Press, 1963.

KLASEN, EDITH. *The syndrome of specific dyslexia: with special consideration of its physiological, psychological, testpsychological, and social correlates*. Baltimore: University Park Press, 1972.

KLAUSMEIER, HERBERT J.; SORENSON, JUANITA S.; & QUILLING, MARY. Instructional programming for the individual pupil in the multi-unit school. *Elementary School Journal*, November 1971, *72*, 88–101.

KLEIN, HOWARD A. Interest and comprehension in sex-typed materials. In June H. Catterson (Ed.), *Children and literature*. Newark, Del.: International Reading Association, 1970. Pp. 59–64.

KLEIN, STEPHEN P. & KOSECOFF, JACQUELINE. Issues and procedures in the development of criterion referenced tests. TM Report 26. Princeton, N.J.: ERIC Clearinghouse on Tests, Measurement and Evaluation, September 1973.

KLEINBERG, NORMAN M. Tachistoscopic vs. pseudo-tachistoscopic training and the Hawthorne effect in improving reading achievement. Unpublished doctoral dissertation, Columbia University, 1970.

KLESIUS, STEPHEN E. Perceptual motor development and reading—a closer look. In Robert C. Aukerman (Ed.), *Some persistent questions on beginning reading*. Newark, Del.: International Reading Association, 1972. Pp. 151–159.

KLINE, CARL L. & KLINE, CAROLYN L. Severe reading disabilities—the family's dilemmas: analysis based on study of 600 consecutive patients. *American Journal of Orthopsychiatry*, March 1973, *43*, 241–242.

KLINE, CARL L. & LEE, NORMA. A transcultural study of dyslexia: analysis of reading disability in 425 Chinese children simultaneously learning to read in English and Chinese. *American Journal of Orthopsychiatry*, March 1970, *40*, 313–314.

KLINE, CARL L. & LEE, NORMA. A transcultural study of dyslexia: analysis of language disabilities in 277 Chinese children simultaneously learning to read and write in English and in Chinese. *Journal of Special Education*, Spring 1972, 9–26.

KLOSTERMAN, SISTER RITA. The effectiveness of a diagnostically structured reading program. *The Reading Teacher,* November 1970, *24,* 159–162.

KNOWLES, B. A. Behavior modification and special education. *Slow Learning Child,* November 1970, *17,* 170–177.

KOHLMORGEN, WILLIAM H. A study of the effects of Delacato's program of neurological organization on reading achievement. Unpublished doctoral dissertation, New York University, 1971.

KOPPITZ, ELIZABETH M. *The Bender-Gestalt Test for young children.* New York: Grune & Stratton, 1964.

KOZOL, JONATHAN. *Free schools* (first rev. ed.). New York: Bantam Books, 1972. Paper.

KRASNOW, ANITA. An Adlerian approach to the problem of school maladjustment. *Academic Therapy,* Winter 1971–72, *7,* 171–183.

KRESS, ROY A. & JOHNSON, MARJORIE S. Martin. In Albert J. Harris (Ed.), *Casebook on reading disability.* New York: David McKay, 1970, Pp. 1–24.

KRIPPNER, STANLEY. Diagnostic and remedial use of the Minnesota Percepto-Diagnostic Test in a reading clinic. *Psychology in the Schools,* 1966, *3,* 171–185.

KRIPPNER, STANLEY. The use of hypnosis and the improvement of academic achievement. *Journal of Special Education,* Fall 1970, *4,* 451–460.

KRIPPNER, STANLEY. Hypnosis as verbal programming in educational therapy. *Academic Therapy,* Fall 1971, *7,* 5–12.

KUBANY, E. S. & SLOGGETT, B. B. The role of motivation in test performance and remediation. *Journal of Learning Disabilities,* October 1971, *4,* 426–428.

KUČERA, HENRY & FRANCIS, W. NELSON. *Computation analysis of present day American English.* Providence, R.I.: Brown University Press, 1967.

KUYPERS, D. S.; BECKER, W. C.; & O'LEARY, K. D. How to make a token system fail. *Exceptional Children,* October 1968, *35,* 101–109.

LABOV, WILLIAM. The logic of nonstandard English. In Johanna S. De Stefano (Ed.), *Language, society, and education: a profile of black English.* Worthington, Ohio: Charles A. Jones, 1973. Pp. 10–44.

LABOV, WILLIAM & COHEN, PAUL. Some suggestions for teaching standard English to speakers of nonstandard and urban dialects. In Johanna S. De Stafano (Ed.), *Language, society, and education: a profile of black English.* Worthington, Ohio: Charles E. Jones, 1973. Pp. 218–237.

LADLEY, WINIFRED C. *Sources of good books and magazines for children: an annotated bibliography.* Newark, Del.: International Reading Association, 1970.

LAFFEY, JAMES L. & SHUY, ROGER (Eds.). *Language differences: do they interfere?* Newark, Del.: International Reading Association, 1973.

LAKE, MARY L. First aid for vocabularies. In Albert J. Harris and Edward R. Sipay (Eds.), *Readings on reading instruction.* New York: David McKay, 1972. Pp. 252–254. Reprinted from *Elementary English,* November 1967, *44,* 783–784.

LAKE, MARY LOUISE. Improve the dictionary's image. *Elementary English,* March 1971, *48,* 363–366.

LANNAY, CLEMENT. La dyslexia: reflection sur un colloque. *Act Paedopsychiatrica,* April 1971, *38,* 119–127.

LAUFER, MAURICE W. Long-term management and some follow-up findings on the use of drugs with minimal cerebral syndromes. *Journal of Learning Disabilities,* November 1971, *4,* 519–522.

LAWSON, CORNELIA V. Children's reasons and motivations for the selection of favorite books. Unpublished doctoral dissertation, University of Arkansas, 1972.

LAWSON, E. A. Note on the influence of different orders of approximation to the English language upon eye-voice span. *Quarterly Journal of Experimental Psychology*, 1961, *13*, 53–55.

LAWSON, LAWRENCE J., JR. Ophthalmological factors in learning disabilities. In Helmer R. Myklebust (Ed.), *Progress in learning disabilities*, Vol. 1. New York: Grune & Stratton, 1968. Pp. 147–181.

LAZAR, ALFRED L. Reading programs and materials for the educable mentally retarded. In Helen K. Smith (Ed.), *Meeting individual needs in reading*. International Reading Association, 1971. Pp. 74–84.

LAZAR, MAY. *Reading interests, activities, and opportunities of bright, average, and dull children*. Contributions to Education, No. 707. New York: Teachers College Press, Columbia University, 1937.

LAZERMAN, AUDREY P. Psycholinguistic characteristics of children with reading disabilities and the effects of remediation on psycholinguistic development and reading achievement. Unpublished doctoral dissertation, Marquette University, 1970.

LEE, DORRIS M. & ALLEN, R. VAN. *Learning to read through experience* (2nd ed.). New York: Appleton-Century-Crofts, 1963.

LERNER, JANET W. A thorn by any other name: dyslexia or reading disability. *Elementary English*, January 1971, *48*, 75–80. (a)

LERNER, JANET W. *Children with learning disabilities: theories, diagnosis, and teaching strategies*. Boston: Houghton Mifflin, 1971. (b)

LERNER, JANET W. Reading and learning disabilities. *Elementary English*, February 1973, *50*, 265–269.

LESSLER, KEN & BRIDGES, JUDITH S. The prediction of learning problems in a rural setting: can we improve on readiness tests? *Journal of Learning Disabilities*, February 1973, *6*, 90–94.

LEVIN, HARRY & COHN, J. A. Effects of instruction on the eye-voice span. In Harry Levin; Eleanor J. Gibson; and J. J. Gibson (Eds.), *The analysis of reading skills: a program of basic and applied research*. Final Report, Project No. 5–1213, Cornell University, 1968. ED 034 663.

LEVIN, HARRY & KAPLAN, ELEANOR L. Grammatical structure and reading. In Harry Levin & Joanna P. Williams (Eds.), *Basic studies on reading*. New York: Basic Books, 1970. Pp. 119–133.

LEVIN, HARRY & TURNER, E. A. Sentence structure and the eye-voice span. Studies in oral reading IX, preliminary draft. Project No. B.R. 5–1213–9—OEC–6–10, September 1966. ED 011 957.

LEVIN, HARRY & WATSON, J. The learning of variable grapheme-to-phoneme correspondence. In Harry Levin, *et al.* A basic research program on reading. Final report, Cooperative Research Project No. 639, 1962.

LEVINE, ISIDORE. The fallacy of reading comprehension skills. *Elementary English*, May 1970, *47*, 672–677.

LEVISON, BEATRICE. Raphael. In Albert J. Harris (Ed.), *Casebook on reading disability*. New York: David McKay, 1970. Pp. 117–134.

LEWIS, JENEVA BELL. A comparison of kindergarten teachers' perceptions of children's preferences in books with the children's actual preferences. Unpublished doctoral dissertation, East Texas State University, 1970.

LEWIS, W. D. & MC GEHEE, W. A comparison of the interests of mentally superior and retarded children. *School and Society*, 1940, *52*, 597–600.

LIBERMAN, A. M.; COOPER, F. S.; SHANKWEILER, D.; & STUDDERT-KENNEDY, M. Perception of the speech code. *Psychological Review*, 1967, *74*, 431–461.

LIBERMAN, ISABELLE Y., *et al*. Letter confusion and reversals of sequence in the beginning reader: implications for Orton's theory of developmental dyslexia. *Cortex*, June 1971, *7*, 127–142.

LICKTEIG, MARY JANE. A comparison of book selection preferences of inner-city and suburban fourth and sixth graders. Unpublished doctoral dissertation, University of Oregon, 1972.

LIDDLE, WILLIAM. An initial investigation of the Wood Reading Dynamics method. Unpublished doctoral dissertation, University of Delaware, 1965.

LIEBEN, BEATRICE. Attitudes, platitudes, and conferences in teacher-parent relations involving the child with a reading problem. *Elementary School Journal*, 1958, *57*, 279–286. Reprinted in A. J. Harris and Edward R. Sipay (Eds.), *Readings on reading instruction* (2nd ed.). New York: David McKay, 1972. Pp. 420–427.

LINVILLE, WILLIAM J. The effects of syntax and vocabulary upon the difficulty of verbal arithmetic problems with fourth grade students. Unpublished doctoral dissertation, Indiana University, 1969.

LOCKMILLER, PAULINE & DINELLO, MARIO C. Words in Color vs. a basal reader program with retarded readers in grade two. *Journal of Educational Research*, March 1970, *63*, 333–334.

LOHNES, PAUL R. Evaluating the schooling of intelligence. *Educational Researcher*, February 1973, *2*, 6–11.

LOHNES, PAUL R. & GRAY, MARIAN M. Intelligence and the cooperative reading studies. *Reading Research Quarterly*, Spring 1972, *7*, 466–476.

LORGE, IRVING. Predicting readability. *Teachers College Record*, March 1944, *45*, 404–419.

LORGE, IRVING. *The Lorge formula for estimating difficulty of reading materials*. New York: Teachers College Press, 1959.

LORGE, IRVING & CHALL, JEANNE. Estimating the size of vocabularies of children and methodological issues. *Journal of Experimental Education*, 1963, *32*, 147–157.

LOWELL, ROBERT E. Reading readiness factors as predictors of success in first grade reading. *Journal of Learning Disabilities*, December 1971, *4*, 563–567.

LUKE, ROBERT A. Federal legislation relating to adult basic education and literacy training. In J. Allen Figurel (Ed.), *Vistas in reading*. Newark, Del.: International Reading Association, 1967. Pp. 372–402.

LYLE, J. G. Reading retardation and reversal tendency: a factorial study. *Child Development*, 1968, *40*, 833–843.

LYLE, J. G. Certain antenatal, perinatal, and developmental variables and reading retardation in middle-class boys. *Child Development*, 1970, *41*, 481–491.

MAC DONALD, JAMES B.; HARRIS, THEODORE L.; & RARICK, G. LAWRENCE. *An experimental study of the group versus the one-to-one instructional relationship in first grade basal reading programs*. Final Report, Project No. 2674. Madison: School of Education, University of Wisconsin, 1966.

MAC GINITIE, WALTER H. An introduction to some measurement problems in reading. In W. H. MacGinitie (Ed.), *Assessment problems in reading*. Newark, Del.: International Reading Association, 1973. Pp. 1–7. (a)

MAC GINITIE, WALTER H. Testing reading achievement in urban schools. *The Reading Teacher*, October 1973, *27*, 13–21. (b)

MAC GINITIE, WALTER H. What are we testing? In W. H. MacGinitie (Ed.), *Assessment problems in reading*. Newark, Del.: International Reading Association. 1973. Pp. 35–43. (c)

MAC GINITIE, WALTER H. & TRETIAK, RICHARD. Measures of sentence complexity as predictors of the difficulty of reading materials. *Proceedings of the 77th Annual Convention of the American Psychological Association*, 1969, *4*, 667–668.

MAC GINITIE, WALTER H. & TRETIAK, RICHARD. Sentence depth measures as predictors of reading difficulty. *Reading Research Quarterly*, Spring 1971, *6*, 364–376.

MACKWORTH, JANE E. Some models of the reading process: learners and skilled readers. *Reading Research Quarterly*, Summer 1972, *7*, 701–733.

MACMILLAN, D. L. & FORNESS, S. R. Behavior modification: limitations & liabilities. *Exceptional Children*, December 1970, *37*, 291–297.

MAGER, ROBERT F. *Preparing instructional objectives*. Belmont, Calif.: Fearon Publishers, 1962.

MAGINNIS, GEORGE H. Measuring underachievement in reading. *The Reading Teacher*, May 1972, *25*, 750–753.

MAKITA, KIYOSHI. The rarity of reading disability in Japanese children. *American Journal of Orthopsychiatry*, July 1968, *38*, 599–614.

MALLINSON, GEORGE G.; STURM, HAROLD E.; & MALLINSON, LOIS M. The reading difficulty of textbooks in junior high school science. *School Review*, 1950, *58*, 536–540.

MALMQUIST, EVE. *Factors related to reading disabilities in the first grade of the Elementary School*. Stockholm: Almqvist and Wiksell, 1958.

MALMQUIST, EVE. *Läs-och skrivsvårigheter hos barn: analys och behandlingsmetodik* (Reading and writing disabilities in children: diagnosis and remedial methods). Lund, Sweden: Gleerup, 1967.

MALMQUIST, EVE. *Lässvårigheter på grundskolans lågstadium* (Experimental studies on reading disabilities at the primary stage). Falkoping, Sweden: Utbildningsforlaget Liber. Research reports from the National School for Educational Research, No. 13, 1969.

MALMQUIST, EVE. Problems of reading and readers: an international challenge. In Dorothy K. Bracken & Eve Malmquist (Eds.), *Improving reading ability around the world*. Newark, Del.: International Reading Association, 1971. Pp. 59–71.

MALONE, JOHN R. Single-sound UNIFON: does it fill the need for a compatible and consistent auxiliary orthography for teaching English and other European languages? Paper presented at the Conference on Perceptual and Linguistic Aspects of Reading, Center for Advanced Study in the Behavioral Sciences, Stanford, California, October 31–November 2, 1963.

MANN, LESTER. Perceptual training: misdirections and redirections. *American Journal of Orthopsychiatry*, January 1970, *40*, 30–38.

MANN, LESTER. Review of the Frostig Developmental Tests of Visual Perception. In Oscar K. Buros (Ed.), *Seventh Mental Measurements Yearbook*, Vol. II. Highland Park, N.J.: Gryphon Press, 1972. Pp. 871–873.

MANOLAKES, GEORGE. The effects of tachistoscopic training in an adult reading program. *Journal of Applied Psychology*, 1952, *36*, 410–412.

A manual for reading clinic teachers. St. Louis: St. Louis Public Schools, 1965.

MARIETTA, DONALD F. Cognitive regulators: an experimental model. *Academic Therapy*, Winter 1971–72, *7*, 185–193.

MARTIN, HAROLD P. Vision and its role in reading disability and dyslexia. *Journal of School Health*, November 1971, *41*, 468–472.

MARTIN, ROBERT L. Interestability of sixth grade basic readers. Unpublished doctoral dissertation, University of Southern California, 1972.

MARTIN, SUE ANN. Techniques for the creative reading or telling of stories to children. *Elementary English,* May 1968, *45,* 611–618.

MARTINIUS, JOEST W. & HOOVEY, ZEECAM B. Bilateral synchrony of occipital alpha waves, oculomotor activity and "attention" in children. *Electroencephalography & Clinical Neurophysiology,* April 1972, *32,* 349–356.

MARTYN, DOROTHY W. Observations of an itinerant teacher. *Academic Therapy,* Summer 1972, *7,* 439–442.

MARWIT, SAMUEL J. & STENNER, A. JACK. Hyperkinesis: delineation of two patterns. *Exceptional Children,* January 1972, *38,* 401–406.

MASLAND, RICHARD L. Lacunae and research approaches to them, III. In C. H. Millikan & F. L. Darley (Eds.), *Brain mechanisms underlying speech and language.* New York: Grune & Stratton, 1967. Pp. 232–237.

MASON, GEORGE E. Extra stimulation in intermediate grade reading. College Reading Association, April 1968. ED 029 752.

MASSAD, CAROLYN E. Interpreting and using test norms. *The Reading Teacher,* December 1972, *26,* 286–292.

MATHEWS, MITFORD M. *Teaching to read: historically considered.* Chicago: University of Chicago Press, 1966.

MATTLEMAN, MARCIENE. *101 activities for teaching reading.* Portland, Me.: Walach, 1973.

MAZURKIEWICZ, ALBERT J. The initial teaching alphabet (i/t/a). In John Money (Ed.), *The disabled reader.* Baltimore: Johns Hopkins Press, 1966. Pp. 161–174.

MC CARTHY, DOROTHEA. Some possible explanations of sex differences in language development and disorders. *Journal of Psychology,* 1953, *35,* 155–160.

MC CARTHY, J. M. Learning disabilities: where have we been? where are we going? *Learning disabilities: selected conference papers.* Arlington, Va.: Council for Exceptional Children, 1969. Pp. 33–39.

MC CLEARY, EMILY K. Report of results of tutorial reading project. *The Reading Teacher,* March 1971, *24,* 556–559.

MC CRACKEN, ROBERT A. *Standard reading inventory.* Klamath Falls, Ore.: Klamath Printing, 1966.

MC CULLOUGH, CONSTANCE M. Flash cards—opiate? *Elementary English,* 1955, *32,* 379–381.

MC CULLOUGH, CONSTANCE M. Components of a reading program for the intermediate grades. In Howard A. Klein (Ed.), *The quest for competency in teaching reading.* Newark, Del.: International Reading Association, 1972. Pp. 67–73.

MC DONALD, ARTHUR S. Television, books, and scholastic performance. In J. Allen Figurel (Ed.), *Reading in a changing society.* International Reading Association Conference Proceedings. New York: Scholastic Magazines, 1959, *4,* Pp. 148–151.

MC DONALD, ARTHUR S. Factors affecting reading test performance. *Ninth Yearbook of the National Reading Conference,* 1960. Pp. 29–35.

MC DONALD, ARTHUR S. Research for the classroom: rate and flexibility. *Journal of Reading,* January 1965, *8,* 187–191.

MC GLANNAN, FRANCES K. Familial characteristics of genetic dyslexia: preliminary report from a pilot study. *Journal of Learning Disabilities,* March 1968, *1,* 185–191.

MC LEOD, JOHN. Prediction of childhood dyslexia. *Bulletin of the Orton Society*, 1966, *16*, 14–23.

MC LOUGHLIN, WILLIAM P. *The non-graded school: a critical assessment.* Albany, N.Y.: State Education Department, September, 1967.

MC NEIL, JOHN D. *Auditory discrimination training in the development of word analysis skills.* Los Angeles: University of California at Los Angeles, 1967. ED 018 344.

MC NEIL, JOHN D. *Behavioral objectives in the teaching of reading.* Professional Bulletin No. 3. Cincinnati: American Book, 1970.

MC NINCH, GEORGE. Determining the reading preferences of third, fourth and fifth grade disadvantaged pupils. *Journal of Reading Behavior*, Spring 1970–71, *3*, 32–38.

MC WHORTER, KATHLEEN T., & LEVY, JEAN. The influence of a tutorial program upon tutors. *Journal of Reading*, January 1971, *14*, 221–24.

MEADE, EDWARD J. Reading: the first R—a point of view. *Reading World*, March 1973, *12*, 169–180.

MEDCALF, ROBERT L. & RATZ, MARGARET. A coding system that makes sense. *Elementary English*, January 1973, *50*, 44–48.

MEIER, DEBORAH. *Reading failure and the tests.* New York: Workshop Center for Open Education, The City College of New York, February 1973.

MICHAL-SMITH, HAROLD; MORGENSTERN, MURRAY; & KARP, ETTA. Dyslexia in four siblings. *Journal of Learning Disabilities*, April 1970, *3*, 185–192.

MILES, J., FOREMAN, P. J.; & ANDERSON, J. The long and short term predictive efficiency of two tests of reading potential. *The Slow-Learning Child*, November 1973, *20*, 131–141.

MILES, W. R. & SEGEL, D. Clinical observations of eye movements in the rating of reading ability. *Journal of Educational Psychology*, 1929, *20*, 520–529.

MILLER, ARTHUR L. A study of reading tastes of children in grades four, five and six in selected schools in the Lamar area school study council. *Dissertation Abstract*, 1967, *27*, 2471A.

MILLER, EDITH F. Stimulate reading . . . with a dictionary. In Albert J. Harris and Edward R. Sipay (Eds.), *Readings on reading instruction.* New York: David McKay, 1972. Pp. 257–260. Reprinted from *Grade Teacher*, February 1962, *79*, 51–52, 106–107.

MILLER, ETTA. Relationships among modality preference, method of instruction, and reading achievement. Unpublished doctoral dissertation, State University of New York at Albany, 1974.

MILLER, GORDON W. Factors in school achievement and social class. *Journal of Educational Psychology*, 1970, *61*, 260–269.

MILLER, WILMA H. The Joplin plan—is it effective for intermediate-grade reading instruction? *Elementary English*, November 1971, *46*, 951–954.

MILLMAN, JASON. Criterion referenced measurement: an alternative. *The Reading Teacher*, December 1972, *26*, 278–281.

MILLS, ROBERT E. An evaluation of techniques for teaching word recognition. *Elementary School Journal*, 1956, *56*, 221–225.

MILNER, BRENDA. Comment. In C. H. Millikan & F. L. Darley (Eds.), *Brain mechanisms underlying speech and language.* New York: Grune & Stratton, 1967. P. 178.

MISHRA, S. P. & HURT, M. JR. The use of the Metropolitan Readiness Test with Mexican-American children. *California Journal of Educational Research*, 1970, *21*, 182–187.

MITCHELL, ADDIE S. Should dialectical differences be considered in reading instruction? In Howard A. Klein (Ed.), *The quest for competency in teaching reading*. Newark, Del.: International Reading Association, 1972. Pp. 151–157.

MOHAN, M. Peer tutoring as a technique for teaching the unmotivated. *Child Study Journal*, Summer 1971, *1*, 217–225.

MONEY, JOHN (Ed.). *Reading disability: progress and research needs in dyslexia*. Baltimore: Johns Hopkins Press, 1962.

MONROE, MARION. *Children who cannot read*. Chicago: University of Chicago Press, 1932.

MOORE, OMAR K. & ANDERSON, ALAN R. The responsive environments project. In R. Hess & R. M. Bear (Eds.), *The challenge of early education*. Chicago: Aldine, 1967. Chap. 13.

MORGAN, W. PRINGLE. A case of congenital word-blindness. *British Medical Journal*, 1896, *2*, 1378.

MORRIS, GREGORY A. A comparison of fourth graders' oral and silent reading behavior in basal reader, science, and social studies materials. Unpublished doctoral dissertation, University of Pittsburgh, 1970.

MORRIS, JOYCE M. *Standards and progress in reading*. London: National Foundation for Educational Research in England and Wales, 1966.

MORRISON, COLEMAN; HARRIS, ALBERT J.; & AUERBACH, IRMA T. The reading performance of disadvantaged early and non-early readers from grades 1 through 3. *Journal of Educational Research*, September 1971, *65*, 23–26.

MORTON, J. The effects of context upon speed of reading, eye movement, and eye-voice span. *Quarterly Journal of Experimental Psychology*, 1964, *13*, 340–354.

MOSS, JOY F. Growth in reading in an integrated day classroom. *Elementary School Journal*, March 1972, *72*, 304–320.

MOTT, JOHN H. Reading interests of adolescents: a critical study of fifty years of research. Unpublished doctoral dissertation, University of Northern Colorado, 1970.

MOUNTCASTLE, VERNON B. *Interhemispheric relations and brain dominance*. Baltimore: Johns Hopkins Press, 1962.

MUEHL, SIEGMAR & FORRELL, ELIZABETH R. A follow-up study of disabled readers: variables related to high school reading performance. *Reading Research Quarterly*, 1973–74, 9, No. 1, 110–123.

MUEHL, S.; KNOTT, J. R.; & BENTON, A. L. EEG abnormality and psychological test performance in reading disability. *Cortex*, 1965, *1*, 434–440.

MURPHY, JOHN F. Learning by listening: a public school approach. *Academic Therapy*, Winter 1972–73, *8*, 167–199.

MYKLEBUST, HELMER R. Learning disabilities: definition and overview. In Helmer R. Myklebust (Ed.), *Progress in Learning Disabilities*, Vol. 1. New York: Grune & Stratton, 1968. Pp. 1–15.

NAIDOO, SANDHYA. Symposium on reading disability. *British Journal of Educational Psychology*, February 1971, *41*, 19–22.

NAIDOO, SANDHYA. The research project, the Word Blind Centre. *Dyslexia Review*, Summer 1972, *7*, 14–18.

NATIONAL ADVISORY COMMITTEE ON HANDICAPPED CHILDREN, Conference sponsored by Bureau of Education for the Handicapped, U.S. Office of Education, Washington, D.C., September 28, 1967.

NEVILLE, DONALD. The relationship between reading skills and intelligence test scores. *The Reading Teacher*, January 1965, *18*, 257–262.

NEVILLE, DONALD. The development of an instrument to predict modality preference for learning to read. IMRID Behavioral Science Monograph No. 16. Nashville, Tenn.: Institute on Mental Retardation and Intellectual Development, George Peabody College for Teachers, 1971.

NEVILLE, DONALD; PFOST, P.; & DOBBS, VIRGINIA. The relationship between test anxiety and silent reading gains. *American Educational Research Journal,* 1967, *4,* 45–50.

NEVILLE, MARY H. Effect of reading method on the development of auditory memory span. *The Reading Teacher,* October 1968, *22,* 30–35.

NEVINS, ROSEMARY V. The effect of training in letter names, letter sounds, and letter names and sounds on the acquisition of word recognition ability. Unpublished doctoral dissertation, State University of New York at Albany, 1972.

NEWCOMER, PHYLISS & HAMMILL, DONALD. Visual perception of motor impaired children: implication for assessment. *Exceptional Children,* January 1973, *39,* 335–337.

NEWPORT, JOHN F. The Joplin Plan: the score. *The Reading Teacher,* November 1967, *21,* 158–162.

NEWTON, MARGARET. A neuropsychological investigation into dyslexia. In Alfred W. Franklin & Sandhya Naidoo (Eds.), *Assessment and teaching of dyslexic children.* London: Invalid Children's Aid Association, 1970. Pp. 14–21.

New York Times. A therapy system for young scored. March 7, 1968.

NIEDERMEYER, F. C. & ELLIS, PATRICIA. Remedial reading instruction by trained pupil tutors. *Elementary School Journal,* 1971, *71,* 400–405.

NIENSTED, SERENA M. Hyperlexia: an educational disease? *Exceptional Children,* October 1968, *35,* 162–163.

NILES, OLIVE (Reviewer). System for objective-based assessment—reading (SOBAR). *The Reading Teacher,* November 1973, *27,* 203–204.

NOLAND, EUNICE C. & SCHULDT, W. JOHN. Sustained attention and reading retardation. *Journal of Experimental Education,* Winter 1971, *40,* 73–76.

NOLEN, PATRICIA A. Reading nonstandard dialect materials: a study at grades two and four. *Child Development,* September 1972, *43,* 1092–1097.

NORN, M. S.; RINDZIUNSKI, EVA; & SKYDSGAARD, H. Opthalmologic and orthoptic examinations of dyslectics. *Skolepsykologi,* 1970, *7,* 333–349.

NORRIE, EDITH. *Laesepaedagogen,* 1954, *2,* 61.

NORRIS, ELEANOR L. & BOWES, JOHN E. (Eds.). *National assessment of educational progress: reading objectives.* Ann Arbor, Michigan: National Assessment Office, 1970.

NORVELL, GEORGE W. *What boys and girls like to read.* Morristown, N.J.: Silver Burdette, 1958.

NORVELL, GEORGE W. The challenge of periodicals in education. *Elementary English,* 1966, *43,* 402–408.

NORVELL, GEORGE W. Revolution in the English curriculum. *Elementary English,* May 1972, *49,* 760–767.

NORVELL, GEORGE W. *The reading interests of young people.* Ann Arbor: Michigan State University Press, 1973.

OAKAN, ROBERT; WIENER, MORTON; & CROMER, WARD. Identification organization and reading comprehension for good and poor readers. *Journal of Educational Psychology,* 1971, *62,* 71–78.

OAKLAND, THOMAS D. Auditory discrimination and socioeconomic status as correlates of reading ability. *Journal of Learning Disabilities,* June 1969, *2,* 325–329.

OBRUTZ, JOHN, *et al.* Re-examination of Koppitz's developmental Bender scoring system. *Perceptual and Motor Skills,* February 1972, *34,* 279–282.

OETTINGER, LEON. Learning disorders, hyperkinesis, and the use of drugs in children. *Rehabilitation Literature,* June 1971, *32,* 162–167, 170.

OFMAN, WILLIAM & SCHAEVITZ, MORTON. The kinesthetic method in remedial reading. *Journal of Experimental Education,* 1963, *31,* 319–320.

OLLILA, L. O. Pros and cons of teaching reading to four- and five-year-olds. In Robert C. Aukerman (Ed.) *Some persistent questions on beginning reading.* Newark, Del.: International Reading Association, 1972. Pp. 53–61.

OLSON, ARTHUR V. Relationship of achievement test scores and specific reading abilities to the Frostig Developmental Test of Visual Perception. *Perceptual and Motor Skills,* February 1966, *22,* 179–184. (a)

OLSON, ARTHUR V. School achievement, reading ability and specific visual perceptual skills in the third grade. *The Reading Teacher,* April 1966, *19,* 490–492. (b)

OLSON, A. V. & JOHNSON, C. D. Structure and predictive validity of the Frostig Developmental Test of Visual Perception in grades one and three. *Journal of Special Education,* 1970, *4,* 49–52.

O'NEIL, WAYNE. Our collective phonological illusions: young and old. In James F. Kavanagh & Ignatius G. Mattingly (Eds.), *Language by ear and eye: the relationships between speech and reading.* Cambridge, Mass.: MIT Press, 1972. Pp. 111–116.

ORTON, JUNE L. *A guide to teaching phonetics.* Cambridge, Mass.: Educators Publishing Service, 1964.

ORTON, JUNE L. The Orton-Gillingham approach. In John Money (Ed.), *The disabled reader.* Baltimore: Johns Hopkins Press, 1966. Pp. 119–146.

ORTON, SAMUEL T. *Reading, writing, and speech problems in children.* New York: W. W. Norton, 1937.

OSBURN, WORTH J. Emotional blocks in reading. *Elementary School Journal,* 1951, *52,* 23–30.

OTTO, WAYNE. *The relationship of reactive inhibition and school achievement: theory, research, and implications.* Occasional Paper No. 4. Madison: Research and Development Center for Learning and Re-education, University of Wisconsin, 1966.

OTTO, WAYNE. Adequate reading instruction: fact or fantasy? *The Slow Learning Child,* March 1972, *19,* 3–11.

OTTO, WAYNE. Evaluating instruments for assessing needs and growth in reading. In W. H. MacGinitie (Ed.), *Assessment problems in reading.* Newark, Del.: International Reading Association, 1973. Pp. 14–20.

OTTO, WAYNE & ASKOV, E. *Rationale and guidelines; the Wisconsin Design for Reading Skill Development.* Minneapolis: National Computer Systems, 1972.

OTTO, WAYNE; BARRETT, THOMAS C.; & HARRIS, THEODORE L. Research in reading. *Journal of Experimental Education,* Fall 1968, *37,* 65–77.

OWRID, H. L. Hearing impairment and verbal attainments in primary school children. *Educational Research,* June 1970, *12,* 209–214.

PARK, G. E. & BURRI, C. The relationship of various eye conditions and reading achievement. *Journal of Educational Psychology,* 1943, *34,* 290–299. (a)

PARK, G. E. & BURRI, C. The effect of eye abnormalities on reading difficulty. *Journal of Educational Psychology,* 1943, *34,* 420–430. (b)

PARK, G. E. & BURRI, C. Eye maturation and reading difficulties. *Journal of Educational Psychology,* 1943, *34,* 535–546. (c)

PARK, GEORGE E. Mirror and reversed reading. *Journal of Pediatrics,* 1953, *42,*

120–128.

PARK, GEORGE E. & LINDEN, JAMES. The etiology of reading disabilities: an histori-cal perspective. *Journal of Learning Disabilities*, May 1968, *1*, 318–330.

PAUK, WALTER. Scholarly skills as gadgets. *Journal of Reading*, March 1965, *8*, 234–239.

PEARSON, GERALD H. J. A survey of learning difficulties in children. *Psychoanalytic Study of the Child*, 1952, *7*, 372–386.

PEDERSEN, KURT. Nogle erfaringer med Frostig-proven—og dens relation til laes-ning (Some experiences with the Frostig test and its relation to reading). *Skolepsykologi*, 1971, *8*, 186–204.

PEISER, IRVING J. Vision and learning disabilities. *Journal of the American Opto-metric Association*, February 1972, *43*, 152–159.

PENN, JULIA M. Reading disability: a neurological deficit? *Exceptional Children*, December 1966, *33*, 243–248.

PENNOCK, CLIFFORD D. Using cloze to select appropriate level instructional ma-terials. In Jane Porter, Research report. *Elementary English*, September 1973, *50*, 940–941.

PETRE, RICHARD M. Pupil response in open structured and close structured reading activities. In Howard A. Klein (Ed.), *The quest for competency in teaching reading*. Newark, Del.: International Reading Association, 1972. Pp 192–197.

PETTY, WALTER T.; HEROLD, CURTIS P.; & STOLL, EARLINE. *The state of knowledge about the teaching of vocabulary*. Cooperative Research Project No. 3128. Champaign: National Council of Teachers of English, 1968.

PIKULSKI, JOHN J. Candy, word recognition and the "disadvantaged." *The Reading Teacher*, December 1971, *25*, 243–246.

PIKULSKI, JOHN J. The validity of three brief measures of intelligence for disabled readers. *Journal of Educational Research*, October 1973, *67*, 67–68, 80.

PLATTS, MARY E. *Anchor: a handbook of vocabulary discovery techniques for the classroom teacher*. Stevensville, Mich.: Educational Services, 1970.

POLLACK, CECILIA. Mass remediation of children's reading problems. *The Reading Teacher*, May 1969, *22*, 714–719.

POMERANTZ, HELEN. Subvocalization and reading. *The Reading Teacher*, April 1971, *24*, 665–667.

POTTER, MURIEL C. *Perception of symbol orientation and early reading success*. Contributions to Education, No. 939. New York: Bureau of Publications, Teachers College, Columbia University, 1939.

POWELL, WILLIAM R. Acquisition of a reading repertoire. *Library Trends*, October 1973, *22*, 177–196.

POWERS, R. B.; SUMNER, W. A.; & KEARL, B. E. A recalculation of four readability formulas. *Journal of Educational Psychology*, 1958, *49*, 99–105.

PRAGER, BARTON B. & MANN, LESTER. Criterion-referenced measurement: the world of gray versus black and white. *Journal of Learning Disabilities*, February 1973, *6*, 72–84.

PRESSMAN, RAYMOND. The relationship of sensory-integration matching abilities and reading instructional approaches to word recognition ability. Unpub-lished doctoral dissertation, State University of New York at Albany, 1973.

PRESTON, RALPH C. & WILLSON, MARGARET F. Fred. In Albert J. Harris (Ed.), *Casebook on reading disability*. New York: David McKay, 1970. Pp. 147–160.

PRICE, UBERTO & LAYTON, JAMES. The national trend and current status of certifica-tion requirements for reading personnel. *Journal of the Reading Specialist*, 1968, *7*, 164–169.

PUMFREY, P. D. & ELLIOTT, C. D. Play therapy, social adjustment and reading attainment. *Educational Research,* June 1970, *12,* 183–193.

PURVES, ALAN C. & BEACH, RICHARD. *Literature and the reader: research in response to literature, reading interests, and the teaching of literature.* Champaign, Ill.: National Council of Teachers of English, 1972.

PUTNAM, RUTH A. Cultivating a taste for non-fiction. *Elementary English Review,* 1941, *18,* 228–229.

RABINOVITCH, RALPH D. Reading and learning disabilities. In S. Arieti (Ed.), *American handbook of psychiatry.* New York: Basic Books, 1959. Pp. 857–869.

RABINOVITCH, RALPH D. Dyslexia: psychiatric considerations. In John Money (Ed.), *Reading disability: progress and research needs in dyslexia.* Baltimore: Johns Hopkins Press, 1962. Pp. 73–79.

RABINOVITCH, RALPH D. Reading problems in children: definitions and classifications. In Arthur H. Keeney and Virginia T. Keeney (Eds.), *Dyslexia: diagnosis and treatment of reading disorders.* Saint Louis: C. V. Mosby, 1968. Pp. 4–6.

RAMSEY, IMOGENE. A comparison of first grade Negro dialect speakers' comprehension of standard English and Negro dialect. *Elementary English,* May 1972, *49,* 688–696.

RAMSEY, WALLACE. The value and limitations of diagnostic reading tests for evaluation in the classroom. In Thomas C. Barrett (Ed.), *The evaluation of children's reading achievement.* Perspectives in Reading, No. 8. Newark, Del.: International Reading Association, 1967. Chap. 6.

RAMSEY, WALLACE Z. *Evaluation of assumptions related to the testing of phonic skills.* USOE Project No. IGO44, Final Report, October 1972.

RAMSEY, WALLACE Z. & BURNETT, RICHARD. Critique of Learning to read: the great debate. *Elementary English,* May, 1969, *46,* 632–634.

Random House dictionary of the English language (unabridged ed.). New York: Random House, 1966.

RANKIN, EARL F. How flexibly do we read? *Journal of Reading Behavior,* Summer 1970–71, *3,* 34–38.

RANKIN, EARL F. & OVERHOLSER, BETSY M. Reaction of intermediate grade children to contextual clues. *Journal of Reading Behavior,* Summer 1969, *1,* 50–73.

RAWSON, MARGARET B. *Developmental language disability: adult accomplishments of dyslexic boys.* Baltimore: Johns Hopkins Press, 1968.

RAWSON, MARGARET B. Perspectives of specific language disability: I. the past—what has been learned? *Bulletin of the Orton Society,* 1971, *21,* 22–34.

REED, DAVID W. A theory of language, speech, and writing. *Elementary English,* December 1965, *42,* 845–851.

REED, JAMES C. The deficits of retarded readers—fact or artifact? *The Reading Teacher,* January 1970, *23,* 347–352.

REED, JAMES C. The ability deficits of good and poor readers. *Journal of Learning Disabilities,* February 1968, *1,* 134–139.

REED, JAMES C.; RABE, EDWARD F.; & MANKINEN, MARGARET. Teaching reading to brain-injured children: a review. *Reading Research Quarterly,* Spring 1970, *5,* 379–401.

REEVES, RACHEL J. A study of the relation between listening performance and reading performance of sixth-grade pupils as measured by certain standardized tests. Unpublished doctoral dissertation, University of Alabama, 1968.

REID, JESSIE F. Learning to think about reading. *Educational Research*, 1966, 9, 56–62.

REID, JESSIE F. Dyslexia: a problem of communication. *Educational Research*, February 1968, *10*, 126–133.

REID, VIRGINIA M. (Ed.). *Reading ladders for human relations* (5th ed.). Urbana, Ill.: National Council of Teachers of English, 1972.

REILLY, DAVID H. Auditory-visual integration, sex, and reading achievement. *Journal of Educational Psychology*, December 1971, *62*, 482–486.

RENTEL, VICTOR M. Concept formation and reading. *Reading World*, December 1971, *11*, 111–119.

RESEARCH FOR BETTER SCHOOLS. *Annual Report*. Philadelphia: Research for Better Schools, May 14, 1971.

RESNICK, LAUREN B. Relations between perceptual and syntactic control in oral reading. *Journal of Educational Psychology*, 1970, *61*, 382–385.

RICHARDSON, ROBERT J. An information system for individualized instruction in an elementary school. *Educational & Psychological Measurement*, 1969, *29*, 199–201.

RIGGS, CORINNE W. (Comp.) *Bibliotherapy: an annotated bibliography*. Newark, Del.: International Reading Association, 1971.

ROACH, EUGENE G. & KEPHART, NEWELL C. *The Purdue Perceptual-Motor Survey*. Columbus: Charles E. Merrill, 1966.

ROBB, J. PRESTON. Neurological aspects of reading disabilities. In J. Allen Figurel (Ed.), *Reading for effective living*. Newark, Del.: International Reading Association, 1958. Pp. 116–119.

ROBBINS, MELVYN P. The Delacato intrepretation of neurological organization. *Reading Research Quarterly*, Spring 1966, *1*, 57–78.

ROBERTS, R. W. & COLEMAN, J. An investigation of the role of visual and kinesthetic factors in reading failures. *Journal of Educational Research*, 1958, 57, 445–451.

ROBERTSON, JEAN E. Pupil understanding of connectives in reading. *Reading Research Quarterly*, Spring 1968, 3, 387–417.

ROBINSON, FRANCIS P. *Effective reading*. New York: Harper & Row, 1962.

ROBINSON, H. ALAN. A study of the techniques of word identification. *The Reading Teacher*, January 1963, *16*, 238–241.

ROBINSON, H. ALAN. Reading skills in solving social studies problems. *The Reading Teacher*, January 1965, *18*, 263–269.

ROBINSON, HELEN M. *Why pupils fail in reading*. Chicago: University of Chicago Press, 1946.

ROBINSON, HELEN M. Perceptual training—does it result in reading improvement? In Robert C. Aukerman (Ed.), *Some persistent questions on beginning reading*. Newark, Del.: International Reading Association, 1972, Pp. 135–150. (a)

ROBINSON, HELEN M. Visual and auditory modalities related to methods for beginning reading. *Reading Research Quarterly*, Fall 1972, 8, 7–39. (b)

ROBINSON, HELEN M. & HUELSMAN, C. B., JR. Visual efficiency and progress in learning to read. In *Clinical Studies in Reading*, II. Supplementary Educational Monographs, No. 77. Chicago: University of Chicago Press, 1953. Pp. 31–63.

ROBINSON, HELEN M. & SMITH, HELEN K. Reading clinic clients—ten years after. *Elementary School Journal*, 1962, *63*, 22–27.

ROBINSON, HELEN M. & WEINTRAUB, SAMUEL. Research related to children's interests and to developmental values of reading. *Library Trends*, October 1973, *22*, 81–108.

ROBINSON, RICHARD D. (Comp.). *An introduction to the cloze procedure: an annotated bibliography*. Newark, Del.: International Reading Association, 1972.

RODENBORN, LEO V. The importance of memory and integration factors to oral reading ability. *Journal of Reading Behavior*, Winter 1970–71, *3*, 51–59.

RODGERS, DENIS C. An investigation of the auditory memory abilities of grade 2 retarded-underachieving readers and competent-achieving readers under conditions of reinforcement and non-reinforcement. Unpublished doctoral dissertation, University of Toronto, 1969.

ROEDER, HAROLD H. & LEE, NANCY. Twenty-five teacher-tested ways to encourage voluntary reading. *The Reading Teacher*, October 1973, *27*, 48–50.

ROELLSE, PATRICIA L. Reading comprehension as a function of three dimensions of word meaning. Unpublished doctoral dissertation, Indiana University, 1969.

ROGERS, CARL R. *Counseling and psychotherapy*. Boston: Houghton Mifflin, 1942.

ROSBOROUGH, PEARL M. *Physical fitness and the child's reading problem*. New York: Exposition Press, 1963.

ROSE, CYNTHIA; ZIMET, SARA G.; & BLOM, GASTON E. Content counts: children have preferences in reading textbook stories. *Elementary English*, January 1972, *49*, 14–19.

ROSEN, CARL L. Visual deficiencies and reading. *Journal of Reading*, 1965, *9*, 57–61.

ROSEN, CARL L. The status of school vision screening: a review of research and consideration of some selected problems. In *The psychology of reading behavior*, 18th yearbook of the National Reading Conference, 1969. Pp. 42–49.

ROSEN, CARL L. & AMES, WILBUR S. Influence of nonstandard dialect on the oral behavior of fourth grade black children under two stimuli conditions. In J. Allen Figurel (Ed.), *Better reading in urban schools*. Newark, Del.: International Reading Association, 1972. Pp. 45–55.

ROSEN, CARL L. & OHNMACHT, FRED. Perception, readiness, and reading achievement. In Helen M. Smith (Ed.), *Perception and reading*, Proceedings of the 12th Annual Convention. Newark, Del.: International Reading Association, 1968. Pp. 33–39.

ROSEN, CARL L. & ORTEGO, PHILLIP D. Language and reading problems of Spanish speaking children in the Southwest. *Journal of Reading Behavior*, Winter 1969, *1*, 51–70.

ROSENTHAL, JOSEPH H. Neurophysiology of minimal cerebral dysfunctions. *Academic Therapy*, Spring 1973, *8*, 291–294.

ROSNER, JEROME. Perceptual skills and achievement. *American Educational Research Journal*, Winter 1973, *10*, 59–67.

ROSNER, JEROME & SIMON, DOROTHEA P. The Auditory Analysis Test: an initial report. *Journal of Learning Disabilities*, August 1971, *4*, 384–392.

ROSS, JOHN J.; CHILDERS, DONALD G.; & PERRY, NATHAN W., JR. The natural history and electrophysiological characteristics of familial language dysfunction. In Paul Satz & John J. Ross (Eds.), *The disabled learner: early detection and intervention*. Rotterdam: Rotterdam University Press, 1973. Pp. 149–174.

ROSS, ROBERT J. An open elementary school. In Willard J. Cagreve & George J. Rinehart (Eds.), *Flexibility in school programs*. Worthington, Ohio: Charles A. Jones, 1972, Pp. 54–61.

ROSSI, GIAN F. & ROSADINI, GUIDO. Experimental analysis of cerebral dominance in man. In C. H. Millikan (Chmn.) and F. L. Darley (Ed.), *Brain mechanisms underlying speech and language*. New York: Grune & Stratton, 1967. Pp. 167–175.

ROSWELL, FLORENCE G. & NATCHEZ, GLADYS. *Reading disability: diagnosis and treatment* (2nd ed.). New York: Basic Books, 1971.

ROWELL, C. GLENNON. An attitude scale for reading. *The Reading Teacher*, February 1972, *25*, 442–447.

ROZIN, PAUL; PORITSKY, SUSAN; & SOTSKY, RAINA. American children with reading problems can easily learn to read English represented by Chinese characters. *Science*, March 1971, *171*, 1264–1267.

RUBINO, CARL A. Psychometric procedures and the detection and exploration of behavioral deficits due to cerebral dysfunction in man: II. *Canadian Psychologist*, January 1972, *13*, 40–52.

RUDDELL, ROBERT B. A longitudinal study of four programs of reading instruction varying in emphasis on regularity of grapheme-phoneme correspondences and language structure on reading achievement in grades two and three. Final Report, Project Nos. 3099 and 78085. Berkeley: University of California, 1968.

RUDDELL, ROBERT B. (Ed.). *Accountability and reading instruction: critical issues:* Urbana, Ill.: National Council of Teachers of English, 1973.

RUDISILL, MABEL. Children's preferences for color versus other qualities in illustrations. *Elementary School Journal*, 1952, *52*, 444–451.

RUDMAN, HERBERT C. The informational needs and reading interests of children in grades IV through VIII. *Elementary School Journal*, 1955, *55*, 502–512.

RUSCH, REUBEN R. Reliability of the Higgins-Wertman Test of Visual Closure. *Perceptual & Motor Skills*, 1970, *30*, 879–885.

RUSSELL, DAVID & KARP, ETTA E. *Reading aids through the grades* (rev. ed.). New York: Teachers College Press, Columbia University, 1961.

SABATINO, DAVID A. & YSSELDYKE, JAMES E. Effect of extraneous "background" on visual-perceptual performance of readers and non-readers. *Perceptual & Motor Skills*, August 1972, *35*, 323–328.

SAEMAN, RUTH ANN. Effects of commonly-known meanings on determining obscure meaning of multiple-meaning words in context. Unpublished doctoral dissertation, University of Wisconsin, 1970.

SAMPSON, OLIVE C. Reading and adjustment: a review of the literature. *Educational Research*, June 1966, *8*, 184–190.

SAMUELS, S. JAY. Letter-name versus letter-sound knowledge in learning to read. *The Reading Teacher*, April 1971, *24*, 609–615, 662.

SAMUELS, S. JAY. Effect of distinctive feature training on paired associate learning. *Journal of Educational Psychology*, April 1973, *64*, 147–158 (a)

SAMUELS, S. JAY. Success and failure in learning to read: a critique of the research. *Reading Research Quarterly*, Winter 1973, *8*, 200–239. (b)

SARTAIN, HARRY W. The research base for individualized reading instruction. In J. Allen Figurel (Ed.), *Reading and realism*. Newark, Del.: International Reading Association, 1969, Pp. 523–530.

SATZ, PAUL & SPARROW, SARA S. Specific developmental dyslexia: a theoretical formulation. In Derk J. Bakker and Paul Satz (Eds.), *Specific reading disability*. Rotterdam: Rotterdam University Press, 1970. Pp. 17–40.

SATZ, PAUL & VAN NOSTRAND, GARY. Developmental dyslexia: an evaluation of a theory. In Paul Satz and John J. Ross (Eds.), *The disabled learner*. Rotterdam: Rotterdam University Press, 1973. Pp. 121–148.

SAUER, FREDA M. The determination of reading instructional level of disabled four grade readers utilizing cloze testing procedure. Unpublished doctoral dissertation, Oklahoma State University, 1969.

SAULS, CHARLES W. The relationship of selected factors to the recreational reading of sixth grade students. Unpublished doctoral dissertation, Louisiana State University and Agricultural and Mechanical College, 1971.

SCANLON, ROBERT G. Individually prescribed instruction: a system of individualized instruction. *Educational Technology,* December 1970, *10,* 44–46.

SCHAIE, K. WARNER & ROBERTS, JEAN. *School achievement of children 6-11 years: as measured by the reading and arithmetic subtests of the Wide Range Achievement Test.* U.S. Department of Health, Education, and Welfare. Public Health Service Publication No. 1000—Series 11—No. 103, June 1970.

SCHAIN, RICHARD J. Neurological diagnosis in children with learning disabilities. *Academic Therapy,* Winter 1971-72, *7,* 139–147.

SCHALE, FLORENCE C. Using special methods of learning, grades IX through XIV. In H. Alan Robinson (Ed.), *Individual differences in reading,* Supplementary Educational Monograph, No. 91. Chicago: University of Chicago Press, 1964. Pp. 41–44.

SCHALE, FLORENCE C. Exploring the potential of the monocularly blind for faster reading. *Academic Therapy,* Summer 1972, *7,* 401–410.

SCHENK-DANZIGER, LOTTE. Probleme der Legasthenie. *Schweizerische Zeitschrift fur Psychologie und Ihre Anwendungen,* 1960, *20,* 29–48.

SCHIFFMAN, GILBERT B. Special programs for underachieving children. In Darrell B. Carter (Ed.), *Interdisciplinary approaches to learning disorders.* Philadelphia: Chilton, 1970. Pp. 69–79.

SCHMITT, CLARA. Developmental alexia: congenital word-blindness, or inability to learn to read. *Elementary School Journal,* 1918, *18,* 680–700, 757–769.

SCHNAYER, SIDNEY W. Some relations between reading interest and reading comprehension. Unpublished doctoral dissertation, University of California at Berkeley, 1967.

SCHNEYER, J. WESLEY & COWEN, SHIELA. *Comparison of a basal reader approach and a linguistic approach in second and third grade reading instruction.* Final Report, Project No. 5-0601. Philadelphia: University of Pennsylvania, 1968.

SCHNICKE, L. F. The relative effects of self-selection and directed reading methods on the development of variability of reading rate in fourth grade. Unpublished doctoral dissertation, University of Wisconsin, 1970.

SCHUBERT, DELWYN. My greatest problem in teaching reading. *Elementary English,* January 1971, *48,* 230–232.

SCHULTE, EMERITA S. Independent reading interests of children in grades 4, 5 and 6. In J. Allen Figurel (Ed.), *Reading and realism.* Newark, Del.: International Reading Association, 1969. Pp. 728–732.

SCHULTE, EMERITA S. Today's literature for today's children. *Elementary English,* March 1972, *49,* 355–363.

SCHULTHEIS, SISTER MIRIAM. *A guidebook for bibliotherapy.* Psychotechnics, 1972.

SEASHORE, ROBERT H. The importance of vocabulary in learning language skills. *Elementary English,* 1948, 137–152.

SECRETARY'S (HEW) ADVISORY COUNCIL ON DYSLEXIA AND RELATED READING DISORDERS. *Reading disorders in the United States.* National Institute of Health, August 1969. ED 037 317. Also available from Developmental Learning Materials, Chicago, August 1969.

SEEGERS, J. C. Vocabularly problems in the elementary school. *Elementary English Review,* 1939, *16,* 157–166, 199, 234, 320; and 1940, *17,* 28–43.

SEELS, BARBARA & DALE, EDGAR (Comp.). *Readability and reading: an annotated bibliography.* Newark, Del.: International Reading Association, 1971.

SERRA, MARY C. The concept burden of instructional materials. *Elementary School Journal,* 1953, *53,* 508–512.

SERWER, BLANCHE L. Linguistic support for a method of teaching beginning reading to black children. *Reading Research Quarterly.* Summer 1969, *4*, 449–467.

SERWER, BLANCHE L. & STOLUROW, LAWRENCE M. Computer-assisted learning in language arts. *Elementary English*, May 1970, *47*, 641–650.

SHANE, HAROLD G. The expanding role of oral reading in school and life activities. In Helen M. Robinson (Ed.), *Oral aspects of reading.* Supplementary Educational Monographs, No. 82. Chicago: University of Chicago Press, 1955. Pp. 1–4.

SHANKMAN, FLORENCE V. Games reinforce reading skills. *The Reading Teacher,* December 1968, *22*, 262–264.

SHANKWEILER, DONALD & LIBERMAN, ISABELLE Y. Misreading: a search for causes. In James F. Kavanagh & Ignatius G. Mattingly (Eds.), *Language by ear and eye: the relationships between speech and reading.* Cambridge, Mass.: MIT Press, 1972. Pp. 293–317.

SHARON, AMIEL T. What do adults read? *Reading Research Quarterly*, 1973–74, *9*, No. 1, 148–169.

SHAW, JULES H. Vision and seeing skills of preschool children. *The Reading Teacher*, 1964, *18*, 33–36.

SHAYON, ROBERT L. *Television and our children.* New York: Longmans, Green, 1951. P. 29.

SHEARER, E. Physical skills and reading backwardness. *Educational Research*, June 1968, *10*, 197–206.

SHEARRON, GILBERT F. Color deficiency and reading achievement in primary school boys. *The Reading Teacher*, March 1969, *22*, 510–512, 577.

SHELDON, WILLIAM D., et al. *Comparison of three methods of teaching reading in the second grade.* OEC 6-10-076. CRP-3231. ED 023-524, 1967.

SHIELDS, DIANNE T. Brain responses to stimuli in disorders of information processing. *Journal of Learning Disabilities*, October 1973, *6*, 501–505.

SHIMRAT, NIUSIA. Lateral dominance and directional orientation in the writing of American and Israeli children. Unpublished doctoral dissertation, Columbia University, 1970.

SHORES, HARLAN J. & HUSBANDS, KENNETH L. Are fast readers the best readers? *Elementary English*, 1950, *27*, 52–57.

SILBERBERG, NORMAN E. & SILBERBERG, MARGARET C. Case histories in hyperlexia. 1968. ED 024 551.

SILVAROLI, NICHOLAS J. *Classroom Reading Inventory* (2nd ed.). Dubuque, Iowa: William C. Brown, 1969.

SILVER, ARCHIE A. & HAGIN, ROSA A. Specific reading disability: follow-up studies. *American Journal of Orthopsychiatry*, 1964, *34*, 95–102.

SILVER, ARCHIE A. & HAGIN, ROSA A. Strategies of intervention in the spectrum of defects in specific reading disability. *Bulletin of the Orton Society*, 1967, *17*, 39–46.

SILVER, ARCHIE A.; HAGIN, ROSA; & HERSH, MARILYN F. *Reading disability: teaching through stimulation of deficit perceptual areas.* New York: Department of Psychiatry and Neurology, New York University Medical Center, 1965. Mimeographed.

SILVER, ARCHIE A.; HAGIN, ROSA A.; & HERSH, MARILYN F. Reading disability: teaching through stimulation of deficit perceptual areas. *American Journal of Orthopsychiatry*, 1967, *37*, 744–752.

SIMMONS, BEATRICE. (Ed.). *Paperback books for children.* Chicago: American Library Association, 1972.

SIMMONS, G. A. & SHAPIRO, B. J. Reading expectancy formulas: a warning note. *Journal of Reading*, May 1968, *11*, 626–629.

SIMONS, HERBERT D. Reading comprehension: the need for a new perspective. *Reading Research Quarterly*, Spring 1971, *6*, 338–363.

SIMONS, HERBERT D. Linguistic skills and reading comprehension. In Howard A. Klein (Ed.), *The quest for competency in teaching reading*. Newark, Del.; International Reading Association, 1972. Pp. 165–170.

SIPAY, EDWARD R. A comparison of standarized reading scores and functional reading levels. *The Reading Teacher*, January 1964, *17*, 265–268.

SIPAY, EDWARD R. Interpreting the USOE cooperative reading studies. *The Reading Teacher*, October 1968, *22*, 10–16.

SIPAY, EDWARD R. Determining word identification difficulties. In Barbara Bateman (Ed.), *Learning Disorders*, Vol. 4. Seattle: Special Child Publications, 1971. Pp. 215–247.

SIROTA, BEVERLY S. The effect of a planned literature program of daily oral reading by the teacher on the voluntary reading of fifth-grade children. Unpublished doctoral dissertation, New York University, 1971.

SKARBECK, JAMES F. The effect of a program emphasizing rate of comprehension at the sixth-grade level. Unpublished doctoral dissertation, University of Maryland, 1965.

SKINNER, CLARENCE E. *Elementary educational psychology*. New York: Prentice-Hall, 1945.

SLINGERLAND, BETH H. *A multi-sensory approach to language arts for specific language disability children: a guide for primary teachers*. Cambridge, Mass.: Educators Publishing Service, 1971.

SMITH, DONALD E. P. & CARRIGAN, PATRICIA M. *The nature of reading disability*. New York: Harcourt Brace, 1959.

SMITH, DONALD E. P.; BRETHOWER, DALE; & CABOT, RAYMOND. Increasing task behavior in a language arts program by providing reinforcement. *Journal of Experimental Child Psychology*, 1969, *8*, 45–62.

SMITH, EDWIN H.; GUICE, BILLY M.; & CHEEK, MARTHA C. Informal reading inventories for the content areas: science and mathematics. *Elementary English*, May 1972, *49*, 659–666.

SMITH, FRANK. *Understanding reading: a psycholinguistic analysis of reading and learning to read*. New York: Holt, Rinehart and Winston, 1971.

SMITH, FRANK & GOODMAN, KENNETH S. On the psycholinguistic method of teaching reading. *Elementary School Journal*, January 1971, *71*, 177–181.

SMITH, HENRY LEE, JR. *English morphophonics: implications for teaching of literacy*. Monograph No. 10, New York State English Council, 1968.

SMITH, M. K. Measurement of the size of general English vocabulary through the elementary grades and high school. *Genetic Psychology Monographs*, November 1941, *24*, 311–345.

SMITH, NILA BANTON. *American reading instruction* (rev. ed.). Newark, Del.: International Reading Association, 1965.

SMITH, NILA B. Research in reading: trends and implications. *Elementary English*, March 1971, *48*, 320–327.

SMITH, NILA B. The quest for increased reading competency. In Howard A. Klein (Ed.), *The quest for competency in teaching reading*. Newark, Del.: International Reading Association, 1972. Pp. 45–56.

SMITH, PHILIP A. & MARX, RONALD W. Some cautions on the use of the Frostig test: a factor analytic study. *Journal of Learning Disabilities*, June/July 1972, *5*, 357–362.

SNAPP, MATTHEW; OAKLAND, THOMAS; & WILLIAMS, FERN C. A study of individualizing instruction by using elementary school children as tutors. *Journal of School Psychology*, March 1972, *10*, 1–8.

SNYDER, ROBERT & POPE, PEGGY. New norms for and an item analysis of the Wepman test at first-grade, six-year level. *Perceptual & Motor Skills*, December 1970, *31*, 1007–1010.

SOUTHGATE, VERA. The language arts in informal British primary schools. *The Reading Teacher*, January 1973, *26*, 367–373.

SPACHE, GEORGE D. A new readability formula for primary-grade reading materials. *Elementary School Journal*, 1953, *53*, 410–413.

SPACHE, GEORGE D. Is this a breakthrough in reading? *The Reading Teacher*, 1962, *15*, 258–263.

SPACHE, GEORGE D. *Good reading for the disadvantaged reader: multi-ethnic resources.* Champaign: Garrard, 1971.

SPACHE, GEORGE D. *Examiner's manual: Diagnostic Reading Scales* (rev. ed.). Del Monte Research Park, Monterey, Calif.: CTB McGraw-Hill, 1972.

SPACHE, GEORGE D. *Good Reading for Poor Readers* (rev. ed.). Champaign: Garrard, 1974.

SPACHE, GEORGE D.; ANDRES, MICAELA C.; CURTIS, H. A.; ROWLAND, MINNIE L.; & FIELDS, MINNIE H. A longitudinal first grade reading readiness program. *The Reading Teacher*, May 1966, *19*, 580–584.

SPARROW, SARA S. Reading disability: a neuropsychological investigation. Unpublished doctoral dissertation, University of Florida, 1968.

SPEARRITT, DONALD. Identification of subskills of reading comprehension by maximum likelihood factor analysis. *Reading Research Quarterly*, Fall 1972, *8*, 92–111.

SPERLING, BARBARA ANN. Pupil team activity, reading interest choices, and reading achievement. Unpublished doctoral dissertation, Ball State University, 1970.

STATTS, ARTHUR W.; MINKE, KARL A.; & BUTTS, PRISCILLA. A token-reinforcement remedial reading program administered by black therapy-technicians to problem black children. *Behavior Therapy*, August 1970, *1*, 331–353.

STANLEY, JULIAN C. (Ed.). *Preschool programs for the disadvantaged: five experienced approaches to early childhood education.* Baltimore: Johns Hopkins University Press, 1972.

STAUFFER, RUSSELL G. A study of prefixes in the Thorndike list to establish a list of prefixes that should be taught in the elementary school. *Journal of Educational Research*, 1942, *35*, 453–458.

STAUFFER, RUSSELL G. (Ed.). *The first grade reading studies: findings of individual investigations.* Newark, Del.: International Reading Association, 1967.

STAUFFER, RUSSELL G. *Directing reading maturity as a cognitive process.* New York: Harper & Row, 1969.

STAUFFER, RUSSELL G. *The language-experience approach to the teaching of reading.* New York: Harper & Row, 1970.

STAUFFER, RUSSELL G. & HAMMOND, W. DORSEY. The effectiveness of language arts and basic reader approaches to first-grade reading instruction—extended into third grade. *Reading Research Quarterly*, Summer 1969, *4*, 468–499.

STAVRIANOS, BERTHA K. A bit of ammunition for Wagner and some answers to Mordock's questions. *Journal of Projective Techniques & Personality Assessment*, 1970, *34*, 87.

STAVRIANOS, BERTHA K. & LANDSMAN, SYLVIA C. Personality patterns of deficient readers with perceptual-motor problems. *Psychology in the Schools*, 1969, *6*, 109–123.

STENSLAND, ANNA LEE. *An annotated bibliography of literature by and about the American Indian.* Champaign, Ill.: National Council of Teachers of English, 1973.

STEPHENS, W. E.; CUNNINGHAM, E.; & STIGLER, B. J. Reading readiness and eye hand preference pattern in first grade children. *Exceptional Children,* 1967, *33,* 481–488.

STEVENS, D. O. Reading difficulty and classroom acceptance. *The Reading Teacher,* October 1971, *25,* 52–55.

STICHT, THOMAS G.; CAYLOR, JOHN S.; KERN, RICHARD P.; & FOX, LYNN C. Project REALISTIC: determination of adult functional literacy skill levels. *Reading Research Quarterly,* Spring 1972, *7,* 424–465.

STODOLSKY, SUSAN S. & LESSER, GERALD S. Learning patterns in the disadvantaged. *Harvard Educational Review,* 1967, *37,* 546–547.

STONE, DAVID R. Speed of idea collecting. *Journal of Developmental Reading,* 1962, *5,* 149–156.

STOODT, BARBARA D. The relationship between understanding grammatical conjunctions and reading comprehension. *Elementary English,* April 1972, *49,* 502–505.

STOTT, D. H. Some less obvious cognitive aspects of learning to read. *The Reading Teacher,* January 1973, *26,* 374–383.

STRANG, RUTH. *Reading diagnosis and remediation* Newark, Del.: International Reading Association, 1968. (a)

STRANG, RUTH. Review of *Learning to read: the great debate. The Reading Teacher,* March 1968, *21,* 575–577. (b)

STRAUSS, ALFRED A. & LEHTINEN, LAURA E. *Psychopathology and education of the brain-injured child.* New York: Grune & Stratton, 1947.

STRICKLAND, DOROTHY S. A program for linguistically different, black children. *Research in the Teaching of English,* Spring 1973, *7,* 79–86. (a)

STRICKLAND, DOROTHY. The black experience in paperback (kindergarten through grade 6). In M. Jerry Weiss, Joseph Brunner, & Warren Heiss (Eds.), *New perspectives in paperbacks.* York, Pa.: Strine, 1973. Pp. 20–23. (b)

SUCHER, FLOYD. Use of basal readers in individualizing reading instruction. In J. Allen Figurel (Ed.), *Reading and realism.* Newark, Del.: International Reading Association, 1969. Pp. 136–143.

SUCHER, FLOYD & ALLRED, RUEL A. *Reading Placement Inventory.* Oklahoma City: Economy Co., 1973.

SWALM, J. E. A comparison of oral reading, silent reading, and listening comprehension. *Education,* 1972, *92,* 111–115.

SWANSON, WILLIAM L. Optometric vision therapy—how successful is it in the treatment of learning disorders? *Journal of Learning Disabilities,* May 1972, *5,* 285–290.

SYMMES, JEAN S. & RAPOPORT, JUDITH L. Unexpected reading failure. *American Journal of Orthopsychiatry,* January 1972, *42,* 82–91.

TANYZER, HAROLD & KARL, JEAN (Eds.). *Reading, children's books, and our pluralistic society.* Newark, Del.: International Reading Association, 1972.

TAYLOR, MARION W. & SCHNEIDER, MARY A. What books are our children reading? *Chicago Schools Journal,* 1957, *38,* 155–160.

TAYLOR, W. L. Cloze procedure: a new tool for measuring readability. *Journalism Quarterly,* 1953, *30,* 415–433.

TERMAN, LEWIS M. & LIMA, MARGARET. *Children's reading.* New York: Appleton-Century-Crofts, 1937.

THOM, E. Sensory integration and initial reading. Unpublished doctoral dissertation, University of Toronto, 1971.

THOMAS, HUGH B. G. Genetic and psychodynamic aspects of developmental dyslexia —a cybernetic approach. *Journal of Learning Disabilities*, January 1973, *6*, 30–40.

THOMPSON, LLOYD J. *Reading disability: developmental dyslexia.* Springfield, Ill.: Charles C Thomas, 1966.

THOMPSON, LLOYD J. Mental retardation and dyslexia. *Academic Therapy*, Summer 1971, *6*, 405–406.

THOMPSON, RICHARD A. *Energizers for reading instruction.* West Nyack, N.Y.: Parker, 1973.

THOMPSON, RICHARD A. & DZIUBEN, CHARLES D. Criterion-referenced reading tests in perspective. *The Reading Teacher*, December 1973, *27*, 292–294.

THORNDIKE, EDWARD L. Reading as reasoning: a study of mistakes in paragraph meaning. *Journal of Educational Psychology*. June 1917, *8*, 323–332. Reprinted in *Reading Research Quarterly*, Summer 1971, *6*, 425–434.

THORNDIKE, EDWARD L. *The teacher's word book.* New York: Bureau of Publications, Teachers College, Columbia University, 1921.

THORNDIKE, EDWARD L. The vocabulary of books for children in grades 3 to 8. *Teachers College Record*, 1936–37, *38*, I, 196–205; II, 316–323; III, 416–429.

THORNDIKE, EDWARD L. & LORGE, IRVING. *The teacher's word book of 30,000 words.* New York: Teachers College Press, Columbia University, 1944.

THORNDIKE, ROBERT L. *Children's reading interests.* New York: Teachers College Press, Columbia University, 1941.

THORNDIKE, ROBERT L. *The concepts of over- and underachievement.* New York: Teachers College Press, Columbia University, 1963.

THORNDIKE, ROBERT L. Dilemmas in diagnosis. In W. H. MacGinitie (Ed.), *Assessment problems in reading.* Newark, Del.: International Reading Association, 1973, Pp. 57–67.

THORNLEY, GWENDELLA. Storytelling is fairy gold. *Elementary English,* January 1968, *45*, 67–79.

TIMKO, HENRY G. Configuration as a cue in the word recognition of beginning readers. *Journal of Experimental Education*, Winter 1970, *39*, 68–69.

TINKER, MILES A. Speed versus comprehension in reading as affected by level of difficulty. *Journal of Educational Psychology*, 1939, *30*, 81–94.

TINKER, MILES A. The study of eye movements in reading. *Psychological Bulletin*, 1946, *43*, 93–120.

TINKER, MILES A. Recent studies of eye movements in reading. *Psychological Bulletin*, 1958, *55*, 4.

TINKER, MILES A. *Bases for effective reading.* Minneapolis: University of Minnesota Press, 1965.

TIZARD, J., et al. (Advisory Committee on Handicapped Children). *Children with Specific Reading Difficulties.* London, England: HMSO., Secretary of State for Education and Science, February 8, 1972.

TOVEY, DUANE R. Relationship of matched first grade phonics instruction to overall reading achievement and the desire to read. In Robert C. Aukerman (Ed.), *Some persistent questions on beginning reading.* Newark, Del.: International Reading Association, 1972. Pp. 93–101.

TUINMAN, J. JAAP. Inspection of passages as a function of passage-dependency of the test items. *Journal of Reading Behavior*, Summer 1973, *5*, 186–191.

TURAIDS, DAINIS; WEPMAN, JOSEPH M.; & MORENCY, ANNE. A perceptual test battery: development and standardization. *Elementary School Journal*, April 1972, *72*, 351–361.

TWELKER, PAUL A.; URBACH, FLOYD D.; & BUCK, JAMES D. *The systematic development of instruction: an overview and basic guide to the literature.* Stanford, Calif.: ERIC Clearinghouse on Media and Technology, March 1972.

TYMCHUK, ALEXANDER J.; KNIGHTS, ROBERT M.; & HINTON, GEORGE G. The behavioral significance of differing EEG abnormalities in children with learning and/or behavior problems. *Journal of Learning Disabilities,* November 1970, *3,* 548–551.

UHL, WILLIS L. The use of the results of reading tests as bases for planning remedial work. *Elementary School Journal,* 1916, *17,* 266–275.

VALMONT, WILLIAM J. Creating questions for informal reading inventories. *The Reading Teacher,* March 1972, *25,* 509–512.

VANDAMENT, WILLIAM E. & THALMAN, W. A. An investigation into the reading interests of children. *Journal of Educational Research,* 1956, *49,* 467–470.

VANDEVER, THOMAS R. & NEVILLE, DONALD D. The effectiveness of tracing for good and poor decoders. *Journal of Reading Behavior,* Spring 1972–1973, *5,* 119–125.

VAN DE VOORT, LEWIS; SENF, GERALD M.; & BENTON, ARTHUR L. Development of audiovisual integration in normal and retarded readers. *Child Development,* December 1972, *43,* 1260–1272.

VEATCH, JEANNETTE. Individual reading guidance: fifth grade. In Alice Miel (Ed.), *Individualizing reading practices.* Practical suggestions for teaching, No. 14. New York: Teachers College, Columbia University, 1958. Pp. 55–63.

VEATCH, JEANNETTE, *et al. Key words to reading: the language experience approach begins.* Columbus, Ohio: Charles E. Merrill, 1973.

VELLUTINO, FRANK R.; STEGER, JOSEPH A.; & KANDEL, GILLARY. Reading disability: An investigation of the perceptual deficit hypothesis. *Cortex,* March 1972, *8,* 106–118.

VENEZKY, RICHARD L. Nonstandard language and reading. *Elementary English,* March 1970, *47,* 334–345.

VENEZKY, RICHARD L. & CALFEE, ROBERT C. The reading competency model. In H. Singer & R. B. Ruddell (Eds.), *Theoretical models and processes of reading.* Newark, Del.: International Reading Association, 1970. Pp. 273–291.

VERNON, M. D. *Backwardness in reading: a study of its nature and origin.* Cambridge, England: Cambridge University Press, 1957, 1960.

VERNON, M. D. *Reading and its difficulties: a psychological study.* Cambridge: Cambridge University Press, 1971.

VERNON, PHILIP E. Ability factors and environment. *American Psychologist,* 1965, *20,* 723–733.

VILSCEK, ELAINE C. & CLELAND, DONALD L. *Two approaches to reading instruction.* Final Report, Project No. 3195. Pittsburgh: University of Pittsburgh, 1968.

VON GLASERFELD, ERNST. The problem of syntactic complexity in reading and readability. *Journal of Reading Behavior,* Spring 1970–71, *3,* 1-14.

VORHAUS, PAULINE G. Rorschach configurations associated with reading disability. *Journal of Projective Techniques,* 1952, *16,* 3–19.

VYGOTSKY, L. S. *Thought and language.* Cambridge, Mass.: MIT Press, 1962.

WAGNER, GUY & HOSIER, MAX. *Strengthening reading skills with educational games.* Riverside, N.J.: Teachers Publishing, 1970.

WAGNER, GUY; HOSIER, MAX; & CESINGER, JOAN. *Word power games.* Riverside, N.J.: Teachers Publishing, 1972.

WAGNER, RUDOLPH F. Specific reading disabilities: the incompatibility of two systems. *Journal of Learning Disabilities*, May 1971, *4*, 260–263.

WALKER, L. & COLE, E. M. Familial patterns of expression of specific reading disability in a population sample. Part I: prevalence, distribution and persistence. *Bulletin of the Orton Society*, 1965, *15*, 12–24.

WANAT, STANLEY. *Graduate programs and faculty in reading*. Newark, Del.: International Reading Association, 1973.

WANAT, STANLEY & LEVIN, HARRY. Linguistic constraints in reader processing strategies. Paper delivered at the Eastern Psychological Association, 1970.

WAPNER, IRWIN. The i/t/a in Lompoc: a longitudinal study. Paper presented at I.R.A. Convention, May 2, 1969. ED 031 387.

WARBURTON, F. W. & SOUTHGATE, VERA. *ITA: an independent evaluation*. London, England: Murray and Chambers, 1969.

WARD, J. The factor structure of the Frostig Developmental Test of Visual Perception. *British Journal of Educational Psychology*, 1970, *40*, 65–67.

WARDHAUGH, RONALD. Is the linguistic approach an improvement in reading instruction? In Nila B. Smith (Ed.), *Current issues in reading*. Newark, Del.: International Reading Association, 1969. Pp. 254–267.

WATTERS, ELISABETH. Reading in a family-grouped primary school. In Helen K. Smith (Ed.), *Meeting individual needs in reading*. Newark, Del.: International Reading Association, 1971. Pp. 29–35.

WAUGH, R. P. Relationship between modality preference and performance. *Exceptional Children*, March 1973, *39*, 465–469.

WEAVER, WENDELL W. & KINGSTON, ALBERT J. Modeling the effects of oral language. *Reading Research Quarterly*, Summer 1972, *7*, 613–627.

WEBER, ROSE-MARIE. The study of oral reading errors: a review of the literature. *Reading Research Quarterly*, Fall 1968, *4*, 96–119.

WEBER, ROSE-MARIE. Some reservations on the significance of dialect in the acquisition of reading. In J. Allen Figurel (Ed.), *Reading goals for the disadvantaged*. Newark, Del.: International Reading Association, 1970. Pp. 124–131.

WEBER, ROSEMARY. Bibliography. In Harold Tanyzer and Jean Karl (Eds.), *Reading, children's books, and our pluralistic society*. Newark, Del.: International Reading Association, 1972. Pp. 81–89.

WECHSLER, DAVID. *The measurement of adult intelligence* (3rd.). Baltimore: Williams & Wilkins, 1944.

WEINSCHENK, CURT, et al. Uber die Haufigkeit der kongenitalen Legasthenie im zweiten Grundschuljahr: II. (On the frequency of dyslexia encountered in the second school year: II). *Psychologische Rundschau*, 1970, *21*, 44–51.

WEINTRAUB, SAMUEL. Research: eye-hand preference and reading. *The Reading Teacher*, January 1968, *21*, 369-373, 401.

WERNER, HEINZ & STRAUSS, ALFRED A. Problems and methods of functional analysis in mentally deficient children. *Journal of Abnormal and Social Psychology*, 1939, *34*, 37–62.

WHIPPLE, GERTRUDE. Characteristics of a sound reading program. In Nelson B. Henry (Ed.), *Reading in the elementary school*. 48th Yearbook of the National Society for the Study of Education, Part II, 1949. Pp. 34–48.

WHIPPLE, GERTRUDE. Appraisal of the interest appeal of illustrations. *Elementary School Journal*, 1953, *53*, 262–269.

WHITCRAFT, CAROL J. Approaching cooperative research in learning disabilities through psycholinguistics. *Journal of Learning Disabilities*, December 1971, *4*, 568–571.

WHITE, JEFFREY & WHITE, MARGARET. Perceptual and psycholinguistic factors in retarded and advanced levels of reading and spelling skills. *Slow Learning Child: The Australian Journal on the Education of Backward Children,* July 1972, *19,* 117–123.

WHITSELL, LEON J. Delacato's "Neurological Organization": A medical appraisal. *California School Health,* Fall 1967, 3, 1–13.

WHITSELL, LEON J.; BUCKMAN, WILMA; & WHITSELL, ALICE J. Jimmy. In Albert J. Harris (Ed.), *Casebook on reading disability.* New York: David McKay, 1970. Pp. 263–288.

WIEDERHOLT, J. LEE & HAMMILL, DONALD D. Use of the Frostig-Horne visual perception program in the urban school. *Psychology in the Schools,* July 1971, 8, 268–274.

WIENER, MORTON & CROMER, WARD. Reading and reading difficulty: a conceptual analysis. *Harvard Educational Review,* Fall 1967, 37, 620–643.

WILLIAMS, JOANNA P. Learning to read: a review of theories and models. *Reading Research Quarterly,* Winter 1973, 8, 121–146.

WILLIAMS, JOANNA P.; BLUMBERG, ELLEN L.; & WILLIAMS, DAVID V. Cues used in visual word recognition. *Journal of Educational Psychology,* 1970, *61,* 310–315.

WILLIAMS, ROBERT T. A table for the rapid determination of revised Dale-Chall readability scores. *The Reading Teacher,* November 1972, *26,* 158–165.

WILLIS, DONALD C. The effect of self-hypnosis on reading rate and comprehension. *American Journal of Clinical Hypnosis,* April 1972, *14,* 249–255.

WILLIS, PERRY W.; MORRIS, BETTY; & CROWDER, JEANE. A remedial reading technique for disabled readers that employs students. *Psychology in the Schools,* January 1972, 9, 67–70.

WILSON, ROBERT M. *Diagnostic and remedial reading for classroom and clinic* (2nd ed.). Columbus: Charles E. Merrill, 1972.

WILSON, THURLOW R. & FLUGMAN, BERT. Management of a class of disruptive students by behavior modification techniques: an exploratory study. Research Report No. 68–10. New York: Office of Research and Evaluation, Division of Teacher Education, City University of New York, January 1969.

WINKLEY, CAROL K. Building staff competence in identifying underachievers. In H. Alan Robinson (Ed.), *The underachiever in reading.* University of Chicago, Supplementary Educational Monograph No. 92, 1962. Pp. 155–62.

WISEMAN, DOUGLAS E. Remedial education: global or learning-disability approach? *Academic Therapy,* Spring 1970, 5, 165–175.

WITHAM, ANTHONY P. An investigation of a controlled reading technique with eighth grade students. Unpublished doctoral dissertation, Wayne State University, 1966.

WITTY, PAUL A. Studies of the mass media—1949–65. *Science Education,* 1966, 50, 119–126.

WITTY, PAUL A. & MELIS, LLOYD. A 1964 study of TV: comparisons and comments. *Elementary English,* February 1965, 42, 134–141.

WOLD, ROBERT M. (Ed.). *Visual and perceptual aspects for the achieving and underachieving child:* Seattle: Special Child Publications, 1969.

WOLF, WILLAVENE; KING, MARTHA L.; & HUCK, CHARLOTTE S. Teaching critical reading to elementary school children. *Reading Research Quarterly,* Summer, 1968, 3, 435–498.

WOODCOCK, RICHARD W. *The Peabody-Chicago-Detroit reading project—a report of the second-year results.* Paper presented at the 4th International i.t.a Conference, Montreal. August 11, 1967.

WOODWORTH, ROBERT S. *Psychology* (rev. ed.). New York: Holt, 1929. Pp. 103–104.

WORLEY, STINSON E. Developmental task situation in stories. *The Reading Teacher*, November 1967, *21*, 145–148.

WRIGHT, LANCE & MCKENZIE, CLANCY. "Talking" group therapy for learning-disabled children. *The Reading Teacher*, January 1970, *23*, 339–346, 385.

WU, JULIA T. A multiple group setting for ability-grouped reading. *Academic Therapy*, Summer 1971, *6*, 355–358.

YARBOROUGH, BETTY H. A study of the effectiveness of the Leavell language-development service in improving the silent reading ability and other language skills of persons with mixed dominance. Unpublished doctoral dissertation, University of Virginia, 1964.

YARBOROUGH, RALPH W. The learning disabilities act of 1969: a commentary. *Journal of Learning Disabilities*, September 1969, *2*, 437–440.

YARINGTON, DAVID J. & BOFFEY, BARNES. Report on a performance curriculum for teacher training. *Journal of Reading*, November 1971, *15*, 115–118.

YNGVE, V. H. Computer programs for translation. *Scientific American*, 1962, *206*, 68–76.

YOAKMAN, GERALD A. *Basal reading instruction.* New York: McGraw-Hill, 1955.

ZAESKE, ARNOLD. The validity of Predictive Index Tests in predicting reading failure at the end of grade one. In William K. Durr (Ed.), *Reading difficulties: diagnosis, correction, and remediation.* Newark, Del.: International Reading Association, 1970, Pp. 28–33.

ZANGWILL, O. L. Dyslexia in relation to cerebral dominance. In John Money (Ed.), *Reading disability: progress and research needs in dyslexia.* Baltimore: Johns Hopkins Press, 1962. Pp. 103–114.

ZEMAN, SAMUEL S. A summary of research concerning laterality and reading. *Journal of the Reading Specialist*, 1967, *6*, 116–123.

ZURIF, E. B. & CARSON, G. Dyslexia in relation to cerebral dominance and temporal analysis. *Neuropsychologia*, 1970, *8*, 351–361.

Appendix A

AN ALPHABETICAL LIST OF TESTS

Pertinent information is given in the list below concerning the tests that have been mentioned earlier in this book. In addition, a few recent tests of interest to reading specialists have been included, although not mentioned earlier. All tests, regardless of type, have been arranged in a single alphabetical order for easy reference. When forms are not mentioned, the test has only one form. Information is based on the publishers' catalogues available when this list was compiled. Many older tests are no longer in print and have been deleted; many new tests and revisions have been added. Since revisions, new forms, new manuals, and so on are issued from time to time, before ordering any test it is desirable to write to the publisher for the current catalogue.

The listings below are very brief and are not evaluative. For detailed descriptions and critical evaluations of reading tests the most useful source is *Reading Tests and Reveiws*, edited by O. K. Buros, Gryphon Press, 1968. This volume includes all the reviews of reading tests that had appeared in the first six *Mental Measurements Yearbooks*. Detailed descriptions and evaluations of psychological tests may be found in those yearbooks and the *Seventh Mental Measurements Yearbook* also published by Gryphon Press. Those interested in learning about currently available tests may wish to subscribe to: The Test Collection Bulletin, Educational Testing Service, Princeton, N.J. 08540. The ERIC Clearinghouse on Tests, Measurements, and Evaluation is also located at ETS.

Before deciding which test to use, it is advisable to make a tentative selection of a few tests that might be suitable and to order a specimen set of each for careful study. For large-scale testing programs it is also desirable to consider the practicality and cost of hand-scoring, use of special answer sheets, and use of the various test-scoring services that are now available.

The names of publishers are abbreviated to save space. Full names and addresses of the publishers are given in Appendix C.

Academic Promise Tests. A scholastic aptitude battery for grades 6–9, with separate tests of verbal, numerical, abstract reasoning, and language usage abilities; gives verbal, nonverbal, and total scores. PSCHOLOGICAL.

Adult Basic Learning Examination (ABLE). *Level I,* grade scores 1.6–6.0; *Level II,* grade scores 3.0–9.0; *Level III,* grades 9–12. Measures adult achievement in basic learning. Contains vocabulary (no reading required) and reading comprehension subtests as well as spelling, arithmetic computation and problem solving. Forms A, B, each level. HARCOURT.

American School Achievement Tests
  Primary I Battery, grade 1, word recogniiton, word meaning, numbers.
  Primary II Reading, grades 2–3, sentence, word, and paragraph meaning.
  Intermediate Reading, grades 4–6, vocabulary, sentence, and paragraph meaning.
  Advanced Reading, grades 7–9, vocabulary, sentence, and paragraph meaning. BOBBS

American School Reading Readiness Test, Revised Edition, Form X. Kindergarten, beginning grade 1. Group administration. Separate norms for those who have and have not attended kindergarten. BOBBS

Ammons Full-Range Picture Vocabulary Test. Preschool to adult. An individually administered test of verbal intelligence in which answer is given by pointing to one of four pictures. Forms A, B. PSYCHOLOGICAL TEST

Analysis of Learning Potential (ALP). *Primary I,* grade 1; *Primary II,* grades 2–3; *Elementary,* grades 4–6; *Advanced I,* grades 7–9; *Advanced II,* grades 10–12. Measure of scholastic aptitude for predicting academic success. Cluster of subtests may be used in predicting school success in reading. HARCOURT

Arthur Point Scale of Performance Tests, Revised Form II. Ages 5–15. An individually administered scale of nonlanguage tests to be used only by trained psychologists. PSYCHOLOGICAL

Aston Index. A battery of tests designed as an early predictor of possible "at risk" children who have a predisposition to dyslexia-type language difficulties. Verbal and perceptual tasks and family history included. ASTON

Auditory Analysis Test. Experimental test which requires the ability to listen to a word, mentally subtract either an initial or final phoneme, and pronounce what is left. *See* Rosner and Simon, 1971.

Auditory Sequential Memory Test. Ages 5–8. Brief test of ability to repeat from immediate memory an increasing series of digits. Forms I, II. WESTERN

Basic Reading Inventory (BRI). Group test for adults who may be functionally illiterate. Contains subtests: sight words, sound and letter discrimination, word meaning (reading), word meaning (listening), and context reading (comprehension). SCHOLASTIC TESTING

Beery-Buktenica Developmental Test of Visual-Motor Integration. Ages 2–15. Measures integration of visual perception and motor behavior by having subjects draw geometric forms. Short and long forms. FOLLETT

Bender Visual Motor Gestalt Test. A clinical test of ability to copy visual designs. PSYCHOLOGICAL

Benton Visual Retention Test, Revised. An individual test of ability to draw designs from memory. PSYCHOLOGICAL

Botel Reading Inventory. Grades 1–12. A group of tests for determining reading instructional levels. Includes tests of phonics, word recognition, word opposites reading, and word opposites listening; mainly group-administered. FOLLETT

Brown-Carlsen Listening Comprehension Test. Grades 9–13. A group test of ability to comprehend spoken English language. HARCOURT

California Phonics Survey. Grades 7 to college. A group test with eight subtests of aspects of phonic knowledge. CALIFORNIA

California Reading Tests, 1970 Edition. *Level 1*, grades 1–2; *Level 2*, grades 2–4; *Level 3*, grades 4–6; *Level 4*, grades 6–9; *Level 5*, grades 9–12. Each level has vocabulary and comprehension subtests. Levels 1 and 2 also have word-attack subtests. Two forms at each level. Also included in the *California Achievement Test* batteries. CALIFORNIA

California Short-Form Test of Mental Maturity, 1963 Revision. Eight levels, kindergarten to college. A group test of intelligence providing separate language and nonlanguage MA's and IQ's as well as total. CALIFORNIA

California Test of Mental Maturity Long Form, 1963 Revision. *Level 0*, kindergarten to grade 1; *Level 1*, grades 1–3; *Level 2*, grades 4–8; *Level 3*, grades 7–9; *Level 4*, grades 9–12; *Level 5*, grade 12 to college. An analytical group intelligence test. Reading and nonreading items are used for testing memory, attention, spatial relationships, reasoning, and vocabulary. Provides separate MA's and IQ's for language (reading), nonlanguage (no reading), and total scores. CALIFORNIA

California Test of Personality. *Primary*, kindergarten to grade 3; *Elementary*, grades 4–8; *Intermediate*, grades 7–10; *Secondary*, grades 9 to college. An analytical group personality questionnaire providing scores on self-adjustment and social adjustment. CALIFORNIA

Carver-Darby Chunked Reading Test, 1972 Revision. High school to adult. The chunked test consists of the same passage (first read as a whole by the student) retyped in 100 chunks (groups of meaningfully related words within a sentence). Within each set of 5 chunks, one has been changed in meaning from the original passage. Yields scores in efficiency, accuracy, and rate. Forms A, B. REVRAC

Cattell Culture Fair Intelligence Tests. Ages 4 to adult. Group tests of general intelligence not requiring any reading and relatively free from educational and cultural influences. *Scale 1*, ages 4–8, one form; *Scale 2*, ages 8–14 and average adults, Forms A, B; *Scale 3*, ages 14 to college and superior adult, Forms A, B. IPAT

Chicago Non-Verbal Examination. Age 6 to adult. A nonverbal group intelligence test requiring no reading; can be given in pantomime to the deaf and non-English speaking. PSYCHOLOGICAL

Children's Apperception Test. Ages 4–10. An individually administered projective test of personality, to be used only by trained psychologists. PSYCHOLOGICAL

Classroom Reading Inventory, 2nd Edition. Grades 2–10. Individually administered test, scored like an informal reading inventory. Consists of: graded word list, graded oral paragraphs, and graded spelling list. WM. C. BROWN

Clymer-Barrett Prereading Battery. Reading readiness test that samples visual discrimination, auditory discrimination, and visual-motor skills. Forms A, B. PERSONNEL

Cognitive Abilities Test.
  Primary I, K–1; *Primary II*, grades 2–3. Group nonreading intelligence test (academic aptitude) using pictorial materials and oral instructions.
  Multi-Level Edition, levels A–H, grades 3–12. Separate batteries: verbal, quantitative, and nonverbal. Also available in one edition. HOUGHTON

Comprehensive Test of Basic Skills, Expanded Edition, Form S. A series of achievement test batteries: *Level A*, K–1, prereading score comprised of 7 tests; *Level B*, Grade 1, word recognition, letter sounds, and reading comprehension; *Level C*, grade 2, vocabulary, sentence comprehension, paragraph comprehension; *Level 1*, grades 2.5–4; *Level 2*, grades 4–6; *Level 3*, grades 6–8; *Level 4*, grades 8-12. Reading vocabulary, reading comprehension, reference skills for Levels 1–4. CALIFORNIA

Cooper-McGuire Diagnostic Word-Analysis Test. Group criterion-referenced tests with subtests in each of 3 sections: readiness for word-analysis, phonic analysis, and structural analysis. CROFT

Cooperative English Tests: Reading Comprehension. Forms 1A, B, C, for grades 12–14; Forms 2A, B, C, for grades 9–12. Provides scores for level of comprehension, rate of comprehension, and vocabulary. ETS

Cooperative Primary Tests. Achievement test batteries for grades 1–2 and 2–3: forms A, B, at each level. Includes a pilot test to give practice in test taking; and tests of listening, word analysis, mathematics, reading, and writing skills. ETS

D.A.T. Verbal Reasoning, Numerical Ability, and Abstract Reasoning Tests. Grades 8–12. These three elements of the Differential Aptitude Tests provide the equivalent of an intelligence or scholastic aptitude measure; only the verbal reasoning test requires any reading. Forms L, M, S, T. PSYCHOLOGICAL

Davis Reading Test. *Series 2*, grades 8–11; *Series 1*, grades 11–13, forms A, B, C, D, each series. Provides two scores, level of comprehension and rate of comprehension. PSYCHOLOGICAL

Detroit Tests of Learning Aptitude. Ages 3 to adult. An individual intelligence test battery containing nineteen subtests, each with separate mental age norms, allowing a flexible choice of tests for diagnostic purposes. BOBBS

Developmental Reading Tests. *See* **New Developmental Reading Tests.**

Diagnosis: an Instructional Aid–Reading. Grades 1–6. Series of criterion-referenced tests (probes) covering a wide range of reading skills. SRA

Diagnostic Reading Tests. A series of survey and diagnostic tests from grade 1 to college.
> *Kindergarten–grade 4.* Reading readiness; Survey section, Booklet I, grade 1; Booklet II, grade 2; Booklet III, grades 3, 4; Section V, Word Attack, Part 1, Oral.
> *Lower Level*, grades 4–8. Booklet I, comprehension and word recognition; Booklet II, vocabulary and rate; Section IV, word attack, oral, for individual administration, silent. Forms A, B, C, D each booklet.
> *Higher Level*, grades 7 to college. Includes a Survey Test of vocabulary, comprehension, and rate, with seven forms, A to H; and a Diagnostic Battery with eight separate booklets: vocabulary, silent comprehension, auditory comprehension, general rate, rate in social studies, rate in science, oral word attack (individual), and silent word attack; forms A, B, each part. COMMITTEE

D-K Scale of Lateral Dominance. A 36-item scale covering handedness, footedness, eyedness, and ear dominance. FOUNDATION

Dolch Basic Sight Word Test. The 220 words of the Dolch Basic Sight Words List arranged on one sheet of paper for testing. GARRARD

Doren Diagnostic Reading Test, 1973 Edition. Grades 2–8. A group test for detailed testing of word-attack skills. Beginning sounds, sight words, rhyming, whole-word recognition, words within words, speech consonants, blending, vowels, ending sounds, discriminate guessing, letter recognition, and spelling. AMERICAN GUIDANCE

Durkin-Meshover Phonics Knowledge Survey. Any grade. Individually administered test of knowledge of phonics, with sixteen subtests. TEACHERS

Durrell Analysis of Reading Difficulty: New Edition. Grades 1–6. A battery of diagnostic tests for intensive analysis of reading difficulties. Includes a set of reading paragraphs, a cardboard tachistoscope, word lists, and a record blank. Provides tests of oral and silent reading, listening comprehension, word analysis, phonics, faulty pronunciation, writing, and spelling. HARCOURT

Durrell Reading-Listening Series. *Primary*, grades 1–2; *Intermediate*, grades 3–6; *Advanced*, grades 7–9. Group tests of listening (vocabulary and sentences) and reading (vocabulary and sentences) standardized on the same population. Replaces the *Durrell-Sullivan Reading Capacity and Achievement Tests*. Forms DE, EF. HARCOURT

Dyslexia Schedule. A school-entrance questionnaire to be completed by parents. Elicits information about children who have been referred because of reading disability. EDUCATORS

EDL Reading Eye, II. A portable eye-movement camera. Accessories include sixty-four reading test selections, grade 1 to adult. EDL

EDL Reading Versatility Tests, Revised. *Basic*, grades 5–8; *Intermediate*, grades 8–12; *Advanced*, college. Covers reading of fiction, nonfiction, skimming, and scanning. Four equated forms at each level. EDL

First Grade Screening Test. A group test for detecting potential learning difficulties. Includes items on social and emotional adjustment as well as intellectual and perceptual abilities. AMERICAN GUIDANCE

Fountain Valley Reading Skills Tests. Grades 1–6. Series of 77 one-page criterion-referenced tests covering 277 behavioral objectives. Skill areas sampled are: phonic analysis, structural analysis, vocabulary, comprehension and study skills. ZWEIG

Frostig Developmental Test of Visual Perception. Ages 4–9. Includes group tests of five aspects of visual perception. FOLLETT

Gates-MacGinitie Readiness Skills Test. Beginning first grade. Listening comprehension auditory discrimination, visual discrimination, following directions, letter recognition, visual-motor co-ordination, auditory blending. A word recognition test is also included to detect early readers. TEACHERS

Gates-MacGinitie Reading Tests. *Primary A*, grade 1; *Primary B*, grade 2; *Primary C*, grade 3; each contains two parts, vocabulary and comprehension; forms 1, 2, each level. *Primary CS*, speed and accuracy for grades 2, 3; forms 1, 2, 3. *Survey D*, grades 4–6; *Survey E*, grades 7–9; *Survey F*, grades 10–12; each contains subtests of vocabulary, comprehension, and speed and accuracy. *Survey D, E*, Forms 1, 2, 3; *Survey F*, Forms 1, 2. TEACHERS

Gates-McKillop Reading Diagnostic Test. Battery of tests for individual diagnosis of disabled readers from nonreader up. Paragraphs for oral reading; word perception, flashed and untimed; phrase perception; syllabication, letter names and sounds, visual and auditory blending, spelling. Forms 1, 2. TEACHERS

Gillingham-Childs Phonics Proficiency Scales. Individual tests of letter-sound correspondences, reading and spelling of real and nonsense words, consonant clusters, vowels, syllable divisions, and so on. EDUCATORS

Gilmore Oral Reading Test, New Edition. Grades 1–8. An individual test of oral reading. Ten reading paragraphs of increasing difficulty, separate record booklet; scored for accuracy, comprehension, and rate. Forms C, D. Older forms A, B also available. HARCOURT

Goldman-Fristoe-Woodcock Test of Auditory Discrimination. Age 4 to adult.

Individual test of ability to discriminate speech-sounds in quiet and in noise. Subject responds to word on tape by pointing to one of four pictures. AMERICAN GUIDANCE

Goodenough-Harris Drawing Test. Ages 3–15. Provides an objective method for scoring children's drawings of the human figure as a measure of non-verbal intelligence. HARCOURT

Gray Oral Reading Tests. Grades 1–12. An individually administered oral reading test with thirteen graded reading passages in each form, separate record booklets; accuracy and rate combined in a composite score. Separate norms for boys and girls. Forms A, B, C, D. BOBBS

Gray Standardized Oral Reading Paragraphs. Grades 1–8. An oral reading test containing twelve graded paragraphs; accuracy and rate combined in one score. BOBBS

Harris Tests of Lateral Dominance, Third Edition. Ages 6 to adult. A set of brief tests of hand, eye, and foot dominance. PSYCHOLOGICAL

Harrison-Stroud Reading Readiness Profiles. A readiness test with five subtests: using symbols, visual discrimination, using context, auditory discrimination, using context and auditory clues; also letter names. HOUGHTON

Henmon-Nelson Primary Battery. Grades K-2. Group intelligence test consisting of 3 subtests: listening, picture vocabulary, and size and number. No reading required. HOUGHTON

Henmon-Nelson Tests of Mental Ability, 1973 Revision. Levels for grades 3–6, 6–9, 9–12. A self-marking group intelligence test that requires reading. HOUGHTON

Illinois Tests of Psycholinguistic Abilities, Revised Edition. Ages 2–10. Twelve individually administered subtests measuring abilities basic in communication. ILLINOIS

Individual Pupil Monitoring System—Reading. Grades 1–6. System of criterion-referenced tests based on stated behavioral objectives in the areas of discrimination, decoding, comprehension, and study skills. HOUGHTON

Instant Word Recognition Test. Self-scoring group test of Fry 600 instant words which covers reading levels grades 1–4. DREIER

Iowa Silent Reading Test—ISRT, 1973 Edition. *Level 1*, grades 6–9; *Level 2*, grades 9–14; *Level 3*, academically accelerated high school and college students. Levels 1 and 2 include subtests of: vocabulary, reading comprehension, directed reading (study skills), and reading efficiency (speed and accuracy). Level 3 does not include a directed reading section. Forms E, F, each level. HARCOURT

Iowa Tests of Basic Skills
  Primary Battery: *Level 7*, grades 1.7–2.5; *Level 8*, 2.6–3.5. Both Standard and Basic Editions contain: Test R, reading comprehension; Test WA, word analysis; and V, vocabulary. Test W, work-study skills only in Standard Edition. Forms 5, 6.
  Levels Edition: *Levels 9–14*, grades 3–8. Tests for all grades in one reusable booklet. Test V, vocabulary; Test R, reading comprehension; Test W, work-study skills. Forms 5, 6. HOUGHTON

Iowa Tests of Educational Development (ITED), 1971 Edition. Grades 9–12. Subtests: reading, language arts, mathematics, social studies, science, and use of sources. Reading score based on vocabulary and comprehension of social studies, science, and literature material. Forms X5, Y5. SRA

Keystone Tests of Binocular Skill. An adaptation of the *Gray Standardized Oral Check Tests* for use with the Keystone Telebinocular. Equivalent oral reading selections are read with each eye separately and with binocular vision. KEYSTONE

Keystone Vision Screening Test Set. Grade 1 and up. Includes a Telebinocular (stereoscopic instrument) and fifteen stereographs providing measures of near and far acuity, muscle balance, depth perception, and fusion; also color vision. Shorter screening tests also available. KEYSTONE

Kindergarten Behavioural Index: A Screening Technique for Reading Readiness, K–grade 1. Rating scale designed to aid in identifying children with potential learning difficulties. AUSTRALIAN COUNCIL. *See* page 36 for a copy of this Index.

Kindergarten Evaluation of Learning Potential: KELP. A teaching program mainly for disadvantaged children, including provisions for evaluation of readiness by the teacher. WEBSTER

Kuhlmann-Anderson Measure of Academic Potential, Seventh Edition. Eight levels one for each grade kindergarten to grade 2, one each for grades 3–4, 4–5, 5–7, 7–9 and 9–13. A group test of general intelligence. Yields verbal, quantitative and total scores. Content below fifth grade is largely nonreading. PSYCHOLOGICAL

Kuhlmann-Finch Scholastic Aptitude Tests. Tests I-VI for grades 1–6, junior high school test, senior high school test. Group intelligence tests, completely nonverbal in lowest two levels, and largely nonverbal in upper levels. AMERICAN GUIDANCE

Leavell Language-Development Program. No age limits. The Hand-Eye Coordinator consists of a slanted surface to which are mounted steroscopic lenses and clips for holding stereoscopic materials which are traced or copied. KEYSTONE

Lee-Clark Reading Readiness Test, 1962 Revision. Kindergarten to beginning grade 1. Contains four tests of visual discrimination of letter symbols, word shapes, and concepts. CALIFORNIA

Let's Look at Children. Materials designed for use in both teaching and assessing the readiness of first-grade children, particularly the disadvantaged. ETS

Lincoln Diagnostic Spelling Tests. *Intermediate*, Grades 5–8; *Advanced*, grades 8–12. Designed to disclose causes or areas of difficulty; pronunciation, enunciation, and use of rules. BOBBS

Lincoln-Oseretsky Motor Development Scale. Ages 6–14. Individually administered test involving a wide variety of motor skills. Unilateral and bilateral motor tasks. STOELTING

A Look at Literature. Grades 4–6. Test of critical reading and appreciation of prose and poetry. Questions focus on: perception of literary qualities and devices, comprehension of meaning, and extension and application of meaning. ETS

Lorge-Thorndike Intelligence Tests, Multi-Level Edition. Grades 3–13. Materials for all grades in a single reusable booklet which contains eight levels of difficulty. Provides verbal, nonverbal, and total scores. A separate level edition is also available. Forms 1, 2. HOUGHTON

Macmillan Reader Placement Test, Revised Edition. Grades 1–6. Individual test containing graded book samples and word lists. MACMILLAN

Macmillan Reading Readiness Test, Revised Edition. End of kindergarten, beginning grade 1. Subtests include a quantified rating scale, visual discrimination, auditory discrimination, vocabulary and concepts, letter names, and visual-motor skills. MACMILLAN

McCullough Word-Analysis Test. Grades 4–6. Group test comprised of seven subtests: initial blends and digraphs, phonetic discrimination (vowels), matching letters to vowel sounds, sounding whole words, interpreting phonetic symbols, dividing words into symbols, root words in affixed forms. PERSONNEL

McGraw-Hill Basic Skills System. Grades 11 to 14. *Reading Test* measures reading rate and comprehension, skimming and scanning, and paragraph comprehension. *Vocabulary Test* samples knowledge of subject-matter words and word parts. *Study Skills Test* measures problem solving ability, underlining techniques, use of the library, and study skills information. CALIFORNIA

Meeting Street School Screening Test. K and grade 1. Individually administered readiness test of gross-motor, visual-perceptual-motor, and language skills. Also includes behavior rating scale. MEETING STREET SCHOOL

Metropolitan Readiness Tests, 1965 Revision. Beginning grade 1. Word meaning, listening, matching, alphabet, numbers, and copying. Forms A, B. HARCOURT

Metropolitan Reading Tests, 1970 Edition.
Primer, grades K.7–1.4. Listening for sounds, word knowledge, comprehension. Forms F, H.
Primary I, grades 1.5–2.4; *Primary II,* grades 2.5–3.4. Word knowledge, word analysis, comprehension. Forms F, G, H.
Elementary, grades 3.5–4.9; *Intermediate,* grades 5–6.9; *Advanced,* grades 7–9.5. Word knowledge, comprehension. Forms F, G, H. HARCOURT

Mills Learning Methods Test, Revised Edition. A series of teaching lessons (visual, phonic, kinesthetic, and combination) with testing to determine immediate and delayed learning and the possible appropriateness of the various methods for the learner. Individually administered. MILLS

Minnesota Percepto-Diagnostic Test, Revised. Ages 5 to adult. A clinical test intended to assist in the diagnosis of neurological dysfunction. Six designs to be copied in different settings. CLINICAL

Minnesota Reading Examination for College Students. Grades 9–16. Measures vocabulary and power of comprehension. Forms A, B. MINNESOTA

Monroe Diagnostic Reading Test. Poor readers, any age. Individually administered battery of tests include oral reading, word recognition and discrimination, mirror reading, other supplementary tests. STOELTING

Monroe Reading Aptitude Tests. Beginning grade 1 and nonreaders to age 9, for measuring readiness for reading instruction. Includes visual, auditory perception and memory; motor control; speed and articulation in speech; language development. Mainly group-administration, some subtests to be given individually. HOUGHTON

Monore-Sherman Group Diagnostic Reading Aptitude and Achievement Tests. Grade 3 and up. Achievement tests include paragraph meaning, rate, and word discrimination; arithmetic and spelling tests also included. Aptitude tests include visual memory, auditory memory and discrimination, motor speed, oral vocabulary. NEVINS

Monroe Standardized Silent Reading Tests. *Test I,* grades 3–5; *Test II,* grades 6–8; *Test III,* high school. Very brief tests of rate of comprehension. Forms 1, 2, 3. BOBBS

Motor-Free Visual Perception Test. Ages 4–8. A visual perception test that does not require motor skills; child points to one of four choices which is the same as stimulus. ACADEMIC THERAPY

Murphy-Durrell Reading Readiness Analysis. Beginning first grade. Includes subtests on visual discrimination, auditory discrimination (phonemes), letter names, and learning rate. HARCOURT

Nelson-Denny Reading Test, 1973 Edition. Grades 9–12, college, adult. Vocabulary and comprehension; also rate. Forms C, D. HOUGHTON

Nelson Reading Test, Revised. Grades 3–9. Vocabulary and paragraph comprehension. Forms A, B. HOUGHTON

New Developmental Reading Tests
Lower Primary, grades 1–2.5; *Upper Primary,* grades 2.5–3.9. Word recogni-

tion, comprehending significant ideas, and comprehending specific instructions. Forms L-1, L-2 (Lower Primary); U-1, U-2 (Upper Primary).

Intermediate, grades 4–6. Reading vocabulary, reading for information, for relationships, for interpretation. Forms A, B. LYONS

Ortho-Rater. Master model for rapid testing of large numbers of adults or adolescents; modified model for school use with children. Available with two sets of slides: a short set for very rapid screening, and a set of twelve tests for more comprehensive visual screening. BAUSCH & LOMB

Oseretsky Tests of Motor Proficiency. Ages 4–16. An age scale of tests of motor proficiency. AMERICAN GUIDANCE

Otis-Lennon Mental Ability Test. Revisions of the Otis series of verbal intelligence tests. *Primary I,* kindergarten; *Primary II,* first half of grade 1, *Elementary I,* grades 1.5–3.9; *Elementary II,* grades 4–6; *Intermediate,* grades 7–9; *Advanced,* grades 10–12. Forms J, K, each level. HARCOURT

Otis Quick-Scoring Mental Ability Tests.
Alpha Short Form, grades 1–4. A group intelligence test requiring no reading. Same booklet is used for a verbal directions test and a nonverbal test.
Beta Test, grades 4–9; *Gamma Test,* high school and college; group tests of the omnibus type requiring reading. Forms Em, Fm, each level. HARCOURT

Peabody Individual Achievement Test (PIAT). An individually administered wide range screening test for kindergarten through high school. Contains subtests on word recognition and reading comprehension (sentences). AMERICAN GUIDANCE

Peabody Picture Vocabulary Test. Ages 2–18. An individually administered test of verbal intelligence. AMERICAN GUIDANCE

Phonics Criterion Test. Survey test of 99 different letter-sound relationships. Individually administered; uses nonsense words. DREIER

Pintner-Cunningham Primary Test, Revised 1965. Kindergarten to grade 2. A group intelligence test requiring no reading. Forms A, B. HARCOURT

Pre-Reading Assessment Kit. Grades K–1. Series of single-page tests which measure achievement in: listening, symbol perception, experience background, and comprehension. Three levels of difficulty in each skill area. Contains items that reflect Canadian culture. CALIFORNIA

Prescriptive Reading Inventory (PRI). *Red Book,* grades 1.5–2.5; *Green Book,* grades 2.0–3.5; *Blue Book,* grades 3.0–4.5; *Orange Book,* grades 4–6. Criterion-referenced tests that measure a wide variety of reading skills. CALIFORNIA

Primary Mental Abilities Test. Five levels: K–1, 2–4, 4–6, 6–9, 9–12. Measurement of readiness to learn in school. All levels sample verbal meaning, number facility, and spatial relations. Perceptual speed tested in K–6, and reasoning ability in 4–12. SRA

Primary Reading Profiles, 1967 Edition. *Level 1,* grade 1.5–2.5; *Level 2,* 2.5–3.5. Each has five subtests: aptitude for reading, auditory association, word recognition, word attack, reading comprehension. HOUGHTON

Psychoeducational Inventory of Basic Learning Abilities. Grades 4–8. Designed to aid in initial evaluation for pupils with suspected learning disabilities. Six areas sampled: gross motor development, sensory-motor integration, perceptual-motor skills, language development, conceptual skills, and social skills. FEARON

Psychoeducational Profile of Basic Learning Abilities. Ages 2–14. A booklet for use by psychologists in summarizing data from various sources concerning motor integration, perception, language, social-personal adaptivity, and intellectual functioning. CONSULTING

Purdue Perceptual-Motor Survey. Ages 6–10. A series of tests for motor control and flexibility, visual-motor co-ordination, laterality, and directionality. MERRILL

Quick Test. Preschool to adult. A shorter test of verbal intelligence, similar to the Ammons Full-Range Picture Vocabulary Test. Forms 1, 2, 3. PSYCHOLOGICAL TEST

Raven Progressive Matrices. A nonverbal test of general intelligence. Individually administered below age 8. *Form 1938*, ages 8 to adult; *Form 1947*, ages 5–11; *Form 1962*, above-average adolescents and adults. English norms. PSYCHOLOGICAL

Reading/Everyday Activities in Life (R/EAL). Ages 10–adult. Measure of functional literacy. Consists of nine reading activities used in everyday life. CAL PRESS

Reading Placement Inventory. Grades 1–9. Consists of a word recognition test and an oral reading test. Scored like an informal reading inventory for determining a child's instructional reading level. ECONOMY

Revised Objective Perceptual Test. A modification of the *Bender* which uses a multiple-choice format. Intended to allow for determining if low *Bender* score is due primarily to perceptual or motor deficit. *See* Fidel and Ray, 1972.

Rorschach Technique. Preschool to adult. A projective test of personality using ink blots, for trained psychologists. PSYCHOLOGICAL

Roswell-Chall Auditory Blending Test. A brief test of ability to hear the sounds of a word pronounced separately and recognize and say the word. ESSAY

Roswell-Chall Diagnostic Reading Test. A short series of tests for analyzing phonic knowledge and skills. ESSAY

School and College Ability Tests—SCAT Series II. Group test of scholastic aptitude. Levels 1–4 cover grades 4–14. Three forms of Level 1 (college); two forms for each other level. Provides verbal, quantitative, and total scores. ETS

Schrammel-Gray High School and College Reading Test. Grades 7–12 and college. Rate, comprehension, and comprehension-efficiency. BOBBS

Screening Tests for Identifying Children with Specific Language Disability (Slingerland). Levels for grades 1–2, 2–3, 3–4, and 5–6. Intended for use in locating children who have or are likely to develop disabilities in reading, spelling, and handwriting. Visual copying, memory, and discrimination; three auditory group tests; one individual auditory test. EDUCATORS

Sequential Tests of Educational Progress—STEP, Series II. *Level 4*, grades 4–6; *Level 3*, grades 7–9; *Level 2*, grades 10–12; *Level 1*, college. A battery of achievement tests including tests of reading comprehension. Forms A, B, each test and level. ETS

Short Form Test of Academic Aptitude (SFTAA). *Level 1*, grades 1.5–3.4; *Level 2*, grades 3.5–4; *Level 3*, grades 5–6; *Level 4*, grades 7–9; *Level 5*, grades 9–12. Index of general academic aptitude. Four subtests: vocabulary, analogies, sequences, memory. Yields language and nonlanguage scores. CALIFORNIA

Silent Reading Diagnostic Tests. Grades 3–6. Group test providing a detailed analysis of many word recognition and phonic skills, with nine subtests. LYONS

Sipay Word Analysis Tests (SWAT). Battery of 16 individually administered word-analysis tests that measure ability in one or more of the three decoding skill areas: visual analysis, phonic analysis (symbol-sound association), and blending. Survey test also available. Answer sheets designed to allow for detailed analysis of learner's performance. EDUCATORS

Slosson Intelligence Test (SIT). Age 4 up. Brief individually administered verbal intelligence tests. Correlates highly with longer tests. SLOSSON

Slosson Oral Reading Test (SORT). Grades 1–12. Very brief individually administered test of word recognition for words presented in isolation. SLOSSON

Southern California Sensory Integration Tests. Ages 4–10. Clinical battery of 17 tests which measure visual, tactile and kinesthetic perception, and several types of motor performance. WESTERN

Spache Binocular Reading Test. Grade 1 and up. Individual test to measure the relative participation of each eye in reading. Uses stereoscopic slides with different words omitted on each side. Three levels of difficulty. For use in a Telebinocular or stereoscope. KEYSTONE

Spache Diagnostic Reading Scales, Revised Edition (DRS). Grades 1 to 8 and disabled readers grades 9–12. An individually administered battery of tests including three word lists, twenty-two graded reading passages, and eight supplementary phonics tests. CALIFORNIA

Spatial Orientation Memory Test, Preliminary Edition. Ages 5–9. Designed to assess development of ability to retain and recall orientation (direction) of visually presented forms. Responses made by pointing to a multiple-choice selection. Forms I, II. LANGUAGE

SRA Assessment Survey: Reading, 1971 Edition. *Primary I*, grades 1–2.5; *Primary II*, grades 2.5–3; *Multilevel Blue*, grades 4–5; *Multilevel Green*, grades 6–7; *Multilevel Red*, grades 8–9.5. Group reading achievement test with vocabulary and comprehension subtests. Forms E, F. SRA

SRA Primary Mental Abilities Test. Levels for K–grade 1; grades 2–4; 4–6; 6–9; 9–12. Provides separate MA's and IQ's for verbal meaning, number facility, reasoning, perceptual speed, and spatial relations, as well as for total score. SRA

SRA Reading Record. Grades 6–12. Ten subtests with short time limits: rate, comprehension, paragraph meaning, directory, map-table-graph, advertisement, index, technical vocabulary, sentence meaning, general vocabulary. SRA

Standard Reading Inventory. Grade 1 and up. Individual tests including recognition vocabulary, oral reading errors, oral and silent comprehension, oral and silent speed. KLAMATH

Stanford-Binet Intelligence Scale, 1972 Norms Edition. Ages 2 to adult. Individual test of general intelligence, for use by trained psychologists. Form L–M. HOUGHTON

Stanford Diagnostic Reading Test. *Level I*, grades 2.5–4.5; *Level II*, grades 4.5–8.5. Group tests with separate measures of comprehension, vocabulary, syllabication, auditory skills, phonic analysis, and rate. Forms X, Y. HARCOURT

Stanford Reading Tests, 1973 Revision.
Primary I, grades 1.5–2.4; *Primary II*, grades 2.5–3.4; *Primary III*, grades 3.5–4.4; *Intermediate I*, grades 4.5–5.4; *Intermediate II*, grades 5.5–6.9. Vocabulary, reading comprehension and word-study skills. Also listening-comprehension subtest.
Advanced, grades 7–9.5. Vocabulary and reading comprehension. Forms A, B, each level. HARCOURT

Stanford Test of Academic Skills (TASK). *Level I*, grades 9–10; *Level II*, grades 11–12; *Level III*, college edition, grade 13. Measure of reading comprehension. HARCOURT

STAR: Screening Test of Academic Readiness. Kindergarten. A group intelligence test. PRIORITY

START: Screening Test for the Assignment of Remedial Treatment. Ages 4–6. Group tests of visual memory, auditory memory, visual copying, visual discrimination. PRIORITY

Study Habits Checklist. Grades 9–13. Yields scores on 37 study skills and habits. SRA

Tests of Adult Basic Education (TABE). Vocabulary and comprehension tests adapted from the 1957 edition of the *California Achievement Tests*. *Level D* for junior high level; *Level M* for upper elementary; and *Level E* for upper primary level. Norms for grades 2–12. CALIFORNIA

Test of Non-Verbal Auditory Discrimination (TENVAD). Ages 6–8. Experimental nonverbal group test of auditory discrimination. Subtests: pitch, loudness, rhythm, and duration. *See* Buktenica, 1971.

Test of Phonic Skills. Contains 19 individually administered subtests, most of which sample symbol-sound association skills. Also has auditory discrimination test which can be administered in 10 dialects. HARPER

Thematic Apperception Test. Ages 6 to adult. A projective test of personality for use only by trained psychologists. PSYCHOLOGICAL

Traxler High School Reading Test, Revised 1967. Grades 10–12. Rate of reading and comprehension of easy material; finding main ideas in factual paragraphs. Forms A, B. BOBBS

Traxler Silent Reading Test, Revised 1969. Grades 7–10. Rate, comprehension, word meaning, paragraph meaning. Forms 1, 2, 3, 4. BOBBS

Tyler-Kimber Study Skills Inventory. Grade 9 to college. Use of reference books, card catalogue, index, interpreting maps and graphs, and so on. CONSULTING

Valett Developmental Survey of Basic Learning Abilities. Age 2–7. A compendium of 233 tasks in seven areas: motor integration, tactile discrimination, auditory discrimination, visual motor co-ordination, visual discrimination, language development, conceptual development. CONSULTING

Van Alstyne Picture Vocabulary Test. Mental ages 2–7. A vocabulary test of sixty items, each requiring only a choice of one out of four pictures. HARCOURT

Walker Readiness Test for Disadvantaged Pre-School Children. Ages 4–6. Individually administered, nonverbal readiness test. Directions available in English, Spanish, and French. Subtests: likenesses or similarities, differences, numerical analogies, and missing parts. U.S.O.E. Bureau of Research, ERIC ED 037 253

Wechsler Adult Intelligence Scale. Age 16 to adult. An individual intelligence scale for use only by trained psychologists. Provides verbal, performance, and full-scale IQ's. PSYCHOLOGICAL

Wechsler Intelligence Scale for Children (WISC). Ages 5–15. An individual intelligence scale for use only by trained psychologists. Gives verbal, performance, and full-scale IQ's. PSYCHOLOGICAL

Wechsler Intelligence Scale for Children—Revised (WISC-R). Ages 6–16. 1974 revision of the WISC. PSYCHOLOGICAL

Wechsler Preschool and Primary Scale of Intelligence (WPPSI). Ages 4–6.5. An individual intelligence scale similar to the WISC. Provides verbal, performance, and full-scale IQ's. PSYCHOLOGICAL

Wepman Auditory Discrimination Test, 1973 Revision. Ages 5–8. Tests ability to distinguish whether two spoken words are the same or slightly different. Scoring now based on correct responses. Forms IA, IIA. LANGUAGE

Wide Range Achievement Test, Revised Edition (1965). Age 5 to adult. An individual test of word recognition, spelling, and arithmetic computation. PSYCHOLOGICAL

Williams Reading Tests, Revised. *Test I,* grade 1; *Test II,* grades 2–3, word recognition and comprehension. *Tests for grades 4–9,* vocabulary in paragraph context. Forms A, B. BOBBS

Wisconsin Tests of Reading Skill Improvement

Word Attack. Grades K–3. Criterion-referenced tests which measure 38 commonly taught word-analysis skills at four levels of difficulty.

Study Skills. Grades K–6. Criterion-referenced tests that assess 77 study skills in three subareas: maps, graphs and tables, and references. INTERPRETIVE

Woodcock Reading Mastery Tests. Kindergarten through grade 12. A battery of five individually administered tests: letter identification, word identification, word attack, word comprehension, and passage comprehension (sentences only). Forms A & B. AMERICAN GUIDANCE

Appendix B

SERIES BOOKS FOR REMEDIAL READING

Many series of books have been written specifically to have mature interest appeal coupled with simplified vocabulary and style. These series have greatly enriched the available resources for corrective and remedial reading.

One of the most difficult, yet most important, things to do when working with a poor reader is to get him interested in reading. Therefore, it is important to choose his reading material with care. In choosing books for a poor or reluctant reader, one should select titles that seem likely to appeal to his interests. These materials should be at or below his independent reading level, at least initially. If a teacher has only a rough idea of a child's independent reading level, it is advisable to start with material which is at least two years below the child's present grade placement. If the first book tried seems to be too easy or too difficult, an adjustment should be made in making the next choice. The reading grade levels shown below are as indicated by the publishers.

Title	Publisher	Reading Grade Level	Interest Grade Level
ANIMAL ADVENTURE SERIES	Benefic	PP–1	1–4

Actions and adventures of animals based on sound scientific knowledge; stories that could actually happen.

| BUTTERNUT BILL SERIES | Benefic | PP–1 | 1–6 |

Adventures of a young boy and his friends in the Ozark Mountains in the 1850s.

| BUTTON FAMILY ADVENTURES | Benefic | PP–3 | 1–3 |

Realistic stories in the life of a large blue-collar family where money is a determining factor.

Title	Publisher	Reading Grade Level	Interest Grade Level
COWBOY SAM SERIES	Benefic	PP–3	1–6

Western content appeals to many boys.

| SAILOR JACK SERIES | Benefic | PP–3 | 1–6 |

Adventure stories aboard an atomic submarine.

| MOONBEAM SERIES | Benefic | PP–3 | 1–6 |

Space-age adventures of a monkey, with adult multi-ethnic characters as co-stars.

| DAN FRONTIER SERIES | Benefic | PP–4 | 1–7 |

Pioneer adventure books depicting early frontier life in the Midwest.

| COWBOYS OF MANY RACES | Benefic | PP–5 | 1–6 |

Depicts adventures of Afro-Americans, Spanish-Americans, and Indian cowboys on the early western frontier.

| FIRST READING BOOKS | Garrard | 1–2 | 1–4 |

Written with the easier half of the Dolch Basic Sight Words and the 95 common nouns. Content deals with pets, birds, and wild animals.

| BEGINNER BOOKS | Random | 1–2 | 1–4 |

The emphasis is on humor and good plot. Several are in rhyme.

| BASIC VOCABULARY BOOKS | Garrard | 1–2 | 1–4 |

Content about folk tales, animals.

| JIM FOREST READERS | Field | 1–3 | 1–7 |

Adventure stories about Jim Forest, young teen-ager, and his forest ranger uncle.

| SPACE-AGE BOOKS | Benefic | 1–3 | 3–6 |

Humor and adventure with scientific space facts.

| WHAT IS IT SERIES | Benefic | 1–4 | 1–8 |

Specific elementary science areas. Emphasis is on basic facts.

| ABOUT BOOKS | Childrens | 1–4 | 2–8 |

Factual science and social studies books that are adaptable for meeting the needs of both able and slow readers.

| BREAKTHROUGH | Allyn | 1–6 | 7–12 |

Series of short original paperbacks containing modern stories, articles, biographies, and poetry.

| PACEMAKER TRUE ADVENTURES | Fearon | 2 | 5–12 |

Variety of true stories in paperback; includes historical figures, escape, spies, and pirates.

| PACEMAKER STORY BOOKS | Fearon | 2 | 7–12 |

Variety of paperback originals, mostly dealing with mystery and adventure.

| PACEMAKER CLASSICS | Fearon | 2 | 7–12 |

Eight abridged and adapted paperback versions including *The Jungle Book*, *Two Years Before the Mast*, and *Tale of Two Cities*. Designed for slow learners.

| TRUE BOOKS | Childrens | 2–3 | 1–6 |

Carefully controlled vocabulary. Social studies and science subjects appealing to most interests; containing well-organized, constructive information.

| DISCOVERY BOOKS | Garrard | 2–3 | 2–5 |

Over 60 true biographies of outstanding women, scientists, explorers, reformers, humanitarians, and statesmen.

Title	Publisher	Reading Grade Level	Interest Grade Level
BOXCAR CHILDREN MYSTERIES	Whitman	2–3	3–8

Series of 17 separate mysteries involving the Alden family who began their adventures by making their home in a boxcar in order to stay together.

| GATEWAY BOOKS | Random | 2–3 | 3–8 |

A wide variety of fact, fiction, humor, and adventure in all content areas.

| STEP-UP BOOKS | Random | 2–3 | 3–9 |

Continuous flow of action will please both the reader who reads beyond his usual age interest and the older reluctant reader who looks for information and an unobtrusive simplified vocabulary.

| ADAPTED CLASSICS | Nat. Assn. Deaf | 2–3 | 6–12 |

Number of titles including some not found elsewhere, such as *Beowolf, Song of Roland, Hunchback of Notre Dame, El Cid,* and *Romeo and Juliet.*

| INTERESTING READING SERIES | Follett | 2–3 | 7–12 |

Designed for remedial work in junior and senior high school. Stories in many areas: history, adventure, biography, sports, science, and fiction.

| THE WILDLIFE ADVENTURE SERIES | Field | 2–4 | 3–9 |

Books portray true-to-life experiences of different wild animals.

| SPORTS MYSTERIES SERIES | Benefic | 2–4 | 4–9 |

Teen-age boys and girls meet and overcome problems in sports and school activities.

| RACING WHEELS SERIES | Benefic | 2–4 | 4–9 |

Adventures of an inner-city boy and his friends who learn about the training, equipment, and driving techniques of auto racing.

| THE MORGAN BAY MYSTERIES | Field | 2–4 | 4–11 |

Well-illustrated mystery books for remedial, supplementary, and individualized reading programs. Includes teen-age characters.

| CHECKERED FLAG SERIES | Field | 2–4 | 6–12 |

Fast-moving stories combine a racing setting with the intrigue of mystery. Different types of cars, races, or motorcycles are featured in each book.

| THE DEEP SEA ADVENTURE SERIES | Field | 2–5 | 3–11 |

Adventure and mystery stories about the sea. Mature characters. Excellent lifelike illustrations.

| WORLD OF ADVENTURE SERIES | Benefic | 2–6 | 4–9 |

Suspense stories built around expeditions.

| AMERICAN ADVENTURE SERIES | Harper | 2–6 | 4–9 |

Action and adventure stories of American pioneers and warriors. Authentic historical background.

| SPACE SCIENCE FICTION SERIES | Benefic | 2–6 | 4–9 |

Explorations of outer space by future space travelers.

| MYSTERY ADVENTURE SERIES | Benefic | 2–6 | 4–9 |

Young-adult boy and girl solve mysteries through deductive reasoning, courage, and determination.

| FIRST BOOKS | Watts | 2–9 | 3–12 |

Factual, straightforward treatments of topics interesting to older children. Over 350 titles in the areas of history, civics, hobbies, sports, the arts, geography, and science.

| JUNIOR SCIENCE BOOKS | Garrard | 3 | 2–5 |

These authentic and well-illustrated books deal with facts scientifically.

Title	*Publisher*	*Reading Grade Level*	*Interest Grade Level*
HOLIDAYS	Garrard	3	2–5
History, customs, and traditions in the United States and other lands.			
FOLKLORE OF THE WORLD BOOKS	Garrard	3	2–8
Twelve books covering folk tales from around the world.			
PACEMAKER FOLKTALE SERIES	Fearon	3	3–6
Ten short paperbacks containing a wide variety of folk tales.			
FRONTIERS OF AMERICA SERIES	Childrens	3	3–8
True stories of pioneer days. Introduction to American history.			
AMERICAN FOLKTALES	Garrard	3–4	2–6
Lively stories about famous folk heroes, Indians and regional lore, and exaggerated adventures.			
STORY OF SERIES	Hale	3–4	3–9
Stories of 38 famous men and women of various ethnic backgrounds who were successful in varying professions.			
WARNER MYSTERY STORIES	Scott F.	3–6	4–6
Series of 14 titles including mysteries and short biographies.			
HI-LO READING SERIES	Pyramid	3–8	5–12
Paperbacks covering a variety of topics from a soul/rock band to the Kennedys.			
REGIONAL AMERICAN STORIES	Garrard	4	3–6
Stories of daring, courage, humor, and gaiety set on the history of America.			
SPORTS	Garrard	4	3–6
Histories of individual sports and biographies of great names in sports.			
EXPLORERS	Garrard	4	3–6
Dramatic historically accurate biographies of exploration, discovery, and conquest; maps trace routes of the explorers.			
PLEASURE READING BOOKS	Garrard	4	3–6
Adaptations of famous stories and legends including Robin Hood, Robinson Crusoe, Aesop, fairy tales, and folk tales.			
AMERICANS ALL SERIES	Field	4	3–9
Concerned with how the young main characters of various ethnic or cultural backgrounds were affected by, and contributed to, the North American culture.			
EXPLORING AND UNDERSTANDING SERIES	Benefic	4	4–9
Each book explores a subject in depth, with special emphasis on science processes.			
SIGNAL BOOKS	Doubleday	4	5–9
Junior high interest in sports, careers, adventure, and mystery.			
EVERYREADER SERIES	Webster	4	7–12
Nineteen simplified classics including short-story collections.			
CHILDHOOD OF FAMOUS AMERICANS SERIES	Bobbs	4–5	4–9
Over 200 biographies stressing childhood of Americans from Washington to Babe Ruth to Gus Grissom.			
HOW AND WHY SERIES	Hale	4–5	4–9
Over 40 titles dealing primarily with science topics; a few social studies books.			
GETTING TO KNOW BOOKS	Hale	4–5	4–9
Informational books about at least 17 different countries.			

THE READING-MOTIVATED SERIES   Field   4–5   4–10
  Fast-moving novels dealing with American history that appeal to both
  reluctant and avid readers.

RALLY SERIES   Childrens   4–5   7–10
  Story characters learn to master minibikes, motorcycles, and midget racers.

ADAPTED CLASSICS   Scott   4–6   4–8
  Sixteen titles including *Around the World in Eighty Days, Captain Courageous, Lorna Doone,* and *Julius Caesar in Modern Prose.*

ADAPTED CLASSICS   Scott F.   4–6   4–12
  Fifteen titles including simplified versions of *Treasure Island* and *Silas Marner.*

WE WERE THERE BOOKS   Hale   4–6   5–9
  Informational books covering historical events in American and ancient
  history.

ALLABOUT BOOKS   Random   4–6   5–11
  Well-written, factual books on many topics of interest to children.

TEEN-AGE TALES   Heath   4–6   6–11
  Mystery, adventure, and action stories about teen-agers and for teen-agers.

TURNER-LIVINGSTON READING SERIES   Follett   4–6   7–9
  Six workbooks containing 138 structured lessons geared toward helping the
  reader to understand basic social behaviors. Titles include *The Money You
  Spend, The Job You Get, The Person You Are.*

VOCATIONAL READING SERIES   Follett   4–6   9–12
  Eight workbooks that upgrade reading skills; content emphasizes real life
  experiences regarding career opportunities.

ADAPTED CLASSICS   Globe   4–10   4–12
  A wide variety of 47 books for secondary schools, simplified and shortened.

RIVERS   Garrard   5   4–7
  Factual stories of the great rivers of the world and the cultures they have
  influenced.

CREATIVE PEOPLE IN THE ARTS AND SCIENCES   Garrard   5   4–7
  Complete life stories of world's creative geniuses.

MYTHS, TALES AND LEGENDS   Garrard   5   4–7
  Adaptations and translations of stories from other lands.

WORLD LANDMARK BOOKS   Random   5–6   5–11
  Events and important people of other lands. Similar to Landmark Books.

LANDMARK BOOKS   Random   5–7   5–11
  U.S. history and important people. Many written by outstanding authors.

TURNER-LIVINGSTON COMMUNICATION SERIES   Follett   5–6   8–10
  Six workbooks geared to help the reader understand facts, concepts, and
  opportunities of modern communication.

TURNER CAREER GUIDANCE SERIES   Follett   5–6   11–12
  Each of six workbooks treats a major aspect of career and job experiences
  such as reading want ads and completing forms.

FUN TO READ CLASSICS   Childrens   5–8   5–12
  Fifteen different titles each for the elementary and junior-senior high sets.
  Designed to aid reluctant readers to understand these classics through use of
  vocabulary definitions, dramatic illustrations, and explanatory information.

Appendix C

A LIST OF PUBLISHERS AND THEIR ADDRESSES

The following list contains, in alphabetical order, the names and addresses of the publishers of the books and tests mentioned elsewhere in this book. It also contains some entries of producers and distributors of audiovisual materials, materials for special education, and so on, although their products may not have been mentioned. Only one office is listed for each publisher. Where an abbreviated name has been used for the publisher, that has been listed in italics, followed by the full name and address. The rapidity of publishing mergers. name changes, and changes of address make it inevitable that some of the entries below will become out of date.

Academic Press, Inc., subsidiary of Harcourt Brace Jovanovich, Inc., 757 Third Avenue. New York, N.Y. 10003
Academic Therapy Publications, 1539 Fourth Street, San Raphael, Calif. 94901
Abelard-Schuman, Ltd. *See* Intext Press
Abingdon Press, 201 Eighth Avenue, Nashville, Tenn. 37203
Addison-Wesley Publishing Co., 2725 Sand Hill Road, Menlo Park, Calif. 94025
Allyn. Allyn and Bacon, Inc., Rockleigh Industrial Park, Rockleigh, N.J. 07647
Almqvist & Wiksell, P.O. Box 62, S-101 20, Stockholm, 1, Sweden
Ambassador Publishing Co., Box 3524, Saint Paul, Minn. 55165
American Book. American Book Co., 450 West 33 Street, New York, N.Y. 10001
American Council on Education, 1 Dupont Circle, Washington, D.C. 20036
American Ed. American Education Publishers, Inc., Education Center, Columbus, Ohio 43216
American Guidance. American Guidance Service, Inc., Publishers Bldg., Circle Pine, Minn. 55014

American Library. American Library Association, 50 East Huron Street, Chicago, Ill. 60611

American Opt. American Optical Co., Box 1, Southbridge, Mass. 01550

American Orthopsychiatric Association, 175 Broadway, New York, N.Y. 10019

Ann Arbor Publishers, 611 Church Street, Ann Arbor, Mich. 48104

Appleton. Appleton-Century-Crofts. *See* Meredith Corp.

Association for Childhood Education International, 3615 Wisconsin Avenue, N.W., Washington, D.C. 20016

Aston. University of Aston, Gosta Green, Birmingham B4 7ET, England.

Audio-Visual. Audio-Visual Research Co., 1317 Eighth Street, S.E., Waseca, Minn. 56093

Australian Council for Educational Research, Frederick Street, Hawthorn E2, Victoria, Australia

Avon Books, 959 Eighth Avenue, New York, N.Y. 10019

Baggiani and Tewell, 4 Spring Hill Court, Chevy Chase, Md. 20015

Baldridge Reading Instruction Materials, Inc., Box 439, Greenwich, Conn. 06830

Bantam Books, 666 Fifth Avenue, New York, N.Y. 10019

Barnell Loft, Ltd., 958 Church Street, Baldwin, N.Y. 11510

Clarence L. Barnhart, Inc., Box 250, Bronxville, N.Y. 10708

Basic Books, Inc., 404 Park Avenue South, New York, N.Y. 10016

Bausch. Bausch & Lomb Optical Co., Rochester, N.Y. 14602

Beckley-Cardy Co. *See* Benefic Press

Beginner Books. *See* Random House

Behavioral. Behavioral Research Laboratories, Box 577, Palo Alto, Calif. 94302

Bell. Bell and Howell Co., Audio Visual Products Division, 7100 McCormick Road, Chicago, Ill. 60645

Benefic. Benefic Press, 10300 West Roosevelt Road, Westchester, Ill. 60153

Berkley Publishing Corp. *See* G. P. Putnam's

Bobbs, Bobbs-Merrill Co., 4300 West 62 Street, Indianapolis, Ind. 46268

Book Lab Inc., 1449 37 Street, Brooklyn, N.Y. 11218

Borg-Warner Educational Systems, 7450 North Natchez Avenue, Niles, Ill. 60648

R .R. Bowker Co., 1180 Avenue of the Americas, New York, N.Y. 10036

Bowmar Publishing Co., 622 Rodier Drive, Glendale, Calif. 91201

Milton Bradley Co., Springfield, Mass. 01101

Wm. C. Brown Co., 2460 Kerper Boulevard, Dubuque, Iowa 52003

Brown University Press, 129 Waterman Street, Providence, R.I. 02912

Burgess Publishing Co., 7108 Ohms Lane, Minneapolis, Minn. 55435

Cadmus Books. *See* E. M. Hale and Co.

California. California Test Bureau/McGraw-Hill, Del Monte Research Park, Monterey, Calif. 93940

Cal Press, Inc., 76 Madison Avenue, New York, N.Y. 10016

Cambridge University Press, 32 East 57 Street, New York, N.Y. 10022

Career Institute, 555 East Lange Street, Mundelein, Ill. 60060

Cenco Educational Aids, 2600 South Kostner Avenue, Chicago, Ill. 60623

Center for Applied Linguistics, 1611 North Kent Street, Arlington, Va. 22209

Center for Applied Research in Education, Inc., 521 Fifth Avenue, New York, N.Y. 10017

Chandler. Chandler Publishing Co., 124 Spear Street, San Francisco, Calif. 94105

Chicago. See University of Chicago Press

Childcraft Education Corp., 150 East 58 Street, New York, N.Y. 10022

Children's Book Centre, 140 Kensington Church Street, London W8, England

Childrens, Children's Press, Inc., 1224 West Van Buren Street, Chicago, Ill. 60607
Chilton Book Co., Chilton Way, Radnor, Penn. 19089
Citation Press, 50 West 44 Street, New York, N.Y. 10036
City College Reading Center, School of Education, CCNY, New York, N.Y. 10031
Clinical. Clinical Psychology Publishing Co., 4 Conant Square, Brandon, Vt. 05733
College Skills Center, 101 West 31 Street, New York, N.Y. 10001
Combined Book Exhibit, Inc., Scarborough Park, Albany Post Road, Briarcliff Manor, N.Y. 10510
Committee on Diagnostic Reading Tests, Mountain Home, N.C. 28758
Communicad, Box 541, Wilton, Conn. 06897
Consulting. Consulting Psychologists Press, 577 College Avenue, Palo Alto, Calif. 94306
Continental Press, Inc., 520 East Bainbridge Street, Elizabethtown, Penn. 17022
Coronet Instructional Media, 65 East South Water Street, Chicago, Ill. 60601
Council for Exceptional Children, 1920 Association Drive, Reston, Va. 22091
Coward-McCann and Geoghegan, 200 Madison Avenue, New York, N.Y. 10016
Craig Corporation, 921 West Artesia Boulevard, Compton, Calif. 90020
Creative Playthings, Inc., Princeton, N.J. 08540
Croft Educational Services, 100 Garfield Avenue, New London, Conn. 06320
Curriculum Associates, 94 Bridge Street, Chapel Hill Park, Newton, Mass. 02158
Curtis Publishing Co., Independence Square, Philadelphia, Pa. 19105
John Day Co. *See* Intext Press
Delacorte Press. *See* Dial Press
Dell Publishing Co., 245 East 47 Street, New York, N.Y. 10017
DLM. Developmental Learning Materials, 7440 Natchez Avenue, Niles, Ill. 60648
Dexter and Westbrook, Ltd., 958 Church Street, Baldwin, N.Y. 11510
Dial/Delacorte Press, 245 East 47 Street, New York, N.Y. 10017
Dick Blick, Box 1267, Galesburg, Ill. 61401
Docent Corporation, 430 Manville Road, Pleasantville, N.Y. 10570
Dodd, Mead and Co., Inc., 79 Madison Avenue, New York, N.Y. 10016
Doubleday. Doubleday and Co., Inc., 277 Park Avenue, New York, N.Y. 10017
Dreier Educational Systems, Inc., 320 Raritan Avenue, Highland Park, N.J. 08904
E. P. Dutton and Co., 201 Park Avenue South, New York, N.Y. 10003
The Economy Co., Box 25308, 1901 West Walnut Street, Oklahoma City, Okla. 73125
Edmark Associates, 655 South Oreas Street, Seattle, Wash. 98108
Education Commission of the States, 186 Lincoln Street, Suite 300, Denver, Colo. 80203
Educational Activities, Inc., 1937 Grand Avenue, Baldwin, N.Y. 11520
Educational Aids, 845 Wisteria Drive, Fremont, Calif. 94538
EDL. Educational Developmental Laboratories, Inc., a Division of McGraw-Hill, 1221 Avenue of the Americas, New York, N.Y. 10020
Educational. Educational and Industrial Testing Service, Box 7234, San Diego, Calif. 92107
Educational Projections Corp., 3070 Lake Terrace, Glenview, Ill. 60025
Educational Progress, P.O. Box 45663, Tulsa, Okla. 74145
Educational Service, Inc., Box 219, Stevensville, Mich. 49127
Educational Solutions, Inc., 80 Fifth Avenue, New York, N.Y. 10011
ETA. Educational Teaching Aids, 159 West Kinzie Street, Chicago, Ill. 60610
ETS. Educational Testing Service, Princeton, N.J. 08540

Educators; EPS. Educators Publishing Service, 75 Moulton Street, Cambridge, Mass. 02138

EFI. Electronic Futures, Inc., 57 Dodge Avenue, North Haven, Conn. 06473

Embossograf Corp. of America, 38 West 21 Street, New York, N.Y. 10010

EBE. Encyclopaedia Britannica Educational Corp., 425 North Michigan Avenue, Chicago, Ill. 60611

ERIC Clearinghouse on Reading and Communications Skills, 111 Kenyon Road, Urbana, Ill. 61801

ERIC Clearinghouse on Tests, Educational Testing Service, Princeton, N.J. 08540

Essay. Essay Press, Box 5, Planetarium Station, New York, N.Y. 10024

Eye Gate House, Inc., 146-01 Archer Avenue, Jamaica, N.Y. 11435

Exposition Press, Inc., 50 Jericho Turnpike, Jericho, N.Y. 11753

Fearon Publishers, 6 Davis Drive, Belmonte, Calif. 94002

F. E. Peacock Publishers, Inc., 401 West Irving Park Road, Itasca, Ill. 60143

Field. Field Educational Publications, Inc., 2400 Hanover Street, Palo Alto, Calif. 94304

Field Enterprises Educational Corp., Merchandise Mart Plaza, Chicago, Ill. 60654

Follett. Follett Educational Corp., 1010 West Washington Boulevard, Chicago, Ill. 60607

Foundation. Foundation for Research in Mental Development, Box 1483, Wilmington, Del. 19899

Four Winds Press, a Division of Scholastic Magazine, 50 West 44 Street, New York, N.Y. 10035

Free Press. *See* Macmillan Publishing Co.

Funk and Wagnalls, Inc., 53 East 77 Street, New York, N.Y. 10021

Gable Academies, 770 Miller Road, Miami, Fla. 33155

Garrard. Garrard Publishing Co., 1607 North Market Street, Champaign, Ill. 61820

Ginn. Ginn and Co., a Division of Xerox, 191 Spring Street, Lexington, Mass. 02173

General Learning Corp., 250 James Street, Morristown, N.J. 07960

George Peabody College for Teachers, Nashville, Tenn. 37203

Globe, Globe Book Co., 175 Fifth Avenue, New York, N.Y. 10010

Golden Gate Junior Books, a Division of Children's Press, 8344 Melrose Avenue., Los Angeles, Calif. 90009

Golden Press. *See* Western Publishing Co.

Grolier Educational Corp., 845 Third Avenue, New York, N.Y. 10022

Grossett and Dunlap, 51 Madison Avenue, New York, N.Y. 10010

Grune and Stratton, Inc., 381 Park Avenue South, New York, N.Y. 10016

Gryphon Press, 220 Montgomery Street, Highland Park, N.J. 08904

Hale. E. M. Hale and Co., 1201 South Hastings Way, Eau Claire, Wis. 54701

Hammond, Inc., 515 Valley Street, Maplewood, N.J. 07040

Harcourt. Harcourt Brace Jovanovich, 757 Third Avenue, New York, N.Y. 10017

Harper. Harper and Row, Inc., 10 East 53 Street, New York, N.Y. 10022

Harvey House, Inc., 5 South Buckout Street, Irvington-on-Hudson, N.Y. 10533

Hastings House, Inc., 10 East 40 Street, New York, N.Y. 10016

Heath. D. C. Heath & Co., 125 Spring Street, Lexington, Mass. 02173

Hoffman Information Systems, 4423 Arden Drive, El Monte, Calif. 91734

Holiday House, Inc., 18 East 56 Street, New York, N.Y. 10022

Holt. Holt, Rinehart and Winston, Inc., 383 Madison Avenue, New York, N.Y. 10017

The Horn Book, Inc., 585 Boylston Street, Boston, Mass. 02116

Houghton. Houghton Mifflin Co., Pennington-Hopewell Road, Hopewell, N.J. 08525

Ideal School Supply Co., 11000 South Lavergne Avenue, Oak Lawn, Ill. 60453

Illinois. See University of Illinois Press

Imperial International Learning Corp., Box 548, Kankakee, Ill. 60901

Initial Teaching Alphabet Publications, 6 East Third Street, New York, N.Y. 10017

IPAT. Institute for Personality and Aptitude Testing, 1602-04 Coronado Drive, Champaign, Ill. 61820

Instructional Communications Technology, Inc., Huntington, N.Y. 11743

IOX. Instructional Objectives Exchange, Box 24095, Los Angeles, Calif. 90024

The Instructo Corp., Cedar Hollow & Matthews Roads, Paoli, Pa. 19301

International Reading Association, 800 Barksdale Road, Newark, Del. 19711

Interpretive. Interpretive Scoring Systems, 4401 West 76 Street, Minneapolis, Minn. 55435

Intext Press, 257 Park Avenue South, New York, N.Y. 10010

Invalid Children's Aid Association, 126 Buckingham Palace Road, London SW1W, England

Jamestown Publishers, Box 6743, Providence, R.I. 02904

Johns Hopkins Press. Baltimore, Md. 21218

Charles A. Jones Publishing Co., a Division of Wadsworth Publishing Co., Inc., 4 Village Green, Worthington, Ohio 43085

Jones-Kenilworth Co., 8801 Ambassador Drive, Dallas, Texas 75247

Judy Publishing Co., Box 5270, Main P.O., Chicago, Ill. 60608

Kenworthy. Kenworthy Educational Service, Inc., Box 3031, 138 Allen Street, Buffalo, N.Y. 14205

Keysone. Keystone View Co., 2212 East 12 Street, Davenport, Iowa 52803

Kids. Kids Publishing, Inc., 777 Third Avenue, New York, N.Y. 10017

Kingsbury. See Remedial Education Press

Klamath Printing Co., 320 Lowell Street, Klamath Falls, Ore. 97601

Alfred A. Knopf. a subsidiary of Random House, Inc., 201 East 50th Street, New York, N.Y. 10022

Lafayette. Lafayette Instrument Company, Inc., Box 1279, Lafayette, Ind. 47902

Laidlaw Bros., a Division of Doubleday and Co., 30 Chatham Road, Summit, N.J. 09701

Lakeshore. Lakeshore Equipment Co., 5369 West Pico Boulevard, Los Angeles, Calif. 90019

Language. Language Research Associates, 175 East Delaware Place, Chicago, Ill. 60611

Lantern Press, Inc., 354 Hussey Road, Mount Vernon, N.Y. 10552

Learn, Inc., 21 East Euclid Avenue, Haddonfield, N.J. 08033

Learning Through Seeing, Inc., Box 368, LTS Building, Sunland, Calif. 91040

Lerner Publication Co., 241 First Avenue North, Minneapolis, Minn. 55401

Lippincott. J. B. Lippincott Co., East Washington Square, Philadelphia, Penn. 19105

Little, Brown and Co., 34 Beacon Street, Boston, Mass. 02106

Lothrop, Lee and Shepard Co., Inc., 105 Madison Avenue, New York, N.Y. 10016

Lyons. Lyons and Carnahan, Inc., 407 East 25 Street, Chicago, Ill. 60616

Love Publishing Co., 6635 East Villanova Place, Denver, Colo. 80222

Macmillan. The Macmillan Publishing Co., 866 Third Avenue, New York, N.Y. 10022

Macrae Smith Co., 225 South 15 Street, Philadelphia, Pa. 19102

Maico Hearing Instruments, 7375 Bush Lake Road, Minneapolis, Minn. 55435

Mast. Mast Development Co., 2212 East 12 Street, Davenport, Iowa 52803

McCormick. McCormick-Mathers Publishing Co., 450 West 33 Street, New York, N.Y. 10001

McGraw-Hill. McGraw-Hill Book Co., 1221 Avenue of the Americas, New York, N.Y. 10020

McKay. David McKay Co., Inc., 750 Third Avenue, New York, N.Y. 10017

Meeting Street School, 333 Grotto Avenue, Providence, R.I. 02906

Melmont Publishers, 1224 West Van Buren, Chicago, Ill. 60607

Meredith Corp., 440 Park Avenue South, New York, N.Y. 10016

Merrill. Charles E. Merrill Publishing Co., 1300 Alum Creek Drive, Columbus, Ohio 43216

Julian Messncr, Inc., 1 West 39 Street, New York, N.Y. 10036

Michigan State University Press, Box 550, East Lansing, Mich. 48823

Mills. The Mills Center, Inc., 1512 East Broward Boulevard, Fort Lauderdale, Fla. 33301

MIT Press, 28 Carleton Street, Cambridge, Mass. 02142

Minnesota. See University of Minnesota Press

Modern Curriculum Press, Inc., 13900 Prospect Road, Cleveland, Ohio 44136

Montana. Montana Reading Publications, 517 Remrock Road, Billings, Mont. 59102

William Morrow and Co., 105 Madison Avenue, New York, N.Y. 10016

C. V. Mosby Co., a subsidiary of the Times Mirror Co., 11830 Westline Industrial Drive, St. Louis, Mo. 63141

National Academy of Sciences, 2101 Constitution Avenue N.W., Washington, D.C. 20418

National Assessment Office, Room 201A, Huron Towers, 222 Fuller Road, Ann Arbor, Mich. 48105

National Association for the Deaf, 814 Thayer Avenue, Silver Springs, Md. 20910

National Association for the Education of Young Children, 1834 Connecticut Avenue, Washington, D.C. 20009

National Computer Systems, 4401 West 76th Street, Minneapolis, Minn. 55435

NCTE. National Council of Teachers of English, 1111 Kenyon Road, Urbana, Ill. 67801

National Foundation for Research in England & Wales. The Mere, Upton Park, Slough, England

Thomas Nelson and Sons, Ltd., 36 Park Street, London W1Y, England

Thomas Nelson, Inc., 407 Seventh Avenue South, Nashville, Tenn. 37203

C. M. Nevins Printing Co., Pittsburgh, Pa.

New Century. See Meredith Corp.

New Zealand Council for Educational Research, Education House, 178 Willis Street, Wellington C-2, New Zealand

Noble and Noble Publishers, 1 Dag Hammerskjold Plaza, New York, N.Y. 10017

Odyssey Press, Ltd., 300 East 42 Street, New York, N.Y. 10017

Ohio State University Press, Hitchcock Hall, Room 316, 2070 Neil Avenue, Columbus, Ohio 43210

Open Court Publishing Co., Box 599, La Salle, Ill. 61301

The Orton Society, Inc., 8415 Bellona Lane, Suite 204, Towson, Md., 21204

F. A. Owen Publishing Co., 7 Bank Street, Dansville, N.Y. 14437

Parents Magazine Press, 52 Vanderbilt Avenue, New York, N.Y. 10017

Parker Publishing Co., a subsidiary of Prentice-Hall, Inc., West Nyack, N.Y. 10994
Penguin Books, Inc., 7110 Ambassador Road, Baltimore, Md. 21207
PDL. Perceptual Development Laboratories, Box 1911, Big Spring, Texas 79720
Personnel Press. 191 Spring Street, Lexington, Mass. 02173
Phonovisual. Phonovisual Products, Inc., 12216 Parklawn Drive, Rockville, Md. 20852
Plays, Inc., Publishers, 8 Arlington Street, Boston, Mass. 02116
Polaski Co., Inc., Box 7466, Philadelphia, Pa. 19101
Prentice. Prentice-Hall, Inc., Englewood Cliffs, N.J. 07632
Priority Innovations. Inc., Box 792, Skokie, Ill. 60076
Psychological. The Psychological Corp., 757 Third Avenue, New York, N.Y. 10017
Psychological Test. Psychological Test Specialists, Box 1441, Missoula, Mont. 59801
Psychotechnics, Inc., 1900 Pickwick Avenue, Glenview, Ill. 60025
G. P. Putnam's Sons, 200 Madison Avenue, New York, N.Y. 10016
Pyramid Books, 919 Third Avenue, New York, N.Y. 10022
Rand-McNally and Co.. Box 7600, Chicago, Ill. 60680
Random. Random House, 201 East 50 Street, New York, N.Y. 10022
Reader's Digest Services, Inc., Educational Division, Pleasantville, N.Y. 10570
Reading Center, University of Missouri, Kansas City, Mo.
The Reading Institute of Boston, 116 Newbury Street, Boston, Mass. 02116
RIF. Reading is Fun-Damental, Smithsonian Institute, Washington, D.C. 20560
The Reading Laboratory, Inc., 55 Day Street. South Norwalk, Conn. 06854
Reilly and Lee Co., 114 West Illinois Street, Chicago, Ill. 60610
Remedial Education Press, Kingsbury Center, 2138 Bancroft Place N.W., Washington, D.C. 20008
Revrac Publications, 1535 Red Oak Drive, Silver Spring, Md. 20910
Rheem Califone, Inc., 5922 Bowercraft Street, Los Angeles, Calif. 90016
Frank E. Richards, Publisher, 324 First Street, Liverpool, N.Y. 13088
Right to Read, 400 Maryland Avenue S.W., Washington, D.C. 20202
The Ronald Press Co.. 79 Madison Avenue, New York, N.Y. 10016
Rotterdam University Press, P.O. Box 66, Groningen, Netherlands
Scarecrow Press, Inc., a subsidiary of Grolier, Inc., 52 Liberty Street, Box 656, Metuchen, N.J. 08840
Scholastic. Scholastic Magazines and Book Services, 50 West 44 Street, New York, N.Y. 10036
Scholastic Testing. Scholastic Testing Service, Inc., Bensenville, Ill. 60106
Scott Education Division, 35 Lower Westfield Road, Holyoke, Mass. 01040
Scott F. Scott, Foresman and Co., 1900 East Lake Avenue, Glenview, Ill. 60025
William R. Scott, Inc., 333 Sixth Avenue, New York, N.Y. 10014
Charles Scribner's Sons, 597 Fifth Avenue, New York, N.Y. 10017
The Seabury Press, 815 Second Avenue, New York, N.Y. 10017
Selected Academic Readings, 630 Fifth Avenue, New York, N.Y. 10017
Silver Burdette Division, General Learning Corp., 250 James Street, Morristown, N.J. 07960
Simon and Schuster, Inc., 630 Fifth Avenue, New York, N.Y. 10020
Singer. L. W. Singer, Inc., a Division of Random House, 201 East 50 Street, New York, N.Y. 10022
Singer Graphlex Division, 3750 Monroe Avenue, Rochester, N.Y. 14603
Slosson Educational Publications, 140 Pine Street, East Aurora, N.Y. 14052
Strine Publishing Co., 391 Greendale Road, York, Pa. 17403

SVE. Society for Visual Education, Inc., 1345 Diversey Parkway, Chicago, Ill. 60614

Special Child Publications, 4635 Union Bay Place N.E., Seattle, Wash. 98105

Spoken Arts, Inc., 310 North Avenue, New Rochelle, N.Y. 10801

SRA. Science Research Associates, Inc., 259 East Erie Street, Chicago, Ill. 60611

Steck. Steck-Vaughn Co., Box 2028, Austin, Texas 78767

Stoelting Co., 1350 South Kostner Avenue, Chicago, Ill. 60623

Syracuse University Press, Box 8, University Station, Syracuse, N.Y. 13210

Teachers. Teachers College Press, Columbia University, 1234 Amsterdam Avenue, New York, N.Y. 10027

Teachers Publishing, a Division of Macmillan Publishing, Inc., 100 F Brown Street, Riverside, N.J. 08075

Teaching Resources Corp., 100 Boylston Street, Boston, Mass. 02116

Teaching Technology Corp., 2103 Green Spring Drive, Timonium, Md. 21093

Technifax Corp., 195 Appleton Street, Holyoke, Mass. 01040

Charles C Thomas, Publisher, 301 East Lawrence Avenue, Springfield, Ill. 62717

3 M Co., Visual Product Division, Box 3344, St. Paul, Minn. 55101

Titmus Optical Vision Testers, 1312 West 7 Street, Piscataway, N.J. 08854

U.S. Government Printing Office, Division of Public Documents, Washington, D.C. 20402

University of Chicago Press, 1130 South Langley Avenue, Chicago, Ill. 60628

University of Illinois Press, Urbana, Ill. 61801

University of Minnesota Press, 2037 University Avenue S.E., Minneapolis, Minn. 55455

University Park Press, Chamber of Commerce Building, Baltimore, Md. 21202

The Vanguard Press, Inc., 424 Madison Avenue, New York, N.Y. 10017

The Viking Press, Inc., 625 Madison Avenue, New York, N.Y. 10022

Harr Wagner. *See* Field Educational Publications

Walach. J. Weston Walach, P.O. Box 658, Portland, Maine 04104

Henry Z. Walck, Inc., 750 Third Avenue, New York, N.Y. 10017

Ward Lock Educational Co., Ltd., 116 Baker Street, London W1M, England

Frederick Warne and Co., 101 Fifth Avenue, New York, N.Y. 10003

Washington Square Press, Inc., a Division of Simon and Schuster, 630 Fifth Avenue, New York, N.Y. 10020

Watts. Franklin Watts, Inc., 845 Third Avenue, New York, N.Y. 10022

Wayne State University Press, 5980 Cass Avenue, Detroit, Mich. 48202

Webster. Webster Division of McGraw-Hill Book Co., 1221 Avenue of the Americas, New York, N.Y. 10020

Weekly Reader, 245 Longhill Road, Middletown, Conn. 06457

Wenkart Phonic Readers, 4 Shady Hill Square, Cambridge, Mass. 02138

Western Psychological Services, Box 775, Beverly Hills, Calif. 90213

Western Publishing Co., 850 Third Avenue, New York, N.Y. 10022

Westinghouse Learning Corp., Box 30, Iowa City, Iowa 52240

The Westminister Press, Witherspoon Building, Philadelphia, Pa. 19107

Whitman. Albert Whitman and Co., 560 West Lake Street, Chicago, Ill. 60606

Wiley. John Wiley & Sons, Inc., 605 Third Avenue, New York, N.Y. 10016

Williams and Wilkins Co., 428 East Preston Street, Baltimore, Md. 21202

Wilson. H. W. Wilson Co., 950 University Avenue, Bronx, N.Y. 10452

Winston. *See* Holt, Rinehart and Winston

Winston Press, 25 Grove Terrace, Minneapolis, Minn. 55403

Winter Haven Lions Research Foundation, Inc., Box 112, Winter Haven, Fla. 33880

Wisconsin Design for Reading Skill Development. See National Computer Systems

Workshop Center for Open Education, 6 Shepard Hall, City College of New York, Convent Avenue and 140 Street, New York, N.Y. 10031

World Publishing Co., 280 Park Avenue, New York, N.Y. 10017

Xerox Education Publications, Education Center, Columbus, Ohio 43216

Zweig. Richard L. Zweig Associates, 20800 Beach Boulevard, Huntington Beach, Calif. 92648

Appendix D

THE HARRIS-JACOBSON READABILITY FORMULAS

This Appendix provides detailed directions for the use of two previously unpublished readability formulas.[1] Formula 1 is for use with materials that are probably below fourth-grade level in difficulty. Formula 2 is recommended when it seems probable that the material is of fourth reader or higher difficulty level.

PROCEDURE

Selecting Samples

Since the readability of the entire book (or single selection) to be measured is estimated on the basis of a small number of samples, it is important that the samples chosen should be representative of the entire book or selection. Even for a single selection, three samples should be taken and their results averaged. For a book, five samples are desirable. The samples should be spread at approximately equal intervals through the material and should be located by opening the book at random to a page within the appropriate part of the book (or selection). For three samples, chose one sample from the first third, one from within the middle third, and one from the final third. For five samples, choose one page at random from each fifth of the work. Do not use the first two paragraphs of a selection, in which there is often a concentration of new vocabulary, and do not count the verbal material in figures or tables.

1. A preliminary report on these formulas was presented at the 1973 Annual Conference of the International Reading Association. A progress report was presented at the Convention of the College Reading Association on October 31, 1974.

Start each sample at the beginning of a paragraph, marking the beginning with a check in the margin. Count 200 consecutive words and continue counting to the end of the sentence that contains the 200th word. Do not count numerals or other nonverbal symbols. Mark the end of the sample lightly in pencil, and write down the page number of the beginning of the sample, and the total number of words in the sample. If one is in a hurry, samples of about 100 words may be used; but these will be less reliable than the recommended length of about 200 words.

Selecting a Formula

Formula 1 is suitable for use with material that is thought to be below fourth-grade level in difficulty, and can be scored and computed by hand.[2]

Formula 2 is recommended when the material is thought to be above third-grade level in difficulty. Although it can be used with primary-grade material, it is less reliable at that range than Formula 1. It may be noted that Formula 1 and Formula 2 are alike except for different weights.

Scoring the Variables

Variable 1. This variable (V1) is the per cent of unique unfamiliar words. For these formulas a word is considered familiar if it is to be found in the Harris-Jacobson Short Readability Word List, which is reproduced on pages 662–675. That word list includes the pre-primer, primer, high first, and second reader level words in the Harris-Jacobson Core and Additional Lists (A. J. Harris and Jacobson, 1972, pp. 60–64) plus the inflected forms which were merged with their roots in developing the Harris-Jacobson word lists. The Short Readability Word List contains 912 root words and 1,880 inflected forms, totaling 2,792 words. The term "unique" means that an unfamiliar word is counted only the first time that it occurs in a given sample; it is not counted if it occurs again in that sample. Proper nouns such as names are not counted as unfamiliar.

In getting the score for V1, start at the beginning of the sample and make a tally mark for each word that is not in the Short Readability Word List.[3] Tally only the first occurrence of an unfamiliar word. With practice, one becomes familiar with the list and relatively few words have to be looked up in it. The fact that one does not have to apply an elaborate set of rules makes it faster and easier to score for this variable than for the corresponding variables in the Spache (1953) and Dale-Chall (1948) formulas.

Count the number of tallies. Divide this number by the number of words in

2. These formulas, and other readability formulas that are too complicated to employ except by computer, can be both scored and computed with special programs devised by Dr. Jacobson. Those interested in computer scoring and computation of readability may communicate with Dr. Milton D. Jacobson, Director, Bureau of Educational Research, University of Virginia, Charlottesville, Va. 22903.

3. Two other word lists were also tried out: a list containing only first-grade words, and a longer list containing first-, second-, and third-grade words. Neither did as well as the present Short List for the levels covered in these formulas, although there were indications that the longer list might be more suitable for formulas that would go up into secondary school readability levels.

the sample and multiply the result by 100 to express it in per cent. Use of a small calculating machine such as are now very common and inexpensive speeds up this and other arithmetic operations in applying the formulas.

Variable 2. This variable (V2) is average sentence length, more precisely described as the mean number of words per sentence.

Count the number of sentences in the sample. If there are headings or sub-headings, each is counted as a sentence. Divide the number of words in the sample by the number of sentences, to three decimal places. The result is the score for V2.

Applying the Formulas

Formula 1. This formula is represented by the following regression equation:

$$\text{Predicted Score} = .094\ V1 + .168\ V2 + .502$$

Sample: 201 words, 14 words not in the Short List, 28 sentences

Step 1. Obtain the V1 score as explained above.
$$14 \div 201 = .0696 \times 100 = 6.96\%$$
Step 2. Obtain the V2 score as explained above.
$$201 \div 28 = 7.179$$
Step 3. Multiply the V1 score by .094
$$6.96 \times .094 = .654$$
Step 4. Multiply the V2 score by .168
$$7.179 \times .168 = 1.206$$
Step 5. Add together the product of Step 3, the product of Step 4, and .502 (a constant). This gives the Predicted Score.
$$.654 + 1.206 + .502 = 2.362 = \text{Predicted Score}$$
Step 6. Using the Formula 1 column in Table 14, find the readability level corresponding to the Predicted Score.
Readability level corresponding to 2.362 is Low Second.

Formula 2. This formula is represented by the following regression equation:

$$\text{Predicted Score} = .140\ V1 + .153\ V2 + .560$$

Sample: 213 words; 49 unfamiliar words; 22 sentences.

Step 1. Obtain V1 score as explained above.
$$49 \div 213 = .230 \times 100 = 23.00\%$$
Step 2. Obtain V2 score as explained above.
$$213 \div 22 = 9.681$$
Step 3. Multiply Step 1 result by .140
$$.140 \times 23.00 = 3.220$$
Step 4. Multiply Step 2 result by .153
$$.153 \times 9.681 = 1.481$$
Step 5. Add the products of Steps 3 and 4, and add .560.
$$3.220 + 1.481 + .560 = 5.261 = \text{Predicted Score}$$
Step 6. Using the Formula 2 part of Table 14, the readability level corresponding to a Predicted Score of 5.261 is Fifth.

TABLE 14. *Readability levels corresponding to predicted scores on two H-J Readability Formulas*

	Predicted Score	
Readability Level	Formula 1	Formula 2
Pre-primer	1.0 –1.53	1.0 –1.63
Primer	1.54–1.74	1.64–1.83
First reader	1.75–1.98	1.84–2.07
Low second	1.99–2.37	2.08–2.42
High second	2.38–2.84	2.43–2.98
Low third	2.85–3.30	2.99–3.70
High third	3.31–3.74	3.71–4.21
Fourth	3.75 and up	4.22–4.80
Fifth		4.81–5.28
Sixth		5.29–5.67
Seventh		5.68–6.05[a]
Eighth and up		6.06 and up

[a] *Scores above sixth grade are based on extrapolation.*

HARRIS-JACOBSON READABILITY
Formula 1 Worksheet

Book title_____ Author_____

Publisher_____ Date of copyright_____

	Samples				
	1	**2**	**3**	**4**	**5**
Pages:	*15, 16*				
A. No. of words in sample	201				
B. No. of words not in list	14				
C. No. of sentences	28				
Step					
1. $V1 = B \div A \times 100$	6.96%				
2. $V2 = A \div C$	7.179				
3. $V1 \times .094$	.654				
4. $V2 \times .168$	1.206				
5. Add Steps 3 and 4 and	.502	.502	.502	.502	.502
= Predicted Score	2.362				
6. Readability level from Table 14	Low 2				

FIGURE **D.1.** *Sample worksheet for the Harris-Jacobson Readability Formula 1. The data for Sample 1 have been entered.*

A worksheet which is laid out to expedite the computation of Formula 1 for five samples is shown in Figure D.1. The same form can be used for Formula 2 by just replacing the numerical constants.

FORMULA DEVELOPMENT, VALIDITY, AND READABILITY

Development of the H-J Readability Formulas

In the process of developing the *Basic Elementary Reading Vocabularies* (A. J. Harris and Jacobson, 1972) six series of basal readers that were in wide use in 1970 were employed. Development of one or more readability formulas that would use these series as a base seemed a logical next step. Readability was narrowly defined, for this purpose, as those characteristics of reading material which make for ease or difficulty in reading comprehension.

Establishing the Criterion. It was assumed that in preparing a series of basal readers covering from beginning first grade through sixth grade, each book in the series would be somewhat more difficult to read than the preceding book in the same series. The average difficulty characteristics of the six series should, then, provide a satisfactory criterion for the development of readability formulas.

Each of the six series included twelve books (three pre-primers, primer, first reader, low second, high second, low third, high third, fourth, fifth, and sixth). At each level from primer up, ten samples were chosen from each reader, approximately evenly spaced through the book. This provided 60 samples at each of those levels. At pre-primer level there was not enough content in one book to provide ten samples, so the three pre-primers were considered as one work. Each sample was slightly more than 200 words, continuing to the end of the sentence that contained the 200th word. Altogether there were 661 samples, totaling about 135,000 words.

Each sample at a given level was given a reading difficulty score using the following scale: pre-primer, 1.2; primer, 1.5; first reader, 1.8; low second, 2.3; high second, 2.7; low third, 3.3; high third, 3.7; fourth, 4.45; fifth, 5.45; and sixth, 6.45. It was understood that some of the samples would be easier and some harder than these values, introducing some inaccuracy into the criterion, but this could not be helped, and its effect would be to lower somewhat the correlations between readability scores and the criterion.

The samples were typed onto IBM cards with computer-readable type and entered into the computer. Each sample was then scored by the computer for ten variables, which had all been used in previous readability studies. One of the requirements was that a variable had to be scorable both by hand and by computer. Three of the variables were dropped after preliminary tryouts.

The correlation matrix for the seven variables and the criterion was computed, and then an iterative multiple-correlation program was applied to produce the best two-variable combination and the best three-variable combination. This was done separately for grades 1–3, grades 3–6,, grades 4–6, and grades 1–6. Since the correlations for grades 1–3 and 1–6 were substantially higher than those for grades 3–6 and 4–6, the former were the ones chosen. In addition to the formulas chosen as the best by the computer program, a number of other combinations of variables were tried, which seemed to have a possible advantage in ease of hand computation. The two formulas presented here were the ones with the best combination of speed and ease of computation with high correlations with the criterion.

Statistical Validity. The two formulas have the same high multiple-correlation coefficient with the criterion, represented by an R of .90 (see Table 15). The relative accuracy of prediction from a correlation is indicated by the square of the coefficient, R^2. R^2 is .81 for Formula 1 and .82 for Formula 2, a difference that is not significant; both indicate a high degree of accuracy.

The standard error of estimate of a predicted score indicates the margin of error to be expected in that score, as compared to the "true" score. Of 100 estimated or predicted readability scores, approximately two-thirds can be expected to be within one standard error of the true score, and the chances are 19 to 1 that the true score is within two standard errors of the predicted score.

TABLE 15. *Multiple correlation coefficients, R^2, and standard errors of estimate for two readability formulas*

	R	R^2	S.E. est.
Formula 1	.90	.81	.384
Formula 2	.90	.82	.714

Using the predicted score for the sample used for Formula 1, which is 2.362, the chances are approximately two to one that the true score is between $2.362 + .384$ and $2.362 - .384$, or between 1.98 and 2.74. The estimated reading level of Low Second is probably but not certainly correct. When several samples are taken and their predicted scores are averaged, however, the margin of error is substantially reduced.

The standard error for Formula 2 is almost twice as large as the standard error for Formula 1, making the latter the preferred formula for primary-grade material. It should be noted, however, that a reading level in grades 2 and 3 covers a half grade. A standard error of .384 is 77 per cent of a reading level for Formula 1, while a standard error of .714 is 71 per cent of a reader level for Formula 2, when used with middle-grade material. Thus the standard errors of estimate for the primary and intermediate levels are approximately equal in terms of reader levels.

At this time the formulas have not been correlated with other possible criteria of reading difficulty, such as the McCall-Crabbs exercises (which were used in constructing the Dale-Chall and Lorge readability formulas), or the measured ability of pupils to comprehend the passages.

Construct validity is the degree to which the measure conforms to a theoretical base. Linguists have emphasized that the ease or difficulty of language is dependent on lexical (word meaning) and syntactic (grammatical) factors. In the past, research by Lorge (1944), Dale and Chall (1948), Spache (1953), and others has shown that the generally most satisfactory measure of vocabulary difficulty is the proportion of words that are outside of a list of common, easy words. The word lists used by those researchers are now quite old, and the Short Readability Word List employed in the present formulas is far more recent, and based on a more solid sampling of basal reader material, than the lists used in previous formulas.[4]

Syntactic difficulty is the other major factor in the difficulty of reading materials. In recent years several attempts have been made to devise linguistically sound measures of sentence complexity. MacGinitie and Tretiak (1971) tried out several of them which had been devised by Allen (1966) and Yngve (1962). They found that none of the measures of sentence depth, when combined with ratio of hard words, gave as high a correlation with the criterion as did the combination of ratio of hard words with average sentence length. The longer a sentence, the harder it is to read, on the average. This does not apply, of course, to the difficulty of single sentences, which may be quite hard or easy, depending on the words in them and the degree of grammatical complexity.

The extant research, then, supports the present research in finding that ratio of hard words (measured by the present Variable 1) and average sentence length (measured by the present Variable 2) provide the best two measures when combined by the technique of multiple correlation. Additional variables add very little to this combination. The present Formulas 1 and 2 use these two same variables, but give them somewhat different weights. Sentence length seems to be somewhat more important in primary materials and word difficulty more important in middle-grade materials.

Reliability

Since the correlation of a measure with a criterion cannot be higher than that measure's reliability, the Rs given in Table 15 represent minimal estimates of the reliability of the two readability formulas, when a single sample is used. When more than one sample is used and the results are averaged, the reliability is raised as indicated by the Spearman-Brown prophecy formula. The use of three samples, which is the minimum we recommend, increases the reliability of Formula 1 from .898 to .964; using five samples increases it to .978. This indicates that three samples are often enough and five samples are quite enough, provided that they have been selected in a way that is representative of the total material.[5]

Speed and Ease of Computation

The Harris-Jacobson Readability Formulas were developed with the use of a computer and can be scored and computed either by hand or by a computer. The Short Readability Word List (pp. 666–675) which is used in getting the score for Variable 1 contains every word that is counted as familiar; any word not in that list is automatically unfamiliar. This eliminates the need to remember or consult and apply rules, and takes little time.

The Spache and Dale-Chall formulas both require the application of many rules in getting a count of unfamiliar words. The Spache Formula requires the application of 10 rules to determine if particular words are familiar or unfamiliar.

4. Since this Appendix was completed, Spache (1974) has come out with a revised readability formula for primary grades.

5. Since this Appendix was completed, the reliabilities of the two formulas have been computed using the split-half method corrected with the Spearman-Brown Formula. The reliability coefficient for Formula 1 is .93; that for Formula 2 is .94.

The particular inflectional endings that are considered to be equivalent to their root words need to be memorized or looked up over and over again.

The Dale-Chall Formula has a total of 19 rules for determining when particular classes of words are to be considered familiar or unfamiliar. Unless one has memorzied the rules and applied them often, considerable time is needed to consult the rules and study the examples given. Although most unfamiliar words are counted each time they occur, certain special classes of items are counted only twice, no matter how often they occur in one sample. The word list used for the Dale-Chall Formula contains more than three times as many root words as the Short Readability Word List, and even with all of the inflected forms included, the latter list contains fewer items than the list used for the Dale-Chall Formula.

It is evident, therefore, that the unfamiliar word count for the Harris-Jacobson Formulas takes considerably less time and effort than the corresponding count for either the Spache or the Dale-Chall Formula.

When the older readability formulas were developed, multiplying or dividing with numbers having two or three places to the right of the decimal point was quite burdensome to many people, and some formulas rounded the weights to simplify the arithmetic, with a little loss of accuracy. The wide availability of inexpensive little calculating machines today makes the number of decimal places an irrelevant factor.

THE HARRIS-JACOBSON SHORT READABILITY WORD LIST

a
able
abler
ablest
about
above
across
act
acted
acting
acts
add
added
adding
adds
afraid
after
again
ago
ahead
air
aired
airing
airplane
airplanes
airs
all
almost
alone
along
also
always
am
an
and
ands
angrier
angriest
angrily
angry
animal
animals
animal's
another
another's
answer
answered
answering
answers
any
anyone

anyone's
anything
apartment
apartments
apple
apples
are
arm
armed
arming
arms
arm's
around
as
ask
asked
asking
asks
at
ate
aunt
aunts
aunt's
away
babies
baby
baby's
back
backed
backing
backs
bad
badly
bag
bags
bake
baked
baker
bakes
baking
ball
balloon
ballooning
balloons
balls
ball's
bang
banged
banging
bangs
bank

banked
banker
banking
banks
bank's
bar
bark
barked
barking
barks
barn
barns
barred
barring
bars
basket
baskets
be
bear
bears
bear's
beautiful
beautifully
because
bed
bedded
bedding
beds
bed's
bee
been
bees
bee's
before
began
begin
beginner
beginning
begins
behind
believe
believed
believer
believes
believing
bell
bells
bell's
belong
belonged
belonging

belongs
beside
besides
best
better
between
big
bigger
biggest
bike
bikes
bird
birds
bird's
birthday
birthdays
bit
bits
black
blacker
blackest
blacks
black's
blast-off
blew
block
blocked
blocking
blocks
blow
blowed
blower
blowing
blows
blowy
blue
blueberries
blueberry
blues
blue's
boat
boating
boats
boat's
bone
boned
bones
boning
book
books
book's

boot
boots
booty
both
bottle
bottled
bottles
bottle's
bottling
bottom
bottomed
bottoms
bought
bounce
bounced
bounces
bouncing
bowl
bowled
bowler
bowling
bowls
box
boxed
boxer
boxes
boxing
boy
boys
boy's
branch
branched
branches
branching
brave
braved
bravely
braver
braves
bravest
break
breaker
breakfast
breakfasts
breaking
breaks
bridge
bridged
bridges
bright
brighter

brightest
brightly
bring
bringing
brings
brook
brooks
brother
brotherly
brothers
brother's
brought
brown
browns
brown's
build
builder
building
builds
bump
bumped
bumper
bumping
bumps
bumpy
bunnies
bunny
bunny's
burn
burned
burner
burning
burns
bus
buses
busier
busiest
busily
busy
bus's
but
buts
butter
buttered
buttering
butters
button
buttoned
buttoning
buttons
buy

buyer	caterpillar	clears	cornered	crow's	dinner's
buying	caterpillars	clever	corners	cry	dirtied
buys	caterpillar's	cleverest	cornfield	crying	dirtier
by	cats	cleverly	cornfields	cup	dirties
cage	cat's	climb	corns	cupcake	dirtiest
caged	caught	climbed	could	cupcakes	dirty
cages	cellar	climber	couldn't	cupped	dish
cake	cellars	climbing	count	cupping	dished
caked	chair	climbs	counted	cups	dishes
cakes	chairs	clock	counter	cut	dishing
calf	chance	clocked	counting	cuts	do
calf's	chanced	clocking	countries	dad	doctor
call	chances	clocks	country	daddy	doctors
called	chancing	close	country's	daddy's	doctor's
calling	chase	closed	counts	dads	does
calls	chased	closely	cover	dad's	dog
came	chases	closer	covered	dairies	dogs
can	chasing	closes	covering	dairy	dog's
candle	cherries	closest	covers	dairy's	doing
candles	cherry	closing	cow	dance	doll
canned	chicken	clown	cowboy	danced	dollar
canning	chickens	clowned	cowboys	dancer	dollars
cannot	chicken's	clowning	cowboy's	dances	dollar's
cans	children	clowns	cows	dancing	dolls
can't	children's	clown's	cow's	dark	dolly
car	choose	coat	crawl	darker	doll's
card	chooses	coated	crawled	darkest	done
cards	choosey	coating	crawler	darkly	don't
care	choosing	coats	crawling	day	door
cared	circus	coat's	crawls	days	doors
careful	circuses	cold	crayon	day's	dot
carefully	circus's	colder	crayoned	dear	dots
cares	cities	coldest	crayoning	dearer	dotted
caring	city	coldly	crayons	dearest	dotting
carried	city's	colds	cream	dearly	down
carrier	class	color	creamed	dears	dragon
carries	classed	colored	creamer	deep	dragons
carry	classes	coloring	creams	deeper	dragon's
carrying	classroom	colors	creamy	deepest	drank
cars	classrooms	come	cried	deeply	dream
cart	clean	comes	cries	deer	dreamed
carted	cleaned	coming	cross	deer's	dreamer
carting	cleaner	cook	crossed	did	dreamily
carts	cleaning	cooked	crosser	didn't	dreaming
car's	cleans	cookie	crosses	different	dreams
cat	clear	cookies	crossing	differently	dreamy
catch	cleared	cooking	crossly	dig	dress
catcher	clearer	cooks	crow	digging	dressed
catches	clearest	cook's	crowed	digs	dresser
catching	clearing	corn	crowing	dinner	dresses
catchy	clearly	corner	crows	dinners	dressing

dressy	eights	fairy's	fielder	fitted	found
dried	elephant	fall	fielding	fitter	founded
drier	elephants	falling	fields	fitting	founding
dries	elephant's	falls	field's	five	founds
driest	elevator	families	fierce	fives	four
drink	elevators	family	fiercely	fix	fours
drinker	else	family's	fiercest	fixed	fourth
drinking	else's	far	fight	fixer	fourths
drinks	emptied	farm	fighter	fixes	fox
drive	emptier	farmed	fighting	fixing	foxes
driver	empties	farmer	fights	flat	fox's
drives	empty	farmers	fill	flatly	friend
driving	emptying	farmer's	filled	flats	friendlier
drop	end	farming	filler	flatter	friendliest
dropped	ended	farms	filling	flattest	friendly
dropping	ending	fast	fills	flatly	friends
drops	ends	faster	find	flew	friend's
dry	end's	fastest	finding	flies	frighten
drying	enough	fat	finds	float	frightened
dryly	even	father	fine	floated	frightening
duck	evened	fathers	fined	floater	frightens
ducked	evening	father's	finely	floating	from
ducking	evenings	fats	finer	floats	front
ducks	evening's	fatter	fines	floor	fronts
duck's	evenly	fattest	finest	floored	fruit
each	evens	feather	finger	flooring	fruits
ear	ever	feathered	fingered	floors	fruit's
earlier	every	feathering	fingering	flower	fruity
earliest	everyone	feathers	fingers	flowered	full
early	everyone's	feathery	fining	flowering	fuller
earn	everything	feed	finish	flowers	fullest
earned	everything's	feeder	finished	flowery	fully
earning	excited	feeding	finishes	flower's	fun
earns	excitedly	feeds	finishing	fly	funnier
ears	eye	feel	fire	flying	funnies
ear's	eyed	feeler	fired	fly's	funniest
earth	eyeglass	feeling	fireman	follow	funny
earthly	eyeglasses	feels	fireman's	followed	game
earthy	eyeing	feet	fires	follower	gamely
earth's	eyes	fell	fire's	following	games
easier	face	felt	firing	follows	garage
easiest	faced	fence	first	food	garages
easily	faces	fenced	firsts	foods	garden
easy	facing	fencer	fish	foot	gardened
eat	fair	fences	fished	footing	gardener
eating	fairer	fencing	fishes	for	gardening
eats	fairest	few	fishing	forest	gardens
egg	fairies	fewer	fishy	forested	gate
egging	fairly	fewest	fish's	forests	gates
eggs	fairs	field	fit	forest's	gave
eight	fairy	fielded	fits	forgot	get

gets	gray's	hangs	hid	housed	I've
getting	great	happen	hide	houses	jar
giant	greater	happened	hides	housing	jarred
giants	greatest	happens	hiding	how	jarring
giant's	greatly	happening	high	how's	jars
girl	green	happier	higher	huge	jay
girls	greener	happiest	highest	hugely	jays
girl's	greenest	happily	highly	hung	jay's
give	greens	happy	highs	hungrier	job
giver	greeting	hard	hill	hungriest	jobs
gives	greetings	harder	hills	hungrily	job's
giving	grew	hardest	hilly	hungry	joke
glad	ground	hardly	him	hunt	joked
gladder	grounded	harp	himself	hunted	joker
gladdest	grounding	harped	his	hunter	jokes
gladly	grounds	harping	hit	hunting	joking
glass	grow	harps	hits	hunts	joy
glasses	grower	has	hitter	hurries	joys
glassy	growing	hat	hitting	hurry	jump
glove	grows	hats	hold	hurrying	jumped
gloved	guess	have	holder	hurt	jumper
gloves	guessed	having	holding	hurting	jumping
go	guesser	he	holds	hurts	jumps
goat	guesses	head	hole	I	just
goats	guessing	headed	holed	ice	keep
goat's	gun	header	holes	iced	keeper
goes	gunned	heading	home	I'd	keepers
going	gunner	heads	homely	idea	keeper's
gold	gunning	hear	homes	ideas	keeping
gone	guns	heard	honey	if	keeps
good	had	hearing	hop	ifs	kept
goodly	hair	hears	hope	I'll	kill
goods	hairs	heavier	hoped	I'm	killed
good-by	hairy	heaviest	hopes	in	killer
good-bye	hall	heavily	hoping	indoor	killing
goose	halls	heavy	hopped	indoors	kills
goose's	hall's	held	hopping	inner	kind
got	hand	helium	hoppy	inside	kinder
grandfather	handed	hello	hops	insides	kindest
grandfathers	handing	help	horn	instead	kindly
grandfather's	handle	helped	horned	into	kinds
grandmother	handled	helping	horns	iron	king
grandmothers	handler	helps	horny	ironed	kingly
grand-	handles	hen	horse	ironer	kings
mother's	handling	hens	horses	ironing	king's
grass	hands	hen's	horse's	irons	kitchen
grasses	handy	her	hot	is	kitchens
grassy	hang	here	hotly	isn't	kite
gray	hanged	hers	hotter	it	kites
graying	hanger	herself	hottest	its	kite's
grays	hanging	hi	house	it's	kitten

kittens	learns	listened	mail's	miller	named
kitten's	leave	listener	make	millers	names
knew	leaves	listening	makes	miller's	name's
knock	leaving	listens	making	mind	naming
knocked	led	little	man	minded	near
knocker	left	littlest	manned	minding	nearby
knocking	leg	live	manning	minds	neared
knocks	legged	lived	man's	mind's	nearer
know	legs	lives	many	mine	nearest
knowing	lemon	living	mark	mined	nearing
knows	lemonade	long	marked	mines	nearly
ladder	lemonades	longed	marker	mining	nears
ladders	lemons	longer	marking	minute	neck
lake	let	longest	marks	minutes	necks
lakes	lets	longing	mark's	minute's	need
lamb	let's	longs	matter	miss	needed
lambs	letter	look	mattered	missed	needier
lamb's	lettered	looked	matters	misses	needing
land	lettering	looking	may	missing	needs
landed	letters	looking	maybe	money	needy
landing	letting	looks	me	money's	neighbor
lands	libraries	lost	mean	monkey	neighboring
land's	library	lot	meaner	monkeys	neighbors
large	library's	lots	meanest	monkey's	neighbor's
largely	lick	loud	meaning	more	nest
larger	licked	louder	means	morning	nested
largest	licker	loudest	meet	mornings	nesting
last	licking	loudly	meeting	morning's	nests
lasted	licks	love	meets	most	never
lasting	life	loved	men	mostly	new
lastly	lifes	lovely	men's	mother	newer
lasts	life's	loves	merrier	mothered	newest
late	light	loving	merriest	mothers	newly
lately	lighted	low	merrily	mother's	news
later	lighter	lower	merry	mountain	next
latest	lightest	lowest	merry-go-	mountains	nice
laugh	lighting	lowing	round	mountain's	nicely
laughed	lightly	lowly	merry-go-	mouse	nicer
laughing	lights	luck	rounds	mouse's	nicest
laughs	like	luckier	met	mouth	night
lay	liked	luckiest	might	mouths	nightly
laying	likely	luckily	mightier	move	nights
lays	likes	lucky	mightiest	moved	night's
lazier	liking	lunch	mighty	mover	no
laziest	line	lunches	mile	moves	noise
lazily	lined	made	miles	moving	noises
lazy	lines	magic	milk	much	noisily
learn	lion	mail	milked	must	noisy
learned	lions	mailed	milking	my	none
learner	lion's	mailing	milks	myself	nose
learning	listen	mails	milky	name	nosed

noses	ovens	pats	pieced	ponds	quacked
not	over	patted	pieced	pond's	quacking
note	overly	patting	pieces	ponies	quacks
noted	owl	paw	piecing	pony	quacky
notes	owls	pawed	pies	pony's	queer
nothing	owl's	pawing	pig	pool	queerest
noting	own	paws	pigs	pools	queerly
now	owned	pay	pig's	poor	quick
number	owning	pay	pile	poorer	quicker
numbered	owns	payer	piled	poorest	quickest
numbering	pail	paying	piles	poorly	quickly
numbers	pails	pays	piling	pop	quiet
oak	paint	peanut	pink	popcorn	quieted
oaks	painted	peanuts	pinks	popped	quieter
oak's	painter	peep	place	popper	quietest
of	painting	peeped	placed	popping	quietly
off	paints	peeping	places	pops	quiets
oh	pair	peeps	placing	pop's	quite
oil	paired	pen	plan	postcard	rabbit
oiled	pairing	penguin	planned	postcards	rabbits
oiling	pairs	penguins	planner	postman	rabbit's
oils	pan	penguin's	planning	postman's	raccoon
oily	pane	penned	plans	prettier	raccoons
old	panes	pennies	plant	prettiest	raccoon's
older	panned	penning	planted	prettily	race
oldest	panning	penny	planter	pretty	raced
olds	pans	penny's	planting	prize	races
on	paper	pens	plants	prized	racing
once	papered	people	plant's	prizes	radish
one	papers	peopled	play	proud	radishes
ones	parade	peoples	played	prouder	rag
one's	paraded	people's	playing	proudest	ragged
only	parades	pet	plays	proudly	ragging
open	parading	pets	please	pull	rags
opened	park	petted	pleased	pulled	rain
opener	parked	petting	pleases	pulling	rainbow
opening	parking	pet's	pleasing	pulls	rainbows
openly	parks	pick	pocket	pup	rainbow's
opens	part	picked	pocketed	puppies	rained
or	parted	picker	pockets	puppy	raining
other	parties	picking	point	puppy's	rains
others	parting	picks	pointed	pups	rainy
other's	partly	picnic	pointer	pup's	ran
our	parts	picnics	pointing	push	ranch
ours	party	picture	points	pushed	rancher
out	pass	pictured	pointy	pushes	ranches
outing	passed	pictures	policeman	pushing	ranching
outs	passes	picture's	policeman's	put	reach
outside	passing	picturing	policemen	puts	reached
outsider	past	pie	policemen's	putting	reaches
oven	pat	piece	pond	quack	reaching

read	rockets	safes	seeing	shook	singer
reader	rocket's	safest	seem	shop	singing
readied	rocking	said	seemed	shopped	sings
readily	rocks	sailboat	seeming	shopping	sister
reading	rocky	sailboats	seemly	shops	sisters
reads	rode	same	seems	short	sister's
ready	roll	sand	seen	shorter	sit
real	rolled	sanded	sees	shortest	sits
really	roller	sander	seesaw	shortly	sitting
red	rollers	sanding	seesawed	shorts	six
reds	rolling	sands	seesawing	should	sixes
remember	rolls	sandy	seesaws	shout	skate
remembered	roof	sang	sell	shouted	skated
remembering	roofed	sat	seller	shouting	skater
remembers	roofer	save	selling	shouts	skates
rest	roofing	saved	sells	shovel	skating
rested	roofs	saver	send	shoveled	sled
resting	room	saves	sender	shoveling	sledding
rests	roomed	saving	sending	shovels	sleds
return	roomer	saw	sends	show	sleep
returned	rooming	sawed	sent	showed	sleeper
returning	rooms	sawing	set	showing	sleepily
returns	roomy	saws	sets	shows	sleeping
ride	rope	say	setter	shut	sleeps
rides	roped	saying	setting	shuts	sleepy
riding	ropes	says	seven	shutter	slid
right	roping	scare	sevens	shutting	slide
rightly	round	scarecrow	shall	side	slides
rights	rounded	scarecrows	shape	sided	sliding
ring	rounding	scarecrow's	shaped	sides	slow
ringed	roundly	scared	shapely	sidewalk	slowed
ringing	rounds	scares	shapes	sidewalks	slower
rings	row	scaring	shaping	sight	slowest
river	rowed	school	she	sighted	slowing
rivers	rower	schooling	shed	sighting	slowly
river's	rowing	schools	shedding	sights	slows
road	rows	school's	sheds	sign	small
roads	rub	sea	sheep	signed	smaller
roar	rubbed	seas	sheep's	signer	smallest
roared	rubbing	seat	ship	signing	smell
roaring	rubs	seated	shipped	signs	smelled
roars	run	seating	shipper	sign's	smelling
robin	running	seats	shipping	silk	smells
robins	runs	second	ships	silks	smelly
robin's	sad	secondly	ship's	silky	smile
rock	sadder	seconds	shirt	sillier	smiled
rocked	saddest	see	shirts	silliest	smiles
rocker	sadly	seed	shoe	silly	smiling
rocket	safe	seeded	shoed	silver	smoke
rocketed	safely	seeding	shoeing	silvery	smoked
rocketing	safer	seeds	shoes	sing	smoker

smokes	spoke	still	summer	tapes	third
smoking	spokes	stone	summers	taping	thirdly
smoky	spot	stoned	summer's	teach	thirds
snapper	spots	stones	sun	teacher	this
snappers	spotted	stoning	sunning	teachers	those
snapper's	spotting	stood	suns	teacher's	thought
snow	spring	stop	sun's	teaches	thoughts
snowed	springing	stopped	supper	teaching	three
snowing	springs	stopping	suppers	tear	threes
snowman	squirrel	stops	sure	teared	three's
snowman's	squirrels	store	surely	tearing	threw
snows	squirrel's	stored	surprise	tears	through
snowy	stamp	stores	surprised	teary	throw
so	stamped	store's	surprises	teeth	throwing
soft	stamper	storied	surprising	telephone	throws
softer	stamping	stories	swam	telephoned	thumb
softest	stamps	storing	sweet	telephones	thumbed
softly	stand	story	sweeter	telephoning	thumbing
some	standing	story's	sweetest	tell	thumbs
someone	stands	straight	sweetly	teller	tie
someone's	star	strange	sweets	telling	tied
something	stare	strangely	swim	tells	ties
sometime	stared	strangest	swimmer	ten	tiger
sometimes	stares	stream	swimming	tens	tigers
son	staring	streamed	swims	tent	tiger's
song	starred	streamer	swish	tented	time
songs	starring	streaming	swished	tenth	timed
sons	stars	streams	swishes	tenths	timely
son's	star's	street	swishing	tents	times
soon	start	streets	swishy	than	time's
sooner	started	stretch	table	thank	timing
sorrier	starter	stretched	tables	thanked	tinier
sorriest	starting	stretcher	tail	thanking	tiniest
sorry	starts	stretches	tailed	thanks	tiny
sound	station	stretching	tailing	that	tip
sounded	stationed	string	tails	that's	tipped
sounder	stations	stringed	take	the	tipper
soundest	station's	stringing	taken	their	tipping
sounding	stay	strings	takes	theirs	tips
soundly	stayed	stringy	taking	them	tire
sounds	staying	strong	talk	then	tired
soup	stays	stronger	talked	there	tires
soups	step	strongest	talker	these	tiring
soupy	stepped	strongly	talking	they	to
spaceship	stepping	such	talks	thing	today
spaceships	steps	sudden	tall	things	todays
spaceship's	stick	suddenly	taller	thing's	today's
splash	sticker	suit	tallest	think	together
splashed	sticking	suited	tape	thinker	told
splashes	sticks	suiting	taped	thinking	tomorrow
splashing	sticky	suits	taper	thinks	tomorrows

tomorrow's	tree's	uncle's	warms	whisper	wishes
tonight	trick	under	was	whispered	wishing
tonights	tricked	unhappily	wash	whispering	with
tonight's	tricking	unhappy	washed	whispers	without
too	tricks	until	washer	whistle	woke
took	tricky	up	washes	whistled	wolf
tooth	tried	ups	washing	whistler	wolf's
toothed	tries	us	watch	whistles	woman
toothily	trip	use	watched	whistling	woman's
top	tripped	used	watches	white	wonder
topped	tripping	user	watching	whiter	wondered
topper	trips	uses	water	whites	wonderful
topping	trot	using	watered	whitest	wonderfully
tops	trots	very	watering	who	wondering
toward	trotted	visit	waters	who's	wonders
towards	trotting	visited	watery	why	won't
tower	trouble	visiting	water's	whys	wood
towered	troubled	visits	wave	wide	wooded
towering	troubles	voice	waved	widely	woods
towers	troubling	voiced	waves	wider	woody
tower's	truck	voices	waving	widest	word
town	trucked	voicing	way	wife	worded
towns	trucking	wag	ways	wife's	words
town's	trucks	wagged	we	will	work
toy	true	wagging	wear	wills	worked
toys	truer	wagon	wearing	win	working
toy's	truest	wagons	wears	wind	works
track	trunk	wags	week	windier	world
tracked	trunks	wait	weekly	windiest	worldly
tracking	try	waited	weeks	winding	worlds
tracks	trying	waiter	week's	window	world's
tractor	turn	waiting	well	windows	would
tractors	turned	waits	wells	winds	write
tractor's	turning	walk	went	wind's	writer
traffic	turns	walked	were	windy	writes
train	turtle	walker	wet	wing	writing
trained	turtles	walking	wets	winged	wrong
trainer	turtle's	walks	wettest	winging	wronging
trainers	tv	wall	wetting	wings	wrongly
trainer's	tv's	walled	we'll	winner	wrongs
training	twice	walls	what	winning	wrote
trains	twin	want	wheel	wins	yard
train's	twins	wanted	wheeled	winter	yards
trap	twin's	wanting	wheeler	winters	year
trapped	two	wants	wheeling	winter's	yearly
trapper	twos	warm	wheels	wise	years
trapping	uglier	warmed	wheel's	wisely	year's
traps	ugliest	warmer	when	wiser	yell
tree	ugly	warmest	where	wisest	yelled
treed	uncle	warming	which	wish	yelling
trees	uncles	warmly	while	wished	yellow

yellowed	yes	you'll	youngest	yourself
yellows	yet	young	your	zoo
yells	you	younger	yours	zoos

Name Index

Name index

Aaron, I. E., 15
Aasen, H. B., 534
Abrams, A. L., 138
Abrams, J. C., 144
Achenbach, T. M., 258
Ackerman, P. T., 244, 245, 252
Adams, A. H., 344
Adams, R. B., 138
Adamson, E. C., 432
Adelman, H. S., 142
Adler, S., 164, 298
Aftanas, M. S., 240
Ahrendt, K. M., 553
Alexander, J. C., 572
Allen, J. E., 3
Allen, M., 147
Allen, R. L., 461, 664
Allen, R. V., 67
Allington, R. L., 388, 411
Allred, R. A., 211
Almy, M., 28
Amatruda, C. S., 263
Amble, B. R., 463
Ames, L. B., 32, 52, 143
Ames, W. S., 410
Amsden, R. H., 520
Anastasiow, N., 190

Anderson, A. R., 66
Anderson, J., 37
Anderson, R. H., 91, 94
Anderson, R. P., 257
Anderson, R. W., 280
Angoff, W. H., 163
Annett, M., 275
Anthony, G. A., 272
Archer, M. P., 541
Arnott, W., 284
Artley, A. S., 78, 87, 506
Ashton-Warner, S., 363
Askov, E., 68, 104
Askov, W., 35
Athey, I., 4, 305
Atkinson, R. C., 66
Attea, M., 217
Auerbach, I. T., 22
Aukerman, R. C., 57, 74
Ayers, F. W., 264
Ayrer, J. E., 165
Ayres, A. J., 280

Bachner, S., 540
Bailey, M. H., 383
Bakwin, H., 142
Balow, B., 345, 392

Subject Index